COLLECTED WORKS OF ERASMUS

VOLUME 50

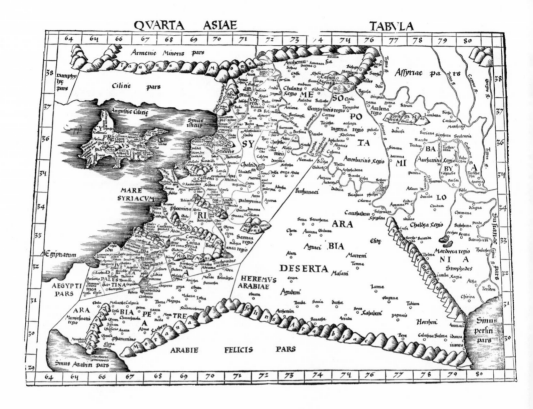

COLLECTED WORKS OF
ERASMUS

NEW TESTAMENT SCHOLARSHIP

General Editor Robert D. Sider

PARAPHRASE ON

THE ACTS OF THE APOSTLES

edited by John J. Bateman

translated and annotated by

Robert D. Sider

University of Toronto Press

Toronto / Buffalo / London

The research and publication costs of the
Collected Works of Erasmus are supported by the
Social Sciences and Humanities Research Council of Canada.
The publication costs are also assisted by
University of Toronto Press.

ISBN 0-8020-0664-7

Printed on acid-free paper

Canadian Cataloguing in Publication Data

Erasmus, Desiderius, d. 1536
[Works]
Collected works of Erasmus

Includes bibliographical references.
Partial contents: v. 50. New testament scholarship:
paraphrase on the Acts of the Apostles /
edited by John J. Bateman;
translated and annotated by Robert D. Sider.
ISBN 0-8020-0664-7 (v. 50)

1. Erasmus, Desiderius, d. 1536. I. Title.

PA8500 1974   876'.04   C74-006326-x

Collected Works of Erasmus

The aim of the Collected Works of Erasmus
is to make available an accurate, readable English text
of Erasmus' correspondence and his
other principal writings. The edition is planned
and directed by an Editorial Board, an Executive Committee,
and an Advisory Committee.

Contents

Preface

The nature and scope of the series of volumes to be published as the New Testament scholarship of Erasmus have been described in the preface to volume 42. That volume also provided introductory studies on the origin and nature of the *Paraphrases*, their publication history, and sixteenth-century translations in English. Those essays should prove useful to readers of this volume.

At a later date, a volume (CWE 41) will appear with a full introduction to the New Testament scholarship of Erasmus, together with translations of shorter works pertaining to that scholarship. Nevertheless, since the *Paraphrase on Acts* stands at the end of the nine volumes to be devoted to the *Paraphrases*, it may not be out of place to say a few words here about Erasmus' achievement. In a letter (Ep 1672) written in 1526 to an admirer who had apparently inquired about the *Paraphrases* on the Gospels, Erasmus explained that he had sought to return scholastic theology, which in his opinion was too much concerned with quibbles, to the true sources of theology and for that purpose had made his revision and new Latin translation of the biblical text, his *Annotations* on it, and his *Paraphrases*. The audience for these publications was, as he said, anyone literate in Latin, but his eye was primarily on students of theology, both clerical and lay. The *Paraphrases* in particular were designed to provide their readers with a summary of evangelical philosophy before they went on to more abstruse studies. Erasmus seems to have envisioned these readers as any of those who were too slow, too busy with other activities, or too fastidious in their literary taste to spend time on the close study of the New Testament and the many problems of interpretation posed by it. The *Paraphrases* thus offered an easy route, as he called it, to the knowledge of apostolic doctrine, which was the necessary foundation of all theological study and indeed of the Christian life itself. Written in an essentially homiletical style, they constitute simultaneously an elucidation 'in terms both plain and clear' of the gospel and an exhortation to live according to its rule. Few if any commentators on the Bible down to

Erasmus' time had so inextricably fused the 'indicative' and the 'imperative'
of the gospel into a unified exposition of the content of the teachings of Jesus
and the early apostles. Erasmus was right to claim, as he did, that in the
Paraphrases he had created something new. Taken together, they constitute
the longest piece of continuous expository writing in his collected works. To
judge from the number of editions of the Latin text and of translations into
the vernacular languages – an activity which Erasmus himself encouraged –
few of his works were as popular with sixteenth-century readers.

The *Paraphrases* were thus designed to entice his contemporaries, especially civil and ecclesiastical leaders, into reading the New Testament, the
spiritual medicine which Erasmus believed his own age desperately needed.
In the letter (Ep 1381) which serves as the preface to the *Paraphrase on Luke*
he develops this thought at length. Thoroughly digested, the medicine of the
gospel will transform its taker totally into itself. But, and Erasmus illustrates
the metaphor from his own case, anyone who reads the gospel carelessly
and perfunctorily will receive little benefit from it; continuous and accurate
reflection on it will bring to one a feeling – Erasmus means this literally
– of power such as can be found in no other book. The medical image
recurs in the letter dedicating the *Paraphrase on Acts* to Giulio de' Medici,
recently consecrated bishop of Rome and pope. Erasmus himself is suffering
from depression brought on by comparison of the nascent church described
by Luke and the corrupt and turbulent church of his own day, racked in
body and mind by the twin diseases of war and doctrinal conflict. Physical
and mental activity was one of the treatments physicians recommended
for melancholy; Erasmus does not say whether the labour of writing the
Paraphrase alleviated his condition, but he had no doubt that an infusion of
the spirit of Christ, which will come directly from reading Scripture, was
an urgent and necessary remedy for the sickness he saw in society. At the
beginning of his *Annotations on Acts* he remarks that it is of the utmost
importance for Christians to become thoroughly familiar with the infancy
of their religion so that they may understand that the same measures which
were responsible for its initial growth must be again employed to bring
about its renewal. The events and characters of the history of the early church
become in the *Paraphrase* permanent models of right and wrong motives and
actions.

At several points Luke, in the act of paraphrasing his own work, pauses
to address his reader, Theophilus, and through him all readers, asking them to
step back and to contemplate for a moment the implications of the narrative or
the speech they have just read. The story of the early church, which cannot be
repeated in its historical particularity, nevertheless becomes in the *Paraphrase*
an example of perennial significance and, to keep the medicinal metaphor,
application. Erasmus does not hesitate to go outside the limits of the biblical

text, though still remaining within the boundaries of the ancient world. Thus the apostles, who are filled with the Spirit, stand in contrast not only to the Jewish leaders who oppose them within the Lucan text, but also to all the orators and philosophers who were the intellectual leaders of the gentile world at large and who constituted what in the letter to Clement VII Erasmus calls 'the world's resistance.' No 'wordly' force could resist the inevitable expansion of the church. Here Erasmus adumbrates in the *Paraphrase* a topic which has become an important theme in the modern study of Luke's Gospel and Acts: the spread of the gospel from its origin in Jerusalem to Samaria, and then to Syria, Asia Minor, Greece, and Rome, and from there to the entire world. Whether for theological motives or not, to get the geography and the chronology right was an important issue for Erasmus. As Professor Sider demonstrates in his notes on these texts, Erasmus tries hard with the information available to him to locate the events of Luke's narrative in the Mediterranean world. He thus applies to biblical studies the concern with geography that was one of the major interests of humanistic historiography and scholarship.

Erasmus develops another interest of humanistic historiography when he describes for the reader the psychological motivation of the actors in the story. Thus at the start of his narrative Luke in the paraphrase states the reasons for what he has recorded of the deeds and teachings of Jesus but also why he has omitted events. Jesus explains why he remained on earth for forty days after the resurrection (1:3). The disciples are driven by 'futile curiosity' to know more about the kingdom of God (1:7); their love for Jesus makes them unable to carry out his order and return to Jerusalem after the ascension (1:10). Judas by contrast preferred the company of criminals to that of the apostles (1:17). The disciples trust not in human judgment but only in prayer (1:24). Even God has an ulterior reason for selecting one of the original twelve to be the betrayer of Jesus: God wants him to be the example of the fate of the bishop who betrays his trust (1:25). The man who succeeds Judas in office as the twelfth apostle does not boast of his election, nor does Joseph the Just, despite the prestige of his relationship to Jesus, begrudge the Lord's choice of Matthias; for to be without such feelings is an essential feature of justice or righteousness (1:26). In the manner of the Roman historian Livy, Erasmus transforms history into drama, and in so doing moves the history of the nascent church from the particular to the universal. He was not suggesting that the institutions of the early church were to be restored – as he observes in the dedicatory letter for the *Paraphrases* on the Epistles to Timothy and Titus (CWE 44), the passage of time had made that futile – but that the attitudes and spirit of the first apostles must be imitated by and renewed in their apostolic successors – courage, perseverance, stern resolve coupled with gentleness, and above all a steadfast commitment to concord.

Many other features of the *Paraphrase* emerge in Professor Sider's notes in addition to the concern with geography. The story of the apostles after the ascension is harmonized with the gospels and with the Epistles of Peter and Paul. The institutions of the Roman world are fully described, as are the persons whom the evangelists encounter in their dissemination of the gospel, not always, to be sure, with complete accuracy. The very text in which Acts came to Erasmus was multiple in form and origin, his Byzantine Greek text representing one ancient text tradition, the Latin Vulgate another, while the divergent citations in the Fathers, which Erasmus so assiduously collected in his *Annotations* on the New Testament, often reflect a third tradition. Echoes of the Vulgate are carefully noted, as are parallel statements or thoughts in Erasmus' own writings. The modern reader is thus constantly made aware of the rich linguistic texture of the paraphrases on individual verses and paragraphs. Erasmus' contemporary critics were incessant in their claim that he had introduced unnecessary innovations in his treatment of the biblical text; his response was that he always remained, as it were, in the mainstream of patristic and later commentary. The truth of that response, whatever one may think of the validity of the criticism, is amply demonstrated in the notes, which show that Erasmus seldom deviated from the traditional interpretation unless he thought that that interpretation required correction. Reading Erasmus against that tradition shows very clearly what he himself contributed to the elucidation and exegesis of the text.

The paraphrase, says Erasmus, was his field, by which he meant that the activity of paraphrasing was part of the art of rhetoric. Luke's work, in conformity with ancient views of historical writing, contains almost equal amounts of narrative and speech. Both gave Erasmus ample opportunity to advance the narrative rapidly and conversely to hold the reader in place as the contents of a speech or the implications of a particular action are drawn out in elaborate detail. There are also 'set-pieces' – 'theses' in the terminology of the art – where the paraphrast pauses to develop an idea close to his heart such as the passage on the tongue. Erasmus had already dwelt at length on this topic in the *Paraphrase on James* (CWE 44) and a few years later devoted to it an entire monograph, *The Tongue* (CWE 29). More important than any of these artistic devices is the rhetorical energy which pervades the text as Erasmus seeks to persuade, or, as he would have said, to captivate, instruct, and move his reader to return to the source itself. It is Professor Sider's special achievement to have found a way to convey in English the persuasive power of Erasmus' Latin.

JJB

Translator's Note

When Erasmus dedicated his *Paraphrase on Acts* to the new pope, Clement VII, he observed that the nascent church in the narrative of Acts provided the true model for the renewal of the church in the sixteenth century.[1] The *Paraphrase* exploits the idealizing portrait of the early church already apparent in the biblical text. The heavenly Spirit is an ever present dynamic source of action, and the leading figures, above all Peter and Paul, are exemplars for the prelates of the church in Erasmus' day. In the book of Acts the common Christian, too, whether an individual like Lydia or the 'multitude,' offered paradigms for subsequent centuries. Nothing, perhaps, seemed more striking in the early church, or more to be desired in the sixteenth century, than the accord of Christians; certainly, in the vision of the *Paraphrase* Christians constitute a harmonious brotherhood where even sharp disagreements can be resolved without rancour.

At the same time the book of Acts includes stories that illustrate patterns of behaviour not to be emulated, and Erasmus draws our attention to these as well. The *Paraphrase* condemns the spirit of greed, ambition, and deceit vividly portrayed, for example, in the paraphrastic narratives of Ananias and Sapphira and of Simon Magus. There are other enemies of the gospel, too, of which especially the spirit of worldly wisdom and the spirit of Judaism appear in the *Paraphrase* in a sinister light. More than once Erasmus speaks of orators, philosophers, and Pharisees in the same breath, all of them representing in different ways human disciplines to be rejected by the church. From the fading Judaism of the early church evident in the biblical text Erasmus constructed a particularly interesting paradigm. In the *Paraphrase* the leaders of the early church are, to be sure, men of unclouded vision, who know well that Jewish practices must come to an end, but they also recognize that radical change requires patience, and they are willing to act on a theory of accommodation according to which some concessions may be granted temporarily for the sake of the 'superstitious.'

The *Paraphrase on Acts* not only betrays Erasmus' characteristic interest in the relevance of the Bible to his own contemporary situation; it reveals also his commitment to a rhetorical culture. If the Spirit is the primary actor in the *Paraphrase*, the rhetorician's search for human motives – whether arising from an individual's character or from the force of circumstances – has the effect of rationalizing sacred history. Moreover, in the paraphrastic narrative rhetorical techniques add precision and colour to scenes and portraits, and heighten dramatic suspense. Occasionally we find highly rhetorical descriptions, like that of the 'tongue' in chapter 2, while rules familiar from classical rhetoric play a fairly obvious role in shaping the paraphrastic expansion of the speeches in Acts. The speeches of defence and apology – of Stephen, of Peter, and of Paul – were particularly susceptible of rhetorical treatment.

However much Erasmus' theological and rhetorical interests shaped the text of the *Paraphrase on Acts*, the genesis of the *Paraphrase* cannot be fully understood without reference to the biblical texts of Acts. Scholars have begun to illuminate the way in which Erasmus used his biblical sources to write the *Paraphrases;*[2] it is not my intent to add to that discussion here. However, it is evident that in the *Paraphrase on Acts* Erasmus sought to accommodate at least three biblical texts – the text of the Vulgate, his own Greek text, and his Latin translation, or rather translations, which represented, in effect, the Vulgate text radically modified to express the Greek with accuracy and elegance.[3] When the *Paraphrase on Acts* was first published in 1524, Erasmus had already produced three editions of his New Testament, the editions of 1516, 1519, and 1522. It was for the edition of 1519 that Erasmus made a translation that would, with only a few exceptions, be standard for the subsequent editions, and it is the version in this edition that is reflected primarily, if not quite exclusively, in the *Paraphrase*.[4] Thus Erasmus was able to weave through the *Paraphrase* threads of Latin from both the Vulgate and his own version. Accordingly, in the *Paraphrase* one hears echoes here and there of the sacred language of the book that was the Bible of the Western church for over a thousand years; but the revered sounds of the ancient language mingle with the decorous elegance and the arresting significations of the novel language of Erasmus' translation.

The *Paraphrase* is, of course, much more than a combination of the text of Acts in an old and a new translation. Paraphrastic expansion gave Erasmus space to create a linguistic texture enriched by borrowings from and echoes of the entire range of biblical literature. I have tried, therefore, both by direct borrowing from translations of the Bible and by echoes of biblical idiom, to impart to this translation of the *Paraphrase* a sense of the sacred language. Notes occasionally call attention to the Latin, either to point to a reflection of biblical idiom as found in the Vulgate or in Erasmus' translation, or to comment on the theological or rhetorical significance of the language of the *Paraphrase*.

In all five editions of his New Testament, those of 1516, 1519, 1522, 1527, and 1535, Erasmus' translation appeared with a Greek text. The primary source for Erasmus' Greek text was manuscripts that belonged to the Byzantine tradition. The Vulgate, on the other hand, generally followed the Alexandrian tradition.[5] In the *Paraphrase on Acts* Erasmus sometimes follows his own Byzantine text, and sometimes the text of the Vulgate. Because the major differences between the two textual traditions are readily discernible, and are moreover finite in number, I have noted at all significant points the text that Erasmus has chosen to follow in a particular passage when the two texts differ. The reader can thus remain alert to the textual traditions that enrich the literary fabric of the *Paraphrase*, and will be able as well to make some judgment about the degree to which Erasmus preferred one text over the other. I have referred the reader to four English translations which reflect these traditions in varying degree: of the older versions, the Douay-Rheims (DV) represents a Vulgate text, while the Authorized Version (AV) represents substantially the Byzantine text of Erasmus. Both the Confraternity Version (Conf) and the Revised Standard Version (RSV) are relatively recent, the former based on the best witnesses to the Vulgate, the latter on the best witnesses to the Greek text.

The text of the *Paraphrase on Acts* has also been shaped – profoundly – by the exegetical tradition.[6] As Erasmus pointed out in his annotation on 1:1 (*primum quidem sermonem*), there were very few commentaries available on Acts. Though he had some notes from Chrysostom's *Homilies on Acts* for his third edition of the New Testament (1522), he did not have the full text of the *Homilies* until 1527. But even where he had these *Homilies* Erasmus seems, with a few exceptions, to have found little inspiration there for his *Paraphrase*. It is rather in the *Gloss*, in Hugh of St Cher (d 1263), who so frequently copies the *Gloss* in his *Postilla* on Acts, and in the commentaries of Nicholas of Lyra (d 1349) that one recurrently finds phrases, images, and ideas that have parallels in the *Paraphrase*.[7] The exegetical tradition as represented by the interlinear *Gloss* appears to have been particularly formative in developing the paraphrastic expansion, often in minor details of explanation: identifying a place name, for example, as a city or an island.[8] One feels also the pervasive influence of the Venerable Bede (d 735). It is not perfectly clear whether for the *Paraphrase* Bede's influence comes through the *Gloss*, where he is frequently cited, or directly from Bede's two commentaries on Acts, the *Super Acta apostolorum expositio* and the *Liber retractationis in Actus apostolorum*.[9] In any case, for allusions to Bede I have included the references not only to the

Gloss, but to Bede's commentaries as well. The *Gloss* also attributes numerous comments to Rabanus, and many of these are echoed in this *Paraphrase*.[10]

The narrative of Acts, set as it is within a framework of constantly changing time and space, challenged the paraphrast to locate and interrelate events much more extensively than is done in the biblical text. From the *Annotations on Acts* we learn that Erasmus consulted a variety of primary sources for his information on matters of this kind. The Bible itself, of course, did provide some information, but Erasmus frequently turned to other sources such as the *Jewish Antiquities* and the *Jewish Wars* of Josephus, and to a 'dictionary' of place-names corresponding to the *De nominibus locorum* of Bede. Erasmus mentions this dictionary several times in the *Annotations on Acts*; his source represented itself as a work of Jerome – fallaciously as he came to think.[11] Equally important, perhaps, were the 'Geographies' of Strabo and Ptolemy, and Pliny's *Naturalis historia*.[12]

In following his sources, Erasmus may confuse the reader. For his *Paraphrase* Erasmus seems to have paid little attention to the significance of the changes in the map of Palestine and of Europe between the time of the New Testament, written in the first century, and that of the *Notitia dignitatum*, a document from the early fifth century.[13] Thus, for example, the reader familiar with the New Testament will be surprised to find that the biblical Damascus is, in the *Paraphrase*, located in 'Phoenicia' – correctly, according to the *Notitia dignitatum*, for in late antiquity Phoenicia was a Roman province in which indeed Damascus lay, as Bede correctly says in the *De nominibus locorum*.[14] However, it is also likely that Erasmus was sometimes careless in following the information he had; he was in any case not always correct.[15] Nevertheless, geography seems to have been not merely an incidental interest in the design of the *Paraphrase*, and the notes attempt, therefore, to explicate geographical allusions worthy of remark.

Not only was Erasmus' mind shaped by his close knowledge of the Bible and his acquaintance with the exegetical tradition; he had also read widely in the literature of classical antiquity. Geographies and encyclopedias were undoubtedly a useful thesaurus, but the poets, philosophers, and rhetoricians of ancient Greece and Rome provided structures of thought, ideas, and language that sometimes lie just below the surface of the paraphrases, sometimes emerge into open view. The speeches in the *Paraphrase on Acts* acquire a special interest by the manifest way in which the biblical text is shaped into a form determined by rules of rhetoric derived from antiquity. Erasmus read deeply in the ancient Christian writers as well. Though the 'Fathers' offered relatively little exegetical material on Acts itself, they had articulated issues and formulated ideas which became part of the heritage of Western Christian thought. I have generally not attempted to determine the 'direct influence' of the early Christian writers on the *Paraphrase on Acts*; references in the notes to the early Christian authors are intended rather to provide a sense of distance through which the formulations of Erasmus in this *Paraphrase* can achieve perspective.

The more one reads Erasmus the more one becomes aware of the intertextuality of his own writings. In the vast variety of his work many of his ideas recur, sometimes with little reformulation. But each new context has the potential to charge a familiar expression with new significance. The notes therefore attempt to locate expressions and reflections found elsewhere in the Erasmian literary corpus, above all in the *Paraphrases* on the other New Testament books and in the *Annotations*. There appears to be a particularly interesting correlation between some formulations in the *Paraphrase on Acts* and comments at corresponding points in annotations added in 1527, as though in writing the *Paraphrase* of 1524 Erasmus was already anticipating ideas to be expressed three years later in the fourth edition of his New Testament. Fruitful comparisons with the ideas of the *Paraphrase* will also be found in the *Adages*, the *Colloquies*, the literary and educational writings, in works of a more or less theological character – for example the *Explanatio symboli* – and in the books written in controversy with critics and opponents. In general the *Paraphrase on Acts* proved to be less provocative than the *Paraphrases* on some of the other books of the New Testament. Nevertheless the running critique of both Lee and Zúñiga on Erasmus' New Testament had implications for the *Paraphrase*. The notes consequently allude to Erasmus' debates with these two critics.[16]

This translation is based on the folio edition of 1535. Against this I have collated the octavo edition of 1534, the folio edition of 1524, and three octavo editions also of 1524. The editions of 1524 are briefly described by Sir Roger Mynors in CWE 42 xxv–xxvi. Of the 1524 octavo editions, the first had its title-page set in italic type (A778), a second appeared later in the year with the title-page set in roman (A779). A third edition has dated title-pages, some copies dated 27 June (A780), others dated 4 July (A781). In spite of the different date on the title-pages, these are copies of the same edition with only the title-page changed.[17]

In the course of these editions Erasmus made few changes in the text of the *Paraphrase*; indeed, as the notes show, he sometimes failed to make a change in the *Paraphrase* even though a particular paraphrase represented a misconception acknowledged in the 1535 edition of the *Annotations*. Moreover, the changes he made are often of little importance. Nevertheless, I thought it would be helpful if the readers of this translation could measure fairly accurately the nature and extent of the changes made, and I have therefore recorded all but a few insignificant changes which the Latin text is essential to appreciate.[18]

I have taken full advantage of the translation of this *Paraphrase* included in *The First Tome or Volume of the Paraphrase of Erasmus upon the Newe Testamente* published in 1548.[19] One will admire the crispness of its language and the unhurried and measured flow of its phrases, but will sometimes wonder at the tendentiousness of the translation. Modern translations require a different style, and this series wishes to avoid paraphrasing the *Paraphrases*. Like every translator I have wanted to represent in a suitably modern idiom something at least of the spirit of Erasmus' Latin style. As a vast expansion on the biblical text, Erasmus' *Paraphrase* gave him space to create a vivacious and energetic style that frequently moves with speed in a syntactical structure where a complex interrelationship of ideas is expressed by careful subordination. It has been necessary to simplify for contemporary readers the typically complex subordination of Erasmus' sentences. It has been my wish, however, to reflect to some degree the vigour and the kinetic energy of Erasmus' paraphrastic style.

The *Peregrinatio apostolorum*, a brief account of the journeys of Peter and Paul that prefaced the *Paraphrase* in the folio and octavo editions of 1524 (but not the editions of 1534 and 1535), will appear with other prefatory writings in CWE 41.

ACKNOWLEDGMENTS

A large part of the translation and annotation of this *Paraphrase* was completed during 1989–90 when I was a fellow-in-residence at the Netherlands Institute for Advanced Study. I am most grateful for the generous financial support from the Royal Netherlands Academy of Arts and Sciences which I received as a fellow, and for the excellent facilities and the gracious ambience of the Institute. I acknowledge with deep gratitude as well the generous support of the National Endowment for the Humanities, which awarded me a translation grant under its Division of Research Programs for the translation and annotation of the *Paraphrase on Acts*. The publication of this volume has also been assisted by the Social Sciences and Humanities Research Council of Canada.

It is a particular pleasure to recall the many ways in which Dickinson College has contributed not only to my work for this volume, but to my endeavours over the years as General Editor of the New Testament Scholarship Series of CWE. From the college I have received financial support for sabbatical leaves and generous funding for travel, research, and clerical aid, and my work has been greatly facilitated by several extraordinary acquisitions by the Spahr Library. The inter-library loan staff at Dickinson College have unfailingly met with cheerful confidence my most challenging demands.

Several people have played indispensable roles in bringing this work to publication. John Bateman, the editor of this volume, read the translation and notes in all of their later stages and saved me from many errors and infelicities. David Smith of the University of Toronto Press offered numerous suggestions for the stylistic improvement of the text, and Mary Baldwin read the proofs with admirable editorial expertise. Secretaries transformed a difficult manuscript into a nicely finished text for the Press: I am deeply grateful for the highly professional work of Pilar van Breda-Burgueño at the Netherlands Institute for Advanced Study and Barbara McDonald at Dickinson College. The skills of the typesetters – Lynn Child, who corrected and coded the computer disks, and Philippa Matheson, who set the Greek – are much appreciated. It is, however, to my wife, Lura Mae, that I owe the most for the successful completion of this work.

RDS

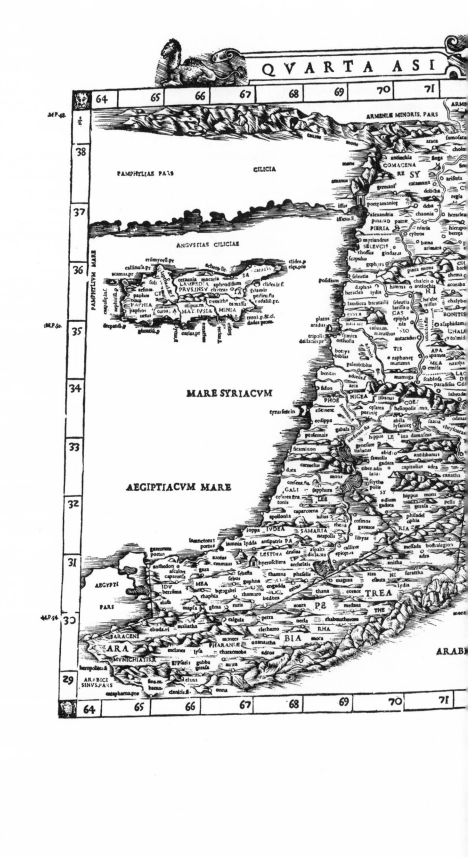

Claudii Ptholemaei Liber Geographiae cum tabulis et vniversali figura
Venice: Iacobus Pentius de Leucho, 20 March 1511
Rare Book Collection, University of Illinois Library, Urbana

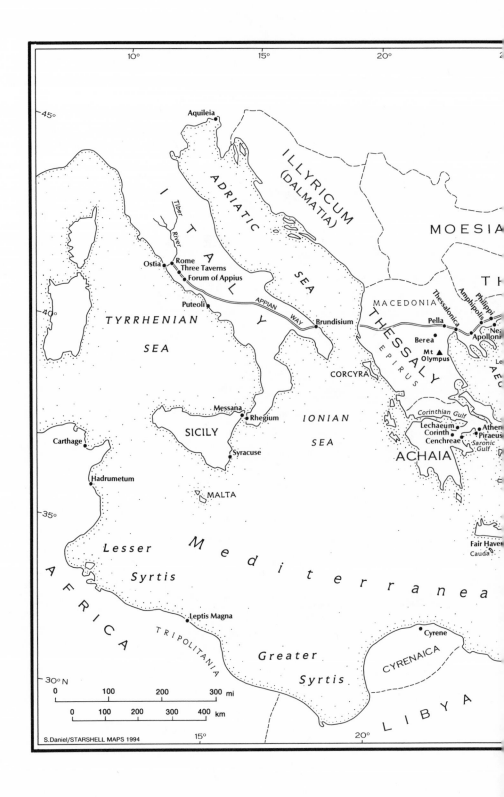

10° 15° 20°

45°

Aquileia

ILLYRICUM (DALMATIA)

ADRIATIC

SEA

I T A L Y

MOESIA

Tiber River

Rome
Three Taverns
Ostia
Forum of Appius

APPIAN WAY

MACEDONIA

Pella

Thessalonica

Amphipolis

Philippi

Ne

T H E S S A L Y

Apolloni

Puteoli

40°

TYRRHENIAN

SEA

Brundisium

Berea

E P I R U S

Mt ▲
Olympus

AE

Le

CORCYRA

Carthage

Messana

Rhegium

IONIAN

SEA

SICILY

Syracuse

Corinthian Gulf

Lechaeum
Corinth
Cenchreae

Athen
Piraeus
Saronic
Gulf.

ACHAIA

Hadrumetum

MALTA

35°

Fair Haven
Cauda

Lesser

Syrtis

M e d i t e r r a n e a

A F R I C A

TRIPOLITANIA

Leptis Magna

Greater

Syrtis

CYRENAICA

Cyrene

LIBYA

30° N

| 0 | 100 | 200 | 300 mi |

| 0 | 100 | 200 | 300 | 400 km |

S.Daniel/STARSHELL MAPS 1994

15°

20°

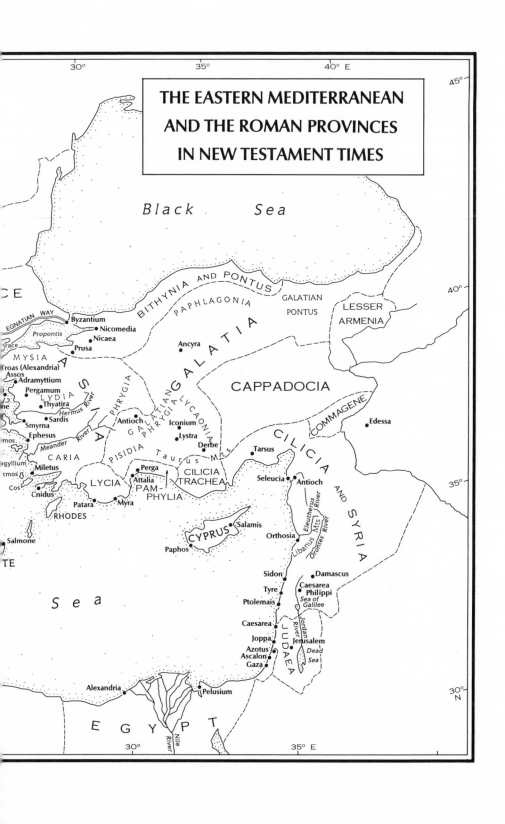

THE EASTERN MEDITERRANEAN
AND THE ROMAN PROVINCES
IN NEW TESTAMENT TIMES

Black Sea

BITHYNIA AND PONTUS

PAPHLAGONIA

GALATIAN PONTUS

LESSER ARMENIA

EGNATIAN WAY

Byzantium

Nicomedia

Propontis

Nicaea

Prusa

Ancyra

GALATIA

CAPPADOCIA

MYSIA

Troas (Alexandria)

Assos

Adramyttium

Pergamum

LYDIA

Thyatira

Hermus River

Sardis

Smyrna

Ephesus

Meander

CARIA

PHRYGIA

GALATIAN PHRYGIA

LYCAONIA

Antioch

Iconium

Lystra

Derbe

Tarsus

CILICIA

COMMAGENE

Edessa

PISIDIA

Taurus Mts.

Miletus

gyllium

tmos

Cos

Cnidus

LYCIA

Perga

Attalia

PAM-
PHYLIA

CILICIA
TRACHEA

Seleucia

Antioch

CILICIA AND SYRIA

Patara

Myra

RHODES

Eleutherus River

Libanus Mts.

Orontes River

Salmone

CYPRUS

Salamis

Paphos

Orthosia

Sea

Sidon

Tyre

Ptolemais

Caesarea

Damascus

Caesarea
Philippi

*Sea of
Galilee*

Joppa

JUDAEA

Jordan River

Jerusalem

*Dead
Sea*

Azotus

Ascalon

Gaza

Alexandria

Pelusium

E G Y P T

*Nile
River*

TE

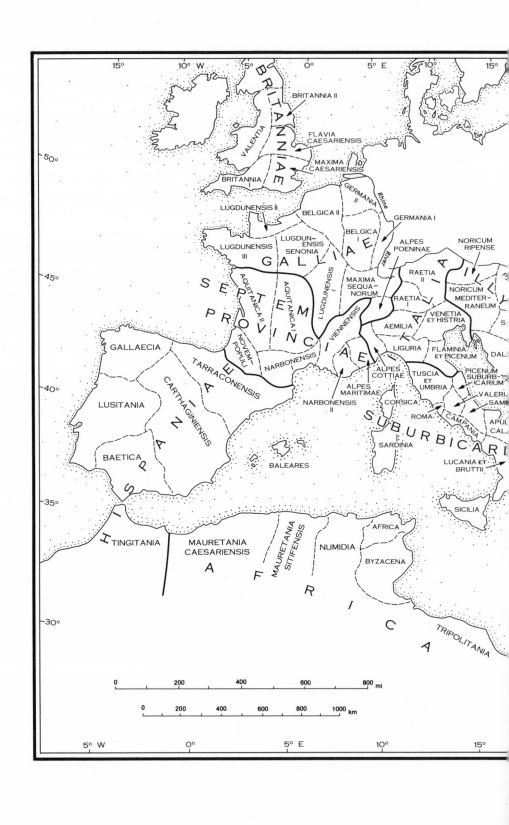

15° 10° W 5° 0° 5° E 10° 15°

BRITANNIAE

BRITANNIA II

VALENTIA

FLAVIA
CAESARIENSIS

MAXIMA
CAESARIENSIS

BRITANNIA

50°

LUGDUNENSIS II BELGICA II GERMANIA II Rhine GERMANIA I

LUGDUN-
ENSIS
SENONIA BELGICA
I ALPES
POENINAE NORICUM
RIPENSE

LUGDUNENSIS
III GALLIAE River

AQUITANICA I MAXIMA
SEQUA-
NORUM RAETIA
II NORICUM
MEDITER-
RANEUM

SEPTEM-

45°

AQUITANICA II LUGDUNENSIS RAETIA
I

VIENNENSIS VENETIA
ET HISTRIA

PROVINC AEMILIA

NOVEM-
POPULI NARBONENSIS LIGURIA FLAMINIA
ET PICENUM DAL

GALLAECIA IAE

TARRACONENSIS

ALPES
COTTIAE TUSCIA
ET
UMBRIA PICENUM
SUBURB-
ICARIUM

40°

CARTHAGINIENSIS ALPES
MARITIMAE VALERI

NARBONENSIS
II CORSICA SAMI

NARBONENSIS ROMA CAMPANIA APUL
CAL.

LUSITANIA H SUBURBICARI

BAETICA I S P A N I BALEARES SARDINIA LUCANIA ET
BRUTTII

35°

A SICILIA

TINGITANIA MAURETANIA
CAESARIENSIS AFRICA

MAURETANIA
SITIFENSIS NUMIDIA

A F BYZACENA

R

30° I

C TRIPOLITANIA

A

0   200   400   600   800 mi

0   200   400   600   800   1000 km

5° W 0° 5° E 10° 15°

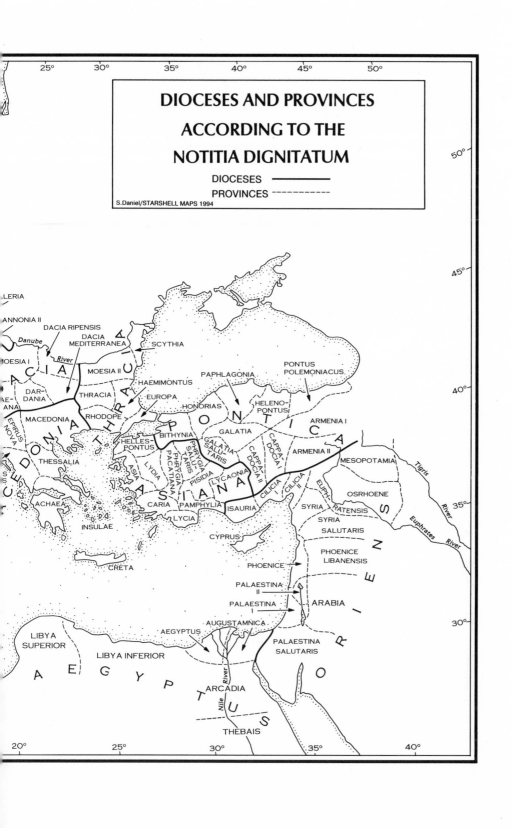

DIOCESES AND PROVINCES
ACCORDING TO THE
NOTITIA DIGNITATUM

DIOCESES ————
PROVINCES ----------

S.Daniel/STARSHELL MAPS 1994

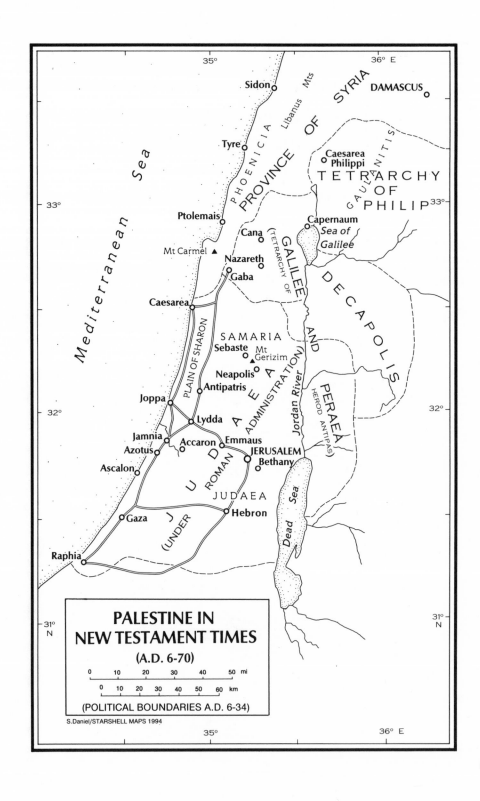

35°

36° E

Sidon

DAMASCUS

P H O E N I C I A

Libanus Mts

P R O V I N C E   O F   S Y R I A

Tyre

Caesarea
Philippi

G A U L A N I T I S

33°

T E T R A R C H Y
O F
P H I L I P

33°

Mediterranean Sea

Ptolemais

Cana

(TETRARCHY OF)

GALILEE

Capernaum

Sea of
Galilee

Mt Carmel ▲

Nazareth

Gaba

D E C A P O L I S

Caesarea

SAMARIA

Sebaste   Mt
▲ Gerizim

32°

Neapolis

Antipatris

J U D A E A   (ROMAN ADMINISTRATION)

Jordan River

P E R A E A

(HEROD ANTIPAS)

32°

Joppa

PLAIN OF SHARON

Lydda

Jamnia

Accaron

Emmaus

Azotus

JERUSALEM

Bethany

Ascalon

JUDAEA

(UNDER

ROMAN

Dead Sea

Gaza

Hebron

Raphia

31°
N

31°
N

PALESTINE IN
NEW TESTAMENT TIMES
(A.D. 6-70)

| 0 | 10 | 20 | 30 | 40 | 50 mi |

| 0 | 10 | 20 | 30 | 40 | 50 | 60 km |

(POLITICAL BOUNDARIES A.D. 6-34)

S.Daniel/STARSHELL MAPS 1994

35°

36° E

PARAPHRASE ON ACTS
In Acta apostolorum paraphrasis

DEDICATORY LETTER

TO HIS HOLINESS CLEMENT,
SEVENTH OF THAT NAME, PONTIFF TRULY SUPREME,
FROM ERASMUS OF ROTTERDAM, GREETING[1]

At one and the same moment, most holy Father, I was writing this paraphrase of the book called Acts of the Apostles and the printers were striking it off; and it is the last task of this kind that I have decided to undertake. As I worked at it my mind was not wholly free from something like melancholy, for I could not fail to compare the very turbulent and corrupt state of the church in our own day with the kind of church of which Luke has given us such a wonderful picture in this book. My gloom was intensified by the news of the death of Adrian vi;[2] for a figure at once so learned and so deeply religious had given us some hope that he might be destined to restore the ruined state of things, Leo the Tenth having been jealously snatched from the world by an early death.[3] Not but what, when I thought of Adrian, my mind had always foreseen that we might be leaning on a tottering wall; for his age and his health never seemed likely to cope with the great turmoil of the world. But it was not long before my spirits were refreshed by letters from several cardinals and learned men,[4] bringing the news that Clement vii had been raised to the summit of human affairs and at the same time giving me a picture of the man you are, so rarely gifted and cast in a heroic mould, as worthy of such a lofty position as you are equal to it. I was at once attracted by your adopted name of Clement, to which men say your character is admirably suited. But what seemed to me above all a most happy omen was your family name of Medici, one of the best known and most popular names in the world. Serious, even desperate, sickness demands some outstanding, some predestined master of the medical art; and no sickness is more dangerous than one in which the patient is very ill in both halves of his being, both in body and in spirit. Surely it is some sickness such as this from which the world now suffers. These chaotic enmities between one monarch and another,[5] so fraught with disaster, so implacable, so long-continued, so far beyond all cure – are they not like some desperate sickness of the whole body? Can we discern any part of the world that is immune from the infection of this dread disease? But even more destructive than that is this pestilence, which with its astounding and insoluble conflict of convictions has overmastered all men's minds.[6]

Great efforts to resolve the conflicts of war which were already spreading have been made by the invincible king of England, Henry, eighth of that name;[7] but it came to nothing. Our own Adrian tried to do the same, and his labours were in vain.[8] Has anything in fact been left untried, has anyone not attempted to reconcile the conflict of convictions which is a sort of sickness of the mind? And down to this day all have laboured in vain, while the disease has constantly grown more severe. But now we have a Medici with his new medicine, and at his appearance, as at some god from the machine, the spirits of all men rise high in hope. Oh may this hope of all Christian people not prove an illusion, if only we might deserve that such should be God's will! At any rate, there are many indications that smile upon our hopes and promise us that here if anywhere we shall find the truth of Homer's saying that 'a physician is a man worth many men.'[9] For it is a greater achievement to heal disorders than to suppress them. For when I contemplate the picture of things as they are today, there come into my mind at once those lines of Virgil:

> As oft in some great city riot spreads,
> The vile mob rages, brands and boulders fly,
> Rage finds them arms,[10]

except that any riot is more disastrous which affects not one city but the whole world and not some vile mob but every class in the community. But then, when I watch how Clement, a Medici, a member of that family of destiny,[11] has been posted at the helm of affairs, there seems to me to be a happy omen in the lines that follow:

> Some grave and reverend senior should they spy
> Of merit proved, they silent fall, and stand
> With pricked ears listening, while his kingly words
> Their spirits rule and soothe their raging hearts.
> So all the roaring of the mighty deep
> Sank, as its lord surveyed the waves, then drove
> His willing steeds beneath an open sky
> And gave free rein to his fast-flying car.[12]

And so, although I had decided to dedicate this work that I had in hand to another person,[13] a man of the highest rank below the papal majesty, when letters[14] arrived from Rome which gave me a lifelike picture of you

and added that your Holiness had actually been heard to express a high
opinion of myself (an opinion which I shall be unable to justify, but at least I
will do my best to show that I have tried), at that point I changed my mind
and preferred to dedicate my new work to the new pontiff. It seemed fitting
too that Luke the physician, the medico, should go to a Medici, and that
the foundations of the newborn church should be offered to the one man
through whom we hope that the church in ruins will be reborn. In those days,
despite the world's resistance, the kingdom of the church grew none the less,
for Christ prospered what was achieved through the leaders of his church;
so too in our own day we hope, nay, we are confident that Christ will not
withhold his blessing from your pious efforts. And may he in his clemency
long preserve our Clement in health and wealth.

Basel, 31 January AD 1524
Erasmus of Rotterdam

THE PARAPHRASE OF
ERASMUS OF ROTTERDAM
ON THE ACTS OF THE APOSTLES

Chapter 1

I have, Theophilus, fulfilled a part of my promise, for in my former book I have traced the contours of the life of Jesus Christ.[1] I began the account further back than the other evangelists – from the conception of John the Baptist, the forerunner of the Lord, since in that narrative too, prophecies were recited that promised the Messiah soon to come.[2] Following this, I made the story fuller by telling some things which had been omitted by the other writers – about the conception of Christ, his nativity, circumcision, and purification.[3] I also touched upon his divine nature, of which he offered some indication when he was twelve years old.[4] I thought these stories should be recorded to make crystal clear, by many proofs, that this was he whom the prophetic oracles had designated, and that not even those early years of Jesus' life had lacked the testimony of godly people and of men inspired by the heavenly Spirit.

Although there is no doubt that the entire life of Jesus was a singular example of perfect piety, nevertheless I passed over the intervening years, and leaped ahead to the time when John began, by his preaching and baptism, to play his role as forerunner of Jesus Christ.[5] I did so, because it was from this time especially that the Lord Jesus began to take up the work of human salvation in accordance with the figures and the riddling allegories of the Mosaic law and in accordance with the oracles of the prophets.[6] In essence, this work consisted of two things: first, of deeds, that is, performing miracles, enduring the pain of the cross, rising again, in which everything that had either been foreshadowed in the Law or promised by the prophets was realized through him; second, in the words by which he gave the world a new and evangelical philosophy.[7] In this way we might be able, from one and the same person, to look for both the ground and the pattern of godly living.[8]

I followed the sequence of these events right to the day when he was taken up into heaven from where he had come.[9] But prior to this, after he

was alive again from the dead, he had instructed both his twelve apostles
and the remaining seventy disciples[10] (whom he had chosen before his death
specifically for this ministry), to go into all the world and preach the gospel
not only to the Jews but to all the peoples of the entire world.[11] This they
were to do when they had received the Holy Spirit, for Christ imparted the
Spirit to them both when he breathed upon their faces and later, when he
sent the Spirit more abundantly from heaven.[12]

First, however, it was necessary to confirm in every possible way the
faith of those who, according to his purpose, should furnish for all mortals
the evidence of his wonderful deeds. The chief point of these deeds was that
everyone be persuaded that Jesus had truly died, and had truly come to life
again on the third day, not in what merely appeared to be a body but in that
same mortal body – now immortal[13] – which he bore on earth, and which had
been buried lifeless in the tomb.[14] Accordingly, he did not think it enough to
present himself alive again to his disciples merely once; he appeared to them
frequently, and not[15] as ghosts usually do, but showing with various clear
proofs that he had assumed again a living body.[16] For this reason, he remained
on earth for forty days, during which, however, he wanted to be visible to no
one except his own. Not only did he present himself to them to be seen with
their eyes, to be heard with their ears, to be touched with their hands,[17] but
he lived with them in close association, and took food with them;[18] and no
other sign of a living body is more certain than this.[19] Meanwhile, he often
spoke with them about the kingdom of God, calling to mind what he had
done and taught before his death so that they might eventually recognize that
everything had happened as he had predicted. At the same time he warned
them what they were either to do or to expect in the future.

Although he had already handed over to them the authority to preach
the gospel he nevertheless forbade them to rush immediately into a duty so
arduous. They were not to depart from Jerusalem, but they were to gather
there, and spending their time together in fasts, hymns, and prayers, to await
the Holy Spirit – a second Comforter who, he had promised before he died,
would be sent to them from the Father.[20]

'By my own mouth,'[21] he said, 'I have promised; do not doubt that
the Father will faithfully fulfil the pledge I have made to you in his name.
My will is the same as my Father's.[22] The task you will be undertaking is a
heavenly, not a human one. You will not teach carnal things, as the Pharisees
have so far taught, but spiritual,[23] and no small persecution will arise against
you because of the preaching of the gospel.[24] Accordingly, you will need to
be strengthened by a power sent forth from heaven in order to be equal to
so great a task, a task which will not be accomplished by human strength but
by the help of the divine Spirit. Thus far we have seen only the prelude[25] to

certain things that are basic to carrying out the gospel. John baptized with water; he did not confer the Spirit, for no human being can confer it. John preached only repentance, because the kingdom of heaven was at hand.[26] Now there is need of more able forces to draw forth the lively strength of evangelical teaching, and to endure the storms from an opposing world. For this, it is not enough that you be cleansed from your sins,[27] but for a new teaching you need a new Spirit – an abundant Spirit, a celestial Spirit, a fiery Spirit. With this Spirit you will be baptized in a few days. This is the baptism John was not able to give[28] but foretold that I would give, for he bore testimony to me, saying, "He will baptize you with Spirit and with fire."[29] Long ago also, God imparted his Spirit to prophets and to holy men, and I have breathed the Holy Spirit upon you. It is the same Spirit, but now it will be poured forth upon the world in great abundance, to renew all things.[30] For its coming, prepare your hearts with sobriety, pious prayers, but above all with simple trust, so that you may be fit instruments of the Spirit, which is about to display its force through you.'

Jesus spoke these words to his disciples, as they were all gathered together, so that he should not leave any disagreement among them. Since[31] they had not yet put aside the dream of an Israelite kingdom emerging, they asked the Lord, inasmuch as he was soon to go away, whether he would, immediately upon sending the Holy Spirit, restore the kingdom to the Israelite people, and whether he would at once display his majesty to the world.[32] They did not yet understand the nature of the spiritual kingdom. On the mountain Peter desired a kingdom to be established. Others also, hearing talk of the resurrection, inquired about the kingdom.[33] Now again, upon hearing the words about sending the Spirit, the kingdom came back into their minds, for they hoped that power over the whole world would be transferred to the Jewish people. And yet it certainly would come to pass that Israel would reign, not that carnal Israel, but the Israel that had truly deserved the name, that is, the one that was truly strong against God,[34] for Jacob won this name by wrestling with an angel.[35] As long as the world relied upon its own works it was no match for the righteousness of God; all were convicted of unrighteousness and fell subject to punishment.[36] But when it began to distrust itself and to trust the evangelical promises, it now stormed, so to speak, the divine righteousness and extorted mercy.[37] This kingdom, in ruins everywhere but especially among the Jews, Christ restored through the gospel. The disciples did not understand this, but dreamed of some good fortune which should free them from all the persecutions of evil people.

This, however, was not to be until the end of the world, and the Lord wanted the time of that event to remain undisclosed to his own since it was not expedient for them to know it. Accordingly, he restrained their futile curiosity[38] with a reply like this:

'Do not ask what it does not help to know. Simply trust, and fulfil your charge. You will be only ministers in this affair; leave its course and its conclusion to the heavenly Father. It is not, then, for you to know in what year and month and hour the kingdom of Israel will come;[39] such things the astrologers in their foolish curiosity investigate. I have imparted to you everything the Father has wanted you to know. What that time is I have not revealed to you because the Father has reserved for himself alone its determination, so that you might always be vigilant in duty.[40] Most assuredly, the kingdom of God will come, and then the godly and the ungodly will be paid the rewards due their deeds. You must always be ready for its advent.[41] And yet, even in the meantime a spiritual kingdom will thrust itself forth. In vindicating and protecting this kingdom, God demands your service; as for the rewards, let them be his concern. So give up your desire to know what you should not; prepare yourselves for events that lie at hand.

'Since your own strength is not equal to these events, the Holy Spirit will be poured out upon you from heaven just as I promised.[42] It will give strength to your souls, will call to mind everything I have taught you, and even supply any further knowledge you might need. Taught by its prompting, strengthened by its support,[43] you will be my witnesses, first in Jerusalem – as the prophet says, "The Law shall go forth from Zion and the word of the Lord from Jerusalem" [Isa 2:3] – shortly thereafter, through all Judaea, then Samaria, which borders on Judaea, finally throughout all the nations of the world wherever the races of mankind inhabit the earth.[44] I came equally for all, I died for all, the grace of the gospel is offered to all.[45] Until now, the Law has held sway among the Jews. It is the Father's will that the reign of the gospel extend as widely as the world extends.'

These were the last words the Lord Jesus spoke to his disciples, who had all gathered together in Bethany. When he had finished speaking and had blessed them, he was borne upward before the eyes of all,[46] until a white[47] cloud withdrew the body of Jesus from their sight. The time had come for them to stop depending on the visual presence of the body, so that they might rather begin to be spiritual and might look upon Jesus now with no other eyes than those of faith.[48] And so when the Lord, concealed by the cloud, was borne into the sky above, the disciples stood there steadfastly gazing upward into heaven.[49] Weak as they still were, they simply could not be torn away from the one they singularly loved.

As they waited to see what further strange events might appear from above, suddenly there were two heavenly messengers there, in human form,[50] clothed in white. Their human form precluded terror; their white garments befitted the messenger of one who was hastening to glory.[51] With friendly words they assuaged the sorrow of the disciples that had arisen from the Lord's departure,[52] and recalled them to duty from useless gazing:

'Men of Galilee,' they said, 'Why do you stand here with your eyes fixed upon the sky? This Jesus who has been taken from you has returned to heaven from where he had come, just as you frequently heard from him that he had come from the Father and would return to the Father, leaving you in the world.[53] He has not been carried off into the air like Elijah,[54] but has been received into the Father's royal dwelling, to sit beside him on his right hand as sharer in his heavenly rule.[55] You have looked upon him as he went to heaven with a body visible indeed but nevertheless immortal.[56] Thus he will come again at some future time, so that those who here have refused to acknowledge his appearance as Saviour, will acknowledge his appearance as judge.[57] He will not return in lowly fashion, but from on high with great glory he will reveal himself to the eyes of all. You few saw him when he departed; everyone will see him when he returns.[58] There is, however, no reason to expect him back now. From him you learned that the gospel of God must first be preached throughout the whole world.[59] This now is your work. You have been told not to stay here, but to remain in Jerusalem to receive there the heavenly Spirit[60] and so to make an auspicious beginning of your heavenly task.'

The disciples obeyed these words. They left the Mount of Olives – whose gentle protection the Lord had enjoyed before his death,[61] and where he had also imprinted his last footsteps when he was about to return to heaven[62] – and returned to Jerusalem. That mountain is a sabbath day's journey from Jerusalem, that is, nearly two miles.[63] From this mountain was the road to the ignominy of the cross, from it also the road to glory. From it Jerusalem could be seen, and sitting on this mount Christ had predicted and[64] lamented the ruin of the city.[65] In this city, slayer of the prophets,[66] the Lord wanted the light of the gospel to arise first, whether because it was so predicted by the prophets[67] or to snatch every pretext of excuse from those who in any case were to perish utterly because of their unbelief.[68] The apostles would rather have continued to look up into the sky where the Lord had gone before them, but for the sake of our neighbour's advantage it is often necessary to descend to things that are essential rather than pleasant for ourselves.[69]

When they came to Jerusalem, they proceeded to an upper room in which those disciples were staying who were especially close to Christ, namely, Simon Peter and John, James and Andrew,[70] Philip and Thomas, Bartholomew and Matthew, James of Alphaeus, Simon Zelotes, who in Hebrew was called the Cananaean, and Judas surnamed Thaddaeus or Lebbaeus, brother of James the Less.[71] In the same upper room several women were staying who had followed the Lord with godly zeal when he set out for Jerusalem and had ministered to him from their means.[72] Mary, too, the mother of Jesus, was among them, with some of his relatives, whom the Hebrews call 'brothers.'[73]

Consider[74] now with me for a little while the first beginnings of the nascent church. The city of Jerusalem, which in Hebrew means 'vision of peace,'[75] pleases them. Those whose native land is this world do not inhabit Jerusalem, nor do they desire to find the tranquillity of the heavenly life. Those whose minds are agitated by worldly passions do not inhabit Jerusalem. The Holy Spirit does not repair to such breasts.[76] The *cenaculum*, which is the higher part of a building, was also agreeable. For the lower parts of a house are usually occupied either by shops or workplaces. But whoever prepares himself as a dwelling for the Holy Spirit must be far removed from sordid cares.[77] This is that holy congregation which the Lord Jesus had chosen out of all.[78] This upper room was the first abode of the church of the gospel.

Now see what is done here. The time is not wasted in quarrels or empty tales, but all continued steadfast with a single heart in holy prayers. Where there is not oneness of heart, there is not the church of Christ; prayers are not pleasing to God where there is not brotherly concord. Only one who has persevered in prayer deserves to be heard.[79] The evangelical congregation prays for the same thing. Where one prays for riches, another hopes for the death of an enemy, one for long life, another for power, where everyone prays for a different thing, there you do not have the supplication[80] of the church. Into the upper room of the apostles flocked the rest of the disciples also. Whoever wishes to be regarded as a disciple of Jesus must be joined to the fellowship of the church.[81]

There had now come together a group of about one hundred and twenty people[82] – so small was the number of those who loved Christ with their whole heart. Peter, who, as a faithful pastor, eagerly desired that the evangelical flock should grow, began at this point to worry about the diminished number of apostles, whom the Lord Jesus had chosen as a band of twelve. For with the death of Judas Iscariot the twelve had been reduced to eleven.

Observe now, Theophilus, the mode of ecclesiastical deliberation. When a very large number of the disciples were present, Peter, assuming the role of bishop, rose in the midst of the assembly of disciples,[83] so that what seemed to pertain to the restoration of the full apostolic order might be established through harmonious agreement.[84] He began from the divine Scripture – an ecclesiastical sermon should begin here.[85] Nothing is decided without a preliminary prayer from hearts united. Then he spoke in this fashion:

'Brethren, you should not attempt some innovation on the basis of human deliberations, but it is necessary to fulfil that which long ago the Holy Spirit spoke beforehand through the mouth of David about electing someone in Judas' place – for even this was predicted in the Psalms, that he would desert his Lord and leave his place free for a successor.[86] For out of all, the Lord Jesus had selected twelve apostles especially, whom he wanted to be witnesses of everything that he had done and taught.[87] You see them all present here, except Judas Iscariot. Even him the Lord Jesus had admitted into the number of the twelve and wanted him to share in the apostolic ministry. He, however, abandoned the fellowship of his teacher and our company. He preferred to be the guide for the criminal band of soldiers who arrested Jesus than to follow Jesus as his guide or to be a companion of the apostles.

'And the outcome of his impious purpose was unhappy! Blinded by avarice[88] he sold and betrayed his innocent Lord for thirty pieces of silver. Then led by penitence for his deed, he brought back his unrighteous reward and threw it at the feet of the priests who had hired him. He himself, mindful of his crime rather than of Jesus' clemency,[89] played his own executioner. He slipped a noose around his throat, and hanging there, he burst in the middle, and all his insides came pouring out. That unlucky money which he had cast at the feet of the priests was, upon their counsel, used to purchase a field for burying strangers, since they regarded it as forbidden to put into the treasury the price of innocent blood betrayed.[90] Such impious scruples of the priests and Pharisees only made both the crime of Judas and their own ungodliness the better known to all who were then living in Jerusalem. So it was that that field was called, in ordinary Jewish speech, Akeldama, that is, "field of blood."[91]

'And so we see fulfilled now in Judas what the Holy Spirit predicted in Psalm 68 concerning the Jews who persecuted Christ with relentless hatred. They refused to repent though called by so many kindnesses; and in their case, too, the prophecy will be fulfilled in its own time. For the prophecy runs thus: "Let their dwelling place be deserted, and let there be no one to inhabit it" [Ps 69:25].[92] The unfortunate Judas lost his place in the apostolic ministry; in the same way the temple will also one day be destroyed, as well as the priesthood and the authority of the scribes and Pharisees, together with Jerusalem itself.[93] The impious Jews will be driven out and the true Jews will follow in their place – those who, circumcised in mind not in body, acknowledge the Messiah whom the former crucified.[94] This too has been predicted by many sayings of the prophets, and we ourselves have heard the Lord Jesus with tears prophesying this of the city of Jerusalem.[95]

'Meanwhile, it remains that someone should be chosen to take Judas' place. For Psalm 108 has predicted this too: "And another will receive his bishopric" [109:8].[96] Our task is simply this, that exercising care over the Lord's flock, we provide for it from the food of evangelical teaching. Judas left his place, but the flock must not for this reason be cheated of its shepherds, nor must the number be diminished which the Lord first of all established, giving them the special designation of 'apostles.' He wanted them to be constant witnesses of his words and deeds, and for this reason he had them as companions who always attended him, even sharing his living quarters. Someone, therefore, must be chosen in place of Judas from those who lived continuously with us all the while the Lord Jesus, in accomplishing the task of human salvation, willed that we should be his close friends and constant followers wherever he went – I mean from the time of the baptism of John whom he presently succeeded[97] right to the day when he returned to heaven. In this way the one chosen can, along with us, be a worthy witness of all that Jesus did and taught, but especially of the resurrection,[98] for [the Lord] did not appear frequently[99] to all his disciples, but only to those whom he had especially selected.'[100]

When this speech had gained approval from the assembled people, they put forward two, selected from the seventy:[101] Joseph who is also Barsabbas,[102] who was given the surname 'the Just' because of the outstanding integrity of his character, and Matthias. Whichever of these two, alike in godliness, more pleased the assembly would receive the office of an apostle. Those, however, who were assembled placed no confidence in their own judgment but beseeching the Lord in communal prayer, said:

'Human beings who judge from what they see and hear can be deceived in their judgment, but you alone, Lord, are the examiner of hearts, for it is in their hearts that persons are truly good or bad. Be not unwilling therefore to show your servants by some sign which of these two you have chosen to complete the number of the twelve apostles and to succeed to the exercise[103] of so great an office,[104] from which Judas has fallen to go to his own place, a place to which you knew he would go, you, whose eyes nothing escapes. It was not by your fault that he withdrew from your fellowship, for you did everything to lead him to repentance. It was not by a mistake in judgment that you received into fellowship a future deserter, but your divine wisdom saw that it was for our advantage that through this traitor your Son should be sacrificed for us and the traitor be an example for us that we should not hold in a negligent and carefree way the office handed over to us.'[105]

After this prayer they proceeded to cast lots, in the Hebrew manner. For by lot Jonah was thrown into the sea; in the same way, Jonathan was caught when he had tasted honey; likewise by lot the priests performed their sacred duties.[106] The Holy Spirit had not yet come, and the apostles still kept some remnants of Judaism – though lots are not dangerous when, whichever of the two they might favour, they designate one who is approved and competent. Moreover the entire affair was not entrusted to the lot. The two most approved were elected by vote; the lot terminated the uncertainty arising from the choice of these two through election, and the lot itself could not be rash when prayer guides its outcome.

This lot, then, which was nothing else than a declaration of the divine will, designated Matthias, though Joseph, in addition to the recommendation suggested by his surname, was commended also through his relationship to Jesus;[107] still Matthias was preferred to him. From this we are shown that in choosing bishops, to whom the stewardship of gospel teaching must be entrusted, no concessions should be made to human feelings; on the contrary, among equals, he should rather be favoured whom no human circumstance commends, so that an action based on a favourable circumstance not become a destructive example. There is also in the names something of a more recondite teaching. Matthias, which is a Hebrew word meaning 'gift of the Lord,'[108] is preferred to Justus. The Pharisees claimed this surname [the Just] on the basis of works, but none is less suitable for the stewardship of the gospel. He alone is worthy to succeed to the office of the apostles who acknowledges and preaches the free gift of God through gospel faith. Justus was not unhappy that his equal had been chosen over himself, and Matthias did not flatter himself that in being added to the eleven apostles, he filled up that sacred number and, as the best man, took the place of the worst.

Chapter 2

Forty-nine days were spent in this way after the Lord's resurrection. Pentecost, that is, 'the fiftieth,' the awaited day, was at hand. This was a day of joy and veneration for the Jews also, whether because of the Year of Jubilee, which returned every fiftieth year, or because the Law was given on Mount Sinai on the fiftieth day after the lamb was slain by whose blood they had gone forth from Egypt unharmed.[1] On a mountain the Old Law was given, written on tables of stone; in an upper room the New Law was given, written by the Holy Spirit on the hearts of believers.[2] In both cases, an elevated place, in both cases, fire.[3] In the one case, however, there was only a mountain, which the people were prohibited even from touching, no doubt because they were gross and earthly,[4] incapable of grasping spiritual things; in the other, a dwelling is on the mountain itself, so that you may recognize the harmony of the church. There Mount Sinai, appropriate to bringing forth the law that was to restrain a rebellious people by a multitude of precepts[5] (for it receives its name from Sina 'precept'); here Mount Sion, which in Hebrew means 'watch-tower,'[6] from which all things earthly are looked down upon, all things heavenly are, through faith, observed as though nearby.[7] There terrifying fire, smoke, conflagration, thunder and lightning; here the Spirit, coming with great force, but bringing eagerness, not terror,[8] and fire that does not incinerate bodies but illuminates minds[9] and brings to the tongues of the simple a rich supply of heavenly eloquence. There a discordant people murmur;[10] here in the same chamber with quiet and concordant hearts they pray, awaiting the gift from heaven.

Such was the day chosen for the heavenly work; such, too, the place into which they had now,[11] in the nine days, become accustomed to come frequently. But now that the fiftieth day had arrived they had all with complete concord come together at the same time to the same upper room to receive the heavenly Spirit. Where the mind is occupied with low and sordid cares, there the Holy Spirit is not found; it has to be in an upper room. Where the breast churns with discord, hatred, and quarrels, there is no place for the Holy Spirit.[12] Gathered together into one place, a lofty place at that, with hearts united,[13] all believe, pray, await.

Lo! suddenly from above there came the gift of God. For all of a sudden there came a sound from heaven as of a wind blowing with mighty force, and it filled the entire room where they were sitting, calm and quiet. This was not that north wind breathing frost from the clouds, nor was it the south wind bearing from the marshes the heat that is baleful to bodies.[14] This was the breath of heaven, coming from where Christ had gone, breathing eternal life into souls, giving strength and vigour to the weak and the faint. This was a sound that did not frighten anyone, but stirred the minds of all to the keen expectation of the promised Spirit.

The one sign was given for the ears, the other was given for the eyes, for these are a person's two chief senses. Tongues appeared, as though in the form of fire, distributing themselves to each of the disciples,[15] and they sat upon the head of each for some time so that we might understand this gift would be everlasting. It was the same Spirit that blew upon the minds of all, the same flame that set on fire the tongue and breast of all.

Without delay, the efficacy of the heavenly gift followed the visible sign. All who were present were suddenly transformed, as it were, into heavenly persons[16] and, filled with the Holy Spirit, began to speak in different tongues. These were not languages they had learned from human conversation, but ones the Spirit had imparted to them from heaven. No member of the human body is more destructive than a wicked tongue, none more beneficial than a good tongue.[17] To sow the seeds of the heavenly doctrine throughout peoples of every language required tongues imbued with heavenly doctrine and aflame with the fire of evangelical love. This was, therefore, the primary sign of evangelical faith, the sign the Lord had promised to them, saying, 'They shall speak in new tongues.'[18] Those who slander, disparage, revile a neighbour, who swear false oaths, engage in filthy talk – these have tongues

burning with the fire of hell, not aflame with the fire of heaven.[19] Those who
dispute about the petty things of this world have not yet received a heavenly
tongue. Formerly the apostles disputed about the bread they had forgotten,
the restoration of the kingdom to Israel, the first seat, the primacy.[20] This was
the human tongue, not yet fit to preach the gospel. Now they speak nothing of
that sort; everything they breathe, whatever they speak, is spiritual, celestial,
fiery.

Sounds are not uttered without breath, without a tongue. Accordingly,
the breath[21] from heaven puts forth a heavenly sound, a tongue of fire carries
off[22] and sets aflame the hearts of the hearers. The tongue of the Pharisees
is cold, the tongue of the philosophers, however erudite, or of the orators,
however fluent, moves no one.[23] This gift comes from heaven; the disciples
are only instruments through which the Holy Spirit puts forth his voice.
A man cannot give this gift to another man, nor does anyone impart it to
himself, but God bestows it upon each person as he sees fit. One upon whom
the gift is bestowed more abundantly has no reason to look down upon
another but should try the more eagerly to be of help to many.[24] The spirit is
a thing of force; fire is something lively and always in motion. The apostles
no longer sleep, as they slept before the Lord's death; they no longer hide,
as they did after the resurrection.[25] They burst forth in public, everywhere
and openly preaching to all free salvation through trust in Jesus, the one
crucified just a little while before.

The city of Jerusalem was indeed an appropriate theatre in which to
begin this play.[26] Because of the city's fame, because of the Passover which
had preceded, and because of their devout regard for Pentecost, there were
many who were then staying in Jerusalem. These were not only from every
part of Syria but also from every territory to which either the storms of war
had scattered the Jews, or some misfortune had dispersed them.[27] Among
these there were many who were deeply devout.

When news of this strange happening had spread to everyone,[28] a
diverse multitude of people came together, puzzled in mind, seeking to know
what this novel event was; for although they had assembled from regions
of such diverse language, nevertheless as the disciples spoke, everyone
understood them just as though they had spoken to each individual in
his own dialect, and not to all in one dialect.[29] For the Hebrew language
also has its differences corresponding to different regions, whether through
proximity to various peoples or some other cause. The Samaritan woman
recognized that Jesus was a Jew from the distinctiveness of his speech,
and Peter's Galilean origin was betrayed by the sound of his speech.[30] The
Greek language likewise is divided into five dialects,[31] and there is no small
difference within languages of other nations. Moreover, many Jews knew

only the language of the people among whom they were born. Hence a sort of profound wonder gripped them all and they began to discuss among themselves[32] how there had occurred something they had never heard of or read about. They said:

'Look! What a strange thing! Aren't all these who speak natives of Galilee? How is it then that we who are so many and who speak different languages, whenever we hear any one of them talking, understand him just as if each were hearing his native language? For this crowd has come together from such different regions: there are Parthians, Medes, Elamites, also those who dwell in Judaea, divided into its many parts,[33] and, besides, Cappadocia, Pontus, and what is properly called Asia,[34] Phrygia, Pamphylia, Egypt, and those parts of Libya which touch Cyrene. There are present those who have their abode in Rome, part of them Jewish in race, part proselyte (that is, those who have been admitted into the Jewish religion),[35] moreover Cretans and Arabians. We who are assembled from so many nations, and have such different languages, hear and understand those who are speaking – speaking not ordinary or human things, but things that are sublime, magnificent, worthy of God.'

Struck by the novelty of the event, all who were lovers of religion spoke to one another in this way, saying, 'What does this strange occurrence mean?' They do not blame what they cannot grasp, as Pharisees usually do,[36] but they seek and desire to learn what they do not know. On the other hand those who were inclined to make unfair and hasty judgments said mockingly, 'They are full of new wine.' You could say that these are disciples of the Pharisees who said of Jesus, 'He has a demon.'[37] Of course, extreme intoxication is very much like madness.[38] One might, perhaps, through madness speak in various languages he had never learned. But no madness enables all to understand what you say. They, indeed, said this in derision, but nothing forbids the truth sometimes to be spoken even in jest. They were completely filled with the new wine which the Lord did not want entrusted to old skins. The old wine of the Mosaic law failed at the wedding of the church, and the cold and tasteless sense of the Law was changed into new wine through Christ.[39] Whatever is carnal is tasteless and weak; whatever is spiritual is lively, effective, and appealing to the taste.[40]

They drank to satiety from the heavenly chalice of which the psalmist says, 'How glorious is my cup that intoxicates.'[41] If one may compare things entirely unlike in kind, the intoxication characteristic of ordinary life gives rise chiefly to four things in people: it brings into the open the secrets of the heart; it brings about forgetfulness of past ills and cheers the heart with the hope of happy things; it adds strength even to the point of scorning life; finally, it makes the tongue-tied fluent.[42] Come now, see whether that new wine of the divine Spirit did not beget something similar in the apostles. What they had concealed through fear, what they had learned in secret, they now[43] publish abroad, and, according to the Lord's prophetic saying, proclaim on the housetops.[44] They forget the old Judaism and, as though newly born, do not remember their former life or recollect the blows in terror of which they had deserted the Lord. Though they are without the support of any human aid, they fear neither governors, nor kings, nor councils; neither prisons, nor torture, nor death, but are always eager and joyful through the evangelical promises.[45] In short, those who were fishermen and simple folk now with eloquence from heaven expose the pride of the Pharisees, refute the propositions of the philosophers, overwhelm the eloquence of the orators.[46]

Nothing is more difficult than to make a speech before a crowd, which is ever a beast with many heads,[47] but especially when it is drawn from different races and tongues. Here then, I ask, observe Simon Peter, a fisherman suddenly become an orator. The crowd was in an uproar. What happened then will always happen, right to the end of the world. In such circumstances especially, it is the duty of the good shepherd to go forth with brave heart into the midst of the people, not to check the murmurers with force or to retort insults, but in a firm rather than a fierce spirit to repel slander with the testimonies of Sacred Scripture and to vindicate the glory of Christ. And so Peter, who earlier in the upper room had stood up, intending to complete the number of apostles, now again stood before the turbulent mob, intending to instruct those who had said, 'What is the meaning of this?' and to stop the mouths of those who had said, 'They are full of new wine.' However, it is not necessary that the bishop always stand when he addresses the people, since Christ himself taught the people while sitting,[48] but whoever undertakes the apostolic office does need to 'stand up' in spirit. Here, meanwhile, recognize Peter's rank and authority. He is the first to speak when circumstances require an evangelical orator. He had sheathed the sword unpleasing to Christ, he had unsheathed the sword of the Spirit.[49] Such should the chief bishop be. Peter rose up, but not alone, for the eleven apostles stood with him so that he should not appear to be usurping absolute power. One alone made the speech, but the one spoke with the voice of them all, just as earlier one in the name of all had professed Jesus Christ the Son of the living God.[50]

Whence came such confidence to a simple and lowly fisherman that he dared even to face so great a crowd? Often in the case of great orators, who produce a speech composed and practised with many a long hour spent under the light of the lamp, when they are about to speak before a packed audience, or before princes, their colour drains, their voice sticks in their throat, their brain becomes numb. In Peter's case it was, no doubt, that heavenly intoxication, that sober inebriation. He stood in the presence of so great a multitude; he took to himself the eleven apostles, not as his defenders but as participating colleagues; he bent his gaze upon the people, an unknown man looking upon an unknown audience; he raised his voice, and without a thing prepared beforehand, he spoke to them, in this already fulfilling the Lord's instructions.[51] He does not speak on his own behalf, but the shepherd protects the flock.[52] He does not make his case with the subtle argumentation of human beings but with the support of divine Scripture.[53] The crowd, attentive, now awaits his address. Let us attend also, since these words are for all.

First, when with a gesture of the hand he had checked the murmur of the crowd, he began with an exordium, which would make them attentive without any rhetorical adulation:[54]

'Men of the Jewish race,' he said, 'you ought to be well informed about the Law and the prophets, and especially you, who live in this city of Jerusalem, the source of religion and of the knowledge of the Law.[55] There is perhaps some reason for your surprise; there is no reason why anyone should slander. Accordingly, all you who are present, lend me attentive ears for a little while, and learn how the matter stands, for this is important to all of you.

'These Galileans whom you see standing beside me are by no means[56] drunk with new wine as some think, since it is the third hour of the day, and usually no one is drunk at daybreak.[57] Rather, in these events you see fulfilled what God through the prophet Joel long ago promised would come to pass. Hear the prophecy and acknowledge the reliability of the promise. Do not slander and misrepresent because you see something unusual, but rather embrace the grace divinely offered you. Joel, inspired by the divine Spirit, saw that God, who had at various times for your salvation imparted his Spirit to Moses and some of the prophets, would at last pour out that same Spirit most abundantly after he had sent his only Son[58] – not upon one or two individuals (as you see in the case of the prophets, where in the course of many centuries few arose), but upon all the nations of the whole world,[59] upon whoever would receive with sincere faith this joyful message which we declare to you at God's command.[60] Joel proclaimed the heavenly oracle thus:

'"It shall be in the last days, says the Lord,[61] that I will abundantly pour out my Spirit upon all flesh, and suddenly your sons and your daughters shall prophesy, your young men shall see visions and your old men shall dream dreams, and upon my servants and my handmaidens in those days I will pour out my Spirit and they shall prophesy. I will show wonders in the heaven above and signs on the earth beneath, blood and fire and vapour of smoke. The sun shall be turned into darkness and the moon into blood before the great and illustrious[62] day of the Lord comes, and all who call upon the name of the Lord shall be saved" [2:28–32].

'These things the prophet Joel foretold to you many centuries ago. You are seeing fulfilled his prediction about the outpouring of the Spirit, and there must be no doubt that God will with equal reliability bring to pass what Joel also prophesied about the calamity to come. There is, however, no reason to despair. The prophet who declares the danger reveals a sure way of salvation: call upon the name of the Lord and salvation is provided for you. But in what way the name of the Lord must be invoked, hear now, men of Israel, and attend carefully to the rest of this speech. Many of you knew Jesus of Nazareth, whom God has displayed to you as the man promised long ago by the oracles of all the prophets. He commended him to you[63] by the many great miracles and wonders which he performed through him before your eyes, for God was in him.[64] I am speaking of something not unknown to you, for the report of his miracles has spread abroad not only throughout all Judaea but also to some neighbouring cities. Since, however, he himself travelled through this whole region, everywhere healing the sick, restoring the disabled, giving sight to the blind, cleansing the lepers, and casting out demons, many of you have seen what I am describing.

'None of these things was done apart from God's plan; thus it pleased God to save the world.[65] Such a man as this you took[66] – handed over to you not by chance or accident, but by the determinate counsel and foreknowledge of God for the salvation of the race of Israel. By the hands of ungodly soldiers you fastened him to a cross, and you killed him – for the soldiers were only the ministrants of the crime; whoever sent him to death killed him.[67] The thing is too obvious to be denied.

'God, who handed this man over to be slain, willing that he be killed by you, also called him back to life on the third day according to the prophetic oracles.[68] In this way, all who have believed the gospel might hope that what had been effected in him by divine power will also happen to themselves.[69] In obedience to the Father's will, Christ patiently bore the shame of the cross, placing all his confidence of salvation not in human support but in the mercy of God. On this account God delivered him from the dead and the pains of death, which as a man he could indeed taste, though since he was free from all sin he could in no way be held bound by them. For death and Tartarus do not have a perpetual authority, except over those who are subject to sin.[70] Accordingly, though death was able to swallow him up, it was not able to keep him once devoured, but on the third day was compelled to vomit him up, just as the whale vomited up Jonah.[71] Accordingly, God willed that an innocent man should suffer all these things on this account, that through him he might redeem us all both from our sins and from the power of death, provided only that we place our whole trust in God, according to the example of Jesus of Nazareth.

'What I am telling you, Israelites, should not seem incredible after David, inspired by the heavenly Spirit, predicted that it would be so. For in Psalm 15 he speaks thus concerning Jesus of Nazareth whom we preach to you:

'"I saw the Lord always before me, for he is on my right hand that I should not be moved. Therefore my heart rejoiced and my tongue was glad; moreover my flesh also shall rest in hope, because you will not leave my soul among the dead nor will you cause your holy one to see corruption. You have made known to me the ways of life; with your presence you will fill me with delight" [Ps 16:8–11].

'You see how clearly David, king and prophet, has portrayed for us what you know has been carried out in Jesus of Nazareth. In God he had placed his entire defence, and relying on the help of him alone, he willingly and gladly suffered all those things that you know he suffered. Rejoicing in his heart, he bore the pains of the body. His tongue leaped for joy, never silent, never concealing the will of God. He suffered himself to be buried, doubting not at all that the Father would call him back to life on the third day and would not allow him to moulder in the grave who was guilty of no wrongdoing and had placed all his hope in God. Whoever places the hope of salvation in his own works or in the protection of this world will not be equal to bearing the pains of death, and once caught by death will not be able to extricate himself. Whoever has eyes continually fastened upon God,[72] who is merciful to all, knows the paths of life, and if ever God seems for a time to turn his face away from him, still he will soon turn again his gaze towards him. He will replace temporary torments with eternal joys; in place of death he will give immortality; for earthly dishonour a heavenly glory. Thus through him there has been shown also to us the path to eternal life.[73]

'There will perhaps be some who suppose that this prophecy pertains to David himself, not to Jesus. I know how highly you think of the patriarch David – not undeservedly, for he was holy and dear to God. But to speak the truth freely to you, my brothers, you must not attribute so much to the patriarch David that you[74] ascribe to him what belongs to the Messiah. The case speaks for itself:[75] this prophecy does not fit David or any other patriarch or prophet. David, as everyone of you knows, is dead and buried, and has never come to life again, since his tomb is with us right to the present day, containing nothing else than the dry and lifeless bones of the dead man. Accordingly David, who knew that he must, like everyone else, be buried and his body decay in the tomb, did not proclaim this prophecy about himself.

But he was inspired by the prophetic Spirit and knew that what God had confirmed for him by oath would happen, namely, that according to the flesh Christ would arise from his own loins, and in the spiritual sense would sit upon his throne to reign forever.[76] Thus prescient, he prophesied concerning those things that you see have now taken place in Jesus of Nazareth, who without question derived his origin according to the flesh from the stock and family of David. Moreover, since it is manifest that in this life Jesus aimed at no earthly kingdom and never sat upon the throne of David, but was treated with utter ignominy, it is clear that some other kingdom was promised of which the oracles of the prophets proclaimed no end.[77] He could not have sat in the seat of David, if, once slain, he had never come to life again. He arose, therefore, and now sits on the throne of David, that is, of the eternal Father, the Lord of all that is in heaven and on earth. This is, no doubt, what David predicted, inspired by the Spirit, foreteller of the future, and what he predicted has come to pass. For although the soul of Jesus descended to the dead, it was not held there, but instead it freed the souls that were held.[78] Thus his body, though lifeless and buried in a tomb, still did not decay therein, but God, who does not know how to be false in what he promises, restored to the body the soul called back from the dead.

'Of this event, we all whom you see standing here are witnesses. We lived in familiar association with him. From him we often heard both that he had to be crucified, according to the prophets, and that he would rise again on the third day. We were both his hearers and onlookers at his death, and we are witnesses of his resurrection: to us he often appeared, not only seen and heard, but also touched with our hands. We recognized his voice, we recognized his face, we saw and touched the prints of his wounds. Finally, he took food together with us so that we might know the body was real and the same as the one buried in the tomb.[79]

'Accordingly, the one who had been cast down by men to the lowest ignominy, him God has raised to the height of eternal glory.[80] One day, at the end of the world, this glory will be openly revealed to all, but in the meantime he is now putting forth in your presence the divine power – putting it forth by the hidden strength of the Holy Spirit which he promised to us from the Father when he was still living on earth.[81] Returning to heaven he has from there abundantly poured out the Holy Spirit upon us according to the prophecy of Joel. Hence this miracle, uncommon among you, that you see and hear us speaking in tongues which you alike understand though you are people of diverse languages assembled here.[82]

'Further, just as the prophecy concerning the resurrection cannot be understood of David (as I have shown), so what was foretold about the ascension into heaven, the session on the right hand of God the Father, the everlasting kingdom, cannot pertain to David, as the Pharisees admitted when they disputed with the Lord.[83] For David never ascended alive again into heaven; and yet, inspired by the prophetic Spirit, he spoke thus in the mystic[84] psalm: "The Lord said to my Lord, sit at my right hand until I make your enemies a footstool for your feet" [110:1]. Accordingly, it is obvious that in this prophecy the discourse is about God the Father, who elevated to heaven Jesus, son of David according to the flesh, Lord according to the Spirit,[85] and bade him sit beside him as sharer in his rule. And so the whole race of Israel should take it as certain that God has raised to his heavenly kingdom this Jesus of Nazareth whom you placed upon a cross, and has set him forth as both Lord of the universe and Messiah; that is, that anointed one whom you await under the name of Messiah, promised by the prophets for so many centuries.'

This speech of Peter cast terror into the minds of his audience. They knew in their conscience that before Pilate they had shouted, 'Crucify, crucify, crucify him!'[86] They recognize from the prophecy that partnership in rule at the right hand of the Father had been given to him until all his enemies should be cast under his footstool.[87] They fear as avenger him who now reigns but whom they had slain, though he had imparted benefits. To recognize the guilt, to fear the punishment deserved, this is the beginning of salvation. And so, pricked in their hearts, they say to Peter and the rest of the apostles, 'What shall we do, brethren?' The matter stands well when the guilty mind does not despair, but seeks a remedy.[88]

Here Peter presents the image of a gentle shepherd.[89] What does he do? He does not rage at them with harsh reproaches, he does not magnify the sin, he does not thrust them away and put them off, he does not prescribe victims and holocausts, but shows the remedy prepared for the conscience-stricken, making no distinction between those who had crucified Jesus and those who had not agreed to the impious deed, for no one was free from sin. Accordingly, he said:

'Repent of your past life,[90] and let each one of you be baptized with water in the name of Jesus Christ, and the remission of all your sins[91] will be granted you by his freely offered kindness. Then, when you have become pure and clean, the gift of the Holy Spirit, which you see poured out upon us, will be given to you. Let no one weigh his merits; everything given is free – only let trust[92] be present. The prophecy of Joel pertains especially to you and to your descendants, whom he calls sons and daughters, servants and handmaidens. Believe God who is the promiser, and receive without cost what has been promised. Nor does the promise of the prophecy pertain to you only who are of the people of Israel, but to all the peoples that are far removed – both from kinship with the tribe of Israel and from the knowledge of God – all whom the Lord our God of his goodness will deign to summon to a share in this gift. This, too, the prophecy has pointed out, adding, "And all who call upon the name of the Lord will be saved." It is not, however, everyone who says "Lord, Lord"[93] that calls upon his name, but the one who places all hope of salvation in his name. It has also been predicted by other prophets that the word of the gospel would penetrate to the very ends of the earth.[94] The Lord Jesus has commanded us also to announce this grace to you first, then to call the gentiles to the same grace,[95] for this call is not made on the basis of human merits, but comes from the freely offered kindness of God.'[96]

With these and very many other words, Peter witnessed to them about Christ, bringing forward the testimonies of the prophets and comparing with them the events which had already occurred. To teaching he added exhortation in order to goad on further those who were hesitating:

'Come, brethren,' he said, 'embrace the kindness of God towards you, a kindness so outstanding, so ready at hand. You know the complaints of all the prophets about the perversity, about the obstinacy of the Jewish people, a people that has always shown itself rebellious to its own Lord God and to the ministers he has sent for their salvation. How often did it resist Moses? How many prophets has it slain? How often has it provoked the wrath of God by its crimes?[97] Hence rightly it is called an exasperating house,[98] and a vine turned to bitterness, which instead of sweet grapes gave its cultivator wild grapes.[99] John made the same complaint, calling Israel a generation of vipers.[100] Often the Lord Jesus made this complaint, offended by the invincible perversity of the many who, though seeing, did not see, though hearing did not hear, though understanding did not understand.[101] They spurned the doctrine that brings salvation; they attributed the kind deeds done through Jesus' miracles to the spirit of Beelzebub.[102] Accordingly, he called it a perverse and unbelieving people.[103] With tears, he declared the destruction of a race which beat, slew, stoned, and crucified all those sent by God.[104]

'Remove yourselves, brethren, from the imminent vengeance of God, cast off the perversity of the Jewish race, which while upholding its own justice wickedly rebels against the justice of God.[105] Through faith and simple obedience eternal salvation is provided for you all. Only then will you be the true Israelites, then will you be the genuine sons of Abraham, then will you be truly Jews if you acknowledge your king, Jesus. Depart from that carnal generation which would rather perish through its own unbelief than be saved. Be born anew into a spiritual and heavenly people which is saved through trust in Jesus.'[106]

This was truly the eloquence of a fisherman, not gained from the precepts of the rhetoricians but infused from heaven[107] and therefore powerful and effective. This was that sword that pierces even to the dividing asunder of soul and spirit,[108] by whose keen blade the hearts of the Jews were pricked. This is the first cast of the net, by which the fisher of men hauled in an abundant multitude.[109] This was the seed of the evangelical word which was to be everywhere sown. The seed, according to Jesus' teaching, does not take root in the hearts of all, but here it at once found good soil that brought forth fruit.[110] For there were baptized and added to the number of disciples (who were at that time very few), about three thousand persons. These truly are the felicitous first-fruits of the evangelical crop. Here too the events described in the New Testament fit the figure in the Old. Moses commanded that the first-fruits be celebrated on the fiftieth day after the Passover; here on the fiftieth day the first-fruits not of grain but of souls are consecrated to the Lord.[111] Through teaching and faith, water had now cleansed them from all sins; they had now drunk of that heavenly Spirit.

Mark now what that heavenly Spirit does in them, for it is not inactive, since it is of fire. Innocence has been freely given; the grace of the Holy Spirit has been freely given. It remains for us to take care that what God has freely bestowed of his goodness, we do not lose through our own thoughtlessness. These are the rudiments of evangelical piety; this is, as it were, the infancy of our new birth into Christ. What is thus far handed down is the milk of teaching; one must progress to solid food.[112] Evangelical pastors ought to have both kinds of food prepared, for the Lord has given them this commission: Go, teach all nations, baptizing them, teaching them to keep whatever I have commanded you.[113] Teach those who are to be baptized the rudiments of the evangelical philosophy; unless one believes these he will in vain be baptized with water. Teach those who have been baptized to live according to my teaching and always to progress to more perfect things.[114]

So those who were numbered among the disciples persevered in the teaching of the apostles (for from this, growth is most abundant) and in taking the token[115] of an unbreakable covenant – they called this the communion.[116] The practice, handed down from the Lord, was like this: bread was broken and a small piece was given to each one; while doing this in memory of[117] the Lord's passion,[118] they gave thanks to the kindness of God, who had purged them from their sins by the blood of his only Son, who had admitted them by the undeserved death of his Son into the inheritance of eternal life. They added holy prayers in which they would ask that the kingdom of the Lord Jesus be daily extended more widely, that his glory come to shine throughout the whole world, that his will be everywhere obeyed.[119] They would ask also that those who had once professed evangelical faith might progress daily to better things through sacred teaching and heavenly grace, and that they might thus live harmoniously together, having peace with their brethren, forgiving an injury if, through human frailty, some wrong had been done, and having peace with God, who is merciful to those who are merciful to their neighbours.[120] In this way, strengthened by the daily help of the divine power, they might withstand all the attacks of Satan until the eternal reward be given after long struggles. In those days, such were the sacrifices made by Christians.[121]

The effect of the miracle of tongues, of the lively exhortation of Peter, of the sudden change in so many people, of so much newness of life, was that now a certain fear gripped the guilty hearts of all. They saw that these events were not a matter of human conspiracy but of heavenly power, for the apostles not only spoke in the languages of all, but also performed many wonderful miracles in Jerusalem[122] by calling upon the name of Jesus – healing the sick, casting out demons, raising the dead. This great fear took hold ever more firmly in the hearts of all; it was in some measure the beginning of a people's change of heart.[123]

Above all, however, that heavenly Spirit produced mutual benevolence and concord in all it inspired. Certainly Jesus had bidden his disciples to be recognized by this special sign, that love for one another held them together.[124] For all who had believed the gospel frequently gathered together in one place and exhorted and comforted themselves by mutual discourse. Many there were, and all were admitted without respect to persons: young, old, women, men, slaves, free, poor, rich.[125] Indeed, the love of Christ implanted in their hearts joined together such disparate people with so much oneness of heart that they regarded all things as common among themselves, which is something rare even among genuine brothers.

To make it easier for them to share their goods among all, those who had estates or other possessions sold them and divided the returns among all as each had need. Thus those who possessed nothing were not in need, and those who possessed much did not live in luxury. They bestowed not as though from their own goods but from a common store. For true love does not know ownership or possessions, and among people of the same mind no one appears as the owner of his own property. Need, moreover, can scarcely arise where each is content with a little, and distribution is made from the common purse to satisfy needs, not wanton desires. The apostles prescribed none of this, but love offered it of its own accord beyond what any law of Moses dared to demand.[126]

Indeed, in the temple also they continued daily in prayers with great unanimity of mind, giving thanks to God, encouraging themselves in mutual discourse, and enticing whomever they could to the evangelical covenant. Then, after the whole day had been spent in such pursuits, they broke bread house by house and ate their meals with each other in turn[127] with incredible joy; and with the most sincere simplicity of heart they praised God by whose kindness they had gained so great a grace. Among all the common folk they were in favour, and were beloved. Who would not love innocent people, ready to do good to all, and in whom was seen such great power of God joined with so much modesty and gentleness?[128]

You will note, here, Theophilus, that the rise of the church happily took its beginnings from concord and joy. There must be concord where the Spirit is, the one who makes peace for all; there must be joy where the conscience is pure, and confidence in the promises of the gospel is sure. Further, though in putting Jesus to death priests, Pharisees, scribes, the foremost of the people were everywhere present, here in the felicitous beginnings of the nascent church there is no mention of them.[129] No one came to this association under compulsion; no force kept them in the compact. Those who were added continued of their own accord, and day by day the Lord drew in first some, then others, whom he had destined for salvation.[130] The grain of mustard was slowly emerging, soon to spread its branches over the whole world.[131]

Chapter 3

Peter and John, with others, used to go together[1] to the temple towards the ninth hour as the day began to decline. This is a time when other people, already drunk, usually play or sleep;[2] it had become the custom of the apostles, however, to be free for holy prayers, fasting until the evening. The two princes of the apostolic order went forth without horse or mule, without a royal bodyguard – but attend the apostolic procession![3]

At the entrance to the temple sat a certain beggar, well known to the people, lame from his mother's womb. So great was the deformity of his body that he was carried by porters. His misfortune, as it happens, provided support for many, since it was for gain that they set him out at the gate of the temple which the people call 'Beautiful' to ask alms from those entering (for this gate was the most crowded).[4] Mendicity has its own talent; it knows that those who go into a temple are so disposed that they give alms quite freely, or wish to seem so disposed.[5] When this man saw Peter and John about to go into the temple, he asked them for alms, for the company attending them suggested that they were people of some substance, and the expression on their faces revealed their essential kindness.

Here the Holy Spirit inwardly suggested to the apostles that it was time to perform a miracle. Accordingly, Peter along with John fixed his eyes upon the cripple and said, 'Look at us!' At their gaze, at these words, the beggar became more eager and turned his eyes upon them, hoping to receive something from them. He had asked for a donation; he expected a donation.

He did not dare to beg that his legs be made whole, since he had no hope that they could do this. And yet he had a feeling that something good was about to happen. Then Peter raised his voice, that sublime voice truly worthy of the supreme Vicar of Christ,[6] and said:

'The silver and gold that you expect are not in my possession. But there is at hand that which comes not from me but from the kindness of heaven, something you need even more; this I give you: in the name of Jesus Christ of Nazareth, rise and walk.'

At the same time, he took the cripple's right hand and raised him up. At once, without delay, his feet and ankles became firm, so that he did not merely arise, but leaped up, stood upon his feet and walked wherever he wished. Delighted by a kindness so unexpected, he entered the temple along with the apostles, walking briskly and jumping for joy, and rejoicing,[7] and praising God from whom, he knew, this good deed had originated. To conceal the kind deeds of God is a matter of ingratitude; to attribute them to human endeavour is impiety.

The entire people, present in the temple in great numbers, caught sight of the man (who had usually been carried by porters) now walking on his feet with a lively step and praising God. They all recognized that he was the same man who was accustomed to sit at the Beautiful Gate to beg. They see him suddenly changed; they hear him giving thanks to God. At this event a vehement astonishment and wonder seized the minds of all.

Peter and John, as the chief of the apostles, had by then become known to many, for the man who had been lame clung to them[8] and proclaimed that through them he had found soundness of body. So when the people saw Peter and John, the whole populace flocked to them. Now they were in the portico of Solomon in which Jesus, that true Solomon, used to walk and where sometimes he disputed with the Pharisees.[9] The novelty of the event had struck the minds of all. When Peter saw the concourse of people – and he could not be unaware of the cause – he again began to speak in this manner:

'Men of Israel, why are you so greatly astonished over this, as though seeing miracles is something that happens to you seldom if at all, or as though you have not seen greater ones in the recent past? Why do you stare at us, as though it was our power or piety that made this lame man, who is known to you all, to walk? What is taking place is not the doing of men, and what you see is not something new but was promised long ago by God through your prophets.[10] You worship religiously the God of Abraham, the God of Isaac, and the God of Jacob,[11] and you glory in having these men as the patriarchs and founders of your race. But you have inflicted the ultimate insult upon the Son of the very God worshipped by the patriarchs, a Son sent to you for your salvation, and sent in lowly guise – made like you – that you might more readily embrace him. And yet God by his own power has glorified the Son who had been cast down by human malice; through him, both in many other ways, and by this deed also, God has put before your eyes innumerable miracles, and has taught the heavenly doctrine. You were in no way moved by these great benefits. After many insults you at length handed him over into the hands of ungodly men to be slain, and when Pilate, a gentile,[12] unfamiliar with the knowledge of the Law, alien from kinship[13] with the patriarchs, had declared him – as your king, as a just and holy man – not guilty, you, who should have recognized him from the prophets, openly and repeatedly denied him at the governor's praetorium, saying, "We have no king but Caesar."[14] You raged against him with such great hatred that you preferred that at your demand Barabbas be given life – a brigand and insurgent, one who had taken the life of others – rather than Jesus, who was bringing life to all.[15] You procured the life of a murderer, you put to death the author and prince of immortal life.[16]

'But this man who was slain by you,[17] God, the author of all life, has called back from the dead and given immortality. Of this we are witnesses, to whom he showed himself alive again, to be seen, heard, and touched;[18] we saw him also ascending into heaven. First came the lowliness which he assumed for the sake of you all. Now, borne aloft to glory by the Father, he exerts power[19] through us, who are nothing else than witnesses of what we have seen and heard. And through the trust which we have in his name, God has restored sound feet to this man whom you see walking and who you know was born lame. No praise here is owed to us, nor should anything be attributed to the merits of us or of this man who has been restored but, as I said, God wanted his Son's name to be glorious among all; he wants all to place their trust and hope of all salvation in it.[20] This trust has in the sight of all of you restored soundness of limbs to this man who was deformed from birth.[21] These things not only prove that he whom you think dead is alive, but also show that all hope of salvation must be placed in him alone.

'There is no reason to despair, brethren; all this has happened through God's permission and plan. Human ignorance excuses your sin to some degree. The weakness of the body prevented you from recognizing his divine power, which not even your leaders knew completely, for if they had known, they would never have resolved to crucify the prince of all glory.[22] Thus it was expedient for the salvation of the human race, thus God had determined from eternity,[23] thus he had predicted through the mouth of all the prophets, that the Messiah whom he would at last send to you for your redemption would endure the ultimate suffering.[24] God is not a liar,[25] but has sent the one he had promised to send; as he willed, so has the one been slain whom he willed to be slain. He willed that this victim be sacrificed to expiate the sins of all. He was sacrificed through you, not without guilt on your part, but the guilt would be removed if only you would repent of your error. Thus it will be that the sin you have committed for the good of all will turn into good for you also.[26]

'Pardon is ready and easy: only repent of your evil deeds, not only this one, but all of them, and turn to the new life.[27] Confess Jesus, whom you formerly denied, as king and ruler of the universe. Him whom you condemned as guilty, acknowledge as the source and giver of all innocence; him whom you put to death, believe to be the author of immortality.[28] Now is the time of forgiveness.[29] Hasten meanwhile to repentance and you will find mercy. Thus when he shall come again to judge the living and the dead,[30] and when the Father, who for your sake sent him once in humble form, shall once more send him from on high in the clouds,[31] you will with good trust endure his face, a face that will be terrible and unbearable to those who have not been penitent.[32] But those who here and now believe in the name of Jesus – the one whom the prophets preached to you many years ago, of whom we bring witness according to the oracles of the prophets – will at that time find themselves refreshed[33] by the just judge. For their sins have been blotted out by repentance; they have submitted themselves to him through faith, and the judge has promised salvation to all through repentance and faith in him.

'Thus far those things have occurred which the prophets had predicted must occur. It must not be doubted that God will fulfil with like fidelity all the rest of the things he has promised. Jesus Christ will return, though he will not return immediately, for the gospel of God must first be preached through all the world.[34] Meanwhile he lives in glory, and sits and reigns in heaven until that time about which Joel and Malachi prophesied,[35] – the time when all things will be restored and perfected, after all the events have been completed of which God spoke through the mouth of all his holy prophets who have lived since the world began.[36] They all prophesied about this one man. The authority of Moses is especially weighty among you, for he was your leader when you left Egypt, wandered through the desert, received the Law. And yet he promised you this Jesus of Nazareth whom you slew, speaking thus in the book of Deuteronomy: "The Lord your God will raise up for you from your brethren a prophet like me; you shall hear him in all things, whatsoever he shall say to you. And it shall be that whoever does not hear that prophet shall be destroyed from the people."[37]

'Acknowledge the prophecy of Moses, acknowledge the true Moses, acknowledge Jesus Christ, born from the stock of David, from the tribe of Judah in the city of Bethlehem according to the oracles of the prophets.[38] With him as your leader, God calls you into eternal liberty;[39] through him God delivers a new law, one that is spiritual and evangelical; through him

God offers remission of all sins and eternal salvation. God wishes all to hear him. Everyone who believes does hear. Whoever has believed will be saved. Whoever refuses to believe will be cast out from the fellowship and the name of the Israelites, and will perish beyond recovery, for there is no hope of salvation outside of Jesus.[40] If you believe Moses, embrace Jesus, whom Moses commended to you by his own prophecy. Moses was not the only one to prophesy of Jesus. All the prophets from the time of Samuel to John the Baptist uttered prophecies describing his birth, teaching, miracles, suffering, insults, the cross, burial, resurrection, the ascension into heaven, the sending of the Holy Spirit upon all believers (all these events have clearly taken place), the spread of the gospel through the whole earth, the glorious return of the Lord at the end of the world.

'If you are the sons of the prophets, a claim in which you not unjustly glory, do not distrust their promises. If you are the sons of the patriarchs, understand that to you belongs the covenant which God made with Abraham, saying, "And through your seed all the families[41] of the earth will receive blessing" [Gen 22:18]. He did not provide this blessing in Isaac, who died and did not come to life again, but in Jesus of Nazareth. Of him Isaac was a type, who of his own accord offered himself for a sacrifice,[42] just as Christ in obedience to the Father was sacrificed on the cross. This is the seed of Abraham through which not only all the Israelites but also all the nations of the whole world will, if they believe the gospel, be freed from the curse of sin and obtain this blessing,[43] so that they might receive the heavenly Spirit and be called children of the living God.[44] The promise of God, therefore, does indeed pertain to all the nations of the world, but he nevertheless wanted you to have the honour of its being offered to you first of all. In accordance with the prophecy of Moses he wanted to raise up from your race and to send to you not just a prophet, but his only Son Jesus to confer the blessing God promised Abraham. But this is the blessing: that everyone who obeys the evangelical word turns from wickedness[45] and confesses Jesus the author of salvation.'

Chapter 4

With these and like words, Peter, the divine orator, and John his colleague were urging the people to embrace the gospel.[1] They flattered no one; rather, they persuaded with the testimony of the prophets, striking terror through fear of the future judgment, then again soothing and enticing with an easily available and a ready pardon, and with the certitude of the promised salvation.

In the midst of their exhortation the priests and the captain of the temple,[2] and with them the Sadducees, came up and broke into their salvific discourse. The priests and the captain took it ill that simple men were in control in the temple, teaching the people where it was proper only for rabbis, Pharisees, and scribes to speak,[3] and that the apostles preached so sublimely about Jesus, whom they had put to death as guilty, and whose name they desired effaced. The Sadducees, for their part, were especially galled because Peter and John were preaching that Jesus was alive again after his death and because they promised a resurrection to all through him,[4] for the Sadducees believe neither that there are angels nor that souls survive after the death of the body.[5] Accordingly, they cannot abide talk of resurrection.

Here is another instance of a battle of ungodly priests against the gospel, as Jesus had predicted to his disciples.[6] But just as malice[7] made the glory of Christ shine more brightly the more it struggled against him,[8] so the more they fight against the heralds of the gospel, the more forcefully the power of the evangelical word breaks forth. What happens? There is no discussion; rather, hands are laid upon the apostles. They are dragged off to prison to be led forth the next day, for evening was then approaching. An impious desire possesses the priests to kill the disciples of Jesus then and there, but fear of the people again stood in the way.[9] A pretext is sought for this nefarious crime, so that what they were doing, they might seem to do justly. But just as their wickedness did not prevail against Christ, except when he himself willed to die, so their conspiracy will avail nothing against the disciples of Christ until that day comes[10] which the heavenly Father had appointed for each. For Christ was in the apostles.

Though interrupted by the priests, the discourse of the two apostles was nevertheless not unfruitful, for many of those who had heard the apostolic word were persuaded and believed. The net expands, the mustard seed grows and branches out, the potency of the evangelical yeast spreads:[11] the number of believers had now grown to as many as[12] five thousand men. Recognize that the gospel is acceptable to the common people; seldom do the mighty of this world come to agreement with it.[13] Recognize the success of the gospel: the chief men are led away to prison; they offer no opposition, nor do the people raise an uproar; they have learned only to trust and to obey Christ.

On the next day, a wicked council assembled, a council that agreed in nothing, except to destroy Jesus and to crush the truth.[14] The priests met with the temple wardens[15] and at the same time the elders of the people with the scribes of Jerusalem. In addition to[16] these were Annas the high priest, and Caiaphas, who clung to the former because of their relationship,[17] also

John and Alexander, then foremost among the priests,[18] and, finally, all who belonged to the priestly class, in which at that time the higher each member was in authority, the more wicked he was.[19] Such anxious diligence on the part of the chief men itself clearly proves that this was no ordinary affair they were concerned to restrain. What was there to fear from a few unknown and unlearned disciples of a man who had been condemned and crucified?

Peter and John were led forth from prison and set in their midst like defendants. What ordinary person would not be dumbfounded when he looked upon the packed ranks of so grand a council?[20] In great pride the pontiffs and priests sat there, the princes of religion; then the officers, as well as the elders of the people; no authority was absent. Indeed, they had already seen the harshness and wickedness of the judges in the case of their teacher, Jesus. And yet they stood there with serene and fearless faces. The Lord Jesus had, of course, predicted that all this would happen and had armed their minds against just such events.[21]

Here again recognize, I ask you, an example of the kind of trial by which Jesus was condemned. He was convicted through interrogation;[22] they too, then, are questioned about the lame man who had been healed: 'By what power or in what name do you do this?' They could have searched this out in the temple before they led them to prison; they could have learned it as the people themselves had, since Peter had given a clear account of this deed. But they preferred to begin with insults. Nor was that followed by any investigation of the truth; rather, they seized the opportunity for injury. This was an indication that the priesthood would soon come to an end, since, full of vices as they were, they had no way to protect their authority except by conspiratorial councils, imprisonment, and death.[23]

At this point what does Peter do, the man who thrice denied the Lord at the threats of a maidservant, a mere woman?[24] Does he become terrified? Does he swoon and lose his wits? Does his voice stick in his throat? None of this! Why so? Doubtless, he had become another person. At that time he had been led by the human spirit: he made great promises,[25] and soon rashly forgetting his promises fled and broke his oath. Now, however, he was filled with the Holy Spirit: he pleaded his case from first to last bravely and extemporaneously, moderating his speech with admirable prudence so that freedom should not end in abuse, or softness[26] smack of adulation or fear, but that the eloquence of the entire speech should have only one object – it is through Jesus that salvation comes to all.[27] Accordingly, Peter spoke as follows:

'Princes of the people, and elders, hear me.[28] I indeed wondered why orders had been given to take us to prison when we were guilty of no crime, for princes do not usually throw people into prison except for evil deeds.

Now if, as I see, no charge is preferred and no crime laid to our account, but we are being investigated about a kindness conferred upon this man once crippled and infirm, now sound and whole, I shall not be loath to give an account to you. For it is our duty calmly to give an account of the evangelical faith to everyone who wishes to learn.[29]

'Since what we teach pertains to the salvation of all, whether princes or populace, be it known therefore to you all – not only you who are foremost but to the whole people of Israel – what has happened to this man. Everyone knows that formerly he used to be carried by porters; now you see him standing with us, whole and sound of limb. He has obtained this kindness not by magical arts,[30] or by human power, or by our merits, but through the invocation of the name of our Lord Jesus Christ of Nazareth, whom you, through Pontius Pilate, sent to the cross a few days ago. But God raised him from the dead, gave him immortality, and set him over all things.[31] Therefore, the power of his name now does the same thing in healing and saving people as he himself used to do when he was present on earth. This is, no doubt, what was predicted in the prophecy of the psalm about the stone that was to be cast aside by men but raised up by God, for he is the stone that was rejected by you, the builders of the synagogue.[32] Hence you cast it away as rejected, but God has made it the head of the corner, to hold together by its strength the whole structure of the church, which is to be built from both peoples, gentiles and Israelites.[33]

'Through him the heavenly Father offers salvation to all, nor is there any hope of salvation for anyone except through Jesus. I know that among you the authority of Moses, of the patriarchs, and of the prophets, is pre-eminent and inviolable.[34] But it pleased the Father that salvation should be provided for all through his Son alone; hence also he wanted him to be called Jesus.[35] No other name has been given under heaven, or will be given, by which we must be saved. There is no reason then why you should be astonished that the invocation of this name has been so effectual in this cripple, when by its power eternal salvation is provided for all who invoke it.'

When Peter spoke these words, all who were in that council were astonished as they observed the freedom and the constancy[36] of Peter and John, which manifested itself even in their very countenance, and the realization struck them[37] that these were uneducated and common folk. They wondered whence came so much confidence, whence so much eloquence, whence the knowledge of the prophets. Then they began to recognize them, that they had been followers of Jesus, and they knew in their hearts that they had slain Jesus through envy. Such undaunted liberty on the part of common and unlettered men filled their hearts with great anxiety, for these men were not moved in the slightest either by the punishment that had been inflicted on the

Lord or by the splendour and authority of so distinguished a council. They sat looking at the man himself as he stood there, known to all the people, a man who, though terribly crippled from birth, now walked with spriteliness. The thing had been done suddenly, not in secret but in front of the entrance to the temple, not with magical arts but through the invocation of the name of Jesus, who they now supposed was dead. The deed was too evident to be denied, and there was no occasion for slander, for what is more popular than to restore health freely to a wretched man? So they made no reply to the apostles. In fact, there was nothing to reply, since they neither wished to approve nor were able to disprove what had been done.

Accordingly, the apostles were ordered, along with the man who had been healed, to withdraw from the council. The men of the council deliberated and compared proposals, saying:

'What shall we do with these men, so unformed by letters and so common? For that this outstanding miracle has been wrought through them is too well known to all who live in Jerusalem for us to be able to deny it. If we deny the deed, our only gain will be shame; if we condemn and punish, we shall seem merciless and unjust, and we shall incite the people against us even more.[38] Nothing remains but to adopt a more lenient plan and take care that this evil, however it arose, does not creep abroad and spread further among the people. For once started, pestilences of this kind usually gain more strength and range more widely if you stir them up than if they are left alone. The right decision therefore is to abstain from punishment, but to frighten them with such severe threats that henceforth they speak to no one, whether Jew or someone from another race, about the name of Jesus.'

A more foolish opinion could not have been expressed, but this one pleased the whole council, and they overwhelmingly sided[39] with this view. They had already observed the constancy and courage of the apostles; they saw that the matter was known to the entire people; they understood that it was the name of Jesus that was so effective and so salvific. With what audacity, then, do they order the name suppressed, or hope that it can be, especially when they themselves through the same name may obtain eternal salvation? Such doubtless are the counsels of princes and pontiffs, of priests and nobles, whenever a council assembles in the spirit of man. Sometimes even in such councils there are present those who perceive what is right, but who also see that if they follow it their reputation will be harmed, their property lost, or that they will suffer some other disadvantage of this kind.

When this resolution had been unanimously approved, the apostles were recalled, and commanded in the name of the entire council not to instruct a single mortal in the doctrine of Jesus, not secretly or openly, not in public or in private, not at home or abroad, or to make any mention at all of his name. Oh foolish wisdom of the world![40] They were not able to keep the dead Jesus in the tomb – and they try to entomb a name,[41] though a name is something that invariably becomes better known after death. When with imposing authority the decision of the council was read, Peter and John replied, bravely indeed, but without disdain:

'Whether it is right in the sight of God to obey your commands rather than those of God, you be judge who keep the precepts of the Law. So God through the mouth of the prophets has predicted, so Christ, God's Son, has commanded us, so the heavenly Spirit, which Christ promised to send us from the Father, prompts our minds and prescribes that we proclaim the name of the Lord Jesus Christ for the salvation of all, witnessing to what we have seen and heard.[42] If you have judged aright, you will submit yourselves also to the divine judgment. If not, regardless of your decision, we, at least, cannot but speak what we have seen with our eyes, heard with our ears, and what God, who is to be preferred to any human being, wants proclaimed among all.'

When they received this reply, so manly[43] and so free, those councillors could resort only to threats and efforts to frighten. Oh deplorable council! They do not have evidence with which to persuade; they do not have arguments with which to refute; they do not have the testimonies of Scripture with which to demonstrate their case.[44] Their entire authority lies in threats. Oh the ever fearful conscience of the ungodly! They longed to punish the innocent, the perverse will was there, but princes fear commoners, officers private citizens, so many fear the few, the armed the unarmed, the learned the unlearned. The apostles do not have a retinue. They do not have ranks of officers sworn to them. But they have something which no earthly power can offer: 'In the name of Jesus, rise and walk.' They have the power to do good; they are unequipped to do harm.[45]

And so for the present the apostles were dismissed from that council laden with threats. The chief men had not laid aside their malicious intent, but had postponed it to seek another opportunity. They did not find a way to punish them, and this because of the people, whom they feared while despising God,[46] for everyone extolled with praises what had been done in the healing of the lame man. And what had happened in the presence of all was the more obvious because the man in whom this miracle had been wrought was more than forty years old. He had been born lame, and he had displayed his debility for so many years as a beggar that no one could say in slander that this deformity was simulated or insignificant.

Peter and John were dismissed from the council and returned to their people, who had gathered in the upper room[47] anxious now about the outcome. They described everything in sequence: the charge levelled by the nobles, and their own reply. Here, indeed, mutual love increased their joy. The disciples rejoiced because the chief apostles had been released; the apostles rejoiced that through the kindness of the Lord this joy had come to the disciples.[48] This is how God blends everything for his servants: he mixes the happy with the sad, so that they might be able to endure, while they in turn give thanks for the happy things and supplicate the Lord for the sad. Therefore, after the assembly had heard the apostles' story, in complete accord they raised their voices to the Lord, by whose kindness the gospel had begun to succeed, and said:

'Lord God almighty,[49] by your word you created the heaven, the earth, and the sea, and whatever is in them; your most holy will no human force can resist, your eternal decrees no human conspiracy overturn. Long ago your Holy Spirit through the mouth of David – our patriarch, your worshipper[50] – foretold that what we now see happening would come to pass, saying, "Why did the gentiles rage and the peoples imagine vain things? The kings of the earth stood up and the rulers were gathered together against the Lord and against his Christ" [Ps 2:1–2].

'We acknowledge the reliability of the oracle. What David, inspired by your Holy Spirit, saw would come to pass, we see in fact both come to pass and coming to pass. For truly in this city,[51] which has a profession of piety, the kings of the earth were gathered together against your holy Son[52] Jesus, the leader, and the teacher of all piety, whom you anointed with heavenly oil – Herod and Pontius Pilate, along with the nations and the peoples of Israel.[53] With impious counsels they plotted to do what you, in your invincible power and eternal wisdom, had determined would be done for the salvation of the human race. Whoever conspires against your Son Jesus, whom you sent, conspires against you.[54] And behold, again a crowded council of the chief men gathers against the holy name of your Son Jesus. But just as you raised from the dead the Jesus they had slain, and took him to heaven to share in your rule, laughing at their councils,[55] so also now look upon their threats, do not let them prevail, but give to your servants strength and confidence, that they might speak out the word of the gospel with the utmost boldness. This is not the word of men, but your word, brought down to us on earth from you through your Son.[56]

'And just as the miracle of the cure of the crippled man has led many to profess the name of Jesus while terrifying the princes who have conspired against the glory of Jesus, so also in the future, let your almighty hand be upon them so that, as others too are healed and like miracles and wonders wrought through the holy name of your Son[57] Jesus, the glory of your gospel may shine forth more widely and brightly, while those will rage in vain who rebel against you and your Son.'

When with one heart they had prayed thus, the place was shaken in which they were assembled. By this sign the Lord showed that their prayers were heard and their hopes would be fulfilled. Nothing is so effective as the supplication of a church in harmony, for it has to be a mighty force to shake the immovable earth.[58] This was no empty sign: the power of the Holy Spirit was renewed and increased in all, then and there, so that not only did they not conceal the evangelical doctrine because of the threats of the nobles, but they proclaimed the name of the Lord Jesus more freely and more courageously,[59] and even more of their number did so than before. Such is the nature of evangelical progress that, just as saffron and some other things are more productive through injury,[60] so it rises up and forces its way out against a world that is bearing down upon it:[61] already, within a few days the number of those professing the name of Jesus had grown large.

That this was not a merely human fellowship you can see from the fact that there was among so many no desire for distinction, no envy, no quarrelling, no contention,[62] but so great was their agreement, so profound their peace that you could say they all were of one heart and one soul. For they now ceased to be led each by his own spirit, which differs so much in different people that you scarcely find two blood-brothers who agree. But all are ruled by the one Spirit of Jesus. Hence among so many people otherwise unlike in sex, age, and fortune, unanimity was so great that they not only had in common all the things usually shared at no cost to the dispenser, such as instruction, counsel, admonition, comfort, exhortation;[63] they also had in common the resources that are shared with others only at a cost to their owner – for which reason it would be hard to find people who maintain their liberality at this point. But among the Christians there was so much sharing of these goods also that no one even called any of the things he possessed his own. Accordingly, the one who gave from his own resources asked no thanks from those with whom he shared, because he judged that what he gave belonged to the one who had need, and he thought himself unjust and a robber if he kept for himself what a brother's need demanded.[64]

For their part, the apostles, who were the nobles, so to speak, of this new city, poor in possessions but rich in the gifts of the Spirit, from day to day increased the multitude more and more. With great strength of heart, and with great power in miracles, they gave witness to the resurrection of our Lord Jesus Christ,[65] for it was first of all through the witness of miracles that people had to be persuaded of this. Many had seen him die, and not a few knew he had been buried. Accordingly, this new people lived most happily under their most courageous leaders; their concord made up for what they lacked in material resources. Although many were poor, still no one among them was in need. As many as were possessors of lands or houses sold them and brought the price of the things sold and laid it at the feet of the apostles. They wanted the wealth they held in common to be distributed at the discretion of those they regarded as fathers. Moreover, the candour of those who brought the profit from the sale of their possessions was matched by the honesty of those who distributed it. Trustworthiness in money-managers is rare. Here distribution was made without respect of persons according to the need of each.

Among this company was Joseph,[66] to whom the apostles gave the surname Barnabas, which in Aramaic means 'son of consolation.'[67] His tribe was Levi, his native land Cyprus. Through his large contributions, this man stood out among the rest; hence because of the joy his addition brought to the multitude he was called Barnabas. He was an example to many to imitate evangelical generosity, for since he had an estate in Cyprus, he sold it, brought the money, and laid it at the apostles' feet as though it were a trifle, to be treated with disdain.[68] Such, however, was the holiness of the apostles that they plucked therefrom for themselves nothing more than the rest received.[69]

Chapter 5

Just as the straightforward candour of Barnabas stirred many to emulate his generosity, so an example was provided to discourage anyone from mixing deliberate deceit with spiritual work.[1] For the Spirit loves simplicity of heart and hates every pretence and disguise. Thus among the twelve apostles the example of Judas was provided so that no one should rely upon himself but persevere in his duty with all diligence.[2] Now there was in this company[3] a certain man named Ananias, who corresponded all too little to his name because he himself responded all too little to the grace of God.[4] He had a wife named Sapphira, a woman like her husband. So when Ananias saw the straightforward and spontaneous generosity of others extolled among everyone, eager for glory more than godliness, he sold his land, and withdrew and set aside a certain portion of the sale price. His wife was aware of this and approved. His intent was to divide the money and with one portion to purchase praise and the impression of piety, but to save the other portion for himself in case some need should arise. Obviously, he distrusted the Holy Spirit, and was looking out for himself more than for the company of brethren. He thought to himself, 'If the rest come to face starvation, I at least have looked out for myself.' This was not the thought of one trusting Christ with his whole heart, for Christ had promised never to fail those who seek the kingdom of God and his righteousness;[5] nor was it the thought of a person who had one heart and one soul with the others.[6]

And so when he had brought to the apostle's feet a part of the money from the land he had sold, Peter, full of the divine Spirit and thus inspired, perceived the impious pretence of the man, and said:

'Ananias, you once dedicated yourself to the Holy Spirit, and you have recognized his power through so many signs. Why, then, has the spirit of Satan again filled[7] your heart so that you have secretly withdrawn some of the money from your estate – as though to mock with a lie the Holy Spirit, who cannot be deceived[8] – and have introduced into this congregation this most pernicious example of all? If we had forced you against your will to sell your land, you would perhaps have some reason to dissemble; now, since you have done this deed of your own accord, what was the point of spoiling a model of generosity with a coating of deceit? Would your estate not have remained entirely yours if you had wished? Even after you had sold it, could you not have kept all the money for yourself? One lauds the candour of those who willingly disclose what they have. We compel no one, however, to do this against his will.[9] Whatever gave you the idea to deceive in this business? You have not lied to men but to God! Now, if you believe that God can be deceived, you think of him irreverently, but if you believe that nothing is concealed from him, either you despise his justice or you suppose that he looks with favour on deceit.'

Ananias realized that his fraudulent intent was in no way eluding the apostles, and smitten by so severe a rebuke, he suddenly collapsed and breathed his last. One perished out of consideration for the welfare of the many. For when the report of this event spread to the rest, it put great fear into all lest they should dare something similar against the Holy Spirit.[10] The young men arose, removed the corpse, carried it out, and buried it. Ananias did not deserve burial, but he had to be removed so as not to pollute a pure and holy congregation.[11]

Here perhaps it will occur to someone to wonder at Peter's harshness towards Ananias, when a little while ago he had with so much gentleness held out the promise of pardon to those who had crucified Jesus, attributing their deed to ignorance and offering eternal salvation to those who repented.[12] Here, because a little bit of money was withheld in an otherwise generous act, a fierce rebuke, and not a hope of pardon is extended. Doubtless the Lord Jesus, who had commanded that everyone be invited to salvation through baptism and the forgiveness of all their sins, wished to show by the destruction of a few how much more serious it is to fall back into sin after the grace and light of the gospel have been received – not now through thoughtlessness and ignorance, but by deliberate pretence.[13] Peter knew that the chief danger to evangelical sincerity would spring from hypocrisy and avarice, and for this reason, a striking example was produced immediately, at the very beginning of the nascent church. Through this example all might be warned that no one who imitated Ananias would escape divine vengeance,[14] even if punishment did not immediately fall upon the guilty person. The issue here was not the loss of money, but the absence of confidence in God and the mockery of the Holy Spirit. Moreover, Peter did not inflict the punishment but poured upon Ananias the acrimony of rebuke to heal him.[15] But because Ananias did not burst into tears, did not utter a word of repentance, he was smitten by the vengeance of God. By the wonderful clemency of God, one was smitten that many might be saved. An example of justice was set forth in the one who perished; the gift of mercy was poured out abundantly upon the many who by his example took care not to sin.

An interval of almost three hours passed, and lo, Ananias' wife entered, not knowing what had happened to her husband, inasmuch as people are usually the last to find out about their own domestic troubles. She was aware of her husband's deceit, ready to claim also for herself a share of false praise. To her impious thoughts Peter answered and said, 'Tell me, woman,[16] did you sell the land for so much and not for more than this price?' She, too much like her husband, shamelessly replied, 'Yes, we sold it for so much.' Then Peter said to her:

'Why have you and your husband conspired to tempt with a lie, not us, but the Spirit of the Lord whom you see working in us? Since you were willing to be your husband's associate in this ungodly deceit, you will also share in his punishment.[17] Behold, the feet of those who have buried your husband are at the door; you also they will carry out.'

At this word the woman immediately collapsed and breathed her last. At the same time the young men entered and found the woman dead; accordingly, they carried her out and buried her beside her husband. It was a harsh example, but salvific, and put forth only once by the apostles. And yet Peter, more kindly than anything, did not inflict punishment here, but inspired by the Spirit, declared it. In those days, Peter knew by the impulse of the divine Spirit what had been done and what would happen. Even if apostolic men[18] are capable of being deceived – for this gift of the Spirit which Peter then possessed is not continual for all[19] – nevertheless, God, whom nothing escapes, will punish those who through deception mock such men. Observe now the good result of a bad event: from the just death of the two, a great fear arose throughout the whole church of the believers;[20] indeed, alarm at this example struck others also who had not yet come to believe.

Moreover, many mighty miracles were wrought among the people by the apostles that it might be clear to all that this was not a matter of human strength but of divine power. All who adhered to the gospel remained with one accord in the portico of Solomon. For they no longer desired to remain hidden, but it was time the candle set on the candlestick gave light to all who entered the house.[21] None of the rest, that is, of those who had not yet through baptism enlisted in service,[22] dared to join them. For they saw a people sacred to God, and from a certain reverence kept away from their assembly, as the profane are accustomed to keep their distance from things consecrated to the temple.[23] The people did not hate them, but respected and revered them because of the extraordinary power of God resplendent in them. And yet the example of Ananias and Sapphira struck terror into many, so that no one joined them under pretence.[24]

Thereupon the multitude of those believing in the Lord daily grew larger and larger, men as well as women, so much so that everywhere they put their sick out in the streets, and those who were unable to walk on their own feet because of the severity of their disease they laid out in public on beds and pallets, so that when Peter approached even his shadow might fall upon one of them as he passed by.[25] Here, doubtless, the promise of the Lord Jesus was fulfilled, who had said of his disciples, 'And greater things than these will they do.'[26] Jesus healed a few people by a touch on the hem of his garment;[27] he healed no one by contact with his shadow. Daily the fame of the miracles spread further so that a great throng of people from the cities round about also hastened to Jerusalem, bringing with them people afflicted with various diseases and tormented by unclean spirits. They all were healed. It is appropriate to note, in the midst of such remarkable success, the invincible modesty of the apostles, who claimed no glory from this for themselves, but gave all the praise to the name of the Lord Jesus.[28]

When in this way the name of Jesus Christ was felicitously gaining fame and the fragrance of evangelical teaching was daily spreading further, Annas the high priest of a false religion did not accept the growth of the true religion. Those who belonged to the party of the Sadducees especially adhered to him more than the others because the apostles bore witness primarily to the resurrection of our Lord Jesus Christ.[29] This witness made the Pharisees more mild, who, against the Sadducees, affirm the resurrection.

It had been decided that the movement which had arisen should be put to sleep by pretending it was not there.[30] But malice overcame counsel and madness drove out fear. For the high priest, moved by satanic envy, along with the Sadducees laid hands on the apostles and put them not now in private custody, as though to await examination, but in the public jail as though caught in manifest crime.[31] They had chosen a prison exceptionally well secured so that the apostles could neither slip out of it nor be rescued by a popular uprising. But the word of the gospel can be neither chained nor imprisoned by human counsels. Jesus, protector of his own, sent his angel, who unlocked the gates of the prison by night, led them out, and said:

'Do not let the malice[32] of the priests confound you; rather, continue in the direction you have begun with so much the more constancy. Go, stand in the temple itself and preach to the people whatever he commanded you to preach among all the nations of the world. There once was a time when he forbade that he be proclaimed[33] as the Christ. Now that time is at hand about which he said to you, "Nothing is hidden which shall not be revealed; and what you now hear in whispers, proclaim from the house-tops." '[34]

The apostles, heartened the more by this exhortation of the angel, came at daybreak into the temple and, in their customary manner, taught the populous crowd. The high priest, however, not knowing what had happened in the night through the angel, came into the council room attended by the Sadducees and those who, he thought, were sure supporters of his view. There the whole council of priests, temple wardens,[35] along with the entire order of elders[36] of the people of Israel had been convened; for they had now determined to take a harsher stand against them, as they had become more annoyed because of the apostles' defiance. Consider here, for a moment, reader, the malicious impudence of the priests, who had no legitimate accusation to bring against the apostles, yet took whatever measures they pleased, in a packed council, so that what was impious might seem just and right from the very fact that it had been decided by the agreement of the entire council.

When the chief men had with proud grandeur each taken his proper seat, officers were sent to lead the defendants from prison and to present them in the assembly. They came to the prison. They found the guards on the alert at the prison gate. They opened the gate,[37] entered, and found none of the apostles, and not a trace of how they had escaped. Accordingly, the attendants return to the council and report what they had seen: 'The prison,' they said, 'we did indeed find securely shut with utmost care and the guards on duty at the gate. But when we opened the gate and entered, we came upon no one there.' This profoundly upset everyone, especially those who were the temple wardens and the chief priests, and now they began to waver in their counsel, uncertain where this affair would end. Meanwhile, as they hesitate, as they deliberate, as they tremble, someone interrupts to upset them even more with his melancholy message. 'Behold,' he says, 'those men whom you shut up yesterday in the prison are now standing in the temple and are teaching great numbers of the people.'

Then, following a decision voted by the priests, the temple wardens – for it was their special responsibility to see that nothing improper was done in the temple[38] – went to the temple, taking along an escort of assistants, since they anticipated violence from the people. They find things as reported: the apostles were standing in the temple preaching a sermon about Jesus to a full crowd. Nevertheless they did not lay hands on them as they had done before, for they saw the numerous crowd of people and were afraid they would be stoned if a riot broke out. But that was not the sort of crowd to offer violence, nor were the apostles such as to want to be defended by force. Unbroken firmness of mind there was, but without ferocity. The apostles see those who had the previous day thrown them into prison. Yet they have no fear, they do not flee, they do not break off from their gospel discourse until the captain of the temple persuades them with calm words to come to the council. The apostles obeyed so they should not seem to despise public authority.[39] The Lord had taught them not to refuse to go when summoned, but to speak undaunted.[40] They come to the council; they are set in the midst of so grand an assembly – two fishermen with[41] a retinue like themselves. Then Annas, chief of all the priests, with great authority, and no less haughtiness, began thus:

'At the last council, did we not[42] emphatically and on the authority of these great men charge you not to continue to teach the people, and not to make any mention of the name of Jesus to any person – whether foreigner or Jew, either in public or in private – a name we want abolished?[43] And here you are, despising the authority of the entire council: not only did you not keep silence, but you have preached even more ardently, so much so that you have filled all Jerusalem with your doctrine, while rumour of the things you are doing has found its way to neighbouring cities also. You wish, then, with malicious zeal to fasten upon us the odium of that man's death, for you proclaim openly that he was slain by us, which cannot be denied; you preach that this same man was just and holy and approved by God; you perform miracles in his name. In effect, you are slandering us before the crowds and condemning us for impiety as the ones who put such a person to death.'

This was the speech of the high priest. It contained no element of a just defence. It only terrified by its authority, in order that what was true and to be proclaimed to all for the salvation of everyone might be silenced to preserve the reputation of the ungodly.

Now on the other side let us hear the fisherman and evangelical pontiff replying in[44] the name of all the apostles with a dauntless intrepidity tempered, however, by mildness:[45]

'Distinguished pontiff,' he said, 'captain,[46] elders, and you other honourable men who sit on this council, in no way do we despise your authority, but we put divine authority before human, and we replied that we would do so when you forbade us to mention the name of Jesus.[47] I do not believe there is anyone in this council who thinks it right that we disregard the commands of God because of human prohibitions and, while fearing your anger, incur the wrath of God. If your commands agreed with the will of God, we would gladly satisfy both you and him. Now since your prohibitions completely contradict his orders, and since we cannot satisfy both, we prefer to obey God rather than men. We do not desire to bring hatred on anyone through the name of Jesus, but to win all to salvation. And it is more expedient for you also to submit your authority to the divine will than to drive us against our will to the point where we fight against it.

'The remission of sins is available to everyone if he embraces the truth of the gospel, comes to his senses again, and repents.[48] As we explained to you earlier, that truth is this: the God of our fathers, whom you worship with us, and we with you,[49] has raised from the dead his Son Jesus, whom you nailed to the cross and killed. Thus it had been determined by the divine plan, thus it had been predicted by the prophets, that one person should die for the salvation of the world.[50] This man was slain by men, as the frailty of his corporeal condition allowed,[51] but God called him back from the dead and by his power has raised him to this glory, that he should be leader and author[52] of salvation for all, but in the first place for the people of Israel. Through him remission of all sins has been provided for all who are penitent for[53] their evil acts and profess his name. We are witnesses[54] of the things whereof we speak: before he died, we lived with him in household companionship, and when after death, he was alive again we heard, saw, and touched him[55] until, with all of us looking on, he ascended into heaven. But if our testimony has little weight with you, the Holy Spirit gives the same witness,[56] the Spirit which as you see he pours out on all who obey the gospel. You hear the strange tongues, you see miracles performed. Nothing here is from us. It is the Spirit of Jesus who exerts his power through his ministers.'[57]

This truly apostolic speech, which should either have terrified them with the fear of punishment or allured them with the hope of ready salvation, exasperated them even more, so much so that they were bursting with anger and took counsel together to kill them. The priests had already become accustomed to homicide, and from slaughtering beasts in the temple they had derived this one advantage, that they more easily cut the throats of men also. No talk here of divine Scripture, no instruction, no reasoning; only, 'So we order, so we wish, either obey or die!'

Gamaliel, of the party of the Pharisees, sat in that council. It was at his feet that the apostle Paul learned the Law;[58] he was a man held in the highest esteem among all the people of Israel because of his singular wisdom and his outstanding knowledge of the Law. When he saw that they were moving towards desperate counsels, he rose and demanded that they ask the apostles to withdraw from the council for a little while. When they had done so, he spoke thus before the session:

'Men of Israel, do not rush into a hasty plan, or rashly make a resolution of which you will later repent in vain, but consider most carefully the decision you are making about these men. Learn from the past what you should resolve for the future. I shall not recall examples from antiquity. What I shall speak of has happened within the memory of you all. Some time ago Theudas arose, a magician and impostor; by making boastful pretensions before the populace and promises of wonderful things, he attracted quite a large number of men to his party, close to four hundred. Since this affair arose from the wicked cunning of a man, it came to an unhappy end, for he himself was punished and all who had joined him – either killed or captured. Thus all were scattered and the movement came to nothing.[59] After him Judas arose, a Galilean, a native of the same country as those about whom you are now deliberating; it was at that time when, as a result of the edict of Caesar Augustus, a census of the whole world was taken. And since this fellow taught what pleased the people, that it was not right for a people dedicated to God to pay tribute to the idolatrous Caesars, he attracted a good part of the populace to himself. The leader of this party himself perished and all who had joined him were scattered.[60]

'My opinion, then, is this: your action will be better considered if you spare these men and let them go, since so far they have harmed no one. For if what they are beginning or attempting has proceeded from human counsel, it will disappear of its own accord, but if God is the author of this remarkable business, it would be both impious to wish to destroy what is being done when God is the originator (for what else is this than to fight against God?), and also imprudent to want to try to achieve what you cannot – for who will resist the will of God?'[61]

This opinion had so much effect on the council that the decision to kill the apostles was deferred to another time, and they supported Gamaliel's recommendation to this extent: they did not entirely spare the apostles, but they called together all twelve of them, and after having them beaten, ordered them to make no mention thereafter of the name of Jesus. Satisfied with this punishment, they dismissed them, hoping that those who had not obeyed commands and threats would be sensible if admonished by physical torture: they judged the apostles – lowly and common in appearance – from the character of barbarians, who are corrected by blows.

However, the force of the evangelical spirit gains strength from evils of this kind. The apostles recognized that the word Jesus had spoken was true, that they would be haled into court and beaten in the synagogues, not because of any wrongdoing, but because of their profession of the salvific name. So they departed from the presence of the council eager and joyful, while the disgrace of the rods, which others thought unbearable, they considered a glory for themselves, because God was acknowledging his apostles, whom he had thought worthy of the honour of having insults inflicted on their persons for the name of his Son.[62] They remembered that Jesus had earlier admonished them, 'Rejoice and be glad, for great is your reward in heaven' [Matt 5:12].[63] This punishment and warning given them by the chief men made them no more reticent to preach the name of Jesus. On the contrary, they actually became more eager:[64] both publicly in the temple and privately in individual homes they taught unceasingly what they had received from the Lord Jesus,[65] and brought to all the joyful message that he was the true Messiah through whom all must be saved.

Chapter 6

During that time, when the number of disciples was daily growing (for those who later came to be called Christians were then called disciples),[1] there arose a murmuring of the Greeks against the Hebrews – the 'Greeks' were Jews born not in Judaea but among the gentiles.[2] The cause of the grumbling arose from piety. For since the apostles took with them some women who ministered to them, the Greeks were grieved that their widows did not receive the same honour, namely, that they be permitted to attend to the apostles and disciples in the daily ministry,[3] for they understood this to be a position of respect. This was the first case of ambition in the church. And yet, that you might understand how discord, however trifling, very much displeases a good shepherd, the twelve apostles at once called together the multitude of disciples – thus decisions taken with the consent of all might have the greater authority[4] – and spoke in this manner:

'We see that some sort of grumbling has arisen among us[5] over the ministry of the women. We must make some provision, therefore, so that we are not repeatedly interrupted by lighter concerns of this kind, since we are surely intended for a higher function. The Lord has enjoined us to teach the gospel; it will not do for us to neglect the responsibility assigned to us and to serve tables. Just as in a body there are various members and each member performs its own duty, so unrest and disorder cannot be avoided in so large a crowd unless different functions are distributed to different persons, and in such a way that all things are directed to the advantage of the whole body. The eye does not see for itself alone, but for all the members; the hands do not labour for themselves only, but for the entire body.[6] Accordingly, brethren, look about from among your number for seven men of proven integrity,[7] full of the Holy Spirit and endowed with exceptional wisdom, to whom we can with your approval delegate this work in which we ourselves are thus far occupied, but not without some cost to our evangelical service.[8] Having thus acquired some relief through their help, we shall devote ourselves to those activities which are especially ours: prayer and the ministry of the word of evangelical doctrine. They will assume the care of feeding bodies; we shall be free to feed your souls.'

This speech pleased the whole multitude. Therefore, seven men were chosen by common agreement of the congregation: Stephen, of outstanding faith and full of the Holy Spirit, Philip, Prochorus, Nicanor, Timon, Parmenas and Nicolaus, a native of Antioch and a proselyte.[9] When these had been elected, the congregation brought them before the apostles so that their authority might sanction what had been done.[10] The apostles poured out prayers to God in their customary way and laid their hands upon them – for sacred ministries were first assigned by this rite , an example taken from the Lord Jesus, who was accustomed to lay his hands on those he blessed.[11] If anyone asks what need there was of these rites for appointing ministers to be in charge of the table, let him know that handling money is indeed a secular and extremely common service, but one that requires an incorruptible fidelity.[12] Judas is a witness – his mind, corrupted by avarice, drove him to betray his Lord. At that time, moreover, since they were prescribing for others too what should be done in matters of this kind, authority also had to be given to them so that everyone would obey them as allies and helpers of the apostles. Besides, the banquets of the disciples were not like those of the common herd, but whenever they took food they did so with great religious devotion. For them, all bread when it was broken represented the body of the Lord, all wine pointed to the Lord's blood.[13] Lastly, both the Lord's body and the blood of the Lord were administered to the multitude by the deacons; and if sometimes they were free in the course of their ministry, these also preached the evangelical word, inasmuch as they were next to the apostles.[14]

By these means it came about that the evangelical doctrine was daily spread further and further, and the number of disciples at Jerusalem was multiplied with great success. For not only did many of the common folk assent to the gospel, but even several from the order of priests, who had previously conspired against Christ and his apostles, were moved by repentance, and laying aside their pride, submitted themselves to the gospel yoke.[15]

Among the deacons the piety of Stephen especially shone out. He conducted himself in his assigned duty in such a way that because of the exceptional gentleness of his character he enjoyed the highest degree of favour[16] among the whole multitude of believers. Towards those who were rebelling against the gospel he displayed a strong and invincible mind, so that rivalling even the powers of the apostles, he performed many great miracles among the people. Since, however, outstanding virtue[17] always draws envy to itself, just as the north-east wind brings the storm-clouds,[18] there arose against Stephen certain ones from various 'societies':[19] one of these is called [the society of] the Libertines, another the Cyrenians, another the Alexandrians, another [the society] of those who had come from Cilicia and Asia, for the Jews had been dispersed above all to these places that are close to Syria.[20] All of them, as though conspiring together, rose up against Stephen and disputed against him. However many, they were not able to withstand the wisdom of one young man and the force within his breast, because the Holy Spirit, with which he was filled, spoke through him.[21]

Recognize at this point the way of the wicked. When they come away from a disputation, inferior in the truth on their side, they take refuge in lies, and overcome by the wisdom of the Spirit, they turn to diabolical deception. For they secretly induced certain men to say that they had heard Stephen uttering blasphemous words against Moses and God. Now among the Jews there is no more capital charge than blasphemy, and none more terrible in the eyes of the people.[22] Recognize here, reader, the same machinations against the servant as there were against the Lord: talebearers are suborned so that those offended should not appear to wish to avenge their own vexation because they had left the disputation defeated. A terrible charge is sought, and religious zeal is a cloak for malice.[23] These sycophants, brought in as they were under cover, so stirred up the people along with the elders and scribes against Stephen that in a concerted attack they seized Stephen and dragged him into the council.

Here witnesses came forth, bribed to act a part and to say:

'This fellow makes no end of spewing out blasphemies[24] against the place[25] sacred and venerable to us all, and against the law of Moses delivered to us by God. For we have heard him say that this Jesus of Nazareth will tear down this place and change the customs Moses delivered to us.'

Stephen had said, on the basis of the apostles' report, that Jesus had predicted that this temple and city would be utterly destroyed by enemies, because of the unbelief of the race.[26] They turned this statement into a malicious charge. You might say that these were the very ones who, in accusing Jesus, said, 'We have heard him say, "I will destroy this temple and within three days I will raise up another." '[27] In the face of this terrible accusation, Stephen, aware of his innocence, was so unshaken that the innocence of his heart shone out even in his very countenance. If the mind is conscious of guilt, the case is fraught with fear. This appearance of self-possession at once exposed the impudence of the false accusers. For those who sat in that council, looking upon him and noting with what boldness he heard the charge cast against him, saw that he was neither downcast nor white with terror – so much so that his aspect seemed to present something superhuman and an almost angelic ardour and majesty.

Then[28] the high priest, in order that here too he might put up a show of a legitimate trial, just as he had done in condemning Jesus,[29] asked the defendant whether he had anything to reply to these charges and whether he admitted the charge laid against him. Then Stephen, inspired by the divine Spirit, began to make his defence in the following manner, seeking the beginning in the distant past.

Chapter 7

'My fellow men[1] – all of you who are present, whether brothers by race or fathers through age and authority – you have patiently heard those who falsely accuse me; hear me also speaking in defence of the truth. We are not insolent towards either God, or Moses, or this temple, but in harmony with Moses we extol the glory of God, and, as we have been ordered by God, we are building a spiritual temple in which God, who is spirit, takes a special delight.[2] It is not blasphemy to set forth to the best of our ability what Moses sketched out in figures; what the prophets, inspired by the Spirit of God, predicted; what the Son of God, sent to earth on this account, both began and entrusted to his followers to complete; what the Holy Spirit now continues for the salvation of all races through those who believe the gospel. But it is impiety, it is blasphemy, to struggle so obstinately against the will of God, a will so manifest, so benign. This, indeed, is what this race began not in recent times to do, but what it already long ago set out to do, and has never ceased doing. Thus it should seem neither strange nor unjust, if it turns out as Jesus predicted it would, namely, that this temple in which you glory, this state in which you rule, the priesthood, the Law, which you misuse for your gain and glory, should be taken from you;[3] and that this glory should be transferred to those who through evangelical faith worship God in a pure way, and keep the spiritual law, and offer themselves a living and holy temple for the Holy Spirit.[4] It was to this that God in so many ways summoned our ancestors; yet he has always been spurned by this rebellious and obstinate people.[5]

'To begin from the first patriarch of this race – if only those who boast that they are his sons would imitate his obedience![6] God, to whom all glory is owed,[7] and whom we devotedly worship with you,[8] long ago appeared to our forefather Abraham when he was in Mesopotamia, before he dwelt in Charan, and said to him, "Go forth out of your country and from your kindred, and come into the land that I shall show you." [Gen 12:1]. Obeying the commands of God, he went out from the land of the Chaldaeans and began to dwell in Charan, ready to move on when a suitable opportunity arose. Again, God brought him from there to this land which you now inhabit; he did so after the death of his father Terah on account of whose old age he had delayed emigration.[9] God brought him to this place, however, as a sojourner and a resident alien, giving him no inheritance here, so that he possessed in this land not even so much as a footprint, unless it was bought with cash. But God promised that he would give the possession of this land to his descendants after his death, though at that time Abraham had no son. Though this seemed incredible, nevertheless Abraham believed and God fulfilled,[10] just as in other things, too, which God has foretold, he has been found true. For at that time, he spoke to him thus:

'"Your seed will be alien residents in a foreign land, and the peoples among whom your descendants will reside will bring them into bondage and will treat them harshly for four hundred and thirty years.[11] At length I shall deliver them from slavery, and the nation to whom they have been in bondage I shall judge and punish," says the Lord. "Then, free from the servitude of men, they shall serve me in this place."[12]

'And he gave circumcision to Abraham as a seal of the covenant, the more to claim his people as his own. Thus, in reliance upon the promises of God, he begot Isaac, and mindful of his agreement, he circumcised the boy on the eighth day after his birth; Isaac in turn circumcised[13] Jacob, Jacob his twelve sons, the patriarchs of our race. Among these were some who were unmindful of the divine covenant and, moved by envy, they devised against their brother Joseph what their descendants devised against Jesus of Nazareth: they cast him into a cistern, then sold him to merchants who took him to Egypt.[14] But just as God raised Jesus when he had been slain and lifted him up when he had been cast down, so at that time he delivered Joseph from all his sufferings, and he caused him, through his character and his skill in divining,[15] to find favour with Pharaoh the king of Egypt, so that he set him over all of Egypt and over his own house.

'But a famine arose throughout the land of Egypt and of Canaan, and severe suffering, so that our fathers found nothing to eat. When Jacob learned that there was an abundance of grain in Egypt he sent our fathers there to bring back grain. When he had sent them there a second time for the same reason, Joseph was recognized by his brothers. It became known to Pharaoh also that he was a Hebrew and that he had a father and eleven brothers living. Joseph therefore sent for his father Jacob and all his kindred to come to Egypt so that they should not be in need. They were seventy-five in number.[16] So Jacob emigrated to Egypt, and he himself died, with his twelve sons, our fathers; and they were buried in the tomb that Abraham had bought for a hundred shekels of silver from the sons of Hamor, the son of Shechem.[17] None of these so far possessed any of the land promised to the descendants of Abraham.

'However, as the time was now at hand when God would fulfil what he had promised to Abraham, the people of the Hebrews grew and multiplied in Egypt until Pharaoh died and another king succeeded him[18] who had less regard for Joseph than was to be expected. This king feared that the Hebrew people would increase too much. He bore down harshly upon our race, and cruelly vexed our fathers, warning midwives by an edict to expose male infants, so that they could not live.[19] At this time Moses was born, against whom these men falsely declare that I have uttered blasphemy.[20] He was a fair child in the eyes of God,[21] who did not allow him to perish; rather he was brought up secretly for three months in his father's house. However, through fear of the royal edict he was put out in the Nile in a little basket daubed with pitch.[22] By chance the daughter of Pharaoh took him up, captivated by the baby's comeliness, and brought him up as a son in her own home. Moses was accordingly regarded as an Egyptian; from his earliest years he was educated in all the wisdom of the Egyptians and was powerful both in words and in deeds.

'Afterwards, when Moses had now completed his fortieth year, it occurred to him to visit his brethren [the sons] of Israel,[23] for he was filled with love towards his own race. While he was staying with them, he saw a certain Israelite suffer an injury at the hands of an Egyptian, and, already then showing the natural characteristics of a good leader,[24] he took vengeance on behalf of the Hebrew by killing the Egyptian. He thought it was already known to the Hebrews that God had determined to save his people through him, and to deliver them from the bondage of Pharaoh. And here Moses was the type of Jesus of Nazareth, whom God has truly chosen to redeem all from the bondage of their sins. But just as the Israelites did not perceive this in Jesus, so they did not perceive it then in Moses.[25] On the next day he was again visiting his people, and came upon two Israelites quarrelling with one another. Interrupting the fight he tried to restore harmony, saying, "What are you doing, men? Since you are brethren and belong to the same race, why do you injure one another?" However, the one who was doing his neighbour wrong thrust the peacemaker away saying, "Why do you meddle in our affair? Who made you a ruler and a judge over us? Do you want to kill me also, as you killed the Egyptian yesterday?" Here at the very beginning there was found among the Israelites the sort of man who was to rebel against Moses, although Moses acted under the inspiration of the Spirit. Hearing this, and perceiving that the matter was not a secret, Moses, in fear of the Egyptians, fled to the land of Madian,[26] where he begot two sons.

'After forty years an angel of the Lord[27] appeared to Moses in the wilderness of Mount Sinai from a bramble-bush which seemed to be on fire.

Moses was astonished at this spectacle and attempted to draw closer to see what this was. But the voice of the Lord forbade him, crying out from the bush: "I," he said, "am the God of your fathers, the God of Abraham, and the God of Isaac, and the God of Jacob."[28] When he heard this name, Moses trembled, and did not dare to look more closely. Then the Lord said, "Take your shoes off your feet, for the place whereon you stand is holy ground." Moses obeyed the Lord. Then the Lord continued to speak: "I have carefully observed[29] the affliction of the people that are in Egypt and have heard the groaning of my people. Therefore, since I have pitied them, I have come down to deliver them. Now, then, attend carefully, and for this cause I shall send you to Egypt" [Exod 3:6-8].

'Notice how clearly Jesus of Nazareth has been represented in Moses. The people of Israel refused Moses, who was still unknown, saying, "Who made you a ruler and a judge over us?" In the same way, Jesus heard from our people, "By whose authority do you do this and who gave you this authority?"[30] They did not yet know that God at that time[31] through pity for our race sent the leader and prince of liberty, and the author of eternal life.[32] And, indeed, God exalted Moses, though despised by his own, and made him leader, ruler, and liberator of his people, and the power of the angel who appeared to him in the burning bush was present to assist him.[33] By Moses' help God led his people out of Egypt, working many miracles and wonders in the land of Egypt, next in the Red Sea, finally, in the wilderness also throughout the forty years. What Moses was to one people, this, truly, Jesus of Nazareth is to all who are willing to follow his leading.

'Lest anyone should think that those who proclaim Jesus of Nazareth are opposed to Moses, this very Moses has already commended Jesus of Nazareth to you, promising so many centuries past that the one would come whom now you see has come to you.[34] For he said, "God will raise up for you a prophet like me from among your brethren; him you shall hear" [Deut 18:15]. He, I say, is that new Moses. As Moses first had spoken with the angel alone near the bush, so later, with the multitude now as witness,[35] he spoke with the angel in the wilderness,[36] on Mount Sinai, and in turn spoke with our ancestors, to whom he conveyed what he had heard from the Lord. For he had received the Law from him to hand over to us, the Law that would confer life upon those who observe it.[37]

'Though the authority of Moses was so great, nevertheless our fathers refused to obey him, and thrust him aside. Forgetting how wretched was the slavery from which they had been freed, they conceived in their heart a longing for Egypt, a longing to forsake their leader and redeemer, who had brought salvation, to spurn the life-giving Law and return to the ways of idolaters. And so, while Moses was speaking with the angel, they said to Aaron, "Make us gods to go before us; as for this Moses who led us out of the land of Egypt, we do not know what has happened to him" [Exod 32:1]. Presently, following the example of the Egyptians, who worship the ox Apis,[38] they made for themselves a calf from molten gold, and sacrificed victims to this lifeless god, spurning the living God by whose mercy they had escaped slavery. And in the course of an outrage so impious they danced and feasted[39] – as though it were a deed well done – turning away from the true God, creator of the universe, and revelling in dumb gods whom they themselves had made for themselves with their own hands.[40]

'In turn, God, offended by this, turned away from them, and allowed them to gratify their own minds,[41] so that at length in imitation of the gentiles they worshipped now not the one God but the whole host of heaven – sun, moon, stars, Mercury, Venus, Saturn – to whom impious tales attribute divinity, though they are bodies created by God to serve human needs.[42] What I am saying cannot be denied. Surely this is what God is vexed at when he speaks through the prophet Amos, saying:

'"House of Israel, did you offer victims and sacrifices to me for forty years in the wilderness? Instead of the temple of the true God you have embraced the tent of Moloch, that is, the idol of the Ammonites,[43] and the star of your God Remphan, that is, Lucifer, or Venus, whom the Saracens worship.[44] You made for yourselves these dumb likenesses to worship, despising the true and living God who alone created the universe. Since, however, your mind is set on these things, I shall carry you away into Babylon[45] that you may again serve idolaters" [Amos 5:25–7].

'I think it has been sufficiently shown that we have blasphemed neither against God, to whom we render unblemished worship, nor against Moses, whose prophecy we embrace. Those blaspheme rather who follow in the footsteps of their ancestors, and have despised God long ago in Moses and today despise both God and Moses in Jesus of Nazareth. As for the Law, we most certainly have not blasphemed against it, we who embrace the one to whom the Law pointed and whom all the prophets promised. Those blaspheme rather who walk in the footprints of their ungodly fathers. The law conveyed by Moses was despised by their fathers, and they now spurn the evangelical law that Jesus brought for all and that does not abrogate the law of Moses but perfects it.[46]

'Now concerning the temple, against which I am said to blaspheme, hear me briefly. I know that this temple, too, was built at God's command to be a figure of the holier temple and to give way to a better one. In the same way the tent of witness gave way to the temple[47] – the tent in which was the ark of the covenant which our fathers carried with them in the wilderness.[48] For God, speaking through Moses, had prescribed the pattern according to which this tent was to be constructed. When Jesus was their leader, our fathers embraced the tent,[49] and they carried it into the possession of the gentiles,[50] whom God drove out from the face of our fathers, right to the time of King David. Since David was a godly man and therefore pleasing to God, he asked God that he might prepare a tabernacle worthy of the God of Jacob. It was Solomon, however, because he was a man of peace,[51] who first[52] built for God this magnificent temple in which you glory, saying, "the temple of the Lord, the temple of the Lord, the temple of the Lord."[53]

'And yet, in truth, this temple is only a figure of the true spiritual temple, the church, which is now being built by Jesus of Nazareth, your king, of whom Solomon was the type.[54] For since God is spirit[55] he does not dwell in buildings made by hands, nor is he who is unmeasurable and fills all things encompassed by walls.[56] This, no doubt, is that which he himself attests, speaking through the prophet Isaiah: "Heaven is my throne, and earth my footstool. What house will you build me? says the Lord, or what is the place of my rest? Has not my hand made all these things?" [66:1–2]. God, therefore, who created the universe had rest in himself before he created all things. If he rests, he does not rest in buildings made by human hands, since, in any case, the sky is his seat and the earth his footstool; but he delights to rest in hearts that are quiet and obedient to the Holy Spirit.[57] Accordingly, it is the one who has a breast befouled with wicked deeds who violates the temple of God. It is the one who gives trouble to those who obey the Holy Spirit who violates the temple of the Lord. Now just as one does not injure Moses by putting Jesus before him, and does not violate the Law which he conveyed by putting the gospel before it, so he does not violate this temple by giving precedence to the spiritual temple in which God has greater delight. It is right that shadows yield to the truth, which is now thrusting itself forward into the light.[58] It is fitting that the carnal yield to the spiritual. This is truly the unchangeable will of God, and he sent his only Son into the world, he sent his Holy Spirit, on this account, that the light of evangelical truth might stream out to all nations.

'You, however, doggedly uphold the carnal. You are rebels against the Spirit of God, who long ago called you a stiff-necked people.[59] And you think you are Israelites and sons of Abraham because you have a little bit of foreskin cut off, when you have a heart uncircumcised, and ears too. Henceforth the true sons of Abraham are those who have a heart cleansed from ungodly desires, who have ears obedient to the precepts of God and purged of the obtuseness of the carnal sense which prevents them from being able to perceive the spiritual sense.[60] Just as your fathers have always resisted the Holy Spirit because of their obtuseness of mind and dullness of hearing, so now you too, in nature no different from your ancestors, do not cease to fight the Holy Spirit – previously in Jesus of Nazareth whom you nailed to the cross, now in his apostles. How many times did your fathers rebel against Moses? – yes! *your* fathers: why should I not call "yours" those whom you imitate.[61]

'Which of the prophets have your fathers not persecuted? They not only beat but even killed those who told you beforehand that the Just One would come, the one through whom alone all would be justified.[62] You hated those who announced his coming, and when he came and fulfilled everything they had predicted, you not only did not embrace him but betrayed him into the hands of Pilate, and through Pilate you killed him – more criminally than if you had perpetrated the deed with your own hands.[63] All these things you do on the pretext of defending the Law, though your ancestors did not keep the Law delivered through angels, nor do you, who not so long ago[64] killed the one whom the Law promised and denoted, and now persecute him even though slain. You begrudge yourselves the gift of eternal salvation that is offered to you, and you invite the destruction which you unjustifiably impute to us and to Jesus of Nazareth.'[65]

This speech, so true, so frank, terribly moved the minds of all who were in the council, so that their hearts were bursting and they gnashed their teeth at him. Stephen, however, was not in the slightest perturbed by them, filled as he was by the Holy Spirit. Ready to endure the worst, and following the example of Jesus Christ, he turned his eyes steadfastly to heaven whence Christians must seek all their help.[66] Soon the distinguished athlete was strengthened for the approaching contest.[67] The sky is parted;[68] he sees the majesty of God, and Jesus whom he confessed standing at the right hand of God. He did not remain silent about this before the ungodly multitude: it is not right that human malice should suppress the glory of God.[69] 'Behold,' he said, 'I see the heavens opened, and the Son of Man standing on the right hand of the divine majesty.'[70]

It is worth the effort here to consider the pattern of this judgment. Charges had been preferred; an answer was given to everything. A young man brought forth the testimonies of the Law and the prophets; the case was won with solid arguments.[71] Nothing was said about God that was not pious, nothing about Moses that was not honourable, nothing about the Law that was not according to the intent of the Law; nothing was spoken with disdain about the temple. And yet those councillors are bursting with anger and grind their teeth like madmen. So little do they tolerate having their own glory diminished and the glory of him proclaimed whose glory alone God wants proclaimed among all. If he had exalted Moses or Abraham, they would have borne it; that Jesus was alive, that Jesus was standing at the right hand of God according to the prophecy of David,[72] this they cannot bear, but turning to frenzy straightaway, they stop up their ears against a discourse so salubrious, and with frantic cries they all rush upon Stephen with a common purpose. And then they cast him out of the city, as though he had been convicted and condemned for blasphemy, in this respect alone mindful of the Mosaic law, and there they stoned him.[73] The witnesses were there like victors, whose role, according to the prescription of Moses, was to begin the stoning.[74] To be freer for the execution, they laid aside their garments[75] and gave them to a young man by the name of Saul who, through ignorance and from zeal for the ancestral law, then still supported the wicked cause.

They soon began to stone Stephen, who did not resist, did not revile,[76] but called upon the one he had seen, and said, 'Lord Jesus, receive my spirit.' You recognize a disciple of Jesus, for so he said on the cross, 'Father, into your hands I commend my spirit' [Luke 23:46]. Then as stones were flying from every direction, he bent his knees to the ground and with a loud voice and much feeling he cried out, saying, 'Lord, do not impute this to them as a sin, for they do not know what they are doing.' How well the servant portrayed his Lord![77] This was his last utterance as he was dying. Then he fell asleep in the Lord:[78] whoever dies in him does not die, but falls asleep to live again unto immortality after a peaceful rest. It becomes all who are truly Christians to die in this disposition. And so Stephen, corresponding to his name, was the first of all to win the martyr's crown[79] and to offer to the Lord the first-fruits[80] of the evangelical sacrifice.[81]

Chapter 8

There were in that crowd some who were not yet persuaded that Jesus was the Son of God. This error to some extent alleviated the dreadful character of the crime, though it did not excuse them from homicide, since, blinded by their own desires, they preferred to punish rather than to learn the truth.[1] Nevertheless, no one was less able to be excused than the priests, scribes, and Pharisees. Again, there were some who erred from honest motives, believing they were offering a sacrifice pleasing to God because they were executing those who were trying to overturn the Law handed down by God.[2] But evangelical charity excuses even things that cannot be excused. Among those who erred without malice was Saul of Tarsus, a young man zealous for the Mosaic law,[3] who, from being a wolf became a sheep, and from being a ruthlessly fierce persecutor became a brilliantly keen advocate of evangelical liberty.[4] He himself indeed at that time threw no stones at Stephen, but he assented to those who had condemned and stoned him, and his intention in protecting their clothes was to be one with those who were throwing stones.[5]

But Jewish malice was not content with the death of one person. A great persecution soon arose against the church at Jerusalem so that they were all scattered hither and yon through the various regions of Judaea and Samaria – all except the apostles, who excelled the others in stout-heartedness.[6] Jewish malice could do nothing against the apostles, nor for that matter could it do anything against the others except by the permission of the Lord Jesus. The Lord Jesus had permitted this so that under pressure of persecution they would flee from city to city.[7] This was not so much a matter of terror on the part of the disciples as of divine dispensation, that as the seed was broadly spread, an abundant harvest of evangelical confession would quickly appear.[8] The twelve apostles alone, as the shepherds, did not give way to this storm but with firm hearts persevered at Jerusalem.

After Stephen's death, certain men who were cultivators of piety took care of his burial, because they realized that he had been destroyed, contrary to his deserts, through hired witnesses. With the same intent Joseph and Nicodemus had cared for the burial of the Lord Jesus.[9] Stephen's death was celebrated in the Jewish manner with great mourning and beating of the breast on the part of the good;[10] for among Christians the death of those who perish for the sake of the glory of Christ is worthy of applause and triumphal celebration.[11] If there are some tears there, they are not shed for the one who has died, but either for the murderers who invoke hell upon themselves, or for the flock deprived of its needed shepherd.

In the midst of this storm Saul, who had given a sample of his zeal in the stoning of Stephen, conceived a profound hatred against the Christians and began to make havoc of the church of God, just as a hungry wolf tears and scatters a flock of sheep.[12] He pursued them when they fled, sought them out in hiding, prowling about one house after another. Wherever he perceived any who professed Jesus Christ, he would force his way in and drag men and women alike off to jail. Clearly, he was more savage than the priests and scribes themselves, none of whom had so far troubled the female sex.[13] He did so as a young man whose will was indeed pious but his judgment awry, and on this account, the Lord restrained his ferocity so that he was not stained with anyone's blood.[14]

While this was going on at Jerusalem, those who had been scattered, though driven from one place to another by fear, nevertheless did not remain silent about Jesus of Nazareth but wandered everywhere through Judaea casting seeds of evangelical discourse,[15] which was the reason the Lord allowed them to be scattered.[16] Among these was Philip, one of the seven deacons, next in order after Stephen.[17] A fugitive from Jerusalem, he went down to the city of Samaria, also called Sebaste.[18] Even before this, some report had arrived there of Jesus of Nazareth.[19] Philip now proclaimed the rest of the story: how Jesus had been crucified and come to life again on the third day; how, after remaining with his disciples for forty days, he ascended into heaven and from there sent the Holy Spirit to his disciples; and that henceforth salvation was provided for all who believed in his name. Now the first harvest of the gospel always begins among the people.[20] Accordingly, the Samaritan people gave heed with one accord to the things Philip was narrating, for his speech won favour, promising salvation to all. Besides, the many miracles performed through Philip built up confidence in his words,[21] for at the invocation of the name of Jesus the demons came forth from many who were possessed by unclean spirits,[22] and in coming forth with a loud cry, they showed that they did so not of their own accord but compelled by the power of the salvific name.[23] Moreover, several paralytic and lame people gained their health. Because of these events, great joy arose among the people in that city. The further the gospel seed moves away from Jerusalem and the closer it comes to the gentiles, the richer is its harvest. See how much the savagery of the Jews has helped. From being a deacon Philip has become an apostle, and instead of a few Jerusalemites, whole cities embrace the teaching of the gospel.

And yet a more noxious bane comes to the church from those who join it with insincere hearts than from those who openly persecute the church. An example of this has been given us that we might the more beware of wolves in sheep's clothing.[24] There was among the Samaritans a certain man by the name of Simon, an impostor and a master in the arts of illusion.[25] Before Philip came there, Simon had practised the art of magic in that city, and with counterfeit miracles and prodigies had deluded the Samaritan populace, a people in any case superstitious and having a propensity for the deceptions of demons.[26] With counterfeits of this kind he was trumpeting himself among the simple and superstitiously credulous populace, boasting that he was someone great – a prophet; all gave heed to him from the least to the greatest. He had, however, done nothing in the name of Jesus, and on this account they were astonished at the wonders he either simulated with illusions or performed with the help of demons, and they said, 'This is the power of God which is called great.' He had lived among them for a considerable time and had long deluded them with his magical arts. Consequently, he had already acquired authority among them all, and many believed what he taught.

Simon saw in Philip the more effective power of performing true miracles through invocation of the name of Jesus. He saw that the Samaritan people had abandoned him and believed Philip, who was bringing to all the joyful news about the kingdom of God and the name of Jesus Christ. He saw that Philip was not proclaiming in some grand way something about himself, as Simon had done, but through his miracles was making the glory of Jesus shine, was promising salvation to all who received baptism and professed that name – and he would also see that many, both men and women, were receiving baptism. Accordingly, Simon himself also at length embraced[27] the evangelical faith, received baptism, and began to cling to Philip. He attached himself to Philip not so much through love of Jesus as from desire for praise and glory, for as he was highly skilled in the arts of magic he perceived that in Philip nothing was done through illusions like his own.[28] Accordingly, when he observed him performing certain things – not trivial miracles like those of magicians generally, such as a serpent flying or a straw crawling like a snake,[29] but demons cast out by a word, paralytics healed with a word – he was exceedingly astonished and wondered by what craft or power those things were done.

The report had now reached Jerusalem and the apostles who had remained there that through Philip Samaria had embraced the evangelical word – an unspiritual people, not entirely free from idolatry.[30] They rejoiced exceedingly, and sent to them Peter and John, the chief of the apostles, so that what had been begun by Philip might through them be approved and completed. When they had arrived and learned that many had been baptized by Philip they gave thanks to God. Now Philip and his companions asked the apostles that those whom they had baptized might receive the Holy Spirit – that those who had already been cleansed from their sins through baptism might receive even more abundantly the gift of God – in the same way as had those who had received the Holy Spirit first in the upper room.[31] For the Holy Spirit had not yet come upon any of them, but they had only been baptized in the name of the Lord Jesus. This power to baptize had been delegated to the deacons, but the imposition of hands through which the Holy Spirit was conferred was reserved for the apostles alone and for their successors.[32] Then the apostles, as they had been asked, laid their hands upon them and they received the Holy Spirit with a visible sign. The Spirit added to their souls a fiery vigour and adorned their tongues with a celestial eloquence.[33]

When Simon, who only recently had been changed from an evil magician into a Christian, and made no better thereby, saw that the apostles conferred a heavenly gift by the laying on of hands, not wanting to lack anything which might contribute to his ostentation and financial profit, he offered them money, and said, 'Give me also this power so that on whomsoever I lay hands, he may receive the Holy Spirit.' The magician supposed that money was all-powerful with everyone. He knew that one who looks for gain must make an investment: he wants to buy what he can sell again for more. And here again is another seed-bed of grave disaster in the church. Ananias and Sapphira had paid the penalty for their deception. This too was a case that had to be at once sharply repulsed, because if it should be accepted it would completely subvert the integrity of Christian godliness.[34] Peter, therefore, showing to all the others what bishops must do to oppose the imitators of Simon, replied:

'It is better that this money of yours, with which you are eager to destroy others, perish along with you, who of your own will already are so utterly lost as to think that the gift of God can be bought with money. God wants us to impart his gift to others without cost, just as he, out of his own kindness, bestows it upon us without charge.[35] You can have no share or partnership with us in this business, which operates on the basis of simple faith toward God. Although your body has been dipped in the water, nevertheless your heart is not right in the sight of God. If you persevere in that wickedness, baptism will not help you at all. Accordingly, repent of that wickedness of yours and beseech God that, if it is somehow possible, your terrible crime will be forgiven. The deed was not in fact perpetrated; yet it was conceived in your mind in such a way that it was no thanks to you that you did not commit the crime[36] and introduce into the church of God the most destructive[37] example of all. The gift of the most gentle Spirit is entrusted to pure and sincere souls. I perceive, however, that your heart is not at all pure, but is infected with the bitter gall of ambition and gain, and is therefore bound in the chains of iniquity.[38] To free yourself from them, you must entreat God with many tears, lest the vengeance of the divine wrath that you have provoked by so great a crime strike you.'

Here Simon, more driven by fear than drawn by repentance for his deed,[39] said to Peter, 'You, rather, entreat the Lord for me that none of the things you[40] have said befall me.' You see, Theophilus, the two contrasting Simons: in the one is shown what must be abjured, in the other what must be imitated. Here, then, after Peter and John had approved and brought to completion through their witness the preaching of Philip, and had taught many of the things they had learned from the Lord Jesus, they returned to Jerusalem. On their way, they preached the gospel in many villages and small towns of the Samaritans, everywhere doing what the Lord had commanded them.[41]

Philip, thirsting intensely for the spread of the gospel, was offered other prey also, for the opportunity to do good is given to the good. An angel of the Lord privately admonished him, saying, 'Rise and go towards the south by the road which leads from Jerusalem to Gaza – I speak of the old Gaza, now a wilderness, bordering the sea.'[42] Philip obeyed the angel and set out; in this you might recognize the alacrity worthy of a bishop whenever someone is to be drawn to the gospel. But like the director in stage plays, so here the angel directs the entrance and the encounter of the *personae*.[43] For it was just at this time that a certain man started out on a journey. He was a eunuch; in body, indeed, castrated and scarcely a man, but with a manly soul,[44] an Ethiopian by race, with black skin, but soon to be clothed in the snow-white fleece of the immaculate Lamb and to change his native skin through the water of baptism.[45] He was a prefect of Candace,[46] the queen of the Ethiopians, and had been put in charge of all her treasures. I am speaking of a race rendered effeminate by luxury (for riches nourish luxury) and clearly deserving to suffer a woman to rule.[47] This eunuch had set out for Jerusalem for the sake of religion: so great was the renown of the temple that even gentiles came there from afar and brought gifts with them;[48] hence the anger of the priests against those who said that someday this temple was to be destroyed.[49] The eunuch had a godly mind, but he was in error when he sought religion in the temple of the Jews, for from their temple religion was soon to migrate to the gentiles. And so, when he was returning home, sitting in his chariot, he did not give his time to reading stories or to sleep, but out of love of religion was reading the prophet Isaiah. He showed us where Jesus must be sought: he does not hide in temples but in the sacred books.[50]

Philip had now arrived at the very same place, and the Spirit again advised him, saying, 'Go near and join yourself to this chariot.' When Philip had run up to the chariot, he heard the eunuch reading the prophet Isaiah, and recognizing immediately his zeal for religion he said to him, 'Do you understand what you are reading?' He replied, 'How should I, a man occupied with secular affairs, be able to understand unless there be someone to explain to me the hidden meaning of the prophet?' And he asked Philip to get into the chariot and sit beside him so they could talk more easily. Philip got in and sat beside the eunuch. Consider here, I ask you, the portrait of the evangelical teacher and of the people of the gentiles eager to learn Christ.[51] The profit cannot fail to be large when one runs up eager to teach, and the other, with a desire to learn, invites him to sit beside him.

Nothing is done here by chance; God guides and directs all. The eunuch had inadvertently come upon that passage in the prophet which portrayed Jesus Christ. It was this: 'He was led as a sheep to the slaughter, and as a lamb before its shearer he was dumb and did not open his mouth. In humiliation[52] his judgment was denied him; who shall declare his generation? For his life is taken from the earth' [Isa 53:7]. When Philip had reread this passage to the eunuch, the latter, more than ever burning with a desire to learn of whom the prophet was speaking, said, 'I beg you, of whom does the prophet say this? Of himself, or of someone else?' Observe the eunuch, willing to be taught. He had heard that Isaiah himself had been cut in two by a wooden saw at the order of king Manasseh,[53] and he was aware that in the nature of prophecy what seemed to be said about this or that person according to the historical sense often referred to another according to the more hidden sense. One who asks questions in this way is willing to be taught![54]

Accordingly Philip, keen to teach an eager learner, opened his mouth and, starting from this passage of the prophet, explained to him the essence of evangelical doctrine: that this was the Son of God through whom God had determined (and through his prophets had promised) to give salvation to all who put their trust in him; that for this reason he wanted him to assume a human body, and be born, now from Mary, a virgin. Moreover, both nativities are ineffable: the one by which he is always being born from the Father, outside of time, and the one by which he was born of a virgin through the activity of the Holy Spirit without the work of a man – assuming a human nature in such a way that he did not lose his divine nature. The prophet, discerning this through the Spirit, was amazed and said, 'Who shall declare his generation?'[55] Further, here was that true paschal lamb, by whose death the Father had destined to free from the bondage of sins and from eternal death not only the Israelites but all races.[56] On this account he gave him over into the hands of the priests, the scribes, the Pharisees, and the leaders of the people, through whom he was led to Pilate, the governor, that he might be crucified by him. Since he was willing to die for our salvation, he made in Pilate's presence no reply that would set him free,[57] but like a sheep offered himself to all their insults and torments; for on that occasion he concealed his majesty and for the sake of mankind cast himself down to the lowest humiliation.[58] The Jews, thinking he was only what he seemed, condemned him and sent him to death. This, surely, is what the prophet says: 'In humiliation, his judgment was taken away.' An innocent man was condemned, a man who will one day return lofty and exalted, and will judge the living and the dead.[59] But God called his Son back to life on the third day. Thereafter for forty days he remained on earth with a body that could be seen and touched, and he repeatedly showed himself to his disciples. Lastly, he was taken away up into heaven while they were looking on. Then, on the tenth day after the ascension, he sent the Holy Spirit from heaven, who breathed upon the minds and tongues of the apostles so that they might fearlessly preach Jesus of Nazareth, prince of salvation and of life, to all the nations of the entire world, a salvation and life attained not through the law of Moses but through faith and baptism. There is not one of these things that has not been denoted by figures in the law of Moses, has not been predicted by the prophets, has not been handed down and promised by Jesus himself.

While Philip was speaking of these and many other things with the eunuch, the latter happened to see a little spring close to the road and said to Philip, 'Why do we put off a matter of such importance. See, here is water; you have instructed, I am ready.[60] What stands in the way of my

Discount: 20%

Rights: WORLD

Nationality of Author(s):Deceased

Domicile of Author(s):

Country of Original Publisher:

Trim Size: 7 x 10

No. of Pages: xix, 7 pp illus., 390

CIP: C74-006326-X

U.K./European Price:£62.00, $107.00

PUBLICATION INFORMATION:

ISBN: 0-8020-0664-7

Price: $95.00

Author: Desiderius Erasmus
Edited by John J. Bateman
Translated & annotated by Robert D. Sider

Title: Collected Works of Erasmus Volume 50,
New Testament Scholarship, Paraphrase on the
Acts of the Apostles

Series: Collected Works of Erasmus, Volume 50

Publication Date: April 22, 1995

being baptized right now?' Then[61] Philip replied, 'Nothing stands in the way, provided you believe with your whole heart the things I have taught.[62] This is the only condition encountered in baptism.'[63] Then the eunuch eagerly replied, 'I believe that Jesus is the Christ promised by the prophets, and the Son of God through whom eternal salvation is offered to all.'[64] Whereupon, Philip ordered the chariot to be stopped.[65] It was a magnificent carriage, worthy of the magistrate of a barbarian queen,[66] but one who wishes to be worthy of baptism must descend, must strip himself of all his fine clothes.[67] They both went down into the water, and Philip baptized the eunuch – the poor baptized the rich; the lowly, the powerful; one fully a man baptized a eunuch; a Jew, an Ethiopian. Not the least respect of persons here:[68] where faith meets, and oneness of heart[69] in Jesus Christ, all things are appropriate. After baptism, he is not a eunuch, or an Ethiopian, but a new creation.[70]

As soon as Philip came out of the water, the Spirit of the Lord carried him away, and the eunuch saw him no more. Nor did he miss his teacher once he had been breathed upon by the Holy Spirit through baptism, but full of joy because he had learned Jesus Christ, he completed his journey so that he might preach the name of Christ among his own Ethiopians also. Then an angel set Philip down in Azotus, the city closest by and the one from which he had come.[71] Proceeding from there, he preached the gospel whenever he came upon a village or town, until he came to Caesarea in Palestine, where he had a house.[72]

Chapter 9

Meanwhile, Saul's cruelty did not confine itself within the walls of the city of Jerusalem. When he perceived that the evangelical doctrine was being spread even farther through the scattering of the disciples, more and more he breathed out against them not only threats and imprisonment now, but slaughter and death, and he went to the high priest so that he might further crush them if he were armed with authority.[1] He asked the high priest for letters of authorization not only in respect to the cities nearby, in which he had already practised his cruelty, but as far away as Damascus, a city of Phoenicia, situated far from Jerusalem.[2] The letters were written to the synagogues of the Jews[3] who were living there, to the effect that they should, on the authority of the high priest, give Saul their help, so that he might bind and bring to Jerusalem whomever he caught belonging to this condemned heresy, whether men or women. Saul was undertaking this from a sincere heart; according to the saying of the Lord, he thought he was doing a service pleasing to God.[4] For this reason, God did not allow him to be polluted with the blood of the innocent, but called him back at the midpoint of his savage course.

For when he had now almost completed his journey and was not far from the city of Damascus, suddenly a light from heaven shone round about him. Falling to the earth in fear,[5] he heard a voice saying to him, 'Saul, Saul, why do you persecute me?' He, wondering who that high and so mighty interrogator was, and uncertain whether it was some angel, or God, timidly replied, 'Who are you, Lord?' Then he: 'I am Jesus the Nazarene whom you believe to be dead, though I live and reign in heaven. In persecuting my disciples and my name, you unwittingly persecute me.[6] But your efforts are in vain. It[7] is hard for you to kick against the goad,[8] for you are struggling not against human beings but against God, whose will no one can resist.[9] Twofold therefore is your sin;[10] nor will you accomplish anything, and you invite evil upon yourself.'

When Saul heard this voice, trembling and astonished he said, 'Lord, what will you have me do?' This was the cry of one going astray not from an evil will, but through ignorance.[11] Such people need only to be taught; it was expedient that the proud and headstrong be cast down, that one who breathed out threats and slaughter be made afraid so that he might become teachable. Then the Lord said to him, 'Arise and go into the city. There you will be shown what you must do.' The Lord smites in such a way that he heals,[12] casts down in such a way that he raises up, takes away sight so that he illuminates.[13] Fierce and raging, Saul was thrown headlong; meek and ready to obey, he was ordered to rise. While this was happening, the men who accompanied Saul on this journey stood there in astonishment, hearing, indeed, the voice of one speaking to Saul, but seeing no one!

Saul, recovering himself, arose: the first step to virtue is to stand erect. Behold, again, a second miracle – though his eyes were open, he saw nothing![14] His companions therefore led him by the hand into the city of Damascus. He was not at once admitted to the gift of the Holy Spirit, in order to offer a prescriptive example to coming generations: the laying on of hands should not be administered to just anyone immediately, but catechumens should first be tested and prepared by fasting and by prayer.[15] Therefore, just as the apostles had remained in Jerusalem for ten days awaiting the Holy Spirit, so Saul remained in Damascus for three days. He saw nothing with the eyes of his body, but the eyes of his mind were meanwhile enlightened. He ate nothing, but his soul in the meantime was fattened on heavenly doctrine.[16]

Now there was at Damascus a certain disciple (for so those who had accepted the teaching of the gospel were still called at that time).[17] His name was Ananias. The Lord had chosen him as the one through whom he would fill Paul with the Holy Spirit. Accordingly, he addressed him in a vision in his sleep, saying, 'Ananias.' He soon perceived that God was calling him, and in response replied, 'Behold, I am here, Lord' – clearly indicating a mind truly Christian and ready for every command.[18] Then the Lord said, 'Arise and go into the street commonly called "Straight," and seek in the house of Judas a man by the name of Saul, a native of Tarsus. For behold, he prays there, earnestly seeking our abundant grace.' At the same time, Saul also, as he prayed, seemed to see a certain man called Ananias enter the house, and put his hands upon him so that he might regain his sight. Thus the Lord prepared them for one another by mutual visions.[19] Ananias, however, frightened at the name of Saul – a name now famous because of his cruelty towards the Christians – replied, 'Lord, I have heard from many people about this man, with what great evils he has afflicted your saints in Jerusalem. Not content with this, he has even come here, armed with cruel letters from the high priests to the effect that he should put chains on all who call upon your name.' To this, once more the Lord replied:

'I know; you sheep fear that ravening wolf.[20] But there is no reason to fear, for I have turned that wolf into the gentlest of sheep. Accordingly, see that you approach him undaunted. I have chosen him for myself as a glorious instrument[21] to carry my name before the gentiles, before kings and the children of Israel. What he has done so far, he has done not through malice, but from zeal for the ancestral law.[22] By erring simply in judgment he has given evidence of the sort of champion he will be for my gospel. Thus far, armed with the bulls of pontiffs, with threats and chains, he has fought against those who profess my name. Henceforth, armed with my Spirit and girded with the sword of the gospel word,[23] he will carry on a war far more bravely against those who hate my name. For the glory of my name he will willingly endure cruelties much worse than those he was just now preparing for you.'

Heartened by these words, Ananias departed and entered the house of Judas. He found Saul praying; putting his hand upon him, he said, 'Brother Saul, the Lord Jesus who appeared to you on the road when you were coming here has sent me to you that you might regain your sight and be filled with the Holy Spirit.' Scarcely had Ananias spoken these words, when instantly something like scales fell from his eyes and he received his sight.[24] Whereupon he arose and was baptized, and after he had taken food he was strengthened. Thus that extraordinary evangelical leader, who would dim the glory even of the other apostles, received the Holy Spirit by the agency of an insignificant disciple before he was baptized. But nothing is done out of order when it is done at the behest of the Lord Jesus, whom Paul had as his catechist.[25] For Jesus handed power over to his apostles in such a way that he reserved for himself the highest authority over the entire business. So Saul, suddenly become a different man,[26] spent some days with the disciples at Damascus. There was no delay. Renouncing the high priest's mandates he began at once in that very place to embark upon the service delegated by Christ. Entering the synagogue of the Jews he began to preach openly and freely, earnestly affirming that Jesus of Nazareth[27] was the Son of God, through whom alone salvation is offered to all according to the oracles of the prophets.

The Jews, who had learned by report about Saul's cruelty towards the Christians, were rejoicing that they had such a champion of the Mosaic law. But when they had heard him preaching with equal zeal the name of Jesus of Nazareth, they wondered what had happened to the man that he had suddenly been changed. They said among themselves, 'Is not this that Saul who a short time ago at Jerusalem had in every possible way assailed those who call upon this name? Now he plays crier and trumpeter for it! Is not this the one who only recently set out for this place with the intention of binding and bringing to the chief priests any he should find here, to have them punished at the will of the chief priests? How has it happened that he has so suddenly cast off the Jew, forsaken Moses, and become a confessor of the crucified?' But Paul (for this name now suited him better after he had been changed from a restless troublemaker into a teacher of moderation and of peace),[28] was in no way frightened by words of this kind from the Jews. Quite the contrary! As he daily gathered greater strength of spirit, he threw into confusion and dismay the Jews living at Damascus. He continually affirmed and demonstrated from the witness of the Scriptures that the Jesus of Nazareth whom he had formerly persecuted in ignorance but now proclaimed[29] was the true Messiah promised to the world, and that no other would arise from whom the Jews should expect salvation.

When for many days Paul had been so bold at Damascus, to the great gladness of the disciples but with much angry muttering on the part of those who had not yet believed, the Jews at last formed a plan to kill him by treachery. O murderous nation! Paul was disputing, demonstrating and, as it were, cutting the throats of the Jews with the testimonies of their Law, as though with their own sword. The Jews had nothing but conspiratorial councils, prisons, the lash, death in various forms. But the Lord had promised his own that not even a hair from their heads would perish without the permission of the Father.[30] The time had not yet come for that distinguished evangelical warrior to perish. He had to fight many battles on behalf of Christ's people, to face danger often in the battle line, to summon to the yoke of Christ many regions and cities subdued by the sacred doctrine.

As God willed, then, it was pointed out to Paul that the Jews were laying an ambush for him, so carefully guarding the gates both night and day that he should nowhere be able to escape without their killing him. They secured the support of King Aretas' governor for this crime, so that if hidden treachery should not succeed, he might still be killed by open force.[31] Accordingly the disciples,[32] unwilling that so brave a champion should perish, judged that the less he feared for himself the worthier he was to be protected. And so they hid him, and at night, putting him in a basket, they let him down from the walls by a rope.[33] Thus sometimes even valiant commanders flee so that, as the proverb goes, they may be able to fight again.[34] O marvellous turnabout of things! He lies hidden and flees who a little before persecuted, full of threats, while those plan to save Paul's life against whom he was previously designing slaughter.

When he had come to Jerusalem he attempted to join the disciples. But everyone feared him, as sheep fear the wolf. To them the old Saul was too well known, while Paul had not yet become known. They did not believe him when he said he was a disciple, remembering, of course, with what great cruelty he had been accustomed to persecute the flock of Christ. They therefore suspected treachery lurking under the name of disciple. But Barnabas, the Levite I mentioned above,[35] who knew what had taken place in Paul, brought him to the apostles. He explained everything to them: how the Lord had appeared to Paul as he was going to Damascus, how he spoke to him, and how he was suddenly changed into a different man and had boldly and freely preached the gospel in the name of the Lord Jesus. The apostles rejoiced, and with their testimony commended Paul to the flock. So he spent quite a few days in Jerusalem, enjoying the companionship of the apostles and the disciples, and freely confessing and proclaiming there the name of the Lord that he had in error persecuted. He had no fear of the reproachful cry of 'apostate' because he had deserted the priests. Indeed he confessed and proclaimed the name not only among the people of Jerusalem. He preached Jesus also to the gentiles who were staying in Jerusalem on account of the city's celebrity, and to the Jews as well who were born among the Greeks,[36] disputing with them and demonstrating from the very testimonies of the Law that Jesus was the Saviour of the world. But they did not endure such liberty, and took refuge in the customary defence against their invincible opponent, seeking a way to slay Paul – that is the way Jewish people 'debate.' And now, while he remained fearless,[37] they began to lay a snare for him. When the brethren perceived this, to prevent anything happening that they would regret, they brought him down to Caesarea Philippi, a city of Phoenicia, and from there in turn they sent him away to his native Tarsus in Cilicia.[38] Paul's wandering and moving about[39] is the progress of the gospel.

Meanwhile the storm of persecution that had arisen now abated. The congregation of disciples[40] spread throughout all Judaea, Galilee, and

Samaria, regions in which the Lord had taught especially and in which he had commanded that the word of the gospel first be proclaimed.[41] On the whole, the congregation enjoyed tranquillity: it was strengthened by mutual concord and paid no heed to human threats. It grew daily and was built up, living in the fear of the Lord, and in the midst of afflictions it was filled with the consolation of the Holy Spirit. This was no doubt what the Lord had promised them: 'In the world you will have affliction, but in me peace and comfort.'[42]

Now it happened that while Peter, like a vigilant and energetic shepherd, went about in all quarters[43] to visit now these people, now those, he came also to the saints who dwelt at Lydda, a city on the coast of Palestine.[44] There he found a certain man named Aeneas who for the past eight years had been confined to his pallet, for he was a paralytic. Peter was mindful of the dominical precept which bade them heal the sick in whatever house they entered,[45] for it is inappropriate that there be diseases of the body in a place where physicians of the soul are present.[46] He said to him, 'May the Lord Jesus Christ heal you,[47] Aeneas. Arise and make your own bed.' Directly upon these words he arose, healed, and made his bed; this was a proof of complete health. When they saw that the man who had been in bed for so many years was suddenly healed, all who lived in Lydda and Sarona (a coastal town near Lydda)[48] also turned to the Lord and professed the name of the Lord Jesus. Thus health of body restored to a single person enticed many to health of soul.

Moreover, at Joppa there was a certain disciple named Tabitha. The name is the equivalent of Dorcas in Greek, *caprea* [roe-deer] in Latin; the Greek is derived from keenness of sight.[49] She abounded in every kind of good work, but especially in the duties of charity by which she supported those in need. Now it happened that at the same time Peter was staying at Lydda, she died from the disease from which she suffered. When they had washed her corpse in the customary way, they laid her in an upper room to be anointed.[50] Since, however, Joppa was not far from Lydda and the disciples had learned that Peter was there, they dispatched two men to him, asking him to hurry and come to them.

Peter went to them without delay, thus giving us an example of the good shepherd. When he had come into the house, they took him to the upper room so that he might be moved to pity by looking on the corpse. Here all the widows – whose special commendation at that time was that they served the needs of the saints[51] – stood beside Peter. They shed tears, which fell not so much for the deceased as for the needy whom Dorcas used to refresh through her services. To have poured forth tears was now in itself to pray. They do not recount the good deeds of the dead woman, but show the tunics and other garments which Dorcas was making to clothe the saints. Death had interrupted her pursuit of doing good.

Here Peter ordered everyone to leave the room, for he remembered the example of Jesus when he cast the crowd of weepers out before he revived the daughter of the ruler of the synagogue.[52] For the widows were only weeping, but weeping hinders prayer. At the same time, he did not want anyone to be present lest the weak sex should be startled by the corpse as it arose, and so he prayed alone, on bended knee. For the vigour of the spirit, through which miracles are performed, is not always present; it is aroused by prayer, as is faith also, without which no miracle is performed.[53] When he had poured forth his prayers and received strength of spirit,[54] he turned to the body and said, 'Tabitha arise!' As though awakened at this voice she looked at Peter, and when she saw him, she sat up. Peter, extending his hand, lifted her up, now alive and alert.

In this way, the weak must be raised up towards godliness. First, there must be prayers to God that he will have mercy on them. Then they must be addressed with teaching, rebuke, and exhortation. Finally, we must with hand extended assist them towards the more perfect things. Peter called back into the room the saints and widows he had asked to leave – they, too, were themselves praying and awaiting the mercy of the Lord – and he presented the woman alive. News of this event spread throughout the whole city of Joppa and led many to confess the name of Jesus. This is the chief benefit of miracles. For it is of little importance otherwise, when so many thousands are born and die in turn, to summon one or two back to life who will a little later die in any case.

As a result of this opportunity, Peter lingered at Joppa for many days. For where would a fisher of men live more gladly than where a huge number are swimming into the net? Meanwhile Peter, prince of apostles, distinguished and esteemed because of such great miracles, lodged with a certain workman, a tanner named Simon.[55]

Chapter 10

None of the apostles had as yet turned aside to the gentiles[1] – it was a favourable opportunity that drew in the Ethiopian eunuch. Nevertheless, for some of the heathen it was a help to have been in the neighbourhood of the apostles. Thus, in Caesarea, formerly called Strato's Tower, a very prosperous city of Palestine,[2] there was a man by the name of Cornelius, a centurion from[3] what is called the Italian cohort. Although he was a pagan by virtue of the religion of his forebears, a soldier by virtue of his office, he was nevertheless a devout man, one who feared God, like one already eager for

Christianity. His entire household, too, was like himself; generally, the rest of the household imitates the head of the house. In two respects, especially, he showed a heart worthy of Christianity: by alleviating the need of the common folk with his great generosity, and by constant supplications to the Lord. He acknowledged the true God – this he had learned by living among the Jews. He knew that God's favour was won especially by dispensing benefactions to the poor and by unremitting prayer. It remained to give to him who had.[4]

At the ninth hour of the day, about dinner time,[5] when he was praying, Cornelius clearly saw in a vision the angel of God coming to him and calling him by name: 'Cornelius' – as though he was well known.[6] Looking at the angel, Cornelius was seized with fear because of the majesty of the unknown figure,[7] and said, 'Who are you, Lord?'[8] The angel replied:

'Your prayers and the alms with which you have solicited the divine mercy have not been lost. What you have invested in fostering the poor, God allows to be reckoned as paid to himself, and he himself will pay back a reward in the name of those who cannot return the favour. You have invested your kind deeds with one who is by no means forgetful. You have done what he wished; he in turn will do for you what you have importunately sought with your constant prayers. God has heard your prayers since your ears were not deaf to the poor.[9] Now, therefore, in order that God may bring to fulfilment his generosity towards you (and this alone remains), you must without delay do this: send some men to the city of Joppa and have them summon a certain Simon, whose surname is Peter – not very noble in the eyes of the world,[10] but in the eyes of God distinguished by his piety. He is staying as a guest with a certain Simon, a citizen of Joppa, a tanner by trade, whose house is by the sea. You will learn from this Peter what you must do to be saved.'[11]

With these words, the angel vanished. At once, then, Cornelius sent two of his household servants, and along with them a soldier – one of those who waited on him, of proven piety and faith; for not only was Cornelius' whole house an imitator of his religion, but there were even among the soldiers some who imitated the religion of their leader.[12] When he had set before them the entire matter about the vision, he told them to go to Joppa. This took place in the evening, and on the next day Cornelius' envoys set out, for at that time the chief shepherd of the church did not disdain a delegation of this kind.[13]

When they were not far from the city of Joppa, at that very time Peter, as his custom was, had gone to the upper room[14] to pray at about the sixth hour – about noon. But when in the midst of his prayers he became hungry, he wanted to take food after a long period of fasting. In the meantime, while food was being prepared at Peter's request, he was carried off in spirit.[15] (This is granted especially to those who pray and fast; to those who are sated and drowsy the mysteries of God are not unsealed.)[16] He saw heaven opened and a sort of vessel, like a great linen sheet tied at the four corners, let down from heaven to earth[17] (foods long ago used to be served on linen sheets).[18] In the vessel was every kind of four-footed beast and creeping thing that lives on the earth, and of fowl that lives in the air,[19] the unclean mingled with the clean. This was no doubt the food that was detestable to the Jews, but which Jesus hungered for when he said to his disciples who were bringing him food, 'I have meat to eat that you know not of.'[20]

While Peter was wondering what the meaning of the strange sight was, a voice rang out and said to him, 'Arise, Peter, sacrifice and eat.'[21] Though the Lord had admonished his own to impart the gospel to all nations,[22] still, that they might do so with greater confidence, he admonished a second time by a vision. Peter, therefore, as a Jew who had hitherto shrunk from foods forbidden by the Law, said, 'Far be it from me, Lord, to eat such foods! For until the present time I have kept religiously the Law of my ancestors; until the present time I have not eaten anything unholy or impure.' To this the same voice that had cried out before, replied, 'What God has made clean, do not you, a man, call unclean.' When the same vision had appeared three times to establish the more its trustworthiness,[23] the vessel was immediately[24] taken up into heaven. Peter came to himself;[25] but while he was hesitating and weighing in his own mind the significance of the vision, whether it was a dream or a token of the divine will, lo, those men whom Cornelius had dispatched were standing at the door of Simon the tanner. Calling out one of the servants, they asked whether a certain Simon surnamed Peter was staying there. However, before it was announced to Peter that some men were asking for him, while he was reflecting privately about the meaning of the vision, the Spirit spoke to him (for God speaks to his saints in various ways)[26] and said, 'Behold, three men are standing in front of the door and are asking for you. Arise, therefore, and go down, and go with them without hesitation, for they have been sent by me, and you will understand the meaning of the vision you are wondering about.'

Peter went down and came to the men[27] and said, 'Here I am, the Simon Peter whom you seek. For what reason have you come here?' Peter does not parade his vision, but demands a confession from the gentiles;[28] for the grace of the gospel should neither be forced upon the scornful nor denied to the eager. The men then replied: 'Cornelius, though officially a centurion, is nevertheless a man of sound character, fearing God, tested and approved[29] not only among his own people but also by the testimony of the whole Jewish race. He has been instructed by an oracle from a holy angel, who appeared to him, to summon you to his house and to hear you prescribe what he must do to gain salvation.' Peter realized that the visions harmonized, and understood what that voice, heard three times, meant: 'What God has made clean do not you make unclean.' He invited them to come in and since it was evening gave them lodging.

This was the beginning of the association of the Jews with the gentiles, who were of their own accord hastening towards partnership in the gospel.[30] But the hesitation of the apostles in this matter stemmed from their concern that it be recognized that the gentiles' admission to the grace of the gospel had been undertaken clearly at God's command, and not rashly. Cornelius invites, but on the admonition of the angel; Peter goes down and meets the messengers, but instructed by a vision. On the one side was a glowing eagerness for the grace of the gospel; on the other an alacrity and promptitude on the part of one who thirsted for the salvation of all races.[31] And so on the next day Peter set out for Caesarea. Some Christians from the city of Joppa accompanied him to be witnesses of whatever should be done, for in their hearts was a presentiment that some joyful event would occur. Meanwhile[32] Cornelius, eager for salvation,[33] awaited the return of his men with Peter. Both his relatives and his closest friends had been called together, so that at one and the same time this deed would have more witnesses and the benefit would be spread among more people.[34]

Now as Peter was going into the house of the centurion, Cornelius was gladdened and, to show his respect, advanced to meet him. He fell at his feet and worshipped him, sensing something about him greater than a human being. So we ought to reverence Christ in his ministers, but in such a way that the glory of God is not attributed to a man.[35] Accordingly, Peter offered an example of how stewards of Christ ought to be free from ambition and not claim for themselves any praise for what they do by the power and the name of Christ.[36] He did not permit the centurion to remain prostrate on the ground, but embraced him, and lifted him up, saying, 'Arise! You are a man speaking with a man. Pay that honour to God, of whom I am only a minister.'[37] And now they entered together in familiar conversation. When they came to the inner part of the house, Peter found many gathered together there.[38] From this, the greedy shepherd now took hope of more abundant fruit.

When, therefore, Peter had sat down,[39] the evangelical orator at one and the same time both addressing the offence taken by his companions[40] and strengthening the faith of the centurion's household, began thus:

'You know that for a Jewish person it is unlawful[41] to join in the daily life of a stranger's household, or even to approach those who are of a different religion and uncircumcised. I, however, though a Jew, have not been afraid to do this. It is not that I have disdained the religion and practices of my people, but I have followed the authority of God, who has shown me by a vision that it is not right to regard anyone, whatever his race, as impure or detestable when God does not hold him to be unclean. For God alone sanctifies all things. Accordingly, trusting to God's command, I have come here without hesitation at your summons. It is yours, therefore, to explain the reason why you have summoned me.'

Peter spoke to everyone that he might gain them all,[42] aware that they had assembled together so that they might hear the word of the gospel. How shrewdly Peter plays the role of pastor! He imparts the mystery of the evangelical doctrine only to those who declare their eagerness to learn.[43] Thereupon Cornelius in the presence of them all explained the circumstances, saying:

'This is the fourth day,' he said, 'since I was at my home, fasting and intent on prayer, until about the ninth hour.[44] And behold, a certain man stood before me. He was majestic in mien, striking in his bright apparel, and he said to me, "Cornelius, your supplication has been heard, and the remembrance of your generosity to the poor is kept in the sight of God. Send, therefore, to Joppa and summon Simon whose surname is Peter. He is a guest at the house of Simon the tanner, close by the sea."[45] Without delay, then, I sent my men to you; nor would I have dared to do so, had I not been ordered by the angel. I am grateful for your kindness, for you have not hesitated to come here. Therefore, we are now all present here with simple and sincere hearts – of this we make God our witness[46] – desiring to hear all that you have been commanded by the Lord[47] to set forth to us. For the angel who aroused this confidence promised me this, and we do not doubt that you will do it, since you, also, by divine command have not disdained to have conversation with us.'

Peter perceived their sincerity, and so at that point he opened his mouth and began to speak in this manner:

'In very truth I perceive that with God there is no respect of persons, but among every people whoever fears him and embraces righteousness is acceptable to him. For I have seen that you, though strangers to our Law, nevertheless worship with us the true and only God: through your holy prayers you offer daily sacrifices to him, and you seek his favour by helping the poor.[48] This is the teaching of the Law and the prophets. Although God long ago promised through the mouth of the prophets that he would send the Messiah, that is, the Christ, he has now at last fulfilled what he promised, making it known to the sons of Israel, not now through prophets but through his only Son Jesus Christ,[49] offering them abolition of sins and reconciliation to himself through faith and obedience to the one he sent. And yet, since he is the God of all,[50] not only of the Israelite people,[51] he wants this grace to be salvific for all who believe the gospel.

'I have no doubt that the report of this affair, which has spread through all Judaea, has reached you also – the report about Jesus who traversed all the regions of Judaea, urging all to repentance, testifying that the kingdom of God was now at hand. But he began the preaching of the gospel especially from Galilee, after he had been baptized by John. John was his precursor and gave testimony publicly about him: that Jesus of Nazareth was the Lamb of God who took away the sins of the world; that God had anointed his Messiah with the Holy Spirit whom he, John, had seen descending upon the Christ in the form of a dove as though from heaven and remaining on his head; and that it was Christ alone who would baptize all who believe, not with water, as he had baptized, but with heavenly power.[52] The Lord Jesus showed this power by his very deeds as he travelled about through all the regions of Judaea, helping everyone, not only by teaching the evangelical philosophy through which souls are healed, but also by healing the sick, casting out demons, cleansing lepers, raising the dead, and, in a word, by lifting up all whom the devil held oppressed.[53] Inasmuch as he alone was free from all sin, he alone was able to crush the tyranny of the devil, who holds sway over those guilty of sin. For God was in his Son, exerting his own might,[54] which no power of Satan can withstand.

'Since all these things have become common knowledge throughout the whole of Judaea, I have no doubt that you too have heard and believed them. But to make your confidence in these events more firm, we who had constant and familiar association with him when he was still a mortal among mortals are witnesses of all that he did in all the territories of the Jews, and also in Jerusalem. The high priests, the scribes, and the Pharisees, with the agreement of the nobles and the people, killed him by nailing him to the cross, thus rendering the vilest thanks for so many kindnesses. God, however, by whose permission all these things were done for the salvation of the human race,[55] called him back to life on the third day after his death and gave him immortality. To strengthen confidence in this fact he presented himself alive – to be heard, seen, touched with the hands – not to the whole people as he had done before his death, but to sure witnesses whom God had chosen beforehand for this purpose: I mean us, to whom he frequently appeared after he had risen from the dead. He remained on earth for forty days,[56] and we ate and drank with him as he ate and drank, so that no doubt could linger in our minds about the reality of the body that was raised.[57] Before he ascended into heaven he commanded us who had been chosen for this task to preach openly to all, testifying that he himself is that one whom God has elevated to the supreme power to be judge of all, the living and the dead, at the end of the world.

'Meanwhile, a sure and easy remedy is offered to all. For what we have said of him, this all the prophets already long ago, and with complete harmony, have testified of him also: that he and he alone is the one through whose name remission of sins is to be given, not only to the Jews, but also to all peoples throughout the entire world, and not through works in which the Jews trust, but through the faith by which the gospel is believed and through the gospel, Christ.'[58]

Peter had not yet finished this sermon when lo, the Holy Spirit descended from heaven with a visible sign and came upon all who heard and believed the apostle's words. This amazed the Jews who had been converted to the evangelical doctrine and had come as companions of Peter from the city of Joppa to be witnesses of what would take place. They were surprised that the grace of the Holy Spirit had been poured out upon gentiles also who had not been circumcised. They supposed that the promise of the prophets pertained to the Israelites alone, although the prophets expressly predicted that the Spirit of God would be poured out upon all who called upon the name of the Lord.[59]

The reality itself accompanied the sign they had seen with their eyes.[60] For they began to speak in different[61] tongues to all those who were listening, extolling with their praises the kindness of God. This sign, so clear, was given to the circumcised who were present so that they should not in the future hesitate to call to Christ even the uncircumcised. It was given to the friends of Cornelius as well so that they should have no doubt that through belief they were equal to the Jews without the help of the Law.[62] The normal order, however, as it was under the control of God, was reversed: first baptism is given to catechumens, then the Holy Spirit through the imposition of hands;[63] here the Holy Spirit was given first without the imposition of hands so that the apostle would not hesitate to add the lesser after God had of his own accord bestowed the greater.[64]

Then Peter, as though he wanted the consent of the Jews to do what he had in any case intended to do, said to his companions, 'Can anyone forbid these to be baptized,[65] even though uncircumcised, who have already received the Holy Spirit just as we ourselves?' They agreed, and he commanded that they be baptized in the name of Jesus Christ.[66] After these events had been brought to a happy conclusion, Peter was preparing to return to Joppa, but they asked him to linger with them for some days, since they desired to be more fully informed about the evangelical precepts. Peter complied, though upon their solicitation, for he knew that the Jews would scarcely tolerate close and familiar association with the uncircumcised.

Chapter 11

The report of this event – that the gentiles also had received the word[1] of God – spread to the other apostles who had remained at Jerusalem, and to the brethren who were in Judaea. It could not easily be concealed, if only because the centurion was well known by virtue of his official status,[2] or because many were baptized at the same time, or because Jews witnessed the event (for the eunuch was baptized on his journey, alone and without a witness, as though he were filching the grace of the gospel from the Jews), or because it occurred in a distinguished city of Palestine.[3]

Peter, however, was not unaware that this would become widely known, and that there would be Jews who would censure the deed. He took every precaution so that it could not be censured justly. God also reassured him: so that no scruple should stick in his mind, the vision was presented thrice. Further, it was through the Spirit that he learned that a delegation from Cornelius was at hand. He does not admit them into his house at once, lest a Jew should seem to be eager for relations with gentiles, but he greets them in front of the door and asks, with witnesses on hand, why they had come. He makes this inquiry for the sake of the Jews who were present, rather than for himself. Then when he learns that the two visions corresponded, he does not set out there except with some Jews of approved faith in his company, who might be witnesses and give consent to the proceedings, so that later they could turn from witnesses into defenders against critics. Again, when they came to the house of Cornelius, Peter did not enter immediately, as though he were longing for a conversation, but sent a man to announce that he was there, so that Cornelius might meet him and bring him in[4] – Peter was not unaware how eagerly he would be received. The centurion fell at his feet and worshipped Peter. This showed to the Jews who were present Cornelius' remarkable readiness of mind. Further, Peter asks in the presence of these Jews why he was summoned, so that the story, heard from Cornelius' mouth, might have more credibility for his Jewish companions. Finally, the Holy Spirit was sent without anyone asking: prayers were not yet poured forth, hands had not been imposed, baptism had not been given. Even so he did not baptize them without addressing the circumcised who were present and showing that it was not right to deny baptism to those upon whom God had bestowed his Holy Spirit.[5]

Such, truly, was that evangelical prudence of Peter, the shepherd. He knew the nature of the Jews, how they prided themselves on account of a little bit of cut off foreskin,[6] how they shunned the uncircumcised. Accordingly, he does everything to avoid the slightest offence.[7] He desired that gentiles should come into the fellowship of the gospel, but, if possible, without the loss of the Jewish race.[8] And so, when Peter happened[9] to return to Jerusalem where the report about Cornelius' baptism had already preceded him, those from the circumcision who had embraced the evangelical doctrine contended with him, saying, 'Why have you entered the house of the uncircumcised, contrary to ancestral tradition, and, not content with this, have shared a table with those who eat food forbidden by the law of Moses?'[10]

Here it was not proper for Peter to be silent, but going back to the beginning, he explained everything in order, as it happened, saying:

'For my part, I should not have ventured to violate the Law handed down from our forefathers, but I obeyed the authority of one greater than the Law. I was in the city of Joppa, fasting and free to devote myself to prayer – let no one suspect this was an empty dream.[11] Spurred by hunger, I had ordered food prepared. Meanwhile I was carried away and saw in an ecstasy[12] a vision like this: a sort of vessel, something like a great linen sheet tied at its four corners,[13] was being let down from heaven and came right to me. When I, in hunger, fastened my eyes upon it, I looked to see what the food was. I saw there various kinds of four-footed creatures, also beasts of prey, and in addition, different species of reptiles and birds[14] which the Law bids us abstain from eating.[15] While I was observing these, a voice also rang out urging me to eat (for I was hesitating), and said to me, "Arise, Peter, sacrifice and eat." To this I then replied, "Far be it from me,[16] Lord; for until the present time, nothing impure or unclean has gone into my mouth." At this, I heard the voice again [17] responding thus: "What God has made clean, do not you, a mere man, call common." This vision was presented three times. Then all those things which I thought abhorrent were taken back into heaven, and I came to myself.

'While I was pondering in my mind what was the meaning of this vision that had been presented so many times, the Spirit at once advised me that three men sent to me from Caesarea were at the door of the house where I was a guest. The same Spirit bade me go with them without hesitation.[18] I obeyed the vision, and under the order of the Holy Spirit I set out for Caesarea, not alone but with these six brethren as companions, that they should be witnesses of all that was being done by the will of God. We entered the house of the man who had summoned us. While all were listening, he told how a few days before, when he was fasting and praying at home, he saw in broad daylight an angel standing near him in a shining garment.[19] The angel said to him, "Cornelius, send some of your servants to Joppa to summon on your behalf Simon surnamed Peter. He will tell you those things through which you may obtain salvation, both you and your entire house." When I saw that the visions harmonized at every point, and then noticed how eager these people were, I began to expound for them the things the Lord Jesus wanted us to preach. I had not yet finished my discourse when, behold, the Holy Spirit descended from heaven upon them as he had descended upon us at the beginning, and they began to speak in different tongues as we at that time spoke. This sign clearly demonstrated that their faith was made acceptable to God.

'And now the events themselves have shown me what was intended by the riddle of the vision I had seen. These were, clearly, those four-footed creatures, creeping things, and fowl[20] that we circumcised abhor but that God has decided to make clean through faith. He does not want us to regard anything as unclean which has been sanctified through evangelical faith.[21] At the same time I remembered the word that the Lord spoke to us when he was about to ascend into heaven: John indeed baptized with water but you shall be baptized with the Holy Spirit.[22] And we indeed do wash the body in water, but water does not confer salvation unless faith obtains from God the baptism of fire.[23] The case spoke for itself.[24] They had already been baptized by that baptism which the Lord Jesus had promised, and the same grace had been conferred through faith upon the uncircumcised that we had received, not because of merits accruing from observing the Law, but because of belief through which we trusted in the Lord Jesus Christ.[25] Who was I, therefore, that I could gainsay the Lord? Should I have denied the baptism of water to those who had already been baptized by the Lord with the Spirit, when the baptism of water is only the sign of a grace to be conferred by God?[26] But now the grace had preceded without our action; and to deny the baptism of water – what else would that have been but to reject what God had done?'

When they heard these things they were silent and glorified God saying, 'The events themselves show, then, that God has granted repentance not to the Israelites only but also to the gentiles, that they might gain eternal life.' And thus Peter joined to the church these 'first-fruits of the gospel' from the gentiles;[27] for hitherto no one had dared this except Philip alone, and then with an angel to prompt him. True, those who had been scattered by the storm of persecution that arose after the death of Stephen went through the villages and cities all the way to Phoenicia and Cyprus (the island facing it), as well as to Antioch, which separates Phoenicia from Cilicia,[28] proclaiming among all the evangelical word they had received from the apostles. They did not, however, dare to share it with anyone except those of the Jewish race alone[29] – not indeed from invidious motives, but out of regard for religion, thinking it was not allowed to give what was holy to dogs, which the Lord had forbidden.[30]

Among those who had believed, however, certain men arose, Cypriots and Cyrenaeans by race, who, when they had come to the city of Antioch, dared to speak to Greeks about Christ, proclaiming the Lord Jesus to them.[31] And they were highly successful, for the favour of the Lord mightily prospered their work, giving strength and courage to the heralds of his name. From these, too, a copious number of people believed the gospel and turned to the Lord. A report of this came to the ears of the church that was in Jerusalem. For this reason, Barnabas the Levite, a Cypriot by race, and a man of apostolic sincerity,[32] was sent there[33] by the apostles, that by being present he might look carefully into what was going on there; if he found that what had been done was of the will of God, he should confirm it with the authority of the apostles. So great was the caution in admitting the gentiles to the gospel. Not that the apostles did not greatly desire this, but they feared that if it were rashly done it might later be annulled by the Jews, or that the gentiles would have little self-confidence, as though they might need the support of the Law. Therefore, when Barnabas came to Antioch and found that through faith and without claiming observance of the Law the Greeks had obtained the same grace of God as the Jews had received, he rejoiced greatly that the number of believers was growing,[34] and exhorted everyone to stand firm in their resolve, and to persevere in clinging to the Lord.[35] For Barnabas was a good man and full of the Holy Spirit and faith. And thus by his preaching it turned out that a further great multitude joined the former number of those professing the Lord.[36]

Since Antioch borders on Cilicia,[37] the very proximity of location invited Barnabas to seek out Paul, who was fitted better than the others (inasmuch as he was chosen by Christ) for the task of making the name of Christ shine among the peoples and the kings of the earth.[38] (When he had fled from Jerusalem the disciples had brought him to Caesarea in Phoenicia, and from there he set out for Tarsus.)[39] When he had found him there, he brought him to Antioch, because he hoped that in a city populous and renowned, but with a mixture of Greeks and Jews,[40] the fruit would be more abundant through an apostle chosen especially for this ministry. And so for a whole year they remained together at Antioch in the church of the believers, a church which had become quite large in number through the conflux of Greeks and Jews. As a result of the teaching of both, that is, of Paul and Barnabas, there was added to this number also a great multitude of people, so that those who were formerly called disciples (the name of 'Christ' was kept muffled because of its odium) began first at Antioch to be called Christians, a term derived from the name of their founder.[41]

At this time certain prophets came to Antioch from the city of Jerusalem. One of them, Agabus by name, rising up in the congregation, indicated to them by the inspiration of the Spirit that there would be a great famine throughout the world. This happened under Claudius Caesar, who succeeded Caligula.[42] Now of those who lived in Jerusalem, part had come to the profession of the gospel from the poor, part had paid into the common chest what they possessed, and part because of their profession of Jesus Christ had lost their goods through the pillaging of the priests.[43] For this reason, therefore, the disciples in Antioch resolved to take a collection from those who had the means, especially from the gentiles who had received the gospel, and to send the money collected to relieve the Christians dwelling in Judaea; in such a way, however, that no one was compelled to contribute but everyone contributed willingly and gladly in proportion to his means.[44] It was done as they resolved. This money was sent through Paul and Barnabas to Jerusalem – to the elders to be distributed at their discretion to those in need.[45]

Chapter 12

While Paul and Barnabas were engaged in this mission, King Herod – who had cut off the head of John the Baptist and had sent Christ to Pilate, robed in a white garment to mock him[1] – was distressed because people of this kind were growing in number daily, and because the name of Jesus, the king of the Jews,[2] was gaining renown through many regions. He thought it a matter of consequence for himself as well that this spreading sect should be destroyed.[3] This was, no doubt, Satan attempting through his instruments what he had attempted before, though he succeeded only in making the name of Jesus more glorious. Herod, therefore, playing without subtlety his part as king, sent his armed guards to afflict some of the congregation who were professing Jesus of Nazareth, the Lord of all.[4] And so he who had learned from the beheading of John to lop off the heads of the pious and those who freely professed the truth cast his hands upon the apostle James, the brother of John, because he was held in a position of special authority among the apostles at that time. He commanded that James, who was steadfast in preaching the name of Jesus, be punished with the sword.[5]

When Herod saw that this barbarous act was not without gratification to the Jewish people, he added crime to crime, and ordered Peter also, as leader among the apostles, to be arrested. He hoped that if the shepherd was removed, the flock would easily be scattered.[6] It was, no doubt, with this in mind that the Jews had earlier killed the Lord Jesus, while keeping their hands off the apostles. He was, however, prevented from immediately killing Peter too by the day of the *azyma*,[7] which in fact fell just then, an exceedingly holy day among the Jews, the time when the Jews had also feared to kill Jesus.[8] And such is Jewish religion in its observance of feast days: they do not fear to propitiate the people with the blood of an innocent man, but they are afraid to violate a feast day, as though one is innocent of homicide who has already decided to kill![9] And so he ordered Peter arrested and thrown into prison. So that he could not possibly escape, as Paul had escaped,[10] he added four squads of four soldiers each to guard him in chains: no one was to be able to rescue him by force.[11] For he had decided that when the feast days were past,[12] he would bring this victim out to the people, who were thirsting for the blood of the innocent. Like people, like king![13]

Meanwhile Peter does not protest the prison – he had been warned of these eventualities by the Lord;[14] nor do the disciples stir up a riot[15] against the impious violence of a tyrant, for they remembered that the Lord had taught them to bless even those who persecuted them.[16] For Herod a prison was not enough, or a pair of chains, or a single squad of armed soldiers – in order, no doubt, that the cruel care of an ungodly king might add to the fullness of the glory of the redeemer Christ![17] Peter, thus guarded, spent the feast day in prison. In the meantime, the church of the disciples, anxious for its pastor, did not cease to ask God for Peter's safety with prayers both day and night.[18]

Now when the feast days were past and Herod was about to bring Peter before the people, then, just in time, on the very night preceding the summons, Peter was sleeping between two soldiers, bound with two chains, while the other soldiers were on sentry duty guarding the gate of the prison, and lo, an angel of the Lord suddenly stood beside Peter, and at the same time a marvellous light illuminated the cell: the gloom both of the prison and of the night was scattered. Tapping Peter on his side, he roused him, saying, 'Arise quickly!' At the sound of these words, the chains fell forthwith from his hands. At once the angel said, 'Dress yourself and bind your sandals upon your feet; leave none of your clothes here.' Peter obeyed, and the angel continued, 'Put on your cloak[19] and follow me.' As the angel went ahead Peter followed and began to leave the prison, not yet aware that what was being done by the angel was really happening; he thought he was seeing a vision as he had before.[20] But when they had passed the first and likewise the second sentry, they came to the iron gate that leads to the city. Though secured with bolts and bars it opened for them of its own accord. And so they went out, and continued until they passed by one district of the city.[21] Immediately the angel disappeared and left Peter just as suddenly as he had stood beside him. Peter, however, looking about and recognizing the part of the city he was then in, came[22] to himself and said, 'Now I see that what has taken place is not a dream, but the Lord, in pity for his own, has sent his angel and delivered me out of the hands of Herod, who had determined to sacrifice me to the Jews. The angel has at the same time mocked the cruelty of the king and the fond hope of the people.'

When he had considered where he might best withdraw to safety, intending to share the joy of this event with his disciples, he proceeded to the house of Mary, the mother of John – not the John who was the brother of James,[23] but the one who was called by his surname Mark. Many were gathered in her house praying together for the release of the shepherd. Peter knocked at the door of the gate[24] that faced the street, and a girl came out to overhear[25] what it was. Her name was Rhoda. When Peter realized that she was at the door, he admonished her to open the door quickly. As soon as she recognized Peter's voice, in astonishment at the unexpected joy, she did not open the door but ran in and announced that Peter was standing in front of the door. But those within were quite aware how diligently Herod had taken care to keep Peter under guard, and they replied to the girl, 'You are out of your mind!' When she continued to affirm that it was so, some said, 'It is not Peter, but his angel imitating his voice.' For it was believed that each had his own angel as a guardian and companion who sometimes appeared in the likeness of the person himself.[26] As Peter in the meantime did not stop knocking, they opened the door. They saw Peter enter, and were dumbfounded. Since the house was ringing with the voices of those who were expressing their joy, Peter signalled to them with his hand that they should be silent and listen quietly, that no one should detect what had happened from the unexpected noise of joyful people.[27] When they were silent, he explained everything to them in order, how the Lord had, through his angel, brought him out of the prison. He said, 'See that James the brother of the Lord' – he was bishop of Jerusalem[28] – 'and the rest of the brethren know this, that they may share in our joy. Thus the God who is best mixes the sad with the joyful, and the joyful with the sad, so that we should not be despondent.'[29] Having spoken thus, Peter went out from there at once and withdrew to another place where he could more safely hide on account of the fear of Herod, whose inflexible cruelty he knew.[30]

Dawn came and the soldiers who had been assigned to guard-duty saw that their captive had escaped, though the doors were closed and the chains untouched. They were mightily disturbed, and wondered what had become of Peter. When Herod asked for Peter, to bring him out for condemnation, and he was not found in the prison, he examined the guards and ordered them to be led away to prison, intending to punish them at his leisure.[31] But God took pity on his own, and checked the madness of Herod, having regard at the same time for the safety both of the apostles and the soldiers. It was not fitting that Peter's safety should provide the occasion for the destruction of the innocent.[32]

For it happened, meanwhile, that Herod had cause to go to Caesarea of Palestine.[33] He was angry with the people of Tyre and Sidon and was already resolved to make war.[34] When this became known, they agreed unanimously to come to him, and having persuaded Blastus, who was the royal chamberlain, they sued for peace, deeming the friendship of a neighbouring king essential for themselves.[35] Since the wealth of the people of Tyre and Sidon grew especially out of the commerce of tradesmen, they made most profit when the territories on their borders were at peace, for they were not able to undertake a war without grave loss when freedom of export and import was interrupted.[36] This affair was settled. A solemn festival was held as a votive celebration for the safety of Caesar, for which reason the chief men of the whole province had assembled there. On the second day of the games, which were provided in abundance,[37] Herod, dressed in a wonderfully made garment woven of silver and gold, addressed the people from an elevated platform. When the folds of the king's robe, catching the light of the sun, reflected its rays like a flash of lightning, everyone was blinded, and the cry arose from the fawning crowd, 'The voice of a god and not of man!' – as though they saw in him something greater than a human being.

Such adulation of the people often contributes to their having tyrants instead of kings, when they attribute divinity to those scarcely worthy of the name of human being. The rulers in turn fawn upon the people with shows and obscene plays, and sometimes even with the slaughter of good men, just as earlier Herod had commended himself to the people by the slaughter of James.[38] Herod did not refuse or abhor an adulation so blasphemous, but was delighted to be regarded as a god though he was but a wretched man, soon to perish.[39]

The divine vengeance soon came upon him, for immediately, in the midst of his address, an angel of the Lord, whom he saw standing behind him as he glanced back, struck him, because he claimed for himself, though a man, an honour which can be shared with no created being. He was suddenly seized by the anguish of a disease more loathsome and more excruciating than almost any other: worms ate away his body and in a few days he died, racked with violent pain.[40] In this way the persecutor of the Lord's flock was removed, and the word of the gospel[41] grew and multiplied.[42]

Barnabas and Saul[43] acquitted themselves of the tasks they had taken into their care from the brethren. The money which had been sent for the support of the needy was handed over and distributed through the apostles. Then the two envoys left Jerusalem[44] and made their way to Antioch, and John, whose other name was Mark, joined them as a companion.

Chapter 13

Now the church of Antioch had flourished, so that it had quite a number[1] rich in the gift of prophecy, others again endowed with the grace of teaching.[2] Among these[3] were Barnabas and Simeon, who was called by the Latin term Niger,[4] also Lucius, a native of Cyrene, and Manahen. This Manahen had been brought up from boyhood with Herod the tetrarch,[5] whose friendship he had forsaken and had gone over to Christ. But chief among these was Saul,[6] who alone excelled in all the apostolic gifts.[7] All of them were serving the good of the church with great zeal, faithfully sharing their gifts for the salvation of all and for the glory of Christ; no sacrifice is more pleasing to God than this.[8] Meanwhile, they were fasting so that they might aid the progress of the church not only with service but with pure prayers[9] also. Then the Holy Spirit, moved by their prayers, signified through the prophets what he wanted done, saying, 'Set apart for me Barnabas and Saul, the two foremost of all, so that they may begin to perform that service[10] to which I have especially called them, that is, to be the teachers of the gentiles,[11] and that I might through them scatter widely abroad the seed of the evangelical word.'

They did as the Spirit commanded. Barnabas and Saul were set apart from the others so that it would be clear to all which ones were being chosen. And when with fasting and united prayer they had entreated the favour of the Lord that the service they were undertaking might turn out prosperously for the church, those among them who were pre-eminent in authority laid their hands upon them[12] and sent them away, to go wherever the Spirit should lead them.

Accordingly, at the impulse of the Spirit, Barnabas and Paul went first to Seleucia, that is, to the headland of Antioch,[13] and from there they sailed to the island of Cyprus. They landed at Salamis, a distinguished city of this island[14] and the first to come in view as one approaches from the east. They did not preach human fables[15] but the word of God; not secretly, but in the synagogues of the Jews, of whom there was a great multitude because of the proximity to Syria.[16] To share in this ministry they had John, also named Mark, whom they had brought with them from Jerusalem. Everywhere they did the Jews this honour, following the mandate of Christ:[17] the gospel was carried first to them, so that a peevish and complaining people should not cry out that they had been despised.[18] Thus they preached as they travelled through the whole island until they came to Paphos, a city sacred to Venus, and furthermost on the western side of Cyprus.[19]

Here they came upon a certain magician by the name of Barjesus, that is to say, the son of Jesus,[20] a Jew by race and by religious profession, and on this pretext claiming for himself, falsely, the spirit of prophecy. He was attached to Sergius Paulus, proconsul of this island, a man in other respects prudent; for men of the kind Barjesus was usually insinuate themselves into friendship with the mighty so that by corrupting them they may bring the more grievous calamity to the affairs of mortals.[21] Accordingly, when the proconsul learned that the evangelical word was being spread abroad through Cyprus, not only did he not oppose it, but even summoned Barnabas and Paul to himself, desiring to learn from them the heavenly doctrine. But Barjesus, the enemy of Jesus the Saviour,[22] tried to withstand the advancing gospel, the craftsman of falsehood strove against the rising truth, and Elymas, an Aramaic name meaning magician and false prophet,[23] fought against the apostles, the true prophets. For, seeing the proconsul eager to learn the evangelical word, and understanding that there would henceforth be no place for his counterfeit arts among those who had learned the genuine truth, he tried to turn the proconsul away lest he put faith in the apostles' words.[24]

Observe here the clash between the cunning arts of human beings and the dynamic force of the gospel. Saul, who was also called Paul,[25] could not abide a man full of the spirit of Satan, a man fighting with malicious arts against the simple truth. Receiving an inrush of the divine Spirit into his whole breast, he fixed his eyes upon the magician and said to him:

'O you who are full of all guile and all villainy,[26] resembling your father the devil, who by trickery and lies formerly enticed man to death; O enemy of all justice and sincerity – in this, too, showing yourself a son of the devil, for he first took innocence away from man – you declare war on justice as it is being reborn. It is not enough for you to have made sport until now of people's simplicity with your deceptive arts. Even now, when God wishes evangelical truth, which knows no deceit, to shine forth through the whole world, you, stubbornly persisting nevertheless in your malicious evil, do not cease to fight against the will of God. You have regard more for your own false glory and base gain than for the salvation of yourself and of many.[27] But that you may understand that the arts of demons have no strength against evangelical truth – behold! you will in a moment feel the power of him whose will you oppose. You boast that you are a prophet and a seer, though in your mind you are blind. Here you delude people who judge from what they see, but God, who knows the blindness of your heart, will soon take away your corporeal eyes.[28] In this way all may see that you are truly blind and unworthy to see this corporeal sun visible to the eyes of all – you who have taken up war against the sun of evangelical truth now dawning upon the world. Such will be the divine vengeance until you repent and come to your senses.'[29]

Scarcely had Paul spoken these words when suddenly a deep blindness like the darkness of night seized the magician, so that he wandered about in bewilderment seeking someone to guide him with outstretched hand. The proconsul had looked on and witnessed these things as they occurred. He was astonished at the instantaneous power of the heavenly doctrine whose force had so easily demolished the empty pretensions of magic, and he believed and professed the name of Christ.[30] Instead of the false prophet Barjesus, he embraced in his heart the true disciples of Jesus.

Such were the events at Paphos. From this city Paul with his companions set sail for Asia Minor,[31] and came to Perga, a city of Pamphylia. But John, also named Mark, left them and returned to Jerusalem from where Barnabas and Paul had taken him. They none the less went through Pamphylia and came to Antioch, a city of Pisidia.[32] There they entered the synagogue where the Jews, as their custom was, usually met, and they sat with the others, ready to hear the reading from the Law and the prophets. When the reading was finished no one arose. Now the leaders of the synagogue saw from their dress that their visitors were Jews from abroad,[33] and they gave every appearance of being upright men, so they signified to them through pages that, if any of them had anything he wished to say to the people by way of instruction or exhortation, he should speak.[34] Then Paul, the heavenly orator, arose to speak. With a gesture of the hand he requested silence[35] and began to speak thus:

'Men of Israel, and you who, following the example of your forefathers, fear God, listen to me as I explain to you the will of God and expound the mystery of this reading, which is repeated every sabbath in the synagogue.[36] God, the protector of the race of Israel, chose for himself our fathers and this people in preference to others.[37] Consequently, when in Egypt they served in hard bondage[38] and Pharaoh took action that they should not increase, while those who remained should be crushed by their labours,[39] God raised them up against the oppressive tyrant by wondrous miracles[40] and led them out of bondage. He did so not through deceptive tricks, or with the help of human defences, but by his own arm raised high, so that all might understand that this race was dear to God. After leading them out, it was with great leniency that for almost forty years he put up with their behaviour in the wilderness,[41] as they repeatedly rebelled and murmured against Moses.[42] Even so, he did not bring upon them the ultimate punishment, in order that what he had promised to the patriarchs he might at length fulfil for their descendants.[43] After forty years he led them into the promised land, and when seven nations had been destroyed in the land of Canaan, he divided among them by lot the land of the Canaanites, after almost four hundred and fifty years.[44] And this was the proof of a mind extraordinarily well disposed towards our race.

'Accordingly when conditions had become peaceful, he gave them judges under whose guidance they might live in tranquillity,[45] until Samuel the prophet, the last of the judges.[46] Under Samuel, they demanded of God a king, though Samuel advised against it.[47] When they persisted in their demand, he gave them Saul, the son of Kish, from the tribe of Benjamin, whom the Lord rejected because of his pride and disobedience.[48] And so under Samuel, a judge of the greatest integrity, and under the ungodly Saul they lived for forty years.[49] Not even at this point was a most forbearing[50] God estranged in heart and mind from his own people, the people he once had chosen, but in place of the bad king whom they had obtained by the force of their impious demands, he raised up David to be their king. God himself bore witness to David's piety saying, "I have found David, the son of Jesse, a man inclined towards me, who will obey my will in everything."[51] For just as an angry God gives a people a foolish and ungodly prince as a very harsh punishment, so when gracious and reconciled, he grants a godly king and one obedient to God in place of the evil king he has removed.[52] To David, God had promised a descendant who would recover the kingdom of Israel and whose kingdom would have no end.[53] Now what has been promised often and for a long time by the oracles of the prophets has been fulfilled.[54] From the stock of David, just as he had promised him, God has brought forth the Saviour of the race of Israel,[55] Jesus – the name corresponding to the reality.[56]

'Just as this Saviour had been promised by the prophets, and had been designated as well by the types and figures of the Law, so he was proclaimed and pointed out by John the Baptist, before he revealed himself to the world. John himself also preceded the Saviour's coming, according to Isaiah's prophecy, and invited the whole people of Israel to baptism and repentance of their former life, crying out publicly that the kingdom of God was now at hand.[57] Now John had been sent from God[58] for this purpose alone, to go before the coming Saviour and to prepare human hearts for his advent. But when John had almost finished his course and many believed that he was the Christ because of his remarkable holiness of life, he publicly refused this title and transferred it to the one to whom it was due, saying: "Why do you think I am the Christ?[59] I am only his messenger. And yet he whom you erroneously believe me to be is not far away. For he will succeed me, later in time but so much greater in power and dignity[60] that I am not worthy to loose the sandals from his feet, a task which in human society is regarded as the lowest form of service. For what is lowest in him is higher than that which is greatest in me."

'We do not, therefore, announce to you something unexpected, but the Saviour promised to the leaders of our race for so many centuries now, awaited for so many ages by our ancestors and even by you, acknowledged by John, who had the greatest authority among the Jews,[61] and commended to all the Jews by John's public testimony. Accordingly, my brothers, you who embrace the Law, who revere the prophets, who derive your race from Abraham, to whom God has promised the seed through which all nations will gain a blessing:[62] if you are truly sons of Abraham, if you truly fear

God[63] – resembling in this the piety of your father Abraham – acknowledge this salvific word which we bring to you, and embrace what the patriarchs were delighted to have been promised but which now has been fulfilled. This salvation is conferred upon all through Jesus, but it is offered first of all to you[64] to whom the prophecies were delivered and from whose race Christ has come forth.[65]

'Do not be moved by the example of the people of Jerusalem and of the rulers of that city. Not recognizing the Messiah sent by God or understanding the utterances of the prophets – though they are read in their midst every Sabbath – they condemned Jesus and through imperception fulfilled what the prophets had predicted. For so it had been determined by the divine counsel,[66] so it had been predicted by the utterances of all the prophets, that one man free from every stain of sin should, like a spotless lamb, be sacrificed for the sins of all.[67] Accordingly, though the priests, Pharisees, scribes, and the chief men of the people along with the people themselves tried everything and still found no reason why he should be killed, nevertheless, with shameless cries[68] they demanded of Pilate that he kill him.[69] And when they had, quite unawares, accomplished all the things the prophets had predicted about him, they took him down from the cross and laid him in a tomb. But the very one whom, as God had willed, the evil will of men had put to death,[70] the power of the same God raised from the dead on the third day according to the oracles of the prophets. Do not suppose that my story is a dream. He was seen, heard, touched; by his body that had come alive again he was recognized during a period of forty days by his disciples who had accompanied him from Galilee when he set out for Jerusalem to die.[71] Almost all of them remain alive to the present time,[72] bringing to the people a faithful witness of the things they saw with their eyes, heard with their ears, and touched with their hands.[73] We, also, performing our apostolic duty[74] at the bidding of the Saviour himself, testify that in raising Jesus from the dead, God has now fulfilled for you and your children[75] the promise he made long ago to your fathers, Abraham and David, and which he declared to your ancestors through his prophets.

'For this Jesus is the Son of God, born from the virgin Mary in respect to his human body, about whom the Father himself testifies in the first mystic psalm, saying, "You are my Son; today I have begotten you" [2:7].[76] That he raised him from the dead, henceforth not to return to corruption but to be immortal – this he promised long ago through the prophet Isaiah thus: "I will give you the holy and sure promises of David" [Isa 55:3].[77] The promise made by the covenant[78] would not have been kept if God had not called Jesus back to immortality. For thus he had promised to David: "Once have I sworn by my holiness; I will not lie unto David. His seed shall endure forever, and his throne as the sun before me, and as the moon perfect forever and a faithful witness in heaven" [Ps 89:35–7].[79] You see, however, that now no one sprung from the stock of David holds his throne; rather, this prophecy pointed to Christ who sits at the right hand of the Father, having received the kingdom that will have no end.[80] And the fifteenth psalm also speaks of the same thing: "You will not allow your holy one to see corruption" [16:10].[81] This prophecy cannot be understood of King David who, it is clear, fulfilled the years of his life, continuing to rule until his death, according to the portion of time God had prescribed; then, as God willed, he died[82] and joined his ancestors, who had all similarly died. But if he who dies sees corruption, then David's sepulchre, which contains his bones and is with us to this very day,[83] cries out that he has suffered corruption. The prophecy does not therefore refer to David but to the one we proclaim to you, whom God raised from the dead before his body felt decay, and to whom he granted immortality.

'Let it be known therefore to you, brethren, that through this Jesus there is offered to you remission of sins and freedom from all the evils from which observance of the Law has thus far been unable to cleanse you. For the Law was imperfect according to the flesh. It was unable to abolish all offences, but punished certain ones, and it did not come to the aid of all peoples.[84] Through this Jesus, however, justice and innocence are offered to all without distinction of persons or of offences, provided they believe the promises of the gospel.

'Beware therefore lest there fall upon you the threat God delivered through the prophet Habakkuk against those who do not believe and who rebel against the word of the gospel: "Behold, you despisers, and be astounded and undone,[85] because I work a work in your days, a work you will not believe if one declares it to you" [1:5]. Who to this day has believed that a man would be born of a virgin? Who would have believed that through the death of one person immortality has been won for all peoples? Who would have believed that one killed and buried would within three days come to life again unto immortality?[86] As he promised, God has worked this incredible work in these your own times. Do not be despisers; do not perish through obstinate incredulity,[87] but believe and embrace the salvation freely offered you.'

When Paul concluded his speech, and the audience had already begun to leave, they asked[88] Paul and Barnabas to speak in the synagogue on the same subject the next sabbath. Now after the assembly was dismissed, many – part of them Jews by birth, part proselytes zealous in their religion[89] – followed Paul and Barnabas, eager to be instructed by the apostles in a more friendly and intimate way. They spoke with these in private and urged them to persevere in that free gift of God which they had begun to embrace and to make constant progress in what had been well begun.[90]

Meanwhile, news of this affair spread far and wide, different ones (as happens) telling different people what they had heard.[91] Indeed, on the next sabbath not only Jews and proselytes but the whole city now gathered in the synagogue to hear the word of the gospel. But most of the Jews had convinced themselves that this grace of the gospel was promised only to those who were sons of Abraham according to the flesh. When they saw a mingled crowd of Jews, proselytes, and gentiles flocking together, they were goaded by envy and became extremely indignant. They contradicted what Paul was saying and did not restrain themselves at times from blasphemous words.[92] Paul and Barnabas perceived their obstinate ill-will and remembered that the Lord had commanded the apostles to depart from that city where they found those who rejected the offer of gospel grace, and even to shake the dust off their feet against the defiant.[93] They said frankly:[94]

'We have done our duty. According to the command of the Lord Jesus, the word of the gospel had to be announced to you first of all – such is the honour bestowed upon you by Christ.[95] But since you yourselves reject such great grace brought to you gratuitously and without charge, and judge yourselves unworthy of eternal life, behold, we turn to the gentiles. We do not do so on our own private authority. The Lord Jesus commanded his own that when the gospel had been preached throughout Judaea, it should thereafter be preached to all nations right to the ends of the earth.[96] This, too, was predicted long ago by the prophet Isaiah, that Jesus would bring salvation not only to the Jewish race but to all the peoples of the world. For in the prophecy the Father speaks to the Son thus: "I have set you to be a light for the gentiles that you should be salvation unto the ends of the earth"' [49:6].[97]

Upon hearing this the gentiles rejoiced – it was not that they were glad about destruction for the Jews, but that they gave thanks for the mercy of God who was turning the unbelief of the Jews to their own salvation.[98] The Jews attacked the salvific doctrine with blasphemies; the gentiles, suddenly changed, embraced it with most eager minds and glorified the word of the Lord.[99] Not indeed all of the gentiles believed the word but as many as the divine mercy had ordained to eternal life, for no one attains to this unless called and chosen by God.[100] And the word of the Lord spread through all that region.

Then the Jews, in envy of the gentiles, stirred up women of religious devotion and high standing, for one quite easily deceives such women through a feigned appearance of piety, while their rank gave greater authority. Then they stirred up the leading men of that city, and through them they raised a persecution against Paul and Barnabas and drove them out of their borders. Here, reader, observe in passing the Jewish art of inciting insurrection against those who sincerely preach Jesus. First, spite spurs on those who feign religion; next, their inward pain breaks out into insolent reproaches; then through serious and responsible women devoted to religion, civil discord arises; through such women the leading men are incited. Thus the apostles are cast out. But Paul and Barnabas, shaking off the dust of their feet against them, set out for Iconium, a city of Lycaonia.[101] The disciples also, happy at the success of the gospel, were filled with joy and with the Holy Spirit.

Chapter 14

When they arrived at Iconium, in their customary manner they went together into the synagogue of the Jews. There, too, they preached the gospel of Jesus Christ, as they had done at Antioch, so that a very great multitude believed, both Jews and Greeks. And here again[1] Jewish spite became the source of sedition. For the Jews, unwilling to obey the evangelical word, did not think it enough that they themselves perish. In order to drag a great many with them into destruction they stirred up and infected the minds of the gentiles against those who had believed.[2]

But the work of the gospel mission gained strength and grew through both adversity and prosperity. In this struggle therefore, Paul and Barnabas remained for some time at Iconium, carrying on their work courageously with the help of the Lord[3] who gave testimony greater than human testimony to his free kindness which was being offered to all through the gospel. For he granted to the weak and insignificant heralds of the gospel that by their hands signs and wonders should be performed which would demonstrate that this undertaking proceeded from the divine will.[4] And so through the work of the Jews the city of Iconium was divided into two parties. The one took the side of the unbelieving Jews, the other supported the apostles. At length, those who were from the gentiles joined with the Jews and the chief men of the city and made an assault[5] upon the apostles, to maltreat them and to stone them. When they learned of this, they fled to Lystra, a city of Lycaonia, which is a part of Pamphylia,[6] and to Derbe. Meanwhile they went through the surrounding region, everywhere[7] sowing the evangelical word, so that in this flight there was more regard for the propagation of the gospel than for the safety of the apostles.[8]

At Lystra there was a certain man with feet so impaired that he was incapable of walking and could only sit, a cripple from his mother's womb. Throughout his whole life he had never been able to walk on his feet.[9] As one of the crowd, he heard Paul speaking of Christ. Paul looked intently at the man and saw in his face his eagerness and his longing, for the man trusted that he could gain wholeness of limbs through the name of the Jesus who had been preached.[10] Paul spoke in a clear voice: 'Rise up upon your feet!' With the very words, the cripple sprang up and walked.

Now the cripple was known to all and had been restored suddenly by a simple word. When, therefore, the crowd had seen such a wonder, they raised their voices high and said in Lycaonian speech, 'The gods have assumed the form of men and come down to us!' This conviction fastened itself more firmly upon the minds of the Lycaonians because of the tale of Jove and Mercury: that when they appeared as men, Lycaon received them as guests – hence, apparently, their name, 'Lycaonians.'[11] And so they called Barnabas 'Jove,' for he carried about himself a singular air of authority, but Paul they called Mercury because he was the chief speaker, and the gentiles believed that Mercury was the messenger of the gods and the tutelary deity of eloquence. Indeed, even the priest of Jove, who lived in the suburbs of the city of Lystra,[12] brought bulls and garlands to the doors of the building where the apostles were, to sacrifice to them. They thought that Jove was especially delighted by the sacrifice of bulls, while both the sacrificers and the victims are usually adorned with sacred garlands.[13] A mixed crowd of men and women followed. Paul and Barnabas[14] inquired into the cause of the affair. They learned that divine honours were being prepared for themselves because they were thought to be gods. They could not endure impiety so great that the honour owed to God was being transferred to human beings.[15] In the Jewish manner, they tore their clothes,[16] and sprang towards the multitude crying out and saying:

'Men, why are you doing this? We are not gods but men like yourselves, mortals, subject to the same misfortunes as you.[17] We do not seek this honour from you. Quite the contrary! We have come to you for this purpose rather, that you, at our instigation, might turn from those false gods which until now you worship with profane rites – gods which are either deceased men, or lifeless statues, or harmful demons[18] – that you might turn from these to the true and living God who created heaven and earth and sea and whatever is contained in heaven, earth, and sea. For there is only one God, creator and ruler of all.[19] It is he who now demands to be known and worshipped by all the peoples of the world so that through him all may gain eternal salvation. In former ages, he allowed all races to live each in the manner it wished, as though he were taking no notice.[20] In this way, after it had become clear that human beings could not be saved by their own help, everyone might be saved through trust in God and through the gospel of God's Son.[21]

'Although most mortals[22] were strangers to the true God through error, worshipping the likenesses of various things instead of God, or worshipping created things instead of the creator,[23] still he did not immediately inflict upon them a just vengeance[24] nor did he cease to call them to the knowledge and love of himself through his constant kindness. For he who created the world for human use also makes the earth fruitful by sending rain from heaven, and causes each year's crops to produce an abundant supply of all that contributes to human life, to refresh us plentifully with the various kinds of food, and to make our[25] hearts merry with the juice of the vine. You do not owe these benefits to your gods, whom you worship until now – Jove, Ceres, or Liber[26] – but to that God whom we proclaim to you.'

Although the apostles said these things before the people they scarcely restrained the crowd from offering sacrifices to them.

While this was taking place at Lystra, certain people – Jews by race, but rebels against the gospel – came there from Antioch of Pisidia and Iconium. They drew the crowd over to their own view, so that they would make an assault upon the apostles, the plan they had tried at Iconium. Paul was stoned, and the Jews dragged him out of the city, thinking he was dead. Such, clearly, are the vicissitudes of human affairs: Paul and Barnabas were taken for gods a little before, when victims were being prepared for them; now Paul is stoned and cast out.[27] (The Jews were more hostile to Paul because his eloquence was drawing many to Christ.) His disciples gathered about him, cast out and left for dead, to attend the corpse. However, coming to himself, Paul arose and entered secretly into the city. On the next day he departed with Barnabas to Derbe, where they had first determined to go.[28]

And when they had preached the gospel in that city and had taught many things,[29] since the seed of the evangelical word had been, as it were, sown, they returned to Lystra, Iconium, and Antioch, strengthening the souls of the disciples they had converted to Christ. They exhorted them to persevere in the faith, and not to be drawn away by any terrors from the trust they had once placed in the Lord Jesus. They were not to be offended because they had heard that Paul was stoned at Lystra, since this was the path Christ had shown for his disciples, that through many afflictions they would enter into[30] the kingdom of heaven.[31] Paul was much too worried to grieve for his own sake – worried that the hardships he was suffering from the ungodly might provide the occasion by which the weak would be estranged from Christ. Meanwhile, he offers an example to bishops: they should imitate industrious farmers who do not think it enough to plant or sow, but who also watch that what begins to spring up successfully reaches maturity.[32]

Since the advance of the gospel demanded that the apostles travel through various regions, presbyters were chosen throughout by popular vote[33] in each city. The apostles set them over the people to carry out the duties of the absent apostles. When common supplication had been made with fasting, they commended them to the Lord, that they should go forward in him whom they had once professed.[34]

This was done at Antioch in Pisidia.[35] They traversed this whole region, and in the same way also Pamphylia, everywhere sowing the gospel where it had not been sown[36] and strengthening those who had once believed – doing so until they returned to Perga. When they had set in order affairs[37] in Perga, they came to Attalia, a city on the coast of Pamphylia.[38] From there they set sail again for Antioch in Syria, whence they had first set sail when the task of preaching the gospel among the gentiles had been delegated to them by the elders, and when by the laying on of hands, by prayer and fasting, they had been commended to the grace of God, so that with his aid their undertaking might have a happy outcome. Accordingly, they returned there, as men ready to give an account of what they had done. They called together the congregation of believers and reported everything the Lord had done with them. They showed that their efforts had been supported by the favour of God, who had opened to the gentiles the door of faith through which they might gain salvation without the burden of the Law.

Chapter 15

Paul[1] and Barnabas, however, stayed for a considerable time with the disciples at Antioch,[2] because in such a populous city a large congregation of believers of different ethnic identities had joined together[3] and the congregation was growing larger every day. There the apostles took pleasure in staying longer where the harvest was more plentiful, for the people of Jerusalem and those who dwell in the part of Syria properly called Judaea[4] were more tenacious of the law of Moses than others. Because they had less contact with gentiles and were closer to the temple, they were less willing to have the gentiles received into the fellowship of the gospel apart from the observance of the Law. They did not understand that once the light of truth had been revealed the Law was to be abrogated insofar as it pertained to shadows, figures, and ceremonies – such as circumcision, the sabbath rest, choice of foods, feast days, distinctions in clothing, vows, fasts, and avoiding things dead,[5] all of which were imposed for a time upon carnal people to accustom them to obey God until the shadows should flee away under the very bright light of truth revealed through the gospel.[6] Accordingly, those who did not understand that the Law was spiritual[7] maintained that what had been prescribed by God, handed down by the fathers, and observed through so many ages by their ancestors, ought to be unending. This conviction arose not so much from malice as from an over-scrupulous regard[8] for the Law, which they destroy in their zealous effort to keep. For this zeal had at first incited even Paul against the Christians.

Now Paul and Barnabas had, with the approval of all, set out for Cyprus, and from there they went to Pamphylia. They preached the gospel openly to Jews, proselytes, and gentiles, making no distinction among them and requiring no observance of the Law. Therefore, when the report of what was being done at Antioch had spread as far as Jerusalem, certain ones from Judaea[9] came to Antioch introducing a new teaching, different from the teaching of Paul and Barnabas.[10] They said to the gentile believers,[11] 'Unless you are circumcised according to the rite prescribed by Moses, you cannot be saved.' This was the beginning of a fight on the part of those who clung tenaciously to the flesh of the Law[12] against those who followed the genuine spiritual liberty of the gospel, a struggle there will always be among Christians. God permitted this conflict to arise so that all disciples of Christ might better understand how deadly is a religion that relies on ceremonies.[13]

When Paul and Barnabas, as doughty champions of evangelical liberty, stoutly resisted this teaching, which was religious in appearance but utterly baneful in fact, sharp dissension arose. The apostles vigorously defended with the testimonies of the prophets the purity of evangelical doctrine, which is spiritual, against the superstitious advocates of the Law, while those, on the other side, in their zeal for the Law handed down from their ancestors, tried to drag the gentiles under the same yoke.[14] They did not know what reproach they were bringing upon Christ, whose grace they thought needed the help of the Law. For he who was the author of the Law was also able to abrogate the Law, though indeed he who perfects does not abrogate.[15] This warfare was much more destructive to the gospel than the violence of Herod or of other princes[16] because it assaulted true godliness under a false image of piety. And so, to prevent the evil of discord from spreading, the disciples were called into council, and it was decided that Paul and Barnabas and some others from this group[17] should set out for Jerusalem and go to Peter and the other apostles and presbyters who then governed the mother church,[18] so to speak, at Jerusalem so that with their authority the issue that had arisen might be resolved. For as yet the chief authority remained in that place from which the evangelical teaching had first gone forth, and with those who had been the first to begin to preach in accordance with the commission given them by Jesus Christ.[19]

Accordingly, Paul and Barnabas took up their journey, and the disciples[20] in large numbers showed their respect by sending them on their way. As they made their journey through Phoenicia and Samaria, everywhere they told how the gentiles had turned to God. So confident were the apostles of what they had done that of their own accord they spoke of it everywhere. They were not proceeding to Jerusalem to learn from apostles whether they had thus far acted rightly or not, but to calm the disquietude of the weak with the authority of more eminent persons.[21] All who had believed the gospel in these parts were filled with great joy – so far were they from raising dissension after the example of the Jews. When they reached Jerusalem, Paul and Barnabas, along with their companions, received a cordial welcome from the congregation there, as well as from the apostles and elders.[22] When these had been convened, Paul and Barnabas set forth all the things God had done among the gentiles through them.

Although the matter won the approval of most of the people, there rose up certain ones from the party of the Pharisees who had indeed believed the gospel, but in such a way as to think the grace of the gospel did not confer salvation without the support of the Law and, consequently, that no gentile was to be admitted into the fellowship of the gospel without the prior imposition of the yoke of the Mosaic law; from this the gentiles utterly recoiled. Now, the Pharisees were eager to seem, in comparison with others, more tenacious of the Law. As teachers of the Law they affirmed that those of the gentiles who had been received had to be circumcised and to be instructed to keep the law of Moses. They did not understand that no one violates the Law so much as those who through zeal for the flesh disregard the spirit of the Law.[23]

How divisive a thing is superstition! Here again strife arose, and the apostles along with the elders assembled to consider what decision should be made in this matter. For since they were most covetous of gain for the Lord,[24] they feared that many of the gentiles would be lost to Christ through their hatred of the Law. On the other hand, they did not think they should give the Jews a likely cause for falling away from the gospel as something in conflict with the holy Law, for the Jews had absorbed a reverence for the ancestral Law too deep to be suddenly torn out.[25] When testimonies and proofs had been brought forward on all sides,[26] and the debate had grown hot, Peter arose and spoke in this manner:

'Brethren, why do you dispute as though something were in doubt, as though it hung upon human judgment to approve or reject what God himself has already approved?[27] You yourselves know that some years ago[28] the same thing happened to me in Judaea[29] that has now occurred in gentile country. This you unfairly attack, for when a similar murmuring[30] arose among you because of the baptism of Cornelius and his family, I set forth for you the whole affair, how I had gone to Caesarea not on my personal authority, but at God's command to preach to the gentiles also the gospel of God,[31] by believing which they might obtain salvation. Now those who at that time heard the gospel word were uncircumcised and unpractised in the observance of the Mosaic law. Nevertheless, God, who judges a person not on the condition of the body but from the desire of the heart[32] – and he alone knows the heart – showed with manifest evidence that he approved their faith, for while they were listening the Holy Spirit was poured out upon them so that they spoke with tongues (as we too had done) even before we baptized them.[33] As far as the grace of the gospel is concerned, God made no distinction between those who are uncircumcised and us who are Jews.[34] For he purified their hearts by faith, unambiguously showing us that this grace was not conferred with the assistance of the Law, but by the commendation of faith – for God does not pour out his Spirit on the impure. They had nothing but a simple readiness to believe when the Holy Spirit came upon them.[35]

'Now, therefore, since God has plainly revealed his will that the gentiles should be admitted to partnership in the gospel through faith alone without the burden of the Law, why do you tempt God and provoke him? For so you do when you try, contrary to his will, to put the yoke of the Law, so heavy,[36] upon the necks of disciples who have not to this point become accustomed to the Law, a yoke neither our fathers nor we who were born under the Law have had the strength to bear. For who of us has kept the Law to the last letter?[37]

'There is, then, no reason why we should hope for salvation by observing the Law. We are confident rather that we shall be saved[38] through the grace of our Lord Jesus Christ.[39] In this respect we are in no better position than the gentiles, upon whom he wanted the same gift bestowed freely as he likewise bestowed freely upon us.'[40]

With this speech of Peter the turbulent dispute was checked between the Pharisees and those who held a contrary view. Therefore, the multitude quietly heard Barnabas and Paul, as they related the many miracles and marvellous signs wrought among the gentiles through themselves, and how God had testified by these miracles and signs that he was pleased that the gentiles should be received into partnership in the gospel without the burden of the Law – just as earlier, when Peter preached Christ in the house of Cornelius, God had revealed his mind by sending the Holy Spirit. When they had finished speaking, James, surnamed the Just, and called the brother of the Lord, to whom the apostles had at that time committed the chief authority,[41] arose and expressed his approval of what they had said, addressing the assembly in the following manner:

'Brethren, since you maintained silence when the others were speaking, listen to me also in silence while I tell you what I think is best to do. Simon Peter[42] has just now related what we all know to be absolutely true, how God took pity upon the human race and, first through Peter himself, had regard for the ruinous misfortune of the gentiles, devoted to idol worship.

From these, too, who seemed not to be a people, he would choose a people acceptable to him and calling along with us upon his name.[43] What God began through Peter, he has carried further through Paul and Barnabas. We have heard what they have done – events long ago predicted by the oracles of the prophets, among whom Amos speaks thus, in the person of God:[44] "After this I will return, and will restore the tabernacle of David which lies fallen, and I will build afresh its crumbled ruins and will set it up, that the people who are left may seek the Lord, and all the gentiles upon whom my name is called, says the Lord who does these things."[45] Whatever God promises to do, this without doubt he does. For before the world was created he had determined what he would do, and when. And whatever he has decided must be best.[46]

'Since, however, we see now coming to pass what he promised, it is my view that the divine will should not be resisted, nor should we cry out against those gentiles who are being converted to the worship of the true God, nor should the burden of the Law be imposed upon them, since evangelical faith is sufficient for salvation for all. Only let them be admonished to abstain from defilements of idols, neither sacrificing nor eating things sacrificed, and to abstain from fornication; the former because of the weak who cannot yet be persuaded that an idol is nothing and that meat sacrificed to idols is no different from any kind of meat sold in the marketplace;[47] the latter because of certain people who do not think fornication is a sin since it is commonly done and is not punished by human laws.[48] Further, because of some rather superstitious Jews who cannot yet be persuaded that to the pure all things are pure,[49] let them abstain from an animal that has been strangled and from blood[50] – not because these things contribute to the salvation of the soul, but because love urges that the weakness of certain brothers be gratified for a time, until they progress to more perfect things. Therefore, nourish brotherly concord with one another by mutual consideration.[51] The Jews should not fear that Moses will cease to have effect, for from times of old until now he has long had those who preach him in the synagogues where on every single sabbath he is read according to custom.'[52]

When all had stood in favour of this decision,[53] the apostles and elders and with them the whole congregation thought they should choose several persons from their group to accompany Paul and Barnabas to Antioch. In fact two were selected of proven integrity:[54] Judas, who was given the surname of 'the Just' because of his devout and virtuous life,[55] and Silas, both of whom enjoyed among the brethren the highest praise for their integrity.[56] Along with the injunctions, they gave them a letter in this vein:

'From the apostles and elders and the brethren[57] converted to Christ from Judaism, to those in Antioch and Syria and Cilicia who have been converted to Christ from the gentiles:[58] Greetings.

'We have learned that certain Jews who set out from here as though they had been sent by us[59] have disturbed the peace you were enjoying in evangelical harmony and have unsettled your minds with their new doctrine, asking you to be circumcised and to keep the Law,[60] though we gave them no such mandate. Therefore, we thought it fitting in accordance with the view of the meeting in which we were assembled together[61] to send to you men chosen from among us, along with Paul and Barnabas, most beloved by us, and justly so, in as much as they have exposed their lives to dangers on behalf of the name of our Lord Jesus Christ. Accordingly, we have sent Judas and Silas, men of utmost reliability. From the reliable report these will give to you, you will be able to learn the same things we are writing about.

'Of these things the substance is this. It seemed good to the Holy Spirit and to us, who through the prompting of the Spirit were in accord, that no additional burden should be imposed upon you beyond those that seemed necessary. These are: first, that you abstain from anything sacrificed to idols, so that you do not appear by eating such food to have any sympathy with the superstition you have renounced once for all; second, that you avoid the blood of an animal and a beast that has been strangled, the eating of which the Law forbids;[62] and last, that you abstain from fornication, which gentiles think permissible. If you keep yourselves from these things, you will do well. Farewell.'

When these matters were concluded in this way, they were dismissed with the letter and its mandates. They came to Antioch, gathered the people together, and delivered the letter, which was read in the presence of all. They rejoiced in such great consolation, because to their own conviction the authority of the apostles, the elders, and the multitude of the Jerusalem believers[63] had been added. Judas and Silas, as the apostles had given them charge, filled in what was lacking in the letter, since they were themselves also prophets, skilled in sacred literature.[64] They exhorted the brethren in copious discourse[65] and strengthened their minds that they might steadfastly continue in things well begun.[66] When, consequently, they had stayed there for some time, they were given an opportunity to return to those who had sent them,[67] and the brothers dismissed them with peace. Since Silas, however, thought he should remain there, Judas returned to Jerusalem alone.[68] Meanwhile Paul also, and Barnabas, stayed in Antioch teaching without discrimination both Jews and gentiles and declaring to all the salvation offered freely to those who believed the gospel, that is, the word of God.[69]

After quite some time, a concern arose in Paul's mind for the disciples whom he had left in Cyprus and Pamphylia, and he said to his colleague Barnabas, 'Let us visit again the brethren in all the cities where we have preached the word of the Lord to see how they are.' Barnabas liked this plan, but wanted[70] John, also named Mark, to be their companion on this voyage – they had taken him with them formerly when they had set out there.[71] On this point Paul disagreed with him. He thought that, inasmuch as John had left them before the work in hand had been completed and had sailed back from Pamphylia to Antioch, he ought not now be taken back into partnership in the work.[72] This dispute became so heated between the two[73] that neither would give in, and they parted company. Not that there was any bitterness between such great apostles, but each strove to get what he thought was best for the work of the gospel. And, in the event, an example was furnished for us that we should not immediately suppose something is to be condemned because it is not in accord with our opinion. Difference of opinion does not harm, provided hearts are united in their purpose to advance the gospel. From the disagreement of the apostles God provided that the gospel should be carried even farther with the two leaders separated than if they had persevered in their original association.[74] And so Barnabas had Mark join him, and sailed to Cyprus, where he had been born.

Paul on the other hand chose[75] Silas, who had stayed at Antioch – as God willed – so that Paul should not lack a colleague of moral weight and endowed with authority.[76] Sent forth by the brethren and commended to the grace of God[77] Paul set out to wherever an evident hope of the success of the gospel called. He went through Syria and Cilicia, where he himself was born,[78] everywhere strengthening the assemblies of the disciples he had won there, and augmenting what he had begun. He instructed them to abide by the decision of the apostles and elders at Jerusalem: to avoid communion with idols, fornication, anything strangled, and blood – otherwise they were free from the burden of the Mosaic law.[79] After these activities in Cilicia, he again arrived at Derbe, and thereafter at Lystra.[80]

Chapter 16

And, behold, there was a certain disciple called Timothy, and his name reflected the reality, for it means 'precious to God.'[1] He was born of a mixed marriage:[2] his mother was a widow who had come to Christ from Judaism; his father was a pagan.[3] The integrity of this Timothy was openly attested by all the brethren who lived at Lystra and also at Iconium. Now, Paul longed for only one thing – that the gospel kingdom should through every opportunity be advanced further from day to day, and he was accordingly everywhere on the look-out for persons suitable for this work. He was like ambitious kings bent upon extending the boundaries of their authority, whose greatest concern is the recruitment of leaders and administrators apt in managing affairs. Moreover, it is not enough that the evangelical leader be endowed with modest gifts; it is not enough that he be of a blameless character; he must also be commended by the attestation of all good people, so that no ugly rumour, however false, should obstruct the work of the gospel. It was Timothy, therefore, both singularly upright and fully approved by the testimony of all the approved, whom Paul desired to have as the companion of his journey.[4]

And when Timothy joined him, Paul circumcised him, not because he thought circumcision conferred salvation, which comes from faith alone, but to avoid any disturbance that might arise from the Jews, of whom there was a large number in those regions.[5] And so he preferred to accept in the case of Timothy the loss of a little piece of foreskin – which when present does not make one more holy, when removed does not make one worse – than that the Jews should be more estranged from the gospel by this circumstance, for he knew how obstinate they were. The apostolic decree made at Jerusalem in the presence of Paul freed the gentiles from the burden of the Law. But circumcision was an acknowledgment of, and a symbol, as it were, of the obligation to keep the whole Law,[6] and the Jews were not yet openly freed from the burden of the Law, which had to come to an end gradually.[7]

Now, it was well known that Timothy was the son of a Jewish mother and a pagan father, and that because of the father's authority he had not been circumcised. For that reason Paul saw that Jews would raise a disturbance (using any excuse that was at all credible), if Timothy, a half-Jew by birth,[8] had not only been received without circumcision into fellowship in the gospel, but was even being admitted to the ministry of the evangelical teacher. Through his zeal for the advancement of the gospel, Paul granted this much to that time,[9] taking thought for the tranquillity of all who had embraced Christ the peacemaker.[10] This was not all he did. To prevent the Jews from being offended, through whatever cities he made his way he gave instructions to those who had come from paganism to Christ that they should observe the decisions made by the apostles and elders at Jerusalem and for the sake of which Judas and Silas had been dispatched to Antioch.[11]

The divine favour[12] was present to aid the efforts of Paul. For the churches of the disciples were confirmed in the evangelical faith and daily increased as the number of believers grew. They travelled through[13] Phrygia and Galatia (regions of Asia Minor) with great profit, though the people were extremely crude and barbaric.[14] Then they desired to set out for the part properly called Asia, but they were forbidden by the Holy Spirit to speak the gospel word there, and they obeyed the hidden counsel of God, against which a human being should not struggle.[15] And so, changing their plan, they took the road to Mysia, which borders on Asia properly so called.[16] From there they turned north and attempted to go to Bithynia. This was a populous province of the Romans, and they were therefore looking for large gains there.[17] But the Spirit of Jesus under whose[18] guidance they were moving did not allow them to go there – it is uncertain why. Accordingly, turning west and travelling first through Mysia, they came to Troas. This is a city on the coast of Phrygia, also called Antigonia.[19]

There a vision appeared to Paul in his sleep that showed him where he was to go. The vision was this: a man, Macedonian in appearance and dress, stood beside him and pleaded with him, saying, 'Come to Macedonia and help us!' This was the angel who watched over that region.[20] Now, Paul had already been prohibited twice by the Holy Spirit from preaching the evangelical word. Hence, as soon as Paul saw the vision we who were his companions rejoiced – for I, too, who write, was then a companion of his journey.[21] At once we bent our efforts to depart for Macedonia, convinced that the Lord[22] had called us to preach the gospel to them and that under the blessing of God success was assured. And so we weighed anchor at Troas, and sailing past the Chersonese, arrived at the island of Samothrace, opposite Thrace;[23] from here, on the next day, to Neapolis, a maritime city in the borderland between Thrace and Macedonia,[24] thence to Philippi.

This city, which is the first you come to travelling from Neapolis into Macedonia,[25] is a colony. We stayed for some days in this city, awaiting an opportunity to begin the work for which we had come. Then on the sabbath day we went out of the city to a place outside the gates,[26] near a river where people were accustomed to gather for prayer.[27] As we sat there we spoke to the women who had gathered there, and proclaimed Jesus of Nazareth to them. Among them was one who was dedicated to religion. Her name was Lydia; she was a seller of purple goods and came from Thyatira, a city in the region[28] of Lydia. Among the many who heard Paul discoursing about Christ, it was she whose heart God opened to heed what Paul was saying. And so, after she had received baptism along with her household, she earnestly entreated Paul and his companions, saying, 'If you have judged me worthy of this honour – to have received me into the fellowship of the gospel through baptism and your teaching[29] – accept from me in turn the honour of staying at my house. Do not think of me as the pagan I was until a moment ago. Think of me rather as that which I have now become through gospel faith and by your ministry.' With such entreaties she constrained the apostles to stay as guests for some time at her place. Meanwhile, an example has been provided for evangelical teachers not to avoid services spontaneously offered by recent converts to Christ, if they extend their offer readily and persistently; otherwise, it might appear that they do not acknowledge the converts as their own. On the other hand, the example shows that they should not thrust themselves upon the converts, lest they appear to demand a reward for communicating evangelical doctrine.[30] But whoever has received a spiritual benefit ought to compel their benefactors to accept a corporeal benefit, should there be a need.[31]

Now, it happened that, as we were going to prayer in our usual manner, a certain slave-girl met us. She had a spirit of divination and brought splendid financial gain to her masters by divining. She followed Paul and us, and kept crying out, saying, 'These men are servants of the most high God who proclaim to you[32] the way of salvation.' She did this for many days, and Paul was annoyed, for he was afraid that he should seem to be acknowledging praise offered by a girl possessed.[33] Turning to face her, he said to the spirit, 'I command you through the name of Jesus Christ to depart from this girl.' At once the spirit came out. When the girl's owners saw that their source of gain was lost, they seized Paul and Silas and dragged them into the forum to the chief men of the city. They stood them before the magistrates and accused them, saying, 'These men have come from other parts and are upsetting the whole[34] city, for they are Jews and are introducing a foreign religion among us and new customs which it is not right for us either to accept or to practise. We live by Roman laws, and these forbid us to accept foreign gods or new cults of the gods.'[35]

Now, among the people the name 'Jew' was hated.[36] Consequently, when they heard this, they rushed together and headed straight for the apostles. To satisfy the furious populous,[37] the magistrates tore the clothes off the apostles[38] and ordered them to be beaten with rods. This punishment did not satisfy the magistrates. After they had inflicted many blows upon them, they cast them into prison, charging the jailer to guard them carefully. Having received such a charge, the jailer, to be the safer, thrust them into the inner prison, and not satisfied with this, he fastened their feet in the stocks. Such were the beginnings of preaching in Macedonia. Either gain or ambition or superstition is always at war with the gospel,[39] but when the world rages most fiercely against the members of Christ, then especially is the solace of heaven at hand to help.[40]

About midnight Paul and Silas, forgetting their beatings, unmindful of the prison, were praying and singing hymns to God, giving thanks to him because he had deemed his servants worthy of the honour of suffering these things on behalf of his name. The others who were in the prison heard them singing with happy voices their praises to God and to his Son Jesus Christ, and they could not imagine what was the source of so much joy in such joyless circumstances.[41] And suddenly there was a mighty earthquake, so that the whole prison was shaken from its foundations and at the same time all the doors of the prison were thrown open and everyone's fetters unfastened. Awakened by this commotion, the keeper of the prison ran in and found all the doors of the prison opened. He conjectured from this that all the prisoners had escaped, and, remembering what kind of charge he had received from the magistrates, he drew his sword and prepared to kill himself – he preferred to perish by his own hand than to be slain by the executioner after many tortures.[42] Paul discerned this even in the midst of the darkness, and cried with a loud voice – enough to make even a thunderstruck person attentive[43] – saying, 'See that you do yourself no harm, since no harm will come to you from us; for we are all here, not one of us has escaped.'

At these words the jailer recovered himself, and ordered his attendants to bring a light. When he discovered that the situation was as Paul had said, and recognized that the event had come about not through human art but by divine power,[44] and at the same time reflected that Paul had seen in the dark what he, the jailer, was doing and why, he went into the inner prison and fell at the feet of[45] Paul and Silas. Disregarding the charge he had received from the magistrates, he led them out of the prison into a more comfortable place and said, 'Sirs, what must I do to be saved?' He wants an exchange of salvation. He had regard for their lives; through them, he wants to have regard for the life of his own soul.[46] They said to him, 'Believe on the Lord Jesus[47] and you will be saved along with your household.' And since the members of his household were already gathered together, immediately in that very place the apostles set forth the gospel teaching to them. You see that any time and any place is suitable for evangelical devotion. That prison, so terribly foul, was a temple for the apostles; the dead of night did not stand in the way of their hymns. The gospel is preached in the prison and booty is taken for Christ; the jail is the magisterial chair[48] of the gospel.

At once, without delay, the keeper of the prison, now a catechumen, hastens to show his gratitude to his catechist, for presently he led them apart and washed off their wounds; this was a duty the jailer knew. Then he himself was washed from the wounds of his soul,[49] along with his own household. After this, he took them to his house, where he was accustomed to pass the time during the day, and he set a meal before them for the refreshment of their bodies – after baptism it was appropriate to share a meal. And the keeper of the prison congratulated himself because he had happened to get prisoners like these through whom he, along with his whole family, had believed the gospel.[50]

Such were the events of the night. But when it was day, the magistrates, having thought the matter over more carefully,[51] sent messengers[52] to the keeper of the prison with instructions to let Paul and Silas go free. The jailer was delighted to hear this both on his own account and on that of the apostles, and reported these words to Paul, that the magistrate[53] had ordered them to be set free. 'Now, therefore,' he said, 'since everything has turned out well, depart, and good luck go with you.' But Paul was eager to make his own innocence more manifest; he also sought an opportunity to have regard for the salvation of many more as well. And so he replied to the messenger:

'They boast that they are Romans. Now it is not permitted by Roman law to punish anyone unless he has been tried and convicted. We are Romans, and they have publicly beaten us with rods, without a hearing, and uncondemned.[54] As though this was not enough, they cast us into prison after beating us. Now they are looking to safeguard their own authority, and are reluctant to admit our innocence; and so they request that we run from prison like guilty men, and steal away secretly. Not so! Let them come themselves, and let them bid us depart, with the same authority as that with which they cast us into prison.'

The messengers reported this reply of Paul to the magistrates. As soon as they had heard that they were Roman citizens, they themselves came to Paul and Silas and begged their pardon, since they had acted contrary to the practice of Roman law because of the uproar of the people. As a mark of honour, they escorted them from the home of the jailer, and asked that they leave the city of Philippi to avoid a riot by the people. The apostles heeded their request. They departed from the prison and proceeded to the house of Lydia, who with her whole household had received the gospel word and whose hospitality they had enjoyed. Accordingly, when they saw her and the rest of the brethren, they encouraged them, telling them what had happened in the prison during the night, and exhorting them to persevere in what they had begun. When they had finished, they left Philippi and departed for another place.

Chapter 17

When they had made their journey through Amphipolis and Apollonia, cities of Macedonia,[1] they came to Thessalonica, the capital of Macedonia.[2] As this was a large and distinguished city[3] there was here a synagogue of the Jews, and from the opportunity thus provided appeared the hope of a richer harvest. Accordingly, Paul went to the meeting of the synagogue in his usual manner, and reasoned with them during three sabbaths, bringing forth from the Scriptures the oracles of the prophets, disclosing the hidden meaning of figures, and adducing the testimonies of the Law. He compared these texts with the events that had taken place and showed that it was by the will and determination of God that Christ thus suffered and rose from the dead for the salvation of the world. Accordingly, since everything that had been predicted through the mouths of the prophets about the future Messiah and everything sketched out in figures found a correspondence in Jesus of Nazareth, he showed the Jews that no other Messiah was to be expected, but that the one he was preaching to them was the Christ.[4]

When Paul had discussed these things in the synagogue on three sabbaths, some of the Jews believed and joined Paul and Silas. From the gentiles a large number of God-fearers believed, including not a few women of rank.[5] On the other hand, certain Jews who were over-zealous for the Mosaic law – whom Paul had once supported – burning with envy,[6] enlisted some mischief-makers who hung about the market-place.[7] (The help of men like this is indeed needed whenever one is operating through agitation and disorder.) They gathered a crowd and set the city in an uproar. During the commotion they assailed Jason's house, and tried to bring Paul and Silas out before the people. But when they went into the house and did not find the persons they were looking for, they dragged Jason himself and with him some disciples to the city prefects, screaming out (for people had once acted thus against Christ[8]) and saying:

'These men, who have hitherto stirred up the world[9] in many places, have come here also to do the same, and Jason has secretly taken men like this into his house. And all these, both the instigators and those who with their hospitality help the instigators,[10] act against the decrees of Caesar when they say that there is a king other than Caesar – for they proclaim a certain Jesus, crucified by Caesar's governor precisely because he claimed to be the king of the Jews.' See how here also they misused the name of Caesar against the gospel.

These words, once heard, stirred up the people and the city magistrates, just as they had moved Pilate also against Christ. For then the unfortunate Jews cried out, 'We have no king but Caesar,' and, 'If you let this man go, you are no friend of Caesar,' and, 'Whoever claims to be a king speaks against Caesar.'[11] On the other hand, true Jews cry out, 'We have no king but Jesus of Nazareth' and, 'Whoever has given himself to Caesar is not Christ's friend.' For Christ alone holds sway over the whole earth.[12] When Jason and the other brethren had brought forward an appropriate means to get themselves excused,[13] the magistrates let them go. The brethren, sensing that people were acting with great hatred against Paul and Silas did not delay, but sent them secretly by night to Berea, a city of Macedonia not far from Pella, the birthplace of Alexander the Great.[14]

Evangelical leaders flee – but to fight none the less in flight. For as soon as they had come to Berea, they entered the synagogue of the Jews, completely undeterred by the uproar raised so many times already by the Jews.[15] But the Jews here were more honourable than the Thessalonians,[16] for they received the evangelical word with the utmost readiness of mind, and every day spent their time searching the sacred books, that they might see how the things they had learned from the apostles' story agreed with the oracles of the prophets and the figures of the Law. Accordingly, many of the Bereans believed, not only Jews[17] but also Greek women of high standing, and not a few men.

Thereupon, rumour reached Thessalonica, conveying to the Jews who had stirred up trouble there the news that the evangelical word had been preached at Berea by Paul, the man whom they had driven out. They set out for Berea, and in their customary way stirred up[18] the populace there also against the apostles. When the brethren realized that danger was imminent, they immediately sent Paul off to go to the sea, for Berea is not far from the sea.[19] Silas and Timothy, however, remained at Berea – it was for Paul the brethren were especially afraid. The brethren who had escorted Paul boarded the boat with him and took him all the way to Athens. There they left him and returned to Berea, with instructions from Paul to Silas and Timothy to follow him as soon as they could.

Though Paul was therefore alone and without his colleagues, nevertheless, when he saw that a city so famous and learned was devoted to the worship of idols, his spirit burned within him, so much that without waiting for his colleagues he went into the synagogue and disputed with the Jews and the devout. Moreover, in the market-place he spoke with all who came his way, whether Jews or Greeks.

Among them were some Epicureans and Stoics, who hold vastly different dogmas. Epicureans, measuring the highest human happiness by the standard of pleasure, believe either that there are no gods or that they have no concern for human affairs. Stoics, besides their other paradoxes, measure human happiness by a single disposition of the mind which they call 'virtue' or 'the morally honourable.'[20] These engaged Paul in vigorous combat, as though he were some philosopher, the founder of a new school. But when Paul had set forth for them the philosophy of the gospel, a philosophy disagreeing widely with all the tenets that please philosophers,[21] some said out of mockery, 'What is that "trifler" trying to say?' – for this was the term of insult the Greeks fastened upon a babbler and a pettifogger,[22] since the heavenly wisdom seemed to them to be folly.[23] But others said, 'He seems to be introducing some new kind of daemon,' because he preached Jesus the author of salvation and Son of God, and the resurrection of the dead. (From the teaching of Plato, the Athenians called the sons of gods 'daemons,' to which they indeed assigned bodies, though immortal.)[24] Since in the market-place opinions about Paul differed, they decided to take him off to the quarter known as Mars. This was the most celebrated place in Athens wherein cases of life and death were investigated in trials held at night.[25] It was a place appropriate to this debate, which offered salvation to those who believed, but death to the unbelieving, and so they said:

'May we know what this new kind of doctrine is of which you speak? For though every kind of philosophy is taught among us, you nevertheless bring to our ears things that are new and hitherto unheard of. We are eager therefore to learn more fully from you in what direction your assertions lead,[26] or what your comments mean.'

Now, this city was devoted, beyond the other Greek cities, to the pursuit of the sciences and of eloquence. Here many people came together from every part of the world for the sake of learning,[27] and both Athenian citizens and the aliens who resided in the place took time for nothing else than to hear or say something new – and this they did more for gratification than for the sake of becoming better through the knowledge they gained.[28] But God, keen for human salvation, snares each person by taking advantage of the things each especially likes, as fishermen or hunters do. And so Paul, who knew how to become all things to all people,[29] and how to accommodate his eloquence to the character of any listener, found a theatre for himself in the midst of the Martian quarter. Surrounded by a close-packed crowd,[30] he began thus:

'Men of Athens, although this city flourishes beyond the others in every kind of literary and scientific activity, I observe nevertheless that when it comes to religion you are in general somewhat superstitious,[31] in spite of the fact that true religion is the chief part of philosophy. For I was walking about to become acquainted with the rituals and practices of your city, and as I was directing my attention to the things you worship and venerate, I found among other things a certain altar with an inscription engraved upon it that mentions an unknown god. Those who allege that I am introducing new and foreign gods are therefore mistaken. On the contrary I proclaim to you the very one whom[32] you worship as unknown, as that inscription on the altar shows.[33] I do this so that you might henceforth worship with true devotion a God who is known, the God whom, as unknown, you have until now superstitiously worshipped.[34]

'Since God is in some sense absolute mind, everywhere present but without being confined to any space, it is not right to think he dwells in temples built by the hands of men or in images crafted by the skill of mortals, nor is it true devotion to worship him with animal victims, as though he either has need of, or takes pleasure in, anything done by human hands.[35] God is in himself boundless and omnipotent, supremely happy and self-sufficient, so that he can neither be harmed by the injuries human beings can do, nor helped by the services they can render. Nevertheless, because he is supremely good and beneficent he has created this marvellous world for the sake of human beings, and whatever is contained in the world he has appointed for the use of the human race. Though he is, as their source, the master and governor of heaven and earth and all they contain, still he himself enjoys the use of none of these things because his eternal felicity has no need to be augmented by any good thing. Rather, he brought forth this well-wrought structure for us to look upon, so that the people dwelling in it might perceive from such a marvellous work the power, the wisdom, and the goodness of the workman;[36] and once he was known, they might love and devotedly worship him by whose kindness they enjoyed so many benefits. But if he is greater than the entire frame of the world and needs none of the things that he created, how much less must we suppose he takes pleasure in temples, statues, or the smell of victims. He is worshipped through purity of mind, since he himself is mind. The slaughter of bulls or sheep does not attract him, who is the source of life for one and all, and who imparts life and respiration to everything that breathes,[37] for the whole race of living creatures has been created by him, and lives through him, each propagating its own kind by breeding.

'To have dominion over all these,[38] however, he has created from one man[39] the whole race of human beings, that they should dwell in every part of the earth. He prescribed for each one the life-span which no one can protract for himself, and distributed the portion of earth which each race would inhabit.[40] Those err who think that the world was created by God but is bereft of his governance, borne along at random and by chance. Nothing at all is done in the world, whether great or small, apart from the providence of the creator.[41]

'Since, however, God cannot in his own nature be grasped by the capacities of human intellect, weighed down, as it is, by the heavy mass of the body,[42] he has endowed human beings with reason so that they might be able to infer one thing from another – the invisible from the visible, the universal from the particular, the eternal from the temporal, the things that are grasped only by the intellect from the things perceived by the senses; and he has set human beings in the midst of the theatre of the world so that from the created things which they see with their eyes, touch with their hands, experience through use, they might trace out and search for[43] the creator. Like the blind who discover by feel what they cannot see, so human beings through reflection upon the marvellous creation of the universe might arrive at some knowledge of God, whom truly to know is utmost felicity.

'And yet it is not necessary to seek God[44] in external things, since we may find him in ourselves, if only each person observes himself and sees within himself the power, the wisdom, and the goodness of the creator.

Though God has disclosed certain traces of his divinity in the heavenly orbs, on the earth, in the sea, and in all living things, yet in none is his divinity more wonderful than in man himself. Even if someone is too dull-witted to be able to comprehend the movements of the stars, the ebb and flow of the sea, the bubbling of springs, the perennial flow of rivers, and the hidden causes of other things, God is not far from each of us, for through him[45] we all live and move and have our being. We owe our existence to him alone who created this world from nothing. Our breathing is a benefit bestowed by no other – if he should desert us, we would die on the spot. To no one else do we owe the fact that the limbs of the living body each performs its own function: eyes see, feet walk, hands work. So God is in each of us and works through us, as a craftsman works through the instrument he himself has made.[46]

'Man, however, reflects God not only as a work reflects the workman, but also as a child reflects its parent, by a certain similarity and kinship of nature. It has been handed down to us in sacred books that God fashioned for Adam, who was the first of the human race, a body from wet clay, in which respect he would have kinship with other living creatures; but with his mouth God breathed into this mud image a tiny bit of celestial breath, through which we might resemble more closely our parent God himself and because of the similarity in nature might recognize him more easily.[47] This was not granted to the other animals. You should not find this absurd, for what has been revealed in mystic literature some of the poets of your own race have also said. Aratus is one of these. In his *Phaenomena* there is this half-line: 'For we also are his progeny.' It makes no difference that he is speaking of Jove; certainly what he called Jove he thought was the supreme God and the procreator of all things, but especially of the human race.[48]

'Since, then, we are the offspring of God in respect to the likeness of the mind planted within us, the opinions we entertain about our parent are not at all correct if we believe that he is like the gold, silver, wood, or stone sculpted by human art, when we ourselves are held to be human beings especially because of the invisible part of us, which is reason.[49] What is more absurd than to suppose that man himself can fashion with his own hands a statue possessing divinity when he is as far as can be from having any claim to the name 'God,' even though he does have some relationship with his parent, God? What is worshipped as God ought to be much superior to the one who worships. Now on how many counts is a human being superior to the image to which divine honours are paid?[50] First, he has received from God this very bodily form. Second, he breathes, lives, moves, and acts. Finally, in his lively force of mind he has a certain likeness to God, his parent. A statue has none of these. But if it is impious to worship a human being as a god, how much further from true piety is it to worship a figure fashioned from matter at the will of the artisan – from the same matter he could have made a stool too, had he wished. This has no likeness to God who is incorporeal. Far from it! Indeed, apart from a certain exquisite bodily form, the product of the imagination, it possesses nothing resembling man, for it does not have even a grain of that part by which a human being bears the image of God.[51]

'Though this is terrible insolence against God, still, because of his love towards the human race, he has not taken revenge; but thus far has, as it were, taken no notice of human ignorance, until the time should come when he had determined to become known to all and to scatter all the gloom and darkness of error.[52] This time is now at hand, when he commands everyone to come to their senses and repent of their former error. To those who so repent[53] he wants forgiveness to be granted, a forgiveness which will not be granted in the future to the insolent, for he has established a day on which he will judge the whole world with a just and unerring judgment, and no one will be allowed to escape it. The reason he has issued his declaration in advance is that no one might be able to allege ignorance as an excuse; and he offers pardon to the repentant so that no one should find mercy lacking in God.[54]

'For both these ends, he has chosen an outstanding man, Jesus of Nazareth. He sent him into the world so that through him everyone might be converted to the worship of the true God. Through him also God will judge the unbelieving and those who rebel against his teaching. Many centuries ago God promised through his prophets that this man would be Saviour and judge. So far God has fulfilled in good faith whatever he had promised: Jesus was born, he taught, suffered and was slain, and, finally, rose from the dead as it had been predicted by the oracles of the prophets. There is no doubt that with similar trustworthiness God will fulfil whatever still remains.'[55]

As Paul was speaking, some of the bystanders began to jeer when they heard him mention the resurrection – though they had received the rest with patient ears, this they thought ridiculous and unbelievable. This was a belief none of the philosophers had handed down, though there were some who said that souls survived after the death of the body, while some even preached that souls migrated from body to body.[56] But others with a less hasty judgment said, 'We will hear you again on this matter.' So Paul dismissed that assembly.

Nevertheless there were among them some who were persuaded to join Paul. These included Dionysius the Aeropagite, who later was installed by Paul and served as bishop of Athens.[57] There was also a certain woman named Damaris, and some others along with these two.

Chapter 18

When this gain in the progress of the gospel had been realized in Athens –
and a slight enough gain it was, since the city was extraordinarily corrupt –
Paul[1] set out from there and went to Corinth. This was the most important
trading centre in all Greece, as wealthy as it was by far the most corrupt of
cities on account of its luxury, lust, and pride.[2] Here he happened to find a
certain man by the name of Aquila, a Jew by religion and a native of Pontus,
which is in the northern part of Asia Minor.[3] Opportunely, he had just come
there from Italy along with his wife Priscilla because the emperor Claudius
had expelled all the Jews from Rome, where a large number of them had
lived.[4] So Paul joined them to avoid being alone; and because they practised
the same trade he lodged in the same house, working at their place with
his hands so that he should not be a burden on anyone.[5] Now, their craft
was to make tents, sewing them from leather.[6] As Peter was not ashamed to
return to fishing when need required, so Paul – such a great apostle who
had done such great things for Christ – was not ashamed to return to the
skins he had left behind for the sake of the gospel.[7] Nevertheless he did not
in the meantime cease from his evangelical ministry. Each sabbath he would
engage both Jews and gentiles alike in disputations in the synagogue.
　　Meanwhile Silas and Timothy, whom Paul had ordered to follow him
to Attica,[8] came from Macedonia. After this, though Paul was troubled and
reluctant (for he regretted the lack of progress he was making in Corinth),
he nevertheless bore witness just as eagerly[9] among the Jews that Jesus of
Nazareth whom he himself was preaching was the Messiah promised by
the prophets,[10] and that there would be salvation through no other. But the
Jews cried out in contradiction – to the point where they did not fear to
spew forth blasphemies against Jesus and Paul. Then Paul, remembering the
gospel precept, shook out his clothes as though in reproach,[11] because he
had brought them without charge the hoped-for message of salvation, and
he said to them:
　　'If you would rather perish than be saved, your blood be upon your own
head, you who are authors of your own death. It cannot be imputed to me
at least, who have performed my duty and[12] am consequently clean. Henceforth, therefore, I shall go to the gentiles, as the Lord has commanded us.'[13]
　　And so he withdrew from companionship with Jews, and moved to
the house of a certain Titus surnamed Justus, a man devoted to religion;[14]
his house adjoined the synagogue. Crispus, the chief of the synagogue –
proximity gave the occasion – along with his whole household believed in
the Lord.[15] With him also many Corinthians who had heard Paul believed
and were baptized. But here, too, the increase did not satisfy the eagerness

of Paul, for the Jews were barking and railing ferociously, and he began to think of leaving Corinth. Then the Lord gave strength to his spirit by a vision in his sleep, saying:

'Do not let the obstinacy of the Jews frighten you, and do not suppress the evangelical word because of them. You must not forsake the salvation of the many because of the invincible malice of the few.[16] Continue without flinching to speak the word of the gospel,[17] relying upon me whom you have as your protector, quite sufficient against any number at all. With me as your protector, no mortal will rise up to hurt you. And so, go nowhere else, since in this city, however corrupt it may be, there are many people whom I have destined for eternal salvation.'[18]

When Paul heard these words, he changed his human plan, and, obedient to the divine plan, remained at Corinth for a year and six months, boldly and freely preaching the evangelical word.[19]

Now at this time Gallio the proconsul governed Achaia (where Corinth is)[20] on behalf of Caesar.[21] The Jews then rose up against Paul with conspiratorial intent, made an uproar, and dragged him off to the tribunal of the proconsul. They brought an accusation against him, saying, 'This fellow persuades people to worship God contrary to the law of Moses, bringing in new rites.'[22] Paul opened his mouth, and was already preparing to respond to this charge, but Gallio, who had realized from the charge laid before him that the controversy between them was over their Jewish religion, looked for the opportunity to free himself from hearing the case. Cutting off Paul's defence, he said to the Jews:

'Acting as proconsul here for Caesar, I am responsible, gentlemen, for civil affairs – that nothing be done against the public laws. Accordingly, if anyone had suffered injury, if any evil deed had been committed which should be punished by the laws, I would justly and as a matter of duty hear you,[23] for the investigation of such cases is my responsibility.[24] If, however, it is nothing of this sort, but a controversy particular to yourselves about the names of factions or about some word in the Jewish religion and about your law,[25] you will better settle it among yourselves, since such affairs do not belong to the office I discharge, nor can they be argued properly before me as judge when I am ignorant of your religion. I will not be judge in such cases.'

With these words the proconsul drove them from the tribunal. However, they beat Sosthenes (the chief of the synagogue) in front of the tribunal, because he had deserted the Jews and, along with his whole family, had joined Paul.[26] They were more angry at him than at Paul, for they were convinced that Paul would have accomplished nothing at Corinth without the support of Sosthenes. The proconsul did not involve himself in this disturbance, pretending not to see what was happening. Since the Romans hated the Jewish name and did not yet distinguish between Jew and Christian, the Roman proconsul did not care what a Jew did to a Jew, knowing that this nation was everywhere given to quarrelling.[27]

Mindful of the divine admonition,[28] Paul delayed there for several days more, even though he saw the fury of the Jews increasing daily. At length, when he perceived that the gospel was sufficiently well established there, he decided to yield temporarily to the rage of the Jews. Therefore, bidding farewell to the brethren, he set out by ship for Syria, accompanied by Aquila and his wife Priscilla. But Paul was aware that the Jews were especially upset because he, a man born in Judaism, appeared to be disregarding the practices of the Law. Consequently, before he set sail from Cenchreae (the Corinthian port)[29] he took a vow in the Jewish manner and shaved his head.[30] This was not a fraudulent pretence on Paul's part, but the indulgence of love. He desired that everyone should be drawn to the gospel, and on this account he accommodated himself, as far as permitted, to the feelings of all so that he might gain all for Christ – he became a Jew to the Jews, to the uncircumcised, uncircumcised.[31] This was granted for a time to the unconquerable superstition of certain people until the evangelical truth should appear more clearly.[32] To shave the head as a result of a vow is not in itself bad, but it is bad to rely on Jewish ceremonies of this sort. In the same way circumcision does not harm one who trusts in Christ, nor does uncircumcision.[33] To submit to these things is sometimes a matter of charity, but only for a time, and while speaking against them whenever the opportunity arises. In other things which are evil in themselves, there must be no concession to the weakness of anyone. On the issue of fornication or idolatry Paul never made concessions to the gentiles.[34] In associating with them, in disregarding choice of foods, in citing their poets he sometimes accommodated himself to them.[35]

And so they arrived[36] first at Ephesus. This is a maritime city in that part of Asia Minor which is properly and without qualification usually called Asia.[37] There he left Aquila and Priscilla, who wished to fix their abode at Ephesus. He himself entered the synagogue of the Jews who dwelt there and disputed with them. When they asked him to stay with them longer, he excused himself, and bidding them farewell, he comforted their hearts with the hope of an early return to them, saying, 'I must by all means celebrate the approaching festival at Jerusalem, but[38] I shall return to you again if God so wills.' After these words, he set sail from Ephesus to go to Jerusalem. He disembarked at Caesarea in Palestine,[39] went up to Jerusalem and greeted the congregation.[40] From there he set out for Antioch in Syria,[41] stayed here for some time, then resumed the journey he had begun, traversing in turn the regions of Galatia and Phrygia, everywhere strengthening the hearts of the disciples wherever any congregation was to be found. So great was the solicitude that lay hold of Paul's mind towards the flock he had gained for Christ.[42]

Meanwhile a certain man by the name of Apollos came to Ephesus, where Paul had left Priscilla and Aquila. He was a Jew by religion, a native of Alexandria, an educated man, possessing uncommon skill in the divine Scripture. This Apollos was half a Christian. He had learned from Christians the rudiments of evangelical doctrine, communicated to others with fervent zeal what he had learned, and diligently taught what he knew about Jesus. But he had not yet been baptized with the baptism of Christ, which conferred a richer grace; he knew only the baptism of John, which taught repentance.[43] He thought this enough, as he had not yet been fully instructed about the things Christ had taught. When Priscilla and Aquila[44] had heard him speaking about Jesus with much spirit,[45] though he had not yet grasped all the mysteries of the evangelical philosophy, they became friends with the man. They saw that he was endowed with such gifts that it appeared he would be an outstanding herald of Christ, and privately they delivered to him more precisely the mysteries of evangelical religion as they themselves had learned them from Paul.[46] They did not repulse the teacher, who was zealous, indeed, but imperfect; the man himself, in other respects distinguished, did not disdain admonition from anyone. These have offered an example that we should courteously give help to those in whom there shines the good hope of better growth. The man has offered a pattern for us. We should be willing to learn from anyone that which, if we fail to know it, will cost us our salvation.

Apollos was baptized in the name of Jesus and received the Holy Spirit. Thereafter, in his eagerness to preach the gospel he desired to go to Achaia, where Corinth is.[47] Though disposed to move in this direction of his own accord, the brethren also spurred him on, and commended him to the disciples in a letter written to the Achaians, asking them to receive him. When he had arrived there, he brought much benefit to those who had believed and was a vigorous champion of the work of the gospel, for the Holy Spirit supported an eloquence joined with sacred erudition.[48] Provided with such weapons, he vigorously beat back the Jews, who fought ceaselessly against the burgeoning growth of the gospel. He openly and publicly showed from the testimonies of the Scriptures that Jesus was the Messiah whom the Jews had awaited for so many centuries, and that everything the prophets had predicted beforehand was congruent with the life of Jesus.[49]

Chapter 19

Just as Priscilla and Aquila had amended in Apollos an imperfect Christianity, so Paul did the same when it was detected in some others. For while Apollos was engaged at Corinth, the capital of Achaia,[1] Paul happened to return to Ephesus after he had travelled through the other regions of Asia Minor – those lying more to the north and east.[2] At Ephesus he found certain of the disciples who were not yet fully Christians, but were interspersed among the rest of the flock of brethren. And so, to improve them, Paul asked whether they had received the Holy Spirit after they believed. Since they had gone astray honestly and not through malice[3] they candidly confessed the truth, and said, 'On the contrary, it has not even come to our ears whether there is some Holy Spirit who is conferred on believers.' Paul replied, 'With what baptism then were you baptized, since you are regarded as Christians?' Here they said, 'The baptism of John; we thought this sufficed for us.' Paul in turn replied:

'No sin has been committed because some time ago, before the light of the gospel appeared, you received the baptism of John. But this does not suffice for eternal salvation. The teaching of John was not an end in itself, but only witnessed to Jesus, the true author of salvation who would come after John. It was a teaching that prepared people's minds so that they might believe in the one who was coming. Likewise the baptism of John did not confer perfect righteousness but only encouraged people to prepare their hearts by repenting of their former life for the physician soon to come, who by his baptism would through faith abolish all sins, and through his own Spirit would enrich the souls of believers with celestial gifts.[4] The Lord Jesus handed down to his apostles this command, to baptize in the name of the Father and of the Son and of the Holy Spirit those who had believed the gospel word.'[5] This is the way those deserve to be taught who have, in all sincerity, gone astray.

When these had been instructed they promptly obeyed their instructor, and were presently baptized in the name of the Lord Jesus. After this, Paul laid his hands upon them and the Holy Spirit came upon them; the reality followed the sign presented to the eyes,[6] for they both spoke in tongues and uttered prophecies about things hidden and yet to come.[7] Now the number of the men was about twelve.

Paul's authority was renewed, so to speak, because as teacher of the gentiles[8] he had imparted the Holy Spirit through the imposition of his hands as the other apostles also had done.[9] Hence, after this event, he went into the synagogue of the Jews who lived there, and spoke openly and freely[10] to all, preaching that the hope of salvation was in Jesus alone. This he did, not for a few days, but for three whole months, debating about the kingdom of God – which is evangelical and spiritual – against those who held tooth and nail to the carnal kingdom of the Law.[11] Now certain persons from the synagogue did not believe the things Paul was declaring in debate but resisted with obstinate hearts, so much so that in the presence of the crowd they openly assailed with insults the evangelical teaching.[12] Then Paul, apprehending the danger that those who had believed might be corrupted by the malice of such people, withdrew from the synagogue of the Jews[13] and separated the disciples from them. Meanwhile, however, he did not cease to preach the evangelical word,[14] but discoursed daily in the school of a certain Tyrannus. He had in mind a pure church, as it were, not spoiled by the yeast of the synagogue,[15] a church which received only the teachable and did not admit troublemakers and blasphemers.

This continued for a period of two years. Paul had so much success that not only the Ephesians but many others also heard the evangelical word.[16] These were in part Jews, in part pagans, and had flocked together from that part of Asia Minor properly called Asia, where Ephesus is.[17] Miracles built up confidence in the spoken word. Many and striking were the miracles God performed through Paul.[18] Not only did he drive out diseases by words or by touch, but even handkerchiefs and aprons which had touched Paul's body were taken to the sick who were unable to come to Paul, and on contact the diseases departed and the evil spirits fled. So great was the trust in the Jesus whom Paul preached.

These events were seen by certain itinerant Jews who go about and cast out harmful spirits for the sake of gain, with fixed rites and set words, boasting that this skill has been handed down to them from Solomon.[19] They attempted on their own to cast out evil demons through invocation of the Lord Jesus – not that they promoted the glory of his name or were motivated by a desire to do good, but because they believed that from this they would get more gain and glory for themselves.[20] Therefore, changing the words with which they usually carried out their exorcisms, they would say to the demons, 'I adjure you by the Jesus whom Paul preaches.' It was especially the seven sons of a certain Jew by the name of Scaeva, a chief priest, who did so. When, however, they attempted in this way an exorcism upon a man subject to an evil demon, the ungodly imp answered the exorcists, 'Jesus I know, through whose name you intend to frighten me, and Paul, Jesus' herald, I know, but who, pray tell, are you who use the name of Jesus and of Paul for gain? – for you are disciples neither of Jesus nor of Paul!' As soon as the words were spoken the man who was subject to the evil demon leaped upon the exorcists and so prevailed against them[21] that only with difficulty did they escape from that house naked and wounded.

News of this spread[22] through the entire city of Ephesus, both among the Jews living there and among the gentiles. Hence great fear took hold of all, and they magnified the name of the Lord Jesus, a name salvific to all persons who sincerely believed, but a name which would not be used to serve anyone's gain or glory. The misfortune of a few meant the salvation of many, for through the example of the sons of Scaeva many were terrified. They now began to believe the gospel when they saw the punishment prepared for those who with an insincere heart called upon the name of the Lord Jesus. They came to Paul, confessing and revealing their sins, so that through repentance they might escape the divine vengeance. For the city of the Ephesians was devoted beyond all other cities to superstitious arts, even as their own proverb witnesses, which speaks of 'Ephesian letters.'[23] Accordingly, there were many there who had in error either practised Jewish exorcisms or had believed them. Indeed many also of those who had practised magic and the clandestine arts brought their books together into a public square and burned them before the eyes of all. So great was the number of these that when their value was calculated, they were found to be worth fifty-thousand denarii. Money was lost[24] but the gospel gained, for by these means the word of the Lord[25] grew exceedingly and prevailed – a saving word to those who embraced it with unfeigned faith, but terrible for those who took it up less honestly.

These were the deeds accomplished auspiciously enough at Ephesus during the two years. Then, admonished by the Spirit, Paul decided[26] that after he had travelled through Macedonia and Achaia, he would set out for Jerusalem. He said, 'I must also see Rome, but not before I have visited Jerusalem again.' With this purpose in mind, he sent on ahead to Macedonia two of his assistants, namely Timothy and Erastus. They were to collect there some alms to alleviate the situation of the poor in Jerusalem; they were also to prepare the minds of the Macedonians for Paul's arrival.[27] Meanwhile, Paul himself stayed in Asia for a while.

At this time, there arose at Ephesus a violent disturbance directed against the gospel.[28] It arose not now from the Jews, as usual, but from those who had imbibed too deeply the superstition of polytheism handed down from their ancestors. The city of Ephesus was, as I have said, intensely devoted to the clandestine arts, and Diana was thought by the gentiles to have some power in sorcery. Hence they say that she too is 'triform,' like Hecate.[29] For this reason she was worshipped at Ephesus with the greatest religious devotion. Love of gain was the first source of this tumult; support was sought in the superstition of the people.

There was at that time in Ephesus a certain man by the name of Demetrius, a silversmith by trade. Since he made silver shrines of Diana – the moon resembles the colour of silver[30] – he brought no small gain to those skilled in his craft. Demetrius therefore called together all those who made money from manufacturing images of Diana and whoever was of the same trade, men who could be expected to support him because of their association in a common craft. Among these, he made an inflammatory speech of this kind:

'Men, it is time that with united efforts we take thought for our own advantage. I have no need to remind you, since you yourselves know that our work is the most profitable in Asia because of the religion of Diana. If her religion fails, our profits will at the same time necessarily dry up. You see and hear – for the matter is in the open – what this wretch Paul has been preaching for two years here: that they are not gods which are made by the hands of men, and that what the art of sculptors or of founders forges from any material at all has no divinity.[31] By preaching of this sort he has persuaded many not only here in Ephesus but also throughout the whole of Asia, and has turned a great number of people away from the worship of the gods.

'Since this work sustains us and our families, what is left but to be reduced to hunger if our source of gain is taken away? For us to sleep in the face of so great a danger would be a case of signal stupidity. But if anyone is little moved by the danger that once our craft has no esteem the splendid profit we now make will fail us, certainly national religion ought to stir us all, since if we allow Paul to act thus with impunity, we see a risk also that the temple of the great goddess Diana will be held of no account, a temple which now is distinguished and holy – and opulent from lavish votive offerings.[32] Once persuaded its protector has no power, who would venerate a temple?[33] And so it will come to pass that the majesty of so great a goddess will gradually come to nothing,[34] a majesty on account of which she is deservedly called great, and which now not only this city and Asia religiously worship, but even the whole world. If, then, you think it prudent to have regard for your own gain, if you think it devout to protect our native gods from injury, now show yourselves men of courage, and hasten to meet the approaching evil.'

This speech so stirred the minds of the superstitious multitude that they all began to bawl out, 'Great is Diana of the Ephesians.'[35] At this inflammatory cry the whole city of Ephesus was filled with commotion. People rushed together and the mingled crowd ran with one accord into the theatre, where the madness of the people usually holds sway.[36] To this place they carried off two Macedonians, Gaius and Aristarchus, Paul's companions. When Paul heard what had happened he wanted to appear before the people, both to help his companions and to persuade the people, but the disciples did not permit it. They judged that it was inadvisable for him to hand himself over to a furious populace when he would gain therefrom no advantage for the gospel. Moreover, certain others also, leading men of Asia who though they had not yet professed the name of Christ were in any case well disposed towards Paul, sent messengers to ask him in their name not to entrust himself to an enraged crowd. Meanwhile a din of varied sounds arose from the people. Some shouted one thing, some another – as usually happens, for the assembled crowd was mixed together from various kinds of people and with different inclinations; many did not even know why they had come together.

Therefore, the situation demanded some popular speaker to bring calm somehow to the present disorder. And so, a certain Alexander was thrust forth from the packed crowd, put forward by the Jews, to quell the disturbance with a speech. No one dared to make a speech before a raging crowd that was a jumble of various prejudices, where anything said was bound to offend some. Compelled, therefore, to stand forth,[37] he demanded attention by a gesture of the hand, and prepared to give an explanation. But the disturbance arose again as soon as the crowd perceived that Alexander was a Jew. Since this nation worships the one God, it detests the gods of the heathen, and so they expected he would say something against the majesty of Diana. Accordingly, with one voice they all began to shout, 'Great is Diana of the Ephesians.' This cry continued for almost two hours. At length, when the town clerk had obtained the silence of the crowd, Alexander said:[38]

'Men of Ephesus, what is the purpose of this shouting? What person is there who does not know that the city of the Ephesians is the worshipper[39] of the great Diana, and of the image that fell from Jove?[40] Since, therefore, no one denies what you affirm, there is no reason to raise this uproar, but you must be quiet and do nothing rashly. You have brought here these two men, who are neither sacrilegious nor blasphemers of your[41] goddess, for to punish crimes of that sort the people might have, perhaps with just cause, gathered together. But if Demetrius, the silversmith, and the other craftsmen who have joined him – for they are the ones who gave rise to this uproar – have any accusation to bring against anyone, there is no need of this theatre, or of a popular gathering, or of disorder. There are laws in this city, there are court days, there are proconsuls to hear cases, to resolve disputes, and to punish evildoers. Let those who have been the cause of this concourse make their mutual accusations before these officials, since their case has nothing to do with the people. However, if this is not a private case, but belongs also to the people, still there is no need to handle the matter in this disorderly way. If you demand anything, it can be settled by a lawful meeting summoned by the proper authorities in the proper way. Now there is danger that because of the uproar made today a charge of rioting may be brought against us before the magistrates, since we are able to advance no good reason why[42] the people have rushed into assembly in the theatre.'

When he had spoken thus, the meeting was dismissed.

Chapter 20

After the uproar had subsided, Paul called the disciples together and exhorted them to continue steadfast in what they had begun.[1] Then he embraced them, took leave, and departed to go to Macedonia.[2] He travelled through the territory of Macedonia, and wherever there was a congregation exhorted them in many words to persevere and advance in evangelical sincerity.[3] Then he came to that region which is properly called Greece, in which Achaia lies.[4] When he had been there three months and was preparing to sail from there to Syria, he became aware that the Jews were laying a plot against him for the voyage.[5] Accordingly, it seemed safer to change the port; he would return to Macedonia and sail again to Syria from the same coast where he had disembarked when he first came to Macedonia.[6] As travelling companions we had Sosipater, the Berean, the son of Pyrrhus,[7] Aristarchus and Secundus, Thessalonians, and along with these, Gaius, from Derbe, and Timothy, also Tychicus and Trophimus, Asians. While Paul stayed in Macedonia, these went on ahead to attend to things necessary for a safe journey, and awaited us in Troas. Going through Macedonia, we came to Philippi. After the days of *azyma*, which[8] immediately follow Passover, we set sail from there and within five days came to those at Troas, where we stayed for seven days.

Here a memorable event occurred. On a certain sabbath,[9] the disciples[10] had as usual met together to break bread. Paul, who everywhere filled the role of pastor, was refreshing their souls with the sacred word,[11] since he intended to depart the next day. He continued speaking late into the night. To prevent the night from causing the breakup of a most delightful discourse, there were many lamps in the upper room where we were then gathered. In the group was a certain young man by the name of Eutychus sitting in a window. Sinking into a deep sleep, as Paul spoke for a long time, he became at length so overwhelmed by the force of sleep that he fell from the third floor prostrate upon the earth. They rushed out, but he was found dead and taken up into the house. When Paul learned of this, he went down and, following the example of Elijah the prophet, bent low and lay upon him, as though warming the lifeless body with his embrace.[12] Having done this, he turned to his disciples, who were upset by the unexpected mischance, and said, 'Do not be alarmed; his life is still in him, for it has not yet entirely left his body.' He consoled them with these words, and went back up to the room, broke bread, and ate. Then for a long time again he conversed with them, right till daybreak, and so at last departed. So hard it is for a loving father to tear himself from his children. Those who had remained with the young man brought him to the upper room alive and well. This in no small measure revived everyone's spirit, for it was not becoming that the word which brings salvation to all should be the occasion for a young man's death.

We, for our part, embarked at Troas, and set sail for Assos, a coastal city below Troas. Paul had arranged that we should go there by ship before him, while he himself would make the journey by land on foot – either because it was safer, or to visit more people. When we met again at Assos, we took Paul on board, and together went on down to Mytilene, a city on the shore of Lesbos.[13] Setting sail from there we arrived the next day off the island of Chios. Again from there on the day after, we pulled in to the island of Samos, and from there crossed to Trogyllium, a city on the shore of Asia, opposite Samos. Here we spent the night,[14] and on the next day arrived at Miletus, a coastal city of Caria.[15]

Although to those who sail along the coast of Asia Ephesus appears before either Trogyllium or Miletus,[16] nevertheless Paul had determined to sail past Ephesus. He feared that he would lose time in Asia if as a result of a plot he should not be permitted to sail safely from there to Syria.[17] He was hastening to spend Pentecost in Jerusalem if at all possible. Still, not to seem to have passed by the Ephesians because of indifference or dislike, he sent from Miletus some persons to summon from the Ephesian congregation the presbyters into whose care he had commended the congregation.[18] When, following his summons, they had come, he spoke to them in this manner:

'I need not speak to you, brethren, of my integrity in the work of the gospel. You yourselves, who have seen, know how I conducted myself throughout the whole time I was with you from the first day I came into Asia. I did not seek from anyone glory or gain for myself, but in handing down the gospel I obeyed the commands of the Lord Jesus and conformed to his will in all things. I have, that is, followed close in the footsteps of the one who cast himself down, who handed himself over to suffering and death to cleanse and establish his church.[19] In like manner I, too, have been engaged in the work of the gospel – with much humility and with dishonour, which I have suffered from the enemies of the gospel; with the many[20] tears that I have shed because of my care for the congregation;[21] with many sufferings that have befallen me from the plots of the Jews, who do not allow the grace of the gospel to be shared with gentiles.

'Nevertheless, none of these evils has shaken my resolve. I have left undone nothing through fear of suffering that pertains to your salvation.[22] I have shown you everything that is to your own advantage. Even at the risk of my life,[23] I have taught you publicly in the synagogues as well as in your homes and in private, however the opportunity arose. I did not preach to you what the Jews wished – circumcision, sabbaths, lustrations – but the repentance for past life that God requires of all in order to grant salvation to all, and trust in our Lord Jesus,[24] in whose gospel whoever believes will be saved, whether Jew or Greek, circumcised or uncircumcised.[25] For this reason I preached indiscriminately to everyone the grace offered to all. I made no distinction of persons,[26] and was not frightened off either by the hatred of the Jews or the cruelty of the gentiles: the Jews assail the gospel through their zeal for the Law, while the gentiles defend the superstition handed down from their ancestors. If any affliction has fallen upon me here, the risk to the congregation has disturbed me more than the humiliation or the pain inflicted upon me, fearing that someone offended by the ills I suffered might be alienated from the gospel. But if I have ever withdrawn myself from dangers, I complied with your own wish, had regard for your welfare rather than my safety.[27] I do not regret this resolve. Indeed, even now – free in body but already bound in spirit[28] – I am setting out for Jerusalem. I do not yet clearly know what will befall me there, except that in every city the Spirit through the mouths of prophets and within me myself[29] proclaims that I will be put in chains and suffer affliction.

'Though I know and believe this, still none of these things deters me from performing my apostolic duty even if I must meet my death. This life of mine is not dear to me, a life which cannot perish since Christ is its protector.[30] It is worth more than life to obey the commands of the Lord and to finish with joy[31] this course of evangelical proclamation, as I have with eagerness maintained it until now. Great is the joy in my heart if the gospel harvest increases through my sufferings. One thing only is dear to my heart, that in the racecourse of the gospel into which the Lord has brought me I should always go forward until I reach the goal, confident of the reward that the judge of the contest, who cannot deceive, will pay out in his own time and according to his own judgment.[32] I did not take this responsibility upon myself, but the Lord Jesus assigned it to me,[33] to preach to Jews and gentiles the most joyful news that God desired to give salvation freely to all through gospel faith. I execute this ministry willingly and gladly whether it is my lot to live or to die. As long as I was permitted to be with you, I took a personal interest in your salvation, teaching, admonishing, exhorting, comforting, rebuking, repeatedly visiting you.[34] But now I know through the inspiration of the Spirit that you will not henceforth see my face – neither you Ephesians nor all you others who dwell in Asia Minor, to whom I came preaching the kingdom of God.[35] I have fulfilled my duty carefully and in good faith.[36]

'Wherefore, now, as I am about to depart from you without hope of return, I call upon you today as witnesses of this, that if anyone perishes – through his own fault or the fault of others – I am free of the blood of all. I have shown to all the true way by which one may reach eternal life. I have disclosed to you the whole counsel of God, both how he wills that the human race be saved and what those must fulfil who continue in steadfast, sincere trust in the Lord Jesus. Thus no one can hide behind ignorance as an excuse. I offered myself as an example,[37] doing and suffering everything that you all might persevere in the unadulterated gospel. No one's death will be able to be imputed to me. I am not plucked from you now of my own accord, nor am I withdrawing from fear of persecution, but as the Spirit of Christ wills, so with foresight and knowledge I set out for the indubitable danger that will be the turning-point of my life.

'What my presence will therefore not be able to provide for you, your own diligence must make good. See that you do not neglect your own welfare, and do not slide back from things well begun. But you who are elders[38] and to whom I have entrusted the care of the multitude, be vigilant both for yourselves, that you be not corrupted by dishonest apostles,[39] and for the whole flock you have undertaken to feed. I have fulfilled with absolute sincerity my own duty, assigned to me by the Lord. You too, in the same manner,[40] with like zeal and like integrity care for the flock over which the Holy Spirit has made you bishops, that is, 'lookers-into';[41] you are to see that the sheep of Jesus Christ lack no salutary food, and that you behave towards the congregation of God not as wolves but as true shepherds. You must not care for it negligently and half asleep, for God thought it so precious that he acquired it for himself with the blood of his Only-Begotten.[42] You must not therefore act in such a way that merchandise so dearly purchased by God should be lost through your negligence.

'Not without cause do I so anxiously give you this admonition. I know that you will not always have Pauls,[43] but after my departure grievous wolves will throw themselves upon you, as upon sheepcotes without the shepherd. They will not spare the flock, but will make every effort to scatter your congregation.[44] The danger here will be that the weak, disheartened by evils, will abandon the gospel.

'Another danger, however, threatens, a much greater one. It is not only that some will come from the outside and with terrors and threats, with crafty persuasions, with a counterfeit form of holiness will try to corrupt your integrity and shake the liberty you have through the gospel of Jesus Christ.[45] But men will also arise from among yourselves; perfidiously betraying your peace, they will speak things that are perverse and do not square with the straight gospel truth. They do so not that the flock of Jesus Christ be kept safe for himself, but to draw disciples away after themselves, to make themselves seem important,[46] fearing no doubt that they will not appear as distinguished teachers unless they teach something new. But novelty is perverse when human beings add to the gospel, which is sufficient in itself. The true pastor prefers that disciples belong to Christ rather than to himself, and from him he takes his food with which to feed them. The others, for the sake of glory and gain, make the disciples of Christ their own disciples.[47] They wish to be the authors of evangelical doctrine, though in fact we are nothing other than its stewards.[48] The more danger threatens, the more carefully you must be on your guard. Remember that during the three years I was in Asia, I did not cease to admonish each of you night and day with tears.

'For the rest, brethren, since I am being torn away from you, I now commend you to God, who will not fail his flock. I commend you also to the evangelical word. The divine favour will lend aid to those who are engaged in this word sincerely and[49] who preach the gratuitous goodness of God towards all people rather than the justice of the Law. We have laid the foundations in accordance with our assigned duty. But God who does all these things through us is able to build upon it to complete what was begun as he wills.[50] As thus far it has been your lot to be admitted into the company of the sons of God[51] through your profession of the gospel, so, persevering in your holy purpose, may you come to the inheritance promised to all those sanctified through the grace of God, whether they are Jews or gentiles.

'You have seen my solicitude, you have seen my labours, you have seen the dangers I have encountered for your sake. Meanwhile, I have striven for no reward from you, neither honour nor gain. Far from that, I did not receive even the necessities of life, as the other apostles did and as I could have done by right.[52] I have coveted no one's gold or silver or apparel. As you know, these hands have supplied my own needs and those of my companions as far as necessary.

'I could have taken this from you. I was not ignorant that the labourer is worthy of his hire,[53] but I preferred to wait for my wages from the Lord. I was eager to offer you an example perfect in every way,[54] so that you who have succeeded to the care of the flock might understand it is the duty of a good pastor to abstain on account of the weak from every human reward, even though avoiding no task in promoting the welfare of the flock. Thus no one would become more averse to the gospel because he was compelled to support his own evangelist;[55] nor would he be the less inclined to obey the admonitions of the pastors because he supposed they had been put under obligation to himself on account of the benefits received. For it is human nature that we somehow have less respect for those on whom we have conferred a benefit.[56] True, it is fair that for those who have imparted to you the riches of the gospel you should provide in turn far cheaper resources;[57] I, nevertheless, knowing that many among you were weak, wanted to give no one any occasion for thinking less highly of us. Be keen to emulate with all your strength this example of mine, and at the same time remember that the Lord Jesus said, "It is more blessed to give than to receive."'

Such were Paul's words. Then, kneeling down, he prayed in his customary way with them all. Great was the weeping that arose among all, so that they fell upon his neck and kissed him as though greedily seizing a supply of what was soon to be torn away. What tortured everyone's mind was the word Paul had spoken that they would see his face no more. After this, they escorted him to the ship, an obligation of courtesy;[58] and as he sailed away they followed him with their eyes as far as they could.

Chapter 21

From there, then, we set sail and presently the growing distance took us from their sight as they stood watching on the shore. We came by a straight course to the island of Cos, the next day to Rhodes, and from there to Patara, a city on the coast of Lycia.[1] Finding a ship departing for Phoenicia, we boarded it and set sail. When the island of Cyprus came in sight we kept it on the left and set our course for Syria. We landed at Tyre, a city on the shore of Phoenicia, as is Sidon also. We should indeed have preferred to go directly to Palestine; since Tyre is a trading centre, however, the skipper had to unload his cargo there.[2] But when in this place too we discovered[3] disciples, we remained with them seven days. There were some there who, under the inspiration of the prophetic spirit,[4] advised Paul not to depart for Jerusalem. Nevertheless, when the seven days were ended we proceeded to set out from Tyre,[5] and all the disciples along with their children and wives escorted us out of the city to the shore. Here we knelt to pray together, then said our mutual farewells. We, for our part, boarded the ship; they returned home. Completing the run from Tyre, we came to Ptolemais, a city situated on the coast near Mount Carmel.[6] Here we greeted the brethren, then remained with them for one day. On the next day we who were accompanying Paul[7] departed and came with him to Caesarea in Palestine. We went to the house of Philip and stayed with him – he was the first to preach the gospel to the eunuch and to the Samaritans, and one of the seven deacons whom the apostles had appointed at Jerusalem.[8]

Philip had four daughters, still unmarried, who were rich in the prophetic spirit, as it is said in the prophecy of Joel.[9] While we were enjoying Philip's hospitality for some days, a certain prophet named Agabus came down from Judaea and found lodgings with us. Taking Paul's girdle, he himself bound his own feet with it,[10] following the practice of the prophets of old, who are accustomed to represent by some sign what they are foretelling.[11] Under the inspiration of the Spirit he said, 'Thus says the Holy Spirit: "So shall the Jews at Jerusalem bind the man to whom this belt belongs and deliver him into the hands of the gentiles."' We were terrified by these words; both we who were Paul's travelling companions and the disciples in that place begged him with many tears not to trust himself to Jerusalem. This was the devoted affection of those who did not wish so excellent a pastor to perish. But the Holy Spirit had uttered within Paul's breast the more certain oracle

that he would go to Jerusalem, and afterwards see Rome.[12] So Paul said to
them:

'Why do you break my heart with your vain tears? The danger that
prophets make known does not move me, but your sorrow brings sorrow to
my heart. What the Spirit wishes to come to pass for the advancement of the
gospel is bound to occur. Chains do not terrify me, for I am now by no means
inexperienced in evils of that sort.[13] So far am I from forsaking the work of
the gospel from fear of chains that I am ready also to die at Jerusalem for the
name of the Lord Jesus. Let Paul be bound provided the word of the gospel
has free course. Let Paul be slain provided the glory of the name of Jesus
lives and flourishes among all![14] I desire life for no other reason than to be
of use to the gospel. It would in any case be a gain for me to finish this life
quickly on behalf of the name of Christ.[15] Accordingly do not lament what
is, in my case, something even to be wished for, if God so wills; and cease
to bring sorrow to my heart with your tears. I cannot but grieve when my
friends are grieving.'

We had nothing to reply to this, and when we saw that his decision to
go to Jerusalem was final, we allowed him to depart, saying, 'The will of the
Lord be done' – an expression belonging to those truly Christian, one that
ought always to be in everyone's heart, even if it is not on the lips, no matter
what is imminent, whether joy or sorrow: the will of the Lord be done.[16] And
so we stayed at Caesarea for some days, then made our preparations[17] for
the journey to Jerusalem. Some of the disciples from the city of Caesarea
accompanied Paul along with us, bringing with them Mnason, a Cypriot,
who was to provide hospitality in Jerusalem.[18] He was a man of proven
piety inasmuch as he had long ago believed the gospel and had persisted
in sincerity of faith for a long time.[19] When we arrived at Jerusalem the
brethren received us with a warm and hearty welcome.

On the next day Paul, accompanied by us, went to the house of James
the Just, who was called the brother of the Lord; for he had been instituted
bishop of Jerusalem by the apostles.[20] All the elders[21] assembled there. Paul
greeted them all, then reported in detail what God had done through his
ministry among the gentiles, among whom he had been preaching the gospel
now for quite a few years. When they heard this they glorified the Lord[22]
who had poured out his grace upon the gentiles also.[23] But Paul had been
denounced among many Jews as a hater of the Mosaic law, who preached the
grace of the gospel in such a way that he attributed less than he should to the
observance of the Law. To improve the situation they said:

'You see, brother Paul, how many thousands of Jews there are here who
have believed the gospel, and they all are possessed by a great zeal for the
Law. There has come to them the rumour (which we know is empty)[24] that

you teach the Jews who live among the gentiles to desert Moses, so that they neither circumcise their children nor observe the practices of their forefathers in choice of foods, in sabbaths, in lustrations, and the rest, customs these Jews who have not been mixed with the gentiles keep most scrupulously. Constrained by the decree of the elders,[25] these somehow accept that the gentiles are not being burdened by the yoke of the Law. But they do not accept that native Jews are being led away from observance of the Law to the practices of the gentiles. Now, then, we must see that no disturbance arises from this.

'So what is to be done? In the first place there is no disguising the fact that a crowd will be assembled,[26] for they will hear that you have come. To free yourself therefore from this suspicion, follow our advice. We have four men who have bound themselves by a vow, according to Jewish custom. Join them and along with them fulfil the rites customary for those who are careful to be purified after a vow; if anything further is to be laid out for sacrifices or gifts, do so along with them until they shave their heads.[27] So it will be that all will know there is nothing in the stories rumour has spread concerning you. When they see you doing the very things certain people declare that you condemn, they will understand that you too preach the grace of the gospel without condemning those who observe ancestral custom and the practices of the Law handed down by God.[28] In this way the murmuring of the Jews will be repressed[29] – and there are too many of them not to take them into account. As for the gentiles who have believed, we wrote long ago on the basis of the decision of the apostles and the people that they should not be forced to observe the Mosaic law provided they abstain from things offered to idols, from blood, from anything strangled, and from fornication.'[30]

Paul complied with the advice of James and the brethren. He joined the four men who had bound themselves by a vow, was purified along with them, entered the temple, and declared that the days of purification were fulfilled. He neglected no ceremony until, in the customary manner, an offering was presented for each one of them.[31] This whole affair was to be completed in seven days. When these were almost fulfilled, some unbelieving Jews who had seen him in Asia and had raised an uproar there[32] saw Paul in the temple. They stirred up all the people and laid hands upon Paul, crying out:

'Here! Help! Men of Israel. Here is the man whom you know from rumour, who travels through all regions, and everywhere teaches a new doctrine – against this people that especially belongs to God, against the Law handed down by God, against this temple sacred to the whole world.[33] This did not satisfy his impiety: he has also brought into the temple men who are Greeks and uncircumcised, and has polluted this holy place.' (They had seen Trophimus the Ephesian in the company of Paul when he was in the city and so had conjectured that Paul had brought him into the temple.)

At this uproar, the whole city was aroused, and the people came running together. They caught Paul and dragged him out of the temple, as though to be thrown to the frenzied mob. At once the gates of the temple were closed so that there should be no place where he might safely withdraw.[34] They sought to kill him, but to do so in the temple was a religious offence[35] – as though to slay the innocent was not everywhere an act of impiety. Meanwhile it was reported to the tribune of the cohort that the whole city of Jerusalem was in tumult. He immediately took soldiers and centurions and ran down to them. When the Jews saw the tribune running towards them with soldiers, they stopped beating Paul.

When the tribune had come closer, he commanded that Paul be arrested and bound with two chains, suspecting that he was some criminal with whom the crowd was so furious. With that, the tribune asked the Jews who he was and what wrong he had done. However, because of the commotion of the mob bawling out different things from different directions, he could not ascertain for certain what it wanted. He therefore ordered Paul to be led, as he had been bound, into the barracks, so that he could discover the truth of the matter within the confines of the fortress,[36] where the crowd was excluded. When they had come to the steps of the barracks, Paul was carried by soldiers on account of the violence of the mob, for they feared the people would use force against Paul before he got into the barracks. Indeed, the crowd of people followed right to those very steps, shouting and crying out, 'Away with this fellow!'

When they came to the entrance of the fortress, Paul, eager to satisfy the riotous Jews, said to the tribune, 'Am I allowed to speak to you?' The tribune replied, 'Do you know Greek?' – for Paul had said this in Greek. 'Are you not,' said he, 'that Egyptian who stirred up a revolt previously as well, and led the four thousand assassins from here[37] into the desert?' To these words Paul responded, 'I am not the person you think. I am a Jew by race; my native land is Tarsus, no obscure city of Cilicia. Meanwhile I ask this of you: let me speak to the people.' When he had given leave, Paul stood on the steps, and with a gesture of his hand indicated to the people that he wished to speak. Immediately there was a great silence and Paul began to speak in the Hebrew tongue.

Chapter 22

'My fellow men, all of you who are here, whether brothers by race or fathers through age and honour,[1] give me your attention, while I clear myself of the charges of which I have been falsely[2] accused before you.'

When Paul had made these preliminary remarks and the crowd heard that he spoke Hebrew, they grew even more silent, whether because every one understood this language, or because everyone is well disposed towards his own language.[3] Then Paul went on to speak thus:

'That you may understand that I have done nothing wicked either against the Jewish people, or against the law of Moses, or against the temple: – I am a Jew, born of Jewish parents in Tarsus of Cilicia, but brought up in this city at the feet of Gamaliel (a man well known to you),[4] and carefully instructed from my earliest years in our ancestral Law. With great zeal I was devoted to that worship of the true[5] God which you too all maintain today, so that through love of the Law[6] I persecuted this evangelical way which I now profess – persecuted not only to the extent of prisons and chains, but right to the point of death. I breathed only threats and slaughter against those who profess the gospel,[7] and bound and dragged off to prison both men and women. That such is the truth, the man who was then high priest is my witness, and with him the whole order of elders.[8] I received from them letters to the Jews[9] and set out for Damascus to bring in chains from there to Jerusalem those who professed the name of Christ, so that they might be punished at the discretion of the priests and elders. Such at that time was my attitude towards them, and for no other reason than my zeal for the Law and the religion handed down from our ancestors, the very reason you too now rage against me.

'Now hear what it was that changed my mind; when you have come to know this, perhaps you too will change your mind. For it happened that while I was on my way and was not far from the city of Damascus, about noon time, suddenly a powerful light from heaven shone round about me. Stricken by this, I fell to the earth and heard a voice from heaven[10] saying to me, "Saul, Saul, why do you persecute me?" When I replied "Who are you, Lord?" I heard again, "I am Jesus of Nazareth whom you persecute." Moreover, my travelling companions had indeed seen the light, and became quite afraid, but they did not hear the voice of the one who was speaking with me.[11] I replied, "What do you want me to do, Lord?"[12] and the Lord responded, "Rise and go into Damascus; there each of the things you must do will be prescribed for you."[13] My eyes were so blinded by the brilliancy of that light that I saw nothing at all, so my companions led me by the hand, and I reached Damascus.

'In Damascus a certain Ananias came to me. He was a devout man and scrupulous in observing the Law,[14] and was approved by the testimony of all the Jews living there. He came to me, stood near, and said to me, "Brother Saul, receive your sight." Immediately I received my sight and saw him. Then he said:

'"The God of our fathers has chosen and prepared[15] you for this, that you should know his will and see that Just One who alone justifies all things, and should hear a voice from his mouth – Jesus was in that light which blinded you and his was the voice you heard[16] – since you will be a witness for him to all people of what you have seen and heard. And now, after God has so willed, why do you delay? Rise, be baptized, and wash away your sins, calling upon the name of him whom you have been persecuting.'

'Some little time after these events in Damascus,[17] I returned to Jerusalem, now a changed man.[18] When I was praying in the temple, I was transported beyond myself,[19] and saw Jesus saying to me, "Make haste, and get quickly out of Jerusalem, since here they will not receive your testimony concerning me." I then replied in this manner:

'"Lord, I have good hope that I shall be successful among the people here because they themselves know that hitherto, through my zeal for the Law, I raged against your disciples, dragging off to prison whomever I could and beating with rods in one synagogue after another those who had believed your gospel. Nor was I content with this. Indeed, when the blood of Stephen was being shed – a man who by his death steadfastly bore faithful testimony to you[20] – I too was standing by those who stoned him, consenting to the death of an innocent man.[21] I even kept the clothes of those who had accused him and who were the first to begin to cast stones at him. When from this they all understand with what feverish zeal for the Law I at one time burned,[22] they will readily realize[23] that I did not rashly change, and many will be found to imitate my example[24] – more willingly in proportion to the greater zeal for the old religion with which I raged against your people."

'When I had spoken, the Lord replied, "Go, I say, obey me, since the time has now arrived when my gospel is going to be spread throughout the whole world. For this purpose have I chosen you, to send you from here to far distant nations."'

Until now the Jews had put up with Paul as he spoke, right to this word, 'I will send you to nations far away.'[25] This statement touched afresh the pain of everyone,[26] because the Jews detest the gentiles with an astonishing hatred. Through this hatred, many even of those who were not spurning the gospel wanted the gentiles absolutely excluded from the grace of the gospel, or, if admitted, they should be admitted only when circumcised, as though one could not be pure and pleasing to God unless he were a Jew.[27] Accordingly, when they heard that the gentiles were preferred to the people of Jerusalem, with great shouts they broke through the sound of Paul's voice as he spoke,[28] saying to the tribune, 'Away with this man from the earth, since it is not right that he should live.' As the Jews were showing unbridled animosity in many ways, crying out and throwing down their garments, and, finally, casting dust into the air, the tribune suspected that some shameful crime had been committed, and that for this reason the whole populace was in an uproar in such a strange way, especially since, after he had given Paul the opportunity to speak, everything that was uttered only made matters worse. He then ordered his soldiers to lead Paul to the barracks and examine him under the lash in order to beat directly out of Paul himself why the populace cried out against him in this way.

In keeping with the tribune's command, Paul was now bound with leather straps, and was on the point of being beaten when he said to the centurion who was standing by and who had been assigned the task of overseeing the examination, 'What? Is it lawful for you to beat with the lash a man who is a Roman, and uncondemned?' As soon as the centurion had heard this, he went quickly to the tribune and reported what he had heard, saying, 'What are you planning to do?[29] For this man whom you ordered to be beaten with rods[30] is a Roman citizen.' On hearing this, the tribune himself went to Paul and said to him, 'Tell me, is it true what the centurion reports to me? Are you a Roman citizen?' Paul affirmed that he was a Roman citizen, and the tribune replied, 'You have mentioned something of great importance. For I procured Roman citizenship for myself only at a very great cost.' Then Paul said, 'In this respect, indeed, my position is better than yours: I was born a Roman citizen; the right of citizenship came to me from my parents.'

At once therefore the men who had prepared to examine Paul by torture left him. Indeed, even the tribune himself was afraid for himself when he learned Paul was a Roman citizen, because he had bound him with straps. So great was the terror of the Roman name among all. On the next day, however, as the tribune desired to know with certainty on what grounds Paul was accused by the Jews, he released him from his chains and ordered the chief priests and the whole council to assemble. He brought Paul forth and had him stand before them so that the matter could be handled by the leaders, away from the agitation of the populace.

Chapter 23

Here Paul fixed his eyes upon the council, and began to speak thus: 'Brethren, I have, right to this very day, conducted myself in all things with a pure conscience in the sight of God who alone judges rightly.' But when the high priest, Ananias, heard an introduction so confident and so bold – simultaneously a declaration of Paul's innocence and a condemnation of the judge and the others who had accused him – he was indignant because Paul, in his preliminary remarks, had not recognized the special position of the high priest and had nothing of the appearance of a guilty man.[1] So the high priest, Ananias, commanded those who stood by to strike Paul on the mouth as he spoke. This was no doubt what the Lord had foretold Paul: 'They will not receive your testimony concerning me.'[2]

At this indignity, Paul was filled with disdain (for such a thing usually does not occur even in pagan courts of justice) and, announcing the punishment that would afterward come from God upon such a manifest tyranny, said, 'God shall strike you, you whitewashed wall! Do you sit thus to judge me after due trial in accordance with the Law, and contrary to the Law order me to be struck before the case has been heard? The Law forbids punishing anyone unless legitimately condemned.'[3] Here, those who stood by said to Paul, 'Do you thus insult the high priest of God?' To such a pitch of tyranny had the Jewish priesthood come that they demanded to be allowed to harm someone contrary to justice and right, and did not permit free speech in others. This was a sign, surely, of the abolition, soon to come, of the priesthood, after it had descended to the lowest depths of wickedness.[4] Then Paul, seeing that he would get nowhere with such a judge, thought only that an occasion should be sought for dissolving that assembly. Accordingly, he replied, 'I did not know, brethren, that he was the high priest. Besides, I know it is written in the book of Exodus, "You shall not speak evil of the ruler of your people"' [22:28].[5]

Though with these words he had in some way placated his admonishers, he sought a device to turn the uproar away from himself, for it is permissible to avoid danger by cunning when no advantage appears to be forthcoming. Accordingly, since Paul knew that the council consisted of two parties, Sadducees and Pharisees, who disagreed with each other, he said in a loud voice in the council so that everyone could hear him, 'Brethren, I am a Pharisee and the son of a Pharisee,[6] and I am on trial for preaching the resurrection of the dead.' When he had said this, a dissension arose between the Pharisees and Sadducees, and through their disagreement the crowd present also split up into different camps. For since the Sadducees believe that the soul perishes along with the body, they do not accept the resurrection, nor do they think there exists either any spirit or angel.[7] The Pharisees, on the other hand, both believe in the resurrection and affirm the existence of angels and spirits.

The crowd, therefore, with a loud cry started to raise an uproar. Meanwhile, some scribes from the party of the Pharisees[8] arose and began to fight on Paul's side, saying, 'We find no evil in this man. But if a spirit or an angel has spoken to him,[9] it is not for us to fight against God.'[10] They said this because on the previous day Paul had described how the Lord had appeared to him in a vision in the temple.[11] So much does it avail, where judgments are predetermined, to belong to this or that party. The Sadducees were shouting on the other side, and when the controversy had already become heated and the affair seemed to be headed towards an outright riot, the tribune, fearing they would tear Paul to pieces, ordered soldiers to go down, snatch Paul from their midst, and bring him back to the barracks.

Now it was time for God to support his athlete[12] with some consolation in the midst of such storms, especially when even fiercer ones were threatening. So during the night the Lord again[13] stood beside him and said:

'Be of good courage, Paul. These storms will not swallow you, for the time of your death is not yet at hand.[14] It remains for you to testify also at Rome just as you have courageously given witness to me at Jerusalem. You have performed your duty in the city that is the capital of Judaea;[15] it remains that you do the same also at Rome, the capital of the world.'

Dawn had now come, and some of[16] the Jews conspired together and called curses upon themselves if they took food or drink before they had slain Paul. So great was the hatred they had conceived against him! Those who had formed this conspiracy were not few in number, but were more than forty. These went to the high priests and elders and set forth to them their intent and purpose saying:

'We have bound ourselves with the strictest oath not to taste any food or drink before we slay Paul. Now you must comply with this purpose of ours, so that what we all want done may be effected the more easily. Signify to the tribune both in your own name and that of the council that he should bring Paul before you again.[17] Use as a pretext that you wish to investigate the case more closely, something the uproar yesterday did not permit. We, however, shall see to it that he does not return to the camp safely, as yesterday; but we are ready to kill him before he approaches the place of the council.'

When a certain young man – Paul's nephew by his sister – heard of this deadly trap, he thought he could not remain idle, but forthwith went to the barracks and told Paul what was impending. On learning this Paul summoned one of the centurions and said, 'Take this young man to the tribune, for he has something to communicate.' The centurion, as requested, took the young man and brought him to the tribune, saying, 'The prisoner Paul asked me[18] to bring this young man to you, because he said he has something he wished to speak about with you.' Then the tribune grasped the young man's hand, went aside with him, and inquired of him, saying, 'What is it you wanted to tell me?' He replied, 'The Jews have conspired to kill Paul, and have agreed to ask you to give the order to have Paul brought into the council again tomorrow. Their pretext will be that they desire to find out something about him they were unable to learn clearly yesterday; in fact, they are up to something else. So take care not to yield to their demand imprudently, for more than forty men, with fixed purpose, are resolved to lay a snare for Paul's life. They have bound themselves with the direst oaths not to eat or drink a thing until they slay him. And they are even now prepared for this crime, awaiting your promise.'[19] When the tribune heard this he dismissed the young man, charging him not to let anyone know that he had given this information to the tribune.[20] For he wished to save Paul's life, but without becoming hated by the Jews.

Accordingly, he called two centurions and said, 'Make ready two hundred soldiers and along with them seventy horsemen and two hundred spearmen to go to Caesarea immediately after the third hour of the night. At the same time get mounts ready to set Paul on, and bring him safely to the governor Felix.' The tribune exercised such great care not because he had regard for the life of one man (for he was not that scrupulous), but he wished to be free of Paul, for he could not have protected him against such obstinate hatred from the whole council, nor did he dare to hand a Roman citizen over to their hatred. For this reason he ordered him to be led forth by night with a large company of soldiers, fearing that if Paul left during the day or in the company of only a few soldiers, the Jews would seize him on the way and slay him, and the criticism from this would thereafter fall upon him who had perfidiously surrendered a Roman citizen.[21] But he also added a letter to Felix to this intent:

'Claudius Lysias to his Excellency, the governor Felix: Greetings.

'This man had been seized by the Jews, and they were on the point of killing him, when I came upon him and rescued him with the help of the army, having learned that he was a Roman citizen. Wishing to know why they were bringing accusation against him, I brought him into their council. I discovered that he was guilty of no crime worthy of prison or death, but they were only casting up certain things at issue in Jewish law. When, presently, I was informed of a plot that the Jews were preparing against him, I at once sent him to you, and at the same time informed the Jews who were accusing him that if they had anything to bring against him, they should declare it before you. Farewell!'[22]

The soldiers, following the tribune's orders, took Paul into their protection and brought him by night to Antipatris. On the next day, since they were not far from Caesarea[23] and there seemed already to be less danger, the soldiers returned to the barracks at Jerusalem, and the horsemen accompanied Paul as far as Caesarea. When they had arrived there and given the letter to the governor, they presented Paul before him also at the same time. Then the governor read the letter and inquired what province he belonged to. When he learned that it was Cilicia, he said, 'I shall hear you when your accusers have come,' and he commanded him to be kept in Herod's headquarters.

Chapter 24

Five days later the high priest Ananias came down to Caesarea with some elders along with the orator Tertullus,[1] who was to plead the case – to such an extent did some kind of obstinate passion to slay Paul possess them! When they approached the governor, they demanded that the defendant be produced, and Felix ordered Paul to be summoned and made to appear. Thereupon Tertullus, who was not the best advocate of a bad case, began to accuse Paul in this way:

'We owe it to you, most excellent Felix, that we have now for some time enjoyed a state of great peace and tranquillity. In many other respects also, affairs are through your foresight administered prosperously and well among this people.[2] We therefore always and everywhere acknowledge and proclaim your kindness towards us, and give you thanks with all the devotion we can. And the very aptness you have for good administration gives us the confident hope that in this case, too, which we now bring, you will have regard for the tranquillity of our nation. But, not to delay you with a too extensive introduction – for you are occupied with many matters of the greatest importance – I beg you out of your kindness and humanity to give us a brief hearing.

'We have discovered this fellow to be a pernicious bane to our nation because he stirs up sedition among the Jews, not only in Syria but in all parts of the whole world, wherever the Jewish race is scattered, making himself the ringleader of a new sect called the Nazarenes.[3] Not content with this, he dared to come to Jerusalem and, taking uncircumcised men into the temple,[4] was not afraid to profane our temple. We arrested him in the very act and wanted to judge him according to our Law; but Lysias, the tribune, came upon us with a large troop of soldiers, took him out of our hands and referred the investigation of the case to you, commanding the accusers to come to you. Accordingly, you can learn directly from the tribune himself that everything we accuse the defendant of is true.'[5]

Thus spoke that orator, as flat as he was fallacious.[6] But the Jews who supported the accusation affirmed that the matter was as Tertullus had described. After this, the governor beckoned to Paul to speak on his own behalf, and he began his defence thus:

'I make my defence on my own behalf the more confidently[7] since I know that you have for many years now lived among this people and are not inexperienced in trying Jewish cases at law. Because the actions these men accuse me of took place recently, you can be very sure that it was only twelve days ago since I, in accordance with the practice of Jewish religion, went up to Jerusalem to worship and, in accordance with a vow I had taken, to purify myself by the established ritual. If this is to violate the temple I acknowledge the crime.[8] They did not discover me in the temple disputing with anyone, or stirring up a crowd of people, neither, indeed, in the synagogues nor in any place in the city. They are not able by any sufficient evidence to prove the charges they cast against me. As to their taunt about the sect of the Nazarenes, I shall not deny its truth, and yet it is irrelevant for the accusers, since that sect has not been condemned among the Jews, nor am I the head of the sect. If, however, you are interested in learning what sect I profess, I shall tell you.

'I worship the God of our fathers, in accordance with the tradition of the Pharisees,[9] which they call a sect. By no means am I the author of a new religion, but a careful observer of the religion handed down from our ancestors, for I believe that everything written in the Law and the prophets is true. Since God has in large part already fulfilled these things as he promised,[10] I have a fixed hope that that too[11] will occur which he promised – I mean that those long since dead[12] will rise, the just and the unjust alike, the just to the glory of immortality, the unjust to everlasting punishment. I do not believe these things light-heartedly; rather, I am persuaded so profoundly that I strive with all my might not to sin in any respect against the law of God but to have a pure and sincere conscience, not only before God, who examines the heart,[13] but also before men, for I know that I must one day stand before the judgment seat of God to receive the reward for my deeds.[14] This I do to this very day. Accordingly, they have nothing in my former life they can accuse me of – should they intend to demonstrate from it that these things too which they now cast up are probably true of me.[15]

'Many years passed without reproach. At length I came to Jerusalem to offer money collected in Asia to alleviate poverty among my people. If to help my people with a good deed is to be pernicious, I acknowledge the accusation. Meanwhile, so that no turmoil could arise from those who were looking for an occasion, I shaved my head, went into the temple, and with the customary rituals completed my purification. I did nothing from which any turmoil or disturbance could arise. I did nothing novel, but used the same rites the whole race uses.[16] If any disturbance was then stirred up, it was stirred up by certain Jews from Asia.[17] Since they are the instigators of this affair they ought to be present at this trial and make their accusation if they have anything against me. It is a sign of a bad conscience that they withdraw from this investigation after they see the case is carried to the governor.[18] If a crime has been committed, it was by them I could have been most effectively convicted or acquitted – though I have no fear of anyone's accusation.

'Or these very people who are present here,[19] let them declare, since I stand in council,[20] if they have found me doing anything other than is right and proper. For in a legitimate trial it is permitted to accuse the defendant, and the defendant also is permitted to make his case. But they have nothing to accuse me of, unless perhaps they wish to throw up that one statement when the tribune brought me out and I was standing among them and saw that nothing was being done fairly, but with obvious hatred everything was aimed at my destruction: I shouted that I was a Pharisee and was a defendant before them because I preached the resurrection of the dead. At these words, they themselves began to raise an uproar, until the tribune snatched me from their hands. I told the truth, and it was fair for the crowd to know why I was endangered in the council, for I saw there was no safety for me among the leaders.'

On hearing this,[21] Felix wanted to defer the case to another time, since he had precise knowledge of the sect of the Pharisees[22] which Paul professed. So he said, 'Since Lysias has a clear knowledge of the course of this affair, I shall hear you when he comes to us.' He gave orders to the centurion to keep Paul in custody but less harshly, so that from time to time he should be granted some freedom and none of his friends should be forbidden to come to him[23] or to supply any needs he had.

After quite a few days Felix came to Caesarea with his wife Drusilla, who was a Jewess, and summoned Paul, desiring to be taught more fully by him about the sect he professed. There Paul disclosed to him what he had before concealed – the way of salvation. This way does not consist in the observances of the Law as the Jews thought, but in trust in Jesus Christ, whom the Jews had crucified though they had awaited him so many centuries. It provides that through baptism all the sins of our former life are once for all abolished, so that those who have been reborn into him may henceforth live pure and holy lives according to the rule of the gospel, doing so until the same Jesus who gave himself for the salvation of the human race returns in exaltation with the glory of the Father, judge of the living and the dead. When Paul had discoursed at length on these things – on the grace of faith, on the justice of the gospel, on the temperance and sobriety of the spiritual life,[24] on the final judgment which no one can escape – Felix shuddered. He was so moved that, though he did not set Paul free (for he feared the Jews, since he knew Paul was exceedingly hateful to them), nevertheless he had him kept in a more humane custody, until an opportunity should arise to free him.

There was another reason, too, why he delayed acquittal: he hoped Paul would pay out a sum of money and put his freedom in his hands.[25] For this reason, he frequently invited Paul to conversation to give him the opportunity to offer money. An established familiarity and the governor's perceived openness might overcome the sense of honour, which, he suspected, would prevent Paul from daring to offer money, for even the laws of the Caesars condemn a judgment won through bribery.[26] In the meantime, while Paul was held at Caesarea during a two-year period, Felix, by the order of the emperor Nero, was succeeded by Porcius Festus.[27] There was at that time, indeed, an opportunity to let Paul go. But Felix was unwilling to depart from the province leaving himself hated:[28] he preferred to gratify the Jews rather

than to set free, out of a sincere conscience, the innocent. He, therefore, left
Paul a prisoner. So difficult it is for the great of this world to follow the right
path in everything.[29]

Chapter 25

Festus accordingly entered his province and after three days went up from
Caesarea to Jerusalem. At the arrival of the new governor, Jewish malice
broke out afresh. For presently the chief priests and the principal men of
the Jews approached him,[1] demanding this favour of the new governor, that
he support them against Paul so far as to summon him to Jerusalem, since
it was inconvenient to pursue the case at Caesarea. They hoped that the
governor, who had recently come into his province and was ignorant of the
affair, would readily gratify them in this. But it had been agreed among
the Jews that if Festus assented to their demand they would lay an ambush
and slay Paul on the way. Festus, however, acting more justly than they
wished,[2] replied that Paul should be kept at Caesarea, but that he himself
would shortly proceed there and hear their case. 'Accordingly,' he said, 'if
there are those among you who are capable of pursuing this case,[3] they may
come along with me to Caesarea. There the defendant will appear in your
presence, and if there is any wrongdoing in this man of whom you speak, let
them accuse him.' After remaining among them for more than ten days,[4] he
went to Caesarea.

On the next day, he took his seat upon the tribunal, and ordered Paul
to appear. When he had been brought in, the Jews who had come from
Jerusalem stood about him directing many grave charges against him, but
they could not prove any of them, because Paul made it clear, as he replied
on his own behalf, that he had committed no offence either against the law of
the Jews which he kept, or against the temple, where without defilement he
had been quietly spending his time, or against Caesar.[5] Festus realized both
the innocence of Paul and the implacable hatred of the Jews towards him.
Eager to gratify the Jews without seeming to hurt the defendant, he said to
Paul, 'Do you wish to go to Jerusalem and stand trial before me there?' – for
he thought this would please the Jews who had earlier demanded it. Then
Paul, not unaware of what the Jews were up to, replied:

'There is no reason why this case should be referred elsewhere, since
nothing stands in the way of my being acquitted or condemned here. I stand
before the tribunal of Caesar in the city of Caesarea; here is where I ought to
be judged. I have done the Jews no injury, as you yourself very well know. If I
have in any way harmed them or in any other respect done anything worthy
of capital punishment, I do not beg to avoid death. But if everything is false
which the Jews cast up against me, no one acting as judge can, contrary to

law, surrender me to their hatred. A judge cannot condemn a defendant as a favour to anyone.[6] I appeal to Caesar.'

Upon these words Festus held a discussion with the council of the Jews[7] and replied to Paul, 'You have appealed to Caesar, to Caesar you will go!' For the Jews preferred that Paul be sent away to Caesar rather than acquitted. They hoped an occasion would be offered to get rid of him at last.

Meanwhile, after several days had passed, King Agrippa along with his wife Bernice came to Caesarea to pay their respects to the new governor Festus. (Agrippa had succeeded to the kingdom of his father Herod, who had been stricken by an angel.)[8] He stayed there for several days, and when an opportunity arose, Festus described Paul's case to the king in the following manner:

'There is a certain man here left a prisoner by Felix, whom I succeeded. When I came to Jerusalem, the chief priests and the principal men of the Jews approached me,[9] asking that I pronounce sentence against him as a favour to them. I replied that it was not the Roman practice to give someone up to death[10] as a favour to another until the defendant met his accusers face to face and had an opportunity to defend himself against the charges made. Therefore, when his accusers came together here, on the next day without any delay I took my seat on the tribunal and ordered the defendant to be brought in. His accusers appeared and made no accusation about the things I surmised. They brought forward against him only certain questions of their own superstition, and about one Jesus who was dead and whom Paul affirmed to be alive again and to live even now. I saw that questions of this sort were not at all appropriate for investigation by me, and was unsure what judgment to give in this case. So I asked him whether he wished to go to Jerusalem and be tried there on these matters, with which priests, scribes, and Pharisees were more familiar. Paul refused this, appealing to Caesar, to be kept for trial by him. I commanded him to be held in custody meanwhile, until an opportunity should arise to send him to Caesar.'

On hearing this, Agrippa replied to Festus, 'I have for some time now heard much about this Jesus and his disciples. For this reason, I myself also should like to hear this man before he goes to Caesar.' At which Festus said, 'Tomorrow you shall hear him.' The next day Agrippa came and with him Bernice, with great fanfare and display,[11] and entered into the audience hall with the tribunes and the principal men of the city. At Festus' command, Paul was brought in. Then Festus, so as not to appear to have brought Paul in to please the king, spoke in this way:

'King Agrippa, and all you men who are here present with us, you see the man about whom the whole multitude of the Jews has approached[12] me, both at Jerusalem and in this place; and they have shouted vociferously that he should not be permitted to live any longer. I made an investigation, however, and found that he had done nothing worthy of capital punishment, but since he himself of his own accord appealed to Caesar, I decided to send him there. I have nothing definite to write to the emperor about him. Wherefore, I have brought him forth to you, and especially to you, King Agrippa, so that he can be examined and I may have something to write. For I think it unfair to send a prisoner without indicating the crimes of which he is accused.'

Chapter 26

Here King Agrippa turned to Paul, who was standing by in chains, and said, 'You have permission to speak on your own behalf, if you have anything to say in your defence.' Then Paul stretched forth his hand and began his own defence thus:

'I believe, King Agrippa, that it is a matter of great importance before what judge a defendant pleads his case. Indeed, whoever has confidence in his own innocence can wish for nothing so much as to find a judge who has either come to know the case inside and out or has the capacity to learn[1] with utmost ease. For in the presence of a judge who does not understand the case in hand the eloquence of the speaker is in vain. And so, though various accusations are brought against me by the Jews, I nevertheless count myself fortunate for this reason, that it is before you I will plead this case today – you to whom both the customs and the controversies of the Jewish people are so very well known. Wherefore I ask you to hear me patiently.

'In the first place, some accuse me of sinning against the Law. How false this is, the life I have lived – all of it, to this very day – sufficiently shows.[2] For although I was born at Tarsus, yet from my earliest years I was brought up among the Jews at Jerusalem. Here I diligently learned the Law at the feet of Gamaliel.[3] The Jews, who have known me for many years, even from the time I first began to live in Jerusalem, know that I have lived a life of purity and religious devotion among the people of my own race and in the most celebrated city of all, if only they would admit what they know! Not only did I assiduously cultivate the Jewish religion, but I also embraced that party which excels the others both in religious zeal and in the most precise knowledge of the Law – I mean the Pharisees.

'It is shameless of them to accuse me (who was and am a Pharisee) of not being a Jew; it is as though someone should deny that a person born in Jerusalem was a Jew. For among Jews it is above all the party of the Pharisees that believes in the future resurrection of the body, and believes also that everyone will receive rewards according to the way he has lived.[4] I have never left the Pharisees' party; on the contrary, I stand even now subject to judgment because of the hope of happiness for those who have lived their lives in godly devotion, a felicity God promised our fathers. But if it is a crime to hope for what God has promised his worshippers, my crime is common to many. With what intent, I ask you, do the twelve tribes of our race worship God earnestly day and night, if not because they hope they will attain the felicity he has promised?[5] He, therefore, is scarcely worthy of the name 'Jew' who does not hope for what God has promised. But it is on account of this hope especially, King Agrippa, that I am now called into court by the Jews.

'I know that to many it seems absurd to say a body lives again, once it is dead and decayed. But many things seem absurd to people which they later find to be absolutely true. If someone should declare that a human being can be called back to life by a human being, he would deservedly appear to speak nonsense. But why should it be thought a thing incredible with you that God, who can do whatever he wishes, should raise the dead? Is he who has given life to all not able to give it back to whomever he wishes?[6] Or do we think him a liar in that he will not fulfil what he has promised?[7] Indeed, it has also been my own experience to have found completely true what I once thought absurd, and what once seemed impious and opposed to our Law I later found was the essence of both godliness and religion. Such had been my experience, even to the point that I myself once had the same attitude towards[8] the disciples of Jesus of Nazareth that the Jews now have towards me. I supposed I was acting with religious devotion if I fought with all my strength against the name of Jesus and inflicted upon its confessors as many evils as I could. This indeed I did at Jerusalem. I threw many saints into prison, obtaining authority to do so from the chief priests, and when they were put to death I brought the sentence.[9] Not only in Jerusalem did I punish them, but through all the synagogues wherever I came upon their assemblies. I was eager to force them, through punishment, even to be blasphemers against that holy name, as I was then.[10] Nor was I content with this. I raged against them with an even greater madness, proceeding even to foreign cities, cities far distant from Jerusalem,[11] to bring punishment upon the confessors of his name.

'I was wholly intent on this cruel business – not from malice but from zeal for the ancestral Law[12] – and I was going to Damascus armed with the authority of the chief priests. At midday, King Agrippa, I saw a light suddenly flash from heaven much more brilliant than the brightness of the sun. It shone round about me and my companions who were there. Stunned by the brilliant flash of light, we all fell to the earth.[13] I heard a voice speaking to me, and saying[14] in Hebrew, "Saul, Saul, why do you persecute me? It is hard for you to kick your heels against the pricks!"[15] Here I replied, "Who are you, Lord?" Then he in turn said:

'"I am Jesus of Nazareth whom you persecute.[16] But arise, stand upon your feet. I have cast you down as a persecutor to raise you up as a preacher of my name. For this purpose I have now appeared to you, that as my chosen one[17] you may witness to and carry out both what you have seen here and what in the future I shall communicate to you through visions.[18] In all of this, I shall be present as your protector, delivering you from the peoples[19] and the barbarous races far distant[20] to whom I now am sending you as my envoy.[21] As you now have been freed from error and, once blind, have been made to see, so I send you, that by preaching the truth of the gospel you may open their eyes, and they may turn to the gospel light from the darkness of the errors and vices in which they are still held; that those who have been slaves of Satan and devoted to idolatry[22] may be transferred to the possession of God who is Lord of all; that those who until this very time have been defiled by every kind of shamelessness may now receive the free remission of all their sins through evangelical faith; that those who until this time have been called 'not a people' – strangers to God, strangers to the entire fellowship of the saints[23] – may now receive their lot among those who have been sanctified, not through circumcision or the observance of the Law, but through trust in me, since they believe the gospel. No other way to sanctification is now available to anyone."

'This took place, King Agrippa, not at night or in our sleep; there were many of us who saw the flash in broad daylight and heard the voice speaking clearly.[24] Hence, as I was certain that this was an act of God from heaven, I was not disobedient to the heavenly vision. I gave up the business I had undertaken and began to act in a far different way, thinking it more important and better to fulfil the mandate of God than that of the chief priests.[25] For I preached the gospel immediately at Damascus, soon at Jerusalem, then through all the regions of Judaea, finally also among various and far distant nations. I preached that they should do penance for their former life and turn from dumb idols to the true and living God, and that once cleansed by baptism they should henceforth do works worthy of those who had truly recovered their senses.[26] It is for this reason that the Jews seized me and tried to kill me when they saw me in the temple.

'To the present time I have not defended myself with human weapons. With God as my protector,[27] at whose command I do what I do, I continue to this very day, witnessing to both the least and the greatest[28] about the things I have been ordered to preach to all without respect of persons.[29] I have devised no new doctrine of my own;[30] I preach nothing else than what Moses and the prophets predicted would come to pass. Indeed, even the Jews are accustomed to debate about Christ from the oracles of the prophets: whether the Messiah would come subject to human evils and to death; whether he would be the first to initiate the resurrection of the body; whether he would proclaim the light of truth first to the people of Israel, then also to the gentiles.[31] Since all this has been predicted about the Messiah by Moses and the prophets, I preach that another Messiah ought not to be[32] expected, for all these things have already been fulfilled in Jesus of Nazareth.[33] I preach that nothing now remains except for everyone, by repentance and newness of life, to prepare for his return when he will come as judge of the whole world.'[34]

Now Festus knew nothing of Judaism. Hence as Paul was making his defence with these and many other words, Festus, thinking his talk about the vision and the resurrection of the body was nonsensical and deranged, said in a loud voice, 'You are mad, Paul. What has befallen many others has happened to you: much learning has deprived you of your wits.' To this Paul replied:

'I am not mad, most excellent Festus. To deviate from the truth through error of mind is madness. I am, in truth, sober, and speak the truth, to know which is true soundness of mind. The king knows these things are so. I speak about them the more freely[35] in his presence because I reckon that none of the things I describe has escaped his notice, for this was not done in a corner but in the open, and the report has subsequently spread throughout all Judaea.'

Thereupon Paul turned to Agrippa and said, 'Do you believe the prophets, King Agrippa? I know that you believe. Whoever believes the prophets cannot fail to believe the gospel, for it proclaims that what the prophets had predicted for the future has now come to pass.' But Agrippa broke into Paul's words and said to him, 'In some small way you do persuade me to become a Christian!' To this Paul replied: 'This, indeed, I desire of God, that not only in a small way but in a large way and not only you but all who hear me today should be such as I am, except for these chains!'[36]

When Paul had spoken thus,[37] the king arose with the governor and Bernice, as well as the others who were sitting with them. They withdrew to discuss the matter, and all came to this opinion, to say that no wrong had been committed[38] by Paul worthy of death or prison chains. Therefore, Paul would have been released, if King Agrippa had not said to Festus, the governor, 'This man could have been discharged had he not appealed to Caesar.'

Chapter 27

And so, in accordance with King Agrippa's recommendation, it was decided that Paul should go to Italy, as he had appealed to Caesar. They delivered Paul, and some other prisoners with him, to Julius, a centurion of the Augustan cohort. We boarded a ship which had come from Hadrumetum, a city in Africa.[1] It was to put us ashore in Asia Minor, since it was to go along the coast of Asia. Aristarchus, a Macedonian from Thessalonica, continued with us; he wanted to be a companion on our sea-voyage also.[2]

Accordingly, the day after we set sail from Caesarea[3] we landed at Sidon. Here the centurion, Julius, who had resolved to treat Paul kindly, permitted him to get off the boat, go to whatever friends he had in Sidon, and be cared for by them. When again we set sail from there, we did not trust ourselves to the open sea, but hugged the shore of Cyprus on the left because the winds were adverse. Cutting along the sea below Cilicia and Pamphylia in this way, we came to Myra on the Lycian shore.[4] Here the centurion found another ship that had come from Alexandria in Egypt and was sailing to Italy, and transferred us to it. When we had sailed for many days with little progress, and with difficulty had arrived at last off Cnidus (for the wind was contrary), we turned our course to the island of Crete, close to a coastal city of that island with the name Salmone or, as some say, Sammonium.[5] We sailed by this city with difficulty and came to another shore of Crete called 'Fair Havens.' Near this place is the city Lasea.[6]

A long time had already been spent on this voyage, and Paul realized that sailing was now beginning to become dangerous. Not only was it impossible for them, due to the contrary winds, to hold the course they desired, but they had also for too long a time not provided their bodies with food.[7] Paul then admonished the sailors saying, 'Men, I perceive that this voyage will be with danger, harm, and much loss not only to the cargo and ship, but to your lives also. It would be best therefore to discontinue the trip.' But the centurion heeded the captain and the owner of the ship rather than the warning of Paul. Since there was no suitable harbour for wintering there, most adopted this plan, that if at all possible they should get as far as Phoenix. This is a harbour of Crete reaching out to the sea in the direction of the south-west and north-west winds.[8]

Meanwhile, when a south wind blew softly, they thought they would achieve their wish to reach Phoenix. So they set sail from the shore of Assos, a city of Crete,[9] and sailed along the Cretan coast. Not much later, however, a sudden violent wind arose. Sailors call it a typhoon, and of all winds they fear it the most. It is also called a northeaster, from the quarter of the world from where it blows, because it blows from the north-east.[10] This wind caught the ship with its violent force. There was no opposing the storm, so we spread our sails to the winds[11] and were borne along at the will of the winds and the waves. We were driven to an island south of Crete called Clauda,[12] and were able with difficulty to secure the skiff as a safety measure in case anything should happen. At length they got it into the ship. They likewise used other helps as well, undergirding the ship with ropes so that it should not easily be shattered if it was driven into shallow water;[13] they feared the wind might drive them onto the Syrtis nearby to the south where the typhoon was carrying them.[14] At the same time they lowered the drag-anchor[15] to retard the velocity of the ship. Assisted by these precautionary measures, we were carried along. But the storm did not abate and we were being tossed about in great danger. So on the following day they betook themselves to their last resort and cast the cargo into the sea, so that the jettison would lighten the ship. The storm persisted further, and on the third day with our own hands we threw overboard even the ship's tackle.[16]

When for many days neither the sun nor the stars appeared and the storm bore down ever more severely, despair of safety had taken hold of everyone. To their despair was added the fact that they had not eaten food for a long time now, since they had been occupied with the difficulties of sailing.[17] Here Paul, taking a stand in their midst, said:

'Men, you should have heeded my advice earlier, when I warned you not to sail from the shore of Crete. You would thus have avoided this distress and loss of goods. Since this cannot be changed, it remains for you to be wise, though belatedly.[18] Do not despair; none of you will perish! The only loss will be the ship. This is not a dream of my own fancy: last night there stood beside me an angel of God, whose minister and worshipper[19] I am. He said, "Do not fear, Paul; you will not perish here,[20] but you must first appear before Caesar. Not only will you escape unharmed, but God has granted to your prayers all who are in the ship with you." Wherefore, I say, be of good cheer, men. I have no doubt it will turn out as God has promised through his angel. But if you ask in what way everyone can be saved – it is necessary that the ship be shattered, and we be cast upon an island, and there we shall be saved.'

But when the fourteenth night had come and we were now sailing in the Adriatic sea, about the middle of the night the sailors looked out into the distance and suspected that some land was coming into sight. Wishing to test whether they could safely land there, they let down a rope with a lead ball attached (the sailors call this a 'missile,' because they 'cast' it),[21] and found the depth twenty feet. After sailing a little further, they sounded again[22] and found it was fifteen feet. When they realized that the depth was decreasing, they feared they were falling[23] upon a rough and rocky stretch. So they cast four anchors from the stern and wished for day to come, to discern with greater certainty what land was becoming visible. The sailors, however, had despaired of the ship, and since they realized they were not far from land, they were eager first of all to look out for themselves. To that end they lowered the skiff into the sea, concealing the fact that they were preparing an escape, and making excuses rather, as though because of the violence of the storm they wished to let down anchors also from the bow. But Paul was not unaware of what they were doing. He also knew that if the rest of those in the ship were to be saved, the services of the sailors would be needed. So he warned the centurion and the soldiers, saying, 'Unless these men stay in the ship, you cannot be saved.' Upon hearing this, the soldiers, using their swords, cut the ropes of the suspended skiff, and let it slip into the sea.

As the darkness of night scattered, day began to appear. Paul urged everyone to take food, saying, 'This is now the fourteenth day that you have continued to fast and have taken no food for your bodies. I urge you therefore to take some food; it is for your welfare, so that you do not perish through · hunger once you are delivered from the storm. There is no reason to think, 'What use is it to eat when we are soon to perish?' For this I promise you: not even a hair will perish[24] from the head of any of you.' When Paul had spoken thus, he took bread in his hands, gave thanks to God in the presence of all, and when he had broken it, imitating the example of the Lord Jesus,[25] he began to eat. Everyone's courage was restored by Paul's words and by his example,[26] and they, too, took food. The total number of all of us who were in the boat was two hundred and seventy-six. Filled with food, they lightened the boat to be able to get closer to land, casting the wheat into the sea. (They were transporting the wheat from Egypt to Italy, for Egypt was the ancient granary of Rome.)[27]

When it had become light, they did not recognize the land they were looking at. But they noticed that it had a sort of bay with a shore extending on either side. They determined to bring the ship to land in this bay if they could. Accordingly, they took up the anchors and trusted themselves to the sea. At the same time they loosened the ropes that tied the steering oars[28] so they could use these, too, to direct the movement of the ship as they wished. Then they hoisted the sails and turned the sail-yards to the wind,[29] thus making for the shore as the wind blew them. But when they were not able to make the shore they were heading for and through the force of the winds had come upon a place jutting out into the sea,[30] they ran the ship aground on it. The bow stuck in the shallow water and remained immobile, but the stern was being broken up by the force of the waves.[31]

There was now nothing else except for each one to look out for himself by swimming. Here, the soldiers' plan was to kill the prisoners so that none should escape after swimming to shore. The centurion suppressed this cruel and barbarous plan, wishing to save Paul, by whose advice they themselves were saved. To prevent anyone from being lost he ordered those who knew how to swim to be first to jump into the sea and swim to land. Those who could not swim made it to land, some supported by planks, some helped by the ship's other gear. In this way it came about that all at length reached land.

Chapter 28

When they drew near the coast, they did not know what island it was, but after they had escaped to land, they learned from the inhabitants[1] that it was called Malta. It is between Epirus and Italy, facing Sicily to the north.[2] The barbarians took pity upon our misfortune[3] and showed us no little kindness, for they kindled a fire and received[4] us all, suffering as we were from both the rain and the cold. Now, Paul had gathered a bundle of sticks and put it on the fire, and a viper which lay concealed therein, until then stiff from the cold, was aroused by the heat; it crawled out and took hold of Paul's hand with its fangs.

When the Maltese barbarians saw the deadly little beast hanging from Paul's hand they said, 'This man must most certainly be some murderer; the storm has cast him out of the sea unharmed, but divine vengeance[5] nevertheless does not allow him to live upon the earth.' On feeling the serpent's bite, however, Paul shook off the beast into the fire, nor did he suffer any harm. Still the natives expected that as the poison coursed through his veins he would become inflamed and swollen, or that he would suddenly fall down dead as the poison penetrated right to the heart. For a long time they waited to see what would happen to Paul. When at length they saw no harm come from the snake's bite, they changed their minds again with the fickleness of barbarians[6] and said he was a god. The Maltese had not yet heard of Jesus, who grants to the confessors of his name that no poison will have the potency and power to harm them, no matter how rapidly it works.[7]

Near that shore where they had come to land were the estates of the chief man of the island, Publius by name. He received us into his house and treated us kindly for three days. At that time, Publius' father was sick with fever and dysentery, so sick that he had taken to his bed. Paul, mindful of the precept of the Lord, went into the sick man, poured forth prayers to God, laid his hands upon him, and healed him.[8] When the report of this deed had spread throughout the island, others also who were sick came to Paul and were healed. Wherefore, as long as we stayed there, the natives extended very many courtesies to us, and when we were preparing to sail on, they put on board the ship the provisions needed for the voyage.

After three months had been spent on the island, we found another ship from Alexandria[9] which had wintered in Malta. This had Castor and Pollux as its figurehead. These the Greeks call the Dioscuri, and believe they bring success to sailing if[10] they light together on the mast. We boarded the ship and set sail from Malta. Later, we landed at Syracuse, a city on the coast of Sicily, and stayed there for three days. Weighing anchor at Syracuse and sailing close to the shore of Sicily, we came to Rhegium, an Italian city in the country of the Brutii.[11] From this city the crossing to Sicily is extremely short. Long ago Sicily was at this point contiguous with Italy, until by the force of the sea running between them the two countries were rent asunder. The channel flowing between them is no more than a mile and a half[12] in breadth; hence also the name Rhegium given the town by the Greeks.[13] With an advantageous wind blowing – a south wind, that is – we were carried from there to Puteoli after one day.[14] Here we found some Christians and were asked to remain for a little while. We complied with their wish and settled in there for seven days; from there we proceeded straight to Rome.

The report had already been conveyed to the brethren at Rome that we were coming (for among the Christians living at Rome the name of Paul was especially distinguished because of the epistle written to them). And so they came out of the city to meet us, coming as far as the Forum of Appius, to the place called 'Three Taverns.'[15] Paul was greatly refreshed at seeing them, realizing that here too there were those who supported the gospel with a sincere heart; and giving thanks to God, he took courage with boldness and good hope. At length, we arrived at Rome. The centurion delivered the other prisoners to the captain of the guard.[16] Paul, however, was allowed to live alone, with only one soldier in attendance to guard him.

Since he was led to Rome as a prisoner along with others, he wished to prevent any of the Jews from suspecting that he[17] was in this condition because of some crime. Accordingly, three days later he called together the leaders of the Jews who lived at Rome and spoke to them thus:

'Brethren, though I have committed no wrong against my people or our ancestral customs, I was taken prisoner at Jerusalem and delivered into the hands of the Romans, taken to Caesarea to the governor Felix, and then to Festus. When they examined my case, they wished to release me, because as they themselves admitted, they found nothing in me worthy of capital punishment. But when the Jews hatefully cried out their opposition, I was forced to appeal to Caesar, not because I was angry with my race on account of this case and am preparing some slanderous charge against them before the Caesar, to increase the hatred that he has towards them,[18] but to protect my innocence. For I wish everyone well who worships God in purity according to the law of our fathers.

'Motivated by such feeling towards you, I asked that you be summoned here in order that I might take comfort from seeing you and speaking with you, for it was not permitted to me, burdened with chains, to go to you. Why, then, does the nation of Israel worship God with so much zeal, despising the idols of the gentiles, except that it looks for the reward of its piety in the resurrection?[19] It is because of this hope, a hope I share with my whole race, that I am bound with this chain that you see. No other charge can be raised against me.'

To this, the Jewish leaders responded in the following manner:

'As to your clearing yourself before us, as though you have been charged by someone, know that no one from Judaea has notified us by letter of anything evil concerning you, nor has anyone coming here from there said anything bad about you. Still, we desire to hear from you yourself what your opinions are. As for that sect recently sprung from Jesus of Nazareth who rose again, we know full well that everywhere and among everyone people cry out against it as being false. It will be a favour therefore if you will instruct us more precisely what your opinion of this is.'

Paul replied that he would gladly do so. A day was set, and the Jews – more than had come before – met Paul again at the lodging where he was staying. He set forth to them the teaching of the gospel, testifying that the kingdom of God was now present and the Messiah was not to be looked for further, and showing that Jesus of Nazareth was the Messiah.[20] He demonstrated this from the figures of the Mosaic law and the oracles of the prophets, and proved that whatever had been foreshadowed in the Law, whatever had been predicted by Moses and the prophets, was fulfilled clearly and completely in Jesus.

When Paul had spoken copiously about these things from morning right on to evening, some of the Jews from the meeting believed Paul's words, some did not. Since they could not agree, they began to depart. But Paul added yet one word to his lengthy speech in order to censure the unbelief of those who did not cease to distrust such manifest testimonies about Jesus from the Law and the prophets. He said:

'Well has the Holy Spirit through Isaiah the prophet spoken prophetically to our fathers[21] about you, whose obstinate unbelief you reproduce. He said, "Go to this people and say to them: you will hear with your ears and not understand, look with your eyes and not see. For the heart of this people has grown dull, their ears have become hard of hearing and they have closed their eyes, lest they should someday[22] see with their eyes and hear with their ears and understand with their heart, and turn, and I should heal them."

'Know therefore that since you spurn this salvation which God offers through Jesus, it will be taken to the gentiles. For he spurns it who does not believe, and he who does not have faith in the gospel is unable to receive this grace. The gift of God has been proclaimed to you first, for so the Lord had commanded.[23] It was right that you above all believe, you who profess the Law and the prophets, but in the face of all these things, you have eyes that are shut, ears that are stopped, a heart made dull, and you cry out against the manifest light of gospel truth. But the gentiles, who do not know God, who do not have the Law or the prophets, will turn from their idols and by faith obtain this divine generosity, which you disdain when offered without cost.'

When Paul had said these words, the Jews left him, engaging in much debate among themselves.[24] But Paul lived for two whole years in the house he had rented,[25] kindly receiving all who came to him, whether Jews or uncircumcised. He preached to them the kingdom of God, and taught them with all confidence the evangelical doctrine, no one hindering.[26] He produced the oracles long ago revealed concerning the Lord Jesus; then he compared with these his deeds, his words, and his promises.

Notes

Translator's Note

xiii

1 Cf the first and last paragraphs of the dedicatory epistle (Ep 1414), 2–4 below.

xiv

2 See John J. Bateman's discussion in the Translator's Note CWE 44 xiv–xvi.
3 Cf Henk J. de Jonge 'The Character of Erasmus' Translation of the New Testament as Reflected in his Translation of Hebrews 9' *Journal of Medieval and Renaissance Studies* 14 (1984) 81–7, and '*Novum testamentum a nobis versum*: The Essence of Erasmus' Edition of the New Testament' *Journal of Theological Studies* NS 35 (1984) 394–413.
4 For the relation between the translations of *1516* and *1519* see Andrew Brown 'The Date of Erasmus' Translation of the New Testament' *Transactions of the Cambridge Bibliographical Society* 8 (1984) 351–80.

xv

5 For a brief description of the Byzantine and Alexandrian textual tradition see Metzger xv–xxiv. On the Greek manuscripts used by Erasmus see Jerry H. Bentley *Humanists and Holy Writ* (Princeton 1983) 124–35 and Erika Rummel *Erasmus' 'Annotations' on the New Testament* (Toronto 1986) 35–42.
6 This appears to be true of all the *Paraphrases*. See CWE 42 xvii–xix; CWE 44 xv; CWE 46 xiii–xiv; CWE 49 xii–xiii.
7 The *Glossa ordinaria* is a compilation of comments and of citations from Christian writers on the words of Scripture. In the *Gloss* a text of Scripture is placed on each page; brief comments appear between the lines of the scriptural text (the interlinear *Gloss*), and more extended comments and citations are found in the margins (referred to hereafter as the marginal *Gloss* or simply the *Gloss*). On the origin and development of the *Gloss* see Beryl Smalley *The Study of the Bible in the Middle Ages* (Notre Dame 1964) 46–66. On Hugh

and Nicholas see CWE 44 134 n12 (dedicatory letter for the *Paraphrase on James*).

8 On the *Gloss* in Erasmus see H.J. de Jonge 'Erasmus und die *Glossa Ordinaria* zum Neuen Testamentum' *Nederlands Archief voor Kerkgeschiedenis* 56 (1975) 51–77.

9 In the *Annotations* on Acts Bede is frequently cited in *1522* – usually, but not always as 'Bede in the *Gloss*'; cf eg the annotation on 27:40 (*levantes artemonem*). A *1527* addition to the annotation on 1:23 (*qui cognominatus est Iustus*) indicates that at that point for that edition Erasmus compared the commentary of Bede with the citation of Bede found in the *Gloss*. Likewise, a comment made in *1516* – 'after I found it annotated by Bede in the *Gloss*' – was changed in *1535* to: 'after I found it annotated by Bede in his scholia on this work. It is reported in the ordinary *Gloss*.' One might deduce that for the *Annotations* Erasmus reported Bede primarily from the *Gloss* until *1527*. It is an easy, if not compelling, inference that likewise for the *Paraphrase on Acts*, published in 1524, Erasmus had his eye on the *Gloss* rather than on the commentaries of Bede.

xvi

10 Rabanus Maurus (d 856), abbot of Fulda and later archbishop of Mainz, was well known throughout the Middle Ages as a biblical exegete. We do not have from Rabanus a commentary on Acts, though he expounds parts of Acts in some of his *Homiliae* (PL 110 9–468), particularly those on the major feast days. For the view that Erasmus relies on the *Gloss* for allusions to Rabanus, see H.J. de Jonge 'Erasmus und die *Glossa Ordinaria*' 59 (see n8 above).

11 Cf the *1535* addition to the annotation on 28:13 (*devenimus Rhegium*) and the *1516* annotation on 28:15 (*usque ad Appii Forum*). In a *1535* addition to the annotation on 27:7 (*Gnidum*) Erasmus noted what he thought was Bede's indebtedness to 'Jerome's' work. M.L.W. Laistner observes in his edition of Bede *Expositio Actuum apostolorum et retractatio* (Cambridge, MA 1939) xxxvii that this 'list of geographical names mentioned in Acts . . . was not infrequently copied by itself in the Middle Ages and was sometimes ascribed to Jerome.' Laistner notes further that the work was printed twice in Migne's *Patrologia Latina*, both among the spurious works of Jerome (PL 23 [1883] 1355–66) and among the works of Bede (PL 92 1033–40), but maintains that 'there would seem to be no real justification for excluding [this geographical glossary] from Bede's genuine works.'

12 Strabo (ca 64 BC–AD 21), an Asiatic Greek who spent a number of years in Rome, wrote a *Geography* which provides a description of Europe and Asia from Britain to India, and of Egypt, Ethiopia, and North Africa. Ptolemy (fl AD 127–48) is popularly known for his astronomical theories. His *Geography* includes extensive lists that locate islands, rivers, and especially cities in relation

to the regions or the provinces to which they belonged. The *Naturalis historia* of Pliny the Elder (AD 23/24–79) is an encyclopedia in thirty-seven books, and provides many details about, for example, the history and sites of cities.

13 The *Notitia dignitatum* was an official document that provided a list of the chief administrators and their spheres of authority in the late Roman empire. See Jones *Later Roman Empire* III 347–80. The map on pages xxiv–xxv above illustrates the political divisions of the empire according to the *Notitia dignitatum*.

14 Cf PL 92 1036D. The *De nominibus locorum* generally presupposes post-Diocletianic political divisions of the Roman empire; see n11 above.

15 See chapter 16 n24.

xvii

16 For the controversies with Lee and Zúñiga see Erika Rummel *Erasmus and his Catholic Critics* 2 vols (Nieuwkoop 1989) I 95–120 (Lee) and 145–77 (Zúñiga).

17 The change in the title-page may have been made to correct the 'Ersami' of the 27 June copies to 'Erasmi' of the 4 July copies. I owe this explanation of a single edition with two-title pages to John J. Bateman.

'A' in citations of these editions refers to H.M. Adams *Catalogue of Books printed on the Continent 1501–1600 in Cambridge Libraries* (Cambridge 1967).

xviii

18 Since LB is still the only edition of the Latin *Paraphrases* widely available, I have noted differences between it and the 1535 edition for the advantage of those who wish to consult the Latin in the text of LB.

19 The history of the publication of the *Paraphrase of Erasmus* has been described by E.J. Devereux in CWE 42 xxxi–xxxiv.

PARAPHRASE ON ACTS

Dedicatory Letter

2

1 Erasmus' dedicatory letter to the *Paraphrase on Acts* (Ep 1414) is addressed to Clement VII. Giulio de' Medici (1478–1534) had been raised in the house of his uncle Lorenzo de' Medici, and when his cousin, Giovanni, Lorenzo's son, became Pope Leo X in 1513, Giulio rapidly rose to positions of power. On Leo's death Giulio 'failed to secure either his own election ... or the confidence of the new pope, Adrian VI' (*Contemporaries* I 309). Adrian's reign, however, was brief, and Giulio became Pope Clement VII in November 1523. Clement was

a friend of humanist learning and showed much favour to Erasmus. He was unable to overcome the papacy's fatal subordination of spiritual to secular interests, and did not, as a consequence, fulfil Erasmus' high hopes of him. This preface appeared in both the folio and octavo editions of 1524, but not in the editions of 1534 and 1535, a circumstance for which there seems to be no satisfactory explanation (see Allen Ep 1414 introduction). The translation given here is, with a single variation (see n6), that of R.A.B. Mynors and Alexander Dalzell in CWE 10 163–6. The notes are based on those of James M. Estes in CWE 9 and 10, and on *Contemporaries of Erasmus: A Biographical Register of the Renaissance and Reformation* ed Peter G. Bietenholz and Thomas B. Deutscher 3 vols (Toronto 1985–7).

2 Adrian VI, born in 1454, was elected to the papacy in January 1522 following the death of Leo X the previous year. He was crowned at St Peter's on 31 August 1522 but died just a little more than a year later on 14 September 1523. Though Adrian endeavoured to establish peace among the warring princes of Europe and was committed to ecclesiastical reform, the circumstances of his time denied him much success in either enterprise.

3 Leo X, born in 1475, died on 1 December 1521, just ten days short of his forty-sixth birthday.

4 These letters are not extant.

5 A reference to the Hapsburg-Valois wars between Charles V and Francis I, which lasted, off and on, from 1521 until 1544. See Ep 1369:67–71.

3

6 This translation reads *hoc* (Allen Ep 1414:27) as an ablative of comparison, and assumes that the sentence alludes to the religious conflicts of the time, when the rise of Lutheranism seemed particularly threatening to the established order.

7 The reference is to Cardinal Wolsey's grandiose but ill-fated plan, embodied in the Treaty of London, 2 October 1518, to establish perpetual peace on the basis of a new international order; see J.J. Scarisbrick *Henry VIII* (Berkeley and Los Angeles 1968) 70–4.

8 Pope Adrian VI had attempted to mediate a peace or at least a truce between Francis I and Charles V in preparation for a united Christian effort against the encroaching power of Islam. However, Adrian's efforts at mediation were undermined by King Francis' demand that the emperor Charles restore Milan as the price of an agreement. See Ep 1353:268–79.

9 *Iliad* 11.514

10 *Aeneid* 1.148–50

11 Cf Ep 335:20–5.

12 *Aeneid* 1.151–6

13 Cardinal Wolsey; see Epp 1415:98–105, 1418:54–8.

14 See n4 above.

Chapter 1

5

1 The language reflects Erasmus' criticism of the Vulgate's 'The first narrative have I made,' a literal translation of the Greek. He himself translated, 'In the former volume have I spoken'; see the annotation on 1:1 (*primum quidem*). Erasmus understood Luke-Acts as a well-defined unity. He saw the two books as parts of one Gospel: in Luke the gospel is, as it were, the seed planted in the soil; in Acts, the seed has sprouted and is gradually bringing forth its own riches. Indeed had Erasmus not feared the critics, he would have broken the traditional sequence of the Gospels for his own edition of the New Testament and joined Acts to Luke (LB VI 433B). See the *1516* annotation on 1:1 (*primum quidem sermonem*) where Erasmus defends the 'unity' of Luke and Acts. For a modern statement of the view that Luke-Acts is a single work whose two parts were separated when they were included in the New Testament see Munck xv–xvii, xxxvi–xli.

2 For the 'prophecies' recited in the account of the birth of John the Baptist see Luke 1:17, citing Mal 4:5.

3 For the 'birth stories' in Luke's gospel see 1:26–38 (conception); 2:1–20 (birth); 2:21 (circumcision); 2:22–39 (purification).

4 See Luke 2:41–51 and the paraphrases on these verses, where Erasmus elucidates the 'divine nature' of the boy Jesus. In his annotation on Luke 2:52 (*et Iesus proficiebat etc*) Erasmus discusses the theological implications of the belief that the divine nature resided in the growing boy.

5 For Erasmus' representation of the place of John the Baptist in the scheme of 'saving history' see the paraphrase on Mark 1:1–4 CWE 49 14–16.

6 The language reflects the view found already in early Christian times that the saving events recorded in the New Testament are prefigured in the Old. See the *Ratio* for the types and shadows of the Law (Holborn 198:33–199:12) and for the prophetic oracles (Holborn 276:8–32, where the imagery of Isa 8:4 is interpreted as a figure of the Magi bringing gifts to the Christ-child). 'Figures' and 'riddling allegories' translate, respectively, *figurae* and *aenigmata*, words already domiciled in early Christian vocabulary. For the early Christian use of *figura* and *aenigma* to designate the foreshadowing in the Old Testament of the events of saving history recorded in the New see T.P. O'Malley sj *Tertullian and the Bible* (Nijmegen 1967) 141–5 (*aenigma*) and 158–64 (*figura*). See also the paraphrases on Gal 4:21–31 CWE 42 118–21, and on the word *aenigma* see CWE 46 55 n16 and CWE 44 236 n15.

7 Cf the *1516* annotation on 1:1 (*primum quidem*): 'Luke has divided the entire life of Christ into deeds and doctrine ... the deeds consist of his miracles, the doctrine of his pronouncements.' For the phrase 'evangelical philosophy'

see the *Epistola de philosophia evangelica* LB VI *4 verso–*5 recto where the evangelical philosophy is seen as the fulfilment of the truth adumbrated in the Law and the prophets, and uniquely embodied in the person of Jesus. The phrase also recalls Erasmus' 'philosophy of Christ' described in the *Paraclesis* Holborn 139–49. Cf CWE 44 158 n23 and CWE 46 34 n131.

8 Cf the *Gloss* (on 1:1) 967C: 'He has shown the pattern of the good teacher, who does what he teaches'; so also Hugh of St Cher (on 1:1) 253 recto C.

9 Nicholas of Lyra (on 1:1) 966F outlined the events embraced in the 'first book' in a sequence similar to that of Erasmus here (paraphrases on 1:1–2), concluding with the ascension: the 'first book' began with the precursor of Christ, then described the conception of Christ, his nativity, life and preaching, death, resurrection, and ascension.

6

10 Erasmus elsewhere also associates the seventy with the twelve apostles. See the paraphrase on Rom 16:7 where, however, he speaks of seventy-two (cf CWE 42 88 and n4), and the annotation on Luke 10:1 (*et alios septuaginta duos*). For the 'commissioning' of the twelve and the seventy (or the seventy-two) see Luke 9:1 and 10:1.

11 A *1522* addition to the annotation on 1:2 (*praecipiens apostolis per spiritum sanctum*) indicates that Erasmus followed Chrysostom in interpreting the 'commandment' (RSV) of 1:2 as the great commission of Matt 28:19; cf Chrysostom *Hom in Acta* 1.3 PG 60 18.

12 The events are recorded, respectively, in John 20:19–23 and Acts 2:1–4. The paraphrase on 1:2 reflects the interpretation of the words 'through the Spirit' represented in Erasmus' translation and clarified in his annotation (cited n11 above), that Christ 'imparted the Spirit to [the apostles] from the resurrection, and so entrusted to them the work of preaching.'

13 Cf Hugh of St Cher 253 recto D who, on the word 'alive' (1:3), comments, 'no more to die.'

14 Both the *Gloss* and Hugh of St Cher note here that the body was Christ's very own and not a phantasmal one; cf the *Gloss* (on 1:3) 968F; Hugh 253 recto D.

15 and not . . . body] Added in *1534*

16 An allusion evidently to Luke 24:36–43; but cf also Chrysostom *Hom in Acta* 1.4 PG 60 19: 'He remained on earth for forty days after the resurrection, in this length of time giving proof that they were looking upon his very self . . . so that they should not suppose it was a ghost that was seen.' This passage is cited in a *1522* addition to the annotation on 1:4 (*et convescens praecepit*) LB VI 435D–E.

17 An allusion to 1 John 1:1. This verse is also cited by Nicholas of Lyra 969B in a note on 1:3 concerning the proofs of the resurrection.

18 The Greek συναλιζόμενος which lies behind the paraphrase on 1:4 here is notoriously problematic. The problem, as outlined by Metzger 278–9, was recognized by Valla (cf *Annot in Acta* 1 [I 847]), and also by Erasmus in the annotation on 1:4 (see n16 above). Three alternative meanings are given for the word: 1/ to stay with, 2/ to assemble, 3/ to eat with (cf AV 'assemble,' RSV 'stay with,' DV and Conf 'eat with'). For his translation, Erasmus chose 'assemble': 'assembling them together in the same place.' The Vulgate had translated *convescens* 'eating with,' a meaning clearly supported, as Erasmus recognized in 1522, by Chrysostom. His paraphrase here adopts the Vulgate translation, but includes in addition the sense of 'staying with': 'he lived in close association with them.' Of modern interpreters, Bruce 68 is equivocal, but notes that 'in its regular sense the meaning will be "being gathered together" with [them]' (cf Erasmus, who renders the Greek in this sense with an active verb, 'gathering them together'); Munck in his commentary (4–5) seems to have understood 'eating with,' but the preceding translation (3) renders 'while he was in their company'; Haenchen adopts 'eating with' in both translation and commentary (135 and 141 n3).

For records of Jesus' eating with disciples see Luke 24:28–43; John 21:9–14.

19 Cf the *Gloss* (on 1:4) 970D–E: 'He declares the signs of the true body ... by appearing, speaking, eating.'

20 Cf John 14:26, cited also by Nicholas of Lyra (on 1:4) 972F.

21 For his paraphrase, Erasmus follows the Vulgate reading, 'You have heard, saith he, by my own mouth' (so DV Conf). His own Greek text read simply, 'You have heard from me' (the preferred reading; cf Haenchen 142 n2 and Metzger 279); he translated, however (from 1516), 'You have heard, he said, from me' (so AV, but with 'he said' in italics, and RSV).

22 Cf John 8:28. Cf also the *Gloss* 971A on the word 'promise' in 1:4: 'Even if it was promised by Christ, it will be fulfilled by the Father, because it is promised in his Word, that is, in Christ.'

23 For the contrast, frequent in Erasmus' *Paraphrases*, between the Law as carnal and the gospel as spiritual, see the Argument to the *Paraphrase on Galatians*, the paraphrase on Gal 2:19 CWE 42 95 and 106–7, and the paraphrase on Mark 1:14 CWE 49 21.

24 For predictions of persecution for professing the gospel see Matt 10:16–23; Mark 13:9–13; and Luke 21:12–19.

25 Erasmus is fond of the image of the 'prelude' or the 'rehearsal,' metaphors taken from the theatre and applied to the events of saving history; cf the paraphrases on John 1:31 CWE 46 31 and Mark 6:7 CWE 49 76, and for an elaboration of the image see the *Explanatio symboli* ASD V-1 218:358–60.

7

26 For the expression here see Matt 3:1–2.

27 Luke 3:3: John preached 'a baptism of repentance for the forgiveness of sins' (RSV). See the characterization of John's preaching in the paraphrases on Mark 1:1–8 CWE 49 14–17.

28 Cf Hugh of St Cher (on 1:5) 253 verso E: 'The Spirit was not given in John's baptism.' See also Acts 19:1–7.

29 Cf Matt 3:11.

30 Cf Ps 104:30 (Vulg 103:30).

31 Since . . . yet] First in 1534; in 1524, 'hitherto they had not'

32 For the majestic appearance of Christ before the world as judge and ruler see Matt 25:31; also Matt 24:30; Mark 13:26; and Luke 21:27.

33 For the allusion to Peter on the mount of transfiguration see Matt 17:1–8; Mark 9:2–8; Luke 9:28–36; for the request that James and John sit at the right and the left hand of Christ in his kingdom see Matt 20:17–28; Mark 10:32–45. Cf Nicholas of Lyra (on 1:5) 974F, who cites the example of James and John, noting that the disciples were still thinking carnally, supposing that Christ's reign would be temporal; cf also the interlinear *Gloss* 973–4 on 'kingdom' (Acts 1:16): the *Gloss* contrasts the spiritual and the temporal kingdom, noting that a spiritual kingdom is meant; so Hugh of St Cher 253 verso F, citing the *Gloss*.

34 On several occasions in his New Testament scholarship Erasmus refers to the meaning of the name Israel. In the *Paraphrase on Romans* (9:6) Erasmus had adopted for the editions of 1517 and 1519 the interpretation of Origen and Jerome that Israel meant 'one seeing God,' but that interpretation was replaced in the edition of 1521 by the interpretation found here, 'one prevailing with God,' which was reinforced in the edition of 1523 by an addition to the paraphrase; cf CWE 42 53 n5. Erasmus reaffirmed the interpretation 'one prevailing with God' in the paraphrase on Mark 7:30 CWE 49 94. The authority for either interpretation is discussed in detail, with references to Origen and Jerome, in the annotation on Rom 9:6 ('for not all'); cf CWE 56 253–4.

35 Cf Gen 32:24–30.

36 See Rom 3:9–20 and the paraphrases on Romans 3 CWE 42 22–6 for an extended exposition of this theme. 'Righteousness' and 'unrighteousness' here translate the Latin *iustitia* and *iniustitia*. The translation accommodates itself to current theological idiom, though it seems probable that in the *Paraphrases* Erasmus intended the words to convey in varying degrees the connotations of 'justice' and 'injustice.' See Sider 'The Just and the Holy' 13–22.

37 The image of 'storming the divine righteousness' alludes to Matt 11:12 and Luke 16:16; see Erasmus' paraphrases on these verses. See also the paraphrase on Mark 7:30, where Erasmus draws upon the same biblical image to express a

similar contrast between faith and works, a setting in which he also explained
the name of Israel as 'a man strong against God'; cf CWE 49 94 and nn25, 26.

8

38 'Futile curiosity': *inutilem curiositatem*. For Erasmus' strictures elsewhere on
'superfluous curiosity' see the *Ratio* Holborn 299–300, where the subtle but
futile investigations of the theologians come under attack; also the *Epistola de
philosophia evangelica* (cited n7 above). For the negative connotations of *curiositas*
in antiquity see eg J.C. Fredouille *Tertullien et la conversion de la culture antique*
(Paris 1972) 412–18. For a discussion of *curiosa* as 'fruitless speculations' see
CWE 44 66 n15.

39 The distinction between 'course and conclusion' on the one hand and 'year,
month, hour,' on the other reflects Erasmus' *1516* annotation on 1:7 (*tempora
vel momenta*) where he distinguishes χρόνος and καιρός, the former referring to
age, year, month, day, hour, the latter to the 'opportunity' or the 'occasion' of
an action, the point at which an action is to be done. On καιρός see *Adagia* I vii
70; see also the index of Greek and Latin words in CWE 56 and Peter Bietenholz
History and Biography in the Work of Erasmus of Rotterdam (Geneva 1966) 39–46.

40 The sentence apparently echoes such passages as John 12:49–50 (Christ speaks
only at the command of the Father) and Matt 24:36 (only the Father knows the
day and the hour).

41 Cf the *Gloss* (on 1:7) 974D: 'He shows that . . . it does not help them to know, but
they should live as though they were to be judged daily'; so also Hugh of St
Cher (on 1:7) 253 verso G. For the representation elsewhere in the *Paraphrases*
of the stern impartiality of the divine judgment see the paraphrases on 2 Thess
1:5–6 and on Matt 25:31–46. On the theme of the divine justice in Erasmus' New
Testament scholarship see Sider 'The Just and the Holy' 1–26.

42 Cf Hugh of St Cher (on 1:8) 253 verso G, who observes that the disciples were
still weak.

43 For the promise of the Spirit see John 16:7–15, especially verse 13, and for the
Spirit as a guide to truth and 'further knowledge' see 1 John 2:20. Hugh of St
Cher (on 1:8) 253 verso G also stresses the Spirit's ministries of teaching and
support in his comments on the words 'power' and 'Holy Spirit.'

44 The paraphrase conflates the 'great commission' as found in Acts 1:8 ('to the
end of the earth' RSV), and in Luke 24:47 and Matt 28:19 ('all nations').

45 For the emphasis upon equal access for all to the gospel, see the paraphrases on
Rom 3:5–31 CWE 42 23–6.

46 For Bethany as the place of the Ascension and for the detail of the blessing see
Luke 24:50–1. In a 1522 addition to his annotation on Acts 1:12 (*sabbati habens
iter*) Erasmus correctly explains that Bethany is on the slope of the Mount
of Olives (cf IDB I 387–8). But the identification of Bethany as the place of

ascension forced Erasmus to define a sabbath day's journey as nearly two miles; see n63 below.

47 That the cloud was white is a detail found neither in Acts nor in the parallel accounts in the Gospels. But for the white cloud on which 'one like a son of man' (RSV) is seated see Rev 14:14, and for the 'bright cloud' on the mount of transfiguration, Matt 17:5. Similarly the Gospels characteristically portray the raiment of heavenly vision as white (cf eg Matt 17:2; Mark 9:3; Luke 9:29; John 20:12; so also Acts 1:10).

48 For the contrast between the vision of the physical world seen with physical eyes and that of the spiritual world seen by the soul see the Fifth Rule of the *Enchiridion* CWE 66 65–84 and especially page 73, where Erasmus suggests that the physical presence of Christ on the earth limited the disciples' understanding. Cf also the paraphrases on Rom 11:7 CWE 42 64 and John 14:12 CWE 46 170.

49 Erasmus called attention in his annotation on 1:10 (*cumque intuerentur in caelum*) to the Greek word ἀτενίζειν: to 'look with eyes intently trained and fixed, like lovers.' The paraphrase follows Erasmus' own translation, 'looking upward into heaven,' rather than a Vulgate variant, found in the Vulgate of *1527*, 'as he went into heaven' (cf Weber II 1698 10n). In a *1527* addition to his annotation Erasmus cited the *Gloss* in support of his own reading (975B–C).

50 Nicholas of Lyra (on 1:10) 975C notes that these were 'angels in the form of men.'

51 Bede in the *Gloss* (on 1:10) 976E notes that 'white garments befit his exaltation' (cf *Super Acta* 1 PL 92 942A); so Hugh of St Cher 253 verso H. On white raiment in biblical narrative see n47 above.

9

52 Cf Bede in the *Gloss* (on 1:10) 976D: 'The angels appeared to bring comfort in the sorrow arising from the Lord's ascension . . .' (cf *Super Acta* 1 PL 92 942B).

53 Cf John 16:28; also John 13:33 and 14:1–7.

54 Cf Bede in the *Gloss* (on 1:11) 976D, who says that the two men in white robes appeared in order to show that Christ had truly gone to heaven, and not merely *as though* into heaven, like Elijah (cf *Super Acta* 1 PL 92 942B). For Elijah's ascent into heaven see 2 Kings 2:11.

55 For the image of Christ at the right hand of God see Rom 8:34; Col 3:1; Heb 1:3 and 13, 8:1, 12:2; also Acts 7:55–6; for Christ as sharer in the divine rule, see Eph 1:20–2. In the *Explanatio symboli* Erasmus describes the phrase 'to sit at the right hand' as a 'trope' that conveys the image of one who shares the divine power both as governor – governing all things *sine sollicitudine* – and as judge (ASD V-1 262:672–91)

56 In the *Explanatio symboli* Erasmus emphasizes that the 'Word' that became flesh 'now incarnate' ascended into heaven, that the Word did not put off the body

assumed, but as he had always shared in his divine nature the glory of the Father, 'so now also with his human nature he sits in the glory of the Father' (ASD V-1 262:661–8).

57 For Erasmus on the theme of the temporal procession from mercy to justice, ie from the incarnation to the Last Judgment, see Sider 'The Just and the Holy' 17–19. For the same theme in late medieval theology see Oberman *Harvest* 46–7, 181–3.

58 Cf Matt 24:30 and Rev 1:7; also Nicholas of Lyra (on 1:11) 977C: 'As he ascended in the glorious form of his humanity, so he will return to judge.'

59 Cf Matt 24:14; also Mark 13:10.

60 For the command see 1:4; for the antithesis in 'not to stay here, but to remain' see Hugh of St Cher (on 1:11) 254 recto A: 'Earlier they were told, "Remain in the city," but here they stand looking at the sky.'

61 The 'gentle protection' (*hospitium*) offered by the Mount of Olives may be an allusion to Luke 21:37. For Christ on the Mount of Olives before his death see Matt 26:30; Mark 14:26; Luke 22:39.

62 Nicholas of Lyra (on 1:12) 977C also notes that Olivet was the mountain from which Christ had ascended into heaven.

63 A sabbath day's journey 'was little more than half a mile' (Munck 7; cf also IDB IV 141). The definition of a sabbath day's journey as two miles supported Erasmus' identification (based on Luke 24:50–1) of Bethany as the place of the ascension (see n46 above). In the *1522* addition to the annotation cited above (n46), Erasmus refers to Jerome's letter to Algasia as his authority for 'two miles' (see Jerome *Epistulae* 121.10 PL 22 1034), giving as additional evidence the information in John 11:18 that Bethany was nearly fifteen stadia from Jerusalem (a stade is a little less than one-eighth of an English mile – see *stadium* 1 in L&s). For Luke's identification of Bethany as the place of the ascension see Bruce 72 and Haenchen 150 n11.

64 predicted and] Added in *1534*

65 Cf Matt 24:1–4, 15–20; Mark 13:1–3, 14–18; Luke 19:37–44.

66 Cf Luke 13:34; also Luke 11:45–51; Matt 23:29–37.

67 Cf Isa 60:1–3; also 42:6, 49:6.

68 That Jerusalem and the Jewish nation were to be destroyed because of disobedience and unbelief is a view which has early witnesses in Christian literary sources. For a Greek source see Justin Martyr *Dialogue with Trypho* 16 PG 6 509A–B; for a Latin source see Tertullian *Adversus Iudaeos* 3.4–6 CCL 2 1345. On Jewish unbelief see the paraphrases on Rom 11:7–9 CWE 42 63–4 and on the inexcusability of the Jews, the paraphrases on John 16:8–10 CWE 46 185–6.

69 Cf the *Gloss* (on 1:12) 978D: 'The return of the disciples from the Mount of Olives signifies the church, which, ascending from the active to the contemplative life, descends again to the active life'; so, similarly, Hugh of St Cher 254 recto B.

For a moralizing interpretation elsewhere in Erasmus of biblical 'mountain' narratives see eg the paraphrases on Mark 9:9 CWE 49 110 and on John 6:3 CWE 46 75–6.

70 In the sequence of these four names – Peter, John, James, Andrew – Erasmus follows the Vulgate and the preferred reading (so DV Conf RSV); in his own text and translation, however, the names appear in the order Peter, James, John, Andrew (so AV). See Metzger 283.

71 In the paraphrase here on 1:13 where the last three names are listed, Erasmus conflates his biblical sources as the following chart shows:

Luke 6:15–16	Matt 10:3–4	Mark 3:18–19
James of Alphaeus	James of Alphaeus	James of Alphaeus
Simon Zelotes	Simon the Cananaean	Simon the Cananaean
Judas of James	[Lebbaeus called] Thaddaeus	Thaddaeus
(Judas Iscariot)	(Judas Iscariot)	(Judas Iscariot)

Acts 1:13 (text)	Acts 1:13 (paraphrase)
James of Alphaeus	James of Alphaeus
Simon Zelotes	Simon Zelotes, in Hebrew called the Cananaean
Judas of James	Judas called Thaddaeus or Lebbaeus, brother of James the Less

It may be noted further that:

1/ Though Erasmus in both translation and paraphrase leaves unqualified the possessive 'of Alphaeus,' he understood 'son of Alphaeus'; cf the annotation on Luke 6:15 (*Iacobum Alphaei*).

2/ 'Cananaean' is an adapted transliteration of an Aramaic word meaning, like the Greek *zelotes*, 'zealot,' 'enthusiast'; cf 'Simon' in IDB IV 357.

3/ In his translations from 1522 and in all editions of his *Paraphrase* Erasmus explicitly interprets the unqualified Greek possessive 'of James' as 'brother of James' (so DV AV Conf), though in his translations of 1516 and 1519 he understood 'son of James' (so RSV and Munck 6). In the annotation on Mark 15:40 (*Iacobi minoris*) Erasmus explains that 'the Less' is apparently to be understood as a cognomen. For the relation of Judas to James see CWE 44 125 n1.

4/ The identification of Judas with Thaddaeus or Lebbaeus, brother of James, is made in the annotations on Matt 10:2–3 (*primus Simon* and *Lebbaeus cognominatus*), though in editions prior to 1535 Erasmus speaks of the 'son of James' rather than the 'brother of James.' For Erasmus' identification of Judas/Lebbaeus/Thaddaeus see CWE 46 173 n32. The identification of the three names is found already in Origen's Preface to his commentary on Romans PG 14 836C–837A. On the readings 'Lebbaeus' and 'Thaddaeus' see Metzger 26 and 81.

10

72 In the text of Acts these women are without any identification. That they are those 'who ministered to Jesus on his way to Jerusalem' Erasmus appears to derive from several passages in Luke; cf Luke 8:2–3, 23:49, 23:55, 24:6–10.

73 Cf Nicholas of Lyra (on 1:14) 979C: 'They are called his brothers according to the Hebrew idiom by which relatives are called brothers.' Jerome, in his controversy with Helvidius, had likewise articulated the view that those designated in the Gospels as 'brothers' of Jesus were in fact his relatives; cf Jerome *Adversus Helvidium de Mariae virginitate perpetua* 15–17 PL 23 (1883) 208B–212A and NCE IX 337.

74 'Consider': *contemplator* (future imperative) 'a word of dignity, strongly didactic in tone' – so T.E. Page in *P. Vergili Maronis Bucolica et Georgica* (London 1898; repr 1963) 206 on *Georgics* 1.187

75 Erasmus alludes to this definition also in the paraphrase on Mark 11:11 (cf CWE 49 138 and n22). For the definition, see Jerome *Liber interpretationis Hebraicorum nominum* CCL 72 136:5, and for the definition in the exegetical tradition see the marginal and interlinear notes in the *Gloss* on 1:12 (marginal 975A, interlinear [Basel 1506–8] 164 verso), and Hugh of St Cher (on 1:12) 254 recto B.

76 Cf Hugh of St Cher 254 recto B on *sabbati* (1:12): 'He who looks upon the glory of the ascending Christ enters by a sabbath day's journey the city of peace … because he who has ceased from evils rests in heaven.' For the quiet heart as the abode of the Holy Spirit, see also the paraphrase on Mark 1:10 CWE 49 19; for the theme in Christian antiquity see eg Tertullian *De spectaculis* 15.2–3 CCL 1 240.

77 Both Bede and Rabanus in the *Gloss* (on 1:13) 978E also interpret the upper room figuratively, Bede as the higher goals of knowledge and virtue, Rabanus as charity (cf Bede *Super Acta* 1 PL 92 942D).
In classical Latin the *cenaculum* designated the upper story, or upper room, of a building. For *cenacula* in the buildings of ancient Rome see Carcopino *Daily Life* 26–7, where two kinds of *insulae* or apartment buildings are distinguished: those whose first floor was a luxurious private dwelling (a *domus* 'house'), and those whose first floor was occupied by shops; in both cases the upper floors were occupied by apartments (*cenacula* 'upper rooms').

78 For the image of the holy congregation chosen by Christ see John 15:16–19 and 1 Pet 2:4–9.

79 Cf Nicholas of Lyra (on 1:14) 979C: 'Perseverance is the unity of hearts in the good which makes prayer worthy of being heard.'

80 Erasmus read (1:14) 'in prayer and supplication' (so AV), the Vulgate simply 'in prayer,' which is the preferred reading of the Greek text (Metzger 284; so DV Conf RSV). In the paraphrase here the variation in language (*preces* 'prayers,' *orat* 'prays,' *deprecatio* 'supplication') is evidently intended to reflect the readings of both the Vulgate and Erasmus.

81 For the language designating the church in this *Paraphrase* see chapter 5 n20.

82 Erasmus follows the Vulgate in 1:15, 'one hundred and twenty people' (*hominum*; so DV Conf RSV), rather than his own text and translation (from 1516), 'one hundred and twenty names' (*nominum*; so AV).

83 Here Erasmus follows his own text and translation of 1:15 (from 1516), 'stood in the midst of the disciples' (AV), rather than the Vulgate and the preferred reading, 'stood in the midst of the brethren' (so DV Conf RSV); see Metzger 285.

84 'Through harmonius agreement': *ex concordi consensu*. For the concepts of concord and consensus in Erasmus' understanding of the church, see James K. McConica 'Erasmus and the Grammar of Consent' in *Scrinium Erasmianum* ed Josef Coppens 2 vols (Leiden 1969) II 77–99.

85 Here and elsewhere in the *Paraphrase on Acts* Erasmus reveals his concern for good preaching. For reflections elsewhere of his interest in preaching see the portrait of the monks in the *Moria* CWE 27 132–5, but see especially the *Ecclesiastes*, a four-part work devoted to preaching (books 1 and 2 ASD V-1; books 3 and 4 LB V 951–1100). For a summary of the contents of the *Ecclesiastes* and a statement of its significance as a study of preaching see Manfred Hoffman *Rhetoric and Theology: The Hermeneutic of Erasmus* (Toronto 1994) 39–59. For Erasmus on preaching see also John O'Malley 'Erasmus and the History of Sacred Rhetoric' ERSY 5 (1985) 1–29.

11

86 A reference to Ps 109:8 cited in the paraphrase on 1:20

87 For the expression see Acts 10:39. For the representation of the apostolic office see n98 below.

88 The theme of avarice holds a prominent place in this *Paraphrase*. Cf eg the paraphrases on the story of Ananias and Sapphira (5:1–11), of the Philippian diviner (16:16–24), and of the silversmith Demetrius (19:23–40).

89 For an exposition of the theme of divine clemency, particularly in relation to divine justice, see Erasmus' *De immensa Dei misericordia* LB V 557–88.

90 Erasmus reconstructs the story of Judas' treachery and death primarily from Matthew: the thirty pieces of silver (Matt 26:15), repentance and return of the money, the hanging, and the deliberation of the priests resulting in their purchase of a burial field for strangers (Matt 27:3–7). Indeed, so strong is the influence of the Matthaean narrative that Erasmus completely disregards the statement of Acts that it was Judas who bought a field with his traitor's money (1:18). On the other hand he follows here (1:18) the Latin tradition in attempting to harmonize aspects of Matt 27:5 (death by hanging) with Acts 1:18 (death by fall); hence here the noose, the hanging, but also the bursting. For the Latin tradition see eg the reading of Augustine in *Contra Felicem Manichaeum* 1.4 PL 42 522: 'Binding his neck [in a noose], he fell upon his face, burst open in the middle and all his bowels came out' – a passage Erasmus cites in the annotation on 1:18

(*et suspensus crepuit*), where he notes the difficulty of the Greek; see Metzger 286. The annotation assumes that Judas died by hanging; neither paraphrase nor annotation takes into account yet another view, that Judas swelled and burst – cf Metzger 286, Bruce 77, Haenchen 160 n5, and *Beginnings* v 22–30.

91 'Akeldama' is an Aramaic word. In spite of an acknowledgment in *1519* that Jerome thought the word Aramaic (annotation on 1:19, *Acheldemach*), Erasmus continued to regard the word as Hebrew; see the *1527* annotation on 1:19 (*et notum factum est*).

92 inhabit it] *habitet in ea*, first in *1535*; in *1524* and *1534*, *inhabitet in ea*. Both *habitet* and *inhabitet* are found in the Vulgate witnesses; cf Weber II 1699 and 20n.

93 Cf Luke 19:43–4, 21:24 and n68 above.

94 For the 'true Jews' and the 'circumcised in mind' see Rom 2:28–9 and the paraphrases on those verses CWE 42 22.

95 For Jesus' prediction of the fall of Jerusalem see Mark 13:2 and Luke 19:41–4.

96 'Bishopric' (as in DV AV) translates *episcopatum*, the word that rendered the Greek ἐπισκοπήν both in the Vulgate and in Erasmus' translation. In his annotation on 1:20 Erasmus explains the word as, among other things, an 'overseership' or 'superintendence.' Cf Haenchen 161 n6, who says the Greek 'here means the apostolic office'; cf also the annotation on Rom 1:5 ('grace and apostleship') CWE 56 18–19 and CWE 44 18 n1, 105 n4.

12

97 On Jesus as successor to John see the paraphrases on John 1:29–37 CWE 46 30–3 and on Mark 1:4–8 and 2:18–21 CWE 49 14–17 and 41–3.

98 In this paragraph (paraphrases on 1:20–2) biblical allusions underlie Erasmus' portrait of the apostolic office; see, for example, Luke 6:12–16 ('choice' of the twelve and their designation as 'apostles'), Mark 3:13–19 (those chosen were to 'be with him'), Luke 24:44–8 (they were to be witnesses especially of the resurrection). See also Acts 10:38–41. On the meaning of 'apostle' see ἀπόστολος in TDNT I (1964), especially 424–30, and *II Corinthians* trans with introduction, notes, and commentary by Victor Paul Furnish, Anchor Bible (New York 1984) 99. Cf also CWE 46 162 n20 and chapter 14 n14 below.

99 frequently] Added in *1534*

100 Cf Nicholas of Lyra (on 1:22) 984F, who observed that witness to the resurrection was especially important since it was revealed only to the apostles and other disciples. For the importance of 'worthy witnesses' to the resurrection, see the paraphrase on Mark 16:14 CWE 49 175; for Erasmus' interest in the 'frequency' of the post-resurrection appearances, see the paraphrase on John 21:1 CWE 46 221.

101 Bede in the *Gloss* (on 1:23) 983A–B notes the report of Clement of Alexandria that these two were from the seventy; cf Bede *Liber retractationis* 1 PL 92 998C. For the seventy see n10 above.

102 'Barsabas' in the Latin text of the paraphrase (LB and the editions *1524–1535*), in some Vulgate witnesses, and in Erasmus' text and translation (so AV in 1:23). Barsabbas is the spelling of the better manuscripts (so RSV and Conf); see 'Barsabbas' in IDB I 359 and Bruce 79.

103 'To complete the number' and 'to succeed to the exercise' represents ambiguously both the Vulgate reading 'to take the place' (so DV RSV Conf) and the reading of Erasmus' Greek text and Latin translation, 'to receive the portion of' (cf AV 'take part of'). A *1527* addition to the annotation on 1:25 (*accipere locum*) indicates that Erasmus understood 'inheritance' here in the sense of 'succession.'

104 The paraphrase explicates the word 'apostleship' (1:25 RSV). Cf the annotation on Rom 1:5 ('grace and apostleship') CWE 56 19: 'I have translated "the fulfilment of the apostolic task," so no one will think that Paul means an office with rank.'

105 For Erasmus' persistent efforts to 'justify the ways of God to men,' exonerating God from all responsibility for human failure, see Sider 'The Just and the Holy' 14–19. On negligent and carefree bishops see the paraphrase on Mark 4:40 CWE 49 64.

106 For Jonah see Jonah 1:7, for Jonathan, 1 Sam 14:24–46, especially verse 42, for the priests, Luke 1:9. Bede in the Gloss (on 1:26) 985A mentions the example of Jonah (cf Bede *Super Acta* 1 PL 92 945B–C), and Nicholas of Lyra (on 1:26) 986E–F mentions the example of Jonathan. Like Erasmus here, both accept only cautiously the use of the lot; for Lyra's long note see 985B–986F.

13

107 Erasmus evidently identifies the Joseph here with the Joseph mentioned in the Vulgate of Matt 13:55 as the brother of Jesus. In his paraphrase on Matt 13:55 Erasmus followed the Vulgate, but in his own text and translation of the verse he read 'Joses,' though 'Joseph' is the preferred reading (Metzger 34).

108 So also the *Gloss* (on 1:23; interlinear 983–4, marginal 983B), and Hugh of St Cher 254 verso F. Cf Jerome *Liber interpretationis Hebraicorum nominum* CCL 72 137, who explains Matthan as 'gift, or, one given,' and Matthaeus as 'one given formerly.'

Chapter 2

1 According to the Old Testament, it was the 'feast of weeks' that was celebrated on Pentecost 'fifty days after passover' (cf Lev 23:5–16). Pentecost was also known as the 'feast of first-fruits' (Exod 23:16, 34:22). In later Judaism it was reckoned to be the anniversary of the giving of the Law at Sinai – a reasonable deduction from the chronological note in Exod 19:1; see Bruce *English Text* 54. For the Year of Jubilee see Lev 25:8–12. Cf n3 below.

2 For the circumstances that surrounded the giving of the Law, as cited throughout this paragraph, see Exod 19:10–25 and 20:18–21. For the tables of stone see Exod 32:15–19 and 34:1–4, 28–9; for the contrast between the two covenants Jer 31:31–3; 2 Cor 3:3–8; Heb 8:6–13.

3 Cf Rabanus in the *Gloss* (on 2:1) 987B: 'On the fiftieth day after the sacrifice of the lamb in consequence whereof the people of Israel went forth from Egypt, the Law was given in the midst of fire. In the New Testament, on the fiftieth day after the resurrection of Christ, the Spirit appearing in fire descended on the apostles. The Law was given on Mount Sinai, the Spirit on Mount Sion; the Law on an elevated place in the mountain, the Spirit in an upper room.'

4 'Gross and earthly': *crassus ac terrenus*, words frequently found in Erasmus' vocabulary of spirituality. Here the two words suggest the limitations imposed by physical density – the intellectual sluggishness and moral recalcitrance of the corporeal condition. Erasmus uses both terms in speaking of the contrast between flesh and spirit; see eg for *crassus*, *Ecclesiastes* III LB V 1024B–C and for *terrenus*, the *Enchiridion* Holborn 48:14–49:5 / CWE 66 47. In the paraphrase on John 14:26 Christ's physical presence is said to be a temporary concession to the *crassitudo* of the disciples, who were still 'terrestrial' men; cf CWE 46 174, where *crassitudo* is rendered 'dullness.' On *crassus* in Erasmus' vocabulary see CWE 42 16 n9, 106 n8; CWE 46 86 n68; and CWE 44 231 n10.

5 For this understanding of the purpose of the Law see the paraphrases on Gal 3:23–4 CWE 42 113–14 and the paraphrase on Titus 1:14 CWE 44 60. The view has its roots in early Christian literature; cf Justin Martyr *Dialogue with Trypho* 19–20 PG 6 516B–520B.

6 Interpretations given in Jerome *Liber interpretationis Hebraicorum nominum* for Sinai and Sion; see CCL 72 77 and 153.

7 Cf the *Gloss* (on 2:1) 988B: 'Whoever desires the Spirit transcends and tramples upon the domicile of the flesh, through the contemplation of the mind'; so Hugh of St Cher 255 recto D.

14

8 Cf the interlinear *Gloss* 987–8 on 'mighty wind' (2:2): 'It frightened no one, as in the case of the Law'; and Nicholas of Lyra 988F: 'They were not frightened … because the Holy Spirit, the heart's comforter, was given to them.' Cf also Heb 12:18–24.

9 Cf the *Gloss* (on 1:3) 990E: 'Fire drives out sluggishness, illuminates ignorance'; so Hugh of St Cher 255 recto D.

10 An allusion perhaps to the story of the golden calf; cf Exod 32:1–24. For the 'murmuring' of Israel elsewhere, see Exod 15:24; 16:2, 7, and 8, 17:3; Num 14:2, 27–9.

11 now] Added in 1534

12 For the quiet heart as the abode of the Spirit see chapter 1 n76; but here cf also Bede in the *Gloss* on the words 'the third hour' (2:15) 995A: 'The grace of the

Spirit is not received unless the mind is raised above the striving of the flesh' (cf Bede *Super Acta* 2 PL 92 948B).

13 The Vulgate's *pariter* in 2:1 may be understood either as 'alike' or 'together.' The interlinear *Gloss* (on 2:1) 987–8 explained, 'having one heart and soul.' The preferred reading of the Greek text is ὁμοῦ 'together' (RSV). However, for his Greek text Erasmus had read ὁμοθυμαδόν, which he translated *unanimiter* 'of one accord' (so AV), though a 1527 addition to the annotation on 2:1 expresses a doubt that ὁμοθυμαδόν is the correct reading (*erant omnes pariter*). The repeated *simul* 'together' (in the phrases 'come together' and 'gathered together') may represent the Vulgate's *pariter* (cf DV Conf); it may, however, also reflect the Greek ἐπὶ τὸ αὐτό, the phrase immediately following the ὁμοῦ of 2:1 and which Erasmus rendered in his translation of 1:15 and 3:1 by *simul* (on ἐπὶ τὸ αὐτό see Bruce 75 and Haenchen 193 n4).

14 The north wind (Boreas) was personified in classical mythology as a deity known for his cold blasts; cf Ovid *Metamorphoses* 6.682–707. On the south wind (Notus) see Ovid *Metamorphoses* 1.264–9, and for the south wind as harmful see Horace *Odes* 2.14.15–16, 3.23.5–6.

15 Erasmus found the Greek syntax of διαμεριζόμεναι 'cloven,' 'parted,' 'distributed' ambiguous in 2:3, allowing either of two readings: 1/ there appeared to them cloven (parted) tongues (DV AV Conf and Erasmus' own translation); 2/ there appeared to them tongues distributed to each (RSV, the Vulgate, and the paraphrase here). See the annotation on 2:3 (*dispartitae linguae*).

16 For the transforming power of the Spirit, changing earthly into heavenly, see eg the paraphrases on Matt 3:11 and John 14:26 CWE 46 174. Cf also n4 above.

17 Cf James 3:3–10, and the colourful paraphrases on the passage in CWE 44 154–6. Erasmus' lengthy treatise on the tongue elaborates themes briefly mentioned here: for the contrast between a good and an evil tongue see *Lingua* CWE 29 262–3; for the evils mentioned just below, especially slander and swearing, see CWE 29 317–67; and for the significance of Pentecost CWE 29 406.

18 Cf Mark 16:17. For the distinction expressed in this paragraph between sign and effective reality see Nicholas of Lyra (on 2:3) 990F, who observed that 'tongues' were to indicate with a visible sign in an exterior way the invisible grace of the Holy Spirit received inwardly, through which the disciples were burning with the love of God and were speaking in all languages for the preaching of the gospel.

15

19 For biblical allusions see James 4:11; Matt 5:22 (slander); James 5:12; Matt 5:33–7 (oaths – though in these passages *all* oaths are condemned); Eph 5:4 (filthy talk); James 3:6 (the burning tongue).

20 For the allusions see Matt 16:5–12; Mark 8:14–21 (the bread forgotten); Acts 1:6 (kingdom restored); Matt 20:20–8; Mark 10:35–45 (first seat); Matt 18:1–5; Mark 9:33–7; Luke 9:46–8 (primacy).

21 In the sequence (in this and the two previous sentences) 'they breathe ... spiritual ... without breath ... breath,' Erasmus plays on the ambiguity of the Latin: *spirant ... spiritualia ... sine spiritu ... spiritus*; the final *spiritus* is at once the heavenly Spirit and the breath from heaven. Similarly above, in the paraphrase on 2:3, 'the same Spirit (*idem spiritus*) that blew,' *spiritus* is both the wind and the heavenly Spirit.

22 'Carries off': *rapit*. Erasmus frequently uses the verb *rapio* 'carry off,' 'transport,' 'ravish' of the effect of the Spirit; cf eg the paraphrase on Matt 3:11; and CWE 42 46 and n9. For the Spirit as fiery, see chapter 8 n33 and the reference there to the *Paraphrase on Mark*.

23 Cf 1 Cor 1:18–24. The passage authenticates the portrait, frequent in the *Paraphrases*, of Pharisee and philosopher, Judaism and the wisdom of the schools as alike antithetical to the gospel; cf eg the paraphrases on Mark 1:14 CWE 49 22; John 1:5 CWE 46 18; Rom 1:16 CWE 42 17; 1 Cor 1:22. For the contrast between the heavenly philosophy and worldly philosophies see the *Paraclesis* Holborn 139:1–145:3. For Pharisees, philosophers, and orators as a trio, see the paraphrase on Mark 4:2 CWE 49 56 and the paraphrase on Acts 2:13 (17 below).

24 Cf Rom 12:3–8 and Erasmus' paraphrases on the passage CWE 42 70–1; cf also 1 Cor 12:1–31, 14:1–5.

25 For the allusions see Matt 26:36–46; Mark 14:32–42; Luke 22:40–6 (apostles sleep); John 20:19 (apostles hide).

26 For images of the theatre in the paraphrases see chapter 1 n25. For the importance in Luke's theology of Jerusalem as the starting point for the church see *The Gospel According to Luke* translated with introduction, notes, and commentary by Joseph A. Fitzmeyer, Anchor Bible 2 vols (New York 1981–5) I 164–71.

27 Cf Nicholas of Lyra (on 2:5) 991C–992F, who notes that Jews from every nation had come to Jerusalem because of the festival; he further explains that Jews had been captured in various wars, and that some had remained in the land of their captivity through love of children born or of possessions acquired there, while others as the result of war had been sold as slaves. For a similar characterization of the Jewish Diaspora see the paraphrase on 1 Pet 1:1 CWE 44 81 and n2.

28 The paraphrase anticipates a *1527* annotation on 2:6 (*facta autem hac voce*) in which Erasmus explicates his interpretation of 'this sound' as the rumour of the events just happened (so DV and AV, but Conf, RSV are ambiguous). In the *1516* edition of his New Testament Erasmus had followed the Vulgate, translating 'when this sound had been made,' but from *1519* he translated 'when this

rumour had spread.' The ambiguity of the expression is attested by modern scholars; cf Bruce 83 (who, however, in *English Text* 59 explains the noise as the loud praises uttered by the disciples – not the rushing wind) and Haenchen 168–9.

29 Here in 2:6 and just below in the paraphrase on 2:8 Erasmus cautiously implies the view expressed in his annotation on 2:8 (*linguam nostram*), that while the apostles spoke their own language, it was the hearers who, by a miracle, understood them, each in his own language. Bede, in the *Gloss* 990F–991A, thinks it preferable to suppose that everyone heard in his own language the apostles speaking in theirs than to suppose that the apostles spoke in the various languages of those present (cf Bede *Super Acta* 2 PL 92 947B–C).

30 For the references to the Samaritan woman and Peter's betrayal see John 4:9 and Matt 26:73. Bede in the *Gloss* (on 2:9) 992E notes the variety of Hebrew dialects among the Jews and refers specifically to the regions of Samaria, Galilee, and Decapolis (cf Bede *Super Acta* 2 PL 92 947D); similarly Hugh of St Cher 255 verso E.

31 In a 1519 addition to his annotation on 2:6 (*linguam nostram*) Erasmus observes that there are five Greek dialects, but goes on to speak only of Attic, Doric, Ionic, and Spartan. By the 'five dialects' Erasmus may have in mind the five literary dialects of the Greek grammatical tradition – Aeolic, Attic, Doric, Ionic, and Koine. For a modern description of Greek dialects see H.W. Smyth *Greek Grammar* rev G.M. Messing (Cambridge, MA 1956) 2–4.

16

32 The paraphrase on 2:7 incorporates two readings adopted by Erasmus for his New Testament: 1/ *all* were amazed; 2/ saying *one to another*. AV represents both readings, the Vulgate has only the former (so DV Conf), RSV has neither. The preferred reading omits both: 'they were amazed ... saying' (RSV); cf Metzger 292.

33 The paraphrase anticipates a 1527 addition to the annotation on 2:10 (*Iudaei quoque*): the Judaea of 2:9, Erasmus believes, refers not to the restricted Judaea embraced by the tribes of Judah and Benjamin, but to a broader territory including Samaria, Decapolis, and Galilee. After the exile, the territory of political control designated by the term Judaea changed in accordance with the vicissitudes of history, sometimes including virtually all of Palestine. In the New Testament, as well as in other contemporary and near-contemporary sources, the term is used in a broad sense to designate most of Palestine, and in the narrow sense to designate what is roughly the territory of the tribes of Judah and Benjamin. For the broad sense see Acts 10:37; Luke 23:5; and (possibly) Luke 4:44; also Strabo *Geography* 16.2.21. For the narrow sense see Matt 4:25; Mark 1:5; Acts 1:8. Cf also Josephus who, in *Jewish War* 3.3.5 (51–8),

names eleven districts into which 'Judaea' was divided. Cf Bruce 84–5 and Haenchen 170; for further definition see chapter 15 n4.

34 Erasmus frequently distinguishes between 'Asia proper,' of which Ephesus was, in the first century, the chief city, and Asia Minor. For the concept of 'Asia Minor' see chapter 13 n31, for 'Asia proper' see chapter 16 n16. Cf also the annotation on Rom 16:5 ('of the church of Asia') CWE 56 426.

35 A similar explanation of 'proselyte' (2:11) is given both in the *Gloss* 993A (citing Bede; cf *Super Acta* 2 PL 92 947D), and by Hugh of St Cher 255 verso F.

36 With this characterization of the Pharisees, compare the paraphrases on John 8:14–15 CWE 46 108–9.

37 Cf John 10:20, where, however, it is not the Pharisees, but 'many of the Jews' who so speak. But for the 'Pharisees' see Matt 12:24; also Luke 7:29–35.

38 For a similar comparison, see the *Moria* CWE 27 119; in the same work Erasmus alludes to Acts 2:13 (CWE 27 149).

39 For the biblical allusions see Matt 9:17; Mark 2:22; Luke 5:37–9 (new wine, old skins); Matt 9:15–16; Mark 2:19; Luke 5:34–5; John 3:29 (wedding); and John 2:1–11 (wedding, tasteless sense of the Law changes into new wine). Much of the language, the images, and the thought in the paraphrase here may be found also in the paraphrase on John 2:11 CWE 46 40. On the tasteless and carnal sense of the Law in contrast to its spiritual and efficacious sense see CWE 42 xxxvi, 11 and n31, and the paraphrases on Rom 8:1–11 CWE 42 45–7.

40 With this passage compare Bede in the *Gloss* 993C: 'Though they laughed, they themselves spoke the truth mystically, because [the apostles] were filled not with the old wine which failed at the wedding of the church, but with the wine of spiritual grace. For now new wine had come into new skins, when the apostles, not in the oldness of the letter but in the newness of the Spirit spoke of the mighty acts of God' (cf Bede *Super Acta* 2 PL 92 948A).

41 For the *calix inebrians* 'cup that intoxicates' see Ps 22:5 Vulgate (according to both the LXX and the Hebrew); the passage is rendered in the RSV (Ps 23:5) 'my cup overflows.'

42 For this list of the effects of wine see Horace *Epistles* 1.5.16–20; also *Odes* 3.21.13–20. Cf also Euripides *Bacchae* 278–83 and 770–4.

17

43 now] In all editions *1524–1535*; in LB 'not,' evidently in error

44 Cf Matt 10:26–7 and Luke 12:2–3.

45 For the hazards as well as the promises, see Matt 10:17–22; Mark 13:9–13; and Luke 21:12–19.

46 Cf n23 above.

47 For the proverbial character of the 'many-headed monster' in classical literature see Plato *Republic* 426E; Herodas *Mimes* 3.89; and Plutarch *Moralia* 341F 'On the

Fortune or the Virtue of Alexander' in Plutarch's *Moralia* IV trans F.C. Babbitt, Loeb Classical Library (London 1936) 469 (the hydra).

48 According to Matthew (5:2) Jesus sat to teach the disciples, though in the parallel passage in Luke (6:17) Jesus appears to have stood. But on Erasmus' comment here, see the different view of Hugh of St Cher 254 recto D who, commenting on Acts 1:15, observes that 'in their midst' is where Jesus is said to have stood (an allusion evidently to the Vulgate of John 20:19, 26; cf AV), and pastors should follow his example.

49 For Peter 'sheathing the sword' see John 18:11; Matt 26:52; for the sword of the Spirit, Eph 6:17.

50 Cf 'Peter's confession' in Matt 16:13–16; Mark 8:27–9; Luke 9:18–20. In the paraphrases on each of these passages, Peter speaks 'in the name of all'; but see especially the paraphrases on Matt 16:16 and 19 for an explanation of Peter's 'rank and authority.' See also the *Peregrinatio apostolorum* LB VII 653–6, where Erasmus demonstrates Peter's primacy among the apostles from the historical record: he is always named first in the list of apostles, he is usually, in the beginning, the first to speak, he is the first to work a miracle, and the first to be thrown into prison. Cf Munck 19.

18

51 Cf Mark 13:11: 'Do not be anxious beforehand what you are to say' (RSV); also Matt 10:19–20 and Luke 12:11–12.

52 Cf the interlinear *Gloss* (on 2:14) 993–4: 'He speaks as a shepherd on behalf of his sheep'; so likewise Hugh of St Cher 255 verso F.

53 For Erasmus' rejection elsewhere of 'subtle argumentation' see the annotation on 1 Tim 1:6 (*in vaniloquium*); see also the note on *curiositas*, chapter 1 n38.

54 In classical rhetorical theory the *exordium*, or beginning of a formal speech, was regarded as an opportune place to enlist the sympathies of the audience on the side of the speaker; flattery of the audience was an obvious way to do so. See Cicero *De inventione* 1.15.20–1.16.23; also Heinrich Lausberg *Handbuch der literarischen Rhetorik* 2nd ed (Munich 1973) sections 263–88.

55 Cf Nicholas of Lyra 994F, who explicates 'Jews' and 'dwellers in Jerusalem' (1:14): 'You who have knowledge of the Scriptures, and especially you who dwell in Jerusalem, wherein there has flourished the study of the Law and the prophets.'

56 by no means] *nequaquam*, first in 1534; in 1524, the less emphatic *non* 'not,' as in both the Vulgate and Erasmus' translation (all editions).

57 Erasmus was evidently puzzled by Peter's inference; see the 1527 annotation on 2:15 (*cum sit hora diei tertia*), where Erasmus notes that the third hour is at least three hours beyond sunrise, when it is not at all strange to see people in some countries drunk. But he justifies Peter's inference by appealing to Paul,

according to whom those who were drunk were drunk in the night (cf 1 Thess 5:7) – at least in that country. The third hour was about 9:00 AM, reckoning from sunrise, and before the Jews had their first meal of the day (Bruce 89; cf Munck 17). Haenchen 178 n9 cites Cicero *Philippics* (mistakenly identified as *Philosophical Discourses*) 2.41.104 as evidence of drinking 'from the third hour.'

58 The language of the sentence suggests an allusion to Heb 1:1–2.

59 world] *orbis*; LB *urbis* 'city,' evidently by mistake. For the thought of this sentence see the *Gloss* (on 2:17) 995B: 'It shows the abundance of the gift that not as of old to prophets and to priests alone was the Spirit to be given, but to everyone everywhere'; similarly Nicholas of Lyra (on 1:17) 995C: '[He will pour out] upon Jews and Gentiles without distinction.'

60 For the command see Acts 1:8; also Matt 28:19; Mark 16:15.

61 In writing 'Lord' Erasmus follows the Vulgate of 2:17 (so DV Conf) rather than his own text and translation (from 1516), 'says God' (so AV RSV).

19

62 'Illustrious': *illustris*. In his translation, Erasmus first (1516) adopted the Vulgate's *manifestus* (cf DV Conf RSV 'manifest'); in 1519, however, he changed to *illustris* (cf AV 'notable'). Cf his annotation on 2:20 (*dies domini magnus et horribilis*).

63 The paraphrase here reflects both the Vulgate reading *approbatum* 'approved,' and Erasmus' own translation (from 1516) *exhibitum* 'displayed.' A 1527 annotation on 2:22 (*virum approbatum*) offers an explanation: Erasmus believed the translator of the Vulgate had read ἀποδεδεγμένον in the sense of 'approve' rather than ἀποδεδειγμένον, which has the sense rather of 'point out,' 'reveal,' 'display.' Erasmus regarded either reading as 'tolerable' (cf DV AV Conf 'approved'; RSV 'attested'). Cf Haenchen 180 n2.

64 Cf 10:38: 'for God was with him' (RSV).

65 Cf 1 Cor 1:21.

66 'You took' is absent from the Vulgate (so DV Conf RSV). According to a 1527 annotation on 2:23 (*praescientia dei traditum*), Erasmus introduced the expression into his own text and translation on the basis of his Greek manuscripts. It appears in AV but is not the preferred reading (Metzger 298).

67 With the sharp accent here on the responsibility of the Jews for the death of Jesus, compare the paraphrase on 7:52 (55 below).

68 For the language here (and elsewhere in this paragraph) see Luke 18:31–3 and 24:18–21, 25–7, 45–7.

69 With the thought here, compare 1 Cor 15:12–19.

70 For sin as the means by which the devil maintains his tyranny see the paraphrases on John 12:31–2 CWE 46 155; also the paraphrases on Rom 5:12–19 CWE 42 34–6.

In the words 'the dead and the pains of death' and 'death and Tartarus' Erasmus has represented both his own translation ('death') and the Vulgate. The Vulgate had rendered 'pains of *hell*' (*inferni*; cf DV Conf 'sorrows of hell'), but Erasmus rightly believed that 'pains of *death*' (as in AV RSV) was the correct reading; cf the annotation on 2:24 (*solutis doloribus*) and Metzger 298. Here in the paraphrase on 2:24 Erasmus did not directly borrow the Vulgate's *infernus*, but rather explicated it by two images, *inferus* 'the dead,' and Tartarus, thus suggesting both inhabitants and place.

In both Greek and Roman mythology Tartarus was held to be a place of punishment in the underworld (Hesiod *Theogony* 711–33; Virgil *Aeneid* 6.539–627). In the Vulgate New Testament the word is used only in 2 Pet 2:4, where it renders the Greek ταρταρώσας [*tartarōsas*] (cf DV 'drawn down to the lower hell').

71 Cf Jonah 2:10; for the story of Jonah interpreted in relation to the death and resurrection of Christ see Matt 12:40.

20

72 Cf Bede in the *Gloss* (1000E), who understands the phrase 'before me' (2:25) as gazing upon God with the eye of the mind (cf Bede *Liber retractationis* 2 PL 92 1001C–D).

73 The *Gloss* (on 2:28) 1001A, in reference to the clause 'You have made known to me,' likewise generalizes from Christ to Christians: 'These words are understood not only of Christ . . . but also of the just who return to life . . . and [who] will rejoice when they see his face.'

74 Here and in the preceding case, 'you' is my interpretation; the subject could equally well be 'we' as in the 1548 *Paraphrase of Erasmus* fol ix recto.

75 For this expression see CWE 46 45 n5 and 60 n57.

21

76 For the allusion see Ps 132:11. For his Greek text of 2:30, Erasmus accepted in 1516 the reading reflected in the Vulgate: '. . . God swore [to David] an oath that someone from the fruit of his loins would sit upon his throne' (cf DV Conf RSV). Here, however, he paraphrases the text he adopted from 1519: '. . . God swore [to David] an oath . . . that of the fruit of his loins, according to the flesh, he would raise up Christ to sit on his throne' (cf AV). A 1527 annotation (*de fructu lumbi eius*) justifies the change. The Vulgate represents the preferred reading; cf Metzger 299.

77 Cf Rabanus in the *Gloss* (on 2:30) 1003A: 'Peter shows manifestly from this psalm that the kingdom of Christ is not earthly, but heavenly.'

78 Cf the interlinear *Gloss* 999–1000 on the words in 2:24 'having loosed the sorrows of hell' (DV Conf, similarly RSV): 'Either by his own resurrection or by the

freeing of the dead'; cf also Bede in the *Gloss* (on the same passage) 999C–1000D, who understands the words to mean that through his descent Christ freed the saints from the abodes of hell (cf Bede *Liber retractationis* 2 PL 92 1001B).

The doctrine of Christ's descent into hell developed with reference to such scriptures as Acts 2:27; Eph 4:8–9; 1 Pet 3:18–20, 4:6, and was firmly established by the second century. Though the purpose of Christ's descent was variously explained, from an early time some exegetes held that Christ descended to liberate the spirits of the saints. For a fuller account see J.N.D. Kelly *Early Christian Creeds* 3rd ed (New York 1972) 378–83. For the significance in Erasmus' thought of the descent of Christ see also the paraphrases on 1 Pet 3:18–20 CWE 44 98–9, Thompson *Inquisitio de fide* 62–4 and the notes on lines 182–193, and CWE 85–6 305–31, 668–87 poem 112.

79 For this sequence of 'evidence' see the paraphrase on 1:3 (6 above).

80 For the vivid antithesis here, and for the general outline of the paraphrastic exposition of 2:31–3, see Phil 2:5–11.

81 Cf 1:8; also Luke 24:49 and John 14:26.

82 The paraphrase reflects an ambiguity expressed in a *1527* annotation on 2:33 (*effudit hunc*) in which Erasmus notes that the word 'this' ('he has poured out *this*' RSV) is ambiguous in the Greek, and may refer to the Spirit (he has poured forth this Spirit; so Conf) or to the gift or to the event. DV and AV, like RSV, retain the ambiguity of the Greek. In the paraphrase here 'this' is both the Holy Spirit poured out and the miracle seen.

22

83 Cf Matt 22:41–6.

84 'Mystic' because tropologically the Psalms speak of the history of salvation. On Erasmus' use of 'mystic,' or 'mystical' see the paraphrases on 1 Tim 3:15 and Heb 1:5 CWE 44 23 and n15; 216 and n12.

85 The interlinear *Gloss* (on 2:34) 1001–2 and Nicholas of Lyra 1002F stress the two natures of Christ – man through the incarnation, but through his divinity sharing the rule with his Father; similarly also the marginal *Gloss* (on 2:36) citing Bede 1004D (cf Bede *Super Acta* 2 PL 92 949D–950B). Cf Rom 1:3–4, and the annotations on these verses ('who was made to him' and 'who was predestined') CWE 56 8–12, where Erasmus argues that the resurrection demonstrated and set forth the eternal divinity of Christ.

86 Cf Matt 27:22–3; Mark 15:13–14; Luke 23:21–3; John 19:6 and 15.

87 Cf 1 Cor 15:25.

88 The 'recipe' here for salvation – to recognize the guilt, to seek a remedy, not to despair – finds frequent expression, if in variant forms, in Erasmus (cf eg the paraphrases on John 5:6–7 CWE 46 65; also the paraphrase on Mark 1:15 CWE 49 23). For the elaboration of the theme, and for the medical image

see the *De immensa Dei misericordia* LB V 557–588, especially 581E; for theme and image in the tradition see the *De vera et falsa paenitentia* (attributed to Augustine) 1.1–5.16 PL 40 1114–18. For fear as the beginning of salvation see Prov 9:10.

89 Erasmus frequently extols in the *Paraphrases* the model of the gentle pastor; cf eg the paraphrases on 1 Tim 3:2–3 and Titus 1:7 CWE 44 18–19 and 58–9. Chrysostom as well had observed the gentleness of Peter, and extolled the benefits of kindness in addressing sinners (*Hom in Acta* 7.1 PG 60 63) – though from Erasmus' annotations we cannot be certain that this homily was available to him for the 1524 *Paraphrase*.

90 In his translation of 2:38, Erasmus adopted the Vulgate's *poenitentiam agite*, but in a brief annotation (*1516*) on the verse (*poenitentiam agite*) he noted that the Greek μετανοήσατε is represented by the Latin *resipiscite* or *poeniteat vos*. It is the latter phrase he adopts in the paraphrase here. For Erasmus' objection to *poenitentiam agere* see the paraphrase on Mark 1:4 CWE 49 15 and n12, and for *resipiscere* see the paraphrase on 1 Tim 2:2 CWE 44 13 and n5.

91 'Your' (2:38) represents the Vulgate (and the preferred) reading (so DV Conf RSV); Erasmus' text and translation omitted the pronoun (so AV; see Metzger 301).

92 'Trust': *fiducia*. On the distinction between *fides* and *fiducia* see CWE 42 xxxvii; and for an elaborate attempt to illustrate the language of faith see the 1527 annotation on Rom 1:17 ('from faith unto faith') CWE 56 42–4.

23

93 Cf Matt 7:21.

94 Cf Mark 13:10; for the 'other prophets' see Isa 49:6, 52:7–10, and less obviously Mic 5:4.

95 Cf Acts 1:8. Both the interlinear *Gloss* (on 2:39) 1005–6 and the marginal *Gloss* 1005A citing Bede specify that the indefinite 'all' of 2:39 refers to the gentiles (cf Bede *Liber retractationis* 2 PL 92 1004D).

96 See the interlinear *Gloss* 1005–6 on the words 'whomever God will call' (2:39): 'by grace, not by merits.'

97 The clauses here anticipate aspects of Stephen's speech; cf especially 7:39, 51–2.

98 'Exasperating house': *domus exasperatrix* – the precise phrase is found in the Vulgate of Ezek 2:8, while the phrase *domus exasperans* is frequently found in Ezekiel (eg Ezek 2:5, 3:9, 12:2, etc; RSV 'rebellious house'). The interlinear *Gloss* 1005–6 on the words 'crooked generation' in 2:40 (RSV) explains: '[A generation that] is perverse and exasperating,' and Hugh of St Cher 256 verso H cites Ezekiel: 'It is an exasperating house.'

99 Cf Isa 5:2–4.

100 Cf Matt 3:7; Luke 3:7.

101 Cf Matt 13:13-15; Mark 4:11-12; Luke 8:10; John 12:39-40; and for a representation of Jesus' attitude in the face of the 'invincible perversity' of the blind see the paraphrases on John 12:35-40 CWE 46 156-7.

102 Cf Matt 12:24.

103 Cf Matt 17:17; Luke 9:41.

104 Cf Luke 19:41-4; Matt 23:29-38; and Matt 21:33-45, especially verses 35 and 39, for the sequence 'beat, slew, stoned, and crucified.'

105 Erasmus uses the word *iustitia* 'justice,' 'righteousness' to refer both to the fulfilment of the commandments of the Law by individuals and to the absolute virtue demanded by the impartial judgment of God. On the range of meanings *iustitia* has in Erasmus' New Testament scholarship see Sider 'The Just and the Holy,' especially 4-8.

106 The language suggests the imagery of 1 Peter; cf especially 1:3-4, 2:2, 2:5, 2:9; but cf also John 3:5; Phil 3:20.

107 'Infused from heaven': *coelitus infusa*. The term *infusa* was common in the scholastic debates concerning the theology of grace; cf Oberman *Harvest* 68-74, 153-4, 169-72; and the annotation on Rom 5:12 ('in whom [or, in which] all have sinned') CWE 56 140 and n13. Cf also the word *infunde* in the ancient hymn *Veni creator*, whose liturgical use in the season of Pentecost is abundantly attested from the twelfth century; on this see John Julian *Dictionary of Hymnology* 2nd ed (London 1907) 1206. Here the language implies a contrast between the learning of the schools and divine inspiration; but cf the paraphrase on 18:27 (115 below), where sacred erudition and the Holy Spirit are represented as a complementary pair.

24

108 The Latin of this clause follows closely the Vulgate of Heb 4:12.

109 Cf Luke 5:1-11; John 21:4-8.

110 Cf Matt 13:3-23; Mark 4:3-20; Luke 8:4-15. The vivid images of sword, net, and seed obscure the biblical text paraphrased – '[gladly] receiving the word' (2:41) – and it remains ambiguous whether Erasmus intended here to represent the 'gladly' of his own text and translation (so AV) or to follow the Vulgate, which omits it (so DV Conf RSV; see Metzger 302).

111 For the feast of first-fruits see n1 above. For the figurative interpretation, see Bede in the *Gloss* (on 2:41) 1006D: 'On the fiftieth day from the Passover, on which day the Law was given, Moses ordered that a festival of first-fruits be established; now, however, with the coming of the Holy Spirit, not bundles of grain but the first-fruits of souls were consecrated to the Lord' (cf Bede *Super Acta* 2 PL 92 950D).

112 For the allusions see Heb 6:1-2 (rudiments of evangelical piety); 1 Cor 3:2 and 1 Pet 2:2 (the milk of teaching appropriate to infancy).

113 Cf Matt 28:19–20.

114 Erasmus elsewhere expressed with greater elaboration the importance of teaching in the preparation for baptism (especially through the catechism): see the paraphrases on Mark 1:5 and 13 CWE 49 16 and 20; on Matt 28:19–20 (which repeat and greatly expand upon the ideas set forth in the paraphrase here); and for Erasmus' 'startling proposal' for catechetical sermons for young adults already baptized, see Payne *Theology of the Sacraments* 172–3. On the catechumenate see chapter 9 n15.

115 'In taking the token': *in sumendo symbolo*. In a 1522 addition to his annotation on 2:42 (*fractione panis*) Erasmus speaks of the 'breaking of the bread' as the *symbolum sacrum* of Christian concord; and a further (1527) addition refers to an ancient custom whereby bishops 'took a part of the broken bread' as a sign of fellowship. In the *Detectio praestigiarum* ASD IX-1 252:433–6 Erasmus felt compelled to explain his controversial paraphrase on 1 Cor 11:25: Christ wanted this feast to be a commemoration (*commemoratio*) and a token (*symbolum*) of an eternal covenant. He explains: 'I do not call the body and blood "tokens"; I call the act of taking [or, eating; Latin *ipsa sumptio*] the token of concord among us and a memorial [*memoriale*] of the sacred death [*sacrata mors*] by which we are redeemed.' On the meaning of *symbolum* see further the *Explanatio symboli* ASD V-1 210:138–212:193, where Erasmus explores various connotations of the word – seal, token of identity, pledge of faithfulness (stressing the inviolability of a covenant). See also Thompson *Inquisitio de fide* 81 and 126 and the notes to lines 57 and 375.

116 Cf the 1527 addition to the annotation on 2:42 (*fractione panis*): 'The [Vulgate] reading lists only three [activities]: teaching, breaking of bread – this they call the communion – and prayers.' Here in the paraphrase on 2:42 Erasmus follows, in the first instance, the Vulgate in reading *three* activities of the Christians – cf Conf: 'They continued steadfastly in the teaching of the apostles and in the communion of the breaking of the bread and in the prayers' (so DV); but his own text and translation adopted a reading that listed *four* activities: teaching, fellowship, breaking of bread, and prayers (so AV RSV and the preferred reading; cf Bruce 99–100, Metzger 302, and Haenchen 191). Consequently, as the paragraph continues, the theme of 'fellowship' ('live harmoniously, having peace') eventually emerges, displaced, however, from its position in the sequence of Erasmus' own text and translation. In this way Erasmus was able to represent both the text of the Vulgate and his own text.

117 'In memory of': *in memoriam*; cf Luke 22:19 (Majority Text) and 1 Cor 11:24–5, where from 1519 Erasmus translated the Greek εἰς τὴν ἐμὴν ἀνάμνησιν by *in mei recordationem* (Luke 22:19), and *in mei commemorationem* (1 Cor 11:24–5) (Vulgate in both texts *in meam commemorationem*); in annotations *in meam*

commemorationem on Luke 22:19 and 1 Cor 11:24 Erasmus explains the Greek as meaning 'for renewing the memory of me.' For the paraphrase on 1 Cor 11:25 see n115 above. For the Last Supper as a 'perpetual memory' of Jesus see the paraphrase on John 13:2 CWE 46 160.

118 This passage specifically was taken by Leo Jud to show Erasmus' sympathy with views of the Eucharist held by the Reformers. But Erasmus replied (*Detectio praestigiarum* [1526] ASD IX-1 252:449–254:486) that since interpreters themselves were ambiguous about whether there was meant here the body and blood of Christ or the bread of fellowship, he had himself endeavoured in the paraphrase to render the passage so that neither sense would be excluded. He notes, however, that Christ himself, in the feeding of the multitude and with the disciples at Emmaus, broke the bread of fellowship without 'consecrating his body and blood,' and the apostles seem to have continued the practice. In the *1527* addition to his annotation on 2:42 (*fractione panis*) Erasmus allows for both interpretations, but clearly favours the view that the words refer to the bread of fellowship, not the Eucharist. See the discussion in Payne *Theology of the Sacraments* 126–33.

119 Erasmus represents the prayers as added (Latin *addebant*) to the communion (cf next note). The three clauses of this sentence may reflect the first three petitions of the Lord's Prayer.

25

120 Cf Matt 5:7, 6:14–15; Eph 4:32. Erasmus appears to represent the prayers and the communion as part of a single ritual, but on this see Haenchen 190–1. With the portrait here of the early church meetings, compare the account in Tertullian *Apology* 39 CCL 1 150–3.

121 For prayers as sacrifices see the paraphrase on 1 Pet 2:5 CWE 44 89; also on Luke 2:47, where 'pure prayers' are the incense 'most pleasing to God.' That prayers are the sacrifices of Christians finds expression in early Christian literature in the interpretation of Mal 1:11 (cf Tertullian *Against Marcion* 4.1.8 CCL 1 546) – though the verse is also interpreted of the Eucharist (Justin *Dialogue with Trypho* 41 and 117 PG 6 564C and 745B).

122 Erasmus follows the Vulgate rather than his Greek text and translation (from *1516*) in including the place-name, Jerusalem (omitted in AV RSV; included in DV Conf [2:43]).

123 'Change of heart': *resipiscentis* (cf n90 above); for the sentiment see the paraphrase on 2:37 (22 above) and n88.

124 Cf John 13:34–5.

125 Cf Gal 3:28.

126 A theme frequently repeated in the *Paraphrases*; cf the paraphrases on Rom 13:8–10 CWE 42 75–6 and n7 and on Gal 5:13–14 CWE 42 124–5. See also 'The

Sober Feast' (Thompson *Colloquies* 456) where it is shown that Aristotle is consistent with Paul in saying that philosophy 'caused him to do of his own accord what most men do by compulsion.' On the theme of common ownership among those who love one another see *Adagia* 1 i 1.

127 Erasmus followed his own translation (from *1516*) which suggested more precisely than the Vulgate a picture of reciprocal meals. Bruce 101 believes the AV 'from house to house' (so DV) reflects the intent of the Greek; cf Conf 'in their houses' and RSV 'in their homes.' Cf the annotations on 2:46 (*circa domos* and *sumebant cibum*).

26

128 The *Gloss* (on 2:47) 1007A–1008D commenting on the words 'having favour with all the people' (RSV) observed that no one could help but love those whom God had flooded with such great grace. Cf also the paraphrase on Luke 2:40 (where the grace of God is said to have been upon Jesus): '. . . his sweetness, affability, and modesty made him loved by all' (LB VII 305B).

129 Cf the paraphrase on Mark 7:1 CWE 49 88: 'For there is hardly any mention of priests except in plans to slay Jesus.'

130 In the last sentence of 2:47 Erasmus' text and translation differed from the Vulgate reading in two important respects. 1/ His text did not take the words ἐπὶ τὸ αὐτό with verse 47, but with 3:1. The preferred reading takes these words with 2:47 (Metzger 304–5), where, however, they are variously rendered: '[the Lord added] in church fellowship' (Metzger 305); 'to the total' (Munck 22); 'to their company' (Conf); 'to their number' (RSV); cf Bruce 75 (on 1:15). 2/ Erasmus' text included the expression τῇ ἐκκλησίᾳ '[the Lord added] to the church.' In the paraphrase the lack of an explicit representation of 'to the church' suggests that here Erasmus favours the Vulgate text, but he favours his own text in representing the expression ἐπὶ τὸ αὐτό in 3:1 rather than in 2:47.

   The Greek τοὺς σῳζομένους is rendered in RSV as 'those who were being saved,' an interpretation with which Haenchen 190 concurs, the meaning Bruce 102 thinks 'probable,' and the sense of Erasmus' *1516* translation. From *1519*, however, Erasmus followed the preferred Vulgate reading (Weber II 1701), giving the sense 'such as were to be saved' (Conf; cf DV AV). The language of 'destination' (but not 'predestination') in the paraphrase clarifies the intent of Erasmus' translation *1519–1535*. On the distinction between 'destination' and 'predestination,' see the annotation on Rom 1:4 ('who was predestined') CWE 56 10–12.

131 For the image of the mustard seed see Matt 13:31–2; Mark 4:30–2; Luke 13:18–19.

Chapter 3

1 The words 'with others ... together' appear to paraphrase the Greek ἐπὶ τὸ
αὐτό (Vulgate *in id ipsum*), a phrase Erasmus included in his Greek text of 3:1
(cf chapter 2 n130). In his translation Erasmus gave the phrase the sense of
'together' (so AV in 3:1); he thought the phrase could refer to either 'place or
time': cf the annotation on 2:47 (*in idipsum*; 3:1 in AV).

2 Erasmus may intend a reference to customs of his own day, in particular, to
a midday meal followed by sport or sleep; the guests in the colloquy 'The
Godly Feast' arrive at 10:00 AM to enjoy leisure before a noon meal (Thompson
Colloquies 49 / ASD I-3 232:44–7). The Roman *cena* normally did not begin until
about 3:00 PM (the 'ninth hour') and often continued long into the evening; cf
Carcopino *Daily Life* 263–76.

3 The language implies a criticism of ecclesiastical pomp in Erasmus' day. For a
satirical portrait of a papal procession see the *Iulius exclusus* CWE 27 192–3.

4 The detail cannot be verified; the identification of the gate is uncertain. In the
'opinion now customary' it is the gate 'which led from the east from the Court
of the Gentiles into the Court of the Women' (Haenchen 198 n12), and it is so
identified in IDB IV 552, 553, 556. For various views see Haenchen 198 n12.

5 The paraphrase on 3:2 implies a criticism of the custom of begging. For
Erasmus' own somewhat unsympathetic view of beggars see the colloquy
'Beggar Talk' (Thompson *Colloquies* 248–54), and the discussion on beggars in
'The Godly Feast' (Thompson *Colloquies* 71). The Latin *templum*, also used to
refer to a church, may sharpen the allusion to the social context of the sixteenth
century. For *templum* as 'church' see the colloquy 'The Godly Feast' (Thompson
Colloquies 70 / ASD I-3 257, where 'church,' 'churches' consistently represent
the Latin *templum, templa*); see also the annotation on Rom 8:33 ('who will make
accusation against the elect of God') CWE 56 230, where Erasmus refers to
public readings in 'churches' (*in templis*).

27

6 Elsewhere, too, in the *Paraphrases*, Erasmus calls attention to the nature and
significance of the voice: cf eg the paraphrases on Acts 16:28 (104 below) and
John 11:43 and 18:6 (CWE 46 146 and 199).

7 The emphasis upon the gestures of rejoicing reflects Erasmus' efforts to express
the force of the Greek participle ἐξαλλόμενος in 3:8; see the annotation on 3:8
(*ambulans et exsiliens*).

8 Standard translations correctly rely upon a Greek text of 3:11 reading 'While
the lame man clung to (DV AV 'held') Peter and John' (so Conf RSV), and this
is the preferred reading of the Vulgate (cf Weber II 1702). Erasmus, however,

had a Vulgate that read 'When they *saw* Peter and John' – the reading of the Vulgate in 1527 (cf the annotation *cum viderent autem etc*). In this paragraph the paraphrase incorporates both readings.

9 According to John 10:22–9 Jesus disputed with the 'Jews' in the portico of Solomon. For Christ as the true Solomon, see the paraphrases on John 2:22 and 10:23 CWE 46 43 and 135; also Bede in the *Gloss* (on 3:11) 1010F: '... the whole world ran to the threshold of the true man of peace' (cf Bede *Super Acta* 3 PL 92 951D–952A); similarly Hugh of St Cher 257 recto D.

10 Cf the *Gloss* (on 3:13) 1011B: 'By mentioning the fathers he encourages belief, avoiding the appearance of introducing something new'; so also Hugh of St Cher 257 recto D.

11 The thrice repeated 'God' of 3:13 represents the Vulgate reading Erasmus followed here (so DV Conf); cf the preferred reading, represented in his own text and translation, 'the God of Abraham and of Isaac and of Jacob' (AV RSV).

28

12 Both in the interlinear *Gloss* 1011–12 and in Hugh of St Cher 257 recto D it is observed at this point (3:13) that Pilate was a gentile.

13 kinship] In 1524 and 1534 *cognatione* (so LB); in 1535, *cognitione* 'knowledge,' no doubt by mistake

14 For the added details here of the praetorium and the denial of Jesus' kingship see John 18:28 and 19:8–15. Nicholas of Lyra (on 3:14) also noted the cry of the chief priests in John 19:15. These details evoke a severe criticism of Jewish behaviour in the paraphrases on John 18:28 and 19:15 CWE 46 204, 210–11.

15 In the elaborate contrast here between taking and giving life, Erasmus emphasizes a stylistic feature he believes belongs to the text of 3:14–15, where the contrast, he notes, is at once 'solemn and pleasant,' a witness to the 'majestic character' of apostolic speech; cf the annotation on 3:14 (*virum homicidam*).

16 Erasmus is fond of the expression *auctor ac princeps vitae* 'author and prince of life' (and variants of it); cf eg the paraphrases on Rom 1:4 CWE 42 15; Acts 7:35; 1 Cor 15:20. For the details here see Matt 27:16; Mark 15:7; Luke 23:19; John 18:40; in Matthew Barabbas is a 'notorious prisoner' (RSV); in Mark and Luke he is said to be guilty of murder and insurrection; in John he is described as a robber.

17 For the emphasis see Hugh of St Cher 257 verso E, following the interlinear *Gloss* (on 3:15) 1011–12: 'The one who hands over is the one who slays'; and cf chapter 2 n67.

18 Cf chapter 2 n79.

19 power] First in 1534; in 1524 'his power' (so LB). For the contrast between the lowliness assumed and the power expressed see Nicholas of Lyra (on 3:15)

1011C, who also contrasts here the humanity assumed in the incarnation and the divine 'omnipotence.'

20 'In it': *in quo*. Either 'in it' referring to the name (so understood in the 1548 *Paraphrase of Erasmus* fol xiii verso); or 'in him' referring to the Son. See next note.

21 No satisfactory solution to the redundancy of the Greek text of 3:16 has yet been found (cf Metzger 311–13). In his annotation on the verse (*et in fide nominis eius*), Erasmus offers three possible interpretations: 1/ the God of our fathers has corroborated his name through trust in the name of Jesus, which trust this man had whom you see and know; 2/ God has made whole this man whom you see and know to have been born lame, because of the trust which either he or Peter had in the name of Jesus; 3/ the name of Christ has strengthened this man, whom you see and know, through trust in his name. Erasmus' paraphrase represents aspects of all three readings. For various explanations of the passage see Metzger 311–13, Bruce 110, and Haenchen 207.

22 Cf 1 Cor 2:8: 'None of the rulers of this age understood this; for if they had, they would not have crucified the Lord of glory' (RSV); the verse is cited by Hugh of St Cher (on 3:17) 257 verso E.

23 For the first clause see John 18:14, where Caiaphas urged that 'it was expedient that one man should die for the people' (cf the paraphrase on the verse in CWE 46 200); for the second see Eph 3:11. Cf also the *Gloss* (on 3:17) 1012E: 'Two things cooperated, your ignorance and God's foreknowledge.'

24 Cf eg the traditional interpretations of Isaiah 53 and Ps 22.

25 For the sentiment and the expression see Rom 3:4, Titus 1:2, and 1 John 1:10; see also the paraphrases on these verses in CWE 42 23, CWE 44 57, and CWE 44 178.

29

26 Cf Rom 8:28; and the paraphrase on Rom 11:15 CWE 42 65: '... if the misfortune of the Jews has worked for good ... how much greater the good if these Jews ... be received back ...'

27 'Turn to the new life': *ad vitae novitatem convertamini*; for the expression see Rom 6:4, where Erasmus' translation has the words *et nos in novitate vitae ambulemus* 'we too might walk in newness of life' (RSV). In his paraphrase on Rom 6:4 CWE 42 37 Erasmus emphasized the moral implications of the expression: 'living now the new life ... progressing from virtue to greater virtue'; but he appears to have recognized that the phrase presupposed baptism as the ontological basis of the moral transformation; thus the phrase connotes both 'newness of life' and 'a new life.'

28 On the sequence 'acknowledge ... believe' see Rom 10:9, 'confess ... believe.'

29 Cf 2 Cor 6:2.

30 The words echo the Nicene Creed.

31 For Christ's coming in the clouds see Matt 24:30, 26:64; Mark 13:26, 14:62; 1 Thess 4:17. For the familiar contrast between the humility and glory of Christ see Thompson *Inquisitio de fide* 66:226–8 / ASD I-3 370:215–17. Nicholas of Lyra (on 3:20) 1013C understood that Christ would be sent in the glorified form of his humanity; see chapter 1 nn56 and 58.

32 'Have not been penitent': *non egerint poenitentiam*. Erasmus adopts here (paraphrase on 3:19) the expression *poenitentiam agere* 'do penance,' 'be penitent,' to which, as a translation of the Greek μετανοεῖν, he elsewhere objected (see chapter 2 n90). The expression here is surprising since both he and the Vulgate translated the μετανοήσατε of 3:19 by the Latin *poenitet* 'repent.' See the annotation on 3:19 (*poenitemini igitur*).
For the terrible face of God's anger see Rev 6:16.

33 The Greek ἀναψύξεως in 3:19 has been translated 'refreshing' (AV RSV) as well as 'refreshment,' but its precise connotation is unclear; see TDNT IX (1974) 664–5; cf Munck 27–8, Bruce 111–12, and Haenchen 208 n8. The Vulgate rendered the word by *refrigerium*; Erasmus in his translation by *refrigeratio* (from 1522), *refrigerium* (1516 and 1519). In the paraphrase here, however, Erasmus adopted the word *refocillatio*, a noun whose verb analogue is used in the Vulgate of the Old Testament to suggest restoration and revival (cf eg Judg 15:19; 1 Sam 16:23; Lam 1:11). In his 1516 annotation, Erasmus explicated the Greek by observing that the righteous would find their *refrigerium* in beholding the divine face, a concept implied in the paraphrase a few lines above, 'you will with good trust endure his face'; cf the annotation on 3:19 (*ut cum venerint tempora*).

34 Cf Matt 24:14

35 Cf Joel 2:28–32; Mal 3:1–2, 4:1–3, 5–6.

36 The paraphrase emphasizes the inclusion of *all* the prophets, reflecting, evidently, Erasmus' own text, based upon manuscripts that read 'all' ('of all his holy prophets' AV); cf the annotation on 3:21 (*per os sanctorum*). The preferred reading omits 'all' (so Conf and RSV). See the paraphrase on the similar text of Luke 1:70.

37 For this text see Deut 18:15, 19 and Lev 23:29.

38 Cf Rom 1:3 and the narrative of the nativity in Matthew, especially 1:20 and 2:5–6. Cf also Nicholas of Lyra (on 3:22) 1014F, who says that by the 'prophet' is understood 'Jesus Christ ... descended from the Jews according to the flesh.'

39 The phrase recalls Gal 5:13.

30

40 Cf Mark 16:16 and John 3:18.

41 all the families] So in all editions 1524–1535; in LB 'all' is omitted.

42 Cf Gen 22:1–14. The typology of Isaac is found in the earliest strata of Christian literature; cf Gal 4:21–31, and Jean Daniélou *From Shadows to Reality: Studies in the Biblical Typology of the Fathers* trans Dom Wulstan Hibberd (London 1960) 115–49. Cf also the paraphrases on Rom 9:7–8 CWE 42 54 and on Heb 11:19 CWE 44 248.

43 Cf Bede in the *Gloss* (on 3:26) 1015A: 'The seed of Abraham is Christ, by trusting whom the blessing is promised to all nations, Jews and gentiles' (cf Bede *Super Acta* 3 PL 92 952B).

44 Cf Hos 1:10.

45 'Wickedness': *malitia* (ablative), representing the πονηριῶν (plural) of the Greek text. In his translation Erasmus had rendered the word first by *malitiis (1516)*, then by *iniquitatibus* (from *1519*); the Vulgate translated *nequitia*. In Rom 1:29 Erasmus rendered the same word (πονηρία) by *versutia* (from *1519*; the word is not represented in the *1516* translation; see CWE 56 61–2 n3). In his annotation on Rom 1:29 ('with wickedness') CWE 56 61 he notes that *malitia* is used not only to mean 'vice' but sometimes to connote perversity, 'when someone is spiteful in return for a service rendered.' Erasmus himself uses the word *malitia* of the perverse will of Pharoah (cf the paraphrases on Rom 9:19–22 CWE 42 55–6, where 'ill will' translates *malitia*) and, in the *Paraphrase on Acts*, frequently of the will and the deeds of the Jews (cf eg the paraphrases on 13:30 and 25:1, 88 and 139 below). Erasmus' annotation on Acts 3:26 (*a nequitia sua*) suggests that in this text he understood the Greek in the sense of *vitia* 'vices.'

Chapter 4

1 In the paraphrase here, the position of Peter is emphasized, but John is not excluded as speaker; cf the interlinear *Gloss* (on 4:1) 1015–16: 'Peter speaks on behalf of himself and John; or, both speak to the multitude.'

31

2 'Captain of the temple' (as in AV and RSV) for the Latin *magistratus templi*, the term used in Erasmus' translation and the Vulgate; cf DV and Conf, 'officer of the temple.' Erasmus' annotation on 1:4 (*et magistratus templi*) shows that he understands this to be a single individual – the form *magistratus* can be either singular or plural (cf the 1548 *Paraphrase of Erasmus* fol xv recto 'rulers') – who was in charge of the temple. Cf Bruce 115: 'This officer ... superintended arrangements for the preservation of order in and around the Temple'; Haenchen 214 describes this magistrate as 'the officer commanding the Temple-police.' See n15 below.

3 For the temple as the setting for instruction see Luke 2:46; Matt 21:23; Mark 14:49; John 18:20. None of these passages, however, indicates that teaching in the temple was limited to rabbis, Pharisees, and scribes; on the scribes as teachers see Emil Schürer *History of the Jewish People in the Time of Jesus Christ* 2 divisions in 5 vols (New York 1897–8) 1st div trans Rev John Macpherson, 2nd div trans Sophia Taylor and Peter Christie II-1 313–26. With the paraphrase here, compare Bede in the *Gloss* (on 4:1) 1015C–1016F, who observes that the priests and the magistrate were angry because though they were regarded as teachers and judges, the multitude had flocked to hear the apostles (cf Bede *Super Acta* 4 PL 92 952C).

4 So, similarly, Bede in the *Gloss* (on 4:2) 1015C–1016F (cf Bede *Super Acta* 4 PL 92 952C).

5 For the Sadducees' belief see 23:6–8 and the paraphrases on those verses (133 below).

6 Cf Matt 10:17–20; Mark 13:9–13; Luke 21:12–15.

7 'Malice': *malitia*, translated just below as 'wickedness' ('just as their wickedness did not prevail'); cf chapter 3 n45.

8 Cf the paraphrase on Rom 5:20 CWE 42 36: '. . . the more sin looms up . . . the more the kindness of God . . . shines forth.'

9 As it did when the chief priests and scribes desired to take Jesus; cf Mark 12:12 and Luke 20:19.

10 comes] The future tense in all lifetime editions; in LB, the imperfect subjunctive

11 For the three images see Luke 5:5–7, John 21:6–11 (net); Matt 13:31–2, Mark 4:30–2, Luke 13:18–19 (mustard seed); and Matt 13:33, Luke 13:20–1 (yeast). For the net and the seed see the paraphrase on 2:40 (24 above).

12 The expression may be intended to accommodate the reading both of the Vulgate, 'The number was five thousand' (cf DV Conf), and of Erasmus (in text and translation from *1516*), 'The number was about five thousand' (cf AV RSV). Cf Metzger 317.

13 See 1 Cor 1:26 for the contrast between the humble and the mighty when confronted by the gospel; cf the paraphrases on Mark 1:9 CWE 49 19, John 7:45 CWE 46 102, and on 1 Cor 1:26–30.

14 Cf Mark 14:53–9.

15 In the paraphrase here on 4:5 it appears that the ἄρχοντας of the Greek text (DV 'princes'; AV Conf RSV 'rulers') are understood to include both the priests and the ' temple wardens' (*magistratus templi*). In fact the ἄρχοντες 'rulers' of 4:5 are the priests; cf Bruce 118 and Haenchen 215. By the plural *magistratus* here Erasmus probably intends to refer to what he elsewhere calls 'military prefects,' whose task, he explains, was to watch over the temple; cf the annotation on Luke 22:52 (*et magistratus templi*). Haenchen 215 n4 observes that there were, in addition to the captain of the temple, other officers, the 'Temple Wardens

– numbering at least seven, and the treasurers, of whom there were at least three.'

16 Though Erasmus understands the first καί 'and' of 4:6 to mean 'in addition to' (cf DV AV), it is probably to be understood as 'including in particular' (so Bruce 118; cf Conf RSV).

17 Caiaphas was Annas' son-in-law and high priest at the time of Jesus' death, according to John 18:13. Annas was high priest from AD 6–15; and at this time the 'senior ex-High Priest' (Bruce 118; cf also Munck 34 and Haenchen 216).

32

18 This is perhaps an inference from the fact that they are mentioned. Nothing is known of John and Alexander as such, though 'John' may be Jonathan, Annas' son and high priest AD 36–7. See Metzger 317–18; also Bruce 118–19, Munck 34, and Haenchen 216.

19 A reference perhaps to the part played by Annas and Caiaphas at the trial of Jesus; cf Matt 26:57–67 and John 18:13–28. The language of priesthood in this sentence may be deliberately ambiguous, intended to point both to the first-century setting of the biblical text and to the sixteenth-century context of the paraphrase: Annas is *summus pontifex*; while the Latin *genus sacerdotale* (so the Vulgate) may in the paraphrase refer either to those who are of priestly class or of priestly family (for the latter see RSV, Bruce 120, and Haenchen 216).

20 Nicholas of Lyra (on 4:7) 1017C observes that both the number and the station of those present were such as to terrify the apostles.

21 Cf Matt 10:17–20; Mark 13:9–11; Luke 12:11–12. Chrysostom cites the latter passage in his commentary on 4:8 (*Hom in Acta* 10.1 PG 60 86).

22 Cf Matt 26:62–6; Mark 14:60–4; Luke 22:66–71.

23 A reference, apparently, to the effect on the priesthood of the destruction of the temple by Titus in AD 70, when 'the priesthood lost its main religious base in society' (ISBE III 969)

24 Cf Matt 26:69–75; Mark 14:66–72; Luke 22:56–62; John 18:16–18. Chrysostom *Hom in Acta* 10.2–3 PG 60 88, commenting on 4:3–6, evokes images of the arrest and trial of Jesus, specifically recalling the story of Peter and the maidservant.

25 Cf Matt 26:33–5; Mark 14:29–31; Luke 22:33.

26 softness] *lenitas*, first in the octavo editions of 1524; in the folio edition of 1524, *levitas* 'smoothness,' 'fluency'

27 Rabanus in the *Gloss* (on 4:11) 1018E observed that in replying to their questions Peter proclaimed Christ.

28 'Hear me' represents a Vulgate reading; though not the preferred Vulgate reading (Weber II 1703 8n), it is found in the Vulgate of the 1527 edition. Erasmus omitted the expression from his text and translation (all editions); cf the annotation on 4:8 (*et seniores Israel audite*). Here in the paraphrase Erasmus omits 'of Israel' after 'elders,' as does the preferred reading of the Vulgate,

though the expression is found in the Vulgate of *1527*, in his own Greek text, and in his Latin translation; cf Metzger 318.

33

29 Cf 1 Pet 3:15.

30 Nicholas of Lyra (on 4:7) 1017C noted that the question 'By what power . . . did you do this?' (RSV) implied that this deed had been done through the power of magic. Cf the *1516* annotation on 4:9 (*in benefacto hominis infirmi in quo iste salus factus est*) where Erasmus elucidates the Greek text with a paraphrase: 'If there is a question about this . . . know that this has been done not by magical art, or by our power, but in the name of the Lord Jesus.' Elsewhere also Erasmus contrasts the power of magic and the power of the gospel; cf eg the paraphrase on Mark 6:13 CWE 49 80. See also CWE 44 168 n22 and 169 n26.

31 Cf Eph 1:20–2.

32 Cf Ps 118:22. Erasmus follows the Vulgate closely here, adding, however, the expression 'of the synagogue' (cf DV).

33 Cf Bede in the *Gloss* (on 4:11) 1018E–F: '. . . the stone was to fit not the one, but the two walls . . . so that from two peoples and two testaments a building of one and the same faith should arise' (cf Bede *Super Acta* 4 PL 92 953A); also Nicholas of Lyra 1018F: 'joining Jews and gentiles as two walls into one church.' For Christ the stone that holds together the two walls, Jews and gentiles, see the paraphrase on 1 Pet 2:7 CWE 44 90.

34 Cf the annotation on 4:12 (*datum hominibus*): 'He adds "among men" because of Moses, in whom the Jews trusted.'

35 Cf Matt 1:21. Jesus (Hebrew Joshua or Jehoshua) means 'Jahweh is salvation' (cf IDB II 869). For the name 'Jesus' elsewhere in the *Paraphrase on Acts* see chapter 13 n20.

36 In both his paraphrases and annotations on Acts Erasmus displays an interest in the noun παρρησία and the verb παρρησιάζομαι. Together the two words appear in the New Testament forty times, twelve times in Acts. Here in 4:13 Erasmus represents both the Vulgate translation – *constantia* 'constancy' (DV) – and his own *1516* translation – *libertas* 'freedom' (from *1519*, 'freedom in speaking'). In his *1516* annotation on 4:13 (*Petri constantiam*) he notes that the Greek παρρησία refers to boldness (*audacia*) or freedom in speaking.

37 and the realization struck them] *compertoque*, first in *1535*; in the previous editions, *iamque comperissent* 'and they had now realized.' In rendering *comperto* in *1535*, Erasmus returned to the Vulgate and his own translation (from *1516*).

34

38 Nicholas of Lyra (on 4:16) 1020F represents similarly the reflection of the council: '. . . by killing or by detaining them we shall incite the whole people against us.'

39 'Sided': *itum est pedibus*, an image from classical antiquity; cf CWE 42 82 n7. Erasmus explicates the image in *Adagia* II vii 12 CWE 34 8–10, and uses it with fine dramatic effect in the colloquy 'The Council of Women' (Thompson *Colloquies* 445 / ASD I-3 632:101–2).

35

40 Cf 1 Cor 1:20; 3:19.

41 Chrysostom, recapitulating his commentary on Acts 4 observes: 'What folly! ... they hoped by their machinations to throw into obscurity the one who had not been restrained by death' (*Hom in Acta* 10.2 PG 60 88).

42 Nicholas of Lyra (on 4:20) 1021C also noted the importance of the divine command: 'Especially since he has commanded us to give witness to this.'

43 'Manly': *masculus*

44 The sequence of evidence, arguments, and witnesses may be inspired by the classical theory of forensic and deliberative rhetoric, which distinguished between inartificial proofs (direct evidence, witnesses) and artificial proofs (arguments); cf Quintilian 5.1.1–9.16 and Heinrich Lausberg *Handbuch der literarischen rhetorik* 2nd ed (Munich 1973) sections 350–5

45 Cf the paraphrase on Mark 3:14 CWE 49 50: 'But because they were fishermen ... who had nothing regal about them ...[God] gave them ... power which no monarch ... can give'; see also the paraphrase on Mark 6:13 CWE 49 80.

46 Cf Nicholas of Lyra (on 4:21) 1021C: '... they were restrained from punishing them only from human fear'; also Hugh of St Cher 258 recto D: 'On account of the people, not on account of God.'

47 For the detail of the upper room see 1:13. In the biblical context here, a small group of believers gathered in a single room may be assumed; cf Haenchen 226.

36

48 Elsewhere also Erasmus emphasizes the theme of mutual rejoicing among Christians; cf the paraphrase on Rom 1:12 CWE 42 16: 'while I rejoice with you in your faith, and you in turn rejoice with me in mine.'

49 The paraphrase here reflects Erasmus' text (from 1516) in 4:24: 'Lord thou art God which hast made' (AV); the text of the Vulgate is the preferred reading: 'Lord, thou art he that didst make' (DV; similarly Conf RSV). See Metzger 321.

50 Erasmus follows the Vulgate text of 4:25: 'Who by the mouth of our father David, thy servant, didst say by the Holy Spirit' (RSV; so also DV Conf). His own text (from 1519) read: 'Who by the mouth of thy servant David hast said' (AV). The text is highly problematic; cf Bruce 126–7, Metzger 321–3, and, for a defence of Erasmus' reading, see Haenchen 226 and nn3 and 4.
In the paraphrase here on 4:25 Erasmus has represented the Greek παῖς 'child,' 'servant' (Vulgate *puer* 'boy,' 'servant') by *cultor*. In his annotation on 4:27 (*adversus sanctum puerum tuum Iesum*), where he argues that the Greek παῖς

referring to Christ should be translated *filius* 'son,' not *puer* 'servant,' he notes that here in 4:25 the word has the sense of *famulus dei*; this is a phrase used in classical literature of the attendant of a god, or a priest of sacred rites (cf Ovid *Metamorphoses* 3.574; Horace *Ars poetica* 239; Virgil *Aeneid* 5.95). Erasmus' interest in the word *cultor* is reflected elsewhere in his use of related forms; see eg CWE 42 16 n8 (*colo*) and CWE 56 33–4 annotation on Rom 1:9 ('whom I serve').

51 The phrase 'in this city,' though found in the Vulgate (so also in DV Conf RSV), is omitted from Erasmus' text and translation (from *1516*; so AV); cf the annotation on 4:27 (*vere in civitate ista*).

52 Here in his paraphrase on 4:27, Erasmus follows his own translation in writing *filius* 'Son,' rather than the Vulgate's *puer* 'servant,' for the Greek παῖς. Zúñiga had objected to his translation on the grounds that it invited interpretations leading either to Apollinarianism, which detracted from the manhood of Christ (in this case, Erasmus might seem to have denied that Christ assumed servanthood); or Arianism, which detracted from the divinity of Christ (in this case, if Christ obeyed as a son rather than a servant, then the Son is not equal to the Father). Erasmus responded not only in his *Apologia ad annotationes Stunicae* ASD IX-2 140–6 and 66:107–10, but also in a large addition to his annotation on the verse (*adversus sanctum puerum tuum Iesum*). Edward Lee had also criticized the translation; for Erasmus' response to Lee see *Responsio ad annotationes Lei* LB IX 205F–207B.

53 In text and translation (from *1516*) as well as in his paraphrase here (4:27) Erasmus followed the Vulgate in reading 'peoples' (so Conf RSV). He acknowledged the reading 'people' (so DV AV), but regarded it as inferior; cf the annotation on 4:27 (*et populis Israel*), where Erasmus understands 'peoples' to refer to the Jews. Haenchen 227 understands the plural 'peoples' to refer to the 'tribes of Israel.'

54 Cf Nicholas of Lyra (on 4:26) 1023C: 'Whatever was done against the Son who was sent, was done against the Father who sent.'

55 Cf Ps 2:4, where the Latin of the Vulgate *irridere* 'laugh at' (cf AV RSV) is apparently echoed in the Latin of the paraphrase here (4:29).

56 Cf Gal 1:11–12.

57 Erasmus noted (*1516*) that here even the Vulgate translated παῖς as *filius* 'Son'; cf the annotation on 4:30 (*filii tui Jesu*) and n52 above. For the meaning of παῖς in Acts see Bruce 107–8 and Haenchen 205 (both on 3:13).

37

58 Cf the *Gloss* (on 4:31) 1024D: 'Great is the power of the prayer of the faithful.'

59 Two words, *liberius* and *fortius*, for the Greek μετὰ παρρησίας, though in his translation of 4:31 Erasmus adopted the Vulgate's *cum fiducia* (cf n36 above). In

his (*1516*) annotation on 4:31 (*cum fiducia*) he explains the Greek phrase here as meaning 'boldly and freely' (*audacter ac libere*).

60 For the saffron flower see Pliny *Naturalis historia* 21.17.34.

61 Cf Nicholas of Lyra (on 4:31) 1024F: '... in a time of persecution the faith and the name of Christ especially grow.' The sentiment is of great antiquity. Cf Tertullian: 'The more we are cut down, the more we grow; the blood of Christians is seed' (*Apology* 50.13 CCL 1 171).

62 For a similar paraphrastic expansion of the biblical text see the 'addition' found in the 'Western' text of 4:32, which adds at this point 'and there was no quarrel [or, division] among them at all'; cf Metzger 325.

63 On the sharing of such 'goods' see the *Gloss* (on 4:32) 1025B: 'The just do not regard as their own the virtues they possess, but theirs for whose use they dispense them'; so similarly Hugh of St Cher 258 verso F. On sharing 'all good things in common,' especially the gifts of teaching and of financial resources, see the paraphrase on Gal 6:6 CWE 42 128.

64 On the possession and use of wealth by the Christian and on Christian liberality see also the colloquy 'The Godly Feast' (Thompson *Colloquies* 69–74) and the paraphrases on Luke 16:9–13.

65 'Lord Jesus Christ' represents the Vulgate text of 4:33 (so DV Conf); 'Lord Jesus' in Erasmus' text and translation (so AV RSV).

38

66 'Joseph' in the Vulgate of 4:36 (so DV Conf RSV); 'Joses' in Erasmus' text and translation (so AV)

67 In *1516* Erasmus had spoken of 'Barnabas' as a Hebrew word, but, challenged by Zúñiga, he conceded in a *1522* addition to his annotation that it might be Aramaic; cf the annotation on 4:36 (*quod est filius consolationis*). The word 'is probably best explained as a Grecized rendering of Aramaic "Barnebous," "Son of Nebo"' (H.J. de Jonge in *Apologia ad annotationes Stunicae* ASD IX-2 149:729n).

68 Cf Bede in the *Gloss* (on 4:37) 1026E, who says that Barnabas was rightly called 'son of consolation' because he 'despised the things at hand,' consoled by the things of the future (cf Bede *Super Acta* 4 PL 92 954B).

69 For Erasmus' strictures on 'profiteering' prelates and priests, see the *Moria* CWE 27 137–8, 140.

Chapter 5

1 The sharp contrast between Barnabas and Ananias as examples of virtue and vice was an exegetical commonplace, to be found in the interlinear *Gloss* (on

5:1) 1027–8, in Nicholas of Lyra 1027C (both in his literal and in his 'moral exposition'), and in Hugh of St Cher 258 verso H. Cf the annotation on 4:37 (*quod est filius consolationis*), where Erasmus notes that the story of Barnabas serves to make the example of Ananias and Sapphira more despicable.

2 Elsewhere in the *Paraphrases* Judas is represented as an example of avarice; cf eg the paraphrases on Matt 26:14; Luke 22:4; John 13:2 CWE 46 160. For the companion themes of reliance on God and vigilance in duty see the paraphrase on 1:7 (8 above).

3 'Company': *multitudine*. Erasmus frequently uses *multitudo* to designate the body of Christians. In his translation he followed the Vulgate without exception in rendering the Greek τὸ πλῆθος in Acts by *multitudo*. In Acts the Greek word refers to the body of believers in 4:32, 6:2 and 5, 15:12 and 30, 19:9 (the Jewish/Christian congregation), 21:22 (variant); cf Bruce 295 (on 15:12) and Haenchen 230 (on 4:32). In Acts the English word 'multitude' invariably represents the Latin in DV, the Greek in AV, a word frequently but not invariably echoed in this translation of the *Paraphrase*; cf the paraphrases on 4:32–6 just above.

4 Cf Bruce 132: 'The name is the OT Hananiah ... "Jah is gracious" ...'; also Haenchen 237 n1: 'Probably ..."Jahweh is merciful"...' Jerome *Liber interpretationis Hebraicorum nominum* CCL 72 143 explains the name as 'the grace of the Lord.'

5 Cf Matt 6:33.

6 Cf the paraphrase on 4:32 just above. This idea is frequently expressed in Erasmus' translation of Acts by the word *unanimiter*; cf 1:14, 2:1 and 46, 4:24, and 5:12.

39

7 Instead of the Vulgate 'tempted' (so DV Conf), Erasmus read 'filled' in both text and translation (so AV RSV). With Erasmus, Bede in the *Gloss* (on 1:3) 1028E (cf *Super Acta* 5 PL 92 954C–D), Hugh of St Cher 259 recto A, and Valla *Annot in Acta* 5 (I 848) all preferred *implevit* 'filled' to the Vulgate's *tentavit* 'tempted.' 'Filled' remains the preferred reading (Bruce 133 and Haenchen 237 n5).

8 Cf Gal 6:7: 'God is not mocked' (RSV). On the theme of deception see the paraphrase on Gal 6:7 CWE 42 128 and the paraphrase on 5:10 below.

9 Cf the interlinear *Gloss* (on 5:4) 1027–8: 'We are not compelled but encouraged to be perfect'; so Hugh of St Cher 259 recto A. Nicholas of Lyra 1028F paraphrases: 'No one compelled you to make a vow.' In his annotation *manens tibi manebat* (1516), Erasmus noted that a double accusation was implied: no one compelled Ananias to sell; and if he wanted to sell, no one compelled him to give the money.

10 Bede in the *Gloss* (on 5:5) 1029C also attempts to explain the severity of the punishment by appealing to its salutary effect upon others (cf Bede *Super Acta* 5 PL 92 955A–B).

11 Nicholas of Lyra (on 5:5) 1029C–1030F reflects a debate then current over Ananias' burial: some thought that Peter permitted burial because Ananias had repented and expiated his crime by his death; Lyra himself disagreed, suggesting that Ananias was buried in a secret and non-sacred place.

12 Cf 2:37–41 and, more specifically with reference to ignorance, 3:17–26.

13 Cf Heb 6:4–6. For the severity with which the early church looked upon post-baptismal sin see Vision 2.2 and Mandate 4.3 in *The Shepherd of Hermas* ed Graydon F. Snyder (London 1968) 35–7, 71–2; also Tertullian *De baptismo* 15.3–16.2 CCL 1 290–1 and *De pudicitia* 12.9–11 CCL 2 1303. Erasmus refused to believe that Heb 6:6 excluded forgiveness after baptism, and interpreted the verse in both paraphrase (CWE 44 227–8) and annotation (*rursum renovari*) to mean that while baptism cannot be repeated, for the once-baptized repentance will bring restoration. Cf also, in general, Erasmus' *De immensa Dei misericordia* LB V 557–88.

40

14 Cf Rabanus in the *Gloss* (on 5:5) 1029A: 'In their beginnings, laws are always commended by punishments ... This man died that others might be frightened by his example'; similarly Nicholas of Lyra 1029C and Hugh of St Cher 259 recto B. For the view that the divine anger sends destruction on some as an example to others, see the paraphrase on Jude 7 CWE 44 127.

15 For the corrective power of rebuke see eg the paraphrase on Titus 1:13 CWE 44 60; for an expression of the theme in early Christianity see Augustine *De correptione et gratia* 16.49 PL 44 946.

16 Some copies of the Vulgate (including the Vulgate of *1527*) read in 5:8: 'Peter said ... "Tell me, woman"' (so DV). Erasmus, in his own text and translation read (from *1516*): 'Peter answered ... "Tell me"' (AV). In the second phrase 'woman' appears in a minority Vulgate reading (Weber II 1705 8n; no witnesses are given for the word either in *Beginnings* III 46 or in Tischendorf II 40). In the first phrase the preferred reading of the Greek text is ἀπεκρίθη (cf *Beginnings* III 46). The normal translation of ἀπεκρίθη is 'answered,' and this is the sense in which Erasmus evidently understood the word here. Hence, in 'answered and said' Erasmus combines two readings to give a characteristic New Testament idiom (cf eg 4:19 AV). However, as the woman had not yet spoken, there were no words to answer, so the paraphrase explains that it is to her impious thoughts that Peter 'answered.' In fact, the Greek here does not mean 'answered,' but 'began to speak to,' or 'addressed' (Bruce 135, Haenchen 238 n6, and *Beginnings* IV 52 8n).

17 Hugh of St Cher had noted (on 5:1) 258 verso H: 'She [Sapphira] who was an associate in the crime, also shared in [Ananias'] death.'

18 On bishops and priests as 'apostolic' see the annotation on Luke 10:16 (*qui vos spernit, me spernit*) and *Ecclesiastes* I ASD V-4 152:400–8; 158:505–17.

19 Erasmus elsewhere expresses the view that the extraordinary gifts of the Spirit evident in the earliest church were appropriate to their own time and circumstances. Cf the statement of Conrad in the colloquy 'The Well-to-do Beggars': 'Miracles were granted [to the apostles] at the time for the sake of unbelievers' (Thompson *Colloquies* 208); cf also the annotation on 10:38 (*quomodo unxit eum*): 'It was not necessary that the gift of tongues be continual; it was enough that it was present when need demanded'; similarly the annotation on 2:8 (*linguam nostram*).

20 It is generally accepted that the Greek word ἐκκλησία appears here for the first time in Acts. In his translation Erasmus renders the word regularly throughout Acts by the Latin *ecclesia* 'church,' with only three exceptions: 2:47 (where, however, the reading is generally rejected; see Metzger 304), 5:11, and 11:26 (from *1519*). In his *Paraphrase*, he represents the word almost equally by 'congregation' (Latin *congregatio*) and by 'church,' occasionally with explanatory qualifications – eg 'congregation of believers,' 'church of believers' – once by 'multitude of disciples' (15:3), and once by 'assembly of disciples' (15:41). In this translation of the *Paraphrase*, the Latin *ecclesia* is consistently rendered by 'church,' the Latin *congregatio* by 'congregation.' Bruce 135–6, Munck 41–2, and Haenchen 239 all comment on this first use of the word ἐκκλησία in Acts. For the distinction between *ecclesia* and *congregatio* in Erasmus see Thompson *Inquisitio de fide* 68:275–82 and the notes on lines 275 and 278–9, where Thompson refers to the *Explanatio symboli*, observing that in the *Explanatio symboli* Erasmus 'expresses a low opinion of *congregatio*, and thinks *ecclesia* much more fitting for Christian use.' For the passages cited from the *Explanatio symboli* see ASD V-1 216:326–217:344 and 272:972–280:222; the latter passage offers an extensive study of the etymology and the theological significance of the two words. Cf also CWE 42 100 n4 and CWE 44 71 n7.

41

21 Cf Matt 5:15; Luke 11:33.

22 For the military image in the context of baptism see the *Enchiridion* CWE 66 26, where, as here, Erasmus uses the classical idiom for enlistment, *nomen dare*, translated here 'enlisted in service' (cf Holborn 24:14). The image arises from the Roman practice of a recruit 'giving his name,' when drafted, to the appropriate officer (cf Livy 2.24.2, 5.10.4), and was thus not without analogy in the baptismal liturgy. For an elaboration of the image of the Christian soldier see also the paraphrase on 2 Tim 2:3 CWE 44 44–5. The image of enlistment as a metaphor of baptism is rooted in Christian antiquity; cf the bibliography cited in CWE 66 26 n18.

23 The observance by the 'profane' of a reverent distance from the presence of the sacred is a practice represented in both biblical and classical literature; cf eg Heb 9:6–8; Euripides *Medea* 1053–5; Virgil *Aeneid* 6.258–9. Cf also W.S. Urquhart 'Profanity' in Hastings *Encyclopaedia* x 378–81.

24 Cf Hugh of St Cher (on 5:13) 259 recto D, who explains that terror at the fate of Ananias and Sapphira kept unbelievers from joining them. The *Gloss* (on 5:13) 1031C follows Bede (cf *Super Acta* 5 PL 92 955B) in noting that the punishment of the two who fraudulently joined the disciples offered an example to others.

25 Some editions of the Vulgate concluded 5:15 with the additional words 'and they might be freed from their infirmities' (so DV and similarly the Vulgate of *1527*; cf Weber II 1705 15n). In the paraphrase here Erasmus followed his own text and translation, which omitted them.

26 Cf John 14:12. The verse is cited here by the *Gloss* (on 5:15) 1032E, and by Hugh of St Cher 259 recto D; it had also been cited by Bede *Super Acta* 5 PL 92 955C and by Chrysostom *Hom in Acta* 12.1 PG 60 100.

27 Cf Matt 9:18–22; Mark 5:25–34; Luke 8:43–8.

28 Cf the similar characterization of Paul in the annotation on Rom 15:19 ('of wonders in the strength of the Holy Spirit') CWE 56 407–8.

29 Both Bede in the *Gloss* (on 5:17) 1033B and Nicholas of Lyra 1033C note that the Sadducees' support of the high priest was motivated by their disavowal of a resurrection (cf Bede *Super Acta* 5 PL 92 955C–D).

30 For the 'decision' see 4:15–17.

31 Nicholas of Lyra observed (on 5:18) 1033C that the apostles were placed in public custody, that is, in prison, where criminals were put, such as homicides and highwaymen; so Hugh of St Cher 259 verso E. Roman practice distinguished between custody during an investigation and imprisonment while awaiting execution (see 'prison' in OCD). For the Greek here, in the sense of 'state prison,' 'close arrest,' see Haenchen 249 n1.
   In the phrase 'laid hands on' (cf DV AV; but RSV 'arrest') Erasmus retains the Latin of the Vulgate, and the idiom of the Greek. For the significance of the idiom in martyr literature see Haenchen 215 (on 4:3).

42

32 'Malice': *malitia*; cf chapter 3 n45.

33 be proclaimed] Passive, in the folio and octavo editions of 1524, in the edition of 1534, and in LB; but in the edition of 1535, active, which does not properly construe. An allusion, perhaps, to Acts 1:4–5; but cf also in the Gospels Jesus' injunction to individuals not to speak of him, eg Matt 8:4; Mark 1:43–4; also Mark 3:12, 5:43, 7:36.

34 Cf Matt 10:26–7; Mark 4:22; Luke 8:17.

35 priests, temple wardens] In all editions *1524–1535*; in LB, 'priests and temple wardens'

36 Erasmus adopted here (5:21) his own translation (from *1516*) *ordo seniorum* 'order of elders' to express the Greek γηρουσία, referring to an official order, or council, not merely to elderly men; cf AV RSV 'senate.' The Vulgate had translated simply by 'elders'; cf DV 'ancients,' Conf 'elders.' From *1522* Erasmus adopted the same translation ('order of elders') for τὸ πρεσβυτέριον in 22:5 (Vulgate *maiores natu*), an idiom he retained in his paraphrase on the verse. See chapter 15 n22 and CWE 44 26 n9.

37 The Vulgate adds the detail (in 5:22) that the guards 'opened the prison' (so DV Conf); the preferred reading omits it (so Erasmus' text and translation, and AV RSV); see Metzger 331.

38 The plural 'wardens' in the paraphrase is noteworthy, since both here in 5:26 and above in 5:24 the word is in the singular in Erasmus' Greek text. In the Vulgate the word is unmistakably singular in 5:26 and is evidently intended as singular in 5:24. Moreover in both verses both Bede in the *Gloss* 1034F and Hugh of St Cher 259 verso F had noted that the word is singular (for Bede see *Liber retractationis* 5 PL 92 1010D–1011A). For these wardens and their distinction from the captain of the temple see chapter 4 nn15 and 2. The captain of the temple appears again in the paraphrase on 5:27.

43

39 On respect for public authority see the paraphrases on Rom 13:1–7 CWE 42 73–5 and n1 and 1 Pet 2:13–17 CWE 44 91–2.

40 Cf Matt 10:19; Mark 13:11; Luke 12:11.

41 With . . . themselves] Added in *1534*

42 Erasmus follows his own text and translation in formulating Annas' first words into a question (so AV). The Vulgate, which understands the words as a statement, represents the preferred reading (so DV Conf RSV; see Haenchen 251 and n2, Metzger 331, and for the manuscript evidence Tischendorf II 45 28n and *Beginnings* III 50).

43 With the emphasis here on the 'name' compare the paraphrase on 4:18 (34–5 above).

44 in . . . apostles] Added in *1534*. The interlinear *Gloss* 1035–6 understood literally the statement in 5:29 that 'Peter and the apostles' spoke: 'Moved by fervour and zeal they do not permit one to speak for all'; so Hugh of St Cher 259 verso G. But Nicholas of Lyra 1035C–1036F thought it more probable that Peter gave the response and the other apostles approved his speech as though it were their own. For Peter as spokesman for all the apostles see the paraphrase on 2:14 (17 above) and n50.

45 Chrysostom *Hom in Acta* 13.1 (on 5:28–9) PG 60 106 twice notes the mildness of the apostles' reply.

46 'Captain': *magistratus*; the form may be either singular or plural; cf n38 above.

47 Cf Acts 4:18–20.

44

48 'Comes to his senses again, and repents': *resipiscat*; cf the paraphrase on 2:38 (22 above) and n90.

49 For the expression 'the God of our fathers whom we worship' see 24:14; see also the paraphrase on Rom 1:9 CWE 42 16.

50 Cf the closely parallel sequence of clauses in the paraphrase on 3:18 (28 above). The prophetic prediction that one would die for the salvation of the world appears to be a loose interpretation of the 'suffering servant' songs of Isaiah; cf chapter 3 n23.

51 'Frailty of his corporeal condition': *iuxta corporis imbecillitatem*, though it might be rendered more literally 'according to the weakness of the body,' which may be intended to recall the biblical expression 'according to the flesh,' an expression Erasmus elsewhere paraphrases as *iuxta carnis infirmitatem* 'according to the infirmity of the flesh' (Rom 1:3); cf CWE 42 15. Erasmus seems to have been aware that the biblical expression 'according to the flesh,' had more than one meaning; cf the paraphrase on Rom 9:3, 'a relationship of nation and race' (CWE 42 53) and on 2 Cor 1:17.

52 For variations on this expression see chapter 3 n16. The expression here reflects Erasmus' exposition in the *1516* annotation on 5:31 (*principem et salvatorem*) of the Greek ἀρχηγός 'leader and author.'

53 For his paraphrase on the words 'to give repentance' (5:31 RSV) Erasmus first introduced his own preferred expression, *resipiscere* (cf n48), then offered here the characteristic Vulgate expression, *poenitentiam agere*; in his translation he followed the Vulgate *ad dandam poenitentiam* 'to give repentance.'

54 Erasmus follows the Vulgate (and the preferred reading; Metzger 332) rather than his own text and translation of 5:32, which read 'we are *his* witnesses' (so AV; but DV Conf RSV 'we are witnesses').

55 Cf the paraphrases on 1:3, 2:32, and 3:15 (6, 21, and 28 above).

56 The paraphrase reflects Erasmus' understanding of the Greek; he observes in a *1516* annotation on 5:32 (*et nos sumus testes*) that the intent is: 'It is not so much we who are witnesses as the Holy Spirit himself, by whose power these things are done.'

57 Cf Nicholas of Lyra (on 5:32) 1036F: 'He who speaks in us witnesses to those things, and by his power signs and wonders are done.'

58 Cf Acts 22:3.

45

59 Bede in the *Gloss* (on 5:37) 1037C–1038D, referring to Josephus, says that Theudas was a magician and a prophet who promised to divide the waters of

the Jordan and provide a crossing (cf Bede *Super Acta* 5 PL 92 956B). So also Nicholas of Lyra 1037C. For the story in Josephus see *Jewish Antiquities* 20.5.1 (97–8).

60 Both the *Gloss* (on 5:37) 1038E (following Bede *Super Acta* 5 PL 92 956B–C) and Nicholas of Lyra 1037C–1038F affirm that Judas objected to Roman taxation on religious grounds. Nicholas of Lyra also identifies the time as that of the census under Caesar Augustus (cf Luke 2:1–3). For the story, set in the time of the census, see Josephus *Jewish Antiquities* 18.1.1 (1–10). Erasmus does not discuss the historical difficulties raised by the narrative in Acts, in spite of the fact that in a *1527* addition to the annotation on 5:36 (*extitit Theodas*), he refers to Eusebius' *Ecclesiastical History* 2.11 PG 20 161C–165A, where Theudas' revolt is assigned to the time when Fadus was procurator of Judaea (AD 44–6). Indeed in the same annotation (from *1516*) he refers the reader to Chrysostom, who (commenting on Matt 22:17) spoke as though both Theudas and Judas stirred up revolt on the issue of taxation (*In Matthaeum homiliae* 70.1 PG 58 655). For the historical difficulties see Bruce 147, Munck 48 and 51, and Haenchen 252 n7.

61 Cf Rom 9:19.

46

62 For the scriptural echoes in this and the previous sentence see Matt 10:17–22; Mark 13:9–13; and 1 Pet 4:13–14. The Gospel sayings are cited in the interlinear *Gloss* (1039–40): in the gloss on 5:40 the saying 'they will deliver you up' is cited; in the gloss on 5:41 the saying 'you will be hated.' Hugh of St Cher 260 recto B likewise cites the Gospel sayings as commentary on 5:40 and 5:41.

63 The interlinear *Gloss* (on 5:41) 1039–40 also quotes Matt 5:12; likewise Hugh of St Cher 260 recto B. Erasmus quotes the Vulgate rather than his own translation.

64 Cf Nicholas of Lyra (on 5:42) 1040E: 'In no way terrified by words or lashes, but eager rather to preach Christ more boldly.'

65 For the expression see 1 Cor 11:25 and 15:3.

Chapter 6

1 See 11:26 for the title 'Christians.' Like Erasmus, the interlinear *Gloss* (on 6:1) 1039–40 explains that 'Christians were at that time called disciples'; so also Hugh of St Cher 260 recto B. For the nomenclature of Christians in the first century see IDB I 571–2, and *Beginnings* V 375–92.

2 The paraphrase here anticipates a *1527* addition to the annotation on 6:1 (*murmur Graecorum*) where Erasmus notes that the Greek word Ἑλληνιστῶν here referred to 'Hellenists,' not 'Greeks,' that is, Jews who, due to their place of origin, were Greek-speakers; on the other hand, the term 'Hebrew' denoted

race, 'Jew' religion. The paraphrase on 9:29 (67 below)identifies 'Hellenist' in the same way as here. The *Gloss* 1039C allowed that 'Greeks' here were either gentiles living then in Jerusalem, or Jews born and raised among the Greeks. On the much-discussed meaning of 'Hellenist' see Bruce 151, Munck 56-7 and 301-4, Haenchen 260 n3 and 267-8, and *Beginnings* v 59-74.

3 Nicholas of Lyra (on 6:1) 1040F offered two explanations for the grievance: 1/ since the Greek women were less educated, they were rejected from the ministry; 2/ the Greeks were discriminated against in the supply of necessary provisions. Hugh of St Cher 260 recto B adopted the first explanation. Modern commentators consistently adopt the second; cf Bruce 151, Munck 55, and Haenchen 261-2.

4 Cf the interlinear *Gloss* 1039-40: 'They seek the consensus of the crowd – which should be taken as an example'; so Hugh of St Cher 260 recto C.

5 us] In all editions *1524-1535*; in LB, 'you'

6 For this comparison with the body see 1 Cor 12:12-27.

7 For integrity 'tested and approved' see 1 Tim 3:10 and the annotation on Acts 6:3 (*boni testimonii*). With the Latin expression here, *spectatae probitatis*, compare eg Cicero's ironic description of Mark Antony, '*Quam spectatus, quam probatus,*' in *Philippics* 2.28.69.

8 'Service' represents the Latin *functio*; its use here anticipates a *1527* addition to the annotation on 6:3 (*super hoc opus*), where Erasmus indicates that the Latin *functio* is a fitting translation of the Greek χρεία. He himself translated (from *1519*) *hoc negotii* 'this work,' also represented here in the paraphrase. For the word *functio* used to describe the apostolic ministry see the annotation on Rom 1:5 ('grace and apostleship') CWE 56 18-19; and cf the paraphrases on Rom 1:5 CWE 42 15, on Titus 1:3 and Philem 1 CWE 44 58 and 71, and on Acts 13:2 (84 below).

47

9 Nicholas of Lyra (on 6:5) 1042F clarifies in a similar way: 'a native of Antioch, and a gentile committed to Judaism.' The paraphrase anticipates a *1527* addition to the annotation on 6:5 (*et Nicolaum advenam*), where the same language as here is used to clarify the biblical expression 'a proselyte of Antioch.'

10 Here, the paraphrase on 6:6 anticipates a *1527* annotation (*et imposuerunt illis manus*) where Erasmus suggests it is Rabanus who observes that in conferring sacred orders the people elect, the bishop ordains – a custom, Erasmus adds, long preserved in the early church. For the distinction between people and bishops see the *Gloss* (on 6:5) 1041B, citing Rabanus. The *Gloss* is cited here also by Hugh of St Cher 260 recto D. For Erasmus on ordination see the *Explanatio symboli* ASD V-1 284:318-23 and 285:348-52. See also Payne *Theology of the Sacraments* 104-9 and Manfred Hoffmann 'Erasmus on Church and Ministry' ERSY 6 (1986) 1-30, especially 16-19.

11 Cf Mark 10:16; also Matt 19:13–15 and Luke 18:15–17.

12 Cf Nicholas of Lyra 1042F commenting on the words 'They chose Stephen, a man full of faith' (6:5): 'Because such a business could be confidently committed to him, and the same must be understood of the others.'

13 For an imaginative contemporary portrait of a dinner enjoyed with similar religious devotion see the colloquy 'The Godly Feast' (Thompson *Colloquies* 46–78, especially 55).

14 The *Gloss* (on 6:6) 1042D, citing Bede, notes that the seven were ordained as ministers both of the sacred altar and of the common table, and that for ministry at the sacred table, the imposition of hands was proper (cf Bede *Liber retractationis* PL 92 1012A–B); so Hugh of St Cher 260 recto D, citing the *Gloss*. In *Ecclesiastes* I Erasmus acknowledged that deacons along with priests shared in the sacred service of the bishop when need demanded (ASD V-4 88: 146–9), but he also recognized the subordinate role of the deacon in the church of his own day, and defined the deacon's special office – [*recitare*] *sacram lectionem*; see *Ecclesiastes* I ASD V-4 134:70–1. On the varied functions and considerable prestige of deacons in the early church see EEC 257–8.

15 For the image of the yoke see Matt 11:29–30, though 'submit to the yoke' was a classical expression implying surrender and abasement (cf eg Cicero *De officiis* 3.30.109; Caesar *De bello Gallico* 1.12.5). On humility as the 'first step towards contrition and confession' see CWE 44 177 n13; also the paraphrase on Mark 1:5 CWE 49 16–17.

16 Erasmus paraphrases the Vulgate of 6:8, 'full of grace' (so DV Conf RSV and the preferred reading; Metzger 339). His Greek text read 'full of faith' (so AV), though he translated 'full of grace' until 1535. For the ambiguity of the biblical word 'grace' in Erasmus' *Paraphrases*, where 'grace' is represented as a divine and saving gift but also a winsome quality of character, see Robert D. Sider '"In Terms Quite Plain and Clear": The Exposition of Grace in the New Testament *Paraphrases* of Erasmus' *Erasmus in English* 15 (1987–8) 23.

17 'Virtue': *virtus*, evidently referring ambiguously here both to Stephen's moral character and his special power. For the double meaning of the word see the annotation on Rom 1:4 ('in power') CWE 56 15–16.

18 For the similitude see *Adagia* I v 62, which refers to Pliny's description of the north-east wind, here *Caecias*, defined by Pliny as east-north-east; cf *Naturalis historia* 2.46.120–1, 18.77.333–5.

48

19 'Societies': *sodalitates*. Though the interpretation of 6:9 as a whole is problematic, modern scholars assume that a synagogue in the conventional sense is intended (cf Bruce 156 and Haenchen 271). Elsewhere Erasmus uses *sodalitas* of the church (cf Hoffmann 5–7 in the article cited n10 above), but there is no

annotation on this verse to illuminate his interpretation here of 'synagogue' as a 'society' or club. The interlinear *Gloss* (on 6:9) 1043–4 had explained 'synagogue' as 'congregation' or 'gathering.'

20 Cf Nicholas of Lyra (on 6:9) 1043C: 'These are the names of regions close to Judaea'; see also, for the Diaspora, chapter 2 n27.

21 The *Gloss* (on 6:10) 1044E quotes Matt 10:19–20 and Luke 21:15; Nicholas of Lyra 1043C–1044E quotes Luke 21:15.

22 Cf Lev 24:13–16, cited by Nicholas of Lyra (on 6:13) 1044F.

23 For the analogous trial of Jesus see Matt 26:59–66; Mark 14:55–64. The analogy between the trial and death of Stephen and that of Jesus is widely recognized: cf Bruce 157, Munck 59. It was well established in the exegetical tradition; cf the interlinear *Gloss* (on 6:11) 1045–6 and Hugh of St Cher 260 verso F.

24 The Vulgate of 6:13 read, 'This man does not cease to speak words against' (so DV Conf RSV and the preferred reading, for which see Metzger 341). Erasmus' Greek text *1516–1535* read, 'This man does not cease to speak *blasphemous* words against' (so AV). 'Blasphemies' in the paraphrase is ambiguous: it may represent Erasmus' text, or it may represent his interpretation of the Vulgate; cf Erasmus' reply to Lee that one can hardly speak words against God and the temple without blasphemy (*Responsio ad annotationes Lei* LB IX 207C). As early as *1516* Erasmus distrusted his own reading, believing that 'blasphemous' was a scribal addition; and in *1522* he was able to add the evidence of Chrysostom, who read 'words' rather than 'blasphemous words'; see the annotation on 6:13 (*non cessat loqui verba*). For Chrysostom see *Hom in Acta* 15.1 PG 60 120, though in *Nicene and Post-Nicene Fathers* 1st series XI (New York 1889) 95 the biblical text is cited according to AV and has 'blasphemous words.'

25 Erasmus follows the Vulgate in paraphrasing in 6:13 'the holy place' (so DV Conf), rather than his own text and translation (from *1516*), which read '*this* holy place' (so AV RSV). The reading is uncertain (Metzger 341); for the textual evidence see Tischendorf II 52 13n.

26 Cf Matt 24:2; Mark 13:2; Luke 19:43–4. Nicholas of Lyra (on 10:14) 1045B cites the logion from the Gospels, noting that Christ did not say he himself would destroy the temple, but predicted that it would be destroyed.

27 Cf John 2:19; Chrysostom *Hom in Acta* 15.1 (on 6:14) PG 60 121 also notes that Christ was accused of intending to destroy the temple.

49

28 In all editions of the *Paraphrase* Erasmus included 7:1–2a in the paraphrases on chapter 6; in doing so he seems to have followed the text of the Vulgate represented in his 1527 edition. For his New Testament (all editions *1516–1535*, both text and translation) Erasmus observed the standard division between

chapters 6 and 7, though, indeed, the annotations on 7:1–2a were, until the final edition of 1535, included with those on chapter 6. Cf 94 n1; also the paraphrase on Titus 2:15 CWE 44 63 and n1.

29 For Caiaphas, see the paraphrase on 4:6 (31 above) and n17.

Chapter 7

1 For the division of the text between chapters 6 and 7 see chapter 6 n28.

2 For the image of the spiritual house acceptable to God see 1 Pet 2:5. For God as spirit see John 4:24.

3 See the paraphrase on 2:40 (23 above) and n104; also the paraphrase on 1:12 (9 above) and n68 and on 4:7 (32 above) and n23.

4 The final clauses of this sentence evoke by a somewhat free association several biblical texts: 'worship God in a pure way' (John 4:23–4; cf also Mal 1:11; James 1:27); 'spiritual law' (Rom 7:14); 'offer themselves a living and holy temple for the Holy Spirit' (Rom 12:1; 1 Cor 3:17, 6:19; Eph 2:21–2).

5 For the theme of the rebellious people, anticipating here 7:51, see Exod 32:9, 33:5; Num 27:14; Isa 63:10.

6 Stress on Abraham's obedience belongs to the exegetical tradition; so the interlinear *Gloss* (on 7:3) 1047–8, and Chrysostom *Hom in Acta* 15.3 PG 60 123. That true sons imitate their father is a recurrent theme in the *Paraphrases*; cf eg the paraphrases on John 8:37–9 CWE 46 115 and nn60, 61; on Rom 4:1 and 12, 8:15 and on Gal 3:8 CWE 42 26, 29, 47, and 110; and on 1 Tim 1:2 CWE 44 5–6.

7 The doxology is frequent in the New Testament; cf eg Rom 11:36, 16:27; Gal 1:5; Phil 4:20; 1 Tim 1:17; 2 Tim 4:18.

8 Cf the paraphrase on 5:30 (44 above) and n49.

50

9 For the age and death of Terah see Gen 11:32. For Chrysostom it was not old age but faithlessness (τῷ ἄπιστος εἶναι) that prevented Terah from moving beyond Charan (*Hom in Acta* 15.3 PG 60 123).

10 For the complementary relationship between promise and fulfilment – a theme central in Erasmus' understanding of faith – see the paraphrases on Rom 4:18–21 CWE 42 31; see also the paraphrase on Acts 3:17 (28 above) and n25.

11 Gen 15:13 foretells 'affliction' for four hundred years; Ex 12:40 records that the entire time of the Israelites' 'sojourn' in Egypt was four hundred and thirty years. For his text and translation of 7:6 (all editions) Erasmus read like the preferred Vulgate 'four hundred years,' but in a 1527 annotation on 7:6 (*annis quadringentis*) he claimed to have found an old edition of the Vulgate that read 'four hundred and thirty years,' and he cited Rabanus (represented in the *Gloss*

1050D), who read 'four hundred and thirty years.' Indeed, the Vulgate printed in Erasmus' 1527 New Testament reads 'four hundred and thirty years,' though the reading is unattested in Weber (cf II 1707 6n) and is not found as a variant in Tischendorf (cf II 54 6n).

12 Cf the interlinear *Gloss* (on 7:7) 1049–50: 'freed from the servitude of men, they will begin to serve.' For the Old Testament scriptures in this paragraph see Gen 15:13–14.

13 At this point in 7:8 the verb is unexpressed in the Greek text, in the Vulgate, and in Erasmus' translation of 1516. In a 1519 annotation on 7:8 (*et Isaac Jacob*) Erasmus argued that 'begot' is to be understood – 'and Isaac begot Jacob' – and so translated henceforth (so DV AV Conf RSV). However, in the second clause of verse 8, though Erasmus read (text and translation) *atque hic genuit Isaac* 'and he [Abraham] begot Isaac,' he expressed in an annotation (*et sic genuit Isaac 1519, 1527*) his preference for the Vulgate reading, 'and *thus* he [Abraham] begot Isaac' (that is, 'under the covenant of circumcision, Abraham begot Isaac'). Thus in the sequence of generations, it is not birth but circumcision that becomes the point of attention. The paraphrase may reflect this reading of the passage. For the circumcision of Isaac see Gen 21:4. The circumcision of Jacob is not recorded in the Bible, but the circumcision of the sons of Jacob is implied in Gen 34:15.

14 For the details beyond the text of Acts (brothers, cistern, merchants) see Gen 37:22–8. These details are recalled also by the interlinear *Gloss* (on 7:10) 1051–2 and Hugh of St Cher 261 recto B; Nicholas of Lyra 1051C notes the brothers, the cistern, and the Egyptian prison. For Jesus' deliverance into the hands of the chief priests and elders at the price of 'thirty pieces of silver' see Matt 26:14–16, 47–57; Mark 14:10–11, 43–53; Luke 22:3–6, 47–54; and for Joseph as a type of Christ, with reference particularly to the thirty pieces of silver and to Christ's death, see Origen *In Exodum homiliae* 1.4 PG 12 300C–D.

15 For Joseph's skill in interpreting dreams and for his prudential foresight see Gen 41:9–49.

16 In a 1535 annotation on 7:14 (*in septuaginta quinque animabus descendit Iacob*) Erasmus observed that the number given in Acts is based upon the Septuagint text of Gen 46:27 rather than the Hebrew, which reads 'seventy.' Cf Bruce 165.

17 In the paraphrase on 7:16 Erasmus follows his own translation and the Vulgate in writing 'Hamor, son of Shechem' (so DV Conf). But his Greek text read Ἐμὸρ τοῦ Συχέμ, a text construed in AV as 'Hamor father of Shechem,' in conformity with the narrative of Gen 33:19 and Josh 24:32 (cf Bruce 166). In fact, the preferred reading of 7:16 is Ἐμμὼρ ἐν Συχέμ 'Hamor in Shechem' (so RSV; cf Metzger 344–5).

The detail of the hundred shekels of silver is added by Erasmus from the accounts of Gen 33:19 and Josh 24:32; both these accounts say that Jacob bought the land, and the latter adds that Joseph was buried in it. In his *1516* annotation on 7:16 (*quod emit Abraham*) Erasmus recognizes the difficulties arising from the conflation here of several stories: 1/ Abraham's purchase for four hundred shekels of a burial plot in Hebron for Sarah (Gen 23:1–20; Jacob requested burial in this plot according to Gen 49:29–33); and 2/ Jacob's purchase described in the accounts cited above. Cf Bruce 165–6.

51

18 In the paraphrase on 7:18 Erasmus follows his own text and translation in omitting 'in Egypt' (so AV); the words are included in the Vulgate (so DV Conf; cf RSV 'over Egypt') and in the preferred reading, for the difficulties in which, however, see Metzger 345–6.

19 For the detail of the midwives see Exod 1:15–16.

20 Nicholas of Lyra (on 1:20) 1054F notes that here Stephen replies to the charge of blasphemy against Moses.

21 The paraphrase on 7:20 follows the Vulgate and Erasmus' translation: Moses was *gratus deo*, a phrase rendered by DV and Conf as 'acceptable to God.' Erasmus' annotation on the verse (*gratus deo*) argues that the Greek ἀστεῖος here must have the sense of χαρίεις, that is, both *gratus* 'pleasing' and *urbanus* 'elegant', 'lovely.' Cf AV 'exceeding fair' (footnote, 'fair to God'). RSV translates 'beautiful before God.'

22 For the details (river, basket) see Exod 2:3. The paraphrastic art invites the added details; cf here the 'Western' text of 7:21, which also includes the detail of the river (Metzger 346–7).

23 In 7:23 Erasmus' text and translation (all editions *1516–1535*) read 'his brethren, the sons of Israel.' The omission of 'the sons' in the paraphrase (*1524* folio and subsequent editions) appears to be an inadvertent error on the part of Erasmus or the compositor of the first edition.

24 Cf the dedicatory letter to Francis I for the *Paraphrase on Mark*: 'When has a king more kingly majesty than when he ... succours the oppressed ...? (Ep 1400:135–7). But cf also the *1519* annotation on 7:25 (*existimabat autem intelligere fratres*) where Erasmus refers to Augustine's question whether the murder was an indication of Moses' character, or a praiseworthy act done at God's command; see Augustine *Quaestiones in Heptateuchum* 2.2 PL 34 597.

25 Cf the *Gloss* (on 7:25) 1055A which shows here how Moses was a type of Christ; so Hugh of St Cher 261 verso F. Cf also the interlinear *Gloss* 1055–6 on the words 'they did not understand' (RSV): 'Obviously, a type of the Jews.'

26 Erasmus' text and translation read, with the Vulgate, 'Madian' (so DV AV Conf). For Madian as 'Midian' (so RSV) see 'Midian' in IDB III 375.

27 Erasmus follows his text and translation of 7:30 (from *1516*), which reads 'an angel of the Lord' (so AV), rather than the Vulgate and the preferred reading (Metzger 347–8), which have simply 'an angel' (so DV Conf RSV).

52

28 The preferred reading of 7:32 does not repeat 'God' in the last two phrases: 'the God of Abraham and of Isaac and of Jacob' (Metzger 348–9; so RSV); but Erasmus followed here the Vulgate and his own Greek text (from 1516): 'the God of Abraham and the God of Isaac and the God of Jacob' (so DV AV Conf).

29 Erasmus recognized that a Hebrew figure of speech lay behind the Greek words (in 7:34), which may be translated literally as 'seeing I have seen' (so the Vulgate and DV). The expression means, he said, 'to see with keen attention'; cf the annotation on *videns vidi*. From 1519 Erasmus translated 'I have seen, I have seen' (so AV), but here in the paraphrase he uses the Latin idiom *etiam atque etiam* to indicate emphasis. Cf RSV 'I have surely seen,' Conf 'I have seen all.'

30 Cf Matt 21:23; Mark 11:28; Luke 20:2.

31 at that time] *tunc* in all editions 1524–1535; in LB, *hunc*, to read 'God . . . sent him'

32 Cf Nicholas of Lyra (on 7:27) 1056F: 'He did not understand that God had made Moses protector and liberator of his people.' For the images of prince and author see chapter 3 n16.

33 Nicholas of Lyra (on 7:35) 1058F also interprets the 'hand' of the angel as the power to assist Moses.

34 Cf Bede in the *Gloss* (on 7:37) 1058E: 'Lest the doctrine of Christ should seem new, Moses . . . preached that Christ would come in the form of a man and give the precepts of life' (cf Bede *Super Acta* 7 PL 92 958D).

35 'With the multitude now as witness': *teste multitudine*. *Multitudo* here represents the Greek (7:38) ἐκκλησία, Vulgate *ecclesia*. In 1516 Erasmus translated '*ecclesia*,' but from 1519, '*congregatio*'; cf DV AV 'church,' Conf 'assembly,' RSV 'congregation.' On terms for the church in Erasmus see the paraphrase on 5:11 (40 above) and n20.

36 The Greek of 7:38 expresses clearly the fact that it is the angel who spoke to Moses. The Vulgate is more ambiguous and would permit the interpretation that Moses spoke with the angel, as here in the paraphrase. For all his editions of the New Testament Erasmus accepted the Vulgate translation.

37 Cf Nicholas of Lyra (on 7:38) 1059C: 'By the words of life are meant the precepts of the Decalogue . . . they are called the words of life because those who kept them did not incur the punishment of bodily death which was inflicted on transgressors, as was said in Galatians 3[:12].' Hugh of St Cher 262 recto A also understands the 'words of life' to be the Law – for it was a preparation for the life to be found in the New Testament. For the Law as 'conferring life' see Deut 32:45–7 and Haenchen 283. Elsewhere, also, Erasmus reflects upon the question of how the Law confers life. Cf the paraphrase on Gal 3:12 CWE 42 110: 'Those who observe [the Law] will indeed obtain life, but not the eternal life which faith promises'; and the annotation on Rom 10:5 ('for Moses wrote') CWE 56 278–80.

53

38 The interlinear *Gloss* (on 7:41) 1059–60 refers to the 'Egyptians who worship the ox,' and Hugh of St Cher 262 recto B refers to Apis worshipped in Egypt in the form of a bull. For Apis see Pliny *Naturalis historia* 8.71.184–6.

39 For the details (dancing and feasting) added by Erasmus see Exod 32:6.

40 For the characterization of gods made by human hands as unable to speak see eg Ps 115:4–8; Jer 10:3–5; Hab 2:18–19.

41 The paraphrase here reflects images from Rom 1:18–28. Cf the paraphrase on Rom 1:24 CWE 42 18: God 'has allowed them to rush headlong into the gratification of the desires of their own hearts.' Here, as in Rom 1:24, 26, 28 Erasmus has paraphrased the biblical 'gave them up' (AV RSV) by 'has allowed,' substituting *passus est* in paraphrase for the *tradidit* of his translation. For the significance of this change see CWE 42 18 n20.

42 The interlinear *Gloss* (on 7:42) 1059–60 explains the 'host of heaven' as 'sun, moon, stars'; so also Hugh of St Cher 262 recto B. Bede in the *Gloss* 1060D explains the phrase as 'the stars' (cf *Liber retractationis* 7 PL 92 1014A). The Christian critique of the divinity ascribed to the elements is found in the earliest writers; cf eg Tertullian *Ad nationes* 2.2.14–6.7 CCL 1 43–51 and Clement of Alexandria *Protrepticus* 2, 4, 5 PG 8 96A, 164A–B, 169B.

43 Cf the *Gloss* (on 7:43) 1060E, citing Bede: 'Although you seem to offer … sacrifices at the tabernacle of God, nevertheless in your whole mind you have embraced the shrine of Moloch … an idol of the Ammonites' (cf Bede *Super Acta* 7 PL 92 959A). For Moloch as an Ammonite god see 1 Kings 11:7.

44 Cf the *Gloss* (on 7:43) 1060E, citing Bede: 'You have given up the true and living God and have taken up the star Remphan as your God. He means Lucifer, to whose worship the Saracens were devoted' (cf Bede *Super Acta* 7 PL 92 959B); similarly Hugh of St Cher 262 recto C. Nicholas of Lyra 1060F likewise identifies the 'star of Remphan' with 'the morning star.' Venus, the morning star, is called Lucifer, the light-bringer.

The Saracens appear in Ammianus Marcellinus (14.4.1–7) as nomads roaming the Arabian peninsula. The term later came to be applied to Arab tribes in general, and eventually to Muslim subjects of the Caliph; cf *Encyclopedia Britannica* 15th ed (1990) vol 10 (*Micropedia*) 445.

The spelling of Remphan varies in the manuscript tradition: Erasmus read Remphan (hence the paraphrase; so also AV), the Vulgate Rempham (DV Conf; cf RSV 'Rephan'). In the Septuagint of Amos 5:26 the word appears as Raiphan. Cf Bruce 174 and Haenchen 284 n1.

45 Erasmus follows his translation of *1516*, 'carry you away into Babylon.' From *1519* he translated 'carry you away beyond (*ultra*) Babylon' (cf DV Conf RSV). The Vulgate had written 'carry you across (*trans*) Babylon.' In 1521 Erasmus debated the reading with Zúñiga (*Apologia ad annotationes Stunicae* ASD IX-2

148), where he defended the translation 'beyond,' noting, however, that some Latin manuscripts read 'into Babylon.' He discussed the reading again in a 1522 annotation on 7:43 (*et transferam vos trans Babylonem*).

46 Cf Matt 5:17.

47 Nicholas of Lyra observes (on 7:44) 1059c that Stephen now turns to the charge of blasphemy against the temple, acknowledging first that the temple had been made in accordance with the divine will. Cf also the *Gloss* 1059B, citing Bede: 'Just as the tent was abandoned in the making of the temple, so also . . . the temple itself had to be destroyed when a better one followed' (cf Bede *Super Acta* 7 PL 92 959C); similarly Hugh of St Cher 262 recto D.

48 The paraphrase goes beyond the biblical text of 7:44 in distinguishing the tent and the ark; cf Hugh of St Cher 262 recto D, who explains that the tent is called a tent 'of witness' because the ark that contained the 'testimony' was in it. For tabernacle and ark distinguished see Exod 25–7, 35:10–12.

54

49 'Embraced': *amplexi sunt*; cf the interlinear *Gloss* 1059–60 on the Vulgate's *suscipientes* 'receiving' (7:45 DV): 'To be venerated and carried on their shoulders.'

'Jesus' (so DV AV), for the Old Testament figure Joshua (so Conf RSV), is a transliteration of the Greek, which appears as *Iesu* in the Vulgate and Erasmus' translation of 7:45. On the identity of the two names see the annotation on Matt 1:21 (*et vocabis nomen eius Iesum*); cf chapter 13 n20.

50 'Into the possession of the gentiles' (so DV and AV), reflecting Erasmus' choice of the Vulgate's translation of the Greek ἐν τῇ κατασχέσει τῶν ἐθνῶν (7:45) for both his translation (all editions 1516–1535) and his paraphrase

51 For Solomon as a man of peace see 1 Kings 5:3–5. For the thought in this and the next sentence see the interlinear *Gloss* (on 7:47) 1059–60: 'Solomon, the figure of the truly peaceable one, built a house for the Lord'; so Hugh of St Cher 262 recto D: 'Solomon in the figure of Christ, the truly peaceable one, built the temple.' Cf the paraphrase on 3:11 (27 above) and n9.

52 first] Added in 1534

53 Cf Jer 7:4, also cited by Hugh of St Cher (on 7:46) 262 recto D.

54 For the comparison of Christ and Solomon see Matt 12:42 and n51 above.

55 Cf John 4:24.

56 Commenting on 'heaven is my throne and earth my footstool' (7:49), Nicholas of Lyra 1060F says that the expression is metaphorical, designating that God is present everywhere in the sky and on earth. Cf the allusion to 7:48 in the paraphrase on John 4:20 CWE 46 57 and n35.

57 Cf Bede in the *Gloss* (on 7:49–50) 1060E–1061A, where the citation from Isa 66:1–2a is expounded by reference to 66:2b: 'On whom does my spirit rest

except on the humble and quiet and those fearing my words?' (cf Bede *Super Acta* 7 PL 92 960A); so Hugh of St Cher 262 recto D–262 verso E. For the 'quiet heart' as the abode of the Spirit see the paraphrase on 1:14 (10 above) and n76, and the paraphrase on 2:1 (14 above).

58 For the temple as an example of Old Testament 'shadows' see the paraphrase on John 4:20 CWE 46 57.

59 Cf n5 above.

60 For the heart cleansed and the ears purged of 'obtuseness,' as well as for the 'obtuseness of mind' and 'dullness of hearing' just below, see Matt 13:15, a verse echoing Isa 6:10. 'Obtuseness' here translates the Latin *crassitudine*, which may reflect the Vulgate of Matt 13:15, *incrassatum*. On *crassitudo* see chapter 2 n4. For the distinction between the carnal and spiritual senses of the Law see CWE 42 45 n2. Cf also Hugh of St Cher (on 7:51) 262 verso E: 'He shows that carnal circumcision ... without the spiritual cannot avail for salvation.'

55

61 Cf the *Gloss* (on 7:51) 1061B: 'Above, speaking with a view to persuasion, he said "our fathers"; now with a view to rebuke he calls them only "their fathers" whom they resemble in malice.' On sons imitating fathers see n6 above.

62 Cf the paraphrase on 22:14 (130–1 below) and n16.

63 On the responsibility of the Jews for the death of Christ see the paraphrase on 2:23 (19 above) and n67.

64 'Not so long ago': *pridem*; for the sense here see Erasmus' *Paraphrasis in Elegantiae Vallae* ASD I-4 282:84–8, where *pridem* is listed with *nuper* and *iampridem*, and distinguished from the latter ('immediately past') as referring to 'time a little further past.'

65 A reference apparently to the prophecies of the destruction of Jerusalem; cf eg Mark 13:2; Luke 19:43–4.

66 A topos of the traditional exegesis of the phrase 'gazed into heaven' (7:55 RSV); cf the interlinear *Gloss* 1061–2, 'where he had looked for help'; so, precisely, Hugh of St Cher 262 verso F; cf Nicholas of Lyra 1062F, 'where he had placed his trust.' Cf Ps 121:1–2; also the paraphrases on John 11:41 and 17:1 CWE 46 145 and 192.

67 The image of the athlete, based on such biblical texts as 1 Cor 9:24–7, 2 Tim 2:5 and 4:7–8, and Heb 12:1–2, is pervasive in the literature of martyrdom from the earliest times: cf eg *The Martyrdom of St Polycarp* 17 and *The Martyrs of Lyons* 42 in *Acts of the Christian Martyrs* introduction and translation by Herbert Musurillo (Oxford 1972) 14 and 74 respectively; and, for Latin literature, Tertullian *Ad martyras* 3.3–5 CCL 1 5–6. Cf also the paraphrase on 1 Tim 6:12 CWE 44 36–7 and n12. For the theme of 'strengthening' see the next note.

68 Cf the *Gloss* (on 7:56) 1062E, citing Bede: 'To strengthen the endurance of the martyr, heaven is opened' (cf Bede *Super Acta* 7 PL 92 960B); cf also Nicholas of Lyra 1062F on the same verse: 'To strengthen him by special grace.'

69 Possibly an allusion to the doctrine of reserve, that holy secrets should not be revealed to the unholy, though in this case Erasmus finds reserve inappropriate. For the doctrine of reserve in early Christianity, see Salvatore R.C. Lilla *Clement of Alexandria: A Study in Christian Platonism and Gnosticism* (Oxford 1971) 142–58.

70 This paraphrase on the biblical 'right hand of God' may be inspired by Erasmus' text of the Vulgate of 7:55, which read 'at the right hand of the power of God.' It is the text of the Vulgate of 1527, but it is not the preferred Latin text; see Weber II 1710. See the annotation on 7:55 (*virtutis dei*), where a 1527 addition affirms that not only the Greek, but even the better Latin manuscripts read 'at the right hand of God.'

71 On the distinction between 'testimonies' and 'arguments' see chapter 4 n44.

72 Cf Ps 110:1; Heb 1:13.

56

73 For the law see Lev 24:13–16. The *Gloss* (on 7:58) 1063B quotes the law that those convicted of blasphemy be stoned outside the city; so Hugh of St Cher 262 verso E.

74 For the part witnesses played in the death of the accused see Deut 17:2–7 and Haenchen 292 n9.

75 Cf Nicholas of Lyra (on 7:58) 1063C, who explains that the witnesses laid aside their clothes 'to kill him more quickly and with less impediment.'

76 Cf 1 Pet 2:21–3; also Isa 53:7.

77 Cf Luke 23:34.

78 'In the Lord' represents an inferior reading of the Vulgate (7:60; Weber II 1710 59n); it appears in the Vulgate of 1527 (so DV). Erasmus rejected the reading for his text and translation (so AV Conf RSV).

79 'Stephen' – Στέφανος in Greek – means 'crown' and is used of the crown of victory at the public games (see LSJ II 2). For the image of the martyr's crown see 2 Tim 4:6–8 and Rev 2:10, and the passages cited in Musurillo, n67 above.

80 'First-fruits': *primitias*; cf Rom 8:23, 16:5; and 1 Cor 15:20. In his annotations on Rom 16:5 ('who is the first of the church of Asia') CWE 56 425 and 1 Cor 15:20 (*primitiae dormientium*) Erasmus explains the Greek term ἀπαρχή both as 'first of all' and as the best of the produce, which is usually consecrated to God.

81 With the last sentences compare the *Gloss* (on 7:60) 1064E: 'Well is it said, "he slept," and not "he died," because he offered the sacrifice of love, and slept in the hope of the resurrection. Saints do not die, since they are changed into something better, and the temporal life is changed into the eternal.'

Chapter 8

1 The self-willed perversity of spiritual blindness is a theme to which Erasmus frequently recurs in the *Paraphrases*; cf eg the paraphrases on John 9 (the story of the man born blind), especially on 9:5 and 9:39 CWE 46 122 and 128; on Mark 3:5 CWE 49 47: 'obstinate in their malice ... they had themselves hearts blinded by earthly desires, so that of their own volition they did not see'; on Rom 10:19 CWE 42 62; and on 1 Tim 1:13 and 6:5 CWE 44 10 and 35. On the relation of knowledge and will in late medieval thought see Oberman *Harvest* 63–5; see also the discussion on faith in the *Explanatio symboli* cited n62 below.

2 For the sentiment see the paraphrase on 9:3 (63 below).

3 Cf Gal 1:14.

4 For the wolf-sheep image see Matt 10:16; Luke 10:3; John 10:12; for the persecutor-preacher contrast see Gal 1:23. Images of Paul as the ravening wolf of Gen 49:27 and as the persecutor turned preacher are found in early Christian literature; cf Robert D. Sider 'Literary Artifice and the Figure of Paul in the Writings of Tertullian' in *Paul and the Legacies of Paul* ed William S. Babcock (Dallas 1990) 102. For the continuity of the wolf image applied to Paul through the medieval period see n12 below.

5 Cf the *Gloss* (on 8:3) 1065A: 'He did not stone, but consented to those who stoned, and so would have perished if God's grace and repentance had not come to his aid, because those who act and those who assent are worthy of death'; so Hugh of St Cher 262 verso H, and Nicholas of Lyra 1065C.

57

6 Cf the interlinear *Gloss* (on 8:1) 1065–6: 'As the shepherds of the flock, the apostles were firmer than the others'; so Hugh of St Cher 262 verso H, and Nicholas of Lyra 1065C.

7 For the dominical saying, cited in the *Gloss* (on 8:1) 1065B and by Nicholas of Lyra 1065C, see Matt 10:23.

8 For biblical images of seed and harvest see Matt 13:1–30; Mark 4:1–29; Luke 8:4–15, 13:18–19. Cf Bede in the *Gloss* (on 8:1) 1065B: 'It was with his consent that the occurrence of tribulation became the seed-bed of the church' (cf Bede *Super Acta* 8 PL 92 960D). That the persecution occurred in accordance with the divine 'economy' is noted also by Chrysostom *Hom in Acta* 18.1 PG 60 142.

9 Cf John 19:38–42. In the synoptic gospels only Joseph of Arimathea is named (Matt 27:57–60; Mark 15:43–6; Luke 23:50–3).

10 Nicholas of Lyra (on 8:2) 1066F also notes that Stephen's death was celebrated 'according to the Jewish manner,' and cites Gen 50:10, Num 20:28–9, and Deut 34:8, all of which record lamentation. For beating the breast see Isa 32:12. For Hebrew customs in general see the article 'Mourning' in *Encyclopaedia Judaica* XII 485–92.

11 The Latin *plausibilis* and *triumphalis* may evoke images respectively of the applause at the conclusion of a theatrical performance (cf eg Quintilian 6.1.52), and of the 'triumph' in which a Roman general celebrated a military victory (for which see OCD). In the New Testament the triumph image is found in 2 Cor 2:14 and Col 2:15. The image is found also in the martyr literature of early Christianity; cf eg θριαμβεύω in *A Patristic Greek Lexicon* ed G.W.H. Lampe (Oxford 1961).

12 The *Gloss* (on 8:3) 1066E notes the ravening wolf image and quotes Gen 49:27, as does Hugh of St Cher 262 verso H (cf n4 above).

13 The interlinear *Gloss* (on 8:3) 1065–6 calls attention to the fact that women too were not spared.

14 The *Gloss* (on 8:3) 1066E observes: 'He dragged them; he did not slay them, because perhaps the Lord restrained his hands so that they should not be stained with the blood of the innocent'; so Hugh of St Cher 262 verso H, and similarly Nicholas of Lyra 1066F.

15 Cf the *Gloss* (on 8:4) 1066E, citing Rabanus: 'Though scattered through fear, they were nevertheless firm in preaching the gospel.'

16 Nicholas of Lyra (on 8:4) 1066F notes that as the good God draws forth good from evil, so here from the evil of persecution God once more drew good – the dissemination of the Catholic faith. Cf the paraphrase on 8:1 above.

17 Cf the *Gloss* (on 8:5) 1066E: 'Among those who sowed [the word] Philip was the first to preach in Samaria. He was the deacon next in order after Stephen. His story is told next after Stephen's as his successor and one of the same rank.' Hugh of St Cher 263 recto A quotes the last two sentences of this gloss: 'He was a deacon ... of the same rank.'

18 The paraphrase anticipates the *1527* annotation on 8:5 (*in civitatem Samariae*) in which Erasmus explains that the reference here is evidently to the city 'Samaria' (from which the region received its name), which was also called Sebaste. In this, Erasmus followed Nicholas of Lyra 1067C, who also thought Samaria referred to the city, not the region. Modern scholars are uncertain about the reference. The biblical text itself is uncertain: either 'the city of Samaria' or 'a city of Samaria' may be read; if the former then apparently either Samaria (Sebaste) or Neapolis, the ancient Shechem, is intended; if the latter, then any city of Samaria (cf Metzger 355–6 and *Beginnings* IV 89 5n; also Bruce 183, Munck 73 5n, and Haenchen 301–2). In spite of his interpretation, Erasmus followed in his own text (from *1516*) the latter reading, 'a city of Samaria' (so RSV; DV AV and Conf read 'the city of Samaria'). For the name 'Sebaste,' given in honour of Augustus to the ancient city of Samaria newly rebuilt by Herod the Great in 30 BC, see IDB IV 186.

19 The *Gloss* (on 8:5) 1067A suggests that the Samaritans were already acquainted with the story of the Samaritan woman (John 4).

58

20 For the response of the common people to the gospel see the paraphrase on 4:4
(31 above) and n13.

21 Cf the *Gloss* (on 8:6) 1067A, citing Rabanus, and noting that faith is inspired
both by the word of preaching and by the 'signs of the powers.'

22 The preferred reading of the Greek text of 8:7 is represented in the Vulgate,
faithfully rendered by DV: 'For many of them who had unclean spirits . . .
went out.' For the Greek text of his New Testament Erasmus adopted not the
preferred reading but that of the Byzantine witnesses, which he translated
freely to give the sense 'The unclean spirits came out of many who were
possessed by them.' The paraphrase thus follows his own translation rather
than the Vulgate and the preferred reading. Erasmus defended his text and
translation in an annotation on the verse (*multi eorum qui habebant spiritus
immundos clamantes voce magna exibant*). For the difficulties of the text and for
the intended sense of the preferred reading of the Greek see *Beginnings* IV 90
7n and Metzger 356–7.

23 For the loud cry of demons as a sign of unwilling departure see the paraphrases
on Mark 1:26 and 9:26 CWE 49 24 and 114.

24 Cf Matt 7:15.

25 In the exegetical tradition, Simon is described as given to the arts of illusion; cf
the interlinear *Gloss* (on 8:9) 1067–8 and Hugh of St Cher 263 recto B.

26 Erasmus represents the traditional view of the Samaritans, based largely on 2
Kings 17. But see the article 'Samaritans' in *Encyclopaedia Judaica* XIV 725–58,
especially 740; also IDB IV 191–7.

59

27 embraced . . . faith] First in 1534; in 1524, simply *credidit* 'believed'

28 Both Bede in the *Gloss* (on 8:13) 1068D–E (cf Bede *Super Acta* 8 PL 92 960D–961A)
and Nicholas of Lyra 1068F question whether Simon truly believed or merely
pretended to believe – pretending, according to the *Gloss*, because he was eager
for glory, hoping to be thought to be the Christ and wishing to develop the
skill of working genuine miracles.

29 For a poetic illustration of magical powers in classical literature see the story of
Medea in Ovid *Metamorphoses* 7.1–424. Medea can disrupt the laws of nature
– eg make streams flow backward, move forests (7:199–206); for her winged
dragons see 7:217–37, 350–403. See also Apuleius *Metamorphoses* 3.15–25 (in
J. Arthur Hanson trans, Loeb Classical Library 44 [Cambridge, MA 1989] I
152–73) where the magical powers of Pamphile are described. For the magical
tricks of Simon in early Christian literature see *The Clementine Homilies* 2.22–34
(*Ante-Nicene Fathers* ed Alexander Roberts and James Donaldson, American
reprint revised with notes and prefaces by A. Cleveland Coxe 10 vols [Grand

Rapids, MI 1950–62] VIII 232–5) where Simon makes statues move, becomes a dragon, and flies; also *The Acts of The Holy Apostles Peter and Paul* (ibidem 480–5).

30 On Samaritan idolatry see n26 above. 'Unspiritual' here translates the Latin *crassam*. For *crassus* see chapter 7 n60; in the 1548 *Paraphrase of Erasmus* the word is rendered here in the paraphrase on 8:14 by 'a sort of carnal [people]' (fol xxxi verso).

31 The translations (DV AV Conf RSV) understand that in 8:15 the apostles asked God ('prayed') that the Samaritans should receive the Holy Spirit. In the paraphrase Philip and his companions asked the apostles 'on their [the Samaritans'] behalf' and the apostles in turn laid hands upon the Samaritans (8:17), who then received the Holy Spirit. This interpretation anticipates a 1527 annotation (*et rogabant pro eis*): 'It is open to question whether the apostles themselves asked God for them, or whether Philip and those who were with him asked the apostles; interpreters seem to assume the latter.' A 1535 addition, however, recognizes that the Greek προσηύξαντο 'asked,' 'prayed' usually implies a prayer to God.

32 Cf Nicholas of Lyra (on 8:15) 1069C: 'Philip was only a deacon and could therefore only baptize. He could not give the Holy Spirit in the visible sign, for this belonged only to the apostles; hence only bishops ... who are their successors impose the hands'; similarly the *Gloss* (on 8:17) 1069B and Hugh of St Cher 263 recto C–D, who contrasts the right of presbyters to baptize with the role of bishops, 'who alone mark the forehead with oil, giving the Holy Spirit.'

33 The paraphrase here may be deliberately ambiguous: is the 'visible sign' the laying on of hands (cf previous note) or the 'celestial eloquence' and the 'fiery vigour'? The interlinear *Gloss* (on 8:17) 1069–70 followed by Hugh of St Cher 263 recto D understands that the gift of tongues was given here as a sign of the Spirit. For 'fiery vigour' and 'celestial' speech as signs of the Spirit see the paraphrases on 2:3–4, where each sign receives both a literal and a spiritual interpretation. For 'fiery vigour' as a sign of the Spirit see also the paraphrases on Mark 1:12 CWE 49 20 and on Rom 12:11 CWE 42 71.

60

34 Nicholas of Lyra (on 8:19) 1070F also assumes that Simon 'wished to buy the power of giving the Holy Spirit with the intention of deriving gain therefrom,' and notes that the vice of simony receives its name from this incident. For Erasmus' criticism of simony in his own day see eg the *Moria* CWE 27 138 and *Iulius exclusus* CWE 27 172.

35 Cf the *Gloss* (on 8:19) 1070D: 'The apostles could not give for money that power when it had been said to them, "Freely you have received, freely give"' [Matt 10:8]; so Hugh of St Cher 263 recto D, also quoting Matt 10:8.

36 Nicholas of Lyra 1071C also notes (on 8:23) that Simon's crime was one of intention.

37 most destructive] *perniciosissimum* in the editions 1524–1535; *periculosissimum* 'most dangerous' in LB, which, however, gives *perniciosissimum* as an alternative reading

38 Cf the *Gloss* (on 8:23) 1071C, citing Bede: 'The Holy Spirit descended in the form of a dove to teach that he is received by the simple in heart. For he who keeps bitterness in his heart, though he may appear to be baptized, has not been freed from the chains of his sin (cf Bede *Super Acta* 8 PL 92 961C); similarly Hugh of St Cher 263 verso E.

Vincula 'chains' anticipates a 1527 addition to the annotation on 8:23 (*et in obligatione*) where the Greek is explained as *vincula*; cf the words *obligatio* in the Vulgate, *colligatio* 'bond' (as in AV Conf RSV) in Erasmus' translation from 1519.

39 Cf Nicholas of Lyra (on 8:24) 1071C: '[Simon] said this, moved more by fear than by the love of grace.'

40 In spite of the response specifically to Peter in the paraphrase on 8:24, Erasmus retains the plural 'you' of the Greek and the Vulgate, as also in the paraphrase on 8:19 above: '[You, plural] give me also this power'; cf the AV of 8:24: 'Pray ye to the Lord.'

41 For the command to preach see Matt 28:19; Acts 1:8.

42 Both the *Gloss* (on 8:26) 1072F, citing Bede (cf Bede *Super Acta* 8 PL 92 961D), and Nicholas of Lyra 1072F distinguish the 'old Gaza' from the 'new Gaza.' Gaza had been destroyed by Alexander Jannaeus (96 BC), but was rebuilt by Gabinius, the Roman governor of Syria (57–4 BC). According to Bede the new Gaza was built in a different place from the old; see *De nominibus locorum* PL 92 1037C. For the geography of 'old' and 'new' Gaza see Bruce 190, *Beginnings* IV 95 26n, and *Encyclopaedia Judaica* VII 339–42.

In describing the city as 'desert' (cf DV AV), rather than the road (so Conf RSV), the paraphrase anticipates a 1527 addition to the annotation on 8:26 (*Gazam*) in which Erasmus explains that the Greek ἔρημος refers to the city – which had been utterly destroyed; on the two alternative interpretations see Haenchen 310 n4.

43 'Director': *choragus*. In Greek the term χορηγός [*chorēgos*] was normally applied to the citizen who bore the main financial burden of staging a play (P-W III-2 2422–3). The *choragus* appears in Plautus, where the figure has been interpreted as the 'one from whom costumes were hired' – so H.R. Fairclough ed *Trinummus* (New York 1909) on line 858; cf also *Curculio* 462–4. But Erasmus may have had in mind rather the type of manager represented by Lucius Ambivius Turpio, who produced and also acted in the plays of Terence; cf the prologue to Terence *Hecyra* (9–57). For images of the theatre in the *Paraphrases* see chapter 1 n25, and for the divine direction of human affairs expressed in the language of stage production see the paraphrase on Mark 7:1 CWE 49 88.

61

44 A passage frequently glossed by the commentators. The interlinear *Gloss* (on 8:27) 1071–2 explains that the eunuch could be called a man 'on account of his manly soul'; so Hugh of St Cher 263 verso F. Nicholas of Lyra 1072F thought he was called a eunuch not because he was castrated, but because of his chaste and honourable character. In a *1516* annotation (*et ecce vir eunuchus*) Erasmus refers to Jerome's observation that one can scarcely be a man and a eunuch at the same time.

45 Cf Bede in the *Gloss* (on 8:27) 1072F–1073A: 'Here the Ethiopian changed his skin because he left the stains of sin in the baptismal font' (cf Bede *Super Acta* 8 PL 92 962A–B); Bede's commentary adds also that the Ethiopian became 'white-robed.' Similarly Hugh of St Cher (on 8:38) 263 verso H, who (on 8:27) 263 verso E had specifically noted that the Ethiopian was dark-skinned. Cf Jer 13:23.

46 In an annotation on 8:27 (*Candacis*) Erasmus explains 'Candace' as the customary name of the queens of Ethiopia – as Pharaoh and Ptolemy were the common names of the kings of Egypt. But cf *Beginnings*: '[The word] is not a name, but a ... title such as Pharaoh' (IV 96 27n). The word appears in Strabo (cf *Geography* 17.1.54) and Pliny *Naturalis historia* (6.35.186), where it is said that 'Candace' is 'a name that has passed on through a succession of queens for many years'; see Pliny *Natural History* II trans H. Rackham, Loeb Classical Library (Cambridge, MA 1942) 477.

47 Cf the portrait of Cleopatra's 'filthy herd' of eunuchs in Horace *Odes* 1.37.9–12; also the portrait of royal luxury in the palace of Queen Dido in Virgil *Aeneid* 1.631–756, 4.129–41. The paraphrase denigrates women; but for a relatively enlightened statement of the equality of the sexes and of admiration for the abilities of women, see the colloquy 'The New Mother' (Thompson *Colloquies* 267–85, especially 270–2).

48 The interlinear *Gloss* (on 8:27) 1073–4 explains that the eunuch came to Jerusalem 'on account of the celebrity of the city and the fame of the temple'; so Hugh of St Cher 263 verso E. Cf Bede in the *Gloss* 1073A: 'He is deservedly called [a man of power] who was so zealous of Scripture that he did not cease to read it on the road, and loved religion so much that he came from the farthest parts of the world to the temple of the Lord' (cf Bede *Super Acta* 8 PL 92 962A). For the nations bringing their wealth to Jerusalem see Isa 60:1–14.

49 Cf chapter 6 n26.

50 Cf the citation from Bede, n48 above. See also Erasmus' colloquy 'The Young Man and the Harlot,' where Sophronius is led to repentance by reading Erasmus' New Testament on his way to Rome (Thompson *Colloquies* 156–7).

51 For the expression 'learn Christ' see Eph 4:20, where the Vulgate has the phrase *Christum discere* that Erasmus uses here.

52 Though in his own text and translation Erasmus read 'In his humiliation' (so AV RSV), he follows here the Vulgate 'In humiliation' (so DV and Conf). In an annotation on 8:32 (*tamquam ovis ad occisionem*) Erasmus observed that the Vulgate here followed the Septuagint exactly.

53 For the legend of Isaiah's martyrdom see IDB II 744. According to the legend Isaiah was 'sawn asunder' with a wooden saw. The story is narrated in *The Ascension of Isaiah*; see *The Apocryphal Old Testament* ed H.F.D. Sparks (Oxford 1984) 775–94. Hebrews 11:37 is probably an allusion to the story. In post-canonical Christian literature an explicit allusion is found as early as Justin Martyr (*Dialogue with Trypho* 120 PG 6 756A).

62

54 Cf the *Gloss* 1074D on the eunuch's question, 'How can I [understand], unless someone guides me?' (8:31 RSV): 'This shows [by contrast] the bravado of those who think they can understand the divine Scripture without a teacher'; so Hugh of St Cher 263 verso G. On the 'senses' of Scripture see CWE 44 115 n28 and CWE 56 33 n4; also chapter 2 n84.

55 Cf the interlinear *Gloss* (on 8:33) 1073–4: 'His heavenly generation cannot be described ... who can explain his carnal generation, how he was born of a virgin without seed'; similarly Bede in the *Gloss* 1074E (cf Bede *Super Acta* 8 PL 92 962D) and Hugh of St Cher 263 verso H. On the 'twice-born' Son of God see the paraphrase on John 1:1–4 CWE 46 16–17. Erasmus' statement of 'evangelical doctrine' in this paragraph follows in outline the pattern of articles in the Nicene Creed.

56 Cf the interlinear *Gloss* on 'lamb' (8:32) 1073–4: 'Behold the Lamb of God who takes away the sins of the world'; cf also Hugh of St Cher 263 verso G, who has a double entry on the word 'lamb': 'Lamb of God, who takes away the sins of the world'; 'Paschal Lamb – Christ our pascha was sacrificed for us.'

57 The exegetical tradition apparently felt the contradiction between the prophetic statement, 'so he opens not his mouth' (8:32 RSV) and the fact that Jesus did speak words, although few, at his trial as recorded in the Gospels. The interlinear *Gloss* (on 8:32) 1073–4, following Bede closely, observed, 'He replied a few words to Pilate and the priests, but nothing to Herod' (cf Bede *Super Acta* 8 PL 92 962D).

58 Cf the *Gloss* 1074E, citing Rabanus on 'in humiliation' (8:33): 'By the passion by which he humbled himself, made obedient even unto death.' Cf also Nicholas of Lyra 1074F, who points more explicitly to the incarnation: 'Through the death which he humbly bore in the humanity he had assumed.'

59 Cf the *Gloss* 1074E on 'in humiliation' (8:33), accurately quoting Bede (*Super Acta* 8 PL 92 962D): 'Because the Judge of all did not receive a fair trial – condemned without fault by the uprising of the Jews and the word of Pilate.'

As this and the preceding notes (54–8) indicate, Erasmus' paraphrase on 8:35 follows closely the exegetical tradition on 8:32–3. Erasmus brings together the hermeneutical tradition on those verses and presents it here within the narrative of 8:35 in a continuous exposition of the essence of Christian teaching. Thus Philip's 'good news of Jesus' (8:35 RSV) is made to 'begin with the prophetic Scripture' (cf 8:35) mystically interpreted according to the tradition. The paraphrase on verse 35 does, however, go beyond the traditional glosses on verses 32–3 to imply the classic formulations of Christian faith as found in the creeds. The emphasis on the humiliation of Christ is characteristically Erasmian; cf eg the paraphrase on John 1:14 CWE 46 22–4, and the Preface to CWE 46 x.

60 On instruction followed by baptism as the proper sequence for Christian initiation see the paraphrase on Mark 1:5 CWE 49 16. Cf also chapter 2 n114.

63

61 The preferred reading omits 8:37 as a 'Western' addition (Bruce 194 and Metzger 359–60). Erasmus retained the verse in text and translation (all editions 1516–1535). In an annotation on 8:37 (*dixit autem Philippus*) Erasmus said that he had not found the passage 'in the Greek manuscript,' but he acknowledged that he had seen it in the margin of 'some Greek manuscript,' and he supposed therefore that the verse had been carelessly omitted by the scribes. In a 1522 addition he added that the passage was not in the Chrysostom he had available then. The verse appears in the Vulgate of 1527 – though it is omitted in the preferred reading of the Vulgate (Weber II 1712 36n). The verse is included in DV AV, in brackets in Conf, in a footnote in RSV. From Erasmus' text and translation Edward Lee took the occasion to criticize reliance on Greek manuscripts (*Responsio ad annotationes Lei* LB IX 207C–E).

62 The paraphrase is careful to include both the *fides qua* and the *fides quae*, the faith by which and the faith which one believes. For the importance of both see the *Explanatio symboli* ASD V-1 206:38–208:73. Cf also the paraphrases on Romans 10:4–17 CWE 42 60–1 and Payne *Theology of the Sacraments* 86–8 and n79.

63 This sentence, included here in Philip's reply, can equally well be understood as Erasmus' gloss on Philip's reply – in which case Philip's reply is limited to the preceding sentence.

64 In the paraphrase on 8:37 the eunuch acknowledges two articles of belief, that Jesus is the Christ and that he is the Son of God. Erasmus' translation was identical to that of the Vulgate: 'I believe that Jesus Christ is the Son of God'; so the standard translations (DV AV Conf and, in a footnote, RSV).

65 Though the subject of 'ordered' is not explicitly stated in the Greek of this passage, it is natural to assume that it is the eunuch, subject of the immediately preceding sentence, a reading that is unavoidable if verse 37 is omitted.

66 For the splendour associated in classical literature with barbarian royalty see eg the portrait of Dido in the *Aeneid* (cf n47 above).

67 Cf the interlinear *Gloss* (on 8:38) 1075–6: 'The one who is to be baptized must humble himself'; so Hugh of St Cher 263 verso H. On humility as the 'necessary first step toward contrition and confession' see CWE 44 177 n13. In early Christian practice, the candidate for baptism laid aside ornaments and clothes before stepping into the baptismal font; cf *The Treatise on the Apostolic Tradition of St Hippolytus of Rome* ed Gregory Dix, reissued with corrections, preface, and bibliography by Henry Chadwick (London 1968) 33–8.

68 Cf Acts 10:34; Rom 2:11; Eph 6:9.

69 oneness of heart] In the editions *1524–1535, consensus*; in LB, *consensu*, apparently by mistake

70 Cf 2 Cor 5:17; Gal 6:15.

71 The paraphrase on 8:39 may reflect the exegetical tradition shaped by Erasmus for the narrative here. In a *1527* annotation on the verse (*spiritus domini rapuit Philippum*) Erasmus observed that Rabanus in the *Gloss* 1075C–1076D seems to have read that the Spirit fell upon the eunuch and carried Philip away. Though Erasmus did not find this particular reading in either his Greek or Latin codices, there are textual witnesses for the slightly different reading 'The Holy Spirit fell on the eunuch and an angel of the Lord carried Philip away' (cf Metzger 360), a reading implied in the witness of some early Christian writers such as Jerome (cf Jerome *Dialogus contra Luciferianos* 9 PL 23 [1883] 173B). The interlinear *Gloss* (on 8:39) 1075–6, apparently following Bede *Super Acta* 8 PL 92 963B, says that an angel 'did these things' and cites Jerome; see Jerome's *Commentarii in Isaiam* 17 (on 63:14) PL 24 617C. That the eunuch returned to his native country to evangelize the Ethiopians is stated by Irenaeus *Adversus haereses* 3.12.8 PG 7–1 902A. That Philip had come from Azotus may be an inference. Of the roads leading from Jerusalem to Egypt, one joined the main coastal road at a point north of Azotus; the traveller who reached Gaza by this road could therefore be said to have come from Azotus (cf *Beginnings* IV 95 26n and Bruce 190).

72 Cf Bede in the *Gloss* (on 8:40) 1076F: 'He means [Caesarea] of Palestine, where Philip is said below [21:8] to have a house' (cf Bede *Super Acta* 8 PL 92 963C); so also Hugh of St Cher 264 recto A. Cf the paraphrase on 21:8 (126 below) and n8.

Chapter 9

1 Cf Nicholas of Lyra (on 9:1) 1076F: 'So that on the authority [of the high priest] he might be more able to harm the faithful.'

2 Cf the interlinear *Gloss* 1075–6 on 'Damascus' (9:2): 'A city of Syria, far away, for he had already inflicted persecution on the cities nearby.' Bede *De nominibus*

locorum PL 92 1036D–1037A describes Damascus as a 'distinguished city of Phoenicia' and adds that it was once the chief city in all Syria, but is 'now' the capital of the Saracens.

In the New Testament Phoenicia is a geographical term referring to the narrow coastal strip west of the Lebanon Mountains between Mount Carmel and the Eleutheros river (roughly, modern Lebanon). It was within the administrative area of the Roman province of Syria. Thus in New Testament times Damascus was not a city of Phoenicia. However, in the Severan administration (early third century) 'Phoenicia' included Damascus, and in the *Notitia dignitatum* (c AD 400) Damascus is within the province of 'Phoenice Libanensis'; see Jones *Later Roman Empire* III 388.

3 For the expression 'synagogue of the Jews' see 14:1, 17:1 and 10 (DV and Vulgate); see also the paraphrase on 19:9 (117 below).

4 For the dominical saying Erasmus follows closely the Vulgate of John 16:2 (cf DV).

64

5 The interlinear *Gloss* (on 9:3) 1075–6 also notes the fear caused by the light; cf Chrysostom *Hom in Acta* 19.3 PG 60 153.

6 Cf Nicholas of Lyra 1076F on 'persecute me' (9:4): 'My members, which Paul persecuted, not Christ in his own person, who was sitting on the right hand of the Father.' Similarly the interlinear *Gloss* 1075–6 on 'me': 'in my members'; and Bede in the *Gloss* 1076F: 'He does not say "members," but "me"' (cf *Super Acta* 9 PL 92 963C).

7 Acts 9:5b–6a (AV; 5b–7a DV) ('It is hard ... the Lord said unto him') are regarded as an insertion into the biblical text, under the influence of 22:10 and 26:14 (Metzger 361–2). Already in 1516 Erasmus suspected as much. In his annotation on 9:5 (*durum est tibi*) he observed that this passage is not found in the Greek codices (changed in 1519 to 'in *most* Greek codices'), and in 1522, when this portion of Chrysostom's Homilies was available to him, he added that Chrysostom had not commented upon it (for a similar comment see the *Responsio ad annotationes Lei* LB IX 207E–F). Nevertheless he included it in his text and translation and paraphrased it here; see *Beginnings* III 84–5 5, 6n, where it is said that Erasmus himself translated this passage into Greek 'from the Latin of the Vulgate and introduced it in his first edition [of the New Testament], 1516.'

8 In the annotation cited in n7 above, Erasmus cites this as a pagan proverb taken from the practice of applying spurs to animals. It does not appear to be among the proverbs of the *Adagia*. For the expression in Greek literature, see Euripides *Bacchae* 795.

9 Cf Romans 9:19. Cf also the interlinear *Gloss* (on 9:5) 1079–80, which explains the 'goad' (DV) as 'the word and power of God'; so also Hugh of St Cher 264

recto B. Nicholas of Lyra 1079C explains the proverb here as 'to resist one incomparably stronger.'

10 The clause refers evidently to what precedes: the sin against the Christians, and the sin against God.

11 For the difference between sins of ignorance and of malice see the paraphrases on 8:1–3 (56–7 above); also the paraphrase on Gal 1:14 CWE 42 101: 'I [Paul] erred in judgment not in heart.' But for the ignorance that arises from an evil will see the paraphrases on Rom 11:7 CWE 42 63–4 and John 16:8–9 CWE 46 185–6.

12 Cf Isa 19:22; Hos 6:1.

13 Cf Bede in the *Gloss* 1080E on the words 'his eyes were opened' (9:8): 'He could not have seen well with the eyes unless he had first been blinded' (cf *Super Acta* 9 PL 92 963D–964A).

14 In writing 'he saw nothing' Erasmus followed the Vulgate of 9:8 (so DV Conf RSV) rather than his text from 1516 and translation from 1519 ('he saw no one'; so AV).

15 The *Gloss* (on 9:9) 1080F also finds the catechumenate reflected in Paul's three days of fasting. In early Christianity the catechumenate often assumed a period of two or three years, including an initial stage in which the catechumen's sincerity was tested, and a more advanced stage of intensive instruction during Lent, followed by baptism at the Easter Vigil. Fasting and prayer before baptism were encouraged. See Tertullian *De baptismo* 20.1 CCL 1 294; Hippolytus *The Apostolic Tradition* 17.1–20.10 in *The Treatise on the Apostolic Tradition of St Hippolytus of Rome* (see chapter 8 n67 above) 28–32; Origen *Against Celsus* 3.51 PG 11 988A–B. The catechumenate as such virtually disappeared during the Middle Ages; see J.A. Jungmann 'Catechumenate' in NCE III 238–40. Elsewhere Erasmus appealed to the catechetical practice of the early church. In *Ecclesiastes* I ASD V-4 188:40–7 I he extols it as the proper norm for his contemporary church, recalling the words of Christ in Matt 18:19, the paraphrase on which insists on instruction and repentance before baptism (LB VII 146A–B). See the introduction by J.N. Bakhuizen van den Brink to the *Explanatio symboli* ASD V-1 186–95; see also Rudolph Padberg *Erasmus als Katechet* (Freiburg 1956), especially 24–7.

16 Cf the *Gloss* (on 9:9) 1080F, which notes that while physically blind for three days Paul was being illuminated by God as he explored heavenly things; also Nicholas of Lyra 1080F, who recorded the common opinion of the Doctors that during the three-day period he was carried off to the third heaven and saw the vision recorded in 2 Cor 12:2–5. For the contrast elsewhere between physical and spiritual sight see chapter 1 n48; see also the paraphrase on John 9:1 CWE 46 121, and for the expression 'eyes of the mind' see CWE 46 121 n2.

17 Cf 6:1 and n1; in this chapter, too, the interlinear *Gloss* (on 9:1) 1075–6, Hugh of St Cher 264 recto A, and Nicholas of Lyra 1075C–1076F all make the equation

between disciples and Christians, and Hugh 264 recto c repeats the observation in his comments on 9:10. Erasmus' paraphrase may also recall the significance the term 'disciple' had in classical antiquity, denoting the follower of a teacher or a learner and devotee of a philosophical or religious sect; cf μαθητής in TDNT IV (1967), especially 416–26.

65

18 Cf the interlinear *Gloss* (on 9:10) 1081–2: 'He acknowledges that he is a servant and ready to obey'; so also Hugh of St Cher 264 recto D.

19 Erasmus' paraphrase assumes two distinct and separate visions, that of Ananias (verses 10–11) and that of Paul (verse 12: 'And he [Paul] saw a man'; so DV Conf). But the text is ambiguous, and it is possible to read verse 12 as a continuation of Ananias' vision: in a vision, the Lord tells Ananias that Paul is praying and has seen a man called Ananias coming to him (so AV RSV). In his translation (all editions 1516–1535) Erasmus, like the Vulgate, allows the ambiguity to remain.

20 Cf the interlinear *Gloss* (on 9:13) 1081–2, which observed that Ananias 'feared the wolf'; so Hugh of St Cher 264 recto D.

21 'Instrument': *organum*, as in his own translation of 9:15 (from 1519), for the Vulgate *vas* 'vessel.' Erasmus frequently uses the word *organum* to designate the minister of the gospel; cf the paraphrase on 2:4 (15 above): 'the disciples are only "instruments"' and the paraphrase on Rom 15:19 CWE 42 85: 'I am nothing other than an instrument.'

22 Cf Gal 1:14.

23 For error in judgment in contrast to malice see n11 above. The phrase 'with the bulls of pontiffs' (*pontificum bullis*) invites an unflattering comparison between the high priests of Jerusalem and the popes of Rome. For the sword of the Spirit as the word of the gospel see Eph 6:17.

24 The AV's 'forthwith' (9:18) was represented neither in Erasmus' text and translation nor in the Vulgate, and hence is omitted in the paraphrase (as in DV Conf RSV); see Metzger 364–5.

25 Nicholas of Lyra (on 9:20) 1083C, echoing Gal 1:12, observed that Paul had received his doctrine not from men but from God. For the inversion elsewhere of the divinely ordained sequence of baptism followed by the reception of the Spirit see the paraphrase on 10:46 (75 below) and n63.

26 For contrasting images of the old and new Paul – the different man – see the paraphrase on Rom 1:1 CWE 42 15 and n28 below.

66

27 From 1516 Erasmus' text in 9:20 read 'Christ' (so AV), and from 1519 he translated accordingly (in 1516 his translation, in spite of his text, read 'Jesus'). Erasmus follows here the Vulgate's 'Jesus,' which is the preferred reading (cf Metzger 364), and that in DV Conf RSV.

28 As Erasmus' annotation on Rom 1:1 ('Paul') indicates, a long line of exegetes had commented both on the meaning of Saul/Paul, and the reason the two names appear in the Acts narrative. Though in the annotation Erasmus himself prefers to think Paul had two names, the paraphrase here suggests the view of Ambrosiaster, who thought the change from Saul to Paul took place as a result of his conversion (CWE 56 3–4). Erasmus' annotation also suggests contrasting meanings for the two names: Saul, 'restlessness,' Paul, 'quietude,' a contrast reflected in the paraphrase on Rom 1:1 CWE 42 15: 'I am Paul, though formerly Saul, that is, I have become peaceful, though formerly restless . . .' For Paul as teacher of peace see eg Rom 5:1; 1 Cor 7:15, 14:33; Eph 2:11–22.

29 For the image of the 'persecutor turned preacher' see the *Gloss* (on 9:22) 1083C; also Nicholas of Lyra 1083C.

30 Cf Luke 21:18; Matt 10:29–30.

67

31 The complicity of the governor is recorded in 2 Cor 11:32.

32 The most ancient authorities read 'his [ie Paul's] disciples' (Metzger 366), and this is the preferred reading of the Vulgate (Weber II 1713 cf 25n; so Conf RSV). But 'the disciples' is thought to be the correct reading (Haenchen 332 and Metzger 366), which Erasmus himself followed in both text and translation (so AV DV). Cf Bede in the *Gloss* (on 9:25) 1085B: 'In the Greek "his" is not found, so that the disciples of Christ in general are understood – for Paul did not yet have disciples' (cf Bede *Super Acta* 9 PL 92 964B); so Hugh of St Cher 264 verso F and similarly the interlinear *Gloss* 1085–6.

33 The detail of the rope is added by Erasmus, implied, he believes, in the Greek χαλάσαντες ('lowering' RSV); see the annotation on 9:25 (*submittentes in sporta*).

34 For the proverb see *Adagia* I x 40. In this adage Erasmus cites Tertullian, who also quotes the proverb in *De fuga* 10.1 CCL 2 1147. The question of flight in persecution was debated in early Christianity. In the *De fuga* Tertullian disallows flight, excepting the apostles, who were to abide by the injunction of Matt 10:23 until the gospel should reach the gentiles. But elsewhere Tertullian himself acknowledges the right of a Christian to flee persecution; cf *Ad uxorem* 1.3.4 CCL 1 375–6 and *De patientia* 13.6 CCL 1 314.

For Paul's flight from persecution see Hugh of St Cher (on 9:25) 264 verso F: 'He does as a soldier does who, shut up in a narrow space, flees to more open terrain in order to slay the more'; also Nicholas of Lyra 1085C: 'He himself agreed [to flee], so that, like a keen soldier . . . he might contend for the Catholic faith more effectively.'

35 Ie in 4:36. Bede in the *Gloss* (on 9:27) 1086E also identifies Barnabas as the Levite mentioned above (cf Bede *Super Acta* 9 PL 92 964D).

The personal allusion to Luke, the author, emerges unexpectedly in this parenthetical reference. For a similar parenthetical intrusion of the persona of the writer see the paraphrase on 8:26 (60 above) and the allusion to 'old Gaza.' The paraphrase on 1:1 (5 above) follows the biblical text in alluding to the author, but see also the paraphrases on 1:14 (10 above) and 2:14 and 47 (18 and 26 above), where the authorial voice intrudes in the paraphrase without warrant from the biblical text. See persona in the indexes of CWE 42 and 49.

36 In the generally accepted reading of 9:28–9, Paul addresses two groups: the Jerusalemites and the Greeks (so AV Conf RSV). But some Vulgate manuscripts insert between these two a third – the gentiles (Weber II 1713 29n). Though Erasmus in his text and translation rejected the reading that included 'gentiles,' he follows it here in this paraphrase; see the annotation on 9:29 (*et disputabat cum Graecis*). Cf Lyra (on 9:29) 1086F, who knew the reading and explained that these were gentiles who had come to Jerusalem to worship. In regard to the term 'Greeks,' Erasmus was able to follow the interlinear *Gloss* 1085–6, which identified these as 'the Jews born among the Greeks,' and this is the position he took in a *1527* addition to the annotation: 'Greeks [*Hellenistae*] refer to Jews born there [ie among the Greeks], for the time for disputing with gentiles had not yet arrived.' See the paraphrase on 6:1 (46 above). On the celebrity of the city as an enticement to visitors see the paraphrases on 2:5 and 8:27 (15 and 61 above).

37 Cf the interlinear *Gloss* (on 9:30) 1085–6: 'He himself did not fear, but consented to the brethren'; so Hugh of St Cher 264 verso H.

38 On Phoenicia see n2 above; for 'Tarsus in Cilicia' see 21:39, 22:3. Erasmus identifies the Caesarea as Caesarea Philippi rather than the port city perhaps under the influence of Gal 1:21. But see Haenchen 333 (on 9:30) and *Beginnings* IV 107 30n.

39 and moving about] Added in *1534*

40 The singular 'congregation' reflects the '*ecclesia*' (singular) of the Vulgate text of 9:31 rather than the text and translation of Erasmus, which read 'churches' (plural; so AV). *Ecclesia* (singular) is the preferred reading of the Greek (Metzger 367); so DV Conf RSV. On the phrase 'congregation of disciples' (paraphrasing 'church') see 5:11 n20.

68

41 Cf Acts 1:8, which is also cited here (9:31) by the interlinear *Gloss* 1089–90.

42 Cf John 16:33.

43 The Greek of the biblical text here is ambiguous, and may mean either that Peter went 'through all quarters' or 'among all people.' As the Vulgate had done, Erasmus himself translated 'all people' (so DV Conf RSV), a translation he defended in his annotation on 9:32 (*dum transiret universos*). Modern

commentators prefer to understand 'all quarters' (Bruce 210, Munck 87, and Haenchen 338 n1; so AV). The paraphrase explicitly adopts the meaning 'all quarters,' but 'now these people, now those' may suggest the interpretation 'all people.'

44 Cf Bede *De nominibus locorum* PL 92 1038B: 'Lydda, a city of Palestine situated on the coast of the Great Sea.' In fact the town (modern Ludd) is inland about eleven miles south-east of Joppa (see 'Lod' in IDB III 148).

45 See Luke 10:5–9, where, however, the 'seventy' are to say 'peace' when they enter a house and heal when they enter the town.

46 For the antithesis between diseases of the body and the physician of the soul see eg Mark 2:9–12.

47 Cf the annotation on 9:34 (*sanet te dominus*). Erasmus' Vulgate (and the Vulgate of 1527) read the Greek verb ἰᾶται here as a subjunctive, and Erasmus so translated and paraphrased. But he recognized the indicative, 'Christ heals you,' as a possible reading (the reading of AV DV Conf and RSV). While some Greek and Latin manuscripts read 'the Lord Jesus Christ' (cf Metzger 367–8 and Weber II 1714 34n; so DV), the preferred reading is simply 'Jesus Christ' (so AV Conf RSV). In all editions of his New Testament Erasmus read ὁ Ἰησοῦς Χριστός, but he translated like his Vulgate 'the Lord Jesus Christ.' In LB VI the translation is corrected to 'Jesus Christ.'

48 Erasmus follows the Vulgate (and the preferred Greek) reading, 'Sarona.' His identification of Sarona as a coastal town near Lydda is a little surprising, since in a 1519 addition to the annotation on 9:35 (*Lyddae et Assaronae*) Erasmus, apparently following the *De nominibus locorum* (cf PL 92 1040) identifies 'Sarona' as the plain between Caesarea and Joppa (ie the Plain of Sharon). But in his own Greek text Erasmus read Ἀσσάρωνα 'Assaron.' If for the paraphrase Erasmus equated Assaron with Accaron (a possibility he considers in the annotation), then he might have found a basis in Jerome for placing this town 'near Lydda,' for in the *De situ et nominibus locorum Hebraicorum* 91 Jerome notes that Accaron is identified either with Caesarea or with a town 'between Azotus and Jamnia,' which perhaps could be construed as 'not far from Lydda.' For Jerome see Paul de Lagarde *Onomastica sacra* 2nd ed (Gottingen 1887; repr Hildesheim 1966) 126–7.

49 Cf Nicholas of Lyra (on 9:36) 1091C (misnumbered 1117C in the 1590 edition I used), who identifies the Greek with the Latin *caprea*; so also Hugh of St Cher 265 recto A. For the derivation see the annotation on 9:36 (*nomine Tabitha*); also LSJ, who, like Erasmus, derive the name from δέρκομαι 'to see' and add, 'an animal of the deer kind (so called from its large bright eyes), in Greece, roe ... in Syria and Africa, gazelle.'

50 The detail of anointing anticipates a 1527 annotation on 9:37 (*quam cum lavissent*) in which Erasmus cites the *Gloss* as evidence that some manuscripts read 'washed with ointments.' Erasmus thought the reading unlikely.

51 For widows who minister to saints see 1 Tim 5:10, and for Phoebe, Rom 16:1–2; for the idiom see eg Heb 6:10. On widows as an order in the early church see EEC 938–9.

69

52 Cf Matt 9:23–5; Mark 5:38–42.

53 On the place of faith and prayer in working miracles, see Matt 17:19–21, 21:21–2.

54 The *1548 Paraphrase of Erasmus* (xxxvii recto) understands 'strength of spirit' here and, just above, 'vigour of the spirit' to be the strength and the vigour of the Holy Spirit.

55 The contrast between prince and tanner suggests an implicit criticism of papal wealth, which is made explicit in the annotation on 9:43 (*apud Simonem coriarium*), particularly in a clause omitted from the last two editions: 'Now the palace of three kings would scarcely suffice to receive the vicar of Peter.'

Chapter 10

1 Cf Matt 10:5.

2 Straton, or Strato's Tower, was a city of apparently Sidonian origin in the fourth century BC, named perhaps after a Sidonian king. In 22 BC Caesar Augustus gave the city to Herod, who greatly enlarged it, 'making it a more magnificent and more beautiful city,' (Bede *De nominibus locorum* PG 92 1036A). Herod then renamed the city Caesarea, and its harbour *Sebastos* (Greek for '*Augustus*'). See Josephus *Jewish Antiquities* 15.9.6 (331–41). In AD 6 the city became the headquarters for the Roman procurators who administered Judaea. Though predominantly pagan, the city had a large Jewish population, and conflict between Jews and gentiles led to the Jewish war against Rome (AD 66); cf Josephus *Jewish Antiquities* 20.8.7–9 (173–84) and *Jewish War* 2.14.3–4 (280–8). It became an important ecclesiastical center in the third century, and in the later organization of the empire it was the capital of Palaestina Prima. See 'Caesarea' in *Encyclopaedia Judaica* v 6–13 and IDB I 479–80; cf P-W III-1 1291–4.

3 'A centurion *from* the cohort' (*centurio de cohorte*) rather than the Vulgate's 'a centurion *of* the cohort' (*centurio cohortis*). Erasmus follows his own literal translation (from 1519) of the Greek ἐκ σπείρης to clarify that the centurion was not the commander of a cohort (theoretically six hundred men) but of a division of the cohort, the 'century' (one hundred men) – so the annotation on 10:1 (*centurio cohortis*).

70

4 Cf Mark 4:25.

5 For the time of the Roman *cena* see the paraphrase on 3:1 (26 above) and n2.

6 Cf the *Gloss* on 'Cornelius' (10:3) 1095B: 'The familiarity of friendship is displayed.'

7 Like Erasmus, Nicholas of Lyra (on 10:4) 1095C also explains the cause of the fear: 'Because of the unusual brilliance issuing from the face of the angel.'

8 The Vulgate readings are divided between 'Who are you, Lord?' and 'What is it, Lord?' (Weber II 1714 4n). Though Erasmus follows his Vulgate in the paraphrase on 10:4, he read in his text and translation 'What is it, Lord?'; so DV AV Conf RSV. For Erasmus' Vulgate text see the annotation on 10:4 (*quis es domine*); the Vulgate of *1527* also read 'Who are you, Lord?'

9 Cf the interlinear *Gloss* (on 10:4) 1095–6, which explains that Cornelius' kindnesses to all reaped a heavenly reward. The marginal *Gloss* 1096D also regarded Cornelius' call as a reward for his merciful deeds. Erasmus frequently stresses the meritorious character of works of piety, especially of generosity to the poor – cf the paraphrases on Matt 3:12, 25:35–40; Luke 3:11, 16:9; Rom 2:13 CWE 42 20 and n6, and the *Divinationes ad notata Beddae* LB IX 494B–C. See Sider 'The Just and the Holy' 22. On the theme of merits preceding justification in late medieval thought see Oberman *Harvest* 189–96.

10 Cf 1 Cor 1:26.

11 This sentence paraphrases a reading poorly attested by both the Greek and Latin witnesses (cf Metzger 370 and Weber II 1714 6 and 6n). Erasmus included the sentence in his text and translation, but in a *1527* annotation (*hic tibi dicet quid te oporteat facere*) he recognized that the words appeared to be spurious, repeated here from 9:6. The sentence is found in DV and AV but not in Conf or RSV.

12 The paraphrase anticipates a *1527* addition to the annotation on 10:7 (*et militem timentem dominum*): 'Lest the reader should be offended because Cornelius employs a soldier for a godly work [the Scripture] adds "devout"' (AV RSV; 'God-fearing' Conf; similarly DV). For portraits of the soldier in Erasmus, see the colloquies 'Military Affairs' and 'The Soldier and the Carthusian' (Thompson *Colloquies* 11–15 and 127–33); also *Adagia* IV i 1: *Dulce bellum inexpertis* LB II 962D–E.

13 With the implicit criticism here of ecclesiastical prelates in Erasmus' time compare the criticism in the paraphrases on 3:1 (26 above, and cf n3) and 9:43 (69 above, and cf n55).

14 'Upper room': *coenaculum*, as in both the translation of and the paraphrases on 1:13 and 9:37, where the Greek word is ὑπερῷον. Here in 10:9, where the Greek is ἐπὶ τὸ δῶμα, Erasmus translated (from *1519*) *in superiora domus* 'the upper part of the house.' In a *1527* addition to an annotation on 1:13 (*in coenaculum ascenderunt*) Erasmus explained the phrase there as 'the upper part of the house' and added that 'there was, possibly, above the *cenaculum* a higher place that [Luke] calls the δῶμα in Acts 10 where Peter went up to pray.' In a *1519* addition to the annotation on 10:9 (*in superiora*) he says that 'Peter evidently

went up to the roof, where people were accustomed to walk, in order to pray under the open sky as being closer to God and farther removed from the din of the street.' Both Bruce 217 and Haenchen 347 understand that Peter went up to the roof and suppose that the roof had an awning. For the paraphrase, it is possible that Erasmus chose the image of the 'upper room' for its rhetorical effectiveness, but cf Chrysostom *Hom in Acta* 22.1 PG 60 172: ἐν ὑπερῴῳ 'alone, and in quiet, as in an upper room.'

71

15 'He was carried off in spirit': *raptus est spiritu*. The 1548 *Paraphrase of Erasmus* understands *spiritu* here unambiguously as the Spirit of God: 'He was ravished wyth the spiryte of god' (fol xxxviii recto). While this is a possible interpretation, I have understood the words in the sense implied in Erasmus' translation, which suggests rather a trance; 'An ecstasy of mind rushed upon him' (cf DV: 'There came upon him an ecstasy of mind'). Modern interpreters understand the Greek to refer to a trance; cf RSV and Bruce 217, who notes the frequent use of the Greek word ἔκστασις as a medical term.

16 The interlinear *Gloss* (on 10:9) 1097–8 also speaks of the 'mysteries' Peter was to see. For 'prayer and fasting' see Luke 2:37, and for the power of prayer and fasting see Mark 9:29 (9:28 in the Vulgate and DV) and Matt 17:21 (17:20 in the Vulgate and DV) – where Erasmus in text and translation read, like the Vulgate, 'prayer and fasting' (for the preferred reading of Matt 17:21 and Mark 9:29 see Metzger 43 and 101). For an affirmative evaluation of 'fasting' see the paraphrases on those verses (for Mark 9:29 see CWE 49 115). For a defence of fasts undertaken voluntarily see the paraphrase on Mark 2:19–20 CWE 49 42 and n47. But for Erasmus' critique of the prescribed fasts of the church, see the colloquy 'A Fish Diet' (Thompson *Colloquies* 312–57), and the bibliography in ASD I-3 495 n1 on the same dialogue; also *De interdicto esu carnium* ASD IX-1, especially 29–50.

17 From *1516* Erasmus' Greek text of 10:11 read 'tied by the four corners and let down' (so AV); his translation of *1516*, however, overlooked the word 'tied' present in his Greek text and followed the Vulgate 'let down by the four corners' (so DV Conf RSV and the preferred reading; see Metzger 371). Erasmus changed his translation in *1519* to correspond to his Greek text, which he followed here.

18 Cf Carcopino *Daily Life* 266: 'Since the time of Domitian it had been the fashion to cover the table with a cloth.' Carcopino cites Martial *Epigrams* 14.138. The historical allusion ('long ago') betrays the voice of Erasmus the commentator.

19 Here in 10:12 Erasmus follows the Vulgate in identifying only three kinds of wildlife: quadrupeds, reptiles, birds (so DV Conf and the preferred reading; see Metzger 371). In his Greek text (from *1516*), however, he followed the

reading that included four: quadrupeds, beasts, reptiles, birds (so AV). His translation in 1516 followed the Vulgate, but was accommodated to his own text in 1519.

20 Cf John 4:31–4 and Erasmus' paraphrases on those verses in CWE 46 59–60.

21 In his annotation on 10:13 (*occide et manduca*) Erasmus observed that the Greek means 'sacrifice and eat'; the Vulgate's translation gave the meaning 'kill and eat.' From 1519 Erasmus translated 'sacrifice and eat,' though in 1516 he had retained the Vulgate's 'kill and eat.'

22 Cf Matt 28:19.

23 Cf Nicholas of Lyra (on 10:16) 1100E, who notes that the vision appeared three times for greater vividness.

24 'Immediately' reflects a reading of 10:16 adopted by the Vulgate; it is in fact the preferred reading (Metzger 371 and *Beginnings* III 94; cf DV Conf RSV). For his Greek text Erasmus followed (from 1516) the Byzantine reading 'again' (so AV), and from 1519 so translated, though in his 1516 translation he had allowed the Vulgate *statim* 'presently' to stand in spite of the Greek text he printed.

25 That Peter 'came to himself' is a detail added by Erasmus here in 10:17, perhaps from 12:11.

26 An echo perhaps of Heb 1:1: 'In ... various ways God spoke ... to our fathers' (RSV).

27 In the paraphrase on 10:21 Erasmus follows the Vulgate in omitting a clause which he added in 1519 to both his text and his translation on the basis of 'some Greek manuscripts'; cf the annotation on 10:21 (*descendens autem Petrus ad viros*). The clause, 'which were sent unto him from Cornelius,' is found in the AV, but the reading is Byzantine and does not represent the preferred text. It is omitted in DV Conf RSV. See Bruce 220 and *Beginnings* III 94.

28 Cf the interlinear *Gloss* (Basel 1506–8) 184 recto: 'He asked ... in order to extract a confession, and left an example of the avoidance of haughtiness.'

29 For the expression 'tested and approved' see the paraphrase on 6:3 (46 above) and n7.

72

30 With this and the contextual sentences compare the *Gloss* (on 10:23) 184 recto A (Basel 1506–8): 'Here begins the association of the apostles with the gentiles, because [Peter] had gone down to them, he who had heard from the angel the command to go into the house of a gentile; on this account he received the gentiles hospitably.'

31 Cf the 'moral exposition' of Nicholas of Lyra 184 recto D (Basel 1506–8). Nicholas, noting Peter's immediate response – 'on the morrow' (10:23) – observed that the gospel preacher ought not to hesitate in the work of saving souls. Cf also the paraphrase on 8:31 (61 above).

32 The paraphrase on 10:24 omits the specific indication of time ('on the following day' RSV) found both in the Vulgate and in Erasmus' New Testament (both Greek text and Latin translation). The detail appears to be one in a series (10:9, 10:23, 10:24) that marks a temporal sequence implied in the 'four days ago'(RSV) of 10:30. For attempts to explain the sequence see Bruce 221–2 and *Beginnings* IV 114.

33 Cf the interlinear *Gloss* (on 10:24) 184 recto D (Basel 1506–8): 'He shows his eagerness and care'; also Nicholas of Lyra 184 recto D (Basel 1506–8) on 'Cornelius waited' (10:24 AV): 'with great eagerness to hear the word.'

34 Cf Nicholas of Lyra 184 recto D (Basel 1506–8) on the phrase 'called together his kinsmen' (10:24 RSV): 'That all might be sharers in the grace of God.'

35 Cf Nicholas of Lyra's comments 184 recto D (Basel 1506–8) on 10:25: 'He knew he was not God, but his messenger'; ... and in the 'moral exposition': 'He shows that reverence is owed to a teacher, especially when he is sent for the salvation of souls.' For the reverence owed to clergy see *Ecclesiastes* I ASD V-4 168:691–170:723, where the village pastor is said to hold a position of dignity higher than that of a monarch. In the same work Erasmus speaks of the office of preacher as 'more truly angelic than human' (ASD V-4 112: 635–8). For the bishop as vicar of Christ see *Ratio* Holborn 202:7–11 and *Moria* CWE 27 139.

36 For 'stewards (*dispensatores*) of Christ' see 1 Cor 4:1–2; 1 Pet 4:10; Titus 1:7 (Vulgate *dispensatores, dispensatorem*). Here it is Peter who is an exemplar of 'freedom from ambition.' Elsewhere Paul is a model: see the paraphrases on Rom 15:17–19 CWE 42 85–6; also the annotation on Rom 15:19 ('of wonders in the strength of the Holy Spirit') CWE 56 408: '... Paul proves that he is an apostle ... by the greatness of the miracles and the success of the evangelical doctrine. And yet he does not arrogantly claim any of these for himself, but ascribes all the glory to God, a man ... proud in Christ, humble in himself'; similarly, *Ecclesiastes* I ASD V-4 50:288–316.

37 Cf chapter 9 n21.

38 Both here in 10:27 and above in 10:25 the paraphrases go beyond the biblical text in referring specifically to the centurion's house. It is not clear, however, that Erasmus intends to convey a picture of a Roman house in Caesarea. In Roman houses a short hallway characteristically led into the central atrium; see eg *Pompeii and Herculaneum: The Glory and the Grief* text by Marcel Brion, photographs by Edwin Smith, trans John Rosenberg (London 1960) 139–41, and for diagrams of Pompeian houses, 61, 75, and 89. Cf Haenchen 350, who assumes a 'gateway' where the centurion met Peter, from where they went into the house talking to one another.

39 For sitting to proclaim the evangelical word see the paraphrase on 2:14 (17 above) and n48. Here in 10:28 Erasmus may, of course, have intended by the detail merely a consideration of hospitality.

40 Ie, as Jews introduced into the house of a gentile. See the paraphrase on 10:22 just above for the 'concern' of the apostles in extending the gospel to the gentiles.

41 'It is unlawful,' following Erasmus' own translation (similarly AV Conf and RSV), a studied attempt to avoid the harsh phrase of the Vulgate 'it is an abomination' (cf DV) – 'hardly a polite way to address a gentile,' Erasmus observed in his annotation on 10:28 (*quomodo abominatum sit*).

73

42 'Might gain them all': *omnes lucrifaciat*. The expression reflects 1 Cor 9:19–22, where a similar idiom is used in the Vulgate.

43 Cf the 'moral exposition' of Nicholas of Lyra on 'Peter opened his mouth' (10:34) 184 verso H–185 recto D (Basel 1506–8): 'He shows that the Catholic teacher who has hearers eager, attentive, and ready to be taught ought to proceed at once to the work of teaching.' Cf also the paraphrases on 8:31–5 (61–2 above), where the eunuch is portrayed as 'an eager learner,' Philip as 'keen to teach.'

44 In two respects the paraphrase on 10:30 reflects Erasmus' Greek text and translation (from *1519*) rather than the Vulgate. Erasmus read, 'Four days ago I sat fasting right to this hour, and I was praying in my house at the ninth hour' (cf AV). The Vulgate reads, 'From the fourth day to this very hour I was praying in my house at the ninth hour'(cf DV). First, here, like the Byzantine text he followed, Erasmus includes the detail of fasting (so AV) not found in the Vulgate and the preferred text; see Metzger 375–7 and *Beginnings* III 96. Second, his translation as well as his paraphrase precludes the interpretation he thinks the Vulgate suggests, that Cornelius fasted for three days – 'from the fourth day right to the present hour'; see the *1519* annotation on 10:30 (*nudius quarto die etc*). In his annotation Erasmus apparently overlooks the fact that the Vulgate does *not* mention fasting, but speaks only of prayer. However, for a three-day fast before baptism see 9:9.
On the other hand, in the clause 'since I was at my home' Erasmus follows the Vulgate, 'I was ... in my house,' rather than his own text and translation (from *1519*), 'I sat ... in my house.' However, in his annotation he acknowledged that 'some' manuscripts read 'I was' (Greek ἤμην) rather than 'I was sitting' (Greek ἤμην), and in *1516* he himself read 'I was.' In fact, the uncompounded ἦμαι 'I sit' is not found in BAG, and 'occurs only in Epic, Tragedy, and Herodotus' (H.W. Smyth *Greek Grammar* rev G.M. Messing (Cambridge, MA 1956) section 789a.

45 In the conclusion of 10:32 the AV adds, 'Who, when he cometh, shall speak unto thee.' Erasmus added these clauses in his Greek text and translation from *1519*. The preferred reading omits them (Metzger 377). They are not in the Vulgate,

hence not in DV or Conf, nor are they in RSV. Erasmus apparently follows the Vulgate here in omitting them.

46 In 10:33 the Vulgate reads 'we are all present in *thy* sight' (Conf; so DV); in *1516* Erasmus read ἐνώπιον τοῦ θεοῦ (the preferred reading; see Metzger 377–8), and translated 'in the sight of God' (so RSV; AV 'before God'). From *1519* he translated the phrase 'God is my witness.' The paraphrase anticipates a *1527* annotation on the expression (*in conspectu tuo*): 'This is the language of one who is affirming [his] simplicity of heart, of which he makes God the witness.'

47 Erasmus follows the Vulgate of 10:33, and the preferred reading (Metzger 378; so DV Conf RSV) in writing 'Lord,' though in his own text (from *1516*) and translation (from *1519*) he read 'God' (as in AV); in his *1516* translation, 'Lord.' Cf n50 below.

48 Cf the interlinear *Gloss* 184 verso (Basel 1506–8), which defines 'does what is right' (10:35 RSV) as 'alms, prayers, fasts.'

49 For the language of this clause see Heb 1:1–2, and for the paraphrase on 10:36 in general and in particular on the word 'peace' (RSV) in the biblical text see Eph 2:13–16.

Here in the paraphrase on 10:36, Erasmus understands the Greek λόγος (Vulgate *verbum*, Erasmus' translation *sermo*, RSV 'word') as the message announced by the prophets and later by Christ, and as Christ himself (cf n52 below). In the paraphrase on 10:37 he understands the Greek ῥῆμα (Vulgate *verbum*, RSV 'word') in the sense of 'report,' a meaning expressed in Erasmus' translation by the use of both *fama* and *rumor*; see the annotation on 10:37 (*incipiens enim*).

74

50 As in 10:33 Erasmus wrote 'Lord' against his own text and translation, which read 'God' (n47 above), so here in 10:36 he wrote 'God' against his own text and translation and the Vulgate, all of which read 'Lord.' With the expression 'God of all' compare the paraphrase on Rom 9:5 CWE 42 53 and n2, and for the Christology implied, the annotation on Rom 9:5 ('who is above all things God' CWE 56 242–52.

51 With Erasmus' paraphrastic exposition here of the phrase 'Lord of all' (10:36), compare the interlinear *Gloss* 184 verso (Basel 1506–8), which observes, 'not of one race.'

52 For the narrative sequence here see John 1:29–34. From his translation of and annotations on 10:36–8 (cf the annotations *verbum misit filiis* and *incipiens enim*) it is clear that Erasmus was quite aware of the textual difficulty of this passage (for which see Metzger 378–9). It also appears that he understood the 'word' of 10:36 as both Christ and the gospel preached, while the 'word' of 10:37 becomes the report about the teaching of Christ. This is the interpretation of the paraphrase, but the paraphrase also invites the reader to see the 'word'

as well in the teaching of the Law and the prophets and in the testimony of John. The interlinear *Gloss* 184 verso (Basel 1506–8) understands 'word' here as the 'incarnate Son,' 'Jesus Christ,' while Nicholas of Lyra 184 verso H (Basel 1506–8) interprets it as the message about justice and the divine goodness.

53 Erasmus evidently intends a verbal play on the contrasting words of the paraphrase, *sublevandis* 'lift up,' 'raise' and *oppressos* 'oppressed.' In his annotation on 10:38 (*omnes oppressos*) he notes that the image implied by *oppressos* is that of someone oppressed by tyranny.

54 The exegetical tradition attempted to protect the phrase 'God was with him' (10:38) from unorthodox interpretations; cf Bede in the *Gloss* 184 verso F (Basel 1506–8), who spoke of human nature joined with the word of God in the womb of the virgin – to avoid the Nestorian doctrine; cf Bede *Super Acta* 10 PL 92 970A–B and Nicholas of Lyra 185 recto B (1506–8 ed), who explained that 'God was with him' through the fullness of grace and the union of the Persons in the incarnation of the Word. Here also the identification of 'him' in the biblical text ('God was with him') with the 'Son' of the paraphrase suggests an effort towards Christological clarification.

55 On the 'permissive will' of God see the paraphrases on 2:23–4 and 8:1 (19 and 57 above).

56 The paraphrase here anticipates a 1527 annotation on 10:41 (*qui manducavimus et bibimus*) in which Erasmus notes that the *Gloss* pointed to Greek manuscripts which included the words 'for forty days.' As they were not in Erasmus' manuscripts, he printed them in none of the editions. Bede in the *Gloss* (on 10:41) 185 recto A (Basel 1506–8) comments on these words, referring to the Greek; cf Bede *Liber retractationis* 10 PL 1019C–1020B. For the 'forty days' see Acts 1:3.

57 For similar lists of the proofs of Christ's resurrection – proofs likewise designed to strengthen confidence and persuade – see the paraphrases on 1:3 and 2:32 (6 and 21 above).

75

58 Contrast the interlinear *Gloss* 185 recto (Basel 1506–8) on 'everyone who believes' (10:43): 'By faith with works.'

59 Cf Joel 2:28–32. The passage is cited also in the interlinear *Gloss* 185 recto (Basel 1506–8) on 'poured out' (10:45), which also explains the amazement of the Jewish attendants on the grounds that 'they did not know that grace belonged to the gentiles.'

60 The biblical text offers no warrant for the claim implicit in the paraphrases on 10:45 and 10:44 that there was a visible sign as well as an audible sign; it speaks only of 'tongues.' Cf the interlinear *Gloss* (on 10:46) 185 recto (Basel 1506–8), which regarded the tongues as the sign of the Spirit's descent. But here Erasmus evidently wished to model the narrative on that of 2:1–4; see the

paraphrase on 2:3 (14 above), which explains the special cogency of the double sign.

61 In both his text and his translation Erasmus read (from *1519*) simply 'to speak in tongues.' This was also the reading of the Vulgate of *1527* (so DV AV Conf RSV). His paraphrase here on 10:46, however, qualifies: 'to speak in "different" tongues,' apparently reflecting the language of 2:4 – *aliis linguis*. Erasmus may suppose that here as in 2:5–11 the 'tongues' were heard as foreign languages.

62 Cf Bede in the *Gloss* 185 recto A (Basel 1506–8), '[Peter] is strengthened by the testimony of the Holy Spirit so that he should not hesitate to give baptism to the gentiles. And this was done so that … his companions, as witnesses, might confound the Jews.' For the equality of Jew and gentile 'without the help of the Law' see the paraphrases on Rom 3:9–30 CWE 42 24–6.

63 For the normal order see Acts 19:5–6; on the importance of due order in sacramental ministries see the paraphrase on 8:36 (62–3) and n60.

64 Cf the *Gloss* (on 10:47) 185 recto B (Basel 1506–8): 'God gave first what was greater, and the order was reversed; surely they cannot prohibit what is lesser.'

65 baptized] First in *1535*; in *1524* and *1534*, 'baptized with water,' a reading observed in a footnote in LB. In a *1516* annotation on 10:47 (*numquid aqua*), Erasmus explained that the sense of the Greek appeared to be 'can anyone forbid these to be baptized with water.' The omission of 'with water' from the 1535 edition may be a printer's error.

66 In writing 'Jesus Christ' Erasmus appears to follow his Vulgate. The textual witnesses for 10:48 vary: 'Lord' (Erasmus' text from *1516* and translation from *1519*, AV); 'Jesus Christ' (Erasmus' translation *1516*, the *1527* Vulgate, Conf, RSV), and 'Lord Jesus Christ' (some Vulgate witnesses; so DV). For the Vulgate variants see Weber II 1716 and 48n; for the Greek text see Metzger 382.

Chapter 11

76

1 'Word': *sermonem*, as in Erasmus' translation in 11:1 (from *1519*), in place of the Vulgate *verbum*, a translation Erasmus had accepted in *1516*. See the paraphrases on 10:36–7 (73–4 above) and n49. On Erasmus' preference for *sermo*, see CWE 46 15 n16 and in the same volume the notes to pages 83–8 passim.

2 Within the Roman army there were considerable differences in rank among the centurions. Theoretically, a legion consisted of ten cohorts, while a cohort consisted of six hundred men divided into six centuries, each with its own centurion; there were thus sixty centurions in a legion. To be *primus pilus* (first centurion of the first cohort), was a coveted honour; nevertheless, the rank of a centurion remained well below that of a legion's commander. See 'centurio' in

OCD and H.M.D. Parker *The Roman Legions* (Oxford 1928) 196–205; also Bruce 214, who compares the status of a centurion to that of a 'non-commissioned officer of today.'

3 Cf chapter 10 n2 for Caesarea as a 'distinguished city.'

4 This messenger appears here without warrant from the biblical narrative, and no such person is found in the paraphrases on 10:24–7. Erasmus has evidently supplied the detail from the logic of the story; see, however, the story of the centurion in Luke 7:1–10, where a go-between appears, sent by the centurion to Jesus.

5 Both the interlinear *Gloss* 1111–12 and Hugh of St Cher 266 verso G provide a list of the considerations that 'explained' Peter's action, the *Gloss* as interlinear comments on 11:8–16, Hugh as part of his introductory outline of the chapter, thus preceding Peter's narrative of events in 11:5–17. The interlinear *Gloss* included among its *excusationes* the character of the vision, the witnesses at the door and the witness of the six brethren (cf 11:12), and the descent of the Holy Spirit.

6 For this expression of disdain see the paraphrase on 7:51 (54 above); also the paraphrase on Rom 2:28 CWE 42 22.

7 On avoiding offence see especially 2 Cor 6:3, but also 1 Cor 10:32 and Mark 9:42.

77

8 The sentence may reflect the theological issue addressed by Paul in Romans 9–11.

9 The expression may be intended to suggest that the return of Peter to Jerusalem was fortuitous, and not compelled by any criticism there. The 'Western' text includes a lengthy statement here in 11:2, showing how Peter's return to Jerusalem was voluntary; see Metzger 382–4 and *Beginnings* III 103.

10 Acts 11:3 in the biblical text is variously punctuated: as a question (DV Conf RSV), a statement (AV), or an exclamation (NEB). Though in his *1516* translation Erasmus followed the Vulgate in reading a question, from *1519* he read the words as a statement, a position he defended in his annotation (*quare introisti*). On the grounds for reading this as a question see Bruce 229 and Metzger 384. Like the interlinear *Gloss* 1109–10 and Hugh of St Cher 266 verso G Erasmus' paraphrase emphasizes that Peter flouted Jewish tradition at *two* points: 1/ in entering the house of the uncircumcised and 2/ in eating with gentiles. Strictly speaking, neither was in itself forbidden to a Jew, but because of the difficulties each entailed, both were contrary to Jewish expectations; see Bruce 222 (on 10:28) and Haenchen 350 n4.

11 Cf the interlinear *Gloss*, which also notes that God would not allow deception in the time of prayer (1109–10).

12 'I was carried away and saw in an ecstasy': *raptus sum et in extasi vidi*. The language suggests a trance; cf the paraphrase on 10:10 (71 above) and n15.

13 For the detail that the sheet was 'tied' at its four corners, see the paraphrase on 10:11 (71 above) and n17.

14 Here in the paraphrase on 11:6, following a solid textual tradition, Erasmus gives four, rather than three kinds of wildlife. No attempt has been made to harmonize with the paraphrase on 10:12 (71 above, and see n19).

15 For the law on clean and unclean foods see Leviticus 11.

16 In the paraphrase here Erasmus repeats exactly the Vulgate of 10:14, *absit*. He thought the point important: in a 1516 annotation on 11:8 (*nequaquam domine*) he criticized the Vulgate for translating the same Greek word (μηδαμῶς) by *absit* in 10:14, but *nequaquam* ('not so' AV) in 11:8. In his translation he wrote *nequaquam* in 10:14 from 1519, in 11:8 from 1516.

17 'Again': *rursum*, for the Greek ἐκ δευτέρου, as in Erasmus' translation of 11:9 from 1516 and reflected apparently in AV; so also DV; in the Vulgate, *secundo* (cf Conf RSV 'a second time'). For the Greek expression see Bruce 232.

18 Scholars are divided over the correct reading of 11:12. In all editions 1516–1535 Erasmus read as in 10:20 μηδὲν διακρινόμενον 'having no doubt,' 'no hesitation' (so the Vulgate DV AV Conf; also Haenchen 345). Some critics prefer μηδὲν διακρίναντα 'making no distinction,' as in RSV; cf Bruce 232 and Munck 98. (For the difference in meaning between the middle διακρινόμενον and the active διακρίναντα see διακρίνω in BAG.) The Vulgate, again 'sporting variety,' wrote *nihil dubitans* in 10:20 and *nihil haesitans* in 11:12; from 1519 Erasmus translated both by *nihil haesitans*, which he retained in the paraphrases on both passages.

19 For the additional details – the few days, fasting and praying, the broad daylight, and the shining garment – see 10:30.

78

20 None of the Latin editions 1524–1535 places a comma after *quadrupedia* 'four-footed [creatures].' The lack of a comma may account for the rendering of the 1548 *Paraphrase of Erasmus* (on 11:15): 'fowerfoted crepyng beastes' (fol xlii verso).

21 For the thought see 1 Tim 4:3–5 and Acts 15:9.

22 Cf 1:5.

23 For the expression 'baptism of fire' see Matt 3:11, and for the 'fire of the Spirit' see the paraphrases on 2:1, 4, and 41 (13–15 and 24 above) and nn9 and 22. For a similar formulation of the 'theology of baptism' see the paraphrase on Mark 1:10 CWE 49 19: 'In the Lord was expressed in corporeal form what happens spiritually to all men who in sincere faith receive the evangelical baptism. The body is bathed with water, and the spirit is anointed with invisible grace.' Cf also the paraphrase on Mark 16:16 CWE 49 175. For Erasmus' hesitation between a causal and a symbolic view of baptism see CWE 42 37 n3 and Payne *Theology of the Sacraments* 163–4. See also the *Enchiridion* CWE 66 71.

24 For the expression see chapter 2 n75.

25 For the language of faith here in the paraphrase on 11:17 (*fides* 'faith,' *credulitas* 'belief,' *confido* 'trust') see the 1527 annotation on Rom 1:17 ('from faith unto faith') CWE 56 42–4.

26 Cf n23 above.

27 For the 'first-fruits from the Jews' see the paraphrase on 2:41 (24 above). Hugh of St Cher (on 11:18) 267 recto B questioned at some length precisely who the 'first-fruits of the gentiles' were. He suggests: 'The eunuch was *simpliciter* the first-fruits of the gentiles, but Cornelius was the first-fruits of the multitude of the gentiles because several believed with him; or, the eunuch was the first-fruits with respect to baptism, Cornelius with respect to fellowship, the kings [Matt 2:1–12] with respect to faith.'

28 It is difficult to account for Erasmus' geography here. Strabo and Ptolemy, both of whom Erasmus knew, place the northern boundary of Phoenicia not at Antioch but either at or just below the Eleutherus river; cf Strabo *Geography* 16.2.21; Ptolemy *Geography* 5.15.4. In New Testament times Eastern Cilicia (which included Tarsus) was attached to the province of Syria, of which Antioch on the Orontes was the capital. Even after the administrative reorganizations of the later empire, Phoenicia and Cilicia were separated not by the city of Antioch, but by one or (later) two provinces with the name 'Syria.'

29 The nature of the adversative relationship intended here in the contrast between preaching to all but (*tamen*) sharing only with the Jews is ambiguous. Erasmus may intend that while mixed audiences heard the proclamation, only Jews were invited to baptism; or that while the proclamation was indeed public, the public was carefully selected to include only Jews. Erasmus' translation in 11:19 ('speaking the word to no one except to the Jews only'), as well as the paraphrases on 11:20–1 which immediately follow, favour the second interpretation. On the other hand, see the paraphrase on 9:29 (67 above), where Paul has already proclaimed the gospel to both gentiles and Jews.

30 Cf Matt 7:6; also Mark 7:24–7.

79

31 As he had done in the 1527 additions to annotations on 6:1 and 9:29, so here in 11:20 Erasmus explains in a 1527 annotation (*loquebantur et ad Graecos*) that the text reads *Hellenistas* 'Hellenists' and refers to Jews of the Diaspora, though he allows, somewhat ambiguously, the possibility that the reference is to pagan Greeks. Elsewhere, the additions of 1527 to the *Annotations* frequently confirm interpretations already adopted in the *Paraphrase on Acts*; not so here, where the paraphrases appear to proceed on the assumption that the Greeks are pagans. *Hellenistas* is the preferred reading. For the meaning of the term see Bruce 235–6, Haenchen 365 n5, and Metzger 386–9. See also the paraphrase on 9:29 (67 above) and especially n36.

32 The details are gathered from 4:36. For Barnabas' 'apostolic sincerity' see the paraphrases on 4:36–5:1 (38 above).

33 The paraphrase here on 11:22 obscures the difference between the Vulgate (as represented in *1527*), 'was sent as far as Antioch' (so DV Conf RSV), and Erasmus' text and translation (from *1519*), 'was sent to go to Antioch' (similarly AV).

34 Cf the interlinear *Gloss* 1113–14 on 'was glad' (11:23): 'Since a great number was converted.'

35 The paraphrase anticipates a *1527* annotation on 11:23 (*permanere in Domino*) which justified Erasmus' translation (from *1516*) 'to persevere in clinging to the Lord' (cf AV RSV); cf the Vulgate 'to continue in the Lord' (so DV Conf), and for 'to the Lord,' as in the preferred reading, rather than 'in the Lord,' see Metzger 390.

36 Both the interlinear *Gloss* (on 11:24) 1113–14 and Nicholas of Lyra 1114F note that a multitude was added 'to the former number of those who believed.'

37 Cf n28 above.

38 For this description of Paul's task see 9:15; also Mal 1:11. Erasmus speaks of 'Paul' for the 'Saul' of the biblical text of 11:25; likewise in verse 30 below.

39 Cf 9:30, to which at this point in 11:25 both the *Gloss* 1114E and Nicholas of Lyra 1114F allude. On Caesarea in Phoenicia, see chapter 9 n38.

40 On Antioch see chapter 15 n3.

41 So likewise the exegetical tradition: the *Gloss* 1115A, citing Rabanus, Nicholas of Lyra 1115B, and Hugh of St Cher 267 recto C all derive the name from Christ, the founder. Here too, the paraphrase anticipates a *1527* addition to the annotation on 11:26 (*ita ut cognominarentur*): 'Just as publicans receive their name from the fact that they collect the public taxes, so Christians received their name from the fact that they professed Christ.'
    It is widely held that the term 'Christian' was a popular rather than an official appellation, and was given to the disciples by the populace of Antioch. For the origin of the name and the extensive literature on the subject see Bruce 238, Haenchen 367 n3; also *Beginnings* v 383–6.

42 Caligula is the nickname (meaning 'Little Boots') given to the boy Gaius by the soldiers when he was with his parents in the military camp on the Rhine. Gaius became emperor in AD 37 and was murdered in AD 41. Claudius was emperor AD 41–54.

80

43 The reasons given here in the paraphrase on 11:29 for Jewish poverty belong to the exegetical tradition. See Bede in the *Gloss* 1116E (cf *Super Acta* 11 PL 92 971C–D) and Nicholas of Lyra 1116E–F for precisely these reasons.

44 Both the interlinear *Gloss* 1115–16 and Nicholas of Lyra 1116E stress the strong desire of the Antiochenes to contribute. For the model of Christian giving described here see 1 Cor 16:2; 2 Cor 8:1–12, 9:7.

45 Cf the similar statement in the paraphrase on 4:35 (38 above) where the importance of the judgment of the apostles in the distribution of money is noted. On the significance in Acts of the term 'elders' see chapter 15 n22.

Chapter 12

1 For the beheading of John the Baptist see Mark 6:14–29; for the mocking of Christ see Luke 23:1–11.

Though the identification of the two Herods is rhetorically effective, it is mistaken. The Herod who beheaded John and mocked Jesus was Antipas, son of Herod the Great; he ruled for 43 years (4 BC–AD 39). The Herod of Acts 12:1 is, in fact, Agrippa I, grandson of Herod the Great and nephew of Antipas. He began his rule in 37 when Caligula granted him the tetrarchy of his uncle, Philip, which included Batanea and Trachonitis; in 39 he was given Antipas' tetrarchy of Galilee and Peraea, to which Judaea and Samaria were added in 41. He ruled his territories as king from 41 to 44. He died in 44 at games given in Caesarea in honour of Claudius. His son, Agrippa II, whom Paul later addressed (Acts 25:13–26:32), was a minor when his father died, but eventually came into possession of the territory once ruled by his uncles and his father. See Bruce 242–3, Munck 115–16, and for a partial genealogical table of the Herods IDB II 587.

Erasmus' mistake is surprising in view of the predominant exegetical tradition. Bede in the *Gloss* 1117A–B (cf Bede *Super Acta* 12 PL 92 971D–972A), Nicholas of Lyra 1117C, and Hugh of St Cher 267 verso E all distinguished the two Herods, as did Chrysostom *Hom in Acta* 26.1 PG 60 197. Here, however, Erasmus was perhaps following the interlinear *Gloss* (1115–16), which, in contradiction to the marginal *Gloss*, did identify the Herod of 12:1 with the Herod 'present at the passion of Christ,' a gloss Hugh of St Cher (ibidem) condemned as erroneous. In *1516* Erasmus' annotation on 12:1 (*misit Herodes rex*) made no comment on Herod. In *1527* he rather peremptorily dismissed the question – there were various opinions, he said, about who this Herod was; for himself he did not think it worth the effort to burden the reader with the problem. But the *1527* addition was replaced in *1535* by a partial genealogy of Herod's family with a brief history of Agrippa I, based apparently on Josephus; cf *Jewish War* 2.9.5–7 (178–83) and *Jewish Antiquities* 18.5.4 (130–42). In spite of the development of his annotation no attempt was made, evidently, to correct the paraphrase in the editions of 1534 or 1535.

2 Cf Luke 23:2–3; Mark 15:26; John 19:19–22.

3 The sentence may allude to a presumed fear of civil unrest. The paraphrase on 5:36–7 (45 above) suggests that the incidents surrounding Theudas and Judas

were intended to be seen as examples of such unrest. For civil unrest in Judaea in the first half of the first century AD see E. Mary Smallwood *The Jews Under Roman Rule: From Pompey to Diocletian* (Leiden 1976) 144–80.

4 'The congregation who were professing Jesus … Lord of all' is an unusually elaborate paraphrase on the word 'church'; cf chapter 5 n20 and the paraphrase on 12:5 (81 below) 'church of the disciples.'

5 'Be punished with the sword': *gladio plecti*; the idiom portrays the martyrdom as a punishment. To be 'killed … with the sword' (RSV) meant beheading (cf Haenchen 382); for the early embellishment of the story of the beheading of James see *Beginnings* IV 134.

6 For the apparent allusion see Matt 26:31 and Zech 13:7.

7 'Day,' subject of the verb *obstitit*, is in the singular in all editions *1524–1534*. It is clear, however, from Erasmus' *1516* annotation on 12:3 (*erat autem dies*) that here he had a Vulgate reading in the singular, though the preferred Vulgate reading is plural (as in the *1527* edition and in Weber II 1718). He himself read the plural in both text and translation (all editions *1516–1535*). In the Vulgate of Luke 22:1 the singular, 'feast day of the *azyma*,' is used to refer specifically to Passover, and this appears to be the interpretation Erasmus adopts here, as the phrase 'exceedingly holy day' indicates – so also, apparently in verse 5 where Peter spent the 'feast day' in prison. Note, however, the plural in the expression 'when the feast days were past' in the paraphrases on verses 4 and 6.

As with 'Pascha' (Passover), the Vulgate adopted the word *azyma* (feast of unleavened bread) without 'translating' it. Except in the case of 1 Cor 5:8, where the use of *azyma* is metaphorical, Erasmus also in his translation everywhere simply transliterated the Greek. In his paraphrases, on the other hand, he usually explains the word; cf the paraphrases on Matt 26:17; Mark 14:1 CWE 49 157; Luke 22:1; and, for its seasonal identification, Acts 20:6 (121 below).

8 Cf Matt 26:1–5; Mark 14:1–2; Luke 22:1–2. See also the interlinear *Gloss* (on 12:3) 1117–18: 'For this reason Herod arrested but did not kill Peter – as the Jews had said also about Christ, "It is not permitted to kill during the Passover"' [cf John 18:31]. So Hugh of St Cher 267 verso F.

9 For the appeasement of the people see the narratives of the trial of Jesus, especially Luke 23:18–25 and John 18:38–40; for guilt through intent, see Matt 5:21–8.

81

10 For Paul's escape from Damascus see 9:23–5 and 2 Cor 11:32–3; the two accounts are interwoven in the paraphrases on 9:23–5 (66–7 above).

11 The purpose of the four squads was not, however, to quadruple the strength of the deterrent force, but to provide for rotation of the guard, each squad serving

as guard for one of the four 'watches'; cf Bruce 244, who cites Vegetius *De re militari* 3.8.

12 Erasmus correctly understands the singular τὸ πάσχα ('Easter' AV) in 12:4 as referring to the entire period of the 'feast of unleavened bread'; see Bruce 244 and n7 above.

13 Proverbial though the statement is in character, I do not find it as the theme of any of the proverbs in the *Adagia*. For its converse, that a people is like its king, see the *Institutio principis christiani* CWE 27 219, and for the popularity of the proverb 'Like king, like people' in the sixteenth century, see Morris Palmer Tilley *A Dictionary of the Proverbs in England in the Sixteenth and Seventeenth Centuries* (Ann Arbor, MI 1950) 356.

14 Cf Matt 24:9.

15 nor ... stir up a riot] *nec tumultuantur*, first in the octavo editions of 1524; in the 1524 folio edition, *ne tumultuarentur* 'that [the disciples] should not stir up a riot' – which construes harshly with the rest of the sentence and is perhaps therefore a careless mistake

16 Cf Matt 5:44 and Luke 6:28; cf also Rom 12:14.

17 Throughout the paraphrases on this chapter Herod appears as the tyrant. For portraits of the tyrant in Erasmus, see especially the *Institutio principis christiani* CWE 27 225–31 and *Adagia* III vii 1: *Scarabeus aquilam quaerit* ASD II-6 400:97–406:258.

18 Cf the interlinear *Gloss* 1117–18, which sees the prayer of the church here in 12:5 as an 'example of prayer for those in danger and especially for the pastors of the church'; so, exactly, Hugh of St Cher 267 verso F.
For his own translation of the adjective ἐκτενής (the preferred reading is ἐκτενῶς adverb; cf Metzger 392–3), Erasmus adopted the Vulgate *sine intermissione* 'without ceasing' (so DV AV Conf), but in his annotation (*sine intermissione*) he explained the word in the sense either of *prolixa* 'extended,' 'copious' or *intenta* 'eager,' 'earnest' (so RSV).

19 For his translation of 12:8 Erasmus retained the Vulgate *vestimentum* 'garment' (so DV; 'cloak' Conf). In the paraphrase, however, he dresses Peter in the *pallium* – τὸ ἱμάτιον 'mantle' (RSV) in the text of Acts – the outer garment worn by Greeks. Tertullian described it in detail and advocated it especially as the garment for Christians; cf *De pallio* 1.1 and 6.2 CCL 2 733 and 750.

20 Cf 10:9–16.

21 In his translation of 12:10 Erasmus retained the Vulgate's *vicum unum* for the Greek ῥύμην μίαν, translated as 'one street' in DV AV Conf RSV. In fact, 'one' is used here as well as elsewhere in the Koine for the indefinite article, hence 'a street'; cf Bruce 246 and Haenchen 384 n7. Though the paraphrase retains the expression *vicum unum* the context here suggests more clearly than in the biblical text the sense *vicus* carries as a street representing a district in the city – a city 'block.'

The paraphrase leaves the topography uncertain. The prison was 'probably the tower of Antonia, where Paul also was detained (21:34–23:30)' (Bruce 246; so Haenchen 384 n6). The fortress of Antonia was just outside the court of the Temple on the north-west, 'from which, steps led to the city and to the Temple' (Haenchen 384 n6).

22 came] In all editions 1524–1535; 'then came' in LB, repeating the immediately preceding 'then,' perhaps by mistake.

82

23 Ie not the apostle John, as in the paraphrase on 12:2 (80 above).

24 'Door of the gate' (so DV and AV) represents the Vulgate's *ostium ianuae*, which Erasmus retains here. His translation, *ostium vestibuli* 'door of the courtyard,' was attacked by Zúñiga (cf *Apologia ad annotationes Stunicae* ASD IX-2 152:794–800 and 797n), and Erasmus attempted to clarify, in a 1522 addition to the annotation on 12:13 (*ad ostium*), the picture he had in mind: the first doorway opening into the courtyard. Cf Haenchen 385: 'a house of some size, with a gateway ... on the street from which the house proper was separated by the intervening courtyard.'

25 'Overhear': *subauscultaret*, as in Erasmus' translation (from 1516), for the Greek ὑπακοῦσαι. Though the preferred reading of the Vulgate is *ad audiendum* 'to hear' (cf Weber II 1718 and 13n), Erasmus' Vulgate, and the Vulgate of 1527, read *ad videndum* 'to see'; cf the annotation on 12:13 (*ad videndum*). In fact, the Greek ὑπακούω 'is the technical term for a doorkeeper's work: "open up"' (Haenchen 385 n1).

26 The *Gloss* (on 12:15) 1121C cites Matt 18:10 and Gen 48:16 as scriptural evidence that each person has his own angel; so also Hugh of St Cher 268 recto A. But see especially Nicholas of Lyra 1121C: 'The saints and Doctors are agreed that individuals each have their own angels assigned to their safety, and sometimes they appear in their likenesses ...' In his paraphrase on Matt 18:10, Erasmus describes the angels as attendants responsible for the care of the 'little ones.' The past tense – 'It was believed' – may suggest the voice of Erasmus the paraphrast rather than the persona of Luke the evangelist. However, belief in guardian angels has been reflected in Christian devotion through the centuries; for the history of this belief see the article 'Anges' by Joseph Duhr in *Dictionnaire de spiritualité* undertaken by Marcel Viller, assisted by F. Cavallera and J. de Guibert SJ; continued by Andre Rayez and Charles Baumgartner SJ, assisted by Michel Olphe-Galliard SJ 15 vols in 18 (Paris 1937–   ) I (1937) 580–619.

27 Cf the *Gloss* (on 12:17) 1121C: 'He bade them be silent so that his arrival should not be known in the city from the loud voices of those who were rejoicing'; so Hugh of St Cher 268 recto B.

28 James is called the 'brother of the Lord' in Gal 1:19. On this James see *Beginnings* V 54–6. Elsewhere Erasmus qualifies the designation 'brother of the Lord'; cf the paraphrase on 15:13 and n41.

29 The phrase 'God who is best' (*deus optimus*) in the paraphrase on 12:17 may have a partial parallel in ancient Roman use (*Jupiter optimus maximus*); here the phrase serves to introduce a theodicy. See the paraphrase just below on 12:19, where God had regard 'for the safety both of the apostles and soldiers'; also the paraphrase on Rom 8:28 CWE 42 50 and Sider 'The Just and the Holy' 14–19, 26.

30 The interlinear *Gloss* 1121–2 (on 12:17) also explains that Peter withdrew on account of his fear of Herod; similarly, Hugh of St Cher 268 recto B. The paraphrase makes no attempt to locate the 'other place' to which Peter withdrew; it has been identified as Rome, as Antioch, and indefinitely as 'another town'; see *Beginnings* IV 138.

31 The English versions – DV AV Conf RSV – explicitly interpret the Greek to mean that the guards were led away to death. Modern commentators regard this as the probable, but not absolutely assured meaning (Bruce 248–9, Munck 114, and Haenchen 386). The medieval exegetical tradition was less certain; cf the interlinear *Gloss* (on 12:19) 1121–2 and Nicholas of Lyra 1122F. In his annotation on the verse (*iussit eos duci*) Erasmus found it unclear whether the guards were led to prison or to punishment. The paraphrase incorporates both possibilities.

32 Cf the *Gloss* 1122F, citing Rabanus: 'That the release of Peter should harm no one, Herod is not permitted to punish the guards'; similarly Hugh of St Cher 268 recto B.

33 The *Gloss* 1122F, Nicholas of Lyra 1122F, and Hugh of St Cher 268 recto B all identify the site of Herod's dramatic death as 'Caesarea of Palestine.' On Caesarea as the administrative centre of the Roman procurators see chapter 10 n2.

34 See the annotation on 12:20 (*erat autem iratus Tyriis*), where Erasmus argues that Herod had not yet declared war but was planning war. But cf Haenchen 386, who argues that Herod could hardly be at war with cities of the Roman province of Syria and suggests that an 'economic war' might have been intended.

83

35 Cf the *Gloss* (on 12:20) 1122F–1123A, citing Bede: 'They regarded the friendship of a neighbouring king essential (cf Bede *Super Acta* 12 PL 92 973B).'

36 Bede *Super Acta* 13 PL 92 973B also noted that the wealth of Tyre and Sidon depended on their income from trade by sea. In fact, both cities were famous for their purple-dyeing industry, though as coastal cities, trade was a major source of their wealth; see, for Tyrian trade especially, P-W VIIA-2 1902–3.

37 For the various kinds of shows or games provided for the populace in the early Christian era see Ludwig Friedländer *Roman Life and Manners under the Early Empire* trans J.H. Freese and L.A. Magnus 4 vols (London 1936) II 1–130.

38 Cf the 'moral exposition' of Nicholas of Lyra 1123B–1124E: 'By this example . . .
   princes and prelates ought to be taught not to accept but rather to discourage
   honours inappropriate to themselves.' On flattery of kings as a vice to be
   avoided see the *Institutio principis christiani* CWE 27 245–53. For the mesmerizing
   effect of shows ('bread and circuses') on the Roman populace see Juvenal
   Satires 10.74–81.

39 For the details Erasmus supplies in this account, see Josephus *Jewish Antiquities*
   19.8.2 (343–6): 1/ Herod was providing shows in honour of Caesar; 2/ it was a
   votive festival on behalf of Caesar; 3/ a large number of distinguished people
   had gathered; 4/ on the second day of the festival Herod entered dressed in a
   radiant robe, 5/ which glittered when reflecting the light of the sun; 6/ Herod
   neither rebuked nor refused the flattery of the crowd.

40 For the detail of the angel and the several days of agonizing pain see the
   Gloss 1123A–1124D; see also Josephus *Jewish Antiquities* 19.8.2 (346–50) where,
   however, Herod sees not an angel but an owl over his head. In the *De immensa
   Dei misericordia* LB V 559B–C Erasmus cites Herod as an example of divine
   vengeance upon arrogance, and suggests that he perished from the 'lousy
   sickness.' For pediculosis as the cause of Herod's death see also the annotation
   on 12:23 (*et consumptus a vermibus*).

41 Though in his Greek text of 12:24 Erasmus printed the preferred reading,
   'word of God' (AV RSV; cf Metzger 397), in all editions *1516–1535* he translated
   with the Vulgate 'word of the Lord' (DV Conf).

42 Cf the interlinear *Gloss* 1123–4: 'The false lord dead, the word of God increased.'

43 Erasmus follows here the Vulgate and the preferred reading of the Greek,
   though in his text and translation he read 'Paul.' Cf the paraphrase on 11:25 (79
   above) and n38; and for the preferred reading of the Greek text see Metzger
   397–8.

44 The paraphrase assumes the Vulgate reading of 12:25 'returned from Jerusalem'
   (so DV AV Conf RSV), though Erasmus himself read (from *1516*) 'to Jerusalem.'
   On the difficulties of the Greek reading here see Bruce 251–2 and Metzger
   398–400, and for Erasmus' uncertainty about the correct reading see the
   annotation on 12:25 (*reversi sunt ab Hierosolymis*).

Chapter 13

1 'Quite a number' reflects the τινες 'some,' 'certain ones' of the manuscript
   tradition Erasmus followed here in text and translation (cf AV). The preferred
   reading omits the word – so the Vulgate DV Conf RSV; see Metzger 400 and, for
   the Vulgate, Weber II 1719.

2 For prophecy and teaching as gifts see 1 Cor 12:1–10, 28–30.

3 'Among these': *inter quos*, paraphrasing the Vulgate's *in quibus*, which is based on a textual tradition reading ἐν οἷς rather than the ὅ τε found in Erasmus' text and which gives the reading 'both Barnabas and Simeon'; cf Metzger 400 and *Beginnings* III 115–16 1n and 117.

4 'Simeon' (so AV RSV) in all editions of the *Paraphrase* except the 1524 octavo (A779), though in Erasmus' text and translation 'Simon' (so DV Conf and the Vulgate of 1527). The preferred reading of the Vulgate is Symeon; cf Weber II 1719 and 1n. On Symeon/Simeon/Simon see chapter 15 n42.
In his 1516 annotation on 13:1 (*Simon qui vocabatur Niger*) Erasmus expresses surprise at the name Niger in the Greek text, as it is a Latin term transliterated directly into Greek in the adjectival form proper to Latin. The Latin word means 'black.'

84

5 Erasmus understands the Greek σύντροφος as 'foster-brother' (DV and Conf) – see the annotation on 13:1 (*collactaneus*). σύντροφος is 'a title of honour given at court to certain youths of the same age as a prince, and retained by adults' (*Beginnings* IV 142). Haenchen 395 explains that 'Manaen' (RSV) was 'an intimate of the tetrarch Herod Antipas: hence he was a courtier of some note'; cf RSV: 'a member of the court of Herod the tetrarch.' On the Herods see chapter 12 n1.

6 In 13:9 Saul is identified as Paul, the name he receives henceforth in the biblical text. In the biblical text of 13:1–8 'Saul' is mentioned by name in verses 1, 2, and 7, and Erasmus in text from 1516 and translation from 1522 in all three verses writes 'Saul.' Before 1522 in his translation of verse 7 Erasmus had written 'Paul,' a variant found in the Vulgate of the 1527 edition (cf Weber II 1719 7n). In the paraphrases on chapter 13, 'Paul' appears first in verse 4 and is used thereafter; cf chapter 12 n43.

7 For Paul's gifts see eg 1 Cor 14:18; 2 Cor 12:11.

8 The paraphrase reflects Erasmus' understanding of the Greek λειτουργούντων (13:2), translated *ministrantibus* in the Vulgate, 'ministering' in DV and Conf (similarly AV), 'worshipping' in RSV. Erasmus himself translated 'making sacrifice' (from 1519) and pointed out in a 1519 annotation (*ministrantibus autem illis*) that the Greek word is used for those engaged in sacred activities. The paraphrase here anticipates a 1527 addition to the annotation: 'No sacrifice is more pleasing to God than imparting evangelical doctrine.' A similar sentiment is expressed in the annotation on Rom 15:16 ('sanctifying the gospel of God') CWE 56 404.

9 'Pure prayers': *puris precibus*. For the phrase see Job 16:17 (Vulgate 16:18, *mundae preces*). Cf also 2 Tim 2:22. For Erasmus' views on fasting see chapter 10 n16.

10 'Perform that service': *fungi munere*; cf chapter 6 n8.

11 With the paraphrase here compare the interlinear *Gloss* (on 13:2) 1125–6: 'Separate them to "serve teaching" alone'; so also Hugh of St Cher 268 recto D. For Paul as 'teacher of the gentiles' see 1 Tim 2:7; 2 Tim 1:11.

12 Erasmus avoids (in 13:3) the bold claim of Nicholas of Lyra 1125C, who argued that it was the bishops of the church of Antioch, already ordained by the apostles, who ordained Paul and Barnabas. Cf the interlinear *Gloss* 1125–6, which noted that hands were laid upon the two 'in the manner of those who are to be ordained.'

13 Seleucia served as the seaport of Antioch. Founded (like Antioch) about 300 BC, it was built on the coast several kilometers above the mouth of the Orontes. Antioch was situated about twenty-five kilometers inland on the Orontes. See IDB IV 264–6, and P-W IIA-1 1184–1200.

14 Though Salamis had been the capital of Cyprus in the earlier Ptolemaic period, its harbour began to silt up, and about 200 BC Paphos became the capital and remained so after Rome annexed the island in 58 BC. Rebuilt as Constantia by Constantius II (AD 317–61), the former Salamis once again became the capital of the island. See 'Salamis' in OCD.

15 For 'fables' see 1 Tim 4:7; 2 Tim 4:4.

16 On the large community of Jews in Salamis and their significance in the history of the city see P-W IA-2 1837. In his annotation on 13:5 (*et cum venissent Salaminam*) Erasmus notes that the Jewish community in Salamis was utterly destroyed during the reign of Trajan; cf Bede *De nominibus locorum* PL 92 1039.

17 Cf Luke 24:47.

18 The interlinear *Gloss* 1125–6 explains the preaching in the synagogues either as a 'mark of respect,' or 'because of the hardness of the Jews.'

19 'Old Paphos,' a site going back to Mycenaean times, had a well-known temple to Aphrodite (Venus), who was thought to have risen from the sea off its coast. In the classical period a new Paphos with a good harbour was built seventeen kilometres to the north and served as the seat of the Roman proconsuls; it was to the new Paphos (generally called simply 'Paphos') that Paul and Barnabas came. 'Old Paphos' with its temple to Aphrodite remained a place of pilgrimage. See 'Paphos' in OCD, P-W XVIII-3 938–41, and IDB III 648; also Bruce 256.

20 Nicholas of Lyra 1126F had also noted the meaning of the name 'Son of Jesus.' For the name see Bruce 256, and for the name in relation to Elymas see n23 below.

21 For Erasmus on the character of magicians see the paraphrases on 8:9–13 (58–9 above). Erasmus speaks briefly of magic in 'The Usefulness of the *Colloquies*' (Thompson *Colloquies* 631 / ASD I-3 746:199–200).

85

22 The clause anticipates a discussion in a *1527* addition to the annotation on 13:6 (*Barieu*): Bede thought the name was Barjeu, not Barjesus, since it was not

appropriate for a magician to be called the 'son of the Saviour'; cf *Super Acta* 13 PL 92 973D. Erasmus disagreed, and in the paraphrase here plays on the contrasting role of the two men with the name Jesus.

23 Erasmus offers the explanation commonly given of both the name *Elymas* and of the Greek text of 13:8 ('for that is the meaning of his name' RSV); cf Bruce 256–7 and Haenchen 398 n2. For Erasmus' uncertainty about the interpretation of 13:6 and 8 see his annotation on 13:6 (*Barieu*).

24 Cf Nicholas of Lyra 1126F on the words 'turn away the proconsul' (13:8 RSV): 'so that he could better keep him under his own influence.'

25 The paraphrase on 13:9 reflects none of the interest in the change of name from Saul to Paul apparent in Erasmus' lengthy annotation on the word 'Paul' in Rom 1:1 CWE 56 3–4. The *Gloss* (on 13:9) 1126E–1127B had commented on the change, citing both Bede and Rabanus, as had Hugh of St Cher 268 verso F and Nicholas of Lyra 1126F.

26 'Villainy': *versutia* 'villainy' (RSV; cf AV 'mischief'), following his own translation from *1519*. In an annotation on 13:10 (*et omni fallacia*), introduced in *1516* and enlarged in *1519*, Erasmus noted that the Greek word ῥᾳδουργία implied a 'propensity to any crime at all.' In *1516* only, Erasmus had followed the Vulgate in translating *fallacia* 'deceit' (so DV Conf). For Erasmus' interest in the language of evil see chapter 3 n45 and chapter 4 n7.

27 many] *multorum* in all editions *1524–1535*; in LB, *tuorum* 'yours'

28 An analogue to the verbal play here on the contrasting images of blindness and sight in the seer may be found in Sophocles *Oedipus Tyrannus*, especially lines 300–462; but cf also the paraphrase on 2 Pet 2:16 CWE 44 118.

29 The exegetical tradition frequently noted the justice of Elymas' blinding in 13:11. Cf the interlinear *Gloss* 1127–8 (on 'sun'): 'since you do not see the sun of justice'; the marginal *Gloss* 1127E: 'He did not deserve to have corporeal eyes who endeavoured to take away from others the eyes of the mind'; and Nicholas of Lyra 1127C, who noted that the penalty corresponded to the sin – physical blindness to the blindness of the mind. In paraphrasing here the biblical words 'for a time' Erasmus implies that a moral purpose motivates the punishment: Elymas is to be blind *until he repents*. For the contrast between physical and spiritual blindness see the paraphrases on John 9, especially 9:1 CWE 46 121; and for the metaphorical interpretation of blindness elsewhere, see especially the paraphrases on Mark 8:22–6 CWE 49 103–4 and on Mark 10:46–52 CWE 49 132–5.

86

30 Cf Nicholas of Lyra (on 13:12) 1127C: 'inferring from the divine power a proof of the doctrine preached by the apostles.'

31 For the geographical concept of Asia Minor elsewhere in Erasmus, see the annotation on Rom 16:5 ('of the church of Asia') CWE 56 426. Orosius *Historia*

1.2 PL 31 679A defined the boundaries of Asia Minor as the Asian peninsula west of Cappadocia and bounded by the Black Sea, the Sea of Marmara and the Dardanelles, the Aegean and the Mediterranean. This is in effect the definition of Erasmus in the annotation on Acts 16:6 (*loqui verbum in Asia*). To the Byzantines 'Little Asia' included a somewhat smaller territory of the peninsula defined by the Diocese of Asiana, for which see Jones *Later Roman Empire* III 387. On the term 'Asia' see *Beginnings* v 229–30, and for the various expressions of the concept of 'Little Asia' in antiquity P-W II-2 1538 and Demetrius J. Georgacas *The Names for the Asia Minor Peninsula* Beiträge zur Namenforschung NF 8 (Heidelberg 1971) 27–35.

For the first clause of 13:13 Erasmus' Vulgate and the Vulgate of 1527 read 'Now when Paul and those who were with him had sailed from Paphos' (so DV). In 1516 and 1519 Erasmus had translated 'When those who were with Paul had sailed from Paphos,' a literal translation of the Greek, which, Zúñiga complained, failed to recognize Greek idiom and seemed to exclude Paul; cf *Apologia ad annotationes Stunicae* ASD IX-2 152:812–19. In 1522 Erasmus changed his translation to read 'When Paul had sailed from Paphos, those who were with him came to Perga.' The paraphrase here appears to favour the Vulgate reading. For the Greek idiom, meaning 'Paul and his company,' see Bruce 259, and for Erasmus' discussion of the idiom see the 1522 annotation on 13:13 (*Paulus et qui cum eo erant*).

32 Erasmus' paraphrase agrees with his text and translation of 13:14 and with the Vulgate in reading *Pisidiae* in the genitive case, apparently making Antioch a city in the province of Pisidia (so DV AV; cf RSV); see the paraphrase on 14:24 (94 below), where Antioch is unambiguously located *in* Pisidia. But Antioch was not part of the province of Pisidia until after Diocletian's reorganization of the Roman provinces c AD 293. In the preferred text, therefore, the word is *Pisidian*, in the accusative case, to mean the Antioch near Pisidia (cf Conf 'Pisidian Antioch'); see Bruce 260, Metzger 404–5, and Timothy D. Barnes *The New Empire of Diocletian and Constantine* (Cambridge, MA 1982) 217. Erasmus appears to have followed sources that placed the city in the province of Pisidia – so the *Gloss* 1127E and Bede *De nominibus locorum* PL 92 1035A; cf the annotation on 13:13 (*venerunt Pergen Pamphyliae*).

33 For the evidence for distinctive Jewish dress from biblical times to Erasmus' own day, see the article 'Dress' in *Encyclopaedia Judaica* VI 212–23 and the bibliography cited there.

34 For Erasmus' amplification on synagogue procedure in the paraphrase on 13:15 see Haenchen 407–8. The introduction of 'pages' may be Erasmus' own imaginative touch.

35 Though the Greek text speaks explicitly only of 'motioning with the hand' (RSV; so AV), the Vulgate had explicated the text: 'motioning with his hand for

silence' (Conf; so DV). Erasmus accepted the Vulgate explication for his own translation (from 1516), which he justified in a 1527 addition to the annotation on 13:16 (*et manu silentium indicens*).

36 The expression anticipates 13:27. On the slight distinction felt here between 'Israelites' and 'God-fearers' see n63 below.

37 Cf the interlinear *Gloss* 1129–30, commenting on the expression '[God] chose' (13:17): 'In preference to other peoples who worshipped other gods.'
The paraphrase apparently attempts to embrace the readings both of the Vulgate, 'the God of the people of Israel' (so DV Conf), and Erasmus' text and translation (from 1516), 'the God of this people.' For a conflated reading, 'the God of this people Israel,' see AV RSV. For the textual problem see Haenchen 408 n4.

38 For the expression see Isa 14:3 (especially the Vulgate). Cf also Nicholas of Lyra (on 13:17) 1129C: '[during their stay in the land of Egypt], in which, after the death of Joseph, they had been subjected to harsh bondage.'

39 For these details see Exod 1:8–22.

40 Cf Nicholas of Lyra (on 13:17) 1129C, who explains 'uplifted arm' by 'wondrous signs.' For the narrative of the miracles see Exodus 7–11 and 14.

41 The interlinear *Gloss* (on 13:18) 1129–30 notes that the 'forty years' 'indicates the long-suffering of God.'

42 Nicholas of Lyra 1129C also glosses the expression 'bore with' (13:18 RSV) by noting the many times the Israelites 'rebelled against the Lord.' For the murmuring and the rebellion see Exod 15:23–16:30; Num 14:1–39.

43 For the promise that Abraham's descendants should inherit Canaan see Gen 15; 17:7–8. The *Gloss* refers to the promise in its commentary on both 13:19 and 13:20 (1130D, 1130E).

44 The paraphrase on 13:19–20 appears to follow the Vulgate: 'He divided their land by lot after about four hundred and fifty years; and after that he gave them judges . . .' The paraphrase, however, implies more clearly the time in the sequence of events – the division of the land concludes a period stretching back 450 years, after which judges were given. But the reading of these verses varies in the witnesses: RSV reads 'He gave them their land as an inheritance, for about four hundred and fifty years. And after that he gave them judges . . .'; AV reads 'He divided their land to them by lot. And after that he gave unto them judges about the space of four hundred and fifty years . . .' For the textual problem see *Beginnings* III 120–1, Bruce 264, Haenchen 408–9, and Metzger 406–7. Bede, in the *Gloss* 1130E, had calculated the 450 years from Abraham to the distribution of the land in Canaan (cf *Super Acta* 13 PL 92 974A–B), similarly Nicholas of Lyra 1130F and Hugh of St Cher 268 verso H–269 recto A, and this conforms with rabbinical opinion – for which, and for a discussion of the time designated by the 450 years, see *Beginnings* IV 150–1.

45 According to the book of Judges, 'the Lord raised up judges for [the people]' (RSV) to deliver them from the oppression of their enemies (Judg 2:18). Here in the paraphrase the judge appears to have had the responsibility to maintain the peace. Cf the dedicatory letter to Francis I for the *Paraphrase on Mark* (Ep 1400 CWE 49 2–12), where Erasmus insists upon the obligation of the king to maintain peace. Cf also Nicholas of Lyra (on 13:20) 1130F: 'He gave them judges for the government of the people' (*regimen populi*).

46 Cf Nicholas of Lyra 1130F on the phrase 'until Samuel' (13:20): 'Inclusively, since he was the last of the judges.' For Samuel as judge see 1 Sam 7:15.

47 Cf 1 Sam 8:4–18.

48 Cf 1 Sam 9:1–10:1, 13:5–14.

87

49 The length neither of Samuel's rule nor of Saul's reign is known; see, for Samuel, 1 Sam 7:15; for Saul, the defective text of 1 Sam 13:1 (RSV), and Josephus *Jewish Antiquities* 6.14.9 (378) and 10.8.4 (143). But the exegetical tradition ascribed the forty years of Acts 13:21 to the rule of both Samuel and Saul: so the interlinear *Gloss* 1129–30, Bede in the *Gloss* 1130E–1131A (cf *Super Acta* 13 PL 92 974B–C), Nicholas of Lyra 1130F, and Hugh of St Cher 269 recto A. Cf Bruce 264–5, Haenchen 409, and, on the problematic text of Josephus *Jewish Antiquities* 6.14.9 (378), see the note in *Josephus* V trans H. St. J. Thackeray, Ralph Marcus, et al, Loeb Classical Library (Cambridge, MA 1934) 357.

50 The interlinear *Gloss* (1129–30) on both 13:21 and 13:22 noted the patience of God.

51 The words cited here in 13:22 are in fact a conflation of passages from Ps 89:20, 1 Sam 13:14, 2 Sam 23:1, and Isa 44:28; see Haenchen 409 and n3. In his translation Erasmus had followed the Vulgate exactly in rendering the 'quotation,' thus offering a literal translation of the Greek (cf DV); the paraphrase gives a free and idiomatic rendition, but without paraphrastic expansion.

52 For the moral mirroring of prince and people see the paraphrase on 12:4 (80–1 above) and n13. For the contrasting portraits of the good and bad king, see the *Institutio principis christiani* CWE 27 223–31 and especially 226, where 1 Sam 8:11–18 is cited as a portrait of the tyrant. On Erasmus' attitude to monarchy see James D. Tracy *The Politics of Erasmus* (Toronto 1978) 23–47.

53 Cf Ps 89:3–4; 132:11–12.

54 Cf the interlinear *Gloss* (on 15:23) 1129–30: 'This was done not suddenly, but after many promises of the prophets'; similarly Hugh of St Cher 268 recto B.

55 The paraphrase 'Saviour *of* the race of Israel' is perhaps surprising, since in his annotation on 13:23 (*eduxit Israel salvatorem*) Erasmus stresses that 'Israel' is in

the dative case: 'brought forth *to* (or, *for*) Israel a Saviour,' a reading reflected in his own translation from *1519*.

'Brought forth' represents the preferred reading of the Greek, ἤγαγε, which is the reading of Erasmus' text and the reading implied by the Vulgate's *eduxit* 'brought out' (cf Conf RSV). Erasmus seems not to have considered the inferior reading ἤγειρε (AV 'raised'), though it appears in a passage of Chrysostom cited in the annotation on 13:23 (*Iesum*); cf *Beginnings* III 122.

56 For the meaning of the name see Matt 1:21. The interlinear *Gloss* (on 13:23) 1129–30 also reflects on the meaning of the name: 'He puts the interpretation with the name – for Jesus means "Saviour."' Though in his text and translation (from *1516*) Erasmus followed the majority reading which includes the name, he was aware of a minority reading from which the name is absent (cf Metzger 408). His annotation on the word (*Iesum*) drew fire from Lee; cf the *Responsio ad annotationes Lei* LB IX 208E–209A.

'Saviour' represents the Latin *servator*, which Erasmus, in his translation of the Greek σωτήρ, everywhere substituted for the Vulgate's *salvator* (except for a periphrasis in Eph 5:23). *Servator* is, as he explains in his annotation on Luke 1:47 (*salutari meo*), the term 'Latin-speakers' prefer; cf CWE 44 xviii.

57 For Isaiah's prophecy see Isa 40.3. For Erasmus' interpretation of John's role as the precursor of Christ, see the paraphrases on Mark 1:4–8 and Mark 1:14 CWE 49 14–17, 21 and on John 1:36 CWE 46 32–3.

58 For the expression see John 1:6.

59 In a *1516* annotation on 13:25 (*quem me arbitramini esse non sum*) Erasmus had observed that the statement of the Vulgate 'I am not he whom you suppose me to be' (Conf; so DV) should be replaced with a question and response: 'Whom think ye that I am? I am not he' (AV). Accordingly in *1519* he changed his text and translation, which he followed here in the paraphrase. He seems to have been unaware of the preferred reading 'what' rather than 'whom' (Metzger 408; cf *Beginnings* IV 152–3 and 25n; also Bruce 266 and Haenchen 409).

60 An allusion to John 1:30; for the interpretation implied here see the paraphrase on John 1:30 CWE 46 30. Cf also the annotation on the same verse (*venit vir*).

61 Cf Matt 21:23–7; Mark 11:27–33; Luke 20:1–8.

62 Cf Gen 22:18.

88

63 In his text and translation of 13:26 Erasmus seems to have distinguished the Jews and the 'God-fearers' ('and those among you that fear God' RSV), but the distinction is effectively eliminated in the paraphrase. Cf the annotation on 13:26 (*et qui in vobis timent*): 'The two personae [you and the God-fearers] are wonderfully mingled, so that they cannot be separated.' Cf the paraphrase

on 13:16 (86 above), where, at the beginning of Paul's speech, Erasmus 'wonderfully mingles' the two groups.

64 Erasmus agreed (text, translation, and paraphrase) with the Vulgate of 13:26 in reading 'to you' (DV AV Conf) rather than the preferred reading 'to us' (RSV); see Metzger 408–9.

65 With this interpretation of the 'word' (13:26 DV AV Conf; 'message' RSV) compare the paraphrase on 10:36 (73 above) and n49. For the prophetic promises and Christ's Jewish descent see Rom 9:4–5.

66 On the divine ordination see the paraphrase on 4:28 (36 above): '... your ... eternal wisdom had determined [what] would be done.'

67 For the mingled allusions see Isa 53; John 1:29; Heb 9:12–14.

68 For the efforts made to find Jesus guilty see Matt 26:59–61 and Mark 14:55–8; for the shameless cries, Matt 27:15–23; Mark 15:8–14; Luke 23:18–23. The interlinear *Gloss* (on 13:28) 1131–2 also observes the shameless cries, citing John 19:15: 'Away with him ... crucify him.'

69 The paraphrase anticipates a *1527* annotation on 13:28 (*ut interficerent eum*): 'We can adopt the sense that Pilate killed him.' This was the sense that Erasmus adopted for his translation from *1516* to *1527*. But as Erasmus himself observed in his annotation, the Greek is ambiguous, reading 'They asked Pilate to have him killed' (RSV). For his final edition of *1535* Erasmus adopted the Vulgate reading, 'They asked Pilate "that they might kill him"' (DV) – a reading that fastens upon the Jews greater responsibility for Jesus' death. Both the interlinear *Gloss* 1131–2 and Nicholas of Lyra 1132F note here that Jesus was killed 'by the hands of the soldiers.' For Erasmus' interest in the problem of locating the responsibility for Jesus' death see the paraphrase on 2:23 (19 above) and n67.

70 Nicholas of Lyra 1132F observes on the words 'they did not recognize him' (13:27 RSV) that the ignorance of the Jews was inexcusable because it proceeded from an evil will, and he repeats the point in a gloss on the words 'voices of the prophets.' Here Erasmus does not labour the connexion between Jewish ignorance and malice; elsewhere it is more explicit. Cf eg the paraphrases on John 15:21–4 CWE 46 181–2 and chapter 3 n45.

71 For the journey to Jerusalem see Matt 20:17–19; Mark 10:32–4; Luke 18:31–4.

72 For the expression see 1 Cor 15:6. The Greek textual tradition is divided on 13:31: some texts read 'who now are witnesses,' others 'who are now witnesses,' still others omit 'now' entirely, reading 'who are witnesses'; cf Bruce 268 and Metzger 410. The Vulgate of *1527* reads 'who to this present are his witnesses' (DV; so Weber II 1721, and cf Conf and RSV); this is the reading the paraphrase somewhat ambiguously acknowledges. In Erasmus' text and translation, however, 'now' is omitted in all editions (so AV).

73 For the sequence of eyes, ears, hands see the paraphrase on 1:3 (6 above) and n17 and the paraphrase on 2:32 (21 above).

74 For the expression see n10 above. Erasmus paraphrases the 'and we' of the Greek of 13:32 (so DV AV RSV) by 'we also' (cf Conf), sharpening the contrast between the 'witnesses' of 13:31 and those of 13:32, namely, Paul, or Paul and Barnabas (see Munck 123). For the command to preach see 13:2; Gal 1:1 and 15–16; also Acts 1:8 (the command to the apostles).

75 Erasmus follows the Vulgate represented in the 1527 edition, 'has fulfilled for your children' (13:33), though the preferred Vulgate reading is 'for our children' (Weber II 1721; so DV and Conf). Erasmus himself read in text and translation (all editions 1516–1535) 'has fulfilled for us their children' (so AV RSV). For the difficulties of the Greek text see Bruce 269, Haenchen 411, and Metzger 410–11.

76 For the reference to Mary at this point see Rom 1:3. Erasmus followed the exegetical tradition in alluding to the incarnation in the interpretation of 13:33; cf the interlinear Gloss 1133–4: 'For that nativity from the Virgin is from God'; so Hugh of St Cher 269 recto D. Bede in the Gloss 1133A insisted that the psalm referred to the incarnation (cf Super Acta 13 PL 92 974C–D), though in the Liber retractationis 13 PL 92 1023B–1023D he records Hilary's view that the reference is to the resurrection of Christ as the 'first-born' from the dead. Nicholas of Lyra 1133C thought the psalm demonstrated the eternal generation of the Son, whose humanity was demonstrated by his life on earth.

The number given to the psalm cited in 13:33 is problematic (see Metzger 412–14). There is evidence that in the early centuries of the Christian era the first two psalms were counted as one psalm and some manuscript evidence to support here in 13:33 the reading 'in the first psalm.' Against the Vulgate ('second psalm' DV AV Conf RSV) Erasmus himself read 'first psalm' in both text and translation, a reading he defended in his annotation on 13:33 (sicut in psalmo secundo scriptum est). Bede in the Gloss 1133A (cf Super Acta 13 PL 92 974D) had noted that some codices read 'first psalm.'

77 In the paraphrase here Erasmus cites the text of Isa 55:3 as it is found in the Vulgate of Acts 13:34. I have adopted the translation of Conf, though DV is a more literal translation of the Vulgate: 'I will give you the holy things of David, faithful.' Erasmus adopted the Vulgate text of 13:34 for his own translation (all editions 1516–1535).

78 'Covenant': pactum, for which see Isa 55:3. The Gloss 1133B citing Bede on 13:34 also alludes to the pactum of Isa 55:3 (cf Bede Super Acta 13 PL 92 975A).

89

79 With two minor exceptions, Erasmus quotes the text of the psalm as it is found in the Vulgate according to the LXX (cf Weber I 882); the English translation here follows the Douay version of Ps 88:36–8 in Challoner's revision (1750).

80 Erasmus echoes the Nicene Creed – 'His kingdom shall have no end'; cf also Matt 22:44; Mark 14:62; and Rev 11:15.

81 Erasmus quotes the psalm cited in 13:35 as he translated in the editions from 1519, rather than from the Vulgate, whose translation he had adopted in 1516.

82 The paraphrase represents Erasmus' understanding of the Greek construction in 13:36, an understanding reflected in all editions of his text and translation, both of which were punctuated to read 'For David, after he had served his own generation, by the will of God fell asleep'; cf his annotation on the verse, *voluntati dei*. But the construction is disputed. RSV reads 'For David, after he had served the counsel of God in his own generation, fell asleep' (similarly Conf); AV reads 'For David, after he had served his own generation by the will of God, fell asleep.' For the ambiguity of the construction see Bruce 270 and Haenchen (who follows Erasmus) 406, 412 and n3. For David's exercise of power until his death, and for his death 'at the prescribed time,' see 1 Kings 1:1–2:11.

83 Cf 2:29.

84 For the Law 'according to the flesh,' ie the carnal part of the Law, see the paraphrases on Rom 8:3 CWE 42 45 and n2 and on Mark 1:14 CWE 49 21. On the punishments of the Law see eg Lev 20:1–21, 24:10–22; Num 15:32–6; and on the inadequacy of the Law see Heb 10:1–4.

85 'Be astounded and undone': *obstupescite ac disperite*. Apart from this clause, Erasmus followed the Vulgate closely both in his translation of 13:41 and here in the paraphrase. In this clause, however, he followed neither his own translation, which read (from 1519) *admiramini et evanescite* 'wonder and vanish,' nor the Vulgate, *admiramini et disperdimini* 'wonder and perish.' See the annotations on 13:40–1 (*quod dictum est in prophetis* and *et disperdimini*), from which it is clear that Erasmus took the word *obstupescite* from the Vulgate of Hab 1:5. But the Vulgate's *disperdere* appears later in the paraphrase in preference to either *disperire* or the *evanescere* of Erasmus' translation; see n87 below.

86 Nicholas of Lyra 1134F also interprets the 'work ... you will not believe' (13:41) as the incarnation, the passion, and the resurrection of Christ. For the 'work' as 'the rejection of the Jews and the acceptance of the Gentiles' see Haenchen 413.

87 The interlinear *Gloss* (on 13:41) 1133–4 observes that people become despisers through incredulity. 'Do not perish' in this clause reflects the Vulgate's *disperdimini* in 13:41; see n85 above.

88 In the paraphrase here Erasmus follows the Vulgate and the preferred reading of 13:42a, where the subject of both clauses is indefinite: 'As they went out, the people begged' (RSV; similarly DV and Conf). In his text (all editions 1516–1535) Erasmus followed a reading of the Byzantine tradition, a reading which from 1516 to 1527 he translated as 'When the Jews went out of the assembly, the

gentiles asked' (so AV). In 1535 he acknowledged the ambiguity of this reading and translated, 'The gentiles asked them [Paul and Barnabas] as they went out of the assembly.' For Erasmus' change of translation in 1535 see the 1535 addition to the annotation on the verse (*exeuntibus autem illis*). On the text see *Beginnings* III 126–7, Haenchen 413 and n6, and Metzger 416–17.

89 The expression reflects an understanding of 13:43 held both by Erasmus and the exegetical tradition. The Vulgate of 1527 translated *colentium deum advenarum* 'strangers who served God' (DV); likewise the Vulgate reflected in the annotation on the verse (*et colentium deum*) – similarly Weber II 1721 '*colentium advenarum*' where, however, *deum* is omitted. Erasmus believed these were proselytes; and this is the interpretation also of the *Gloss* 1135A and of Valla *Annot in Acta* 13 (I 850). In 1516 Erasmus translated 'religious strangers,' but thereafter 'religious proselytes' (so AV).

90 The interlinear *Gloss* 1135–6 interprets 'to continue' (13:43 RSV) as striving for the end implied in a good beginning. For this image elsewhere in Erasmus, particularly (but not exclusively) in the sense of progress in the Christian life, see eg the paraphrases on John 8:31 CWE 46 113; Gal 3:2–3 CWE 42 108–9; Rom 8:28–30 CWE 42 50–1; also on Mark 6:9 CWE 49 79.

90

91 Erasmus' paraphrastic expansion here on 13:44, which notes the spread of the good news, has a parallel in the paraphrastic 'Western' text: 'And it came to pass that the word of God went throughout the whole city' (Metzger 418). Bede *Liber retractationis* 13 PL 92 1023D attests this addition in the Greek text known to him.

92 Erasmus follows the Vulgate reading of 13:45, 'contradicted . . . and blasphemed' (so Conf; similarly DV and RSV), rather than his own text and translation (from 1516), which repeats the word 'contradict': 'contradicted . . . contradicting and blaspheming' (similarly AV). The shorter reading is preferred (Metzger 418–19).

93 Cf Mark 6:11; Luke 9:5.

94 'Frankly': *libere*. Compare the Vulgate *constanter*, DV 'boldly,' Greek παρρησιασάμενοι, Erasmus' translation *sumpta fiducia* 'with assured self-confidence.' See the paraphrases on 2:29 ('to speak the truth freely') 20 above and 9:27 ('boldly and freely') 67 above. On the significance of the biblical word see chapter 4 n36. For his translation of the word in 13:46 see his annotation on the verse (*constanter*).

95 Cf Matt 10:5–6; Luke 24:47; also Rom 1:16 and the paraphrase on Acts 3:26 (30 above).

96 Cf 1:8.

97 Here, as in his translation, Erasmus cites the prophetic words for the most part as they are found in the Vulgate of Isa 49:6, where, however, the text reads,

'you should be my salvation' rather than 'you should be salvation.'
In Isaiah the words are addressed by the Lord to his 'servant,' who is given as a light to the gentiles. In Luke 2:32 the 'light to the gentiles' is Jesus. But the *Gloss* (on 13:47) 1137A, citing Bede, notes that 'what is said specifically of Christ, the apostles believe was said for themselves' (cf Bede *Super Acta* 13 PL 92 975A–B). Nicholas of Lyra 1136F–1137B understood the 'light to the gentiles' as the 'faith of Christ,' received by the gentiles through the preaching of the apostles.

98 Cf Rom 11:11–20.

99 'Of the Lord' is the reading of the Vulgate and of Erasmus' text and translation (so DV AV Conf). It is also the preferred reading, though 'of God' has strong support (so RSV); cf Metzger 419.

100 For the phrase 'called and chosen' see Rev 17:14. On the distinction elsewhere in Erasmus between 'called' and 'chosen' see the paraphrase on Matt 20:15–16, and the annotation on Rom 1:1 ('called an apostle') CWE 56 5–6.

91

101 Cf Bede *De nominibus locorum* PL 92 1037D: 'The most distinguished city of Lycaonia; there is another in Cilicia' – a distinction Erasmus makes in his annotation on 14:1 (*factum est autem in Iconio*). F.V. Filson 'Lycaonia' in IDB III 189 suggests that the reference in Acts 14:5–6 to only Lystra and Derbe as 'cities of Lycaonia' implies Iconium was 'sometimes reckoned as part of Phrygia'; see Bruce 279 and Munck 128. See also the comments of Haenchen 419 n1 (on Iconium): 'Ethnically Phrygian, politically part of the province of Galatia'; and Hans Conzelmann: 'Iconium ... was reckoned partly with Phrygia ... and partly with Lycaonia' (in his *Acts of the Apostles* trans J. Limburg, A. Kraabel, and D.H. Juel, ed E.J. Epp, C.R. Matthews, Hermeneia [Philadelphia 1987] 107). For the shifting political geography of Lycaonia see Jones *Cities* 128–36.

Chapter 14

1 Ie as in Pisidian Antioch; cf the paraphrase just above on 13:50. For Jewish malice see chapter 3 n45; 'spite' here, as in the paraphrase on 13:50, translates *livor*.

2 Cf Chrysostom *Hom in Acta* 30.1 PG 60 222: 'They stirred up the gentiles also, since they themselves were not enough.' Erasmus had at least a portion of Chrysostom's homily on this chapter in 1522; see the annotation on 14:6 (*et universam in circuitu regionem*). 'Stirred up and infected' represents the Latin *concitaverunt et corruperunt*, which follows Erasmus' translation from 1516. Erasmus endeavoured to justify his translation in a 1527 annotation on 14:2 (*suscitaverunt et ad iracundiam concitaverunt*).

3 Both phrases in this clause of 14:3 are problematic. 'Carrying on their work courageously' (*fortiter rem gerentes*) follows closely Erasmus' translation (from 1519) for the Greek παρρησιαζόμενοι (on which see chapter 13 n94). Haenchen 420 n6 thinks the word here describes 'the Christian missionaries' confidence in a dangerous situation' (cf DV 'dealing confidently'; Conf 'acting fearlessly'), but for the view that the word here implies 'preaching' see TDNT V 882. BAG cites Acts 14:3 for the meaning 'speak freely'; cf AV RSV 'speaking boldly.' 'With the help of the Lord' follows exactly Erasmus' translation (from 1519). The Vulgate had here rendered the Greek ἐπί by *in* – 'in the Lord' (so DV AV Conf; cf RSV 'for the Lord'). For the use of ἐπί here see παρρησιάζομαι 1 in BAG. For Erasmus' attempt to explain the significance of ἐπί followed by the dative (as here) see the annotation on Rom 5:12 ('in whom [or, in which] all have sinned') CWE 56 140–1.

4 With this sentence compare 1 Cor 2:1–4.

5 Erasmus adopted the expression of the Vulgate *impetum facere* 'to make an assault' (DV AV), though the sequence of events in Acts indicates rather that a 'movement' (Conf) or an 'attempt' (RSV) was made (cf Haenchen 420–1).
By the expression *primores civitatis* 'chief men of the city' Erasmus may intend to suggest the city magistrates; cf 13:50, where Erasmus in paraphrase uses a similar expression to refer to what are apparently the city magistrates (so Bruce 276). In fact, however, here in 14:5 the ἄρχοντες are Jewish, or both Jewish and gentile, leaders; cf *Beginnings* IV 162 5n and Bruce 278.

6 Lycaonia may be defined both as an ethnographical and a political-administrative concept. As the former, it can be located north of the Taurus Mountains and east of Pamphylia, while Pamphylia was south of the Taurus range. As the latter, its boundaries frequently changed throughout antiquity, though always with some connection to ethnic realities. In the Roman provincial system Lycaonia was, until late antiquity, included within various provinces – Cilicia, Galatia, Cappadocia – but was never, evidently, a part of Pamphylia. The *Notitia dignitatum*, in late antiquity, lists Lycaonia as a separate province, and the two are clearly distinguished by Pliny *Naturalis historia* 5.25.95–26.96. There is then no reason to think that Lycaonia was either ethnographically or politically a part of Pamphylia. Cf P-W XIII-2 2253 (for Lycaonia) and P-W XVIII-3 355–6 (for the boundaries of Pamphylia); also Jones *Cities* 124–47 and Jones *Later Roman Empire* III 387.

7 Among the translations DV and Conf include in verse 6 the words 'and there they preached the gospel' (whose paraphrase begins here); in AV and RSV these words constitute a separate verse 7, thus adding a verse to the chapter. Henceforth in the paraphrases on this chapter verses are cited according to the number assigned in AV and RSV.

8 Cf the interlinear *Gloss* 1139–40 on 'preached' (14:7 RSV): 'They fled so they could preach the gospel'; also the marginal *Gloss* 1139A, citing Rabanus: 'The flight of the apostles was not more from fear than from their love of the word of God'; similarly Hugh of St Cher 270 recto A. For the image of sowing the word, based on the parables of sowing, see Matt 13:1–23; Mark 4:1–20; Luke 8:4–15; cf also the paraphrases on 14:22 and 24 (93–4 below).
The 'Western' text added two clauses at the end of 14:7: 'The whole multitude was moved by their doctrine; and Paul and Barnabas stayed at Lystra'; cf *Beginnings* III 131 and Metzger 419–20; also Bede *Super Acta* 14 PL 92 975C. Erasmus omitted them from his own text, as from the paraphrase. They are not added in DV AV Conf or RSV, but they are found in the *Vulgate* of 1527, and their omission from Erasmus' text drew harsh criticism from Edward Lee; see the *Responsio ad annotationes Lei* LB IX 209B–E and Erasmus' discussion in his annotation on 14:6 (*et universam in circuitu regionem*).

9 The exegetical tradition acknowledged the biblical emphasis on the severity of the cripple's condition, which made the miracle seem the greater. Cf the interlinear *Gloss* (on 14:8) 1139–40; also Hugh of St Cher 270 recto A and Bruce 280.

92

10 The biblical text of 14:9 says that Paul 'saw' the man's faith. How? Erasmus rationalizes – Paul recognized it from the cripple's expression; but cf Nicholas of Lyra 1140F, who noted that Paul looked with both physical and mental vision, since 'faith cannot be seen by corporeal eyes.'

11 The origin of the name Lycaonian is obscure, though various attempts were made in antiquity to derive Lycaonian from a mythological Lycaon (P-W XIII-2 2253–4). In Ovid's *Metamorphoses* Lycaon was the king of Arcadia who received Jupiter into his house to test his divinity by placing before him the roasted flesh of a human being and was in punishment turned into a wolf (Greek λύκος [*lykos*] 'wolf') (1.209–43). In a contrasting narrative Jupiter once again visited the human race, but now with Mercury. Both were turned away by everyone else but received hospitality from Baucis and Philemon, who were as a reward granted their wish to die together (8.618–724). Even some modern scholars have appealed to the Philemon-Baucis myth to explain the Lycaonians' hasty identification of Paul and Barnabas with Jupiter and Mercury; cf Bruce 281–2 and Haenchen 426–7.

12 In his translation of 14:13a Erasmus followed fairly closely the Vulgate, where the Latin has some ambiguity: grammatically the one who 'was before the city' (DV) might be either Jupiter or his priest. The language of the paraphrase here implies that it is the priest who lives outside the city, and

this is the interpretation of the paraphrase adopted in the 1548 *Paraphrase of Erasmus* (fol li recto). In the Greek text, however, there is no ambiguity: the reference is clearly to Zeus, whose temple is before the city; cf Bruce 282 and Haenchen 427.

13 Cf the *Gloss* (on 14:13) 1141B: 'It is the custom of the gentiles that those who sacrifice in honour of the gods wear garlands; at the same time, the victims too are garlanded'; similarly Hugh of St Cher 270 recto B.

14 The paraphrase on 14:14 omits the word 'apostles,' probably inadvertently rather than to avoid calling Barnabas an apostle – as evidently is the case in some witnesses to the 'Western' text (cf Metzger 423–4). Erasmus himself had no hesitation elsewhere to call the pair 'apostles'; see the paraphrase on 14:18 below, and cf the paraphrases on 16:32–40 (104–5 below), where Paul and Silas are 'apostles.' On the meaning of 'apostle' in Acts see the paraphrases on 1:21–2 (12 above) and n98 and Munck 11–12. Erasmus here inverts the order of the names in the biblical text (Barnabas and Paul). For the order of the two names in this *Paraphrase* see especially the paraphrases on chapter 13.

15 Cf the interlinear *Gloss* (on 14:14) 1441–2: 'They do not patiently bear the injury that the honour owed to God was being conveyed to themselves.'

16 For the custom, as represented in the Bible, see Mark 14:63; also Num 14:6; 2 Sam 13:31; Joel 2:13.

17 In the first part of this sentence, Erasmus, like Nicholas of Lyra 1142F, contrasts human mortality with divinity; the second part reflects his interest in bringing out the full force of the Greek ὁμοιοπαθεῖς 'of like nature' (14:15 RSV), and the paraphrase follows closely his own translation (from *1519*), 'men subject to the same evils as you.' It is not, he said in his annotation on the verse (*mortales sumus similes vobis*) a matter merely of mortality, but of all the sufferings to which human beings are subject (cf AV 'of like passions'). The Vulgate read 'We also are mortals, human beings like you' (Conf and similarly DV). Erasmus follows Valla *Annot in Acta* 14 (I 851) in his explanation of the Greek word.

18 In early Christian apologetic the pagan gods were frequently characterized as dead men and lifeless statues, while the demons were regarded as spirits that fostered the worship of idols; cf Athenagoras *Legatio* 26.1–28.10 in Schoedel *Athenagoras* 65–71 and Tertullian *Apology* 12.1–7 and 23.1–19 CCL 1 109–10 and 130–3. Early Christian writers sometimes cited the Greek Euhemerus (late fourth century BC) as a pagan witness to the view that the gods were dead men; cf eg Lactantius *Institutiones divinae* 1.11, 13–15 PL 6 174A–175A, 188B–194A, and *De ira* 11 PL 7 111A–112B. For demons as equivalent to gods, see Everett Ferguson *Demonology of the Early Christian World* (New York 1984) 33–5. From its earliest period ancient Christianity acknowledged the existence of pagan demons; cf eg 1 Cor 10:20. See chapter 17 n24.

19 With this expression, compare Cicero *De republica* 3.22.33: 'One God ... master and ruler of all' (cited by Lactantius *Institutiones divinae* 6.8 PL 6 661A).

20 Cf 17:30; also Rom 3:25–6.

21 On the salvific purpose of God's forbearance see the paraphrases on Rom 3:25–6 CWE 42 25. Perhaps surprisingly, the paraphrase on Acts 17:30 (111 below) says little on the theme.

22 With the implied contrast here between 'most mortals,' who have been idolaters, and the few who have not, compare the tension between 'all have sinned' and 'very many have sinned' in the account of human sinfulness in the paraphrases on Rom 5:17–19 CWE 42 35 and n16. For saints among pre-Christian pagans, see the colloquy 'The Godly Feast' (Thompson *Colloquies*, especially 65–8), and for Socrates, in particular, 'in [whose] life you will find things that accord with the life of Christ,' see *Ratio* Holborn 210–11. For the theme of pagan saints in humanist literature of the Renaissance see the bibliography cited in *Colloquia* ASD I-3 254:710n.

23 Cf Rom 1:23–5.

24 Cf Chrysostom (on 14:17) *Hom in Acta* 31.1 PG 60 227–8: 'They ought to have been punished.'

93

25 The textual tradition of the Vulgate (for 14:17) offers several alternative readings: 'giving rains ... filling our hearts' (DV); 'giving rains ... filling your hearts' (Conf and the preferred Vulgate reading) – for these readings see Weber II 1722 and 16n; while the Vulgate of 1527 reads 'giving rains ... filling their hearts.' Erasmus' Greek text (all editions 1516–1535) read 'giving us rains ... filling our hearts' (AV). The preferred reading of the Greek text is represented by RSV 'gave you rains ... satisfying your hearts'; cf *Beginnings* III 134. In the paraphrase here Erasmus follows the reading of his own Greek text and from 1519 his Latin translation.

26 For an appreciation in classical literature of the benefits of Ceres (Greek Demeter, goddess of grain and harvest) and Liber (Greek Bacchus, god of wine) see Euripides' *Bacchae* 272–85.

27 Cf the dramatic change in the Maltese attitude to Paul in the paraphrase on 28:6 (148 below).

28 This statement of intent is without warrant in the biblical text. As Derbe constitutes the final point in this missionary journey, Erasmus may wish to imply that the travels of Paul and Barnabas were not haphazard but well planned from the beginning.

29 'Many things': *multa*; Erasmus' translation (14:21) agreed (all editions 1516–1535) with the Vulgate *multos* 'many people' (so DV AV Conf RSV), a reading uniformly supported by the witnesses; cf *Beginnings* III 136–7.

30 enter into] In all editions *1524–1535*; in LB, 'enter'

31 An allusion to Matt 5:10, under the influence of which, evidently, the kingdom 'of God' (14:22) became in paraphrase the kingdom 'of heaven.'

32 Cf Nicholas of Lyra's 'moral exposition' of Paul's return to Lystra (on 14:21) 1144F: 'By this he gives a pattern to preachers of the church, that they should be concerned not only for the conversion of sinners from evil, but also for their strengthening in good things – like a good gardener who after the planting of a tree is careful to water it until he has made its roots strong.' For the image of sowing see n8 above.

33 Cf the annotation on 14:23 (*et cum constituissent illis*), where Erasmus insists that we are to understand here a choice by vote. Though the Greek word χειροτονέω usually does imply a vote, the context here suggests appointment by Paul and Barnabas; cf BAG and Haenchen 436. On the importance for Erasmus of the vote for ecclesiastical position see the paraphrase on 1:26 (12–13 above). On 'presbyters' see chapter 15 n22.

34 Cf the paraphrase on 13:43 (89 above) and n90.

94

35 The reference in the paraphrase (on 14:24) to Antioch in Pisidia recalls the last place mentioned (in 14:21) on the return journey. In the biblical text, however, the intervening verses show that the same things happened in all the cities on this journey. For Antioch in Pisidia see chapter 13 n32.

36 The words appear to echo Rom 15:20.

37 A reference evidently to choosing and establishing presbyters over the churches as described in 14:23.

38 Attalia was 'the chief port of Pamphylia' (Bruce 286), situated on the coast at the western end of Pamphylia.

Chapter 15

1 In all editions, the paraphrases on chapter 15 begin with 14:28, though in his text and translation Erasmus maintains the traditional division between the two chapters. There is a similar shift in the traditional division in Titus where, in the *Paraphrase*, 2:15 becomes part of chapter 3. In the case of Titus, there is some manuscript support for such a division (cf CWE 44 63 and n1), though the division was congenial to the theological design of the *Paraphrase* at this point; see R.D. Sider ' "In Terms Quite Plain and Clear": The Exposition of Grace in the New Testament Scholarship of Erasmus' *Erasmus in English* 15 (1987–8) 18. In the case of *Acts* modern critical texts acknowledge only the traditional division between chapters 14 and 15 (cf *Beginnings* III 138–9 and Tischendorf II

127), though Chrysostom *Hom in Acta* 32.1 PG 60 233 cites 14:28 with 15:1. But the logic of narrative and argument is probably sufficient to explain Erasmus' division of these two chapters in the *Paraphrase on Acts*; cf chapter 6 n28 and *Beginnings* IV 169.

2 The interlinear *Gloss* (on 14:28) also recalls the place (Antioch, named in 14:26); cf the paraphrase on 14:24 (94 above) and n35, where in a similar way Erasmus endeavours to keep the place clearly before his reader.

3 Capital of the Roman province of Syria (organized in 64 BC), Antioch had become by the first century AD a major city with an ethnically mixed population, including many Jews. It was known for its beauty and fine buildings; cf Glanville Downey *A History of Antioch in Syria* (Princeton 1961) 163–201, and for the Jews in Antioch 107–11 and 192–5. For the church there, represented as large and successful, see the paraphrases on 11:26 and 13:1 (79 and 83 above).

4 Erasmus uses the term Syria somewhat loosely to designate a geographical area – not only here in the paraphrase on 14:28, but elsewhere as well; cf the paraphrase on Acts 24:5 (136 below) and CWE 46 91 n6. By 'Judaea proper' he apparently refers to the ethnic 'Judaea' of New Testament times, a geographical area 'almost a square, *ca* forty-five miles on a side' from the Dead Sea to the coast, and north and south from just above Jerusalem to Masada and from Joppa to Gaza – of which the capital city was Jerusalem (IDB II 1012). But in the New Testament literature the term 'Judaea' sometimes refers to a much more extended area; cf chapter 2 n33. Moreover, from AD 6–41 and 44–66 'Judaea' was also a Roman procuratorial province, which included the territories of Samaria, Judaea, and Idumea, with its capital at Caesarea. As a province with its own governor it was technically independent of the Roman province of Syria, though the governor of Syria occasionally exercised surveillance over it. See *A History of the Jewish People* ed H.H. Ben-Sasson (Cambridge, MA 1976) 248 and Yohanan Aharoni and Michael Avi-Yonah *The MacMillan Bible Atlas* (New York 1968) 156.

5 Erasmus is fond of such lists of 'ceremonies'; cf eg the paraphrases on Rom 4:16, 9:32, and Gal 4:3 CWE 42 30, 58, and 115, also on Mark 2:19 and 12:34 CWE 49 42 and 147–8. These lists generally reflect practices familiar from the New Testament, but for parallels from patristic literature see CWE 42 30 n9 and 58 n25. 'Things dead' translates the Latin *morticina*, referring evidently to dead animals (see *morticinus* in L&S and OLD); cf Lev 11:31–40. Erasmus includes 'clothing' among the 'ceremonies' listed in the paraphrases on Gal 4:3 and Mark 2:19. Dress had been a matter of considerable personal concern to Erasmus, since he claimed a papal dispensation from wearing the habit of his order; see his letter to Servatius Rogerus (Ep 296:181–218). See also the allusions to dress in his letter to Paul Volz (Ep 858:468–591 / CWE 66 19–22), and cf Ep 447:490–599. On fasts see chapter 10 n16.

6 Erasmus elsewhere uses similar imagery to contrast Law and gospel; cf the
Argument to Galatians CWE 42 95 – the Law is 'flesh, shadows, appearances,' the
gospel 'spirit, light, truth' – and the paraphrases on Rom 10:3 CWE 42 59. For the
Law as a pedagogue see the paraphrases on Rom 10:3 and Gal 3:24 CWE 42 113–14.
For the disciplinary purpose of the Law in early Christian literature see chapter
2 n5. 'Carnal' in this sentence represents *crassus*, on which see chapter 2 n4.
7 For the Law as both spiritual and carnal see the paraphrases on Rom 8:3 and
Gal 5:4–5 CWE 42 45 and 122.
8 'Over-scrupulous regard' translates *superstitio*. For the 'unconquerable
superstition of the Jews' see the Argument to Romans in CWE 42, especially
8–9 and n28 and the paraphrases on Gal 2:10–12 CWE 42 104–5; cf also the
paraphrases on Rom 14:1–2 CWE 42 77–8.

95

9 The paraphrase on 15:1 offers here a slightly different nuance from the standard
text; the textual tradition, both Greek and Latin, is uniform in reading 'certain
ones came down from Judaea' (cf DV AV Conf RSV). Cf the Argument to Romans
CWE 42 8, which offers a summary interpretation of Acts 15: 'certain Jews came
to Antioch.'
10 For 'the new and different teaching' see Gal 1:6–9. The paraphrastic narrative
may also echo Acts 11:22.
11 Cf the interlinear *Gloss* (on 15:1) 1145–6, which also defines the 'brethren' as
'gentile believers.'
12 In the *Enchiridion* CWE 66 70 Erasmus explains the phrase 'flesh of the Law' (*caro
legis*) in terms of Jewish 'legalistic' practices and the spirit of pride in one's
religious accomplishments, and he associates the 'flesh of the Law' with the
'superstition' of the Jews: '[Paul] expresses contempt for the flesh [of the Law]
and the superstition of those who preferred to be Jews in public'; cf Holborn
73:4–5: '[Paulus] contemnit carnem legis et superstitionem.' Cf also *Enchiridion*
CWE 66 83, where Erasmus says that '. . . in the old Law, in the new . . . there is
externally something we can call the flesh, and internally there is the spirit.'
See nn6 and 7 above.
13 The 'moral exposition' of Nicholas of Lyra 1145–8 also applied this incident to
the situation of Christians in general: the Judaizers signify those who 'impose
upon the Catholic people heavy regulations and so turn the liberty of the
Christian religion into a harsh servitude.' Throughout his *Paraphrases* Erasmus
frequently attacks religion which 'relies on ceremonies' (cf 'ceremonies' in
the Index of Theological Terms in CWE 42 187 and 49 232). His criticism of
ceremonies appears also in the *Methodus* (1516) and the *Ratio* (1519, 1522);
cf Holborn 157:15 and 239:23–241:10. For similar criticism elsewhere see the
colloquies 'The Godly Feast' and 'A Fish Diet' (Thompson *Colloquies* 68–9;

320–1; in the latter, with reference to the apostolic age); cf also the *Enchiridion* CWE 66 70–5.

14 The Vulgate text of 15:2 read only 'dissension' (similarly DV Conf), Erasmus' text and translation 'dissension and debate' (RSV; so AV and the Greek witnesses, for which see *Beginnings* III 138–9). Erasmus appears here to follow his reading in representing the encounter not merely as dissension, but also as a debate between the apostles and those 'on the other side.' For the image of the yoke see Acts 15:10 and Gal 5:1.

15 Cf Matt 5:17.

16 'Herod' is presumably the Herod of 12:1–19, properly, Agrippa I, who, however, in the paraphrases on those verses is represented as Herod the tetrarch (cf chapter 12 n1). The allusion to 'other princes' is perhaps deliberately ambiguous, capable of generalization regardless of the historical era. For early Christian lists of persecuting emperors see Tertullian *Apology* 5.3–4 CCL 1 95 and Lactantius *De mortibus persecutorum* 2–7 PL 7 193–206.

17 Though not the preferred Vulgate reading, Erasmus' Vulgate and the Vulgate of *1527* read 'some from the others' (cf DV 'certain others of the other side'); cf Weber II 1723 2n. This reading was explained by the interlinear *Gloss* 1145–6 as 'those on the other side of the question,' so that both sides sent representatives from Antioch. Erasmus, however, in text from *1516* and translation from *1519* read 'certain others of them'; see his annotation on 15:2 (*et quidam alii ex aliis*). Though the paraphrase is ambiguous about who constitutes 'this group'(*hoc numerum*), in the Argument to Romans Erasmus clearly adopts the traditional view that the 'others' were 'adversaries' (CWE 42 8).

18 'Mother church': *metropolis ecclesiarum*: ie the 'capital of churches.' *Metropolis* is frequently used of a capital city, as in the interlinear *Gloss* – cf eg the glosses on 8:26 (1071–2) where Jerusalem and Gaza are each said to be a 'metropolis,' Jerusalem of the Jews, Gaza of the Philistines.

19 For the commission see 1:8 and Luke 24:46–8.

20 'Disciples' paraphrases *ecclesia* of the Greek and Latin texts; cf chapter 5 n20.

96

21 Cf the Argument to the Epistle to the Galatians CWE 42 95: 'There [Paul] talked over his own gospel with the leading apostles, not because he had now come to doubt the preaching of so many years, but because he believed that from the approval of those whose authority was very great, others might be strengthened'; in this sentence, as the context makes clear, Erasmus refers to Gal 2:1–10. The parallelism with the paraphrase here suggests that Erasmus equates the events described in Acts 15 with those in Gal 2:1–10. The 'more eminent persons' are thus Peter, James, and John (Gal 2:6–9), though in the Argument to Galatians Erasmus cites Peter alone as having 'added nothing' (cf Gal 2:6).

22 In an annotation on 15:4 (*ab apostolis et senioribus*) Erasmus explains that the Greek πρεσβύτερος [*presbyteros*] implies rank, the Latin *senior*, age; similarly the annotations on 20:17 (*maiores natu*) and 1 Tim 5:17 (*qui bene praesunt presbyteri*). In his translation of Acts (from 1522) Erasmus generally used *seniores* 'elders,' to refer to Jewish leaders, *presbyteri* to refer to Christian leaders, though for exceptions see 11:30 and 15:22, where πρεσβύτεροι used of Christian leaders is rendered by *seniores*. In his *Paraphrase on Acts*, however, he follows as a rule the Vulgate, which writes *seniores* everywhere except in 14:22 (14:23 RSV), 15:2 (*presbyteri*) and 20:17 (*maiores natu*); to this rule, Erasmus made exceptions only in 20:17 and 25:15, where for the Vulgate's *maiores natu* (20:17) and *seniores* (25:15) the *Paraphrase* has *presbyteri* and *primores* 'chiefs.' Cf CWE 44 11 n34 and 165 n25. For the expression 'order of elders' see chapter 5 n36.

23 For the reputation of the Pharisees as more devoted to the Law than others see Josephus *Jewish War* 1.5.2 (110); for their disregard, as represented in the New Testament, of the spirit of the Law see Matt 15:1–20 and 23:1–28.

24 Cf 1 Cor 9:19–22.

25 For a similar expression of the apostolic concern to gain the gentiles without losing the Jews see the paraphrase on Gal 2:10 CWE 42 103–4.

26 The interlinear *Gloss* (on 15:6) 1147–8 observed that the meeting considered the opinions of both sides. For the rhetorical distinction between testimonies and proofs see chapter 4 n44 and the paraphrase on 7:56 (55 above).

27 For a similar sentiment see the paraphrase on 11:17 (78 above).

28 Only once thus far in the biblical narrative of Acts has the passage of time been measured in terms of 'years' (11:26). The reference to 'years' here in the paraphrase on 15:7 may reflect a general sense of the time required for the events between Cornelius' conversion and the Council of Jerusalem. But in the sequence of the biblical narrative the conversion of Cornelius (chapter 10) follows shortly after the conversion of Paul (chapter 9). If one assumes that the two events are temporally proximate and identifies the meeting of Gal 2 with that of Acts 15 (cf n21 above), one can find in Gal 1:15–2:1 some basis for the 'years' referred to here.

29 On Judaea, see n4 above: Caesarea, the scene of Cornelius' conversion, was the capital of the province of Judaea; Joppa, the place of Peter's vision, belonged to the geographical area called Judaea.

30 'Murmuring': *murmur*, as in the Vulgate and the paraphrase on 6:1 (46 above); cf the similar *obmurmurantes* in the paraphrase on 11:2 (76 above) where the word is translated 'critics.' With Erasmus' use of the word, compare the Vulgate of Exod 15:24, 16:2, 7, and 8, and 17:3.

31 Cf Nicholas of Lyra 1148F on the words 'God made choice' (15:7 RSV): 'As though to say, "I did not go to preach to Cornelius ... on my own authority, but I was sent by God."'

97

32 For the expression see 1 Sam 16:7.

33 The interlinear *Gloss* (on 15:8) 1147–8 also notes that in the event of Cornelius' conversion speaking in tongues was the evidence that the Holy Spirit had been poured out.

34 The interlinear *Gloss* (on 15:9) 1147–8 also characterizes 'us' and 'them' as the circumcised and the uncircumcised.

35 Cf the *Gloss* (on 15:9) 1148F, citing Bede: 'They do not need to be made clean through circumcision of the flesh whose hearts are purified by a faith so great that they deserve to receive the Spirit even before baptism' (cf Bede *Super Acta* 15 PL 92 976D). Cf the paraphrase on 11:15 (78 above) for the same sentiment.

36 For the 'yoke of the Law … so heavy' see the interlinear *Gloss* 1149–50, which explains *iugum* 'yoke' (15:10) as the *gravitas* – the 'heaviness,' or 'burden' – of circumcision and the Law. On the burden of the Law, see also Matt 23:4; Luke 11:46; and (by implication) Matt 11:28–30. For the expression 'tempt and provoke' see Ps 78:56, especially in the Vulgate according to the Hebrew (Ps 77:56; Weber I 869); cf also Heb 3:9 and Ps 95:9.

37 Cf the interlinear *Gloss* 1149–50 on the words 'our fathers' (15:10): 'We were not able … to observe all the things that are in the Law.'

38 Erasmus translated (in all editions *1516–1535*) the Greek aorist passive infinitive of 15:11 as a future, 'shall be saved' (AV RSV); the Vulgate had translated it as a present infinitive, 'are saved' (Conf; cf DV). Thus Erasmus follows here his own translation; for the verb as either past, present, or future, see *Beginnings* IV 174 11n and Bruce 294–5.

39 Erasmus follows his own text and translation (from *1516*) and the Vulgate of *1527* in writing 'Lord Jesus Christ' (so DV AV). The Vulgate witnesses are divided (Weber II 1723 and 11n); the preferred reading of the Greek is 'Lord Jesus' (so Conf RSV). For the two readings see *Beginnings* III 142–3.

40 Cf the interlinear *Gloss* (on 15:11) 1149–50, which explains *gratia* as 'the free gift of God without the works of the Law.'

41 Nicholas of Lyra (on 15:13) 1149C–1150F explained that James, not Peter, spoke at this point because he was bishop in Jerusalem and Peter therefore deferred to him in his own diocese in bringing the question to resolution.
On James see the paraphrase on 12:17 and n28. For the title 'Just,' applied to James at least as early as the second century, see Bruce 296. Though in the paraphrase on 12:17 (82 above) Erasmus had introduced James as 'the brother of the Lord,' he qualifies here: he is 'called' the brother of the Lord. As his annotation on Gal 1:19 indicates (*Iacobum fratrem*), Erasmus follows a line of exegetes who explained the designation in ways that left unchallenged the doctrine of Mary's perpetual virginity: James, actually a cousin of the Lord, was called a brother according to a Jewish custom (Jerome); it was a designation

given to James out of respect (Theophylactus). Cf the paraphrase on Gal 1:19
CWE 42 101: 'James surnamed the Just ... was called a brother of the Lord
because of the distinguished holiness of his life.' Cf also the annotation on
James 1:1 (*Iacobus apostolus*).

42 Erasmus' Vulgate and the Vulgate of *1527* read (in 15:14) 'Simon' (DV and
Conf) though the Vulgate witnesses are divided between 'Simon' and 'Simeon'
(Weber II 1724 14n). Erasmus in text (from *1516*) and translation (from
1519) read 'Symeon' (AV and RSV). In the annotation on 15:14 (*Simon narravit
quemadmodum*) Erasmus proposed that 'Symeon' represented a Hebrew
pronunciation, 'Simon' a Greek pronunciation of the same name. However, for
the 'complicated reality' of the relation between the two names, see *Apologia ad
annotationes Stunicae* ASD IX-2 155:831n and CWE 44 111 n1; on Simon/Simeon
in John cf CWE 46 35 n139.
Simon is 'surnamed Peter' in Acts 10:18 and 11:13, though Simon Peter is found
predominantly in John (but cf Matt 16:16; Luke 5:8; 2 Pet 1:1).

98

43 For the imagery see Hos 1:8–10 and 1 Pet 2:10 (people of God); Zeph 3:9; Zech
13:9; and Joel 2:32, cited in Acts 2:21 (calling upon the name).
With the words of the paraphrase, 'a people calling upon his name' (15:14)
compare the translations 'a people for his name' (AV RSV), 'a people to his
name' (DV), 'a people to bear his name' (Conf). The Vulgate read a dative – 'to
his name' or 'for his name' – following the preferred Greek text, which has a
dative without a proposition (*Beginnings* III 142); Erasmus read the dative with
the preposition ἐπί, and translated (from *1516*) 'in his name.'

44 Erasmus regarded the proper identification of the persona speaking in a biblical
text as one of the 'keys' to the interpretation of Scripture; cf his annotation
on Rom 7:24 ('from the body of this death') CWE 56 195; also *Ratio* Holborn
196:29–198:32, and the paraphrase on Rom 9:32 CWE 42 59.

45 For the quotation see Amos 9:11–12 (LXX). The paraphrase on the quotation as
cited in 15:16–17 reflects the Latin of both the Vulgate and Erasmus' translation.
The expression 'upon whom my name is called' is, in paraphrase, identical
to the Latin in both the Vulgate and Erasmus' translation. For the Greek
expression see ἐπικαλέω in BAG: '... *someone's name is called over someone* to
designate the latter as the property of the former ...'

46 The paraphrase on 15:18 represents Erasmus' text and, with minor variations,
the text of the Vulgate. Including 15:17b this text reads: 'saith the Lord, who
doeth all these things. Known unto God [Vulgate, the Lord] are all his works
[Vulgate, his work] from the beginning of the world' (AV); similarly DV and
Conf. For the Greek the preferred reading of 15:17b–18 is: 'says the Lord,
who has made these things known from of old' (RSV); cf *Beginnings* IV 176

17n, Haenchen 448 n5, and Metzger 429. With Erasmus' paraphrase compare the interlinear *Gloss* 1151–2 on the verse: 'He foreknew from eternity what he would do'; and for the sentiment that what God has decided is best see the paraphrase on 12:17 (82 above) and n29.

47 Cf 1 Cor 8:4, 7, 10–11.

48 Cf Nicholas of Lyra 1152F on 'fornication' (15:20): 'The gentiles commonly believed this was permissible; for this reason it was necessary to prohibit it.' In the paraphrase on 15:29 Erasmus specifically names the gentiles as those who regard fornication as permissible.

'Fornication' translates *scortatio* here. In his translation (from *1519*) and in his paraphrase on the verse, Erasmus replaces the Vulgate's *fornicatio* with *scortatio* for the Greek πορνεία. As he tells us in his annotation on 1 Cor 5:1 (*inter vos fornicatio*), *fornicatio* was not used by the better authors, and he preferred to translate the Greek word either by *scortatio* or by *stuprum*. While *stuprum* can refer quite generally to lewdness and unchastity, *scortatio* is a formation based on *scortor* and *scortum*, words well attested in classical usage in reference to harlotry (cf L&s). Erasmus seems unaware that the probable reference in this part of the Jerusalem decree is to the prohibited degrees of relationship in marriage outlined in Lev 18:6–18 (cf Bruce 300 and Haenchen 449; but for other possibilities see Metzger 431). For a light ecclesiastical penance given to 'whoring' see the colloquy 'The Young Man and the Harlot' (Thompson *Colloquies* 153–8, especially 157).

49 For the biblical allusion see Titus 1:15. For the view that the regulations of the Jerusalem decree were a temporary concession to Jewish 'superstition' see the Argument to Romans CWE 42 8; on this interpretation, according to Erasmus in the Argument, the Jerusalem decree offers a general principle applicable to later times. Cf CWE 42 8 and n20.

50 In the three passages where the Jerusalem decree is given (here in 15:20, also in 15:29 and 21:25) Erasmus in text and translation, as well as in paraphrase, gives four prohibitions: against idolatry, fornication, eating things strangled, and blood; in this he agreed with the Vulgate of *1527* and the preferred Vulgate reading (but for 15:29 cf Weber II 1724 and 29n). It is not until *1527* that his annotations on these verses show that he is aware of one of the readings with only three prohibitions (idolatry, fornication, blood); cf the annotations on 15:29 (*ab immolatis similacrorum*) and 21:25 (*ab idolis immolato etc*). On the complexity of the text, see Bruce 299–300, Haenchen 449 n6, and Metzger 429–34 ; all three accept as the correct reading the fourfold prohibition.

51 With the sentiment expressed here compare the paraphrases on Romans 14 CWE 42 77–83. Nicholas of Lyra (on 15:20) 1152F observed that the foods prohibited were in fact permissible, but gentiles were asked to abstain that association with Jews might be amicable; for essentially the same interpretation see Munck 140.

52 Erasmus fails to paraphrase the words 'in every city' found in the biblical text of 15:21 – perhaps inadvertently: they are in his own text and translation, as well as in the Vulgate. *Bede's quotation in Exposition of Luke on 6:6 omits phrase*

53 For the Latin idiom translated here see chapter 4 n39.

54 For the same Latin idiom (*spectata probitas*) see chapter 6 n7; and for similar expressions see the paraphrases on 6:5 (*spectata fides* 'outstanding faith') 47 above, 21:16 (*spectata pietas* 'proven piety') 127 below, also 10:22 (*spectatus ac probatus* 'tested and approved') 71 above and 22:12 (*vir pius ac ... probatus* 'a devout man and ... approved') 130 below. See also chapter 16 n4.

55 The paraphrase on 'Judas, called Barsabbas' (15:22 RSV) may suggest that Erasmus understood the surname to mean 'the Just.' It is more probable that Erasmus has erroneously identified the Joseph Barsabbas of 1:23, called 'the Just,' with Judas Barsabbas here. The two names do not refer to the same person, though it is not impossible that the two were brothers (cf 'Judas' in IDB II 1008) or otherwise related (Munck 143). 'Barsabbas' does not mean 'the Just' but perhaps either 'son of the sabbath' (ie born on the sabbath) or 'son of the elder'; cf Bruce 79.

56 Erasmus stresses the moral excellence of the delegation; cf Nicholas of Lyra (on 15:22) 1153C, who rationalized the choice by noting the general distinction of the delegation – 'most distinguished after the apostles, so they would be believed and their embassy enjoy the greater authority.'

99

57 Erasmus follows his own text and translation of 15:23: 'apostles and elders and brethren' (so AV); but the Vulgate gives the preferred reading, 'apostles and elders, brethren' (cf DV Conf RSV). On the difficulty of the Greek expression see Bruce 302 (who understands 'the elder brethren') and Haenchen 451 and n4.

58 For the phrase 'from Judaism' see the interlinear *Gloss* 1153–4, which also specified that the 'elders, brethren' were 'from the Jews.' For the phrase 'converted to Christ' see the *Gloss* (on 10:23) 1153A, which noted the kindness in calling 'brethren' those gentiles who had become like the Jews 'sons of God.'

59 Here the paraphrase on 15:24 represents Erasmus' text and translation, as well as the text of the Vulgate (Weber II 1724), reading 'certain which went out from us' (AV; so DV); in the Greek the preferred text omits the word ἐξελθόντες to give the reading 'some persons from us' (RSV; so Conf); cf *Beginnings* III 146–7.

60 The paraphrase on 15:24 follows the text Erasmus adopted from *1516* which briefly recapitulates here the demand of the 'Judaizers': '[certain ones troubled you] saying, Ye must be circumcised and keep the Law' (AV). The Vulgate (and the preferred reading) omits the clause (so DV Conf RSV; cf Metzger 436). In a *1527* annotation (*quibus non mandavimus*) Erasmus justified his text by an appeal to the Greek manuscripts and to Bede (cf *Liber retractationis* 15 PL 92 1024C).

61 The translator of the Vulgate understood the Greek ὁμοθυμαδόν (15:25) to mean 'together,' hence 'assembled together' (DV Conf); Erasmus thought it meant 'of one accord,' hence 'assembled with one accord' (AV; cf RSV). The paraphrase here appears to adopt both meanings: 'the view of the meeting' and 'assembled together'; but cf the paraphrase on 15:28 below, where Erasmus' interpretation intrudes: 'Through the prompting of the Spirit [the brethren] were "in accord."' BAG adopts Erasmus' interpretation for 15:25, but accepts the Vulgate's interpretation as 'a weakened meaning' possible elsewhere.

62 For the law against eating blood see Lev 17:10–14 and Gen 9:4. For this law as including animals strangled see Bruce 300.

63 Erasmus retains the Vulgate's *multitudo* for the Greek πλῆθος invariably in his translation and characteristically in his paraphrases on Acts; cf chapter 5 n3. In the paraphrases here on 15:30–1 the complementary image of the apostles and elders sharpens the sense the word carries of the body of believers, the Christian *plebs*; cf the paraphrases on 4:33 and 6:5 (37 and 47 above); also on 6:2 (46 above), where the importance of the multitude in ecclesiastical decisions is emphasized. For the view that Erasmus was a 'champion of lay Christianity' see Payne *Theology of the Sacraments* 104.

64 Though Erasmus sometimes understands prophets to be those who reveal the future – cf eg the annotation on Titus 1:12 (*proprius eorum propheta*) – here he includes among their gifts the interpretation of Scripture; for the same view see the paraphrase on 1 Cor 12:28, where prophets are defined as 'either those who disclose the future or those who explain mysteries (*explicent occulta*), and on 1 Cor 13:2, where it is said to be through prophecy that one might hold 'all the hidden meanings (*arcani sensus*) of divine Scripture.' See also the annotation on 1 Cor 14:1 (*sectamini charitatem, aemulamini spiritualia*): 'Here, by prophecy Paul means not the prediction of the future, but the interpretation of divine Scripture'; likewise in *Ecclesiastes* 1 Erasmus says: 'I call prophets those who explain the mysteries of "arcane" Scripture' (ASD V-4 106:530). On the significance of the preacher as prophet see John W. O'Malley SJ 'Erasmus and the History of Sacred Rhetoric: The Ecclesiastes of 1535' ERSY 5 (1985) 24.

65 'Copious discourse': Erasmus borrows the phrase from his own translation (from 1516). For the *sermo copiosus* of the preacher, see *Ecclesiastes* III LB V 967A; and for Erasmus' praise of the 'abundant style' more generally see *De copia* book 1 chapter 1 CWE 24 295.

66 Cf chapter 13 n90.

67 Here in 15:33 Erasmus follows the Vulgate '[returned] to those who had sent them' (RSV, also DV Conf) rather than his own text and translation, which read (from 1516) '[returned] to the apostles' (AV). The Vulgate represents the preferred reading (Metzger 439).

68 Here, too, Erasmus appears to have followed his Vulgate and the Vulgate of 1527, which included the longer text of 15:34: 'But it seemed good unto Silas to remain there: and Judas alone departed to Jerusalem'(DV). For his own text and translation (from 1516) Erasmus accepted only the first half of the verse (so AV), though his 1516 annotation (*manere ibi*) indicates that he regarded even the first half as somewhat doubtful. Nicholas of Lyra 1155C noted that neither clause was found in the Greek or in the corrected Latin copies. In fact, the Vulgate witnesses are divided (Weber II 1724 33n), and the preferred reading of both the Latin and the Greek manuscripts omits both clauses (so RSV; Conf brackets the verse); cf Metzger 439.

69 The paraphrase on 15:35 fails to represent the words 'with many others also' (RSV) – perhaps an oversight: the words appear in Erasmus' text and translation (from 1516) and in the Vulgate. Erasmus' text and translation and the Vulgate read 'word of the Lord' for 'word of God.'

100

70 Erasmus follows the Vulgate 'wanted' (DV Conf RSV), based on the Greek ἐβούλετο. He himself thought that the correct Greek reading was ἐβουλεύσατο 'determined' (AV); cf the annotation on 15:37 (*Barnabas autem volebat*). For the (preferred) reading ἐβούλετο see *Beginnings* III 150.

71 For John's part in the first missionary journey see 12:25, 13:5 and 13.

72 Erasmus' paraphrase on 15:38 stays close to the biblical text and avoids the reproach found in the exegetical tradition: Nicholas of Lyra 1156F thought John had departed either through 'fear of the dangers' or through a 'love too carnal' for his mother; the *Gloss* 1156D also accused John of timidity, citing Bede (cf *Super Acta* 15 PL 92 977C).

73 The paraphrase on 15:39 reflects Erasmus' criticism of the Vulgate's lacklustre translation (*dissensio*) of the colourful Greek word παροξυσμός [*paroxysmos*]; cf DV 'dissension' and AV Conf RSV 'sharp contention.' See the annotation on the verse (*facta est autem dissensio*) and Erasmus' own translation (from 1516), *acris disceptatio* 'sharp contention.'

74 With Erasmus' attempt here to justify the quarrel between Paul and Barnabas, compare Nicholas of Lyra (on 15:39) 1156F: '[The dissension] was not contrary to charity because each of them had regard for the good, but was moved by different considerations; so it happened that the fruit of their preaching was the greater because they preached the more widely'; similarly Hugh of St Cher 271 verso F. Modern scholarship remains divided on the cause of the quarrel; cf eg Haenchen 475–7 and Bruce *English Text* 318–19.

75 'Chose': *adscito sibi*. The phrase reflects Erasmus' debate with Zúñiga, who had objected to the former's use of *allego* in his translation of 15:40. Erasmus replied that *allego* is the word used customarily to designate admission into the senate (*dicuntur allegi in senatum qui eo asciscuntur*) – an appropriate connotation for

the Greek ἐπιλεξάμενος; cf *Apologia ad annotationes Stunicae* ASD IX-2 154:841–3.
On the meaning of the Greek word ('choose for oneself') see Haenchen 474.

76 For Silas' moral authority see the paraphrase on verse 22 (98 above) and n56
above.

77 'Sent forth ... commended': '*dimissus ... commendatus*,' the two words used in
the interlinear *Gloss* (on 15:40) 1157–8 to explain the Vulgate's *traditus* ('being
delivered' DV); so Hugh of St Cher 271 verso F. 'Grace of God' is found in
the Vulgate of *1527* and in Erasmus' own text and translation from *1516* (so
DV AV), though 'grace of the Lord' (Conf RSV) is the preferred reading of
both the Greek and the Latin manuscripts; cf Metzger 440 and Weber II 1725
and 40n.

78 Paul's birthplace, Tarsus, was in Cilicia; cf Acts 22:3.

79 In the paraphrase here Erasmus follows a Vulgate reading which includes a
clause at the end of 15:41, 'commanding them to keep the precepts of the
apostles and the ancients' (DV; similarly the Vulgate of *1527*, and Conf – though
in brackets). The clause was rejected by Erasmus for his text from *1516*, though
it was not until *1527* that he defended his decision; cf the annotation on 15:41
(*praecipiens custodire praecepta apostolorum et seniorum*). The clause is omitted in
the preferred reading of the Greek text (Metzger 440; so AV RSV). The Vulgate
witnesses are divided; cf Weber II 1725 41n.

80 Erasmus includes in his paraphrase of chapter 15 the first clause of 16:1; cf n1
above.

Chapter 16

1 'Precious to God': *deo pretiosus*, a Latin equivalent for the Greek τίμιος [*timios*]
'precious' and θεῷ [*theō*] 'to God' – perhaps a correction to the interlinear *Gloss*
1159–60 and to Hugh of St Cher 271 verso F, where the name is explained as
'generous,' 'beneficent' (*beneficus*). The name is well attested in pre-Christian,
classical sources; see τιμόθεος in BAG, and for the expression 'precious to God'
in early Christian literature see τίμιος 1b.

2 'Mixed marriage': *ex impari matrimonio* – an 'unequal' marriage, with an echo
of 2 Cor 6:14 (cf AV), in his annotation on which (*nolite iugum ducere*) Erasmus
notes that Jerome calls marriages between Christians and pagans *imparia*

3 The Vulgate witnesses to 16:1 are divided between the reading *viduae* 'widow'
and *Iudaeae* 'Jewish' (Weber II 1725 1n). The Vulgate of *1527* read 'widow,' the
reading also of the copy used for the annotation on 16:1 (*filius mulieris viduae
fidelis*). Erasmus' Greek text (from *1516*) read ἰουδαίας 'Jewish.' The paraphrase
reflects both readings.
   In his paraphrase on the last part of the verse, Erasmus' *ethnicus* 'pagan'
appears to favour the Vulgate, which spoke of Timothy's father as a *gentilis*

'gentile.' His own text and translation (all editions 1524–1535) read *Graecus* 'Greek.' In early Christian literature *gentilis* had acquired the sense of 'pagan' (see *gentilis* II B 2 b in L&S), as had *ethnicus* (cf L&S).

101

4 Cf the 'moral exposition' of Nicholas of Lyra 1159C: 'From this it is evident that a companion of the gospel preacher should have a good name, and be suitable in knowledge and life to help.' For the importance in this *Paraphrase* of the concept of an integrity 'witnessed and approved' see chapter 15 n54; cf also the paraphrases on 1 Tim 3:2 and 7 CWE 44 18 and 21.

5 The number of Jews was an easy inference from the narrative of 14:1–23, but for an indication of the large Jewish population of Asia Minor see Josephus *Jewish Antiquities* 14.10.8–26 (213–67), 16.6 (160–78).

6 An echo, perhaps, of the text of 15:24 according to Erasmus (and AV); cf chapter 15 n60.

7 On the need for the gradual, rather than the sudden, abolition of the Law see the paraphrases on Gal 2:9–10 CWE 42 103–4. Hugh of St Cher (on 16:3) 271 verso G also notes the distinction between the earliest New Testament times when keeping the Law was a matter of indifference and the somewhat later period when legal prescriptions had entirely ceased. For 'gradualism' as a principle of divine revelation see the references under 'gradualism' in the index to CWE 46.

8 Erasmus describes Timothy as a half-Jew by virtue of his parentage. Among Jews, however, though he would have been regarded as illegitimate, he was nevertheless a Jew, taking his mother's nationality (Munck 155); cf Bruce *English Text* 322: 'Paul regularized his status (and, in Jewish eyes, legitimized him) by circumcising him.'

9 to that time] *ei tempori* in the editions 1524–1535; in LB, *ei tempore* 'to him at that time'

10 For 'Christ the peacemaker' see Eph 2:14–16. For this interpretation of the circumcision of Timothy, see the Argument to Romans CWE 42 8–9.

11 For the decrees of the council as prohibitions designed primarily (but not exclusively) to forestall the 'offence of the Jews' see the paraphrase on 15:20 (98 above).

12 'Favour': *favor*. For this word in the sense of the divine grace see R.D. Sider ' "In Terms Quite Plain and Clear": The Exposition of Grace in the New Testament Paraphrases of Erasmus' *Erasmus in English* 15 (1987–8) 23.

13 through ... Asia Minor] First in 1534; in 1524, 'through Phrygia and the Galatian region' – the reading in 16:6 both of the Vulgate and of Erasmus' text and translation (so DV AV Conf; also Haenchen 483, though some scholars prefer 'through the Phrygian and Galatian regions,' eg Bruce 309–10 and

Metzger 441; cf RSV). The textual change in *1534* may indicate that Erasmus (correctly) understands the biblical words as a reference to ethnic regions – north of Iconium lived the Galatians, west, the Phrygians. On the other hand, his geography, here as elsewhere, may be influenced by a picture of the post-Diocletianic organization of the empire. In the first century AD the province of Galatia extended south to include Lycaonia. In the fourth century, much of the southern portion of first-century Galatia had been made into independent provinces (Lycaonia and Pisidia), while two provinces of 'Phrygia' were established west of the now relatively small northern province of Galatia Salutaris. In any case, it would appear from the *Peregrinatio apostolorum* that Erasmus assumes a 'north-Galatian' visit on this tour since he postulates (LB VII 655–6) that the sequence 'Phrygia and Galatia' inverts the order of Paul's journey: first he went north to Galatia, then west to Phrygia. On these territories and their names see Haenchen 483 n2.

14 The Galatians were descendants of Gallic tribes that crossed into Asia in 287 BC and within a few years settled in central Asia Minor. Jerome says that the Galatians came not from the Grecized Celts of southern Gaul, but from the 'wilder' tribes of Gaul; cf *Commentarius in epistulam ad Galatas* (introduction to book 2) PL 26 381A. For their reputation for stupidity see the Argument to the Epistle to the Galatians and the paraphrase on 3:1 CWE 42 94–6 and 107–8.

102

15 For the 'hidden wisdom of God' see 1 Cor 2:7. Cf also the *Gloss* 1160E, citing Bede: 'Terrible is God in his counsels on behalf of the sons of men' (cf Bede *Super Acta* 16 PL 92 978A); so, exactly, Hugh of St Cher 271 verso H.

16 For parallels to the expressions 'Asia properly so called' and, just above, 'the part properly called Asia' see the paraphrases on 18:19 (114 below) and on 14:28 (94 above, in chapter 15); see also chapter 15 n4. In his annotation on 16:7 Erasmus says that the 'Asia' referred to is not 'Asia Minor' but the smaller Asia 'adjoining Ephesus' (*loqui verbum in Asia*), meaning, apparently, the Roman province of Asia. But Erasmus might have been unclear about the extent of its boundaries in the New Testament period. Erasmus knew the *Geography* (second century AD) of Ptolemy, to whom he refers in the *Peregrinatio apostolorum* LB VII 655–6. (Indeed, he wrote a preface for the first edition of the Greek text of the *Geography*; see Allen Ep 2760.) Ptolemy defines the regions that comprise 'Asia properly so called' (ἡ ἰδίως καλουμένη Ἀσία), but his definition includes both 'Lesser Mysia' and 'Greater Mysia' (see the *Geography* 5.1.1–34), whereas Erasmus here in the paraphrase on 16:7 seems to exclude 'Mysia' from Asia. On the other hand, Strabo *Geography* 2.5.24 uses the expression 'Asia properly so called' to name the entire peninsula. In fact, Mysia was included in the Roman province of Asia until the Diocletianic reforms; after the reforms, however,

much of 'Mysia' became the separate province of Hellespontus, which then indeed did border on the greatly reduced province of Asia to the south.

17 Bithynia was north-east of Mysia. It became a Roman province in 74 BC. In Pompey's settlement of the East it was joined with the western portion of 'Pontus,' the two forming a single province; but Bithynia was again a separate province in late antiquity. Pliny *Naturalis historia* 5.43.148–9 lists the many cities of Bithynia, the most distinguished of which, both in the imperial period and in late antiquity, were Nicomedia and Nicaea (on which see David Magie *Roman Rule in Asia Minor* 2 vols [Princeton 1950] 1 305–6). Life in Bithynia in the earlier imperial period is relatively well known from the letters of the younger Pliny (see letters 17A–121 in *Epistulae* 10), as well as from some of the discourses of Dio Chrysostom (see eg *Orationes* 38–48).

18 whose] The *1524* folio edition and most of the *1524* octavo editions have the plural *quorum*, but the Froben octavo of *1524* (A779) has, correctly, the singular *cuius*, the reading of *1534, 1535*, and LB.

19 Though in his text of 16:8 Erasmus always read παρελθόντες 'passing by' (AV Conf RSV and the preferred text; cf Metzger 442), he retained the translation of the Vulgate *cum pertransissent* 'when they had passed *through* [Mysia]' (so DV). Here in the paraphrase on 16:8 Erasmus uses the word *peragro*, as in the paraphrase on verse 6, 'travelled through Phrygia.'
Erasmus had already identified 'Phrygia' as bordering upon Galatia in central Asia Minor. In Erasmus' picture here (as in the *Peregrinatio apostolorum* LB VII 655–6), Paul and his companions pass west through Phrygia, then Mysia, coming finally to the 'coast of Phrygia.' Both Strabo (*Geography* 2.5.31) and Ptolemy (*Geography* 5.2.4, 14) identify the region known as the Troad (where the city 'Troas' is located) with a 'Phrygia': Strabo says that the Troad is a part of 'Phrygia on the Hellespont,' while Ptolemy identifies the Troad with 'Lesser Phrygia' – to be distinguished from 'Greater Phrygia' bordering on Galatia. Bede explains that the city 'Troas' is also called Antigonia (*De nominibus locorum* PL 92 1040), and Strabo (*Geography* 13.1.26) says that Antigonia was founded by Antigonus, but changed its name to Alexandria (its full name was Alexandria Troas) to honour Alexander; cf Bruce 311 and 'Antigoneia' 6 in P-W I-2 2405.

20 In Nicholas of Lyra 1161C the man is identified as a Macedonian by his appearance and dress; cf Munck 157–8. For the angel, see the *Gloss* (on 16:9) 1161A: 'The angel of that race is likened to a Macedonian, whether through his native tongue or particular appearance'; similarly Hugh of St Cher 272 recto A. On angels see chapter 12 n26. For the concept in biblical literature of angels that are guardians of the tribe see George B. Caird *Principalities and Powers* (Oxford 1956) 1–30. The idea was common in early Christianity; cf eg Irenaeus *Adversus haereses* 3.12.9 PG 7 903B (commenting on Acts 17:26), where Deut 32:8 [LXX] is cited.

21 Cf the interlinear *Gloss* 1161–2: 'Here Luke shows that he was a companion of Paul.' Erasmus stresses the persona of the narrator, on which see further the references under persona in the indexes to CWE 42 and 49. On the various interpretations of the 'we' passages in Acts see Haenchen 489–91.

22 'The Lord' in Erasmus' text of 16:10 from *1516*, and in his translation from *1519* (so AV); but 'God' is the preferred reading (Metzger 444; so the Vulgate DV Conf RSV).

23 Chersonese, from a Greek word meaning 'peninsula,' refers here to the peninsula on the north-western side of the Dardanelles – the modern Gallipoli peninsula. The name 'Samothrace' associates the island with Thrace – the Thracian Samos – an allusion Erasmus may intend by locating it 'opposite Thrace'; cf P-W IA-2 2224.

24 Erasmus' annotation on 16:11 (*Neapolin*) reveals some uncertainty about the identification of Neapolis. In *1516*, he located the city in Caria in Asia (cf Bede *De nominibus locorum* PL 92 1039). Though Zúñiga ridiculed the misidentification, a Neapolis is in fact listed among the cities of Caria in Ptolemy *Geography* 5.2.19; for Zúñiga see the *Apologia ad annotationes Stunicae* ASD IX-2 156:864–70. In *1522* Erasmus added to the note the observation that some people locate the city in Thrace, while in *1527* he cited Ptolemy for his view that it was more probably located in Macedonia (cf Ptolemy *Geography* 3.13.9). In fact, the boundary between Thrace and Macedonia was not constant in antiquity, but in New Testament times Neapolis, and Philippi as well, were in the Roman province of Macedonia (see Kraeling *Bible Atlas* map 20). Erasmus' uncertainty suggests the vague 'borderland' as a translation for Latin *confinium*.

25 The Greek text of 16:12 is problematic (Metzger 444–6; cf Bruce 312–13, Munck 161, and Haenchen 494). Erasmus' translation 'the first city of the region of Macedonia' leaves the meaning of 'first' ambiguous – either first in location (for one travelling from Neapolis into Macedonia), or first in importance (so DV AV Conf and RSV). The paraphrase assumes the former meaning, found also in the exegetical tradition represented by the interlinear *Gloss* 1161–2, Hugh of St Cher 272 recto B, and Nicholas of Lyra 1161C. The Roman Via Egnatia took one directly from Neapolis to Philippi. On Philippi as a colony see Haenchen 494 n2.

26 'Out of the city ... outside the gates' combines the reading of the Vulgate ('outside the gate' DV Conf RSV 16:13) and of Erasmus' text and translation (all editions *1516–1535* 'out of the city'; so AV). Though Erasmus scorned the Vulgate translation – see the annotation on 16:13 (*foras portam*) – his own reading is regarded as the inferior one; cf *Beginnings* III 154.

27 prayer] First in *1534*; in *1524*, 'preaching.' Cf the interlinear *Gloss* 1161–2, which noted that the place was suitable for 'preaching or for prayers'; so also Hugh of St Cher 272 recto B and, similarly, Nicholas of Lyra 1162F.

The difficulties of the Greek text here in 16:13 are 'well-nigh baffling' (Metzger 447). The Vulgate read 'where there seemed to be prayer' understanding the verb in the sense of the Greek ἐδόκει (cf DV Conf), while Erasmus in text and translation read 'where prayer was accustomed [*solebat*, representing the Greek ἐνομίζετο] to be' (so the paraphrase, also AV). The preferred reading is 'where we thought [ἐνομίζομεν] there was prayer' (so RSV). In his annotation on 16:13 (*ubi videbatur oratio esse*) Erasmus allows the possibility that even *his* Greek text could be construed 'where it was thought there would be prayer.' Cf Bruce 314.

28 in the region] Added in *1534*. Cf Bede *De nominibus locorum* PL 92 1040: 'Thyatira, a city of Lydia, a province of Asia.'

29 On the importance of teaching for baptism see chapter 2 n114.

103

30 Cf the *Gloss* (on 16:15) 1162E: 'Here two examples are given, one of constraining guests, the other of going in to those recently converted'; similarly Hugh of St Cher 272 recto B.

31 Cf 1 Cor 9:11.

32 'You' also in the Vulgate and the preferred reading of 16:17 (Metzger 448; so DV Conf RSV); 'us' in Erasmus' text and translation (all editions 1516–1535; so AV)

33 Cf the interlinear *Gloss* (on 16:17) 1163–4, which notes that the unclean spirit praised the servants of God; similarly Hugh of St Cher 272 recto D. The 'moral exposition' of Nicholas of Lyra 1162F is more emphatic: 'Paul refused to have himself and his companions praised by a demon speaking in the girl.'

34 the whole] First in *1535*; in *1524* and *1534*, 'this.'

35 Cf the *Gloss* (on 16:21) 1164E, citing Bede: 'The Romans had already decreed that no new god should be received unless approved by the Senate' (cf Bede *Super Acta* 16 PL 92 978D); similarly Nicholas of Lyra 1164F. For Roman attitudes towards and legislation against foreign cults see W.H.C. Frend *Martyrdom and Persecution in the Early Church* (New York 1967) 77–93. For the Roman character of life in Philippi, a Roman colony, see Munck 161. In fact what the objectionable 'customs' were is uncertain; cf Haenchen 496.

36 On anti-Semitism in the Hellenistic world see Victor Tcherikover *Hellenistic Civilization and the Jews* trans S. Applebaum (New York 1970) 357–77. On Erasmus' attitude to the Jews see CWE 42 9 n23, CWE 46 8 n18, and CWE 44 60 n20.

37 The passion of the mob is also noted by Nicholas of Lyra (on 16:22) 1164F.

38 In the paraphrase on 16:22, as in the Vulgate, the magistrates tear the clothes off Paul and Silas. In Erasmus' translation (from *1516*) the magistrates tear their own clothes. In a *1527* annotation (*scissis tunicis eorum*) Erasmus argues that the Greek is ambiguous, allowing for either interpretation. In fact, the paraphrase represents the correct interpretation; cf Bruce 317 and Haenchen 496 and n7.

39 For superstition see the paraphrase on 15:6 (96 above); for ambition, the paraphrases on 6:1–2 (46 above); for gain, the paraphrases on 8:18–19 (59–60 above).
40 For a similar formula see the paraphrase on 4:3 (31 above) and n8.

104

41 Though in all his editions of the New Testament Erasmus translated, like the
Vulgate, 'they praised God' (16:25 DV), in his annotation (*adorantes laudabant
deum*) he observed that the Greek implies that they praised God in hymns (RSV;
cf AV Conf). For happiness associated with hymn-singing, see the paraphrase
on Col 3:16. For the theme of joy in suffering expressed in this paraphrase see
Rom 5:3; also James 1:2, to which the *Gloss* (on 16:26) 1166D alludes: 'One who
praises God with Paul and Silas in prison thinks it all joy when he falls into
various trials'; similarly Hugh of St Cher 272 verso E.

42 The 'tortures' are a rhetorical touch, added by Erasmus, but rooted in the
exegetical tradition. Nicholas of Lyra (on 16:27) 1165C also notes the 'harsh
and despicable death' the jailer would suffer if he did not kill himself. Bruce
248–9 (on 12:19), citing Justinian's Code, explains that 'a guard who allowed
a prisoner to escape became liable to the same punishment as had awaited
the prisoner'; cf Munck 114. In the ancient Roman legal system torture was in
theory used primarily to extract evidence from witnesses. Criminals could,
however, be subjected to cruel forms of death, as in the case of some of the
Christian martyrs. For a brief account of the use of torture in antiquity and the
Middle Ages see Edward Peters *Torture* (Oxford 1985).

43 The exegetical tradition was concerned both with Paul's unexpected ability to
see in the dark and with the loud voice. The *Gloss* (on 16:28) 1166D–E noted
that a loud voice is used to reveal the knowledge of hidden things – for Paul
knew the jailer even in the darkness; similarly Hugh of St Cher 262 verso E.
Nicholas of Lyra 1165C observed that Paul knew 'through the Spirit' why the
jailer wanted to kill himself. The paraphrase on 16:29 continues to reflect this
tradition. For the significance of the voice elsewhere in Erasmus see chapters
3 n6 and 8 n23; see also the paraphrases on 7:57 and 60 (56 above) and the
paraphrases on John 11:43 and 18:6–8 CWE 46 146 and 199.

44 Nicholas of Lyra (on 16:29) 1165C explains that the jailer trembled because he
recognized that 'the earthquake had happened by divine power.'

45 In his annotation on 16:29 (*procidit Paulo et Silae ad pedes*) Erasmus recognized
that the Vulgate's phrase *ad pedes* 'at the feet of' (DV) was not strictly speaking in
the Greek (cf AV Conf RSV 'before'), but he thought it was added appropriately
to avoid ambiguity, and he retained it both in his translation (though, from
1519, in small letters, which LB italicizes) and here in the paraphrase. Though
well attested in the Latin witnesses, Weber II 1726 29n cites the phrase as a
variant; cf Metzger 449.

46 Cf the *Gloss* (on 16:33) 1166E, citing Bede: 'A fine exchange; through those on whom he had inflicted the marks of wounds he lost the marks of sins' (cf Bede *Super Acta* 16 PL 92 979A).

47 'Lord Jesus' (16:31) is the reading of the Vulgate and Erasmus' own text (so DV Conf RSV and the preferred reading); 'Lord Jesus Christ' (AV) is the reading of the Western and Byzantine texts. Cf *Beginnings* III 158–9 and Bruce 320.

48 'Magisterial chair': *cathedra*; Erasmus may intend an allusion to the teaching function of the bishop, on which see the paraphrase on 1 Tim 3:2 CWE 44 18–19 and n2, and on John 6:11 CWE 46 77 and n15. See also Payne *Theology of the Sacraments* 107–9.

49 Cf the interlinear *Gloss* (on 16:33) 1165–6: 'washing he was washed'; similarly Chrysostom *Hom in Acta* 36.2 PG 60 259: 'He washed them and was himself washed; he washed them from their wounds and was himself washed from sins.' Cf also n46 above.

50 The syntax of πανοικεί 'with his whole household' in the Greek text is ambiguous, as is its translation in the Vulgate (*cum omni domo sua*), but in a *1516* annotation on 16:34 (*cum omni domo sua*) Erasmus explains that it should be taken with 'believe' ('believe with his whole house'; so his translation from *1519* and AV), not with 'rejoice' ('rejoice with his whole house'; so his translation of *1516*, and DV Conf RSV). Cf Bruce 321: 'Grammatically it may be taken with either ['believe' or 'rejoice'], in sense it no doubt goes with both.'

51 Cf Nicholas of Lyra (on 16:35) 1166F: 'When the impulse of passion subsided, the magistrates reflected that Paul and Silas had been unjustly beaten.'

52 Erasmus represented the Greek ῥαβδούχους both here and in his translation (from *1516*) by *viatores* (rather than the Vulgate *lictores* 'lictors'), and in his annotation on 16:35 (*miserunt magistratus lictores*) explained that while *viatores* normally carried rods (as did the lictors), their chief function was to deliver messages from the magistrates. In classical literature, *viatores* appear as officers of various magistrates, but especially of the tribune of the plebs, sometimes with power of arrest; cf Livy 2.56.13 and Aulus Gellius 13.12.6. For an explanation of the name see Pliny *Naturalis historia* 18.4.20–1. See also A.H.M. Jones *Studies in Roman Government and Law* (Oxford 1960) 154–5.

105

53 'Magistrate' here is in the singular, following neither the Vulgate nor either the text or translation of Erasmus; hence possibly an inadvertent mistake.

54 Cf Bruce 322: 'By the Valerian and Porcian Laws ... Roman citizens were exempted from all degrading forms of punishment.' For the Porcian and Valerian laws see under *lex* and *provocatio* in OCD.

Chapter 17

1 cities of Macedonia] Added in *1534*. In identifying places as cities or regions Erasmus had precedents in the exegetical tradition, especially as it is represented in the *Gloss*; thus the interlinear *Gloss* (on 17:1) 1167–8: 'These are the names of cities'; similarly Nicholas of Lyra 1167C. For other examples see the interlinear *Gloss* (on 17:10 and on 14:24–5) 1169–70 ('Berea, a city') and 1143–4, where Pisidia and Pamphylia are identified as regions, Attalia as a city; also Hugh of St Cher (on 16:11–12) 272 recto B, who notes that Neapolis and Philippi are 'names of cities.' Cf Erasmus' additions to the paraphrases on 16:6 and 14 (see chapter 16 nn13 and 28).

2 Thessalonica was founded in 316 BC, and became the capital of the Roman province of Macedonia organized in 146 BC. The city enjoyed great prosperity, and eventually became (in the Byzantine Empire) a city second only to Constantinople (cf 'Thessalonica' in OCD and IDB IV 629).

3 'Large and distinguished' represents the Latin *celebritatem*, a word whose adjectival analogue, *celeber*, Erasmus used elsewhere in these paraphrases to describe cities and provinces – eg Athens (17:16) 107 below, Caesarea (11:1) 76 above, Antioch (11:26, 14:28 in chapter 15), 79, 94 above, Corinth (18:1) 112 below, Jerusalem (26:5) 141 below, and Bithynia (16:7) 102 above. The adjective can mean both 'populous' and 'renowned' (L&S) and appears to be used in this *Paraphrase* to designate a major city or province; cf the translation 'noble' in the 1548 *Paraphrase of Erasmus* (fol lix recto).

106

4 Cf the *Gloss* (on 17:2) 1168E, citing Bede: 'Paul not only preached the mystery of Christ, but taught that in Jesus all things were fulfilled' (cf Bede *Super Acta* 17 PL 92 979A–B).

5 Erasmus follows his own text and translation in understanding three groups here (in 17:4): Jews, God-fearing gentiles, and the leading women (so AV RSV), rather than the Vulgate, which implied four: Jews, God-fearers, gentiles, and the leading women (so DV Conf); cf *Beginnings* III 162–3.

6 This paraphrase on 17:5 is apparently intended to explicate two meanings of the Greek ζηλώσαντες: 1/ being zealous and 2/ being jealous; see ζηλόω C in BAG, and also CWE 42 118 n14. Erasmus does not, however, follow his own text and translation (from *1516*), 'Jews which believed not' (AV), but the Vulgate and the preferred reading, simply 'Jews' (so DV Conf RSV); cf Metzger 453.

7 In his paraphrase on 17:5 as in his translation (from *1516*) Erasmus attempted to catch the image of the market-place that seems implicit in the Greek ἀγοραίων: these men were not merely from the undefined rabble – 'lewd fellows of the

baser sort' (AV) – but loafers who spent their time in the market-place; cf the annotation on 17:5 (*zelantes autem Iudaei*). But the precise connotation of the word is disputed; cf *Beginnings* IV 204 5n, Bruce 326, and Haenchen 507 n8.

8 Cf Luke 23:1–24. For the comparison of other heroic figures with Christ see the paraphrases on 4:3–7 (Peter and John) 31–2 above, 7:1 (in chapter 6) and 54–8 (Stephen) 49 and 55-6 above, 12:1–3 (James and Peter) 80 above.

9 'World' is the reading of Erasmus' text and translation and the preferred reading of the Vulgate (cf Weber II 1727 and 6n; so AV Conf RSV); 'city' is the reading of the *Vulgate* of *1527* (so DV). Erasmus considered the Vulgate's *urbem* 'city' a mistake for *orbem* 'world'; cf the annotation on 17:6 (*hi qui urbem concitant*).

10 Nicholas of Lyra (on 17:7) 1169C also observed that those who had received Paul and Silas were regarded as 'sharers in the evil deed.'

11 For the allusions to Jesus see John 19:12–15 and 19–22; also n8 above.

12 On the words 'another king' (17:7 RSV) see the *Gloss* 1170D: 'The apostles [were saying] that Christ was indeed the king of the Jews, that is of those who confess'; also Nicholas of Lyra 1169C, who explained the same words: 'That is, not subject to Caesar but rather to his Lord.'

13 'Had brought forward an appropriate means to get themselves excused': *idoneam excusationem attulisset*. Nicholas of Lyra 1169C commented on the Vulgate's phrase 'having taken satisfaction' (17:9 DV) that 'satisfaction' was taken through a *rationabilis excusatio* – 'whether by buying a release or in some other convenient way.' For *excusatio* in the legal sense of an 'exemption' see *The Digest of Justinian* 27.13.1–46 trans Alan Watson from the Latin text ed Theodore Mommsen and Paul Krueger 4 vols (Philadelphia 1985) II 787–94.

14 The last phrases of the sentence anticipate a *1527* addition to the annotation on 17:10 (*dimiserunt Paulum et Silam*), in which Erasmus similarly explained that Berea was a city of Macedonia, 'not far from Pella, birthplace of Alexander the Great.' Pella, on the Via Egnatia west of Thessalonica, had become the capital of Macedonia under Archelaus king of Macedon (c 413–399 BC). It was replaced by Thessalonica as the capital of the Roman province in 146 BC (see n2 above). A major road led from Pella to Berea located some kilometres south-west. There is no evidence that Paul went on the Egnatian Way as far as Pella; see the account of Paul's journey from Philippi to Berea in Kraeling *Bible Atlas* 441.

107

15 Cf the interlinear *Gloss* (on 17:10) 1169–70, which also noted that on entering Berea the apostles did not 'cease to speak because of the persecution of the Jews.'

16 The paraphrase here anticipates almost verbatim a translation of the Greek Erasmus offered in a *1527* addition to the annotation on 17:11 (*qui cum venissent in synagogam Iudaeorum introierunt*). This differed from his New Testament

translation, which assumed that the Greek εὐγενέστεροι 1/ referred to social class and 2/ was followed by a partitive genitive: the Berean Jews came from the highest class of those who lived at Thessalonica. But the 1527 addition recognized that the Greek εὐγενέστεροι might refer to a quality of mind; hence in the paraphrase the Latin *generosiores* 'more honourable' – primarily in disposition, possibly also in social class. Both the interlinear *Gloss* and Nicholas of Lyra had recognized the ambiguity of the Vulgate's *nobiliores*; the *Gloss* 1169–70 commented, 'in class or in mind,' Nicholas 1169C, 'in class or in mind, or in both ways.' As in the paraphrase here, the 1527 addition to the annotation read the Greek genitive τῶν 'those' not as a partitive but as a comparative: more honourable than those in Thessalonica. Bruce 328 regards the Greek εὐγενής as equivalent to the Latin *generosus* 'noble,' 'liberal,' but Haenchen 508 explains the word as meaning 'fair.' See also *Beginnings* IV 206–7 11n.

17 The explication in this and the previous sentence may recall the commentary of Nicholas of Lyra 1170F, who explained the 'Scriptures' (17:11) as 'the Law and the prophets' and noted that the 'many who believed' were Jews.

18 The paraphrase (on 17:13) follows Erasmus' text and translation, which omits the Greek καὶ ταράσσοντες, reading simply 'stirred up the people' (AV), rather than the Vulgate and the preferred text, 'stirred up and incited the people' (DV Conf RSV); cf Metzger 454.

19 Berea is inland about twenty-five miles from the sea (Kraeling *Bible Atlas* 441). In the paraphrase Erasmus followed the Vulgate of 17:14, 'to go to the sea' (DV Conf RSV), rather than his own text and translation 'to go as though to the sea'(cf AV), which implies that the direction was a ruse (cf Metzger 455).

20 Cf the *Gloss* (on 17:18) 1171B, citing Bede: 'Epicureans ... placed human happiness in pleasure alone of the body, the Stoics in virtue alone of the soul' (cf Bede *Super Acta* 17 PL 92 979C). The Epicureans did not deny, but rather affirmed that the gods exist; they insisted, however, that the gods did not concern themselves with human affairs. See Cicero *De natura deorum* 1.16.43–20.56; also Epicurus' 'Letter to Menoeceus' and Sovereign Maxim 1 in Diogenes Laertius 10.123–4 and 139 (*Lives of Eminent Philosophers* II trans R.D. Hicks, Loeb Classical Library, [New York 1925] 649–51 and 663). For the Stoics' theory of virtue as the sole good, see Cicero *De finibus* 3.6.20–1. For a list of Stoic paradoxes see Cicero *Pro Murena* 61 and for Cicero's discussion of six paradoxes see the *Paradoxa stoicorum* 1–52.

21 Erasmus contrasts the 'philosophy of faith' with secular philosophy in the *Explanatio symboli* ASD V-1 236:906–237:951. See also Erasmus' formulation of the 'philosophy of Christ' in the *Paraclesis* Holborn 139–49.

22 The paraphrase on the words 'What is this babbler trying to say' (17:18 Conf) reflects Erasmus' scholarship on the clause. In the first place, he follows his translation (from 1519) in transliterating the Greek σπερμολόγος; taken literally,

the clause here in the paraphrase reads, 'What is that *spermologus* trying to say'? Secondly, his 'explanation' of *spermologus* in the paraphrase reflects his exposition in the annotation on 17:18 (*seminiverbius*), an annotation to which he made additions and changes in each of the editions. In the annotation he objects (*1516*) to the Vulgate's strange coinage *seminiverbius* and thinks *verbisator* 'sower of words' (adopted in the *1516* translation) would have been better. (Indeed the exegetical tradition had explained the Vulgate term as 'sower of words'; cf eg the *Gloss* 1172D and Nicholas of Lyra 1172F.) But he finds (*1519*) that Hesychius (fifth-century AD lexicographer) had explained the word as 'trifler,' literally 'one who collects seeds,' a metaphor from the life of birds; so modern scholars: Bruce 333, Haenchen 517 n11, and cf σπερμολόγος in BAG. Erasmus says that the word has the sense of 'babbler,' and he thinks Demosthenes used the word to refer to one who would say anything for gain (cf *De corona* 18.127). In *1522* he adds that such a person is called a pettifogger by way of insult, and in an addition of *1535* he offers further grounds for translating the Greek as 'pettifogger' (*rabula*).

23 Cf 1 Cor 1:20–7, 3:19–20. See the 'moral exposition' of Nicholas of Lyra 1172F: '... those who are wise through worldly wisdom ... regard the preachers of the church as sowers of empty words.'

24 For the teaching of Plato on demons see *Apology* 27D, *Timaeus* 40D–E (demons are the bastard children or the descendants of the gods), and *Epinomis* 984D–E (demons are of an ethereal substance). The doctrine of demons was widely adopted in early Christian apologetic, where knowledge of these beings was characteristically traced to Plato; see Athenagoras *Legatio* 23.5 in Schoedel *Athenagoras* 55–7; Justin Martyr *Apology* 5, 14 PG 6 336A–C, 348A–B; Tertullian *Apology* 22–3 CCL 1 128–33. For the doctrine of demons in the history of Greek thought see A.C. Pearson 'Demons and Spirits (Greek)' in Hastings *Encyclopaedia* IV 590–4; for the doctrine in early Christian thought see 'Demons' in EEC 259–61. See also chapter 14 n18.

108

25 In his annotation on 17:19 (*ad Areopagum*) Erasmus justifies his translation of Areopagus as Mars' Quarter on the grounds that the term refers to an area of the city where people other than judges lived. However, 'the Areopagus here [in 17:19] is much more likely to mean the Council [of the Areopagus] than the place' (*Beginnings* IV 212 19n). In archaic and classical Athens, the court of the Areopagus tried homicide cases (cf Aeschylus *Eumenides* 681–5), though it did not always conduct its trials on the Areopagus. 'No quite satisfactory account of the [Council of the] Areopagus in the Roman period exists' (*Beginnings* IV 213), but in this period it may have 'concerned itself with cases of forgery, maintaining correct standards of measure, supervision of

buildings, and matters of religion and education' (ISBE I [1979] 288); cf Bruce 333 and Haenchen 519 n1. In his commentary on this passage Chrysostom *Hom in Acta* 38.1 and 2 PG 60 268 and 270 observes both in the initial exposition and in the recapitulation that the Areopagus was the place murder trials were held. It is stated in Lucian that the court heard its cases by night (*Hermotimus* 64 and *De domo* 18), but 'there is no passage in any classical author that permits us to accept this opinion' (E. Caillemer in *Dictionnaire des antiquités grecques et romaines* 5 vols in 9 ed Charles Daremberg and Edmond Salio with Edmond Pottier and George Lafaye [Paris 1873–1919] I [1873] 398).

26 For the expression at this point see the interlinear *Gloss* 1171–2, which explains the clause 'what these things mean' (17:20) as 'in what direction they lead.'

27 Cf Nicholas of Lyra (on 17:21) 1173B, who notes that in Paul's time foreigners went to Athens for learning, as in his own day they flocked to Paris.
Athens became in the fifth century BC a distinguished centre of learning, attracting teachers such as Protagoras and Prodicus from other Greek states. For the part played by such teachers in the intellectual life of Athens see W.K.C. Guthrie *A History of Greek Philosophy* 6 vols (Cambridge 1962–81) III (1969) 35–48. The four philosophical schools begun in Athens in the fourth century – Academics, Peripatetics, Stoics, and Epicureans – maintained a strong tradition in the city in subsequent centuries and enjoyed an international clientele. In the first century BC many young Romans went to Athens to complete their education – Cicero's son Marcus and the poet Horace, for example; Cicero himself had studied there.

28 The interlinear *Gloss* (on 17:21) 1173–4 also contrasts the strength of curiosity with the lack of any good result.

29 Cf 1 Cor 9:22. The passage is cited, and the same point made, in the annotation on 17:22 (*superstitiosos vos video*).

30 The picture here of Paul addressing a large crowd as in a theatre may catch an emphasis of the biblical narrative, but an address before the Council of the Areopagus would in fact presuppose a relatively small audience; cf Haenchen 518–19.

31 'In general somewhat superstitious': *fere superstitiosiores*, a phrase Erasmus took from his own translation (from *1516*), which reflected, he believed, the Greek ὡς δεισιδαιμονεστέρους, a formulation intended 'to soften the odium of the word.' Cf the annotation on 17:22 (*superstitiosos vos video*). The Vulgate of *1527* rendered the Greek by *quasi superstitiosos* 'as it were superstitious,' with the adjective in the positive degree. In fact the preferred reading of the Vulgate has the adjective in the comparative degree, 'somewhat superstitious'; cf Weber II 1728 and 22n. Though the Latin *superstitiosus* often has the meaning 'over-scrupulous,' the context here, in which the intellectual enlightenment of the Athenians is contrasted with their religious attitude, suggests that Erasmus

intended the negative connotation implied by the English 'superstitious.' The Greek word, however, means 'religious' in a 'cautiously appreciative' sense (Haenchen 520 n7).

32 'Whom' follows Erasmus' text and translation from 1516 (so AV) rather than the Vulgate 'what' (DV Conf RSV), which is the preferred reading (*Beginnings* III 166).

33 Cf the interlinear *Gloss* 1173–4 on the words 'ignorantly worship' (17:23 AV): 'as the altar confesses.'

34 Similarly the explication of the interlinear *Gloss* (on 17:23) 1173–4: 'That this might be a God who is known'; likewise Hugh of St Cher 273 recto B

35 Nicholas of Lyra 1175C also explained the phrase 'served by human hands' (17:25) as the sacrifices offered by human beings.
   In the paraphrases on 17:24–8 Erasmus develops the programme inherent in the biblical text of combining Stoic and Epicurean ideas (cf Bruce 336). Many of the ideas in these paraphrases are expressed in Cicero *De natura deorum*, where Velleius the Epicurean enunciates the doctrine that God is supremely happy, unable to be harmed by injuries inflicted by human beings (1.17.45 and 1.19.51). From the doctrine of the Stoics, presented by Balbus, the following views are relevant here: 1/ that God is reason, or mind, everywhere present, all-powerful, and rules all things (2.2.4, 2.11.30); 2/ he has created the world for the sake of human beings and whatever is in it is for the use of the human race (2.53.133, 2.61.154–263.159); 3/ the frame of the world was created for human beings to look upon (2.62.155); 4/ the world is ruled by providence (2.32.81, 2.34.87, 2.53.132); 5/ God has disclosed traces of his divinity in the stars, the sea, the fountains, the rivers (2.39.98–2.44.115); 6/ but in nothing is God's divinity more evident than in the excellence of human nature, its perfection both of body and of mind (2.54.134–2.61.153).

109

36 For the three divine attributes of power, goodness, and wisdom see the *Explanatio symboli* ASD V-1 235:879–83 and 238:980–2, Thompson *Inquisitio de fide* 56:64–58:85, *Institutio principis christiani* CWE 27 220 / ASD IV-1 150:454–5, and the *De immensa Dei misericordia* LB V 560D–561E, where Erasmus expounds homiletically these three attributes.

37 Erasmus follows his own text and translation of 17:25 (from 1516): 'He gives to all life and breath through all things'; cf the preferred reading: 'He gives to all life and breath and all things' (DV AV Conf RSV). For his text Erasmus had adopted the Byzantine reading κατὰ πάντα in place of καὶ τὰ πάντα; cf *Beginnings* III 168.

38 For the phrase see Gen 1:26, 28.

39 Erasmus follows the Vulgate of 17:26 and the preferred reading (Metzger 456), 'from one man' (Conf; similarly DV RSV 'from one'). In text and translation

(from *1516*) Erasmus followed the reading of his Byzantine witnesses 'from one blood' (so AV); cf *Beginnings* III 168.

40 In interpreting the prescription of 'time' Erasmus appears here in the paraphrase on 17:26 to follow the interpretation of Nicholas of Lyra 1176F, who understood the phrase in terms of the length of life allotted to individuals – people lived longer before the Flood than after. However, in his annotation on the verse (*definiens statuta tempora*) Erasmus understood the prescription in terms of periods of human history – of the duration of empires, also of the periods of divine 'grace.' Like the interlinear *Gloss* 1175–6, the paraphrase interprets 'the boundaries of their habitation' (RSV) as the 'borders of the individual races.'

41 In contrast to the Stoics who thought the world providentially ordered (n35 above), Epicureans believed that worlds came into being by the accretion of atoms apart from a divine plan and were sustained by the forces of nature rather than divine governance. Though the Epicureans believed that the gods existed, they did not affirm that the world was created by the gods; cf Cicero *De natura deorum* 1.19.51–1.20.54 and Lucretius *De rerum natura* 5.416–31.

42 For the retarding effect of the body on the capacities of the mind, see Plato *Phaedo* 65A–67C, 81C; Virgil 6.719–21, 730–2. See also the paraphrase on Rom 8:20 CWE 42 48 for the weight of the body as an impediment to the 'sons of God.' With the expression here of the limitations of the intellect, compare the paraphrase on Rom 1:19 CWE 42 17: 'God, indeed, as he wholly is, can by no means be known by human intelligence.'

43 'They might trace out and search for': *vestigarent ac scrutarentur*. For Erasmus' interest in these verbs and their related forms, see the annotations on Rom 11:33 ('incomprehensible' and 'untraceable') CWE 56 317.

44 Here, and in the preceding sentence, Erasmus follows both the Vulgate (of 17:27) and his own translation (from *1516*) in writing 'God' (so DV Conf RSV), though in his text (all editions *1516–1535*) he printed τὸν κύριον 'the Lord' (AV), an inferior reading (Metzger 456–7).

110

45 'Through him' represents Erasmus' own translation of 12:28 (from *1519*); cf the English translations 'in him' (DV AV Conf RSV). He noted more than once that in the New Testament the Greek preposition ἐν 'in' sometimes has an instrumental force; cf the annotation on Rom 1:4 ('in power') CWE 56 15–16.

46 The exegetical tradition on 17:28 attempted to explain the way in which God was the 'efficient cause'; cf Nicholas of Lyra 1176F: 'He causes in us living ... and so is more intimate to us than ourselves' and Hugh of St Cher 273 recto D: 'God is the efficient cause in a way different from the other causes, which are extrinsic.'

47 Cf the interlinear *Gloss* (on 17:28) 1177–8: 'The human race was produced not from nature but by the breath of God ... we are quite rightly called "his race"'; similarly Hugh of St Cher 273 verso E. For the biblical account see Gen 2:7.

48 Aratus (c 315–240/39 BC) of Soli in Cilicia spent some time in Athens, and under the influence of Zeno became a Stoic. His *Phaenomena* is a poem on astronomy, with a proem (1–18) to Zeus, in which the half-line cited in 17:28 is found (line 5); cf *Arati Phaenomena* ed Ernestus Maass 3rd ed (Berlin 1964). The poem was famous in antiquity and was repeatedly translated into Latin – Cicero was among the translators; cf *Cicéron: Les Aratea* ed and trans Victor Buescu (Bucharest 1941; repr Hildesheim 1966). There was considerable interest in the work in the Renaissance. The fragments of Cicero's translation, which do not include line 5, were published in Venice in 1488 (see Buescu 141–2), and fresh translations appeared in the sixteenth century – in 1521, for example, Philippus Melanchthon published his *Arati Phaenomena graece et latine* in Wittenburg (cf Buescu 26). The line quoted had already been attributed to Aratus by early Christian writers, eg Clement of Alexandria *Stromateis* 1.19 PG 8 807A, Jerome *Epistulae* 70.2 PL 22 665, to whom Erasmus refers in his annotation on this passage (*ipsius enim et genus sumus*), and Chrysostom *Hom in Acta* 38.1 PG 60 269. For the argument that the verse belongs to Epimenides see *Beginnings* V 246–51.

49 Cf Nicholas of Lyra (on 17:29a) 1177B: 'We have a relationship or similarity to him inasmuch as we have the capacity to understand, even as he, and by virtue of which we are made in his image.'

50 Cf Nicholas of Lyra (on 17:29b) 1177C: '[Gold and silver] are below human beings since they are without reason and without sense. God, however, is above human beings – hence it is said that the worship owed to God must not be offered to idols.' Similarly the *Gloss* 1177A–B and Hugh of St Cher 273 verso E.

111

51 Cf Gen 1:26–7 and n49 above. The view that it is by virtue of the mind that human beings are made in the image of God found expression in the early Christian era. For a reproof of idolatry in terms similar to those found here see Clement of Alexandria *Protrepticus* 10 PG 8 212C–213C.

52 For a similar contrast between the past when God 'overlooked' human sin and the present 'appointed time' when God has made known his righteousness see the paraphrases on 14:15-17 (92–3 above) and on Rom 1:18 and 3:25–6 CWE 42 17 and 25.
'Has, as it were, taken no notice': *velut dissimulavit*; Erasmus used the same phrase in the paraphrase on 14:16 (14:15 in LB). Here in 17:30 he translated the Greek ὑπεριδών by *cum dissimularit* (from 1519; in 1516, *cum dissimulasset*),

replacing the Vulgate's *despiciens* 'looking down on'; cf the annotation on the verse (*despiciens deus*): '[The Greek means] "as though to take no notice," and, when you see, to act as though you do not see.' For Zúñiga's criticism of Erasmus' translation here see the *Apologia ad annotationes Stunicae* ASD IX-2 156:871–82.

53 Here, as in the previous sentence, *resipiscere* replaces the Vulgate's *poenitentiam agere* (cf DV 'do penance' 17:30). On *resipiscere* see chapter 2 n90.

54 On the themes of judgment and mercy in Erasmus' New Testament scholarship see Sider 'The Just and the Holy' 15–19.

55 For Nicholas of Lyra 1178F the 'assurance' (17:31 RSV) was of the future resurrection, of which the resurrection of Christ was the pledge. For the theme of the reliability of God based on past events see the paraphrases on 13:23–41 (87–9 above).

56 For the survival of the soul after the death of the body see Plato *Phaedo* 77C–81A. The Pythagoreans believed in the transmigration of souls. For expressions of similar views in the Roman world see Virgil *Aeneid* 6.719–51 and Cicero *De republica* 6.24.26–6.26.29 (from the 'Dream of Scipio').

57 The paraphrase anticipates a *1527* addition to the annotation on 17:34 (*in quibus et Dionysius*) in which Erasmus cites Eusebius as authority for this information about Dionysius; cf the *Ecclesiastical History* 3.4.10 and 4.23.1–3 PG 20 221A and 384B–385A. Already in *1516* Erasmus had in this annotation followed Valla *Annot in Acta* 17 (I 852) in refusing to identify Dionysius the Areopagite with the Platonizing Dionysius, who, Erasmus noted, 'was the author of the books we have *Concerning the Hierarchies* and *Concerning the Divine Names.*'

Chapter 18

112

1 Though in a paraphrastic expansion it is to be expected that a proper name will replace the pronoun in the biblical text, in this case the name 'Paul' reflects Erasmus' own text and translation from *1516* (so AV), though the preferred reading omits the proper name in 18:1 (so DV Conf RSV); cf Metzger 460.

2 Though Corinth had been destroyed by the Romans in 146 BC, it had been refounded by Julius Caesar in 44 BC, and became the capital of the province of Achaia in 27 BC. Through its access to Lechaeum on the Corinthian Gulf and Cenchreae on the Saronic Gulf it was, in effect, a port city. Thus both its political role and geographical position assured its importance in the time of Paul (cf CWE 42 7 n15), and Erasmus could justly speak of it as *celeberrimus* (cf chapter 17 n3). It was famous in antiquity for the dissolute style of living prevalent in it (cf Κορινθιάζομαι in LSJ: to 'Corinthicize' was to

practise fornication), but Erasmus' characterization of it as 'most corrupt' may rather be based on a sentiment expressed by Cicero that maritime cities, due to the intermingling of morals and manners of an international population, are subject to corruption and transformation; cf *De republica* 2.4.7. See the Argument to 1 Corinthians LB VI 657–8: '[Corinth was] the most important and the wealthiest trading centre of all Achaia; it is generally the case that morals in cities of this kind are most corrupt because not so much morals as vices are generally imported from every race.' It is presumably on the same grounds that Athens is also said here to be 'extraordinarily corrupt.'

3 Bede describes Pontus as a 'region ... bordering the Pontic [Black] Sea' – hence in the northern part of Asia Minor (cf *De nominibus locorum* PL 92 1039). In his annotation on 18:2 (*Ponticum genere*) Erasmus identifies the Pontus from which Aquila came as a part of Asia (*1516*; in *1535*, Asia Minor) to distinguish it from the Pontic Sea. Cf chapter 16 n17.

4 On the Jewish population in Rome cf E. Mary Smallwood *The Jews under Roman Rule: From Pompey to Diocletian* (Leiden 1976) 121–2: 'Rome ... eventually had one of the largest Jewish communities in the Empire.' The paraphrase leaves untouched the complex historical problems 18:2 raises; cf Bruce 342–3 and Haenchen 65–7.

5 Cf Nicholas of Lyra (on 18:3) 1179C: 'Paul practised this trade to maintain himself, so that he should not be a burden on those to whom he preached (see 1 Cor 9:6, 15–18).

6 The paraphrase on 18:3 here may owe something to Erasmus' critic Zúñiga, who challenged Erasmus' translation (*1516, 1519*) *texere aulaea* 'wove curtains' (or 'canopies'). Zúñiga argued that the image was one of 'making tents from leather'; see *Apologia ad annotationes Stunicae* ASD IX-2 156:884–158:894.

7 Both the *Gloss* 1180D and Hugh of St Cher 273 verso F had at this point (18:3) compared Peter and Paul, but following a mystical interpretation (Peter withdrew us from the world through the nets of faith; Paul erects an umbrella protecting us from sin). For Erasmus' allusion to Peter see John 21:3. In expressing admiration for Paul, the paraphrase reflects additions of *1519* and *1522* to the annotation on this verse (*scenofactoriae artis*), additions that implicitly rebuke contemporary prelates for their wealth and arrogance: 'O true priest [ie Paul], truly – and with his own gifts – great! We, with our retinue, resources, wealth, and our threats wish to seem great'; cf also the annotation on Rom 15:19 ('of wonders in the strength of the Holy Spirit') CWE 56 407–8.

8 Cf 17:15.

9 For his New Testament text of 18:5 Erasmus adopted (from *1516*) the inferior reading συνείχετο τῷ πνεύματι, which he translated *coartabatur spiritu* ('was pressed in the spirit' AV). He follows his translation for the paraphrase, and his annotation (*instabat verbo Paulus testificans*) shows that he understood the phrase

to refer to an action undertaken unwillingly and reluctantly. The preferred reading has λόγῳ 'word' (Vulgate) rather than πνεύματι 'spirit' and gives the sense 'pressing on eagerly with the word,' hence 'occupied with preaching' (RSV; similarly DV Conf); cf Metzger 461–2. But Erasmus' understanding of the text leaves problematic the connection between Paul's reluctance and his readiness to witness ('he was pressed in the spirit and testified to the Jews' AV). The paraphrase explains the connection; it assumes that Paul's preaching in Corinth had met with little success, but in spite of small progress Paul continued to 'witness eagerly.' In the 1548 *Paraphrase of Erasmus* the translators, apparently troubled by the difficulty of the connection, forced the sense of the Latin: 'This done Paul because he was much sory that he had don very lytle good there, was constreined by the spirite neverthelesse, to preach yet diligently Jesus of Nazareth to the Jewes' (fol lxii verso).

10 Cf Nicholas of Lyra 1180F, commenting on 'Jesus was the Christ' (18:5): 'Promised in the Law and the prophets.'

11 For the 'gospel precept' see Matt 10:14 and Mark 6:11, and on the sign of reproach see the paraphrases on these verses (for Mark 6:11 CWE 49 79).

12 and . . . clean] Added in 1534

13 Cf Matt 28:19; Acts 1:8, 26:16–18.

14 In the paraphrase on 18:7 Erasmus follows the Vulgate and the preferred reading (Metzger 462–3) in giving the man two names, Titus Justus (so DV Conf; 'Titius Justus' RSV). His own text and translation (from 1516) read simply 'Justus' (so AV). Did Erasmus intend to suggest that Paul moved from the house of Aquila and Priscilla to that of Titus Justus (as the 'Western' text implies; cf Metzger 462)? Modern scholars understand from the text that Paul moved his preaching headquarters (not his residence) from the synagogue to Titus Justus' house; see eg Haenchen 535, 539. In the paraphrases on the remainder of this chapter and elsewhere (cf eg the paraphrase on Rom 16:3 CWE 42 88) Erasmus implies that Paul had only the most cordial relationship with Aquila and Priscilla.

15 The punctuation of the 1535 and earlier editions of the *Paraphrase* has been followed in the translation of the paraphrase on 18:8 in the 1548 *Paraphrase of Erasmus*: 'Than Crispus whiche was chief of the Synagoge by reason that he dwelled nere, beleved in the lorde . . .' (fol lxiii recto). But Nicholas of Lyra (on 18:7) 1180F had observed that the proximity of Justus' house to the synagogue became the occasion through which Paul was able to 'produce more fruit' (because the people assembled in the adjacent synagogue); Erasmus, then, may wish to say that the proximity of Justus' house to the synagogue provided the opportunity through which the head of the synagogue and his household believed. For what is known about the position of the head of the synagogue in the life of the Jewish community see *The Jewish People in the First Century* ed

S. Safrai and M. Stern with D. Flusser and W.C. van Unnik 2 vols (Philadelphia 1974–6) II 933–7.

113

16 For 'Jewish malice' see chapter 3 n45.

17 The interlinear *Gloss* (on 18:9) 1181–2 likewise explicates the verb 'speak': 'the gospel.'

18 On the divine 'destination' of believers see the paraphrase on 13:48 (90 above) and the paraphrase on Rom 8:29 CWE 42 50. See further the annotations on Rom 8:29 ('whom he foreknew') CWE 56 225–8 and on Rom 1:4 ('who was predestined') CWE 56 10–12; also the annotation on Eph 1:5 (*qui praedestinavit nos*).

19 Erasmus introduces into the paraphrase here on 18:11 and on the preceding verse characteristic descriptors of Paul's preaching: *fortiter ac libere* 'boldly and freely' and *constanter* 'without flinching.' In other passages in this *Paraphrase* these adjectives have been used to explicate the sense of the Greek παρρησία / παρρησιάζομαι, on which see chapter 4 n36.

20 Corinth is similarly located by the interlinear *Gloss* 1181–2 and Hugh of St Cher 273 verso H; cf chapter 17 n1.

21 During the reign of Claudius (AD 41–54) Achaia was a 'senatorial province' (from AD 44), and the governors of senatorial provinces were theoretically responsible to the Senate (P-W I-1 194).

22 Erasmus follows Nicholas of Lyra (on 18:13) 1181C in interpreting 'the law' here as the law of Moses – an interpretation suggested by Gallio's reply. But it is possible that the text of Acts means 'Roman law'; cf Bruce 347, Munck 178, and Haenchen 536.

23 For the Greek ἀνέχομαι 'bear with' (18:14 DV AV Conf RSV) in the sense of 'hear patiently' cf Bruce 347, who cites 2 Cor 11:1.

24 The administration of justice was one of the major tasks of a provincial governor. For the governor's responsibilities in the civil affairs of the provinces see F.F. Abbott and A.C. Johnson *Municipal Administration in the Roman Empire* (Princeton 1926) 202–4.

25 Erasmus' Vulgate and the Vulgate of 1527 read 'about a word and the names of your law' (cf Weber II 1729 15n); hence here in 18:15 Erasmus follows his own text and translation (from 1516), 'about a word and names and your law.' His annotation (*de verbo et nominibus legis vestrae*) explains further his understanding of the clause: 'He has contrasted "words" with "deeds"; "names" are questions about clean and unclean and about genealogies; the law means "Mosaic ceremonies."'

26 Erasmus omits the detail of Sosthenes' arrest – 'And they all seized Sosthenes' (18:17 RSV) – perhaps inadvertently; the detail is found in his own text and

translation as well as in the Vulgate. In Erasmus' text and translation it is 'the Greeks' who beat Sosthenes; in the paraphrase it is the indefinite 'they'; cf the Vulgate's indefinite 'all,' which is the preferred reading (Metzger 463). The context also implies that these are Jews. The exegetical tradition, on the other hand, had noted that it was gentiles who beat Sosthenes: so the interlinear *Gloss* 1181–2, the marginal *Gloss* 1181C, and, by implication, Nicholas of Lyra 1181C.

114

27 For the negative attitude of Romans towards Jews see eg Juvenal *Satires* 6.542–7, 14.96–106 and Tacitus *Histories* 5.3–5. Cf chapter 16 n36; also the Argument to the Epistle to the Romans CWE 42 9. For the view that before AD 70 Christians were not distinguished from Jews see W.H.C. Frend *Martyrdom and Persecution in the Early Church* (New York 1967) 121–6. Suetonius *Claudius* 25.4 may indicate that no distinction was made between Christians and Jews in the time of Claudius.

28 Cf 18:9–10.

29 The identification is common to the exegetical tradition: cf the *Gloss* 1182F and Nicholas of Lyra 1182F. For Cenchreae as the Corinthian port see n2 above.

30 In his annotation on 18:18 (*qui sibi totonderat caput*) Erasmus observes that from the syntax of the Greek we cannot determine whether it was Paul or Aquila who shaved his head. The question is still discussed; cf Haenchen 545–6. The paraphrase leaves unexplained the nature of the vow, though the allusion to Jewish anxiety associates the vow here with that in 21:22–6. The vow as stated here has perplexed commentators, both modern (cf Haenchen 543 n2) and ancient (cf Chrysostom *Hom in Acta* 40.1 PG 60 281, who notes that the vow is taken 'in the Jewish manner' but lacked the sacrifice).

31 Cf 1 Cor 9:20–1.

32 Cf the *Gloss* (on 18:18) 1182F–1183A citing Bede: 'In order not to scandalize the Jewish believers, Paul acted the part of a Jew to gain the Jews' (cf Bede *Super Acta* 18 PL 92 981D); also Nicholas of Lyra 1182F: 'It was not right that legal rites should cease absolutely at once lest some should think that Jewish rites like gentile practices had always been wrong. Hence it was permitted to those converted from Judaism to observe the Law for an intermediate time between the passion of Christ and the spread of the gospel.' Hugh of St Cher 274 recto B has a similar comment. Cf the paraphrase on 16:3 (101 above, the circumcision of Timothy) and n7; also the Argument to the Epistle to the Romans CWE 42 8–9, where both the circumcision of Timothy and Paul's vow are justified, like the Jerusalem decree itself, as a concession to the 'unconquerable superstition' of the Jews and out of consideration for the times. Cf also the annotation on Acts 21:21 (*neque secundum consuetudinem ingredi*).

33 Cf 1 Cor 7:18–19.

34 Cf 1 Cor 5:11; Gal 5:19–21; Col 3:5–6; and the paraphrase on Acts 15:41 (100 above).

35 Cf 1 Cor 10:23–33, Gal 2:12–14 (choice of foods); Acts 17:28, 1 Cor 15:33, Titus 1:12 (citation from pagan authors). On the doctrine of accommodation, see the Argument to Romans CWE 42 8 and n20 and the paraphrase on Rom 12:16 CWE 42 72 and n9.

36 'They arrived': *perventum est,* thus without identifying the person; in the Vulgate and Erasmus' own text and translation 'he' (DV AV Conf); in the preferred reading of the Greek text 'they' (RSV; cf Metzger 464)

37 Cf chapter 16 n16.

38 These words ('I must ... Jerusalem, but') are taken virtually without change from Erasmus' translation (from *1516*). He found them in his Greek manuscripts, and so printed them in his text; see the annotation on 18:21 (*iterum revertar ad vos*). They appear in AV, but are not found in the Vulgate DV Conf or RSV; the preferred reading of the Greek text omits them (*Beginnings* III 176–7 and Metzger 465; see n40 below).

39 Bede *De nominibus locorum* PL 92 1036A–B differentiates two Caesareas: Caesarea in Palestine and Caesarea Philippi. For Caesarea in Palestine cf chapter 10 n2.

40 That Paul went to Jerusalem is a natural inference from the inclusion in 18:21 of the 'Western' addition (see n38). But there is no textual evidence in 18:22 that he did so. Without support from the Vulgate, DV translates 'he went up *to Jerusalem*'; so Conf (without italics) – cf AV ('he had ... gone up') and RSV ('he went up'). On the question of where Paul went in 18:22 see Bruce 350, Munck 181, and Haenchen 547–8.

41 As in the case of Caesarea (see n39 above) Bede *De nominibus locorum* PL 92 1035A also identifies two Antiochs: Antioch in Syria and Antioch 'in Pisidia.' For Antioch in Syria see chapter 15 n3.

42 For Paul's exemplary solicitude for the flock see the paraphrases on 14:21–2 (93 above), and for the image of the flock, Acts 20:28–9.

115

43 For John's baptism see Matt 3:11 and Luke 3:16. On the 'richer grace' of Christ compared with the repentance preached by John see the paraphrase on John 1:16 CWE 46 25.

44 In his Greek text of 18:26 Erasmus printed the names of this couple in the order of the 'Western' text, 'Aquila and Priscilla' (so AV), but in all editions he translated, with the Vulgate, in the order of the preferred text, 'Priscilla and Aquila' (cf Metzger 466–7); in LB Erasmus' translation is corrected to fit his Greek text. The names appear on several occasions in the New Testament, most frequently in the order 'Priscilla and Aquila.' See *Beginnings* III 178–9.

45 In 18:26 the Greek text uses παρρησιάζεσθαι of Apollos' preaching, which Erasmus' translated *libere loqui* 'to speak freely' and represented here in paraphrase by *loquentem magno spiritu de Iesu* 'speaking with much spirit about Jesus'; cf n19 above. The failure to note in the paraphrase that Apollos spoke 'in the synagogue' may be inadvertent.

46 For the distinction between the rudiments of evangelical doctrine (paraphrase on 18:25 just above) and the mysteries of evangelical religion see 1 Cor 2:6–3:4. In his annotation on 18:25 (*hic erat edoctus*), however, Erasmus observed that the word 'catechumen' is derived from the verb κατηχέω used there, and it may be that by the distinction made in the paraphrase Erasmus thought also of the stages in the catechumenate of early Christianity (cf chapter 9 n15).

47 Cf Nicholas of Lyra 1184F on 'when he arrived' (18:27): 'That is at Achaia, where Corinth is.'

48 The 'for' clause explicates the biblical words 'through grace'(18:27). These words ('through grace') are omitted in the Vulgate (so DV and Conf), but are included in all editions of Erasmus' text and translation (cf AV RSV).

49 In his annotation on 18:28 (*contulit multum his qui crediderunt*) Erasmus questions the point of reference for δημοσίᾳ (Vulgate *publice*) 'in public': the word could be taken with 'confuted' (18:28a) or with 'showing' (18:28b), though he thought it should be taken with 28a, not 28b. In text (from *1516*) and translation (from *1519*) he put a comma both before and after the word, leaving ambiguous its relation to the two verbs. In his translation of *1516*, however, and here in the paraphrase he clearly takes the word with 28b. DV AV Conf RSV all take the expression with 28a; but both Munck 182 and Haenchen 549 take it with 28b.

Chapter 19

1 Cf chapter 18 n2.

2 The paraphrase is only slightly more specific than the biblical text 'upper country' (19:1 RSV), but implies the territories Paul had visited before and to which he returned according to 18:23.

116

3 On the sentiment (to err sincerely, not with malice) see the paraphrase on 8:1 and 9:3 and 6 (56 and 63–4 above).

4 Cf the *Gloss* (on 19:4) 1185B, citing Bede: 'John did not remit sins, but taught repentance . . . a penitent people accepted this washing as a sign of their own devotion' (cf Bede *Super Acta* 19 PL 92 982B); similarly Hugh of St Cher 274 recto D; also Nicholas of Lyra 1186F: 'The baptism of John was a sort of attestation of repentance, and of the disposition for the baptism of Christ in which justifying

grace is given.' This contrast between the baptism of John and the baptism of Jesus is found in the very early exegetical tradition. Tertullian, referring to Acts 19:2, speaks of John's baptism as preparatory, through repentance, to the heavenly baptism of Christ through which sins were forgiven and celestial gifts offered; cf *De baptismo* 10.2–5 CCL 1 284–5. (The coincidence with Erasmus' paraphrase reflects the common tradition rather than direct influence, as the *De baptismo* was not published until 1545). The thought of the paraphrases here finds more elaborate expression in the paraphrase on Mark 1:4 CWE 49 14–16.

5 For the command see Matt 28:19 and Mark 16:15–16. Though the biblical text of 19:5 indicates that these disciples were baptized in the name only of 'the Lord Jesus,' the medieval commentators, whom Erasmus apparently reflects here, stressed the importance of the Trinitarian formula in baptism; cf eg the interlinear *Gloss* 1185–6 and the marginal *Gloss* 1185B, citing Rabanus: 'That is not baptism which is not given in the name of the Trinity'; also Hugh of St Cher 274 recto D and Nicholas of Lyra 1186F, who explains why in the earliest church baptism was given (as in the biblical text of 19:5) only in the name of 'the Lord Jesus.'

6 On the expression see the paraphrase on 10:45 (75 above). The interlinear *Gloss* (on 19:6) 1185–6 observed that speaking in tongues is the 'customary sign' of having received the Holy Spirit; similarly Hugh of St Cher 274 recto D.

7 See the interlinear *Gloss* 1185–6 on 'prophesied' (19:6): 'By teaching or by predicting things to come.' On the role of prophets as biblical expositors see the paraphrase on 15:32 (99 above), where Judas and Silas are 'prophets, skilled in sacred literature.'

8 For Paul as 'teacher of the gentiles' see chapter 13 n11.

9 For 'the other apostles' see 8:14–17.

10 Representing the Greek ἐπαρρησιάζετο (19:8), which Erasmus' translation renders 'spoke freely'; cf chapter 18 n19.

11 On the kingdom of God as the evangelical doctrine opposed to the Mosaic law see the paraphrase on Mark 1:15 CWE 49 22–3; on the characterization of those who hold *mordicus* ('tooth and nail,' 'doggedly') to the carnal law see the paraphrase on Rom 8:8 CWE 42 46.

12 The exegetical tradition explained 'the way' of 19:9 as 'evangelical teaching'; cf the interlinear *Gloss* 1187–8, Hugh of St Cher 274 verso E, and Nicholas of Lyra 1187C. See n28 below.

117

13 Erasmus is fond of the expression; cf chapter 9 n3.

14 See Nicholas of Lyra 1187C on 'argued daily' (19:9 RSV): 'To set forth the evangelical truth.'

15 For the images here see Eph 5:25–7 (pure church); Mark 8:15 and 1 Cor 5:6–8 (yeast).

16 'Evangelical word,' sometimes 'evangelical doctrine,' occasionally simply 'gospel,' are by far the most common expressions in the *Paraphrase on Acts* for the expressions 'word,' 'word of God,' 'word of the Lord' in the biblical text; cf the paraphrases on 4:31 (37 above), 6:4 (47), 8:14 (59), 8:25 (60), 12:24 (83), 13:5 and 7 (84), 13:44 and 46 (90), 17:13 (107), 18:11 (113).

17 Cf the paraphrase on 18:19 (114 above) and chapter 16 n16. The interlinear *Gloss* 1187–8 identifies 'Asia' here in 19:10 as 'Asia Minor.'

18 Nicholas of Lyra 1188F glosses both words of the phrase 'extraordinary miracles' (19:11 RSV); he explains 'extraordinary' as 'many and excellent' and says of 'miracles' that they were to 'confirm the teaching.'

19 The *Gloss* (on 19:13) 1188D–E, citing Bede, refers to Josephus as authority for the view that Solomon discovered and taught the art of exorcism (cf Bede *Super Acta* 19 PL 92 983A); so Hugh of St Cher 274 verso F. For Solomon's skill see Josephus *Jewish Antiquities* 8.2.5 (42–9); also the *Wisdom of Solomon* 7:15–22.

20 For the motif of gain and glory among magicians, see the narrative of Simon Magus and the paraphrases on 8:12–13, 18–24 (58–60 above).

21 The paraphrase anticipates a 1527 addition to the annotation on 19:16 (*daemonium pessimum*) wherein Erasmus explains that the Vulgate translator seems to have read 'both' (Vulgate DV Conf) instead of 'them' (AV). But it is likely that the ἀμφοτέρων of the preferred text is used here in the sense of 'all' (RSV); cf Bruce 359, Haenchen 564 n5, Metzger 470–2, and ἀμφότεροι in BAG.

22 'spread': *divulgata est. Divulgare* is the word used by the interlinear *Gloss* (on 19:17) 1189–90 to explain the Vulgate's *notum factum est* 'became known.'

118

23 Cf *Adagia* II viii 49 CWE 34 67, where Erasmus explains the proverb as referring to 'certain magic characters and words, by the use of which [the Ephesians] emerged successful in business of every kind.' The 'Ephesian letters' are thought to be six magical words. Their meaning was obscure even in antiquity; Clement of Alexandria *Stromateis* 5.8 PG 9 72C–73A records the interpretation of a certain Androcydes, a Pythagorean, who understood the words to mean darkness, light, earth, year, sun, and true voice. See P-W V-2 2771–3 and Bruce 360.

In his annotation on 19:18 (*confitentes et annunciantes actus suos*) Erasmus noted that the confession of the Ephesians was a public confession. The annotation drew fire from Lee, to which Erasmus replied with a lengthy critique of the ecclesiastical practice of auricular confession; cf *Responsio ad annotationes Lei* LB IX 255–62. For the wide ramifications of this particular debate see Payne *Theology of the Sacraments* 183–7.

24 The denarius was a Roman silver coin, but the Latin term had been transliterated and used frequently in the Greek text of the Gospels (eg Matt 20:2, 9, 10, 13; cf RSV where the English retains the word 'denarius'). The Vulgate had

rendered the Greek ἀργυρίου here in 19:19 by *pecuniam denariorum* 'money to
the sum of [fifty thousand] denarii.' In his translation Erasmus omitted the
Vulgate's *denariorum*, and rendered 'money to the sum of fifty thousand.' The
paraphrase, like the Vulgate, uses both words – 'money' and 'denarii' – but in
a new configuration. Erasmus' annotation on the verse (*pecuniam denariorum
quinque milium*) indicates that he understood the Greek to mean 'fifty thousand
pieces of silver' (or, 'fifty thousand in cash').

25 'Word of the Lord' reflects Erasmus' Greek text of 19:20 (from 1516), but not his
translation, which, in spite of his text, followed the Vulgate in reading 'word of
God.' 'Word of the Lord' is the preferred reading of the Greek text (Metzger
472), 'word of God' the preferred reading of the Vulgate (cf Weber II 1731 20n).

26 The paraphrase on 'resolved in the Spirit' (19:21 RSV) reflects the same
ambiguity as the interlinear *Gloss* 1189–90: 'By the Holy Spirit, or by his own.'
Nicholas of Lyra 1190F, on the other hand, understood 'the Holy Spirit, not
[Paul's] own' – as is evidently the assumption in the paraphrases on 21:13–14
(126–7 below). On the ambiguity of the Greek see Bruce 361 and Haenchen 568
and n2.

27 Cf the interlinear *Gloss* (on 19:21) 1191–2: 'Meanwhile he sends deputies to
prepare alms which he would take to Jerusalem'; so Hugh of St Cher 274
verso H. For the 'collection' see 1 Cor 16:1–10 and 2 Cor 8; for Timothy as an
emissary of Paul sent in advance to 'prepare minds' see 1 Cor 4:17 (where the
reference is to the Corinthians alone), and cf Phil 2:19–24. But the circumstances
of Timothy's deputization to Macedonia and Greece are obscure; cf *Beginnings*
IV 244 22n and Bruce 361.

28 'Gospel' paraphrases 'way' (19:23 AV Conf RSV; 'way of the Lord' DV); see the
paraphrases on 19:9 (116 above) and on 22:4 (130 below), where the 'way'
is paraphrased as 'evangelical teaching' and 'evangelical way'; similarly the
paraphrases on 'the way of the Lord' in 18:25 and 26, where the biblical
expression is represented by the phrases 'evangelical doctrine,' 'evangelical
philosophy,' 'evangelical religion' (115 above). In 9:2 (63 above), however, 'the
way' is paraphrased as 'condemned heresy.' See also chapter 24 n9.

29 Both here in the paraphrases on 19:24–41, and in his translation Erasmus
follows the Vulgate – and Roman mythology – in identifying the Artemis
(RSV) of the biblical text with Diana (DV AV Conf). For the designation
in antiquity of the Ephesian temple as the temple of Diana see eg Pliny
Naturalis historia 14.2.9 and Caesar *De bello civili* 3.33. In Roman mythology
Diana was generally regarded, like the Greek Artemis, as the twin sister
of Phoebus Apollo (Ovid *Metamorphoses* 6.204–17). In Roman mythology
Diana was also identified with the moon (Ovid *Metamorphoses* 15.196–8) and
regarded as a goddess of witchcraft and sorcery (Horace *Epodes* 5.47–54),
and so the equivalent of 'three-formed' Hecate (Ovid *Metamorphoses* 7.177,

194). But the actual relationship between the Roman Diana and the Greek and the Ephesian Artemis is a matter of discussion. Erasmus himself distinguished Diana, goddess of the hunt, from the Ephesian Artemis, the 'many-breasted one'; cf the annotation on 19:27 (*et destrui incipiet maiestas eius*). See *Beginnings* v 251–6, Bruce 363, Haenchen 575 (on 19:34), and IDB I 242.

30 The explanation is unlikely since the Ephesian Artemis was not a moon goddess; cf n29 above. The word 'silversmith' in the preceding sentence (cf 19:24 DV AV Conf RSV) conceals a vigorous debate between Zúñiga and Erasmus over the proper way to render the Greek into Latin. The paraphrase adopts Erasmus' translation (from 1519): *faber argentarius* 'silversmith' (in 1516, *aurifaber* 'goldsmith'). The Vulgate had rendered the Greek by *argentarius*, which, Erasmus argued, designated a 'money-changer' (cf *Apologia ad annotationes Stunicae* ASD IX-2 158:904–13). Similarly, in place of the Vulgate *aedes* 'temples' (DV), Erasmus translated (from 1516) *delubra* 'shrines' (AV Conf RSV). In fact, no silver images of Artemis but only terracotta shrines have been found (Haenchen 571–2).

119

31 Cf Nicholas of Lyra 1192F on 'persuaded' (19:26 RSV): 'saying there is no divinity in them'; cf also 17:29 and the paraphrase on that verse (110–11 above). For the 'two years' see 19:10.

32 The temple of Artemis at Ephesus was regarded as one of the seven wonders of the world (cf *Beginnings* v 251–6); for its magnificence see Strabo *Geography* 14.1.22–3 and Pliny *Naturalis historia* 16.79.213–15. For votive offerings as a source of great and varied temple wealth in antiquity see Arthur Fairbanks *A Handbook of Greek Religion* (New York 1910) 92–6 (cf also Mark 12:41–4).

33 In Nicholas of Lyra 1192F, Demetrius poses the problem stated in 19:27 in a slightly different way: 'In making images that have no power we are convicted of falsehood.'

34 Erasmus accepted for both his text and translation of 19:27 the reading of the Vulgate 'her magnificence will be destroyed' (so DV AV Conf); cf the preferred reading (*Beginnings* III 186 and 27n): 'she will be deposed from her magnificence' (RSV).

35 Here, as in his translation, Erasmus follows exactly the Vulgate in representing the cry of the Ephesians, rendered in both DV and Conf by 'Great is Diana of the Ephesians.'

36 Cf the *Gloss* (on 19:29) 1193B citing Bede: 'The theatre is the place of deranged counsel' (cf Bede *Super Acta* 19 PL 92 984B); similarly Hugh of St Cher 275 recto A. Both Bede and Hugh refer the expression to Arator's *De actibus apostolorum*; cf 2.713–18 PL 68 215.

120

37 For his text of 19:33 Erasmus adopted the reading προεβίβασαν, which he rendered (from *1516*) by the Latin *protraxerunt*, the verb he uses in the paraphrase here and just above ('Alexander was thrust forth'). In a *1519* addition to the annotation (*detraxerunt Alexandrum*), he explains the Greek as meaning 'to compel to appear,' 'to be thrust forth.' The paraphrase appears to stress the sense of compulsion. But the preferred reading is συνεβίβασαν 'they instructed' (Haenchen 574 and Metzger 473); cf RSV 'prompted,' but Conf 'called upon.'

38 In his annotation on 19:35 (*et cum sedasset scriba turbas*), Erasmus comments that the subject of 'said' is ambiguous: either the town clerk or Alexander. In fact, the town clerk is intended; cf Bruce 367, Munck 195, and Haenchen 570 (translation) and 574 (notes).

39 Erasmus retained the Vulgate's *cultrix* for νεωκόρος of 19:35, though we learn from the *Apologia ad annotationes Stunicae* ASD IX-2 158:915–160:937 that Zúñiga had to correct his etymology of the Greek word, which means 'temple-keeper' (RSV; cf νεωκόρος in BAG). *Cultrix* 'worshipper' (DV AV Conf) has the connotation also of 'one who cares for' (L&S).

40 The Vulgate had understood the Greek τοῦ διοπετοῦς as 'Jupiter's offspring' (so DV Conf); in his annotation on 19:35 (*Jovisque prolis*) Erasmus correctly noted that the Greek refers to something fallen from heaven (so AV RSV). He thought the object was an image of Diana; in fact, a reference to a sacred stone, or meteorite, is probably intended (cf Bruce 367, Munck 196, and Haenchen 575 and n5).

41 From *1516* Erasmus read and translated 'your' goddess (19:37), though the preferred reading is 'our' goddess (Metzger 473). Erasmus' reading facilitates the interpretation that Alexander, the Jew, is the speaker (cf n38 above).

42 The Greek of 19:40 is generally construed 'there being no reason about which we can give an account' (so AV RSV; Bruce 368, Munck 194, and Haenchen 576). This is the sense of Erasmus' translation (from *1519*) and the paraphrase here. The Vulgate, however (and Erasmus *1516*), had understood, 'there being no man guilty of whom we may give account of this concourse' (DV; cf Conf: 'since there is no culprit whom we can hold liable for this disorderly gathering').

Chapter 20

1 Nicholas of Lyra 1195C, on 'exhorted' (20:1 RSV), comments: 'That they should remain in the good begun.' For this theme in the exegetical tradition, see the paraphrase on 13:43 (89 above) and n90.

2 The paraphrase on 20:1 represents a combination of the Vulgate and Erasmus' translation. The Vulgate was based on the Alexandrian text, with five verbs,

which it understood as follows: [Paul] 1/ sent for, 2/ exhorted, 3/ took leave (ἀσπασάμενος), 4/ departed, 5/ to go (cf DV Conf RSV). Erasmus' text, following the Byzantine tradition 1/ read 'called together' in place of 'sent for'; 2/ omitted 'exhorted'; Erasmus 3/ translated ἀσπασάμενος as 'embrace' rather than 'take leave'; and 4/ like the Vulgate read 'departed to go': 'After Paul had called the disciples together and embraced them, he departed to go to Macedonia' (cf AV). For the text see *Beginnings* III 190–1.

121

3 Nicholas of Lyra 1195C explained the 'exhortation' (20:2 AV) in similar terms: 'That they should remain firm in the faith.'

4 Nicholas of Lyra 1195C also attempted to explain the apparent anomaly of 20:2: 'By "Greece" is meant another part of Greece, for Macedonia, too, is often said to be in Greece.' For the Romans, 'Greece' included Epirus and Macedonia, though for the Greeks 'Hellas' (the Greek word in 20:2) included the mainland territory below Macedonia, southward from Mt Olympus (cf ISBE II 557). After AD 44, the Roman province of Achaia included most of this territory. Cf Haenchen 581 n2, quoting Theodor Zahn, '"Hellas . . . does not have the same meaning as Achaia . . . but describes Greece proper" without Thessaly.' Haenchen himself, however, says that 'Hellas' here stands for Achaia (581).

5 for the voyage] First in 1534; in 1524, 'on the voyage'

6 Cf 16:11–12. Nicholas of Lyra 1196F (but on 20:6) likewise observes the symmetry: Paul leaves Europe from the point at which he entered.

7 Instead of Sopater (as in Erasmus' text and translation of 20:4, from 1516), the name is given in a minority Vulgate reading as Sosipater (eg in the Vulgate of 1527; not, however, in Weber II 1732; cf Rom 16:21). The Vulgate also identifies Sopater as '[the son] of Pyrrhus' (DV Conf RSV, but not AV or Erasmus' text and translation). The exegetical tradition generally explained the phrase 'of Pyrrhus' to mean 'the son of Pyrrhus' – so the *Gloss* 1195B, Nicholas of Lyra 1195C, and Hugh of St Cher 275 recto D; cf Metzger 475.

8 which . . . Passover] Added in 1534
Nicholas of Lyra (on 20:6) 1196F also explained that the days of *azyma* immediately followed Passover. The days of *azyma* continued for a week after Passover eve. Cf chapter 12 n7. In the *Peregrinatio apostolorum* LB VII 657–8 Erasmus observed that Paul seems to have spent Passover day at Philippi.

9 In his annotation on 20:7 (*una sabbati*) Erasmus indicates that he understands the day to be Sunday: *una* 'one' here means *prima* 'first,' he says (cf the Vulgate of Luke 24:1, where *una sabbati* means 'first day of the week'). The exegetical tradition likewise understood 'Sunday' here; cf the interlinear *Gloss* 1195–6, Nicholas of Lyra 1196F, and Hugh of St Cher 275 recto D. For his translation

Erasmus followed closely the Greek, writing (from 1519) *uno die sabbatorum*. For his paraphrase he wrote *quodam die sabbatorum*. Elsewhere in the Vulgate, *die sabbati* and *die sabbatorum* mean the sabbath; for the phrase with *sabbati* (singular) see the Vulgate of Luke 4:16, 13:14 and 16, with *sabbatorum* (plural), Acts 13:14.

10 'Disciples' represents Erasmus' reading of 20:7 (text and translation; so AV) rather than the Vulgate's 'we' (DV Conf RSV). Cf *Beginnings* III 192.

11 Cf Nicholas of Lyra (on 20:7) 1196F: '[Paul] first refreshed them with the bread of the divine word.'

12 For the allusion to Elijah see 1 Kings 17:17–24.

122

13 In this and the preceding sentence, the paraphrase at two points reflects problems of translation rather than text. 'We met' (20:14) represents Erasmus' translation for a Greek text more literally rendered 'he met us' (DV AV Conf RSV). His translation is exactly that of the Vulgate of 1527, *cum convenissemus* 'when we met' – though Weber II 1733 gives only the reading 'he met us.' The preceding sentence, paraphrasing 20:13, evidently reflects Erasmus' ambiguity about the meaning of the words προελθόντες ἐπὶ τὸ πλοῖον, translated by the Vulgate and Erasmus as 'go on board the ship,' 'embark' (DV Conf), but also receptive of the interpretation 'going before to the ship' (AV; cf RSV) or, as Erasmus apparently interprets here, 'going before by,' or 'on the ship.' (On προελθόντες as 'going before' see 20:5 AV).

14 Erasmus follows his own text and translation (from 1516) of 20:15, which adds 'and tarried at Trogyllium' (AV); he assumes the night was spent at Trogyllium. The Vulgate omits the clause (Weber II 1733); so DV Conf RSV. The clause is omitted in the preferred reading (Metzger 478).

15 The attempt to give geographical precision to the places mentioned in 20:13–16 followed the exegetical tradition (cf chapter 17 n1). But in the identification of the places mentioned here the exegetical tradition was untrustworthy. Mytilene, for example, was identified as 'an island opposite Asia ... or a city on the island of Cyprus' (interlinear *Gloss* 1197–8), as 'the name of an island' (Nicholas of Lyra 1198F), as 'an island or a city near Asia' (Hugh of St Cher 275 verso F). In 1527 Erasmus added comments in three successive annotations (*Mytilene, et sequenti die venimus contra Chium,* and *transnavigare Ephesum*), in which he located the sites in terms very similar to those used here in the paraphrases, which thus appear to anticipate the annotations. There is one difference: the second annotation correctly identifies Trogyllium as a 'promontory' (likewise the *Peregrinatio apostolorum* LB VII 657–8) – not, as in the paraphrase, a city – and Erasmus cites Ptolemy and Strabo as his sources; for Trogyllium see Strabo *Geography* 14.1.12–13 and Ptolemy *Geography* 5.2.8.

16 For the same observation see the *1527* addition to the annotation on 20:16 (*transnavigare Ephesum*).

17 The reason given here (paraphrase on 20:16) for avoiding Ephesus – a Jewish plot – may derive from 20:3 and 19. That Paul avoided Ephesus for the sake of his own security seems probable; cf Haenchen 588, who cites 2 Cor 1:8–10 and Rom 15:30–1.

18 On 'congregation' see chapter 5 n20; on 'presbyters' chapter 15 n22. The interlinear *Gloss* (on 20:17) 1199–1200 explained the Vulgate's *maiores natu* as '"presbyters" – as it is found in the Greek'; similarly Hugh of St Cher 275 verso F.

19 For echoes of biblical images in this sentence see 1 Cor 11:1 (Paul, an imitator of Christ); Phil 2:5–8 (lowered himself); Eph 5:26 (cleanse the church).

20 The paraphrase adopts the reading of Erasmus' text and translation, '"many" tears' (20:19; so AV), rather than the Vulgate's 'tears' (DV Conf RSV); cf *Beginnings* III 194.

21 Cf 2 Cor 11:28, 'care of all the churches' (AV).

22 Cf Nicholas of Lyra (on 20:19) 1199F: 'I have left nothing undone that pertains to your salvation.'

23 Cf 2 Cor 1:8; also 1 Cor 15:32.

24 Vulgate 'Lord Jesus Christ' (20:21 DV AV RSV Conf); Erasmus' text and translation 'Lord Jesus' (cf Bruce 378).

25 Cf Rom 1:16 and Col 3:11.

26 Nicholas of Lyra (on 20:21) 1199C stresses that the preaching was without distinction of persons. For the thought and the expression see Rom 3:21–4; Acts 10:34; Rom 2:11.

123

27 For a similar justification of the Apostle's avoidance of danger, see the paraphrases on 9:23–5 (66–7 above); also on 19:30–1 (119 above).

28 A reversal of the familiar contrast – the body bound, the spirit free; cf eg Cicero *De finibus* 3.22.75.

29 The interlinear *Gloss* (on 20:22) 1199–1200 interpreted Spirit ambiguously as either the Holy Spirit or Paul's own mind; so Hugh of St Cher 275 verso H; cf chapter 19 n26. The marginal *Gloss* 1199A, on the other hand, citing Bede, insisted that the revelation came to Paul through the prophets, not through himself (cf Bede *Super Acta* 20 PL 92 985D). See the paraphrase just below on 20:25, where Paul credits his knowledge solely to the 'inspiration of the Spirit.'

30 The translations of 20:24a differ widely, eg: DV (following the Vulgate) 'But I fear none of these things, neither do I count my life more precious than myself' (so Conf); AV (following the Textus Receptus) 'But none of these things move me, neither count I my life dear unto myself.' Erasmus' Latin translation read

'Nothing moves me, nor is my life dear to me.' The differences in interpretation arise in the first instance from the textual variants, but also from the idiomatic character of the Greek (for the problems see *Beginnings* IV 260 24n). The paraphrase clearly follows Erasmus' translation of the second clause; for the first clause it skilfully blends the different emphases given in the translations of the Vulgate and of Erasmus ('deters' represents the Latin *deterreo* 'frighten from,' 'deter'). Cf the annotation on 20:24 (*nihil horum vereor*), where Erasmus asks how the translator of the Vulgate could say that Paul did not fear when he knew what was coming? He did indeed fear, but disregarded his fears.

31 'With joy' (20:24 AV), a reading of the witnesses of the Byzantine tradition (*Beginnings* III 196), follows Erasmus' text and translation; the Vulgate omits the phrase (so DV Conf RSV).

32 For the image of the athlete in New Testament and early Christian literature see chapter 7 n67.

33 Cf Gal 1:1 and the paraphrase on it in CWE 42 97.

34 Cf Phil 1:19–26, where Paul is prepared to live or die, but expects to live for the welfare of the Philippians.

35 Erasmus follows the Vulgate and his own text and translation in reading 'kingdom of God' (20:25 DV AV Conf); in the preferred reading of the Greek text, simply 'kingdom' (so RSV; cf Metzger 479).

36 For the sentiment see the paraphrase on 2 Tim 4:7 CWE 44 52; for the expression 'in good faith' see the annotation on Rom 1:17 ('from faith unto faith') CWE 56 42–5.

37 For the exemplary Paul see 1 Cor 4:16 and 11:1; Phil 3:17. The exegetical tradition emphasized, in its comments on this speech, Paul's exemplary role; cf eg the interlinear *Gloss* (on 20:18) 1199–1200: 'Paul does not glory but offers himself an example to be followed'; similarly Hugh of St Cher 275 verso G; and cf n40 below.

124

38 Cf the interlinear Gloss (on 20:28) 1201–2: 'Here he addresses the elders [*maiores natu*].' The elders addressed are clearly the 'presbyters' of 20:17, though here in the paraphrase Erasmus has adopted the term *seniores* generally used in the Vulgate for the Greek πρεσβύτεροι; cf n18 above.

39 Nicholas of Lyra 1201C calls the 'grievous wolves' (AV) of 20:29 'false apostles'; cf 2 Cor 11:13.

40 The 'moral exposition' of Nicholas of Lyra 1199–1200 stressed that in Paul's speech to the Ephesian elders his own solicitude provided an example for them; cf n37 above.

41 'Lookers-into': *inspectores* 'those who look into, examine,' or 'who look over.' The exegetical tradition attempted to translate the Greek ἐπίσκοποι [*episcopoi*]

'bishops' (20:28) into Latin terms. The *Gloss* 1201A, citing Bede, gave as an equivalent *superinspectores* 'over-lookers' (cf Bede *Super Acta* 20 PL 92 986A), the interlinear *Gloss* 1201–2 *speculatores* 'observers,' and Hugh of St Cher 276 recto A followed the interlinear *Gloss*. I have avoided 'overseers,' wishing not to obscure the etymological function of the exegesis. See Erasmus' definition of the word 'bishop' in his paraphrase on 1 Tim 3:1 CWE 44 18, where see n1. See also the explanation of *episcopos* in the *Moria* CWE 27 137, where the term is said to signify 'work, care, concern' and (with a pun on the word) 'no careless lookout.'

42 The interlinear *Gloss* 1201–2 stressed the great price paid – the blood of Christ (10:28) – therefore, as here, a precious acquisition; cf 1 Pet 1:18–19.
In all editions (1516–1535) Erasmus read in text and translation 'through his own blood,' like the Vulgate (so DV AV Conf). But the preferred text reads 'through the blood of his own' (RSV; cf Metzger 480–2). The evidence suggests that the paraphrase represents Erasmus' paraphrastic expansion on his own reading, rather than a reflection of the preferred text. For the difficulties of text and interpretation here, see *Beginnings* IV 262 29n and V 372.

43 Erasmus was evidently fond of the idiom; cf the annotation on Rom 1:16 ('for I do not feel ashamed of the gospel') CWE 56 41, where he speaks of the 'Platos, the Pythagorases, the Zenos, the Aristotles.'

44 See John 10:12 for the image of the sheep scattered after the shepherd has fled.

45 For the images see Gal 2:4 (threaten your liberty in Christ); Gal 5:7–8 (crafty persuasions); Matt 23:27–8 and 2 Tim 3:5 (counterfeit holiness).

46 The expression, in Erasmus' Latin, is identical to that of the Vulgate of Gal 2:6, which speaks of those 'who seemed to be somewhat' (AV). For the self-sufficiency of the gospel, with no novelties added, see Galatians 1–2.

47 For the images in this and the preceding sentence see 1 Cor 3:1–11 (pastors seek disciples for Christ, not themselves); John 21:15–17 (feeding the flock); 1 Pet 5:2–3 (not for gain).

48 For the image of stewards see 1 Cor 4:1–2.

125

49 and] Added in 1534

50 For the images in this and the preceding sentence see 1 Cor 3:5–10 (laid the foundations on which God builds); Col 1:29 (God works through us).

51 Cf the paraphrase on Rom 8:15 CWE 42 47: 'You have been adopted into the number ... of the sons of God'; also, for the idiom, the paraphrase on James 2:25 CWE 44 153: 'Rahab merited being counted in the register of the godly.'

52 Cf 1 Cor 9:3–8; and for Paul's 'right' not to work for his living see the annotation on 1 Cor 9:6 (*hoc operandi*).

53 See Luke 10:7 for the allusion; for the thought see also 1 Cor 9:7–10 and 1 Tim
5:17–18. In the paraphrases on 1 Tim 5:17–18, Erasmus offers a justification
of the right of 'ministers of the word' to receive pay (cf CWE 44 31), but in
his annotation on 1 Tim 5:18 (*non alligabis os*) he excoriates clergy who take
advantage of this right in such a way that they live in the lap of luxury.

54 The interlinear *Gloss* (on 20:35) 1203–4 explained 'all things' as 'examples,'
especially of working, and Nicholas of Lyra 1203C observed here that Paul was
an example of perfection. On Paul as an example see n37 above.

55 Nicholas of Lyra (on 20:35) 1203C noted that Paul frequently abstained from
charging expenses so that those to whom he preached might not, on account of
his avarice, draw back from hearing the preaching. Cf also 1 Cor 9:12.

56 Cf the annotation on 20:35 (*oportet suscipere infirmos*): 'Would that those might
find this example pleasing who in a manner so unworthy of a priest demand
the tithes from the people, quite forgetful of their duty.' For Erasmus' criticism
of the clergy's scramble for wealth see eg the *Moria* CWE 27 137, 140 and the
Iulius exclusus CWE 27 186.

57 Cf Rom 15:27; 1 Cor 9:11.

126

58 Cf the paraphrase on 15:3 (95 above).

Chapter 21

1 The *Gloss* 1205A had called Patara an island. In Bede *De nominibus locorum* PL
92 1039 Patara is a 'city of Lycia, a province in Asia.' Lycia was established by
Claudius as a Roman province (with Pamphylia) in AD 43. It became a separate
province in the early fourth century; cf Jones *Cities* 106–9.

2 On the location of Tyre and Sidon see the interlinear *Gloss* (on 21:2 and 3)
1205A–B, at which point Phoenicia is identified as a province of Syria where
Tyre and Sidon are, and Tyre is identified as a city of Phoenicia (so Hugh of
St Cher 276 recto D). On Phoenicia see chapter 9 n2. Palestine, distinguished
from Phoenicia, refers evidently to the area of the later Roman provinces of
that name (cf chapter 10 n2). On Tyre as a trading centre see chapter 12 n36.

3 Modern scholars, reading in 21:4 ἀνευρόντες δὲ τοὺς μαθητάς (with the article,
'*the* disciples') understand that the party actively sought out the Christian
community in Tyre (*Beginnings* IV 265–6 4n and Haenchen 600 and n7); cf
RSV 'having sought out the disciples' (similarly Conf). But Erasmus read a
text without the article, 'finding disciples' (DV AV), and in translation (from
1519) replaced the Vulgate's *invenio* with *reperio*, the word he uses here in
the paraphrase. Elsewhere Erasmus indicates that *reperio* is used to refer

to what one finds unexpectedly; cf *Paraphrasis in Elegantias Vallae* ASD I-4 310:848–50.

4 The interlinear *Gloss* (on 21:4) 1205B offered an alternative interpretation of 'spirit': 'Either their own or the prophetic spirit'; Nicholas of Lyra 1205C observed that they spoke through the spirit of prophecy – not the Holy Spirit who told Paul to go to Jerusalem, but the prophetic spirit by which they knew that if he went to Jerusalem he would endure persecution. For a similar ambiguity see chapter 19 n26.

5 The interlinear *Gloss* (on 21:5) 1205B also clarifies the location here: 'from Tyre.'

6 Cf Bede *De nominibus locorum* PL 92 1039: 'Ptolemais a city . . . on the coast near Mount Carmel.'

7 What text was Erasmus following in this paraphrase on 21:8a? The evidence is ambiguous. The Vulgate read 'we departed and came' (DV Conf RSV), and this is the preferred reading of the Greek text (Metzger 482–3). For his Greek text Erasmus followed (from 1516) the Byzantine witnesses, reading 'those who were with Paul departed and came' (*Beginnings* III 200 8n). In spite of the Greek text he printed, Erasmus' translation read (from 1516) 'we who were with Paul came.'

8 For the allusions see 8:26–40 (eunuch), 8:5–13 (Samaritans), 6:1–6 (institution of deacons). With the identification of Philip here, compare the interlinear *Gloss* (on 21:8) 1206D: 'Not the apostle, but the evangelist who preached the gospel in Samaria and to the eunuch'; so Hugh of St Cher 276 verso E.

9 The interlinear *Gloss* (on 21:9) 1206E also cites Joel; cf Joel 2:28–9 and Acts 2:17–18.

10 In the paraphrase on 21:11 Agabus binds only his feet, not his hands as well. In all editions of Erasmus' text and translation and in the Vulgate Agabus binds both his 'hands and feet.' The omission of 'hands' in the paraphrase is not, therefore, evidently based on a textual reading; perhaps it is due to the rationalization of the narrative: Erasmus pictures the 'girdle' (*zona* in the Vulgate and the paraphrase) as a belt (*cingulum* in Erasmus' Latin translation, from 1519); he stresses in the paraphrase that Agabus himself binds his own feet (*ipse sibi*) – could he also bind his own hands? But on the kind of 'girdle' implied see Haenchen 601 n5.

11 Cf Nicholas of Lyra (on 21:11) 1206E: 'He imitated the manner of the ancient prophets who sometimes prophesied not only with words but by palpable deeds.' Nicholas cites Jer 27:1–11; for other examples see 1 Kings 22:11–12 (Zedekiah); Jer 13:1–11 (Jeremiah); Ezek 4–5 (Ezekiel).

127

12 Cf the paraphrase on 19:21 (118 above) and n26; cf also 23:11 (134 below).

13 For Paul's hardships see 16:19–24; 2 Cor 11:23–7.

14 Cf 2 Thess 3:1, where Paul desires that the word of the Lord 'may have free course, and be glorified' (AV; cf DV 'may run and may be glorified').

15 Cf Phil 1:20–3.

16 The paraphrase may suggest an allusion to the third petition of the Lord's Prayer (cf Matt 6:10), and to Jesus' prayer in Gethsemane (cf Mark 14:36), hence a prayer especially appropriate to those 'truly Christian'; cf also James 4:15.

17 Erasmus read in 21:15 (from *1516*) ἀποσκευασάμενοι, which he translated *sublatis sarcinis* 'taking up our baggage' – a translation which may be reflected in AV 'we took up our carriages.' But the preferred reading is ἐπισκευασάμενοι 'making preparations' (so the Vulgate, which Erasmus follows here; likewise DV Conf RSV). Cf Bruce 389 and Haenchen 607 and n1.

18 Here in the paraphrase on 21:16, and in his translation, Erasmus understood the Greek in the sense of the Vulgate, 'bringing with them Mnason with whom we should lodge' (so DV AV Conf). But the Greek probably means 'bringing us to the house of Mnason with whom we should lodge' (so RSV); cf Bruce 389–90 and Haenchen 607 and n6.

19 Cf the interlinear *Gloss* 1207–8 on 'early disciple' (21:16 RSV): 'from long ago a man of faith'; also Nicholas of Lyra 1207C: 'long since approved [*probatum*] in faithfulness.' On the phrase 'proven piety' see chapter 15 n54. The paraphrase stresses the fact that Mnason had long been a faithful Christian, but cf James Hardy Ropes, for whom it is Mnason's long-time residence as a Christian in Jerusalem that is 'of real consequence to the narrative' (*Beginnings* III 204 16n).

20 For James similarly described, see the paraphrase on 15:13 (97 above) and n41. Nicholas of Lyra (on 21:18) 1207D also identified this James as brother of the Lord and bishop of Jerusalem. The paraphrases here pass over the question of James' own convictions about the Mosaic law, a question Erasmus raised in his annotation on 21:21 (*neque secundum consuetudinem ingredi*). A *1522* addition to that annotation attempts to explain James' apparent support for the Mosaic law: James thought the Law should be kept only to the extent needed to avoid offending the Jews, an explanation Erasmus reiterated in the *Responsio ad annotationes Lei* LB IX 210A–B.

21 'Elders': *seniores*; see chapter 15 n22.

22 'Lord' in Erasmus' text and translation of 21:20 from *1516* (so AV); 'God' in the Vulgate and the preferred reading (so DV Conf RSV); cf *Beginnings* III 204

23 The clause apparently echoes 10:45b.

24 On rumour see *Adagia* I vi 25.

128

25 'Elders': *maiorum*, normally with the meaning of 'forefathers,' as in 'practices of their forefathers' a few lines above. So the 1548 *Paraphrase of Erasmus*: 'Restrayned by an acte made of their forefathers' (fol lxxii recto). But the

reference seems to be to the decree of the 'apostles and elders' in 15:22–9, who can hardly be called 'forefathers.' Perhaps *maiorum natu* was intended, a phrase used in the Vulgate for 'elders' (cf chapter 15 n22).

26 Paraphrasing 'the multitude must needs come together' (21:22 AV; cf DV Conf) – 'a Western addition that gained rather wide circulation' (Metzger 484) and is found in both the Vulgate and Erasmus' text. The preferred reading, however, omits the words (cf RSV).

27 It is not clear from either the paraphrases or the annotations on this chapter that Erasmus understands the vow to be that of the Nazarites (Num 6:2–21). Cf Nicholas of Lyra 1208F, who says that Paul was to be purified in the temple with some Nazarenes. For the added detail of 'sacrifices or gifts' see 21:26. On the difficulties raised by the description of the vow in 21:22–7 see Haenchen 611–12.

In his translation of 21:24, Erasmus, like the Vulgate, followed the imperative 'pay' (RSV Conf) with a purpose clause: 'Pay their expenses so that they may shave their heads'; here in the paraphrase he continues with a temporal clause, 'until [*donec*] they shave their heads,' though the words may be intended to convey a final sense as well.

28 Cf the *Gloss* (on 21:24) 1209A, citing Bede: 'Paul the mighty preacher of grace ... swiftly avoided the false charge [that he was an enemy of the Law] by performing the very rites he seemed to condemn' (cf Bede *Super Acta* 21 PL 92 987C).

29 For the 'murmuring' of the Jews see the paraphrase on 13:18 (86 above) and n42. Erasmus uses the word (*murmur*) also of the Hellenists in the paraphrase on 6:1 (46 above).

30 On the fourfold prohibition see chapter 15 n50. The clause 'that they should not be forced to observe the Mosaic law' (21:25) paraphrases an addition in Erasmus' text and translation ('that they observe no such thing' 21:25 AV); the words are not found in the Vulgate or in the preferred reading of the Greek text (so DV Conf RSV); cf Metzger 485.

31 The verb in the past tense attempts to clarify the noun 'completion' in the Greek (and in the Vulgate and Erasmus' translation): 'Announced the *completion* of the days of purification' (21:26 Conf). It is commonly assumed that Paul announced when the days of purification *'would be fulfilled'* (RSV); so Bruce 394. For the problematic sequence of events in the narrative see Haenchen 611–12. The lack of any paraphrase for 'on the next day' may be inadvertent: the phrase is found in the Vulgate and in Erasmus' text and translation.

32 Cf eg 13:50, 14:4–5; and (for Ephesus) 19:9 and 23.

33 For the people 'peculiar to God' see Deut 14:2, 26:18; 1 Pet 2:9. For the rhetorical exaggeration that the temple was sacred to the whole world see 2 Macc 3:12 and the analogous claim of Demetrius for the temple of the Ephesians in Acts

19:27. Elsewhere, also, Jewish literature recorded the respect paid to the temple by gentile rulers eg Josephus *Jewish Antiquities* 11.8.5 (329–39) (Alexander the Great) and 14.4.4 (72–3) (Pompey).

129

34 Cf the interlinear *Gloss* (on 21:30) 1211–12, which explained that the gates were shut so that Paul could not flee; similarly Hugh of St Cher 276 verso H.

35 Nicholas of Lyra 1211C observed that the gates were shut (cf n34 above) so that the temple should not be polluted by Paul's death; similarly Haenchen 616–17. In explaining that killing in the temple was a religious offence, Erasmus may have in mind the right of sanctuary – on which see 'Asylum, right of' in Hastings *Encyclopaedia* II 161–4.

36 In his translation of 21:34 Erasmus followed the Vulgate in rendering παρεμ-βολήν by *castra* 'barracks' (Conf RSV; 'castle' DV AV); in his paraphrase he uses both *castra* and *praesidium* 'fortress.' For the tower of Antonia as palace, fortress, and barracks see IDB I 153–4 – though Erasmus does not in his annotations on this chapter anywhere identify the 'fortress' as the tower of Antonia, to which the biblical account evidently refers (cf *Beginnings* V 478–9 and Bruce 397).

37 For the detail that it was from Jerusalem that the Egyptian led his company see Josephus *Jewish Antiquities* 20.8.6 (169) (but cf his *Jewish War* 2.13.5 [261–3], where the Egyptian is said to have gathered his followers from the country). See also Bruce 398.

Chapter 22

1 Cf the opening remarks of Stephen in the paraphrase on 7:1 (49 above).

2 falsely] Added in *1534*

130

3 On the reasons given in the exegetical tradition for the silence of the crowd (22:2) see the interlinear *Gloss* 1211–12: 'That the whole people might understand, or that they might be more quiet'; likewise Hugh of St Cher 277 recto B; also Nicholas of Lyra 1213C: 'Because they knew by this that he was a Jew, and because they understood their own language better than another.' Erasmus offers a more obviously rhetorical rationale: Paul evokes good will (*captatio benevolentiae*) by using the language preferred by his audience. On *captatio benevolentiae* see chapter 2 n54; also CWE 46 45 n4.

4 Cf 5:34.

5 true] Added in *1534*

6 The paraphrase on 22:3 incorporates both the reading of Erasmus, 'zealous for God' (the preferred reading, represented in AV RSV; cf Metzger 485), and that of the Vulgate, 'zealous for the Law' (DV Conf).

7 For 'breathing threats and slaughter' see 9:1.

8 Erasmus does not identify the man who was high priest at the time of Paul's conversion, either here or in the paraphrases on 9:1–2 (63 above), but see the paraphrase on 4:6 (31–2 above) and nn17 and 18, especially the reference to Bruce 118, where a list of high priests AD 6–66 is given; cf Haenchen 637 n6. Ananias, high priest 47–59 (ISBE I 121) is identified in 23:2 as high priest at the time of the events recorded in Acts 22–3. On 'order of elders' see chapter 5 n36; on 'elders' see chapter 15 n22. The Vulgate had rendered the Greek τὸ πρεσβυτέριον here in 22:5 by *maiores natu* ('the ancients' DV, 'the elders' Conf). In the paraphrase Erasmus adopts his own translation, 'order of elders' (from 1522; previously, 'order of presbyters'), thus keeping clear the reference to a council.

9 The paraphrase anticipates a 1527 annotation on 22:5 (*ad fratres*) in which Erasmus clarifies that 'letters to the brethren' (RSV) means 'letters to the Jews'; if 'brethren referred to the Christians, we would have to translate "letters *against* the brethren."'

10 In Acts the biblical text speaks of the 'voice from heaven' in the account of Peter's vision (11:9), but not in any of the three accounts of Paul's conversion.

'To the earth' (in 'I fell to the earth') follows the Vulgate's *in terram* rather than Erasmus' translation *in solum* 'to the ground.' Elsewhere Erasmus seems to have thought the distinction between γῆ 'earth' in 9:4 and ἔδαφος 'ground' here to be important. See the annotation on 22:7 (*et decidens in terram*).

11 The annotation on 22:9 (*et qui mecum erant lumen quidem viderunt*) reveals the depth of Erasmus' concern over the apparent contradictions in the three accounts of Paul's conversion, the most problematic of which was the difference between 9:7 (the companions heard a voice) and 22:9 (the companions did not hear a voice). In his annotation Erasmus cites two 'solutions' to the problem: first, that in 9:7 the companions heard the sound but did not distinguish the words; second, that in 9:7 the companions heard not the voice of the one speaking to Paul but the voice of Paul as he responded. Both solutions are cited by Bruce 199, who prefers the latter. Erasmus makes no attempt in the *Paraphrase on Acts* to solve the problem, and though the paraphrase on 9:7 (64 above) might allow the first solution, it clearly rejects the second.

The paraphrase on 22:9 reflects a reading of the 'Western' text and of some Byzantine witnesses that add the words 'and became afraid.' Erasmus found the words in his Greek manuscripts and adopted them for his text from 1516 (so AV). They are omitted in the Vulgate and in the preferred reading, hence also in DV Conf RSV; cf *Beginnings* III 210 and Metzger 486.

12 In Erasmus' translation, as in the Vulgate, the Greek here in 22:10 is rendered by 'What shall I do, Lord?' The idiom in the paraphrase here echoes, then, not his translation of 22:10 but the expression in 9:6 that Erasmus inserted from the

Vulgate into his own text and translation: 'Lord, what will you have me do?'
See chapter 9 n7.

13 As in 9:6 (Vulgate 9:7), so here in 22:10 the paraphrase 'interprets' the same
Greek verb λαληθήσεται – there by *doceberis* 'you will be shown,' here by
praescribetur 'it will be prescribed.' In both cases, Erasmus translated with the
Vulgate 'it will be told you.'
From 1516 Erasmus followed in his text the majority reading 'all that has been
appointed for you to do' (RSV; so AV Conf), though in 1516 only he translated
with the Vulgate 'what you must do' (DV) – the reading he follows here. The
expression 'what you must do' appears also in the earlier account of Paul's
conversion; cf 9:6 and the paraphrase on 9:6 (64 above).

14 The Vulgate text of 22:12, 'a man according to the Law' (DV), is obviously
defective, as Valla *Annot in Acta* 22 (I 853) had observed. Erasmus found the
correct reading of 22:12 in some of his Greek manuscripts, which added the
word εὐλαβής, a word he understood as 'devout' or 'scrupulous.' See the
annotation on 22:12 (*Ananias quidam vir secundum legem testimonium habens*).

15 Erasmus believed that the Greek προεχειρίσατο in 22:14 had the sense of
'prepare,' 'make ready' – God had prepared Paul by the events of the Damascus
road to place his faith in Christ; cf the annotation on the verse (*praeordinavit
te*). See also the annotation on 3:20 (*qui praedicatus est vobis*), where Erasmus
also defined the word as 'prepare,' and the *Responsio ad annotationes Lei* LB IX
210C, where he claims that 'predestine' refers to one who is deciding, the word
here to one who is setting about to do something. But the Greek word has been
variously interpreted: 'appointed' (Bruce 403 and 112; so RSV, and cf 22:14
Conf); 'appointed' or 'forechosen' (Haenchen 203, 208, and cf 626; cf 22:14 AV
'chosen,' DV 'preordained'). See *Beginnings* IV 280 14n and 37–8 20n; see also
προχειρίζω in BAG and LSJ.

131

16 The paraphrase anticipates a 1527 addition to the annotation on 22:14 (*ut videres
iustum*) in which Erasmus acknowledged that the light and the voice referred
to Jesus, the 'Just One.' From 1516 in text and translation he had read not 'the
Just One,' but 'the just thing,' understanding it as Paul's new vision of the
gospel. The Vulgate reading was ambiguous, and could be understood as either
'the Just One' or 'the just thing.' Cf the interlinear *Gloss* 1215–16 on 'the just':
'Christ or the gospel'; likewise Hugh of St Cher 277 verso E. For 'the Just One
justifying all people' see the paraphrase on 7:52 (55 above).

17 For the time see 9:22–6 and Gal 1:16–18.

18 Paul's sudden transformation as a result of his conversion is a repeated theme
in the *Paraphrases*; cf the paraphrases on 9:19, where the Latin, as here, is *factus
alius* (65 above), on Gal 1:23 CWE 42 101–2, and on Rom 1:1 CWE 42 15.

19 'I was transported beyond myself': *raptus sum extra me*. Nicholas of Lyra 1215C explains the Vulgate expression 'stupefaction of mind' in 22:17 by the word *raptus*, and Erasmus elsewhere in the *Paraphrases* uses forms of *rapio* in describing ecstatic experience; see chapter 10 n15.

20 The clause is evidently intended as an explanation of the Greek word 'martyr' in the text of 22:20 (cf AV). Though the word originally had the sense of 'witness' (RSV; cf Luke 24:48 and Acts 1:22), 'before the end of the second century' it came to signify one who died for confession of the faith; cf EEC 575. Bruce 405 regards the use of the word in the biblical text of 22:20 as 'a step in the direction of the later meaning.'

21 For the stoning see 7:58; on Stephen's innocence see the paraphrases on 6:8–15 and on chapter 7 (47–8 and 49–56 above), which both affirm and demonstrate his innocence. The paraphrase on 20:20 follows here Erasmus' text and translation, which read 'consented to his death' (so AV). The Vulgate and the preferred reading have only 'consented' (DV; 'approved' Conf RSV); cf *Beginnings* III 212.

22 Cf Phil 3:6.

23 will realize] *perspicient*, in all editions 1524–1535; LB reads *perspicientes* 'realizing,' which leaves the sentence without a main verb.

24 Cf the interlinear *Gloss* (on 22:19) 1215–16: 'The example of my conversion will be enough for them'; similarly Hugh of St Cher 277 verso F. On Paul as example see chapter 20 n37.

25 Like Erasmus here in the paraphrase on 22:22, the interlinear *Gloss* 1215–16 explained that the offensive word was 'I will send you to the nations'; likewise, Hugh of St Cher 277 verso F.

26 The pain (*dolor*) and grief of the Jews is noted in comments on 22:23 by the interlinear *Gloss* 1215–16 and Nicholas of Lyra 1216F.

27 With this description of Jewish attitudes compare the Argument to the Epistle to the Romans CWE 42 8–9.

28 Cf the 'moral exposition' in Nicholas of Lyra (on 22:22) 1215C–1216F: 'When they heard the gentiles were preferred to themselves, they were terribly upset.'

132

29 Here in the paraphrase on 22:26 Erasmus appears to follow the Vulgate and his own translation. The Vulgate read simply 'What are you about to do?' This is the preferred reading of the Greek text (Metzger 487); so DV Conf RSV. Erasmus' Greek text, following the Byzantine witnesses, read 'Look, what are you about to do?' – a text which can, however, be understood in the sense of the AV 'Take heed what you do.'

30 The paraphrase may imply a distinction between the 'lash' (Latin *flagra*, verses 24, 25), used here for the purposes of examination, and the 'rods' (Latin *virgae*, verse 26), used by magistrates to punish criminals (cf *virga* I B 3 in L&S). On the

use of torture to extract evidence see chapter 16 n 42, and on the 'rods' see the paraphrase on 16:37 (105 above, where 'rods' also represents the Latin *virgae*) and n54.

Chapter 23

1 For the topics appropriate to the *proemium* or introduction of a speech, particularly the praise of the judge, see Quintilian 4.1.5–16; see also chapter 22 n3. For the characteristic boldness of Christian defendants before Jewish councils see the paraphrases on 4:8–9, 13 (Peter) 32–3 above and 6:15, 7:54 (Stephen) 48, 55 above, and for boldness serving as a declaration of the innocence of the defendant and the condemnation of the accusers see the paraphrase on 6:15 (48 above).

2 Cf 22:18.

133

3 Cf Lev 19:15 and Deut 25:1–2.

4 See the paraphrase on 4:7 (32 above) and n23.

5 Both ancient and modern commentaries have addressed two questions arising from the narrative of 22:3–5: 1/ How could Paul have cursed anyone, not to say the high priest? 2/ How could Paul say he did not know the high priest? The *Gloss*, Hugh of St Cher, Nicholas of Lyra, and Erasmus' own annotations illuminate his paraphrases here. The *Gloss* 1217C says that Paul's words were a prophecy, not a curse, a prophecy referring to the Jewish priesthood. Nicholas of Lyra 1218F affirmed that the priest's attempt to offer the appearance of justice without its substance evoked the curse. Hugh of St Cher 278 recto A argued that Paul knew that a man who so symbolized injustice could not be the true high priest. In his annotation on 23:3 (*percutiat te deus paries*) Erasmus does not deny Paul's 'human affections.' Paul had uttered his words not out of any 'common irritation' but burning with the spirit of an apostle because of the injustice of the high priest. His words were, however, a rebuke and not a curse. His apparent admission that he cursed the high priest was an effort to alleviate a dangerous situation – as was his statement that he did not know the high priest. To save the situation Paul could say that he did not know Ananias was the high priest, because he did not recognize as priest the one who had not granted even the justice that is to be found in a pagan court, since such a man was in fact a tyrant rather than a priest. Edward Lee, however, was unwilling to accept this solution; cf *Responsio ad annotationes Lei* LB IX 210D–F.

6 Erasmus follows his own text and translation from *1516*, 'the son of a Pharisee' (23:6 AV), rather than the Vulgate, 'a son of Pharisees' (so DV Conf RSV).

7 For the Sadducees' belief that the soul perishes along with the body see Josephus *Jewish Antiquities* 18.1.4 (16); see also the paraphrase on 4:2 (31 above).

8 The paraphrase on 23:9 conflates the reading of Erasmus' text and translation
  (from *1516*) and that of the Vulgate: 'scribes from the party of the Pharisees'
  (Erasmus; so AV); 'some of the Pharisees' (Vulgate; so DV Conf). Cf the reading
  of the Codex Vaticanus: 'some of the scribes from the party of the Pharisees'
  (RSV), and see *Beginnings* III 216.

9 to him] Added in *1534*

10 The paraphrase follows Erasmus' text and translation of 23:9 (from *1516*),
  which includes the last clause (cf AV 'let us not fight against God'); but as
  Erasmus suggested in a *1527* addition to the annotation *quid si spiritus locutus
  est ei aut angelus,* the words are probably added from 5:39 (so Metzger 487). The
  clause is omitted by the Vulgate DV Conf RSV.

11 Cf 22:17–21.

134

12 For the image see the paraphrase on 20:24 (123 above) and n32.

13 For previous visions see 22:17–21; also 16:9, 18:9–10.

14 An echo apparently of 2 Tim 4:6, but cf also Phil 1:21–6.

15 For the capital of Judaea see chapter 15 n4.

16 Erasmus retained in the text and translation of 23:12 (from *1516*) the Vulgate's
  quidam 'some of' (so DV AV Conf) but the preferred reading omits it – simply,
  'the Jews' (so RSV); cf Metzger 488.

17 'Tomorrow' in Erasmus' text and translation of 23:15 (cf AV), is omitted from
  the Vulgate (so DV Conf RSV), as here in the paraphrase. Cf *Beginnings* III 218.

18 In Erasmus' text and translation of 23:18, 'called me and asked me' (so AV
  Conf RSV). Though both verbs are found in the Greek witnesses and in the
  preferred reading of the Vulgate (Weber I 1738), Erasmus evidently follows
  here the reading represented in the Vulgate of *1527,* which has simply 'asked
  me' (DV).

19 Taken literally, the Latin of the paraphrase on 23:21 reads 'what you will
  promise,' suggesting that Erasmus understood the biblical text to mean 'a
  promise' (so DV AV Conf RSV). But the Greek word here probably means
  'consent'; for this meaning of ἐπαγγελία, see *Beginnings* IV 292 21n, Bruce 415,
  and Haenchen 647.

135

20 In the expression 'charging him to tell no one' (23:22), Erasmus regarded the
  Greek infinitive ἐκλαλῆσαι 'to tell' as an imperative and so translated, 'charging
  him, "Tell no one"' (so AV RSV) – see the annotation on the verse (*quoniam haec
  nota fecisset sibi*). Here in the paraphrase Erasmus follows the Vulgate, which
  rendered the Greek as an indirect command, 'charging him that he should tell
  no one' (DV Conf); cf Bruce 415, Haenchen 647. On the infinitive as imperative
  see the annotation on Rom 12:15 ('to rejoice') CWE 56 338.

21 The explication of the tribune's motives (23:24) is found in a minority reading
   represented by some Vulgate witnesses, including the Vulgate of 1527; cf Weber
   II 1739 24n. It appears in DV and (bracketed) in Conf, but not in Erasmus' text
   and translation or in AV or RSV, and it is omitted in the preferred reading
   of the Greek text; cf Metzger 488–9. Erasmus follows the minority Vulgate
   reading here, but with adaptation: in the Vulgate the tribune fears the charge
   of bribery. Erasmus may reflect Nicholas of Lyra 1223C–1224F, who inferred
   from the tribune's letter that the tribune sought rather to enjoy the favour of
   the governor through his concern for a Roman citizen; cf Munck 230.
22 'Farewell' (23:30), found in the Vulgate of 1527 and Erasmus' text and
   translation (so DV AV Conf), is omitted in the preferred reading of the Greek
   (so RSV; cf Metzger 489–90), and is not the preferred reading of the Vulgate; cf
   Weber II 1739 and 30n.
23 The journey from Jerusalem to Antipatris was about forty miles, the journey
   from Antipatris to Caesarea only about twenty-five (IDB I 152).

Chapter 24

1 With the paraphrase on 24:1 compare the readings of the biblical text: 'some
   elders' (DV Conf RSV); 'a certain Tertullus' (DV AV Conf RSV). For the paraphrase
   Erasmus adopted the Vulgate's 'some elders' rather than the reading of his own
   text, 'the elders' (so AV); but as he read with the Vulgate 'a certain Tertullus'
   the omission in the paraphrase of 'a certain' is evidently either inadvertent or
   deliberately artistic.

136

2 For his text of 24:2 Erasmus followed the Byzantine witnesses, reading
   κατορθωμάτων γενομένων, which he translated 'affairs are administered well,'
   as in the paraphrase here; cf Haenchen 652, who indicates that the Greek has
   the sense of 'ordered conditions' – 'ordered conditions prevail'; also AV, which
   renders, 'very worthy deeds are done.' The preferred reading is διορθωμάτων
   γενομένων 'reforms are being made'; cf RSV 'reforms are introduced'; similarly
   DV Conf. See Beginnings III 222.
3 The paraphrase on 24:5 follows Erasmus' text (from 1516) and translation (from
   1519), 'author of the sect of the Nazarenes' (so AV RSV), rather than the reading
   of the Vulgate, 'author of the sedition of the sect of the Nazarenes' (cf DV Conf
   and Weber II 1739).
4 The interlinear Gloss (on 24:6) 1227–8 similarly explained the profanation of the
   temple – 'by taking gentiles into it'; similarly Hugh of St Cher 278 verso G and
   Nicholas of Lyra 1228F.

5 The paraphrase follows the text of Erasmus and of the Vulgate to include
  verses 6b–8a. If this passage is included, then the words of verse 8b – 'by
  examining him yourself' – seem to imply that Felix is asked to examine the
  tribune, Lysias, to discover the facts of the case. The preferred reading omits
  these verses, so that Felix is asked to examine Paul himself (cf Haenchen 653
  and n4 and Metzger 490). The verses were missing in most of Erasmus' Greek
  manuscripts, and he knew from the *Gloss* that Bede found them missing in
  the old Latin codices (cf Bede *Super Acta* 24 PL 92 990B). But Erasmus affirms
  they were commonly included in the copies of the Vulgate available in his
  day; moreover, he had found them written in tiny letters in the margin of
  just one Greek manuscript he had seen, and he therefore included them in his
  text and translation; cf the annotation on 24:6 (*quem et apprehensum voluimus
  … iubens accusatores eius ad te venire*) and the *Responsio ad annotationes Lei* LB
  IX 211C–E. Though the verses appear in the Vulgate of 1527 they are not the
  preferred Vulgate reading; cf Weber II 1739 6n. On the importance of 'a single
  Greek manuscript' for Erasmus' textual criticism cf H.J. de Jonge 'Erasmus
  and the *Comma Johanneum' Ephemerides Theologicae Lovaniensis* 56 (1980) 381–9
  and Erika Rummel *Erasmus' 'Annotations' on the New Testament* (Toronto 1986)
  132–4.
6 The paraphrase calls attention to the rhetorical character of the speech in
  the biblical text. In language familiar to classical rhetoric, Tertullus in the
  paraphrase speaks of a 'too extensive introduction' (*proemium*; cf chapter 23
  n1), while the term 'flat' (*frigidus*) was used in rhetorical texts to describe
  ineffective speech; cf Cicero *De oratore* 2.63.256 and Quintilian 8.5.30. Cf Bruce
  421: 'Tertullus begins his speech with a great flourish, after the rhetorical
  fashion of the times; the rest of the speech … does not fulfil the promise of the
  exordium, and it tails away in a lame conclusion.'
7 'Make' (cf AV RSV) rather than 'shall make' (cf DV Conf); 'more confidently' (cf
  AV) rather than 'confidently' (cf DV Conf RSV). In both cases the paraphrase
  follows Erasmus' text of 24:10 rather than the Vulgate.
8 Both the interlinear *Gloss* (on 24:11) 1227–8 and Hugh of St Cher 278 verso H
  emphasize the intent to worship by adding the contrast, 'not to violate the
  temple.' For the purification see 21:26. In the paraphrase on 24:11 Erasmus
  transforms Paul's response as found in the biblical text into a version of
  the 'absolute defence' as defined by classical rhetoric, in which a defendant
  proudly claims that the crime charged is honourable; cf Quintilian 7.4.4. For a
  similar line of defence see the paraphrase just below on 24:17.

137

9 Both here (24:14) and below (24:22) Erasmus understands the 'way' as the
  teaching and the practices of the Pharisees, a view stated in his annotation

on 24:14 in *1516* and confirmed by an addition in *1535* (*secundum sectam quam dicunt haeresim*). The exegetical tradition expressed uncertainty about the meaning of the 'way' in 24:22; cf eg Hugh of St Cher 279 recto A: 'The way of truth that was in Paul; or of the unrighteousness they were committing against Paul.' On the 'way' elsewhere in this *Paraphrase* see chapter 19 nn12 and 28.

10 For Nicholas of Lyra 1229C, too, 'believing all things' (AV 24:14) included belief that the prophecies were fulfilled in Jesus.

11 too] In all lifetime editions *1524–1535*, but omitted from LB

12 'Those long since dead' represents Erasmus' reading of 24:15 (from *1519*), 'the resurrection of the dead, both the just and the unjust' (so AV); in the preferred reading, simply, 'the resurrection both of the just and the unjust' (Vulgate DV Conf RSV; cf Metzger 491).

13 For the 'pure conscience' see 1 Tim 3:9 and 2 Tim 1:3; for God the examiner of the heart see Ps 26:2 and Jer 17:10.

14 For the image see Rom 14:10–12.

15 For the classical rhetorical topos of inference from one's past life as evidence of the crime charged see Cicero *De inventione* 2.11.35–6; Quintilian 5.10.28 and 7.2.33–4.

16 Cf the interlinear *Gloss* (on 24:18) 1229–30: 'In shaving his head, he kept the Law.'

17 The paraphrase here follows Erasmus' earliest explanation (*1516*) of the Greek syntax of 24:18–19. According to the preferred text the second sentence of this passage appears to contain an anacoluthon, represented in RSV: '[18] they found me purified in the temple, without any crowd or tumult. But some Jews from Asia – [19] they ought to be here before you . . .' In *1516* Erasmus recognized the anacoluthon, and thought the sentence should be completed by supplying what was intended: 'But some Jews from Asia [stirred up the disturbance, not I]; they ought to be here' (cf n18 below). In *1522* he had Chrysostom's homily on the passage, which offered the reading of the Byzantine witnesses – without an anacoluthon – as in AV: 'Certain Jews from Asia found me purified in the temple, neither with multitude, nor with tumult, who ought to have been here . . .' Though he acknowledged Chrysostom's interpretation in a *1522* addition to his annotation on the verse (*quidam autem ex Asia Iudaei*), Erasmus left his own text and translation unchanged, which the paraphrase here represents. For Chrysostom's interpretation see *Hom in Acta* 50.2 PG 60 346; for the text and variants see *Beginnings* III 224 and IV 303 19n; and for the syntax see Haenchen 651, 655–6.

18 Cf Nicholas of Lyra (on 24:19) 1230F: 'By their absence he shows that they [rather than Paul] are guilty of the riot in the temple.'

19 Nicholas of Lyra 1230F also explicated the words 'these same people' (24:20) by adding 'who are present here.'

20 The present tense, 'I stand,' in the paraphrase on 24:20 follows the Vulgate and Erasmus' translation and implies a reference to the present trial before Felix,

not a reference to the earlier encounter (in 23:1–10) with the Sanhedrin. But in the biblical text the earlier event is, in fact, clearly meant (so AV Conf RSV and, perhaps ambiguously, DV). (Erasmus' Latin translation, *stem* 'I stand,' is corrected in LB to *starem* 'I stood,' no doubt to clarify the allusion to the past.)

138

21 These words represent Erasmus' text of 24:22 (so AV). The preferred text omits them (so the Vulgate DV Conf RSV); cf *Beginnings* III 226.

22 Cf n9 above.

23 'To come to him' represents Erasmus' text of 24:22 (so AV). The preferred text omits the words (Vulgate DV Conf RSV); cf *Beginnings* III 226.

24 For temperance and sobriety as the fruit of the Spirit see Gal 5:21–2; also the annotation on Rom 12:3 ('to be wise unto sobriety') CWE 56 327–8.

25 The clause reflects Erasmus' Greek text (from 1516) of 24:26, which adds 'that he might set him free' (cf AV). The clause is omitted in the preferred text (so Vulgate DV Conf RSV); cf *Beginnings* III 226.

26 Cf eg the Lex Julia 'On Extortion,' for which see *The Digest of Justinian* 48.11, trans Alan Watson from the Latin text ed Theodor Mommsen and Paul Krueger 4 vols (Philadelphia 1985) IV 830–1.

27 Nero was emperor AD 54–68. Porcius Festus succeeded Felix as procurator of Judaea possibly about AD 60, though the dates of his administration are uncertain (cf IDB II 265–6).

28 Perhaps an allusion to Jewish hostility to Felix due to his mismanagement of affairs in Judaea, to which both Josephus and Tacitus bear witness; see, respectively, *Jewish Antiquities* 20.7.1–8.8 (137–81) and *Annals* 12.54. Josephus *Jewish Antiquities* 20.8.9 (182) reports that the Jews sent a delegation to Rome to bring charges against Felix after his term of office was completed.

139

29 Cf the 'moral exposition' of Nicholas of Lyra 1230F: 'Felix represents the unrighteous judge who puts off a judgment on behalf of the innocent to curry favour with the opposite party.' On the many temptations of the mighty to do wrong, see the dedicatory letter prefacing the *Paraphrase on John* and addressed to Ferdinand (Ep 1333:147–95 / CWE 46 5–6).

Chapter 25

1 Erasmus recognized that the Greek ἐνεφάνισαν meant 'informed against' (AV RSV; cf Conf) rather than 'went to' (DV) or 'approached,' as in the Vulgate. He himself translated (from 1519) with the sense 'informed against,' but he follows the Vulgate here in his paraphrase on 25:2; cf the annotation on the

verse (*adieruntque eum principes sacerdotum*). Erasmus also follows the Vulgate here in writing 'chief priests' in the plural (so DV Conf RSV), which in his own text (from *1516*) and translation (from *1519*) is in the singular (AV).

2 The statement may reflect the relatively favourable picture of Festus in Josephus; see *Jewish Antiquities* 20.8.9–11 (182–96) and *Jewish War* 2.14.1 (271).

3 Cf AV (25:5) 'let them which are able' (similarly DV). Erasmus' annotation on the verse (*potentes*) suggests that he did not fully appreciate the technical meaning of the Greek, which has the sense 'let the men of authority' (RSV; similarly Conf); cf Bruce 430, Haenchen 665 and n7, and δυνατός 1a in BAG.

4 Though from *1516* Erasmus followed in text and translation the reading of the Byzantine witnesses, 'more than ten days,' it was not until *1527* that he attempted to justify his reading in an annotation on 25:6 (*dies non amplius quam octo aut decem*). But the reading of the Vulgate, 'not more than eight or ten days,' is also the preferred reading of the Greek text (so DV Conf RSV); cf *Beginnings* III 228.

5 Here in the paraphrase on 25:8 Erasmus follows his own translation (from *1516*) in rendering Paul's response in the third person. In the Greek text Paul's reply is given in the first person: 'neither ... have I offended at all' (RSV, similarly DV AV Conf). The Greek here follows an idiom frequently found in the New Testament, where direct speech is introduced with the conjunction 'that' appropriate to indirect discourse: 'Paul replied that "Neither ... have I offended"' (so the Vulgate of 25:8, translating the Greek literally); for the idiom see ὅτι 2 in BAG. Elsewhere Erasmus renders the same construction in direct speech, omitting the conjunction 'that'; cf eg his translation of Rom 3:8 and Rom 4:17 and the annotations on those verses ('let us do evil' and 'that I have made you the father of many nations') CWE 56 97 and 117–18.

140

6 The interlinear *Gloss* (on 25:11) 1233B likewise contrasted the judge's duty with the temptation to offer a favour; similarly Hugh of St Cher 279 verso E.

7 In the biblical text the 'council' refers not to the Sanhedrin but to the governor's advisors (Haenchen 668). Erasmus' interpretation is the same as that of Chrysostom *Hom in Acta* 50.3 PG 60 355: 'Do you see how he favours them? For it is a favour to consult the accusers.' Nicholas of Lyra 1233F understood 25:12 more accurately: 'He took counsel with the experts who were there to assist him.'

8 For this Agrippa, see chapter 12 n1. The *Gloss* (on 25:13) 1233E, citing Bede *Super Acta* 25 PL 92 990D–991A, identifies Agrippa's father as the man stricken by an angel; for the allusion see Acts 12:23. Bernice was the sister, not the wife, of Agrippa. She was correctly identified by Nicholas of Lyra 1233F as sister to Agrippa, but the interlinear *Gloss* (on 25:13) 1232–3 equivocated: either Agrippa's wife, or 'some man.' Rumours of an incestuous union with her

brother are attested by Josephus in *Jewish Antiquities* 20.7.3 (145–6) and taken as fact by Juvenal in *Satires* 6.156–60; cf P-W III-1 287–9.

9 Cf n1 above. Here in 25:15 Erasmus again follows the Vulgate in writing 'approached,' though from *1519* he had translated 'informed against,' as in 25:2. 'Chief priests,' in the plural, represents Erasmus' text and translation and the reading of the Vulgate.

10 'To death' may represent the reading of 25:16 found in Erasmus' text and translation from *1516* (so AV); the words are omitted from the Vulgate (so DV Conf RSV; cf *Beginnings* III 230). These words, however, make an obvious gloss on the expression 'give up' (RSV), a gloss found in Nicholas of Lyra 1233F; cf the similar gloss on 'asking for sentence' (25:15) in the interlinear *Gloss* 1232–3 and Hugh of St Cher 279 verso F.

11 For the Greek φαντασία [*phantasia*] 'pomp,' 'pageantry' (25:23), the Vulgate had written *ambitio* (cf DV 'pomp'; so AV Conf RSV). The exegetical tradition favoured the word *apparatus* 'display' (the *Gloss* 1233B, Hugh of St Cher 279 verso F–G, and Nicholas of Lyra 1234F). Though Erasmus translated it by *apparatus*, his paraphrase evokes more extensively images both of sight and sound, *strepitus et apparatus*; cf his annotation on 25:23 (*cum multa ambitione*).

12 Erasmus adopts for his translation, and uses here in the paraphrase on 25:24, the Vulgate's *interpellavit* for the Greek ἐνέτυχον. In his annotation on the verse (*interpellavit me*) he explains the word as meaning here 'approach' or 'accost'; cf DV AV 'dealt with.' But the Greek word also has the meaning of 'plead with' (Conf) or 'petition' (RSV). See the annotation on Rom 8:26 ('the Spirit makes request') CWE 56 222.

Chapter 26

141

1 to learn] *discere*, in all editions 1524–1535; in LB, *dicere*, which, if not an inadvertent mistake, might have been intended in the sense 'to pronounce judgment.'

2 For the argument see chapter 24 n15.

3 Cf 22:3; Nicholas of Lyra (on 26:4) 1235C also notes that Paul was instructed by Gamaliel.

4 For the Pharisees' doctrine of rewards and punishment see Josephus *Jewish War* 2.8.14 (162–3).

142

5 The hope promised the fathers in the biblical text (26:6–7) is generally understood as the Messianic hope 'bound up with the hope of resurrection' (Haenchen 683, and similarly Munck 241; cf Bruce 441, who cites Luke 1:55,

72 and Rom 9:4–5). But the exegetical tradition appears to equivocate in its interpretation of 'hope' in 26:6–7. The interlinear *Gloss* (on 26:6) 1235–6 explained it as the 'hope of rising again,' but the interlinear *Gloss* (on 26:7) 1235–6 explained it as the 'hope in the risen Christ.' For Hugh of St Cher 280 recto A, it is by implication the hope of our resurrection. Nicholas of Lyra (on 26:6) 1235C explained the hope as that 'concerning the coming of Christ and the resurrection and the beatification [*beatificatio*] which must come to pass through him.' The paraphrase, though to some extent ambiguous, invites the interpretation that those of godly devotion will achieve felicity in their resurrection; the promise in this case may refer to such passages as Ezek 37:1–14.

In 26:7 'worship' (Conf RSV), rather than 'serve' (DV AV), reflects Erasmus' repeated attempts to correct the Vulgate's translation of the verb λατρεύω; cf the annotation on 26:7 (*duodecim tribus*): '[The Greek word], as I have often already said, signifies the worship of divinity.' Cf the annotation on Rom 1:9 ('whom I serve') CWE 56 33–4.

6 The arguments are conventional, found already in early Christian literature. For the argument that he who created has power to re-create, see Tertullian *Apology* 48.5–6 CCL 1 166; *De resurrectione mortuorum* 11.10 CCL 2 934; and Athenagoras *De resurrectione mortuorum* 3.1 in Schoedel *Athenagoras* 94. For the theme that the power of God must not be compared to that of a man see Athenagoras *De resurrectione mortuorum* 9.1–2 (ibidem 108–10), a passage that also addresses the question of the relation between God's power and his will. On the relation between God's power and his will in medieval theology see Oberman *Harvest* 36–8.

7 Cf the paraphrase on Rom 3:4 CWE 42 23: God, who 'cannot lie, is prepared to fulfil whatever he has promised.' See also chapter 3 n25.

8 towards] *in* first *in 1535; in 1524 and 1534, erga*

9 In his translation as well as in his paraphrase on 26:10, Erasmus left the Vulgate unchanged – 'I brought the sentence' (DV). He thought that it was not clear from the biblical text whether Paul conveyed the sentence decreed by the council, or by his own vote condemned Christians; cf the annotation on the verse (*detuli sententiam*). Nicholas of Lyra 1236F thought Paul conveyed the council's decision to those who carried it out, but Rabanus in the *Gloss* 1237A understood that Paul voted for the death of Christians. Cf RSV 'cast my vote against'; so Bruce 443 and Haenchen 684.

10 For Paul as blasphemer see 1 Tim 1:13.

11 Cf the interlinear *Gloss* 1235–6 on 'foreign cities' (26:11): 'Not only those nearby in Judaea' (1235–6); similarly Hugh of St Cher 280 recto B.

12 The same view is expressed in the paraphrase on 22:5 (130 above). For the exoneration of Paul the persecutor see also the paraphrases on 8:1 and 9:3 (56 and 63 above).

13 Cf chapter 22 n10. The Greek word here in 26:14 is γῆ, as in 9:4.

14 'Speaking to me and saying' in 26:14 represents the reading found in Erasmus' text and translation (so AV), but not in the Vulgate, which reads simply 'saying to me,' as in DV Conf RSV; see *Beginnings* III 236.

143

15 For this proverb see chapter 9 n8.

16 The paraphrase on 26:15 represents an interesting conflation of Erasmus' text with that of the Vulgate of 1527: 'And he said, I am Jesus whom you persecute' (Erasmus; so AV); 'And the Lord said, "I am Jesus of Nazareth whom you persecute"' (Vulgate). But 'of Nazareth' is a minority Vulgate variant, not cited in Weber II 1743; hence DV: 'And the Lord answered, "I am Jesus whom thou persecutest"' (so Conf RSV).

17 chosen one] *delectus* in all editions 1524–1535; in LB, *deiectus*. The word appears to be a paraphrase on the Greek προχειρίσασθαι (26:16). In his annotation on the verse (*ut constituam te ministrum*) Erasmus notes that the Greek word means 'to prepare'; but for the meaning 'to choose' see chapter 22 n15 and the paraphrase on 22:14 – 'chosen and prepared.'

18 For the 'visions' see eg 22:17–21; Gal 1:11–12; 2 Cor 12:1–4.

19 Though Erasmus knew that 'people' (in the singular, referring to the Jews) represented the Greek text, in the paraphrase he follows the Vulgate minority, reading 'peoples' (Weber II 1743 17n), the reading also of the Vulgate of 1527 and his own translation of 1516; cf the annotation on 26:17 (*eripiens te de populis et gentibus in quas*).

20 On this theme, that the gospel is to be offered to distant and barbarous races, see the paraphrases on Rom 1:14–16 CWE 42 17, where the 'distant races' are the Scythians and the Britons.

21 For Paul as ambassador see Eph 6:20; cf also the image in 2 Cor 5:20. 'Envoy' represents the Latin *legatus*, a word that has something of the connotation of *apostolos* in Greek; cf CWE 46 162 n20.

22 At two points the paraphrase on 26:18 explicates the biblical text very much as does Nicholas of Lyra 1237C, who explains 'darkness' as the darkness 'of errors' and the 'power of Satan' as the 'slavery of idolatry.' But for the extended image of the devil's slave, once dedicated to idolatry, now transferred to Christ, see the paraphrase on Rom 6:16–17 CWE 42 39.

23 For the image 'not a people' see 1 Pet 2:10; for the image 'strangers' see Eph 2:12, 19.

24 The paraphrase draws the details from 22:9, 26:13 (Paul's companions saw the light), and 9:7 (the companions heard the voice). Thus the paraphrase boldly solves the problem of the discordant details in the parallel narratives at this point; cf chapter 22 n11.

25 For the sentiment, see 4:19.

26 The paraphrase on 26:20 both adopts the characteristic Vulgate translation for the Greek μετανοεῖν 'do penance' (DV) and introduces Erasmus' preferred rendering, 'recover one's senses' (cf chapter 2 n90). For Erasmus' interpretation here of 'deeds worthy of repentance' (RSV) see the annotation on Matt 3:8 (*fructum dignum poenitentiae*), to which, indeed, he refers in his annotation on Acts 26:20 (*digna poenitentiae opera*).

27 Cf the expression of Nicholas of Lyra 1237C on the words 'help that comes from God' (26:22 RSV): '[God] protecting me.'

28 The phrase may echo Jer 31:34.

29 For the command to preach to all see 9:6 and 15, 22:10 and 15; Gal 1:16. For the expression 'without respect of persons' see eg Rom 2:11; Eph 6:9; James 2:1; and Acts 10:34.

30 Cf 1 Cor 15:3.

144

31 The statement that Jews are accustomed to debate the issues enunciated appears to reflect Erasmus' interpretation of the Greek syntax; see the annotation on 26:23 (*si passibilis Christus*) where Erasmus takes the Greek conjunction 'if' in the sense of 'whether.' Hence his translation (from 1516): 'Saying nothing else than what the prophets and Moses have predicted would occur, whether Christ would suffer ...' He explains in his annotation: 'For [Paul] carried on debate from the prophets to show that their prophecies referred to Christ.' Indeed the Gospels reflect Jewish debate about the Messiah (cf eg Matt 11:2–6; John 1:44–6), and early Christian writers attest to continuing Jewish debate with Christians, for which see Robert D. Sider *The Gospel and Its Proclamation* (Wilmington 1983) 43–4. For the evidence for Messianic discussion in Jewish literature of the period see *Judaisms and Their Messiahs at the Turn of the Christian Era* ed Jacob Neusner, William Scott Green, and Ernest S. Frerichs (Cambridge 1987).

32 to be] *esse*, added in *1535*

33 Similarly Nicholas of Lyra 1238F on 'saying nothing but' (26:22): '[all these things] have been fulfilled in Jesus of Nazareth.'

34 For the place of divine judgment in the sequence of events to be fulfilled see the paraphrase on 17:31 (111 above).

35 The Vulgate had rendered the Greek παρρησιαζόμενος in 26:26 by *constanter*, Erasmus by *libere*. Cf the paraphrase on 13:46 (90 above) and n94. The comparative *liberius* of the paraphrase is apparently intended to strengthen the force of the word.

36 In the dialogue between Agrippa and Paul the short sentence in 26:28 represented in the paraphrase here appears to be open to different interpretations: 1/ 'soon you will convince me to play the Christian' (Haenchen 689); 2/ 'in a short

time you think to make me a Christian' (RSV); 3/ 'in a short while thou wouldest persuade me to become a Christian' (Conf); 4/ 'you make little business of persuading me to play the Christian' (*Beginnings* IV 322, and for the difficulties in interpreting the Greek in this sense see 322 28n). Nicholas of Lyra 1239C noted two ways to read the text: 1/ scarcely do you persuade me to be a Christian; 2/ you do persuade me a little, but not completely – the interpretation Nicholas preferred. Erasmus explains his understanding of the passage in his annotation (*in modico suades*): 'I do not think Agrippa meant he was close to having the desire to be a Christian, but rather that Paul's speech had inclined him a little in that direction.' Erasmus' text had read (with the Vulgate) '*become* a Christian'; there is no reflection therefore in the paraphrase of the difficulties of interpretation raised by the preferred reading, 'to make' or 'to play' the Christian (cf Metzger 496).

37 The clause represents the reading of 26:30 in the Greek text adopted by Erasmus from *1516* (so AV). It is not found in the Vulgate (nor in DV Conf RSV). See *Beginnings* III 238.

38 The past tense represents the reading in 26:31 of the Vulgate of *1527* (so DV Conf), but not the preferred Vulgate reading (Weber II 1743 31n). Erasmus' own text and translation, from *1516*, has the present tense; cf RSV 'This man is doing nothing to deserve death' (similarly AV).

Chapter 27

145

1 Erasmus follows the exegetical tradition in representing the Vulgate's 'Hadrumetine ship' as a ship from Hadrumetum in North Africa (modern Sousse, Tunisia); so the *Gloss* 1241A (citing Rabanus), Hugh of St Cher 280 verso G, Nicholas of Lyra 1241C, and Bede *De nominibus locorum* PL 92 1037C. But he himself read (from *1516*) 'Adramyttine ship' and in his annotation on 27:2 (*navim Adrumetinam*) noted that Stephanus of Byzantium (probably sixth century AD) derived the adjective 'Adramyttine' from the name of the town Adramyttium (a coastal town of Mysia); cf Bruce 452: '[a ship] of Adramyttium, in Mysia, opposite Lesbos.'

2 Aristarchus had accompanied Paul before; cf 19:29; 20:3–4.

3 The paraphrase recalls for the reader the point of departure; similarly the interlinear *Gloss* (on 27:3) 1241–2, 'after departing from Caesarea.' Cf chapter 17 n1 and below, where precision is given to the details of the biblical narrative, eg verse 7: Crete, an island; Salmone, a coastal city.

4 Erasmus correctly replaced the Vulgate's 'Lystra' (so DV) – a city of Lycaonia, as he observed in his annotation on 27:5 (*venimus Lystram quae est Lyciae*) – with Myra (AV Conf RSV), a city of Lycia.

5 For the biblical Salmone as Sam(m)onium see Strabo *Geography* 10.4.2–3; Ptolemy *Geography* 3.17.5; Pliny *Naturalis historia* 4.12.58; and P-W IA-2 1986–9. The sources cited generally speak of Sammonium as a promontory – Cape Sammonium – but Bede identifies it as a 'coastal city of Crete'; cf *De nominibus locorum* PL 92 1039 and Erasmus' annotation on 27:7 (*iuxta Salmonem*).

6 Following his own text of 27:8 (from *1516*), Erasmus corrected the Vulgate's Thalassa (DV Conf) to Lasea (AV RSV); cf Haenchen 699 and n4 for the corruption of the Vulgate.

7 The paraphrase reflects Erasmus' understanding of 27:9 at least in the editions of the New Testament from *1519–1527*, when he had translated 'because they had already gone too long without food.' He had defended this translation in an annotation introduced in *1522* (*eo quod ieiunium iam praeterisset*), where he acknowledged that he was following the interpretation of Nicholas of Lyra 1242F–1243C. But in a *1535* addition to the annotation he reconsidered; he was encouraged by the interpretation of Chrysostom *Hom in Acta* 53.1 PG 60 368, who thought the Jewish fast was intended here, and he now recognized the force of the καί 'also,' which indicated that sailing would be dangerous on two counts, both because of the weather and also because the season had arrived when sailing was difficult. For similar interpretations see *Beginnings* IV 328 and Bruce 455. Accordingly, in *1535* Erasmus returned to his translation of *1516* and to that of the Vulgate, modifying them slightly for the sake of clarification; the paraphrase, however, remained unchanged. Scholars agree that the fast refers to the Day of Atonement; cf Munck 250 and Haenchen 699–700.

8 Erasmus thought it one of those small points of great importance (cf Ep 373:84–118) to note that the Greek in 27:12 refers to 'winds' and not to countries; cf the annotation on the verse (*ad Africum et ad Corum*). He does not sense, however, the difficulties scholars have felt in bringing precision to the meaning of the Greek; cf the translations: 'looking towards the southwest and northwest' (DV; cf AV Conf); 'looking northeast and southeast' (RSV, with the alternative 'southwest and northwest' in a footnote). See also *Beginnings* V 338–44 and Kraeling *Bible Atlas* 455; cf Bruce 457 and Haenchen 700 n7.

9 Erasmus followed the Vulgate in understanding the Greek ἆσσον (27:13) as a place name; cf DV 'when they had loosed from Asson.' His annotation (*cum sustulissent de Asson*) shows that he was uncertain precisely how to construe the Greek (where 'from' is missing), and the literary sources he was able to cite located Asson or Assos in Asia, not in Crete. (No Cretan Asson or Assos is found in Ptolemy or in Strabo; and cf P-W II-2 1748–50). In fact, the Greek here is the comparative of the adverb ἄγχι 'quite close' – they sailed 'quite close' to Crete (AV Conf RSV); cf Bruce 458.

10 The paraphrase on 27:14 is clarified by the annotations on the verse (*ventus Typhonicus* and *qui vocatur Euroaquilo*). In terms of the direction from which

the wind blows it is a 'northeaster.' Insofar as it is 'sudden and tempestuous,' however, it is called a 'typhoon' (cf in 27:14 the Greek τυφωνικός [*typhōnicos*]), a wind especially destructive to ships, as Pliny says in *Naturalis historia* 2.49.131–2, a passage Erasmus appears to have plagiarized. Though Erasmus printed *Euroclydon* (AV) in his Greek text (from 1516), he invariably translated *Euroaquilo* (DV Conf), as here in the paraphrase. Neither word is elsewhere attested in literary use. As Erasmus states in his annotation, *Euroclydon* must be intended to suggest the great waves stirred up by the wind; while *Euroaquilo*, a compound of Greek and Latin, defines the direction of the wind. It is reasonable to assume that the word referred to the 'northeaster' (RSV) though strictly speaking, *Euros* (a Greek word) is a south-east and *Aquilo* (Latin) is a north-east wind; cf *Beginnings* V 344. For the preferred reading, Εὐρακύλων [*Eurakylōn*], see Metzger 497.

11 For the proverbial character of the expression see *Adagia* I iv 33.

12 The Vulgate witnesses read *Caudam*, *Cauda*, and *Claudam* (Weber II 1744 16n). Erasmus, following his Greek text, translated in all editions *Clauda* (cf AV), like the Vulgate represented in the lemma of the 1519 annotation on 27:16 (*quae vocatur Clauda*) – though the Vulgate of 1527 is *Cauda* (DV Conf RSV). A 1535 addition to the annotation recognizes *Cauda*. Cf *Beginnings* III 242 reading.

146

13 Erasmus' annotations on 27:16–17 do not tell us how, precisely, he envisioned the sailor's work of 'securing the skiff,' getting it into the boat, using helps, and undergirding the ship with ropes. His translation does not depart very far from the Vulgate, and the paraphrase here does little to clarify the picture at the crucial points. In translating the paraphrase I have therefore followed the interpretation of Conf RSV and Bruce 459. Cf the 1548 *Paraphrase of Erasmus*: '. . . we had muche worke to get a boate, whereby we mighte succour our selves, if any thynge chaunced otherwyse then well. And whan at the last we had drawen the boate up into the shippe, they used other policies to preserve the ship for lest that the chaunce to breake by beating her selfe on the shalowes and flattes, they gyrded the shyppe about with ropes' (fol lxxxiii verso). For another way of understanding the Greek, see *Beginnings* IV 331–2 (translation), and for the difficulties presented by the Greek see Haenchen 703 n1.

14 Erasmus correctly identifies the Syrtis as the 'quicksands' (DV AV cf Conf) 'to the south,' ie the Greater Syrtis off the coast of North Africa west of Cyrene (Bruce 460).

15 In the translation (from 1519) of 27:17 as in the paraphrase Erasmus replaced the Vulgate's *submisso vase* ('let down the sail-yard' DV) with *demisso vase*. Modern scholars are unable to offer a convincing interpretation of the Greek represented by these words; cf *Beginnings* IV 333 17n, Bruce 460–1, and

Haenchen 703 n2 (who doubts that Luke understood every detail reported). The exegetical tradition was uncertain what the Latin meant: the interlinear *Gloss* 1243–4 explained the phrase as 'lowering the skiff,' as did Nicholas of Lyra (1244F); but Bede in the *Gloss* 1244E explained it as 'letting down the sail-yard' (DV) (cf Bede *Super Acta* 27 PL 92 992B). The 1548 *Paraphrase of Erasmus* rendered the paraphrase 'they let downe a certayn vessell to staye the shippe' (fol lxxxiii verso); certainly, the paraphrastic expansion here on the biblical text suggests an action intended to retard the ship. For the interpretation 'lowering the drag- (or, drift-) anchor' see Bruce 460, Munck 248, 250, and Haenchen 703.

16 In the paraphrases on chapter 27 Erasmus generally follows the biblical text in distinguishing the passengers ('we') and the crew ('they'); but not quite always: for the biblical text of 27:17, '*they* were carried along,' the paraphrase substitutes 'we.' Here, however, in 27:19, where 'we,' the passengers, throw overboard the tackle, it is a question of a textual reading: Erasmus followed the Byzantine text (first person, so AV), rather than the preferred text (third person, Vulgate DV Conf RSV); cf *Beginnings* III 244.

17 Similarly Nicholas of Lyra 1245C, who adds 'fear' as a reason for the fast: 'Partly from fear, partly from the constant occupation of the soldiers.'

18 The expression is proverbial; cf *Adagia* I i 28.

19 Nicholas of Lyra (on 27:23) 1246F explained 'whose I am' (AV) as 'apostle and minister'; for 'worshipper' see chapter 26 n5.

20 The exegetical tradition on 27:24 noted that since Paul was to appear before Caesar, he had nothing to fear from the present danger of the sea; cf the interlinear *Gloss* (1245–6) and Hugh of St Cher 281 recto C.

21 With the description compare Nicholas of Lyra (on 27:28) 1247C: 'the *bolis* is an instrument ... with lead or tin attached to a cord'; for the explanation, see the annotation on 27:28 (*submittentes bolidem*) where Erasmus derives the word *bolis* 'missile' from the Greek *ballein* 'to throw,' 'cast.'

22 Erasmus' text, like the Greek witnesses generally, reads in 27:28 'they sounded again' (so AV RSV); cf *Beginnings* III 244. The Vulgate omits the clause (so DV Conf); cf Weber II 1745.

23 The paraphrase on 27:29 follows Erasmus' text, 'they were falling,' a reading supported by a small minority of the Byzantine witnesses; cf Tischendorf II 236 29n. The Vulgate and the preferred reading of the Greek text have 'we were falling' (DV AV Conf RSV); cf n16 above.

147

24 'Perish' follows the Vulgate of 27:34 (so DV Conf RSV) and the preferred reading of the Greek text, rather than the reading of Erasmus' text and translation, 'fall' (so AV); cf *Beginnings* III 246.

25 For the example of Jesus see Matt 14:19, 26:26; Mark 6:41, 14:22; Luke 9:16, 22:19; 1 Cor 11:23–4. For the importance of Christ's example before eating see the colloquy 'The Godly Feast' (Thompson *Colloquies* 55–6).

26 The interlinear *Gloss* 1247–8 and Hugh of St Cher 281 recto D both note that Paul's action in 27:35 is exemplary. For Paul as example see chapter 20 n37.

27 Tenney Frank says that Rome received from Egypt '20,000,000 modii of grain which supplied the annona [grain distribution] of the capital for a third of each year'; cf *An Economic Survey of Ancient Rome* 5 vols (Baltimore 1933–40) v (*Rome and Italy of the Empire*) 282.

28 Cf *Beginnings* IV 337–8 40n: 'Ancient ships had a rudder, or rather, a steering oar, on each side.'

29 The paraphrase here reflects Erasmus' debate with Zúñiga on the meaning of the Greek ἀρτέμων. In his annotation on 27:40 (*levantes artemonem*) Erasmus had in 1516 defined the word as the sail-yard. Challenged by Zúñiga, he acknowledged (1522) that the word might refer to the sail (see *Apologiae ad annotationes Stunicae* ASD IX-2 160:941–162:971). The paraphrase incorporates both definitions. The Greek word is not found in other Greek literary sources (*Beginnings* IV 338), but it is now understood as the 'foresail' ('hoisting the foresail to the wind' RSV); cf Bruce 467, Munck 251, and Haenchen 708; and for the word in a broader context Lionel Casson *Ships and Seamanship in the Ancient World* (Princeton 1971) 240 and n70.

30 The Vulgate had transliterated rather than translated the Greek διθάλασσον [*dithalasson*] as *bithalassum*. Erasmus translated the word *bimaris*, lying between two seas, and in an annotation defined the word as an isthmus, referring by way of illustration to Corinth; cf the annotation on 27:41 (*in locum bithalassum*). The paraphrase suggests he may have had in mind a narrow neck of land jutting out into the sea. Though the meaning of the Greek word is not quite certain, most scholars understand a 'sandbank' (BAG), or a 'shoal' (Haenchen 708; cf RSV), but see Kraeling *Bible Atlas* 457–8.

31 The Vulgate of 27:41 reads 'by the force of the sea' (DV Conf); the Byzantine witnesses, which Erasmus follows, read, as here in the paraphrase, 'by the force of the waves' (AV); the preferred reading is simply 'by the force' (*Beginnings* III 248; cf Metzger 500), which Haenchen 708 n5 thinks should be understood as 'the force of the impact.'

Chapter 28

148

1 Erasmus follows his own text and translation in 28:1, where the subject of the verbs is 'they' (AV); in the Vulgate and preferred reading it is 'we' (DV Conf

RSV); cf *Beginnings* III 248. On the importance of the 'we' here (signifying only the Christians) cf Haenchen 712–13. Like Nicholas of Lyra 1249C, Erasmus notes the source of the voyagers' knowledge about the island's name – they learn 'from the inhabitants.'

2 Epirus, a region in north-west Greece and a Roman province in the time of Septimius Severus, was divided in late antiquity into two provinces – Epirus Nova (New Epirus) and Epirus Vetus (Old Epirus); (cf Jones *Later Roman Empire* III 386). What we call the Adriatic Sea divides Epirus from Italy. However, the Sea of Adria of Acts 27:27, near which Malta lies, is not our Adriatic Sea but the sea between southern Greece and Italy (Kraeling *Bible Atlas* 456–7). See Ptolemy *Geography* 7.5.3 and 10, and 3.15.1 and 2, where the Adriatic Gulf, our Adriatic Sea, is distinguished from the Sea of Adria. In a *1516* annotation on 28:1 (*quia Mitilene insula vocabatur*) Erasmus affirmed that Malta 'was an island between Epirus and Italy.' In *1535* he corrected the mistake in his annotation – 'an island between Africa and Sicily' – but left the paraphrase unchanged.

3 Cf Nicholas of Lyra (on 28:1) 1249C: 'out of compassion.'

4 The paraphrase on 28:2 anticipates a *1527* annotation (*reficiebant nos omnes*), justifying the translation (from *1516*) *recipiebant* 'received' (AV; cf RSV 'welcomed') rather than the Vulgate's *reficiebant* 'refreshed' (DV Conf). For the meaning 'brought us all to it [ie the fire]' see *Beginnings* IV 341 2n, Haenchen 712 (translation), 713 (note), and Bruce 470, who, however, prefers the Vulgate's reading, 'refreshed.'

5 For his translation, Erasmus retained (from *1516*) the Vulgate's *ultio* 'vengeance' (DV AV) for the Greek δίκη 'justice' (Conf RSV) here in 28:4. For the 'divine vengeance' see Ps 94:1; Rom 12:19; Heb 10:30. Erasmus seems to be unaware of the construction favoured by modern scholars who understand 'justice' here as a pagan deity (cf Bruce 471, Munck 255, but also Haenchen 713 n5).

6 Cf the fickleness of the Lycaonians in the paraphrase on 14:10–18 (92–3 above).

7 Cf Mark 16:18; Luke 10:19.

8 For the dominical precept see Matt 10:8 and Luke 10:8–9.

149

9 For the first ship see 27:6.

10 if ... mast] Added in *1534*. The Greek text of 28:11 speaks of the *Dioscouroi* ('the Twin Brothers' RSV; cf Conf), the Vulgate of the *Castores* (DV); in his translation (from *1516*) Erasmus named the twins, Castor and Pollux (AV). Pliny *Naturalis historia* 2.37.101 comments on the phenomenon known as St Elmo's Fire, noting that the 'twin stars' that light on the sail-yards are 'Castor and Pollux,' promising a successful voyage. Bede in the *Gloss* 1252D explains the Vulgate's 'Castores' as Castor and Pollux who, if they appear together on the ship, signify a prosperous voyage (cf *Super Acta* 28 PL 92 993D). In their *Annotations* both Valla and Erasmus identify the Castores and explain their

significance for sailors; for Valla see *Annot in Acta* 28 (1 855), for Erasmus see
the annotation on 28:11 (*cui erat insigne castrorum*).

11 The people living in the toe of Italy became known as the Bruttii when they
asserted independence from the Lucani in 356 BC. Though they disappeared as
a separate nation after they supported Hannibal in his war with Rome (late
third century BC), the territory they had occupied continued under Roman
rule to be known as Bruttium. Rhegium was founded as a Greek colony
and remained Greek-speaking throughout imperial times (see 'Bruttii' and
'Rhegium' in OCD).

12 mile and a half] Printed in abbreviated form M.D.P. in 1534 and 1535 and in
the Froben octavo A779 of 1524; in the folio edition of 1524 and other octavo
editions of the same year, M.D.M.P.

13 For the geographical information about Rhegium and the Strait of Messina see
the annotation on 28:13 (*devenimus Rhegium*), an annotation that presupposes
the information available in Bede *De nominibus locorum* PL 92 1039, including
the derivation of the name: the Greek ῥήγνυμι [*rhēgnymi*] meaning 'break.' This
derivation of the name was common in antiquity; cf Strabo *Geography* 6.1.6.

14 The biblical text of 28:13 defines the temporal sequence with two references
to time: 'after one day' and 'on the second day' (RSV). Haenchen explains: 'In
Rhegium after a day's wait in the harbour a south wind comes up, which
brings the travellers at the exceptional average speed of five knots ... to Puteoli
... in two days.' Both references to time are found in Erasmus' Greek text;
he translated '... we came to Rhegium, and, a south wind springing up after
one day, we came on the next day to Puteoli.' The paraphrase, omitting the
reference to 'the next day,' indicates that the travellers arrived at Puteoli 'after
one day,' intending, apparently, that they arrived there on 'the next day.' For
the south wind as advantageous see Ovid *Tristia* 1.10.33–4 and *Metamorphoses*
8.3 and the paraphrase on 27:13 (145 above).

15 Erasmus' Greek text of 28:15 reads 'the Forum of Appius and Three Taverns';
but the Vulgate of 1527, omitting 'and,' reads 'the Forum of Appius at Three
Taverns.' In the paraphrase here, Erasmus is evidently following a Vulgate text
with this reading. This reading suggests that the Three Taverns was in or near
the market town called *Appii Forum*. In fact the Three Taverns was ten miles
north of *Appii Forum* on the Appian Way; cf Cicero *Ad Atticum* 2.10, where a
considerable distance between the two is implied.

16 The paraphrase on 28:16 follows Erasmus' text (from 1516) by including the
clause 'The centurion ... guard' (so AV); it is not found in the Vulgate or
the preferred reading (see DV Conf RSV; cf Metzger 501). An addition to the
annotation on 28:16 (*ut venimus autem Romam permissum est Paulo manere*)
justifies the inclusion in Erasmus' text.
'Captain of the guard' renders the phrase *princeps exercitus*. Erasmus, in the
annotation cited, identifies this figure as a 'tribune.' In the biblical text it is

possibly the prefect of the praetorian guard that is meant (cf Bruce 476 and Haenchen 718 n5).

17 he] *eum*, added in 1534; in earlier additions the pronoun is implied by the syntax.

18 Though some of the actions of the emperors in this period might suggest their hostility in repressing the Jews (cf eg the paraphrase on 18:2 and n4), other actions reveal the emperors' concern and even esteem for the Jews; for the evidence see Emil Schürer *A History of the Jewish People in the Time of Jesus Christ* (chapter 4 n3 above) II-2 235–6 (Tiberius), I-2 96–103 (Caligula), I-2 98–9, II-2 236–8, 266 (Claudius), II-2 238 and n74 (Nero). For Roman attitudes towards Jews see chapter 18 n27.

150

19 The interlinear *Gloss* 1253–4 interprets the 'hope' of 28:20 as the 'hope of the resurrection'; similarly Hugh of St Cher 282 recto B. Nicholas of Lyra 1253C explains it as the hope of Christ promised in the Old Testament and of the resurrection to be fulfilled at Christ's second coming. For the 'hope' interpreted as the hope of the resurrection see the paraphrases on 26:7–8 (142 above) and n5.

20 Cf Nicholas of Lyra 1254F on the words of 28:23, 'concerning Jesus' (AV): 'that is, Jesus of Nazareth who is truly the Christ.'

21 Erasmus' text, translation, and the Vulgate of 28:25 read 'our fathers' (DV AV Conf); the preferred reading of the Greek text is 'your fathers' (RSV); cf Metzger 502.

22 Erasmus translated (from 1516) the μήποτε of the Greek text of 28:27 by the Latin *ne quando* 'lest at some time'; the Vulgate had rendered it 'lest perhaps' (so DV Conf), but the meaning here is simply 'lest' (AV RSV). Cf μήποτε 2bα in BAG.

151

23 Cf Acts 1:8.

24 Erasmus printed 28:29 in all editions, but in a 1527 annotation (*et cum haec dixissent exierunt ab eo Iudaei multam habentes inter se quaestionem*) he added that he had not found the sentence in some old [Latin] manuscripts. The verse is present in Byzantine witnesses; cf *Beginnings* III 254 and Metzger 502.

25 'Rented quarters' is the generally accepted meaning of the Greek in 28:30 (so DV AV Conf and Haenchen 724), but this meaning is not attested elsewhere for μίσθωμα (cf BAG), hence RSV 'at his own expense' (so Bruce 480).

26 This translation of the paraphrase on 28:31 reflects Erasmus' understanding of the verse apparent in his own translation and in his annotation (*sine prohibitione*). However, the punctuation in all editions 1524–1535 of the *Paraphrase* suggests rather the translation 'taught them with all confidence, no one hindering the evangelical doctrine.'

THE SEQUENCE AND DATES OF THE PUBLICATION OF THE PARAPHRASES

The Epistles

Romans	November 1517
Corinthians 1 and 2	February 1519
Galatians	May 1519
Timothy 1 and 2, Titus, Philemon	November/December 1519
Ephesians, Philippians, Colossians, and Thessalonians 1 and 2	January/February 1520
Peter 1 and 2, Jude	June/July 1520
James	December 1520
John 1–3, Hebrews	January 1521

Gospels and Acts

Matthew	March 1522
John	February 1523
Luke	August 1523
Mark	December 1523/February 1524
Acts	February 1524

The Epistles were originally published by Dirk Martens in Louvain, except for Timothy, Titus, and Philemon, which were published by Michaël Hillen in Antwerp. The Gospels and Acts were all originally published by Johann Froben in Basel.

WORKS FREQUENTLY CITED

This list provides bibliographical information for works referred to in short-title form in this volume. For Erasmus' writings see the short-title list following.

Allen	P.S. Allen, H.M. Allen, and H.W. Garrod eds *Opus epistolarum Des. Erasmi Roterodami* (Oxford 1906–47) 11 vols, plus index volume by B. Flower and E. Rosenbaum (Oxford 1958)
ASD	*Opera omnia Desiderii Erasmi Roterodami* (Amsterdam 1969–)
AV	*The Holy Bible: Authorized Version* (1611)
BAG	*A Greek-English Lexicon of the New Testament and Other Early Christian Literature*, a translation and adaptation of the fourth revised and augmented edition of Walter Bauer's *Griechisch-deutsches Wörterbuch zu den Schriften des Neuen Testaments und der übrigen urchristlichen Literatur* by William F. Arndt and F. Wilbur Gingrich (Chicago 1957); 2nd ed revised and augmented by F. Wilbur Gingrich and Frederick W. Danker from Walter Bauer's 5th ed, 1958 (Chicago 1979)
Bede *De nominibus locorum*	Bede *Expositio de nominibus locorum vel civitatum quae leguntur in libro Actuum apostolorum* PL 92 1033–40
Bede *Liber retractationis*	Bede *Liber retractationis in Actus apostolorum* PL 92 995–1032
Bede *Super Acta*	Bede *Super Acta apostolorum expositio* PL 92 937–96
Beginnings	*The Beginnings of Christianity, Part I: The Acts of the Apostles* ed F.J. Foakes Jackson and Kirsopp Lake (London 1920–33) 5 vols
Bruce	*The Acts of the Apostles* Greek text with introduction and commentary by F.F. Bruce 2nd ed (Grand Rapids, MI 1952)

Bruce *English Text*	*Commentary on the Book of Acts: English Text* with introduction, exposition, and notes by F.F. Bruce (Grand Rapids, MI 1954)
Carcopino *Daily Life*	Jerome Carcopino *Daily Life in Ancient Rome* trans E.O. Lorimer (New Haven 1940)
CCL	*Corpus Christianorum series Latina* (Turnhout 1953–)
Chrysostom *Hom in Acta*	John Chrysostom *In Acta apostolorum homiliae* PG 60 13–384
Conf	*The New Testament: The English Text of the Confraternity of Christian Doctrine* (Washington 1941)
CWE	*Collected Works of Erasmus* (Toronto 1974–)
DV	*The Holy Bible Translated from the Latin Vulgate* (the Old Testament first published at Douay 1609, the New Testament first published at Rheims 1582), with notes by Bishop Challoner (New York 1943)
EEC	*Encyclopedia of Early Christianity* ed Everett Ferguson with Michael P. McHugh, Frederick W. Norris, and David M. Scholer (New York 1990)
Encyclopaedia Judaica	*Encyclopaedia Judaica* ed Cecil Roth, Geoffrey Wigoder, et al (New York 1972) 16 vols
ERSY	*Erasmus of Rotterdam Society Yearbook*
Gloss	*Biblia sacra cum glosa ordinaria . . . et postilla Nic. Lyrani addit. Pauli Burgensis et Mt Thoringi replicis . . .* (Paris 1590) VI also: *Textus biblie cum glossa ordinaria, Nicolai de Lyra postilla, moralitatibus eiusdem, Pauli Burgensis additionibus, Matthie Thoringi replicis* (Basel 1506–8) V [for notes in chapter 10]
Haenchen	Ernst Haenchen *The Acts of the Apostles: A Commentary* trans Bernard Noble and Gerald Shinn from the 14th German edition (1965), rev R.McL. Wilson (Philadelphia 1971)

Hastings *Encyclopaedia*	*Encyclopaedia of Religion and Ethics* ed James Hastings with John A. Selbie and Louis H. Gray (New York 1924–7) 12 vols plus index volume
Holborn	*Desiderius Erasmus Roterodamus: Ausgewählte Werke* ed Hajo Holborn and Annemarie Holborn (Munich 1933; repr 1964)
Hugh of St Cher	*Hugo Cardinalis de Sancto Caro Postilla super bibliam* (Basel 1504) VI
IDB	*Interpreter's Dictionary of the Bible* ed George Arthur Buttrick et al (New York 1962) 4 vols
ISBE	*International Standard Bible Encyclopedia* revised edition by Geoffrey W. Bromiley with Everett F. Harrison, Roland K. Harrison, William Sandford Lasor, and W. Edgar Smith (Grand Rapids, MI 1979–91) 4 vols
Jones *Cities*	A.H.M. Jones *The Cities of the Eastern Roman Provinces* (Oxford 1937)
Jones *Later Roman Empire*	A.H.M. Jones *The Later Roman Empire 284–601* (Oxford 1964) 3 vols with supplementary maps
Kraeling *Bible Atlas*	Emil G. Kraeling *Bible Atlas* (New York 1956)
LB	*Desiderii Erasmi Roterodami opera omnia* ed J. Leclerc (Leiden 1703–6; repr 1961–2) 10 vols
L&S	Charlton T. Lewis and Charles Short *A Latin Dictionary* (Oxford 1879; repr 1975)
LSJ	*A Greek English Lexicon* compiled by Henry George Liddell and Robert Scott, revised and augmented by Sir Henry Stuart Jones, 9th ed with supplement (Oxford 1968)
LXX	*Septuaginta: id est Vetus Testamentum Graece iuxta* LXX *interpretes* ed Alfred Rahlfs (Stuttgart 1935) 2 vols
Metzger	Bruce M. Metzger *A Textual Commentary on the Greek New Testament* (New York 1971)

Munck | *The Acts of the Apostles* introduction, translation, and notes by Johannes Munck, rev William T. Albright and C.S. Mann, Anchor Bible (New York 1967)

NCE | *The New Catholic Encyclopedia* ed W.J. McDonald, J.A. Morgan, et al (Washington 1967) 15 vols

NEB | *The New English Bible with the Apocrypha* (Cambridge 1970)

Nicholas of Lyra | see *Gloss*

Oberman *Harvest* | Heiko Oberman *The Harvest of Medieval Theology: Gabriel Biel and Late Medieval Nominalism* rev ed (Grand Rapids, MI 1967)

OCD | *Oxford Classical Dictionary* ed N.G.L. Hammond and H.H. Scullard 2nd ed (Oxford 1970)

OLD | *Oxford Latin Dictionary* ed P.G.W. Glare (Oxford 1982)

Paraphrase of Erasmus | *The First Tome or Volume of the Paraphrase of Erasmus upon the Newe Testamente* (1548), a facsimile reproduction with an introduction by John N. Wall Jr (Delmar, NY 1975)

Payne *Theology of the Sacraments* | John B. Payne *Erasmus: His Theology of the Sacraments* (Richmond, VA 1970)

PG | *Patrologiae cursus completus . . . series Graeca* ed J.-P. Migne (Paris 1857–86) 162 vols

PL | *Patrologiae cursus completus . . . series Latina* ed J.-P. Migne (Paris 1844–84) 221 vols

P-W | *Paulys Realencyclopädie der classischen Altertumswissenschaft* new ed August Friedrich von Pauly, Georg Wissowa, and Wilhelm Kroll (Stuttgart and Munich 1893–1967; 2nd series 1914–72)

RSV | *The Bible: Revised Standard Version* (Old Testament 1952, New Testament 1946)

Schoedel *Athenagoras* *Athenagoras: Legatio and De resurrectione* ed and trans William R. Schoedel, Oxford Early Christian Texts (Oxford 1972)

Sider 'The Just and the Holy' Robert D. Sider 'The Just and the Holy in the New Testament Scholarship of Erasmus' ERSY 11 (1991) 1–26

TDNT G. Kittel *Theological Dictionary of the New Testament* ed and trans G.W. Bromiley (Grand Rapids, MI 1964–76) 10 vols

Thompson *Colloquies* *The Colloquies of Erasmus* trans Craig R. Thompson (Chicago and London 1965)

Thompson *Inquisitio de fide* *Inquisitio de fide: A Colloquy by Desiderius Erasmus 1524* ed with introduction and commentary by Craig R. Thompson 2nd ed (Hamden, CT 1975)

Tischendorf *Novum Testamentum Graece* ed Constantinus Tischendorf 8th ed (Leipzig 1869–72) 2 vols; *Prolegomena* (vol III) ed C.R. Gregory (Leipzig 1894)

Valla *Annot in Acta* Laurentius Valla *Annotationes in Acta apostolorum* in *Opera omnia* (Basel 1540; repr Turin 1962) 2 vols, I 847–55

Weber *Biblia sacra iuxta vulgatam versionem* ed Robertus Weber with Bonfatio Fischer OSB et al, 3rd ed (Stuttgart 1983) 2 vols

SHORT-TITLE FORMS FOR ERASMUS' WORKS

Titles following colons are longer versions of the same, or are alternative titles. Items entirely enclosed in square brackets are of doubtful authorship. For abbreviations, see Works Frequently Cited.

Acta: Acta Academia Lovaniensis contra Lutherum *Opuscula* / CWE 71

Adagia: Adagiorum chiliades 1508, etc (Adagiorum collectanea for the primitive form, when required) LB II / ASD II-4, 5, 6 / CWE 30–6

Admonitio adversus mendacium: Admonitio adversus mendacium et obtrectationem LB X

Annotationes in Novum Testamentum LB VI / CWE 51–60

Antibarbari LB IX / ASD I-1 / CWE 23

Apologia ad Caranzam: Apologia ad Sanctium Caranzam, or Apologia de tribus locis, or Responsio ad annotationem Stunicae . . . a Sanctio Caranza defensam LB IX

Apologia ad Fabrum: Apologia ad Iacobum Fabrum Stapulensem LB IX

Apologia adversus monachos: Apologia adversus monachos quosdam Hispanos LB IX

Apologia adversus Petrum Sutorem: Apologia adversus debacchationes Petri Sutoris LB IX

Apologia adversus rhapsodias Alberti Pii: Apologia ad viginti et quattuor libros A. Pii LB IX

Apologia contra Latomi dialogum: Apologia contra Iacobi Latomi dialogum de tribus linguis LB IX / CWE 71

Apologiae contra Stunicam: Apologiae contra Lopidem Stunicam LB IX / ASD IX-2

Apologia de 'In principio erat sermo' LB IX

Apologia de laude matrimonii: Apologia pro declamatione de laude matrimonii LB IX / CWE 71

Apologia de loco 'Omnes quidem': Apologia de loco 'Omnes quidem resurgemus' LB IX

Apologia qua respondet invectivis Lei: Apologia qua respondet duabus invectivis Eduardi Lei *Opuscula*

Apophthegmata LB IV

Appendix respondens ad Sutorem LB IX

Argumenta: Argumenta in omnes epistolas apostolicas nova (with Paraphrases)

Axiomata pro causa Lutheri: Axiomata pro causa Martini Lutheri *Opuscula* / CWE 71

Carmina: poems in LB I, IV, V, VIII / CWE 85–6

Catalogus lucubrationum LB I

Ciceronianus: Dialogus Ciceronianus LB I / ASD I-2 / CWE 28

Colloquia LB I / ASD I-3

Compendium vitae Allen I / CWE 4

Conflictus: Conflictus Thaliae et Barbariei LB I

[Consilium: Consilium cuiusdam ex animo cupientis esse consultum] *Opuscula* / CWE 71

De bello Turcico: Consultatio de bello Turcico (in Psalmi)

De civilitate: De civilitate morum puerilium LB I / CWE 25

Declamatio de morte LB IV

Declamatiuncula LB IV

Declarationes ad censuras Lutetiae vulgatas: Declarationes ad censuras Lutetiae vulgatas sub nomine facultatis theologiae Parisiensis LB IX

De concordia: De sarcienda ecclesiae concordia, or De amabili ecclesiae concordia (in Psalmi)

De conscribendis epistolis LB I / ASD I-2 / CWE 25

De constructione: De constructione octo partium orationis, or Syntaxis LB I / ASD I-4

De contemptu mundi: Epistola de contemptu mundi LB V / ASD V-1 / CWE 66

De copia: De duplici copia verborum ac rerum LB I / ASD I-6 / CWE 24

De immensa Dei misericordia: Concio de immensa Dei misericordia LB V

De interdicto esu carnium: Epistola apologetica ad Christophorum episcopum Basiliensem de interdicto esu carnium LB IX / ASD IX-1

De libero arbitrio: De libero arbitrio diatribe LB IX

De praeparatione: De praeparatione ad mortem LB V / ASD V-1

De pueris instituendis: De pueris statim ac liberaliter instituendis LB I / ASD I-2 / CWE 26

De puero Iesu: Concio de puero Iesu LB V / CWE 29

De puritate tabernaculi: De puritate tabernaculi sive ecclesiae christianae (in Psalmi)

De ratione studii LB I / ASD I-2 / CWE 24

De recta pronuntiatione: De recta latini graecique sermonis pronuntiatione LB I / ASD I-4 / CWE 26

Detectio praestigiarum: Detectio praestigiarum cuiusdam libelli germanice scripti LB X / ASD IX-1

De taedio Iesu: Disputatiuncula de taedio, pavore, tristicia Iesu LB V

De vidua christiana LB V / CWE 66

De virtute amplectenda: Oratio de virtute amplectenda LB V / CWE 29

[Dialogus bilinguium ac trilinguium: Chonradi Nastadiensis dialogus bilinguium ac trilinguium] *Opuscula* / CWE 7

Dilutio: Dilutio eorum quae Iodocus Clithoveus scripsit adversus declamationem suasoriam matrimonii

Divinationes ad notata Bedae LB IX

Ecclesiastes: Ecclesiastes sive de ratione concionandi LB V

Elenchus in N. Bedae censuras LB IX

Enchiridion: Enchiridion militis christiani LB V / CWE 66

Encomium matrimonii (in De conscribendis epistolis)

Encomium medicinae: Declamatio in laudem artis medicae LB I / ASD I-4 / CWE 29

Epistola ad Dorpium LB IX / CWE 3 / CWE 71

Epistola ad fratres Inferioris Germaniae: Responsio ad fratres Germaniae Inferioris
    ad epistolam apologeticam incerto autore proditam LB X / ASD IX-1

Epistola ad graculos: Epistola ad quosdam imprudentissimos graculos LB X

Epistola apologetica de Termino LB X

Epistola consolatoria: Epistola consolatoria virginibus sacris LB V

Epistola contra pseudevangelicos: Epistola contra quosdam qui se falso iactant
    evangelicos LB X / ASD IX-1

Euripidis Hecuba LB I / ASD I-1

Euripidis Iphigenia in Aulidae LB I / ASD I-1

Exomologesis: Exomologesis sive modus confitendi LB V

Explanatio symboli: Explanatio symboli apostolorum sive catechismus LB V /
    ASD V-1

Ex Plutarcho versa LB IV / ASD IV-2

Expositio concionalis (in Psalmi)

Formula: Conficiendarum epistolarum formula (see De conscribendis epistolis)

Hyperaspistes LB X

In Nucem Ovidii commentarius LB I / ASD I-1 / CWE 29

In Prudentium: Commentarius in duos hymnos Prudentii LB V / CWE 29

Institutio christiani matrimonii LB V

Institutio principis christiani LB IV / ASD IV-1 / CWE 27

[Julius exclusus: Dialogus Julius exclusus e coelis] *Opuscula* / CWE 27

Lingua LB IV / ASD IV-1A / CWE 29

Liturgia Virginis Matris: Virginis Matris apud Lauretum cultae liturgia LB V /
    ASD V-1

Luciani dialogi LB I / ASD I-1

Manifesta mendacia CWE 71

Methodus (see Ratio)

Modus orandi Deum LB V / ASD V-1

Moria: Moriae encomium LB IV / ASD IV-3 / CWE 27

Novum Testamentum: Novum Testamentum 1519 and later (Novum instrumentum for the first edition, 1516, when required) LB VI

Obsecratio ad Virginem Mariam: Obsecratio sive oratio ad Virginem Mariam in rebus adversis LB V

Oratio de pace: Oratio de pace et discordia LB VIII

Oratio funebris: Oratio funebris in funere Bertae de Heyen LB VIII / CWE 29

Paean Virgini Matri: Paean Virgini Matri dicendus LB V

Panegyricus: Panegyricus ad Philippum Austriae ducem LB IV / ASD IV-1 / CWE 27

Parabolae: Parabolae sive similia LB I / ASD I-5 / CWE 23

Paraclesis LB V, VI

Paraphrasis in Elegantias Vallae: Paraphrasis in Elegantias Laurentii Vallae LB I / ASD I-4

Paraphrasis in Matthaeum, etc (in Paraphrasis in Novum Testamentum)

Paraphrasis in Novum Testamentum LB VII / CWE 42–50

Peregrinatio apostolorum: Peregrinatio apostolorum Petri et Pauli LB VI, VII

Precatio ad Virginis filium Iesum LB V

Precatio dominica LB V

Precationes LB V

Precatio pro pace ecclesiae: Precatio ad Iesum pro pace ecclesiae LB IV, V

Psalmi: Psalmi, or Enarrationes sive commentarii in psalmos LB V / ASD V-2, 3

Purgatio adversus epistolam Lutheri: Purgatio adversus epistolam non sobriam Lutheri LB IX / ASD IX-1

Querela pacis LB IV / ASD IV-2 / CWE 27

Ratio: Ratio seu Methodus compendio perveniendi ad veram theologiam (Methodus for the shorter version originally published in the Novum instrumentum of 1516) LB V, VI

Responsio ad annotationes Lei: Liber quo respondet annotationibus Lei LB IX

Responsio ad collationes: Responsio ad collationes cuiusdam iuvenis gerontodidascali LB IX

Responsio ad disputationem de divortio: Responsio ad disputationem cuiusdam Phimostomi de divortio LB IX

Responsio ad epistolam Pii: Responsio ad epistolam paraeneticam Albert Pii, or Responsio ad exhortationem Pii LB IX

Responsio ad notulas Bedaicas LB X

Responsio ad Petri Cursii defensionem: Epistola de apologia Cursii LB X / Allen Ep 3032

Responsio adversus febricitantis libellum: Apologia monasticae religionis LB X

Spongia: Spongia adversus aspergines Hutteni LB X / ASD IX-1
Supputatio: Supputatio calumniarum Natalis Bedae LB IX

Tyrannicida: Tyrannicida, declamatio Lucianicae respondens LB I / ASD I-1 / CWE 29

Virginis et martyris comparatio LB V
Vita Hieronymi: Vita divi Hieronymi Stridonensis *Opuscula* / CWE 61

Index of
Biblical and Apocryphal References

References to the Old Testament and Apocryphal books are complete. References to the New Testament do not include allusions to the *Paraphrases* or *Annotations* on the New Testament. For these see the General Index, under Erasmus, original works.

Index of Classical References

Index of
Patristic and Medieval
References

The *Gloss* and the *Postillae* of Hugh of St Cher and Nicholas of Lyra are the commentaries most frequently cited in the notes. Inasmuch as the numerous citations from these commentaries follow closely the sequence of the narrative of Acts, this index does not list them in detail. The index attempts to be complete for other authors.

Acts of the Holy Apostles Peter and Paul 59 n29

Arator *De actibus apostolorum* 119 n36

Athenagoras
- *De resurrectione mortuorum* 142 n6
- *Legatio* 92 n18, 107 n24

Augustine
- *Contra Felicem Manichaeum* 11 n90
- *De correptione et gratia* 40 n15
- *Quaestiones in Heptateuchum* 51 n24

Bede, the Venerable
- *De nominibus locorum* 60 n42, 63 n2, 68 n44, 69 n2, 84 n16, 86 n32, 91 n101, 102 nn19, 24, 28, 112 n3, 114 nn39, 41, 126 nn1, 6, 145 nn1, 5, 149 n13
- *Liber retractationis* (1:23) 12 n101; (2:24) 21 n78; (2:25) 20 n72; (2:39) 23 n95; (5:24) 42 n38; (5:26) 42 n38; (6:6) 47 n14; (7:42) 53 n42; (10:41) 74 n56; (13:44) 90 n91; (15:24) 99 n60
- *Super Acta* (1:10) 8 n51, 9 n52; (1:11) 9 n54; (1:13) 10 n77; (1:26) 12 n106; (2:6) 15 n29; (2:9) 15 n30; (2:11) 16 n35; (2:13) 16 n40; (2:15) 14 n12; (2:34) 22 n85; (2:41) 24 n111; (3:11) 27 n9; (3:25) 30 n43; (4:1) 31 nn3, 4; (4:11) 33 n33; (4:36) 38 n68; (5:3) 39 n7; (5:5) 39 n10; (5:13) 41 n24; (5:15) 41 n26; (5:17) 41 n29; (5:36) 45 nn59, 60; (7:37)

52 n34; (7:43) 53 nn43, 44; (7:44) 53 n47; (7:49–50) 54 n57; (7:56) 55 n68; (8:1) 57 n8; (8:13) 59 n28; (8:23) 60 n38; (8:26) 60 n42; (8:27) 61 nn45, 48, 50; (8:32) 62 n57; (8:33) 62 nn55, 59; (8:39) 63 n71; (8:40) 63 n72; (9:4) 64 n6; (9:8) 64 n13; (9:25) 67 n32; (9:27) 67 n35; (10:38) 74 n54; (11:29) 80 n43; (12:1) 80 n1; (12:20) 83 nn35, 36; (13:6) 85 n22; (13:9) 85 n25; (13:19–20) 86 n44; (13:21) 87 n49; (13:33) 88 n76; (13:34) 88 n78; (13:47) 90 n97; (14:7) 91 n8; (15:9) 97 n35; (15:38) 100 n72; (16:6) 102 n15; (16:21) 103 n35; (16:33) 104 n46; (17:3) 106 n4; (17:18) 107 n20; (18:18) 114 n32; (19:4) 116 n4; (19:13) 117 n19; (19:29) 119 n36; (20:23) 123 n29; (20:28) 124 n41; (21:24) 128 n28; (24:6–8) 136 n5; (25:13) 140 n8; (27:17) 146 n15; (28:11) 149 n10

Chrysostom. *See* John Chrysostom

Clement of Alexandria
- *Protrepticus* 52 n42, 111 n51
- *Stromateis* 110 n48, 118 n23

Clementine Homilies 59 n29

Dionysius the Pseudo-Areopagite
- *Concerning the Divine Names* 111 n57
- *Concerning the Hierarchies* 111 n57

Index of Greek and Latin Words Cited

Index of Place-Names

This index undertakes to identify primarily those references to passages and notes that have some importance for the geographical conceptualization of the text.

General Index

For specific citations of the works of classical, patristic, and medieval authors listed here, see the Index of Classical References and the Index of Patristic and Medieval References.

149; Christians worship with Jews
49; gentiles worship 73; pagan 107–
8, 110; Peter is worshipped 72, 76;
God alone worshipped 92; pure 49;
through purity of mind 109; David
a worshipper 36; Paul a worshipper
146; proper translation of Greek
word 142 n5. *See also* the Index
of Greek and Latin Words, *cultor,*
cultrix

yeast. *See under* metaphors and
figurative language
yoke. *See under* metaphors and
figurative language

Zeno, philosopher 110 n48
Zúñiga, Diego López, critic of Erasmus
xvii n16, 36 n52, 53 n45, 82 n24, 86
n31, 100 n75, 102 n24, 111 n52, 112
n6, 118 n30, 120 n39, 147 n29

This book

was designed by

ANTJE LINGNER

based on the series design by

ALLAN FLEMING

and was printed by

University

of Toronto

Press